22nd International Conference on Cognition and Exploratory Learning in Digital Age (CELDA 2025)

Porto, Portugal
1-3 November 2025

ISBN: 979-8-3313-2984-6

Printed from e-media with permission by:

Curran Associates, Inc.
57 Morehouse Lane
Red Hook, NY 12571

Some format issues inherent in the e-media version may also appear in this print version.

Printed with permission by Curran Associates, Inc. (2026)

For permission requests, please contact International Association for Development of the Information Society (IADIS) at the address below.

International Association for Development of the Information Society (IADIS)
Rua Sao Sebastiao Da Pedreira
No. 100, 30, 1050-209
Lisbon, Portugal

Phone: 351 21 3151373
Fax: 351 21 3151244

secretariat@iadis.org

Additional copies of this publication are available from:

Curran Associates, Inc.
57 Morehouse Lane
Red Hook, NY 12571 USA
Phone: 845-758-0400
Fax: 845-758-2633
Email: curran@proceedings.com
Web: www.proceedings.com

CELDA 2025

22nd International Conference
on Cognition and Exploratory Learning in Digital Age

1-3 November
Porto, Portugal

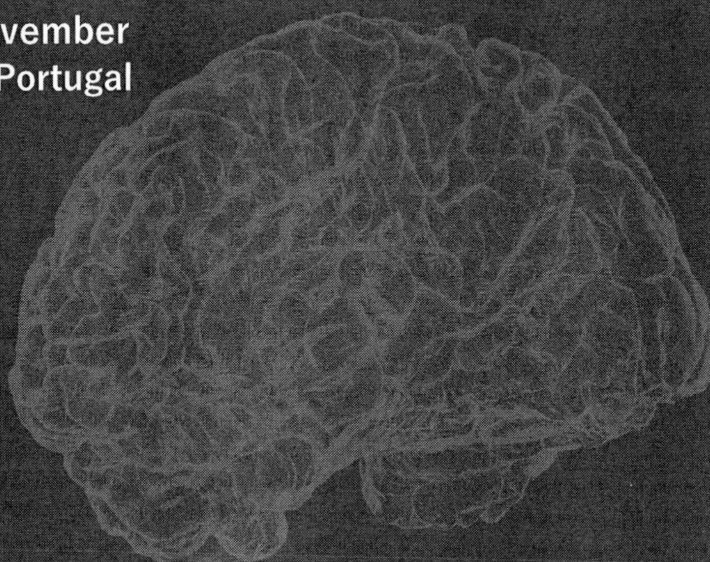

PROCEEDINGS

Edited by

Demetrios G. Sampson
Dirk Ifenthaler
Pedro Isaías

iadis
international association for development of the information society

Image credit: Designed by Freepik

PROCEEDINGS OF THE 22nd INTERNATIONAL CONFERENCE on

COGNITION AND EXPLORATORY LEARNING IN THE DIGITAL AGE (CELDA 2025)

PORTO, PORTUGAL

NOVEMBER 1 - 3, 2025

Organised by

iadis

international association for development of the information society

As a member of Crossref (a non-profit membership organization for scholarly publishing working with the purpose to make content easy to find, link, cite and assess) each published paper in this book of proceedings will be allocated a DOI (Digital Object Identifier) number for its fast and easy citation and indexation.

Edited by Demetrios G. Sampson, Dirk Ifenthaler and Pedro Isaías

Associate Editor: Luís Rodrigues

TABLE OF CONTENTS

SHORT PAPERS

REFLECTION PAPERS

FOREWORD

These proceedings contain the papers of the 22nd International Conference on Cognition and Exploratory Learning in the Digital Age (CELDA 2025), held in Porto, Portugal, from 1 to 3 November 2025 and organized by the International Association for Development of the Information Society (IADIS).

The CELDA conference aims to address the main issues concerned with evolving learning processes and supporting pedagogies and applications in the digital age. There have been advances in both cognitive psychology and computing that have affected the educational arena. The convergence of these two disciplines is increasing at a fast pace and affecting academia and professional practice in many ways.

Paradigms such as just-in-time learning, constructivism, student-centered learning and collaborative approaches have emerged and are being supported by technological advancements such as simulations, virtual reality and multi-agent systems. These developments have created both opportunities and areas of serious concerns. This conference aims to cover both technological as well as pedagogical issues related to these developments. Main tracks have been identified. However innovative contributions that do not easily fit into these areas will also be considered as long as they are directly related to the overall theme of the conference – cognition and exploratory learning in the digital age.

The following areas are represented in the submissions for CELDA 2025:

- Acquisition of Expertise
- Assessing Progress of Learning in Complex Domains
- Assessment of Exploratory Learning Approaches
- Assessment of Exploratory Technologies
- Cognition in Education
- Collaborative Learning
- Educational Psychology
- Exploratory Technologies (Simulations, VR, i-TV, etc.)
- Just-in-Time and Learning-on-Demand
- Learner Communities and Peer-Support
- Learning Communities & Web Service Technologies Pedagogical issues related with Learning Objects
- Learning Paradigms in Academia
- Learning Paradigms in the Corporate Sector
- Life-long Learning
- Student-centered Learning
- Technology and Mental Models
- Technology
- Learning and Expertise
- Virtual University

The CELDA 2025 Conference received 78 submissions from more than 28 countries. Each submission was reviewed in a double-blind review process by at least two independent reviewers to ensure quality and maintain high standards. Out of the papers submitted, 42 were accepted as full papers for an acceptance rate of 54%; 20 were accepted as short papers and 2 were accepted as a reflection papers. Authors of the best published papers in the CELDA 2025 proceedings will be invited to publish extended versions of their papers in a book from Springer.

In addition to the presentation of full, short and reflection papers, the conference also includes one keynote presentation from an internationally distinguished researcher. We would therefore like to express our gratitude to this year keynote speaker: Professor Marcus Specht, Learning Sciences in Higher Education at the Research Center for Higher Education of the Future (CATALPA) at the Fernuniversität in Hagen, Germany.

A successful conference requires the effort of many individuals. We would like to thank the members of the Program Committee for their hard work in reviewing and selecting the papers that appear in this book. We are especially grateful to the authors who submitted their papers to this conference and to the presenters who provided the substance of this meeting. We wish to thank all members of our organizing committee.

Last but not least, we hope that everybody enjoyed the presentations and we invite all participants for next year's edition of the International Conference on Cognition and Exploratory Learning in the Digital Age.

Pedro Isaías, Universidade Aberta (Portuguese Open University), Portugal
Conference Chair

Demetrios G. Sampson, University of Piraeus, Greece
Dirk Ifenthaler, University of Mannheim, Germany & Curtin University, Australia
Program Co-Chairs

November 2025

PROGRAM COMMITTEE

CONFERENCE CHAIR

Pedro Isaías, Universidade Aberta (Portuguese Open University), Portugal

PROGRAM CO-CHAIRS

Demetrios G Sampson, University of Piraeus, Greece
Dirk Ifenthaler, University of Mannheim, Germany & Curtin University, Australia

COMMITTEE MEMBERS

Ah-Choo Koo, Multimedia Univerisity, Malaysia
Alice Barana, University of Turin, Italy
Allan Jeong, Florida State University, USA
Andrea Guidi, Rome Fine Arts Academy, Italy
Annika Wilmers, Frankfurt University of Applied Sciences, Germany
Anthony Y. H. Liao, Asia University, Taiwan
Barbara Lockee, Virginia Tech, USA
ChanMin Kim, Penn State University, USA
Charalampos Karagiannidis, University of Thessaly, Greece
Chien Sing Lee, Sunway University, Malaysia
Chien Ching Lee, Singapore Institute of Technology, Singapore
Chun-Wang Wei, Kaohsiung Medical University, Taiwan
Dana-Kristin Mah, Leuphana University, Germany
Dirk Tempelaar, Maastricht University, Netherlands
Fabio Roman, University of Turin, Italy
Farshad Badie, Berlin School of Business & Innovation (BSBI), Germany
Flavio Manganello, National Research Council, Italy
Francesco Floris, University of Turin, Italy
Giuliana Guazzaroni, MI, Italy
I-Fang Liu, National Central University, Taiwan
Jay Loftus, Michigan State University, USA
Joan Ann Swanson, Franklin Pierce University, USA
Joe Klunder, UC-Irvine, USA
Josef Buchner, St. Gallen University of Teacher Education, Switzerland
Josef Guggemos, University of Education Schwäbisch Gmünd, Germany
Julie-Ann Sime, Independent Researcher, United Kingdom
Karl-Heinz Gerholz, University of Bamberg, Germany
Katja Buntins, University of Duisburg-Essen, Germany
Kristian Träg, University of Duisburg-Essen, Germany
Kuo-Liang Ou, National Tsing Hua University, Taiwan
Kyparissia Papanikolaou, School of Pedagogical and Technological Education, Greece
Lence Miloseva, Goce Delcev University, Macedonia
Mahani Abdul Malik, Open University Malaysia, Malaysia
Maiga Chang, Athabasca University, Canada
Marc Egloffstein, University of Mannheim, Germany
Michael Magee, University of Calgary, Canada

KEYNOTE LECTURE

CHALLENGES AND PERSPECTIVES ON THE DEVELOPMENT OF HUMAN LEARNING WITH AI

Professor Marcus Specht
Learning Sciences in Higher Education at the Research Center for Higher Education of the Future (CATALPA) at the Fernuniversität in Hagen, Germany

Abstract

The talk will connect perspectives from the learning sciences on human learning with the emerging changes and challenges brought about by the rise of generative AI and new technologies. It will then examine current approaches to technology adoption in education and propose a living lab approach for the interdisciplinary development of learning innovations. This approach emphasizes the integration of new technologies with continuous scientific evaluation and research.

Full Papers

EXPLORING THE AFFORDANCES AND CONSTRAINTS OF SCRATCH IN MATHEMATICS EDUCATION: A STUDY THROUGH THE LENS OF AFFORDANCE THEORY

Said Hadjerrouit
University of Agder, Department of Mathematical Sciences, Faculty of Engineering and Sciences, Kristiansand, Norway

ABSTRACT

The integration of programming into mathematics education in Norway introduces additional workload for students, who must adapt to new challenges in their learning processes. This study investigates how student teachers perceive the affordances and constraints of using the programming language Scratch as a tool for learning mathematics. Drawing on Gibson's Affordance Theory and employing a qualitative research design approach, the study analyzes activity reports from three student groups. The results reveal students' perceptions of various affordances and constraints across technological, mathematical, and pedagogical dimensions. Based on the results, conclusions are drawn, limitations are acknowledged, and future directions are suggested to improve the quality of the study.

KEYWORDS

Affordances, Affordance Theory, Constraints, Programming, Mathematics Education, Scratch

1. INTRODUCTION

In recent years, block-based programming languages like Scratch (https://scratch.mit.edu/) have been receiving increasing attention in mathematics education. Scratch's intuitive design and accessibility make it potentially an effective programming tool for beginners. However, research on block-based programming languages is still in its early stages, particularly regarding the evaluation of their affordances and constraints. This study is grounded in Gibson's Affordance Theory (Gibson, 1979). Previous studies have applied this theory to explore the affordances of specific digital tools in mathematics education (Hadjerrouit & Nnagbo, 2023; Hadjerrouit, 2000). By analyzing how students interact with these tools, the studies have identified affordances at technological, mathematical, assessment, and socio-cultural levels, providing insights into how such tools can support mathematical learning. While these studies demonstrate the application of Gibson's Affordance Theory in integrating digital tools into mathematics education, the extent of its use in a programming environment is still emerging. This study proposes a framework that categorizes Scratch's affordances according to three dimensions: Technological, pedagogical, and mathematical. It seeks to investigate the extent to which Scratch affords students' mathematical learning. This study aims to address this research question: *How does Scratch afford students' mathematical learning at the technological, pedagogical, and mathematical level?*

2. LITERATURE REVIEW

In the past decade, there has been a significant increase in research exploring the integration of Scratch into mathematics education. Several studies report on the incorporation of Scratch into mathematics curricula such as geometry (Baccaglini-Frank et al, 2020; Hernandez-Zavaleta et al, 2023), algebra (Chiang & Qin, 2018; Kilhamn et al, 2022), arithmetic (Fang et al., 2023; Germia & Panorkou, 2020), problem-solving (Rodríguez-Martínez, González-Calero, & Sáez-López, 2019). The studies highlight that the user-friendly graphical design of Scratch encourages exploration and creativity, allowing students to experiment with mathematical concepts in a low-stakes and playful environment. At the same time, several studies point out challenges, such as the need for adequate teacher training and the alignment of Scratch activities with established curricular outcome. Other research gaps remain such as longitudinal impact, diverse educational contexts, and comparative studies.

The research literature draws on various theories, including computational thinking (Gökçe & Yenmez, 2023; Kurt & Çakıoğlu, 2024; Sáez-López, Sevillano-García & Vazquez-Cano, 2019), constructionism (Ng, Leung, & Ye, 2023), constructivism (Tijani, Callaghan, & de Villers, 2020), creative mathematical reasoning (Olsson & Granberg, 2024), Chevallard's praxeologies (Kilhamn et al, 2022), variation theory (Olteanu, 2022), beliefs (Dilling, Köster & Vogler, 2024), Vygotsky's theory of cognitive developmental (Hernandez-Zavaleta et al, 2023), instrumental approach (Gueudet & Joffredo-Le Brun, 2021) and Theory of Didactical Situations (Daher, Baya'a & Jaber, 2022). Gibson's affordance theory is rarely referenced explicitly in mathematics education research literature, with a few exceptions (Calder, 2018; Humble & Mozelius, 2023).

3. THEORETICAL FRAMEWORK: AFFORDANCE THEORY

The notion of affordance was proposed by Gibson (1979). It refers to the relationship between an object's physical properties and the characteristics of a user that enables specific interactions. Specifically, Gibson used the term "affordance" to describe the action possibilities offered to an animal by the environment with reference to the animal's action capabilities. A typical example is a tall tree that has the affordance of food for a giraffe because it has a long neck. Gibson's notion of affordance has three characteristics. Firstly, affordances imply a complementarity between an observer (whether an animal or a human) and the environment. Secondly, affordances exist independently of the observer, but they must be perceived to be acted upon. Finally, affordances and constraints are complementary, not opposites.

In the computer world, the notion of affordance refers to the fundamental properties of an object that determine how it could be used Norman (1988). Accordingly, an affordance is the design aspect of an object, which suggests how it should be used and a visual clue to its function. Examples of affordances are user interface elements, which directly suggest suitable actions: Clickable geometrical figures, draggable sliders, pressable buttons, selectable menus for figures, etc. Moreover, Turner and Turner (2002) specified a three-layer articulation of affordances: Perceived, ergonomic, and cultural affordances. Kirchner et al (2004) described a three-layer definition of affordance: Technological affordances to cover usability issues, educational affordances to facilitate teaching and learning, and social affordances to foster social interactions.

In mathematics education, Hadjerrouit and Nnagbo (2023) presented a model with three levels (technological, pedagogical, and mathematical) of affordances of Numbas, a computer-based assessment system. In the context of programming, a few articles utilize Gibson's affordance theory (Calder, 2018; Humble & Mozelius, 2023). In a recent article, Hadjerrouit (2024) highlighted that the emergence of affordances depends on a coherent combination of mathematical thinking, computational thinking (CT), and programming. Drawing on these studies, this research proposes a framework that supports the exploration of affordances in the context of programming at three levels: Technological, pedagogical, and mathematical.

4. METHODOLOGY

This research uses a case study design approach (Yin, 2018). The participants were master's degree teacher students taking a course on digital tools in mathematics education. Data was collected through activity reports from 12 participants divided into 3 groups of 3-4 students each. Thematic analysis (Braun and Clarke, 2006) was used to analyze the data from the activity reports. Specifically, thematic analysis involves generating codes directly from the data, identifying, defining and naming the themes, drafting a report, and categorizing the themes within pre-defined categories. This process emerges inductively from the empirical data (and the codes derived from it and deductively from three predefined categories and sub-categories of affordances: a) Technological (ease-of-use, understandability of commands and graphics); b) Pedagogical (feedback, level-of-difficulty, motivation, collaboration); and c) Mathematical (mathematical knowledge, understanding, and problem-solving). To explore students' perceived affordances, they were asked to complete the following mathematical tasks (Figure 1) and to record their reflections on affordances and constraints in activity reports.

a) Write a program to draw the geometric pattern. This task is about motion and drawing.

b) Write a program that prompts the user to enter the radius and diameter of a circle. Then, calculate and display the area and circumference of the circle, the surface area of a sphere volume. This task focuses on using variables and functions.

c) Write a program that generates three random numbers. The program should display the three random numbers, for example, like this: "*The first random number is 6*", "*The second random number is 4*", and "*The third random number is 8*". Finally, the program should determine and print the largest of the three random numbers. This task is about making decisions.

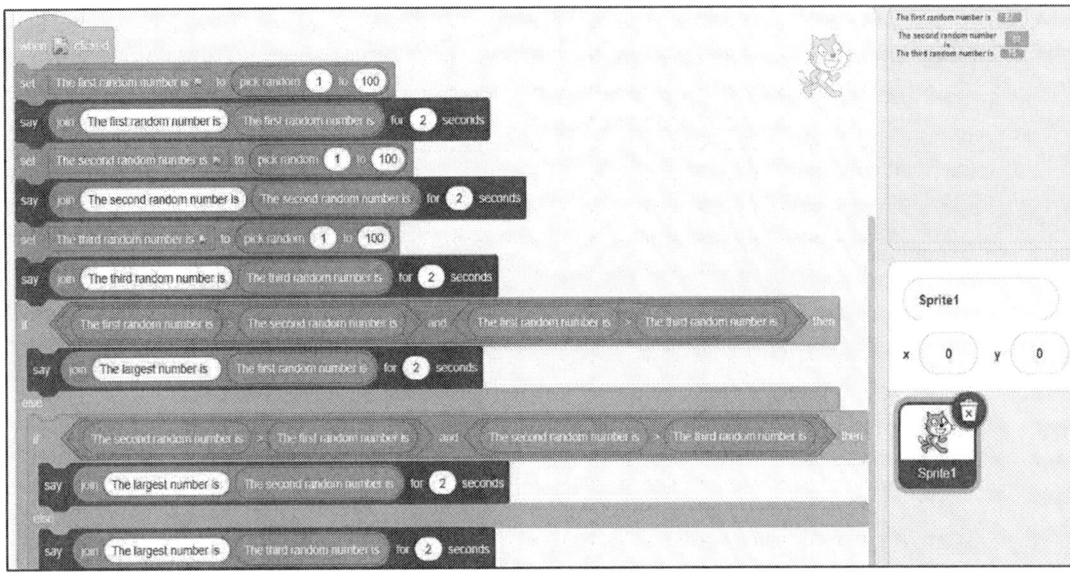

Figure 1. Mathematical task c) and its corresponding example of Scratch program

5. RESULTS

5.1 Group 1

Technological affordances and constraints: ***Ease-of-use, understandability of commands and graphics***

In terms of affordances, the group perceived that Scratch is easy to use, as the various commands available are understandable and easily accessible, and they only need to "drag them into place." In terms of constraints, the group found it challenging to combine the different commands so that the program does what they want. This is not always perceived as intuitive as this comment reveals: "*The program is limited to the available commands, meaning that users cannot do exactly as they wish. Some understanding of how programming works is necessary to create something meaningful.*" There are also certain commands that are not as obvious, e.g., the wheel that can be used to rotate a figure in the right direction, but it was not easy to see it was there just by looking. Clearly, Scratch commands should be easier to discover. The group also perceived that Scratch has a colorful, childlike look with simple character designs and somewhat "choppy" animations.

Pedagogical affordances and constraints: ***Feedback, level of difficulty, motivation, and collaboration***

The group perceived varying levels of motivation as some wanted to complete the tasks to experience a sense of achievement, while others simply wanted to finish quickly and resorted to YouTube videos for explanations on how to solve tasks 1b and 1c. They stated that "*the more familiar one becomes with Scratch, the better they can figure things out and gain greater control over their own learning.*" Moreover, the group perceived collaboration in Scratch as possible, but its effectiveness depends on the specific task.

One constraint is that Scratch is limited to the available commands, meaning that users cannot do exactly as they wish. Clearly, some understanding of how Scratch works is necessary to create something meaningful. Another constraint is that Scratch does not provide feedback: *"(...) when creating commands involving, for example functions and variables, users need to manage the mathematical aspects on their own. This means that if an error is made in a formula within Scratch, the users must identify it themselves. If they do not have a strong grasp of mathematics, such mistakes can be difficult to detect, as Scratch does not provide feedback on errors during programming. A teacher can pre-program something that gives feedback to students, but when students program on their own, they do not receive any form of feedback."* Besides this constraint, the group perceived that the level of difficulty in Scratch can be adjusted. Users can create simple programs (e.g., making a character move forward) or more advanced ones (e.g., using variables, formulas, and if/else functions).

Mathematical affordances and constraints: ***Mathematical knowledge, understanding, & problem-solving***

This group perceived the affordance of combining mathematical thinking with programming. Based on the idea that mathematical knowledge is useful for solving tasks in Scratch, the group think that this knowledge makes it easier to determine whether mistakes have been made, or something is done correctly, as they already know what the expected outcome should be. The group also perceived the necessity to grasp the basics of programming to complete the tasks as this comment indicates "(...) *to use Scratch effectively (...), students should first have the necessary mathematical knowledge required for the tasks and also possess a basic understanding of how to program."* Another perceived is computational thinking (CT) in terms of the decomposition of the task and the problem-solving approach step by step. They perceived that this structured approach made it simpler to identify errors and understand what went wrong. Additionally, the overall workload was reduced when they had a clear plan before starting to code in Scratch.

One constraint is that Scratch alone did not enhance their understanding of mathematics. They concluded that they had to be familiar with the mathematical concepts required for solving the tasks: *"This makes Scratch less suitable for learning new mathematical concepts. If the goal is to acquire new mathematical knowledge, other mathematical programs or traditional methods like pen and paper may be more effective than Scratch."*

5.2 Group 2

Technological affordances and constraints: ***Ease-of-use, understandability of commands and graphics***

This group perceived that Scratch is an intuitive and easy program to use, but they recognize the challenges an inexperienced coder might face when using Scratch without guidance from a competent person. In this case, Scratch may be perceived as not intuitive, as it does not provide guidance beyond tutorial videos. Furthermore, the group disagrees about the level of interactivity. Based on their previous coding experience, two students appreciate feedback or error messages when a code is unsatisfactory, as this comment reveals: *"In the few hours we have spent using the program, this kind of feedback has been completely absent."* However, the third student thinks that the interactivity is high and that Scratch aids in learning programming. Finally, the group perceived the quality of the animations and graphics as user-friendly, and that the colors provide users with immediate recognition and encourage further exploration, concluding that these *"are simple, but the quality is good."*

Pedagogical affordances and constraints: ***Feedback, level of difficulty, motivation, and collaboration***

In terms of feedback, the group perceived the potential of Scratch to allow users to choose how simple or complex they want to make their solutions. However, many may not recognize the potential to expand their tasks, as this is limited by the user's experience and understanding of Scratch. While working on tasks 1, 2, and 3, the group did not perceive that they received any useful feedback to help them understand the program: *"For example, when entering a radius in task 2, there is no (...) feedback if a user inputs letters instead of numbers. We also found no guidance beyond the separate tutorial videos on how to use the program (...)"*. Furthermore, the group felt motivated to complete the tasks because they could constantly see what they were creating and receive immediate visual feedback in the graphics window. This encouraged them to expand on the tasks and add extra features such as backgrounds, speech bubbles, and other elements.

Finally, the group does not think that Scratch inherently supports collaboration, unless the teacher designs tasks that require students to work together. However, the group found it very helpful to complete the tasks collaboratively, as it allowed them to ask each other questions and learn from one another.

Mathematical affordances and constraints*: Mathematical knowledge, understanding, & problem-solving*

In terms of mathematical knowledge, the group thinks that it is helpful when visualizing geometric shapes and formulas. Using Scratch, however, they did not apply mathematical knowledge in new ways. The tasks were designed in a way that allowed them to structure their code based on their existing knowledge to connect with functions such as <If> and <If not>. In terms of CT (decomposition and step-by-step approach to problem-solving), the group used two different approaches. Two wrote the code from *top to bottom*, while one first identified which functions, blocks, or codes were needed to sort the information (Task 3). They pointed out that these approaches reflect how people function in daily life, where some read texts from beginning to end, while others jump between topics and multiple sources simultaneously.

Regarding mathematical understanding, the group did not immediately see the advantages of using Scratch instead of traditional teaching methods. Clearly, they *"are skeptical about whether Scratch provides mathematical insights that would otherwise be unattainable."* Instead, they believe that *"existing mathematical knowledge is necessary to learn how to program rather than Scratch being a tool for learning mathematics."*

5.3 Group 3

Technological affordances and constraints*: Ease-of-use, understandability of commands and graphics*

The group perceived the programming language as very clear and easy to use, and in many ways, its functions are intuitive. This can be seen in the comment: *"It quickly becomes apparent that you can move blocks from the command palette to the empty window beside it, which will then trigger an action on the "stage" to the right. The palette is also well-organized, with categories such as sounds, actions, variables, etc., making it easy to find what you need."* Moreover, they perceived Scratch as very user-friendly and has an interface that allows users with different levels of experience to program. However, some found it difficult at times to locate certain commands if they did not already know their names or where they were located, as it was not always obvious which category they belonged to. Nonetheless, all agree that *"once you become familiar with the menu, it is quick and easy to navigate. The commands are simple to use once you understand their meaning and function."* Finally, the group perceived Scratch as visually very appealing, allowing users to choose between realistic backgrounds and "sprites" (characters) or more cartoon-like figures and backgrounds. The animations are decent but somewhat choppy in movement.

Pedagogical affordances and constraints*: Feedback, level of difficulty, motivation, and collaboration*

With Scratch, students can work on tasks at an adapted level, based on their prior knowledge and abilities. This allows for good differentiation. However, in some cases, it is not easy to simplify tasks, especially when a specific final product is required. For example, in the tasks we worked on, there was little flexibility. On the other hand, an open-ended task, such as creating a mathematical game would be more adaptable to different levels, as students can decide how complex they want to make it.

The group thinks that Scratch provides some feedback in the sense that users can notice errors when the output does not match their expectations, allowing them to learn from mistakes. When coding tasks, there is no direct error message if the code is incorrect. Users only see that something is not working as intended, but it would be challenging for the program to determine what should have been done in cases of incorrect coding. Clearly, the lack of feedback was very demotivating, especially when errors were not immediately obvious. However, if users discover and correct the error on their own, it can lead to a deeper understanding of the code.

Scratch offers good opportunities for collaboration, as students can discuss their work and provide feedback to each other when mistakes occur. However, only one person at a time can actively interact with the program. Collaboration can still take place if a classmate sits beside the user, discussing problem-solving together. Alternatively, each student can work on their own computer and compare solutions, discussing challenges as they arise. If a student struggles with a task, another student can suggest solutions and explain why the code is not working as intended. Since students have different backgrounds in coding and mathematics, they can benefit from helping each other. Once students understand the code, they can program independently.

Mathematical affordances and constraints: *Mathematical knowledge, understanding, & problem-solving*

The group thinks that Scratch can help develop a more relational understanding of mathematics by allowing students to explore shapes and algorithms, provided they are able to apply their mathematical knowledge both when interpreting and completing tasks, as this comment reveals: "*Understanding mathematical concepts in geometry, such as angles, degrees, radius, circumference, and volume, provides a solid foundation for solving Task 1. In Task 2, we needed to know the formulas for circumference and area of a circle, as well as the volume and surface area of a sphere. In Task 3, knowledge of inequalities was essential.*"

The group also found that it is easiest to start coding immediately rather than planning in advance, so pre-planning did not seem necessary: "*For example, in Task 3, where we had to make a character say the highest number, it was easier to directly code the inequalities (...) and adjust them based on the output, rather than drafting a plan beforehand*". Moreover, the group thinks that translating mathematical knowledge into code helps deepen understanding. By presenting mathematics in a new way, Scratch requires students to apply their mathematical skills in a different format, reinforcing their comprehension.

6. DISCUSSION

The results show that the students perceived a range of affordances and constraints across technological, pedagogical, and mathematical dimensions. While its intuitive design and accessibility make it a powerful introductory tool for programming, its constraints raise important questions regarding its educational value.

6.1 Technological Affordances and Constraints

One of Scratch's primary technological affordances is its drag-and-drop interface, which simplifies programming syntax and reduces the cognitive load required for learning to code. This accessibility allows beginners to experiment with programming concepts without the intimidation of text-based syntax errors. Additionally, its colorful and engaging interface fosters an inviting learning environment. However, its perceived "childish" aesthetic may deter older students or those seeking a more professional programming experience. Despite Scratch's emphasis on ease-of-use, some features remain non-intuitive. The rotation wheel, as indicated by group 1, is not immediately discoverable, potentially hindering users attempting to manipulate sprite movements. Furthermore, Scratch lacks detailed debugging feedback, providing no explicit error messages. While this encourages trial and error, it can also frustrate learners who struggle to identify issues in their code. The small working window and manual saving process further limit the overall usability of the platform, making long-term or complex projects more cumbersome.

6.2 Pedagogical Affordances and Constraints

From a pedagogical perspective, the immediate visual feedback from the Scratch's graphical interface may enhance engagement and allow students to iteratively refine their programs. This experiential learning aligns well with constructivist approaches, which emphasize learning through doing. However, the lack of direct error messages presents a significant constraint, as debugging is an essential programming skill. Beginners may struggle to identify and fix problems without guidance, potentially leading to frustration. As a result, feedback from teachers to students regarding their performances, challenges and difficulties is essential to identify their misunderstandings and misconceptions of mathematical concepts, and ways to implement them using Scratch.

Moreover, while Scratch potentially supports collaboration (Quevedo Gutiérrez & Zapatera Llinare, 2021), it does not inherently promote teamwork, requiring teachers to design collaborative activities. Motivation levels are mixed. While some students are engaged by the problem-solving nature of programming, others approach Scratch in a task-oriented manner, aiming to complete activities with minimal effort. This suggests that while Scratch has potential as a pedagogical tool, its effectiveness depends heavily on the educational context and the extent to which teachers integrate guided discovery and inquiry-based learning approaches.

6.3 Mathematical Affordances and Constraints

Scratch enables students to apply mathematical concepts such as variables, coordinates, and geometric transformations in a practical, visual context, but it only allows limited mathematical operations (Dilling, Köster & Vogler, 2024). Moreover, Scratch does not inherently facilitate deep understanding of new mathematical concepts. Instead, prior mathematical knowledge is often necessary to use Scratch effectively, positioning it as a reinforcement tool rather than a primary educational medium for mathematics.

Furthermore, Scratch's design aligns more with procedural knowledge rather than conceptual understanding. While students can visualize mathematical relationships through programming, Scratch does not inherently promote higher-order thinking at the upper levels of Bloom's taxonomy. This constraint suggests that while Scratch has value in connecting coding with mathematics, it should be supplemented with additional teacher-led strategies to enhance conceptual learning (Olsson & Granberg, 2024). By lowering the barrier to entry for coding, Scratch potentially supports broader participation in programming. However, arguments on Scratch's effectiveness as an educational tool vary. While some teachers see it as an invaluable introduction to programming, others argue that alternative platforms, such as mBot (Sáez-López, Sevillano-García, & Vazquez-Cano, 2019) or Alice (Yildiz Durak, 2020) provide more engaging experiences. The choice of programming tools ultimately depends on the learning goals, student demographics, and teaching approaches. Nevertheless, Scratch remains a widely used tool that supports CT and problem-solving in an accessible format.

7. CONCLUSIONS, LIMITATIONS AND FUTURE WORK

Scratch's intuitive and visually appealing interface supports beginners' programming experiences. It offers the potential to make mathematical concepts more accessible by enabling students to create dynamic simulations, thereby linking mathematics with computational thinking and programming (Kurt & Çakıoğlu, 2024; Molina-Ayuso et al., 2022; Ng, Leung, & Ye, 2023; Xie et al., 2023). However, constraints such as limited debugging tools present challenges. Pedagogically, Scratch facilitates experiential learning but requires careful design to maximize engagement and collaboration. Mathematically, it reinforces existing knowledge rather than introducing new concepts, positioning it as a complementary rather than primary educational tool.

The paper has some limitations. The sample size ($N = 12$) is relatively small. A larger and more diverse sample size would have been preferable to provide deeper insights into the affordances and constraints of Scratch. The participants are student teachers, which may introduce a bias, as their perceptions could differ from those of younger students less familiar with mathematical and pedagogical concepts. From a methodological standpoint, the thematic analysis used in the study relies on predefined categories, which may limit the emergence of new themes from the data. A more flexible approach could allow for the identification of novel categories and unexpected insights. The article focuses primarily on Scratch without comparing its affordances and constraints to those of other educational programming tools. Including such a comparison could provide a more comprehensive perspective. Finally, the paper could be set around the use of Scratch to teach a simple vs complex procedural mathematics problem and the results of student outcomes compared.

Gibson's Affordance Theory has been applied to only a limited extent in the context of programming within mathematics education. Hence, further research is needed to comprehensively understand how the theory can inform the use of programming. The use of AI tools, such as ChatGPT, to generate or suggest Scratch programming blocks represents a promising area of research, both in terms of affordances and constraints.

REFERENCES

Baccaglini-Frank, et al. (2020). Teachers' Perspectives on the Intertwining of Tangible and Digital Modes of Activity with a Drawing Robot for Geometry. *Educ. Sci. 10*(12), 387; 1-21.

Braun, V., & Clarke, V. (2006). Using Thematic Analysis in Psychology. *Qualitative Research in Psychology, 3*(2), 77–101. https://doi.org/10.1191/1478088706qp063oa

Calder, N. (2018). Using Scratch to Facilitate Mathematical Thinking. *Waikato Journal of Education, 23(*2), 43-58.

Chiang, F. kuang, & Qin, L. (2018). A Pilot Study to Assess the Impacts of Game-Based Construction Learning, Using Scratch, on Students' Multi-Step Equation-Solving Performance. *Interactive Learning Environments, 26*(6), 803–814.

Daher, W.; Baya'a, N. & Jaber, O. (2022) Understanding Prospective Teachers' Task Design Considerations through the Lens of Didactical Situation. *Mathematics 10*, 417, 2-14. https://doi.org/10.3390/math10030417

Dilling, F., Köster, J. & Vogler, A. (2024). Beliefs of Undergraduate Mathematics Education Students in a Teacher Education Program about Visual Programming in Mathematics Classes. *Int. J. Res. Undergrad. Math. Ed. 10*, 700–731.

Fang, X., et al. (2023). Integrating Computational Thinking into Primary Mathematics: A Case Study of Fraction Lessons with Scratch Programming Activities. *Asian Journal for Mathematics Education 2*(2), 220-239.

Germia, E. & Panorkou, N. (2020). Using Scratch Programming to Explore Coordinates. *Mathematics Teacher: Learning & Teaching* PK–12, *113*(4), 293-300.

Gueudet, G. & Joffredo-Lebrun, S. (2021). Teacher Education, Students' Autonomy and Digital Technologies: A Case Study about Programming with Scratch. *Review of science, mathematics and ICT education 15*(1), 5-24.

Gibson, J.J. (1979). *The Ecological Approach to Visual Perception*. Houghton Mifflin, Boston.

Gökçe, S. & Yenmez, A.A. (2023). Ingenuity of Scratch Programming on Reflective Thinking towards Problem Solving and Computational Thinking. *Educ Inf Technol 28*, 5493–5517. https://doi.org/10.1007/s10639-022-11385-x

Hadjerrouit, S. (2024). Programming and Computational Thinking in Mathematics Education: An Affordance Theory Perspective. In I.E. Faggiano et al. (2024). *Mathematics Education in Digital Age. Proceedings of MEDA4*, 191–198.

Hadjerrouit, S. & Nnagbo, C.I. (2023). Analyzing Affordances of the E-assessment System Numbas in Mathematics Education from an Activity Theory Perspective. In: Sampson, D. G., Ifenthaler, D. & Isaias, P. (Eds.). *20th Proceedings of CELDA 2023.* IADIS Press, 199–206.

Hadjerrouit, S. (2020). Exploring the Affordances of SimReal for Learning Mathematics in Teacher Education: A Socio-Cultural Perspective. In: Lane, H.C., Zvacek, S., Uhomoibhi, J. (eds.). *Computer Supported Education, CSEDU 2019. Communications in Computer and Information Science, 1220*, 26-50. Springer, Cham.

Hernández-Zavaleta, J. E., Brady, C., Becker, S., & Clark, D. B. (2023). Vygotskian Hybridizing of Motion and Mapping: Learning about Geometric Transformations in Block-Based Programming Environments. *Mathematical Thinking and Learning*, 27(1), 25–59. https://doi.org/10.1080/10986065.2023.2191074

Humble, N. & Mozelius, P. (2023). Making Programming Part of Teachers' Everyday Life: Programming Affordances and Constraints For K-12 Mathematics and Technology. *International Journal of Information and Learning Technology, 40*(1), 98-112.

Kilhamn, C., Bråting, K., Helenius, O. & Mason, J. (2022). Variables in Early Algebra: Exploring Didactic Potentials in Programming Activities. *ZDM Mathematics Education 54*, 1273–1288. https://doi.org/10.1007/s11858-022-01384-0

Kirchner, P., Strijbos, J.-W., Kreijns, K., & Beers, B.J. (2004). Designing Electronic Collaborative Learning Environments. *Educ. Technol. Res. Dev. 52*(3), 47–66.

Kurt, G. & Çakıoğlu, Ö. (2024). Insights on the Role of Scratch in Fostering Computational and Mathematical Thinking: The Case of Prime Factorization. *Digit Exp Math Educ 10*, 76–107.

Molina-Ayuso, Á. et al. (2022). Introduction to Computational Thinking with Scratch for Teacher Training for Spanish Primary School Teachers in Mathematics. *Educ. Sci.*, *12*, 899, 1-13.

Norman, D.A. (1988). *The Psychology of Everyday Things*. Basic Books, New York.

Ng, OL., Leung, A. & Ye, H. (2023). Exploring Computational Thinking as A Boundary Object between Mathematics and Computer Programming for STEM Teaching and Learning. *ZDM Mathematics Education 55*, 1315–1329.

Olsson, J. & Granberg, C. (2024) Teacher-Student Interaction Supporting Students' Creative Mathematical Reasoning during Problem Solving Using Scratch. *Mathematical Thinking and Learning*, *26*(3), 278-305.

Olteanu, C. (2022) Programming, Mathematical Reasoning and Sense-Making. *International Journal of Mathematical Education in Science and Technology, 53*(8), 2046-2064.

Quevedo Gutiérrez, E., & Zapatera Llinares, A. (2021). Assessment of Scratch Programming Language as a Didactic Tool to Teach Functions. *Educ. Sci. 11*, 499. https://doi.org/10.3390/educsci11090499

Rodríguez-Martínez, J. A., González-Calero, J. A., & Sáez-López, J. M. (2019). Computational Thinking and Mathematics Using Scratch: An Experiment with Sixth-Grade Students. *Interactive Learning Environments, 28*(3), 316–327.

Sáez-López, J.M., Sevillano-García, ML. & Vazquez-Cano, E. (2019). The Effect of Programming on Primary School Students' Mathematical and Scientific Understanding: Educational Use of mBot. *Education Tech Research Dev 67*, 1405–1425. https://doi.org/10.1007/s11423-019-09648-5

Tijani, F., Callaghan, R., & de Villers, R. (2020). An Investigation into Pre-service Teachers' Experiences while Transitioning from Scratch Programming to Procedural Programming. *African Journal of Research in Mathematics, Science and Technology Education, 24*(2), 266–278. https://doi.org/10.1080/18117295.2020.1820798

Turner, P., & Turner, S. (2002). An Affordance-Based Framework for CVE Evaluation. In: People and Computers XVII – *Proceedings of the Joint HCI-UPA Conference*, 89–104. Springer. https://doi.org/10.1007/978-1-4471-0105-5_6

Yin, R. K. (2018). *Case Study Research and Applications: Design and Methods* (6th ed.). Thousand Oaks, CA: Sage.

Yildiz Durak, H. (2020). The Effects of Using Different Tools in Programming Teaching of Secondary School Students on Engagement, Computational Thinking and Reflective Thinking Skills for Problem Solving. *Tech Know Learn 25*, 179–195.

Xie, Z. et al. (2023). Bridging K–12 Mathematics and Computational Thinking in the Scratch Community: Implications Drawn from a Creative Learning Context. *IT Professional, 25*(2), 64-70.

DIGITALLY SUPPORTED SCENARIO-BASED LEARNING FOR IMPROVING MATHEMATICS EDUCATION AND PERCEPTION IN SECURITY AND DEFENCE

Marina Marchisio Conte[1], Giulia Boetti[1], Fabio Roman[1], Enrico Spinello[2],
Nikolaos V. Karadimas[3], Linko Nikolov[4], Paulina Owczarek[5] and Andrada Livia Cirneanu[6]
[1]*Department of Molecular Biotechnology and Health Sciences, University of Turin, Via Nizza 52, 10126 Torino, Italy*
[2]*Italian Army Officers School, Via Arsenale 22, 10121 Torino, Italy*
[3]*Department of Military Sciences, Hellenic Army Academy, Dirrachiou 16, 16672 Vari, Greece*
[4]*Department of Communication Networks and Systems, National Military University "Vasil Levski", Karel Shkorpil 1 str., 9700 Shumen, Bulgaria*
[5]*Faculty of Security, Logistics and Management, Military University of Technology, ul. Gen. Sylwestra Kaliskiego 2, 00-908 Warszawa 49, Poland*
[6]*Faculty of Integrated Armament Systems, Military Engineering and Mechatronics, Military Technical Academy "Ferdinand I", 39-49 George Cosbuc, Sector 5, Bucharest, Romania*

ABSTRACT

The provision of a profitable education in Mathematics is important at a cross-curricular level, since this subject finds room in a plethora of academic paths, not limited to the most scientific or technological curricula. In particular, this applies to the security and defence area, where several skills related to mathematical reasoning, such as problem solving and critical thinking, are pivotal. To make students comfortable with Mathematics, even when it is not their specialisation, a central role is played by a proper design of the content they have to study, along with teachers providing adequate instruction based on it. In this sense, using scenarios and digital tools has already proved to be effective in some contexts, but most research has been performed outside higher education. In this research, we investigate the implementation of scenario-based learning with the support of digital tools within an international school, which involved university students in mathematical problem-solving activities based on real-world scenarios relevant to the security and defence area. Findings from quantitative and qualitative analyses reveal that scenario-based learning, when combined with problem solving and technology-enhanced environments, can foster deeper learning and enhance students' ability to apply mathematical concepts to real-world situations. This research is part of the activities undertaken within the European project DIMAS, whose goal is to increase interest in studying Mathematics in the field of security and defence and to provide more understandable Mathematics problems and Mathematics applications using digital tools.

KEYWORDS

Digital Education, Mathematics Education, Scenario-Based Learning, Security and Defence Education

1. INTRODUCTION

Mathematics is a fundamental subject that is typically incorporated in the first-year curriculum of numerous bachelor's degrees. Indeed, Mathematics modules are present in a wide range of curricula, including Economics, Finance and science-related subjects such as Biology, Biotechnology and Chemistry. The inclusion of these modules is indicative of the fundamental role of Mathematics in providing essential tools for data analysis, modelling, and the resolution of complex problems in these disciplines. Furthermore, Mathematics modules are also present in several humanities bachelor's curricula, including Psychology and Strategic Sciences. These modules provide students with quantitative and statistical tools for analysing data and interpreting research results and are also crucial for developing 21st-century skills. By focusing on the security and defence area, the teaching of Mathematics becomes particularly relevant to boost the development of essential skills in this field, such as problem solving, critical thinking, and leadership. The challenge in designing and teaching these modules is to ensure that Mathematics is made attractive in contexts where students are not specifically specialising in mathematical disciplines. The use of scenarios and digital technologies can effectively support the teaching and learning of Mathematics (Cirneanu and Moldoveanu, 2024; Engelbrecht and Borba, 2024; Molina-Toro et al., 2019). However, while there is a consistent body of research on the use of digital technologies in Mathematics higher education (Barana et al., 2023; Molina-Toro et al., 2019), relatively little attention has been given to scenario-based learning in higher education, despite its potential to make Mathematics more accessible, especially in contexts where it is perceived as difficult. In this paper, we present an international experience conducted within the Erasmus+ project "Digital Mathematics Applied in Security and Defence Education" (DIMAS). This experimentation involved 16 university students in the security and defence field, who participated in an immersive week. During this period, they were presented with a series of scenarios that required applying mathematical concepts to military problems, with the support of digital tools. In this research article, we report and analyse the perception of students regarding the proposed activities, specifically focusing on the use of digital technologies and the learning process through scenarios, considering their effects on learning Mathematics and the development of problem-solving and critical thinking skills. While our study took place within the military setting, we found more general outcomes also applicable to different premises. The paper is structured as follows: Section 2 presents the theoretical framework of our research; Section 3 depicts the research context presenting the DIMAS project and the learning, teaching, and training activity taken into account; Section 4 presents the research question and the methodology; Section 5 reports the analysis results, with the related discussion; Section 6 contains some concluding remarks and inspiration for future work.

2. THEORETICAL FRAMEWORK

Scenario-based learning (SBL) is a didactic approach that provides students with practical experiences and contexts, allowing them to apply their theoretical knowledge to real-life problem-solving situations. In several experimental studies, the SBL has been shown to be effective in terms of students' achievement in Mathematics from primary school (Aslan, 2019) through middle school (Altıntaş et al., 2023; Usta and Söylemez, 2020; Zhou et al., 2024) to high school (Hassan et al., 2023). In (Hassan et al., 2023), the authors identify four types of SBL, considering on what the design is based:

- project-based: students collaborate on assigned projects, applying previously acquired knowledge to produce a final product that integrates theory and practice;
- case-based: learners work in small groups to analyse multiple related cases, practising problem solving within structured, topic-relevant scenarios;
- context-based: knowledge is grounded in students' real-life experiences, enhancing relevance and understanding by connecting learning to familiar, authentic situations;
- problem-based: students face unfamiliar problems requiring research, reflection, and new learning to find solutions, fostering scientific and logical thinking skills.

In each case, the common element is the active and central role of students: the scenario is designed to be familiar and make the subject matter more practical, and students must actively engage in solving it. This type of methodology can be particularly effective in the field of security and defence, as it allows the incorporation of simulations, case studies, and real-life exercises to acquire the necessary skills to deal with complex and dynamic issues typical of this field (Barana et al., 2024; Cirneanu and Moldoveanu, 2024), such as problem solving and critical thinking (Barana et al., 2023).

Critical thinking and problem solving are key competencies promoted by educational frameworks, such as the Partnership for 21st Century Learning (Partnership for 21st Century Skills, 2009). These skills are also explicitly addressed in DigComp 2.2, the Digital Competence Framework for Citizens (Vuorikari et al., 2022), which emphasises the ability to identify needs and problems, resolve conceptual and practical issues in digital environments, use digital tools to innovate processes and products, and keep up to date with the digital evolution. Given their acknowledged importance for active citizenship, it is essential to integrate these skills into educational programs alongside core academic content, thereby fostering their development systematically and intentionally (Fissore et al., 2020). As pointed out in the DigComp 2.2, digital technologies can not only support the learning process, but also foster the development of such skills in students. This is also recognised in the field of mathematics education, in which the use of a problem-solving approach within a digital learning environment, along with teaching methodologies and technologies, allows students of a non-mathematical science to better learn mathematics (Marchisio et al., 2022).

The use of technologies and specifically mathematical software, such as advanced computing environments (ACE), e.g., Maple, can facilitate the development of problem-solving skills thanks to the opportunity of symbolic and numerical calculation, graphical representations, and interactivity (Fissore et al., 2021), which lift students from mere mechanical computation in favour of deeper understanding. As highlighted in (Fissore et al., 2021), students perceive that engaging with contextualised mathematical problems makes the subject more relevant and applicable to real-life situations. This perceived relevance fosters a deeper understanding and equips them with versatile problem-solving skills to better address future challenges.

3. RESEARCH CONTEXT: THE DIMAS PROJECT

The DIMAS project, in which our experimentation took place, aims to address the challenges of teaching and learning Mathematics in digital environments within the security and defence area. Despite the methodological and technological potential of these educational formats, student engagement remains limited in the currently implemented teaching methodologies. Given the key role of Mathematics across all disciplines—including security and defence—enhancing mathematical competence is crucial for improving educational outcomes and employability. Specifically, the project aims to foster interest in Mathematics by designing more accessible problems and relatable applications using contemporary digital tools. The initial phases of the project have included surveys to identify needs and define key mathematical areas relevant to defence and security, as well as students' and teachers' attitudes (Marchisio Conte et al., 2025). This information shaped the creation of real-world problem scenarios, followed by the use of digital mathematics tools for analysis and training. A series of learning, teaching, and training activities (LTTAs) will be used to test this methodology. Outputs of the project include a handbook of scenarios, interactive materials, and pilot courses to support both teachers and learners.

3.1 The Learning, Teaching and Training Activity

We now present the event in which we developed our research. Planned as the second learning, teaching, and training activity of the project DIMAS, after a first event taking place in Athens during the summer of 2024 and limited to teachers, this LTTA #2 was conducted in Warsaw from the 19th to the 23rd of May, 2025, involving 16 students and 13 instructors coming from the partner institutions. The title of the initiative, "Course-specific digital Math applications", reflects what we proposed to learners during that week: a series of scenarios where they had to apply mathematical concepts to problems in the military setting with the support of digital tools. Specifically, students worked on scenarios related to logistics, military leadership, electronic warfare and cybersecurity, artificial intelligence, and technical systems, all of which tailored to the area of security and defence. These settings were prepared by the various partners participating in the project, with students working on them in international groups, fostering proficient collaboration from both educational and transversal perspectives. The digital support included a dedicated digital learning environment and specific software devoted to Mathematics, such as Maple and Matlab, along with more generalist programs (e.g., Microsoft Excel). Students were able to arrive in Poland prepared for the activities thanks to an introductory online meeting held a week before the beginning of the event, where they were instructed about its goals and activities.

4. RESEARCH QUESTION AND METHODOLOGY

Inspired by the opportunities enabled by the DIMAS project and the relative LTTA #2, we were interested in providing an answer to the following research question (RQ): *how can scenario-based learning be beneficial in fostering interest in Mathematics and the ability to apply its concepts in practice, with a proper support from methodologies and digital technologies?* Aiming at evaluating the factors implied by this RQ, we followed a twofold path. On the one hand, we proposed to students a survey assessing quantitative and qualitative features, acting in accordance with a mixed method research approach (Creswell and Plano-Clark, 2017). In particular, our interest is focused on factors we were able to compare between an initial and a final questionnaire, administered respectively before and after the LTTA. For the quantitative part, we employed a 5-point Likert scale, where 1 represented the lowest possible score and 5 represented the highest. The numerical data were then analysed by means of both descriptive and inferential methods, looking for statistical significance of the variations by computing proper p-values. On the other hand, we collected observations about how students worked during the event, discussing it in relation to their commitment and the goals of the LTTA. These findings were linked to the qualitative part of the final questionnaire, aiming at comparing our perceptions as researchers with students' impressions. Despite having 16 students participating in the event, our samples for the two paths are slightly smaller because not all students filled both questionnaires or took part in every scenario. However, these samples include international participants, with about one-third of women, an expected proportion in a military setting, where the share of women has been constantly increasing over time. Specifically:

- for the quantitative inquiry, the sample size is 14 (9 males, 5 females), of which 5 from Greece, 3 from Poland, 2 from Bulgaria, 2 from Italy, and 2 from Romania;
- for the inquiry with the observations, the sample size is again 14 and has the same gender distribution, but with 6 students from Greece and 2 from Poland.

Additionally, all the people in the latter group but one responded to the final questionnaire (the exception is a Greek student), resulting in 13 students eligible for comparisons between our perceptions and theirs.

5. RESULTS AND DISCUSSION

Let us start from some aspects we asked students to evaluate both before and after the event. In a first question, learners were invited to express their agreement with the following statements related to learning Mathematics, and ranging from interest to usefulness and engagement:

- (1A) I am interested in the things I learn in Mathematics
- (1B) Learning Mathematics is worthwhile for me because it will improve my career (prospects, chances)
- (1C) I think Mathematics is useful to learn
- (1D) Using real-world scenarios can enhance my understanding and engagement with mathematical concepts

Table 1 shows the differences in evaluations relative to the two moments, by considering the 14 students answering both questionnaires. Here and in the subsequent tables, we computed the p-value by performing an exact Wilcoxon-Pratt signed-rank test, on the paired data.

Table 1. Evaluation of agreement with statements concerning learning Mathematics

Item	Avg. before	Std. before	Avg. after	Std. after	Diff. in avg.	p-value
1A	4.00	0.68	4.29	0.83	0.29	0.109
1B	3.79	0.43	4.14	0.86	0.35	0.063
1C	4.00	0.68	4.71	0.47	0.71	0.004
1D	4.07	0.47	4.57	0.51	0.50	0.046

We observe that the ratings were generally high before the event, but increased even further after the LTTA, with the increments showing some statistical significance: moderate in the case of the first two items and marked in the case of the latter ones. This suggests that the event served as a catalyst in boosting these positive perceptions of Mathematics, which were already present to a certain extent before the LTTA. In a subsequent question, we invited students to assess how they agreed with a list of statements regarding problem solving and critical thinking, reading as follows; Table 2 displays their results:

- (2A) When confronted with a problem, I give up easily
- (2B) When confronted with a problem, I do more than what is expected of me
- (2C) I put off difficult problems

- (2D) I like to solve complex problems
- (2E) I often find myself questioning things I hear or read in courses to decide if I find them convincing
- (2F) When a theory, interpretation, or conclusion is presented in class or in the readings, I try to decide if there is good supporting evidence
- (2G) I treat the class material as a starting point and try to develop my own ideas about it
- (2H) I try to play around with ideas of my own related to what I am learning in courses

Table 2. Evaluation of agreement with statements concerning problem solving and critical thinking

Item	Avg. before	Std. before	Avg. after	Std. after	Diff. in avg.	p-value
2A	2.00	0.96	1.50	0.52	-0.50	0.047
2B	3.50	1.02	3.93	0.83	0.43	0.063
2C	2.43	1.16	2.21	0.97	-0.22	0.344
2D	3.71	0.91	4.07	0.73	0.36	0.031
2E	3.43	1.02	3.43	0.85	0.00	-
2F	3.50	0.94	3.64	0.74	0.14	0.344
2G	3.64	0.84	3.86	0.77	0.22	0.188
2H	3.50	0.85	3.86	0.86	0.36	0.094

Here, we detected scores slightly lower than those regarding learning Mathematics, but again, the event allowed students to improve their feelings about it. Note that two items, i.e. (2A) and (2C), corresponded to statements formulated negatively: the best outcomes occur if learners *do not* give up easily and *do not* put off problems, so the LTTA decreasing their ratings consisted of a positive effect. The only exception to these improvements lies in item (2E), where it seems that the event did not particularly impact that aspect. Under the inferential point of view, the most significant variations were observed among the items in the first half, which refer to problem solving, rather than those in the second half, referring to critical thinking. This can be a consequence of the fact that it could be faster to reevaluate the insights about the former with respect to the same concerning the latter, given the LTTA duration. Another question related to problem solving asked to rate typical actions performed while implementing a resolution process, with students being asked to provide a score about their consideration for each of the following ones, and Table 3 collecting the results:

- (3A) Creating a list of steps to solve it
- (3B) Using math
- (3C) Trying to simplify the problem by ignoring details that are not needed
- (3D) Looking for patterns in the problem
- (3E) Breaking the problem into smaller parts
- (3F) Working with others to solve different parts of the problem at the same time
- (3G) Looking at how information can be collected, stored, and analysed to help solve the problem
- (3H) Creating a solution where steps can be repeated
- (3I) Creating a solution where some steps are implemented only in certain situations

Table 3. Evaluation of actions typically performed when solving a problem

Item	Avg. before	Std. before	Avg. after	Std. after	Diff. in avg.	p-value
3A	3.79	0.58	3.79	0.89	0.00	-
3B	3.71	0.61	3.93	0.47	0.22	0.227
3C	4.00	0.78	3.93	1.00	-0.07	0.227
3D	3.92	0.47	4.14	0.53	0.22	0.250
3E	4.14	0.53	4.14	0.36	0.00	-
3F	3.50	0.65	3.43	1.40	-0.07	0.488
3G	3.79	0.70	4.07	0.62	0.28	0.156
3H	3.86	0.53	3.64	0.74	-0.22	0.266
3I	3.64	0.63	3.64	0.74	0.00	-

These findings show a less noticeable impact of the event on the actions students used to solve problems. Some more generic items such as using math (3B), looking for patterns (3D) and information handling (3G) saw a slight increase in the scores with low statistical significance, while more specific ones as listing steps (3A), applying *divide et impera* (3E) and devising conditional steps (3I) remained basically unchanged after the LTTA; furthermore, the other three items had their score decreased, albeit slightly and not significantly. While this can be mitigated by the fact that the starting scores were in general higher than those in Table 2, the results suggest that the event was more successful in enhancing students' mindset toward solving problems, rather than in acting on the ways they actually solve them. We also highlight that these items refer to computational thinking (CT) in problem solving, and we did not develop activities specifically targeted to fostering CT, so some selective improvements can be deemed as already satisfactory. A final quantitative question concerned the benefits of using technology while doing Mathematics, by looking again for students' agreement with some statements on the topic, which follow along with the relative results in Table 4:

- (4A) Using technology is beneficial during Mathematics activities
- (4B) Using specific software for solving mathematical case studies is beneficial
- (4C) Using artificial intelligence digital tools is beneficial to solve mathematical case studies

Table 4. Evaluation of agreement with statements concerning the use of technology in Mathematics

Item	Avg. before	Std. before	Avg. after	Std. after	Diff. in avg.	p-value
4A	4.14	0.77	4.36	0.50	0.22	0.281
4B	4.07	0.83	4.50	0.52	0.43	0.055
4C	3.93	0.83	3.79	0.80	-0.14	0.340

It can be seen that the scores relative to the use of technology in a generic sense and to the usage of specific software devoted to Mathematics increased after LTTA, the latter with statistical significance, while the score associated to using AI digital tools slightly decreased. This can have a twofold explanation: on the one hand, the activities of the event considered artificial intelligence (a scenario was explicitly devoted to its use in security and defence), but to a lesser extent with respect to mathematical software, so students were less prone to give credit to AI. On the other hand, AI tools are still a novelty compared to other digital instruments, thus hindering at least a bit the students from fully understanding their potential.

We will now report direct observations of the researchers for the scenarios for military leadership, specifically focused on game theory, to have insights into how students approached problem-solving tasks in a progressively structured sequence within a scenario-based learning framework. 14 students took part in this activity, 9 males and 5 females. They were divided into four groups (A, B, C, and D), which were heterogeneously composed in terms of nationality, i.e., in each group, all participants came from different countries, except two groups with two students from Greece which were the two groups composed by four people instead of three, and each group had at least one woman. Each task was performed using Maple. Only the basics of Maple were used, as the majority of students had never used it before: the intent of this activity was also to introduce students to this ACE. The activity was implemented in two phases: a first phase led by the instructors, which alternated theoretical parts with group work, and a second phase consisting of group work in the independent resolution of a scenario similar to the one presented in the first phase.

The first phase began with a contextual introduction that utilised real-world examples from newspaper articles, effectively capturing students' attention and supporting the relevance of the topic. This preparatory phase encouraged students to engage with the topic of game theory and its usability, as a connection to real life can be perceived as positive (Usta and Söylemez, 2020). The first theoretical concepts were then introduced, presenting the *battle of the sexes*, a classical game theory example. A first task was proposed in which the students had to "play" a game contextualised in the Marshall Plan, which is relevant in the security and defence context. Students engaged in the initial game activity without any prior knowledge of strategic concepts such as Nash equilibria or other formal approaches. The outcomes varied across groups, but in several cases students demonstrated an intuitive approach to informal problem-solving strategies in the absence of explicit instruction. The Nash equilibria were then introduced. A second task was proposed, in which students were presented with a specific situation related to the Marshall Plan. They were asked to construct the corresponding payoff matrix and identify any Nash equilibria. Groups A, B, and C successfully built a consistent payoff matrix and correctly identified the equilibrium. In contrast, Group D did not construct an accurate matrix, as they failed to recognise the relevant information in the task premises.

This divergence highlights how students' interpretation of contextual information can impact their ability to model a strategic situation correctly. Lecturers then introduced Pareto optimality, followed by a third task designed to allow students to explore these concepts using interactive components designed by instructors in Maple. The activity then progressed to a fourth task, in which students were asked to play based on a given payoff matrix. This task functioned as a conceptual trap: in reality, the most convenient solution could only be identified through the use of mixed strategies. These become necessary, particularly in the absence of Nash equilibria derived from pure strategies, and are also relevant when multiple equilibria are present, as in the case of the battle of the sexes. Group responses to this task revealed different levels of understanding. Groups A and D concluded that no Nash equilibrium existed in the matrix. Group C correctly (and intuitively) identified the Pareto optima, while Group B reported that they could not clearly determine what might happen because they did not know the context. Despite the apparent uncertainty, Group B accurately identified the absence of a clear strategy for decision-making—an observation that anticipated the formal introduction of mixed strategies. Following this, the theoretical foundations of mixed strategies were presented, and students were asked to re-perform Task 4 using this new knowledge. Group A arrived at the correct solution, probably through intuition, because they did not set up the correct system of equations to implement mixed strategies, while trying to apply the principle of indifference of expected payoff. During the class discussion, it emerged that groups had found one equation but had overlooked the second, which requires that the sum of the probabilities relative to the two playable actions equals one ($p + p' = 1$). With guidance from the instructors, the groups successfully completed the system and reached a consistent solution. The whole-class discussion revealed a general misunderstanding regarding mixed strategies: the instructors revised the explanation and presented the correct system more explicitly to boost students' comprehension. These observations underscore how scenario-based learning, especially when involving progressively structured problem-solving tasks, can reveal both students' intuitive reasoning processes and the conceptual difficulties that arise without adequate scaffolding (Zhou et al., 2024). The episode also illustrates the value of classroom discussion in diagnosing misunderstandings and adapting instructions in real time, as well as the relevance of student-centred activities to improve the learning process (Aslan, 2019).

The second phase then began, in which the groups worked independently on tasks assigned using Maple to solve them: two groups worked on a scenario based on the Battle of Leuctra, and two groups on a scenario related to an underhand deal. The groups had one and a half hours to work independently on the assigned tasks. At the end of the group work, a class presentation and discussion of the results took place. From the discussion, the students' comprehension of the topic presented clearly emerged.

The impressions from students further support these observations. In a qualitative question from the final questionnaire, we asked them to explain their views and motivations concerning appreciation, effectiveness, and relevance of the game theory scenario. Some noteworthy responses were:

- "The real-life scenarios helped me visualise math problems. Game theory scenarios were well constructed and made learning different concepts much easier. Translating real-life scenarios into numbers was much easier than understanding the material while using raw numbers."
- "The scenario provided a clear and practical framework for applying key game theory concepts such as payoff matrices, Nash equilibrium, and dominant strategies. Working through real decisions and outcomes helped consolidate theoretical knowledge."
- "I believe I learned the mathematical topics covered in the game theory-related scenario to a great extent because the structure and content were clear and well-presented. The tasks helped me understand key concepts and apply them in a meaningful context."

As it can be seen from the students' answers, they recognised how working with the scenario was helpful in providing a better understanding under various directions, ranging from being more able to handle the theory to managing numbers and concepts in the proper ways. Feedback from other qualitative questions in the same questionnaire confirms what emerged in the above question.

Summing all up, according to the results obtained from the quantitative analysis, this activity showed that the scenario-based learning approach—structured around significant contexts, problem-solving activities, and the integration of digital tools—can effectively support both conceptual understanding and active engagement. This is in line with existing literature, e.g. (Aslan, 2019; Hassan et al., 2023), which, however, only focuses on first-level education. The use of progressively challenging tasks encouraged students to develop and refine their strategies, moving from intuitive reasoning to formalised mathematical thinking.

Moreover, the digital components of the activities allowed for dynamic interaction with the content, promoting experimentation, immediate feedback, and collaborative exploration. These findings suggest that scenario-based learning, when combined with problem solving and technology-enhanced environments, can foster deeper learning and enhance students' ability to apply mathematical concepts in real-world situations. Furthermore, the impact of these outcomes can be extended far beyond the security and defence setting, since the features allowing for prompting the presented benefits are not exclusive to that premise. Indeed, the approach can be generalized to other settings characterized by interdisciplinarity and practical applicability, sharing these traits with military education but possibly being themselves not related at all to armed forces.

6. CONCLUSIONS AND FUTURE WORK

This research allowed us to explore how scenario-based learning, equipped with a proper support from methodologies and digital technologies, can be beneficial in fostering interest in Mathematics and the ability to apply its concepts in practice, thus generally answering the research question. We found out how setting up several scenarios as part of a learning, teaching, and training activity planned inside a project devoted to dealing with the challenges of Mathematics didactics in digital environments, and contextualizing them in the security and defence area, given the nature of the program, generally incremented students' ratings of many aspects related to learning Mathematics and using methodologies and technologies, in several cases with important statistical significance. At the same time, both researchers' and students' perceptions agreed on the benefits this methodology provides in different areas, and translating into a better understanding and handling of mathematical concepts and methods, along with their implementation in concrete practical applications. As limitations, it should be noted that we based our analysis on a moderate size sample; furthermore, since the LTTA took place during this year, we were not able to collect evidence of long-term benefits. This suggests, as future work, to perform analogous inquiries on events involving a larger number of participants, provided that similar modalities and the same attention to the various needs are preserved. Concerning the legacy of this event, it will be possible to assess its impact over a broader timespan by tracking the proficiency of the students participating over time and comparing it with their peers not taking part in the LTTA, with the latter substantially acting as a group control. Another direction toward which this research can be expanded is exploring in more detail why gains in critical thinking were less significant compared to other ones, see Table 2 and its relative commentary. A way to perform this exploration can consist of designing tasks that explicitly require evidence evaluation and reasoning, in addition to problem solving. Namely, structured debates may be introduced, requiring students to defend or challenge mathematical models with evidence, and reflective essays or learning journals could also be used. These tasks would push students to justify their choices, test the strength of their assumptions, and consider alternative approaches: for our purposes, embedding such elements in scenario-based learning would make evidence evaluation a deliberate part of the problem solving process. Finally, since Table 4 showed us that students perceived less benefit from AI-based tools than from traditional mathematical software, it would be valuable to design future scenarios by making AI indispensable for their handling. To make two distinct examples, AI-driven simulations could model cybersecurity attacks, or large language models could be used to generate alternative solving strategies for students to evaluate. In this way, AI would not only support problem solving but also require students to judge the validity, reliability, and ethical aspects of AI-generated solutions.

ACKNOWLEDGEMENTS

The research activity described in this paper was carried out within the Erasmus+ Key Action 2 Strategic Partnership N. 2023-1-BG01-KA220-HED-000156664 "Digital Mathematics Applied in Defence and Security Education – DIMAS"; the GNSAGA group of INDAM – "Istituto Nazionale di Alta Matematica Francesco Severi"; the National Recovery and Resilience Plan (NRRP), D.M. 118/2023 by the Italian Ministry of University and Research (MUR), funded by the European Union–NextGenerationEU; and the project EDVANCE – Digital Education Hub per la Cultura Digitale Avanzata, funded by the European Union-NextGenerationEU, Componente 1, Investimento 3.4 "Didattica e competenze universitarie avanzate".

REFERENCES

Altıntaş, E. et al. (2023). Scenario-based teaching in teaching algebra in gifted education. *In Journal of Gifted Education and Creativity*, Vol. 10, pp. 345–366.

Aslan, S. (2019). The impact of argumentation-based teaching and scenario-based learning method on the students' academic achievement. *In Journal of Baltic Science Education*, Vol. 18, No. 2, pp. 171–183. https://doi.org/10.33225/jbse/19.18.171

Barana, A. et al. (2023). Fostering problem solving and critical thinking in mathematics through generative artificial intelligence. *In Proceedings of the 20th International Conference on Cognition and Exploratory Learning in Digital Age (CELDA 2023)*. Madeira Island, Portugal, pp. 377–385.

Barana, A. et al. (2024). Detecting blended learning, collaborative learning and internationalisation in military education: a systematic literature review. *In Proceedings of the 18th International Conferences E-Learning and Digital Learning 2024 and Sustainability, Technology and Education 2024*. Budapest, Hungary, pp. 137–144.

Cirneanu, A.-L. and Moldoveanu, C.-E. (2024). Use of Digital Technology in Integrated Mathematics Education. *In Applied System Innovation*, Vol. 7, No. 4, 66. https://doi.org/10.3390/asi7040066

Creswell, J.W. and Plano-Clark, V.L. (2017). *Designing and Conducting Mixed Methods Research, 3rd edition*. Sage Publications, Thousand Oaks, USA.

Engelbrecht, J. and Borba, M.C. (2024). Recent developments in using digital technology in mathematics education. *In ZDM Mathematics Education*, Vol. 56, No. 2, pp. 281–292. https://doi.org/10.1007/s11858-023-01530-2

Fissore, C. et al. (2020). Digital competences for educators in the Italian secondary school: a comparison between DigCompEdu reference framework and the PP&S project experience. *In International Conference E-Learning 2020*. Zagreb, Croatia, pp. 47–54. https://doi.org/10.33965/el2020_202007L006

Fissore, C. et al. (2021). Development of Problem Solving Skills with Maple in Higher Education. *In Corless, R.M., Gerhard, J., Kotsireas, I.S. (Eds.), Maple in Mathematics Education and Research. MC 2020, Communications in Computer and Information Science*, Vol. 1414, pp. 219–233. https://doi.org/10.1007/978-3-030-81698-8_15

Hassan, A.K. et al. (2023). The Impact of a Scenario-Based Learning Model in Mathematics Achievement and Mental Motivation for High School Students. *In International Journal of Emerging Technologies in Learning (iJET)*, Vol. 18, No. 7, pp. 103–115. https://doi.org/10.3991/ijet.v18i07.39263

Marchisio, M. et al. (2022). Teaching Mathematics to Non-Mathematics Majors through Problem Solving and New Technologies. *In Education Sciences*, Vol. 12, No. 1, pp. 34–51. https://doi.org/10.3390/educsci12010034

Marchisio Conte, M. et al. (2025). Empowering Mathematics education in security and defence: technological tools and methodological strategies for motivation enhancement. *In IEEE 49th Annual Computers, Software, and Applications Conference (COMPSAC)*. Toronto, Canada, pp. 131-140. https://doi.org/10.1109/COMPSAC65507.2025.00025

Molina-Toro, J.F. et al. (2019). Research Trends in Digital Technologies and Modeling in Mathematics Education. *In EURASIA Journal of Mathematics, Science and Technology Education*, Vol. 15, No. 8, em1736. https://doi.org/10.29333/ejmste/108438

Partnership for 21st Century Skills, (2009). *P21 framework definitions*. Washington, DC, USA. Available at: http://www.battelleforkids.org/networks/p21

Usta, N. and Söylemez, S. (2020). Effectiveness of Utilizing Scenario-Based Instruction to Teach" Functions" to High School Students in Mathematics Classes. *In International Online Journal of Education and Teaching*, Vol. 7, No. 4, pp. 1791–1821.

Vuorikari, R. et al. (2022). DigComp 2.2 - the Digital Competence Framework for Citizens: with new examples of knowledge, skills and attitudes, EUR. Publications Office of the European Union, Luxembourg. https://doi.org/10.2760/115376

Zhou, L. et al. (2024). Scenario-Based Teaching Enhances Mathematical Core Competencies—A Study on Cultivating Mathematical Thinking Ability of Middle School Students under the Background of the New Curriculum Standards. *Proceedings of the 2024 5th International Conference on Mental Health, Education and Human Development (MHEHD 2024)*. Kaifeng, China, pp. 758–772.

LECTURE AS CODE: A DEVOPS-DRIVEN TEACHING APPROACH FOR AI-SUPPORTED LEARNING

Nane Kratzke[1]
University of Applied Sciences Lübeck, Institute for Interactive Systems (ISy)
Mönkhofer Weg 239, 23562 Lübeck, Germany

ABSTRACT

Background: Traditional methods of managing educational materials are repetitive and often lack scalability. Integrating DevOps principles into educational content creation would provide a more streamlined approach to delivery.
Objective: This solution proposal report shares initial experiences and introduces the concept of Lecture as Code (LaC), which applies DevOps practices such as version control, automation, modularity, and scalability to educational content management.
Methods: Using tools like Markdown, Kubernetes, and AI-driven technologies such as Large Language Models and AI frameworks like Langchain and Chainlit, LaC automates content creation, delivery, and chatbot integration for interactive student support.
Results: Evaluation across computer science courses showed increased student engagement, reduced teaching time, and consistent content quality. Automated Item Generation (AIG) and chatbot support led to higher weekly participation and lowered dropout rates to below 13%.

KEYWORDS

Lecture as Code, DevOps, Education, Automation, Automated Item Generation, AIG, AI in Teaching, Adaptive Learning, Chatbot Integration, AI-powered Education Tools

1. INTRODUCTION

The digitalization of education and the integration of artificial intelligence (AI) have opened up new possibilities for the efficient creation, management, and scaling of teaching materials. This paper presents an exploratory investigation into the novel application of DevOps principles within the educational domain—an area that remains somewhat uncharted in academic research. By conceptualizing educational content as code, the proposed Lecture-as-Code (LaC) framework offers a novel and maybe thought-provoking approach to creating, managing, and deploying teaching materials. The paradigm enables automation, modularity, and version control in developing educational resources, aligning instructional design with modern software engineering practices. The aim is to relieve teachers of redundant tasks, ensure consistent quality of materials, and enable adaptive learning for students. LaC applies DevOps principles (Leite, et al., 2019) (Jabbari, et al., 2016) to create, manage, and deploy educational content. At its core, LaC treats teaching materials—such as slides, videos, tests, and chatbot interactions—as code, which can be versioned, modularized, and automated. The approach leverages tools and practices from software development and IT operations to streamline the production and maintenance of educational resources. The key principles include:

- Educational content is managed through version control systems, which enable change tracking, collaborative editing, and rollback capabilities.
- Automation: Deployment pipelines are used to automatically generate and update content, such as screencasts, slides, tests, and bots

[1] nane.kratzke@th-luebeck.de

- Modularity: Content is broken down into reusable modules, allowing educators to combine and repurpose them efficiently

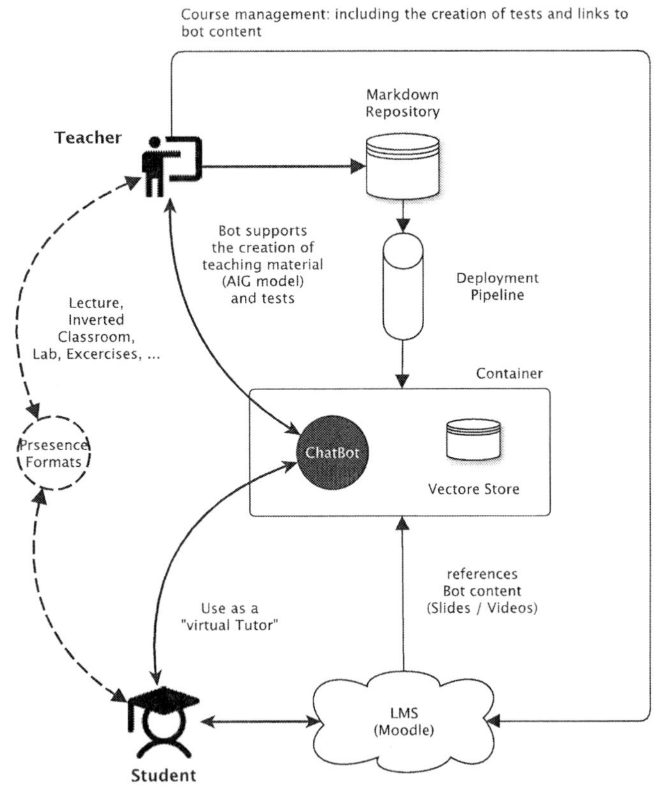

Figure 1. AI-based Automated Item Generation Architecture

The guiding research question of this paper aimed to gain and report on **practical experience** with the Lecture-as-Code (LaC) approach: ***How can the application of DevOps principles to educational content creation be practically implemented in a real-world teaching environment, and what initial effects does it have on teacher workload and student engagement?***

The concept of Lecture-as-Code can be viewed as a modern application of Automated Item Generation (AIG), introduced in the 1960s (Bormuth, 1970). While Bormuth's work mainly centered on the systematic automation of test item creation, recent advancements in DevOps practices and AI language models (such as GPT, Codex, and Copilot) have broadened the scope well beyond testing. Lecture-as-Code applies these core DevOps principles to developing, maintaining, and deploying comprehensive educational resources, including lecture materials, course content, interactive learning tools, and tests. By incorporating AI-powered tools into this framework, Lecture-as-Code not only automates and scales educational content production but also updates Bormuth's original vision, turning the creation of educational materials into a structured and scalable process. This method connects educational theories from the mid-20th century with modern software engineering practices, addressing a wider range of teaching and learning needs.

2. RELATED WORK

Especially, Automated Item Generation (AIG) is not a new concept (Haladyna, 2012) and was first introduced by John R. Bormuth in the 1960s (Bormuth, 1970). However, modern language models such as GPT have significantly improved the efficiency and quality of generating educational and assessment content (Circi et al., 2023). Similar approaches to automating teaching materials can also be seen in projects like OpenAI's Codex and GitHub Copilot. The use of ChatBots in teaching has also been examined in various studies—both before the launch of ChatGPT (Okonkwo & Ade-Ibijola, 2021; Wollny et al., 2021) and afterward (Hwang & Chang, 2023)—to name a few recent examples. However, little research has been done on the intersection of DevOps and education. Most studies focus on how to teach DevOps and what needs to be considered for teaching it (Fernandes et al., 2022; Pang et al., 2020; Fernandes et al., 2020). The author is only aware of two studies (Airaj, 2017; Mekic et al., 2024) that use DevOps to make teaching more efficient, as in this case. But even in (Mekic et al., 2024), the focus was on a DevOps curriculum. In other words, most research views DevOps as something to be taught rather than a tool to achieve other educational goals.

3. SOLUTION PROPOSAL

The idea presented in this paper is based on applying principles from Infrastructure as Code (IaC) to teaching, which at first seem to have little in common. Infrastructure as Code (IaC) involves managing and provisioning infrastructure through configuration files that machines can interpret (Rahman, et al., 2019), instead of manual hardware setup or interactive configuration tools. It depends on machine virtualization—a form of automation that is just as hard to automate as teaching, where, in an educational setting, "generative AI" can serve as this virtualization role. Markdown functions as the main format for describing teaching content (in fact, we can see Markdown as a unique kind of machine-readable setup), which can then be automatically transformed into different media formats.

- **Slides**: Generation of presentations from Markdown documents.
- **Screencasts** and **videos**: Automatic creation of educational videos based on Markdown documents.
- **Bots**: AI-supported tutor systems designed to assist students through ChatBots using a retrieval-augmented generation (RAG) approach (Gao et al., 2023).
- **Tests**: Automated creation of test questions through ChatBots utilizing large language models.

The infrastructure relies on containers, deployment pipelines, and AI-supported processing systems orchestrated through Kubernetes (Carrion, 2022) in a cloud-native manner (Kratzke, 2023). The architecture shown in Figure 1 demonstrates this AI-supported teaching framework based on modern software engineering principles, integrating automation and flexibility in delivering educational content. It includes the components and technologies listed in Table 1.

Table 1. Overview of applied technologies, tools, and frameworks used for different components of the architecture

Technology	Tool/Framework	Remarks
Content creation	GitLab (git)	Version Control System
	VSCode	Code / Content editor
	Markdown	Lightweight Markup Language
	MARP Plugin	VSCode Plugin for the Markdown presentation system
Slide+Video generation	MARP	Markdown Presentation System
	MoviePy	Python library for video editing
	OpenAI TTS-1-HD	Text-to-Speech (OpenAI)
Bot generation	Python	Programming Language
	Chainlit	Python library to implement conversational AI agents
	Langchain	A composable library to integrate LLMs into AI apps
	OpenAI GPT-4o-mini	Large-language model (OpenAI)
Vector Store	Chroma	AI-native vector database for semantic retrieval of documents
	OpenAI Embeddings (Ada-002)	Numerical representations of texts for semantic retrieval
	Document Loader (pyMuPDF)	Load PDF documents into LangChain Document format
Bot deployment	Orchestration	Kubernetes (Container Orchestration)
	Container	Docker (Container Image Building)
	Continuous Deploymement	GitLab Pipelines (automatic deployment of bot/content updates)
LMS	Moodle	Learning Management System

Educator Workflow and Content Creation: Educators play a key role in the initial stages by developing educational materials, including lecture content and assessments, within a *code repository* (Markdown repository). The Markdown content can be created and versioned using standard code editors. We have had excellent experiences with the combination of VSCode, MARP, and Git (see also Figure 3). This repository serves as a structured, version-controlled storage system for all course materials, aligning with *Infrastructure as Code* (IaC) principles. The Markdown repository functions as an *Automated Item Generation (AIG)* model, producing content and assessments that are processed through a *Deployment Pipeline* for seamless delivery and integration into both online and physical learning environments.

Content Delivery and AI Integration: After content passes through the deployment pipeline, it is containerized and stored in a *Vector Store*. This store enables efficient storage and retrieval of structured educational resources, such as slides, videos, and other text-based content. A *ChatBot* connects to the Vector Store, acting as a *virtual tutor* for students and a *teaching assistant* for educators. The chatbot uses AI capabilities to answer questions, provide support, and deliver relevant educational content interactively. It can be enhanced with external materials like textbooks or supplementary resources (see Figure 2), expanding its knowledge base and support capabilities. Additionally, the ChatBot can be configured with different profiles to assist with content revision, answer questions, and offer practice materials. It can also help educators create and validate test content. Students can use the ChatBot for practice, exam preparation, and self-assessment. These customizable features offer a flexible, goal-oriented approach to using ChatBots, catering to the diverse needs of students and educators. Based on the teaching materials provided and semantically indexed in the Vector Store, the ChatBot can identify gaps in its knowledge base and either decline assistance or refer to specialized ChatBots configured for specific tasks. This ChatBot's "character" can be set up using a simple text-based format (YAML, see Listing 1 and 2 in the Appendix).

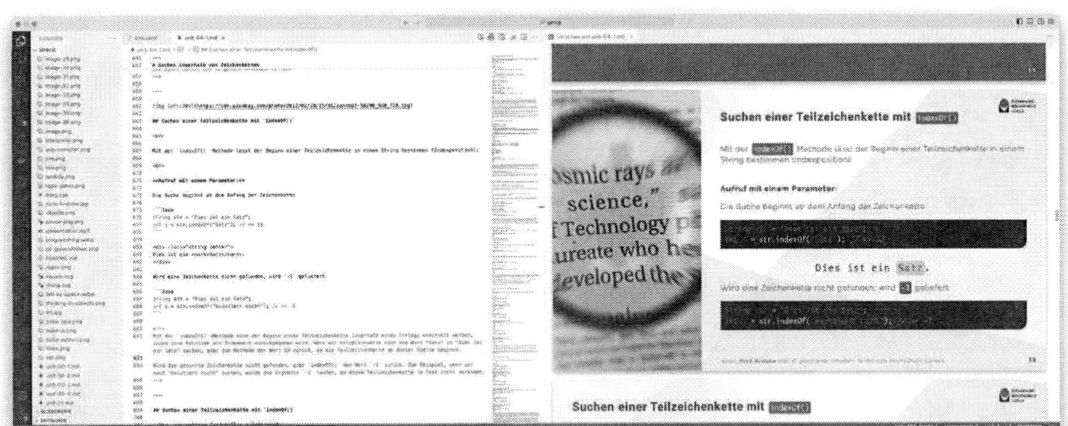

Figure 2. llustrative screenshot of the Markdown editor (from the teacher's perspective). On the left is the Markdown code; on the right is the rendered result. Comments in Markdown (marked in green) are interpreted as speech text and can be used to generate videos with a text-to-speech engine. We used VSCode with the MARP (Marp-Team, 2024) and Git plugins. Other editors and plugin combinations are possible and depend on the educators' preferences

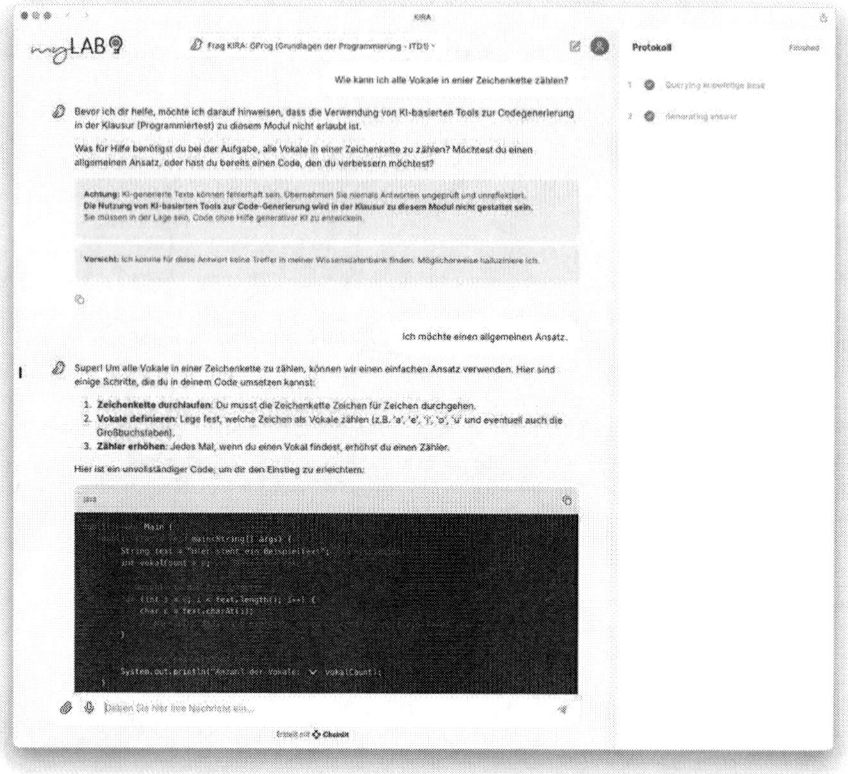

Figure 3. Illustrative screenshot of the ChatBot (student default profile for a beginner programming course, in German)

Learning Management System (LMS) Integration: The content stored in the vector database and accessed through the chatbot can be linked to a *Learning Management System* (LMS), such as *Moodle*. As a result, established LMS platforms can still serve as the main hub for delivering structured materials, assessments, and multimedia content to students. Students can access the chatbot via a designated link on their learning platform. This resource can be used during various classroom activities, including lectures, group discussions, workshops, and practical exercises, to increase engagement and support learning. The chatbot is designed to provide ongoing assistance, customize learning experiences to individual needs, and grant access to relevant content as needed.

Learner Interaction and Feedback Loop: When students use the chatbot as a *virtual tutor* to access course content and ask questions, traditional face-to-face teaching methods work alongside the AI-based approach, creating a comprehensive learning experience. This interaction can be fed back into the repository by the educator, allowing for iterative improvements and updates to course materials based on student performance and feedback.

4. EVALUATION AND RESULTS

This concept has developed gradually and iteratively across various courses, especially in computer science programs at Lübeck University of Applied Sciences. It has been included in small master's programs (Cloud-native Programming and Cloud-native Architectures, 1st and 2nd semesters, since 2021) with about 20 students, as well as in bachelor's programs (Web and Cloud Programming, 4th semester, since 2022) with approximately 70 students. The data used in this study were collected from a bachelor's program in Information Technology and Design (Foundations of Programming, 1st semester) during the winter semester of 2024/25. The course had around 60 students.

Table 2. Course schedule: "Fundamentals of Programming" (Java, Winter Semester 2024/25)

Week	Topics
40	*Administration (not covered by this study)*
41	Introduction to Programming and **Programming Paradigms**
42	**Hello World** (first hands-on programming)
43	**Computational Thinking**
44	**Datatypes** (and most essential operators)
45	**Methods**
46	**Strings** (and first loops)
47	**Arrays** (and first loops in loops)
48	**Operators** and **Expressions** (in-depth)
49	More on **Control-Flow**, **Exceptions** and **Loops** (in-depth)
5ß	(Simple) **Classes**
51	**List** and **Maps**
52 – 01	*Christmas holidays (not covered by this study)*
02 – 04	*Test-Exam, Wrap-Up (not covered by this study)*
05	*Exam (Final Programming-Test, not covered by this study)*

The course was structured as an inverted classroom: students received weekly content (see Table 2) in the form of slides and automatically generated videos. This content was reinforced during a weekly lecture, which featured concrete programming tasks in an inverted classroom style, enabling students to work on these tasks. The lecture duration was reduced from 90 to 60 minutes because participants had to review the content beforehand. Each week's content was assessed via weekly Moodle tests (multiple-choice), which contributed a small portion to the final grade (about 2.5%). A practical programming course was held simultaneously, where students completed three to four programming tasks weekly and could ask questions during scheduled practical sessions. Students also had access to a ChatBot that stored the module's content (slides and programming textbooks available online from the university library) in its knowledge base. The ChatBot could be used to help solve tasks in both the practical course and the inverted classroom.

The acceptance of AI-generated videos varied significantly. Videos (not necessarily AI-generated) were much better accepted in higher semesters, as shown by the confidential evaluation feedback for those courses. Overall, in the first semester, such videos should only serve as a supplement at most, and the content should always be explicitly discussed in weekly face-to-face classes or flipped classroom sessions. Reducing lecture time from 90 to 60 minutes was more of a hindrance in this context. However, an important benefit of incorporating AI into teaching was the reduced lecture time, which created opportunities for more interactive formats like the flipped classroom model. Additionally, the weekly Moodle tests, which were also generated by AI, showed an unexpectedly high level of continuous participation. We will focus more on these tests in the discussion, as they provide more reliable data and are less influenced by subjective impressions.

5. DISCUSSION

Figure 4 (left) shows the number of tests completed throughout the semester, highlighting total completed tests (grey bars) and active participants (dark grey bars). Each student was allowed up to three weekly test attempts, with only the best attempt counting toward their final grade. A total of 885 tests were completed, each consisting of 15 randomly selected questions.

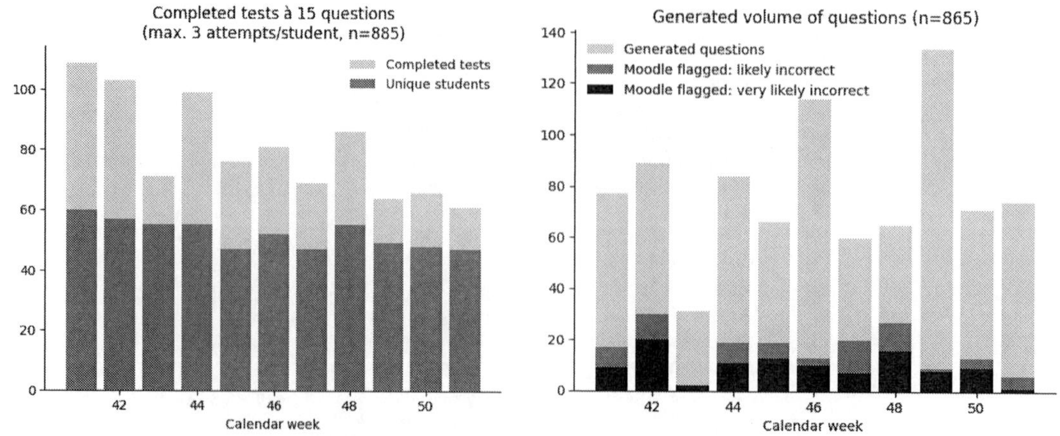

Figure 4. **On the left:** Tests completed during the semester. Test participation remained surprisingly steady, as shown by the dark bars. The first two weeks probably served as a 'settling in' period. However, just before Christmas, interest appeared to decline slightly. **On the right:** Generated questions per calendar week across the lecture topics. A sample review of questions from weeks 42, 45, and 48 (weeks with the highest estimated error rates, according to Moodle) showed that only four of 49 flagged questions (or 8%) were incorrect, which is about 2% of the total question pool for those weeks

The grey bars show the total weekly tests taken, while the dark grey bars represent the number of active participants. Their close alignment indicates strong engagement, as students often make multiple attempts to improve their scores. Overall, Figure 4 emphasizes the effectiveness of automated testing systems in encouraging continuous student participation and establishing structured learning routines. The number of active students dropped from 60 at the start of the semester to 52 by the end. Therefore, this approach fostered consistent study habits and lowered dropout rates to less than 13% by semester's end.

Figure 4 (right) shows the number of AI-generated test questions per calendar week. These questions are categorized into generated questions (grey bars), questions likely to be incorrect (grey bars), or very likely to be incorrect (dark grey bars), as verified by Moodle. Throughout the semester, 865 questions were created, aligned with weekly lecture topics. The Moodle evaluation system assessed question quality using difficulty and discrimination indices to measure clarity, appropriateness, and the ability to distinguish between different student knowledge levels. The number of questions generated was influenced by teacher prompts (e.g., "Create questions about loops in Java") and the system prompt described in Listing 2 (Appendix). This process ensured the questions matched the course topics for each week. The weekly volume of questions varied depending on the complexity and scope of the topics. An evaluation of questions from weeks 42, 45, and 48—weeks with the highest estimated error rates by Moodle—showed that only four out of 49 questions (about 8%) flagged as **incorrect** were actually wrong. This accounts for roughly **2%** of the total questions for those weeks. This low error rate indicates that the AI-generated questions are generally reliable and accurate; however, a human review is recommended to cross-check the questions, given the approximate 2% error rate.

6. THREATS TO VALIDITY AND LIMITATIONS

This study aimed to ensure the reliability and validity of its findings by addressing both internal and external validity concerns. Internal validity was supported by an iterative development process that has been refined over several semesters. By consistently applying the Lecture-as-Code (LaC) methodology across different cohorts and course sizes, the study minimized confounding factors, including curriculum inconsistencies and student biases. External validity was considered by evaluating LaC in various academic settings, including small Master's seminars and large-scale Bachelor's lectures, demonstrating a level of adaptability to different instructional formats. However, several significant limitations must be considered when interpreting the results:

Disciplinary Bias: The current implementation and evaluation focused solely on computer science-related programs. These students typically have a higher tolerance and familiarity with DevOps tools, which may skew the results and limit how well the findings apply to fields that are less centered on technical workflows. However, the chatbot component of the approach is currently (Summer Semester 2025) being evaluated in courses with about 400 students across a range of disciplines, including Analog Electronics, Fundamentals of Technical Optics, User Experience Design, IT Security, and Environmental Simulation during the summer semester of 2025. Unfortunately, due to the editorial deadline, these evaluation results could not be included in this paper.

Technical Barriers: The use of advanced DevOps infrastructure (e.g., Kubernetes, GitLab CI/CD, and vector databases) can create a steep learning curve for non-technical educators, thus limiting the wider adoption of LaC without substantial support, training, or the development of specialized tools that encapsulate all the complexities into an end-user friendly form.

AI Evaluation and Oversight: Although AI-generated test questions were manually reviewed and showed a low error rate (2%), this figure is based on a sample of questions flagged by Moodle (about 8%). Relying on Moodle's internal metrics adds uncertainty. It's still unclear whether Moodle might produce false negatives (i.e., fail to detect flawed AI-generated content). This should be considered when interpreting the error assessment.

Inconclusive Dropout Data: This study observed lower dropout rates compared to previous semesters in non-LaC settings, where rates ranged from 25% to 40%. However, these figures were reconstructed from older data and were not systematically collected. Future research should use more rigorous statistical methods to verify the effect of the LaC approach.

Anecdotal Claims: Several statements throughout the study, such as the different acceptance levels of AI-generated videos or improvements in engagement, are currently anecdotal or based on limited informal feedback (e.g., free-text responses from internal course evaluations). These would benefit from triangulated evidence, such as standardized student surveys, interviews, A/B testing, or pre- and post-assessments.

7. CONCLUSIONS

Despite the limitations mentioned, the exploratory nature of this study offers valuable firsthand insights into the implementation and practical challenges of the Lecture-as-Code paradigm. The findings establish a foundation for future, more rigorous research aimed at refining and expanding this approach. The paper does not fully address non-technical risks related to AI integration, such as ethical issues, potential biases in generated content, data privacy concerns, or the pedagogical effects of automating parts of the learning experience. Future research should explicitly consider these broader factors. For example, in an ongoing evaluation study, we are investigating how bots can be used as AI tutors using the current LaC approach, which has access to teaching materials and employs a Retrieval Augmented Generation (RAG) method.

However, the present study already shows that AI processes improve efficiency but also introduce challenges. **Human oversight remains crucial for quality assurance**. More research is necessary to evaluate acceptance criteria, especially for AI-generated content such as educational videos. The current reliance of the Lecture-as-Code approach on code-focused version control systems increases technical barriers for educators' management and reduces acceptance rates.

The Lecture-as-Code architecture applies DevOps principles to educational content delivery by utilizing version control and CI/CD. By integrating Automated Item Generation (AIG), AI chatbots, and Learning Management System (LMS) platforms, content creation becomes more flexible and scalable from a single Markdown repository. Test generation shows a **2% error rate**, highlighting the need for human oversight while also demonstrating the increasing reliability of the large language models involved. For example, automatic generation of multiple-choice questions for self-assessment supports innovative teaching methods, like flipped classrooms, which boost student engagement. Although it has minimal impact on final grades, 52 out of 60 participants completed the tests, resulting in a **dropout rate of less than 13%**. However, as discussed in the study's limitations, further research is needed to explore the broader applicability of the Lecture-as-Code approach and to enhance its integration with existing educational technologies.

ACKNOWLEDGEMENT

This work was partially funded by the German Federal Ministry of Research, Technology, and Space ('Innovative Hochschule,' support code 03IHS245A). I thank David Engelhardt, Louis Grümmer, Sören Gode, and Kjell Treder for supervising our students in the labs, and Jonas Flodin, Max Sternitzke, and Patrick Willnow for managing our Kubernetes, GitLab, and LLM platform. This study (and many other innovative approaches) would not have been possible without their tireless effort. Additionally, I thank Mathias Beyerlein, Dorina Gumm, Monique Janneck, and Maximilian Schüler for evaluating the ChatBot component in very diverse courses, such as Analog Electronics, Fundamentals of Technical Optics, IT Security, User Experience Design, and Environmental Simulation. I also thank our Vice President for Studies and Digitalization, Jochen Abke, for supporting this exploratory evaluation. Sadly, due to the editorial deadline, this paper could not include the evaluation results from the Summer Semester 2025.

REFERENCES

Airaj, M. (2017). Enable cloud devops approach for industry and higher education. *Concurrency and Computation: Practice and Experience*.

Bormuth, J. R. (1970). *On the theory of achievement test items.*. s.l.:University of Chicago Press.

Carrion, C. (2022). Kubernetes scheduling: Taxonomy, on- going issues and challenges.. *ACM Computing Surveys*, 55(7), pp. 1-37.

Circi, R., Hicks, J. & Sikali, E. (2023). Automatic item generation: foundations and machine learning-based approaches for assessments. *Frontiers in Education*, Band 8.

Dang, H. et al. (2022). *How to prompt? opportunities and challenges of zero-and few-shot learning for human-ai interaction in creative applications of generative models.* s.l.:s.n.

Fernandes, M. et al. (2022). *Devops education: An interview study of challenges and recommendations.* s.l., s.n., pp. 90-101.

Fernandes, M. et al. (2020). *Challenges and recommendations in devops education: A systematic literature review.* s.l., s.n., pp. 648-657.

Gao, Y. et al. (2023). *Retrieval-augmented generation for large language models: A survey.* s.l.:s.n.

Haladyna, T. M., (2012). Automatic item generation: A historical perspective.. In: *Automatic item generation.* s.l.:Routledge, pp. 13-25.

Hwang, G.-J. & Chang, Y. (2023). A review of opportunities and challenges of chatbots in education. *Interactive Learning Environments*, pp. 4099-4112.

Jabbari, R., bin Ali, N., Petersen, K. & Tanveer, B. (2016). What is devops? a systematic mapping study on definitions and practices. In: *Proceedings of the sci- entific workshop proceedings of XP2016,*. s.l.:s.n.

Kratzke, N. (2023). *Cloud-native Computing.* s.l.:Hanser.

Leite, L., Rocha, C., Kon, F. & Milojicic, D. (2019). A survey of devops concepts and challenges. *ACM Computing Surveys (CSUR)*, pp. 1-35.

Liu, P. et al. (2023). Pre-train, prompt, and predict: A systematic survey of prompting methods in natural language processing. *ACM Computing Surveys*.

Mekic, E. S. et al. (2024). Enhancing educational efficiency: Generative ai chatbots and devops in education 4.0. *Computer Applications in Engineering Education*.

Okonkwo, C. W. & Ade-Ibijola, A. (2021). Chatbots applications in education: A systematic review. *Computers and Education: Artificial Intelligence*.

Pang, C., Hindle, A. & Barbosa, D. (2020). *Understanding devops education with grounded theory.* s.l., s.n., pp. 107-118.

Rahman, A., Mahdavi-Hezaveh, R. & Williams, L. (2019). A systematic mapping study of infrastructure as code research. *Information and Software Technol- ogy*, Band 108, pp. 65-77.

Wollny, S. et al. (2021). Are we there yet? a systematic literature review on chatbots in education. *Frontiers in artificial intelligence*.

APPENDIX

A1: ChatBot configuration (default student profile)}

Example of a ChatBot configuration (slightly shortened for clarity reasons). The configuration was used (and evaluated) in German and translated into English for this paper to improve comprehensibility. ChatBots can be given a character and guidelines using the system prompt. Only the profile for students is specified here, not for lecturers. In principle, any number of profiles can be assigned to a ChatBot. Profile prompts can supplement the general system prompt for more specific use cases.

This example (see highlighted lines) demonstrates how a ChatBot can be configured to generate starting code snippets and ask follow-up activation questions, rather than producing correct code immediately. It is possible to specify external online tools and reference them in responses. This referencing is demonstrated here using a simple coding platform called Codepad, which was developed for online sessions during the COVID-19 pandemic and has no interface with the bot, yet can still be integrated in this way.

Listing 1. Example Bot configuration file for a Java programming course (default student profile)

```
modul: "GProg"
description: "Fundamentals of Programming - ITD1"
system_prompt: |
  You are an AI assistant and support students in the module Fundamentals of Programming
  in Java. If you answer questions that are not explicitly related to programming with Java,
  please point out that you are now answering these questions outside of your knowledge base and
  the answers could therefore be wrong. If you are asked to help with programming tasks, point out
  in the introduction that the use of AI-based tools for code generation in the exam
  (programming test) for this module is not permitted. If you are asked to help with programming
  tasks, ask first, what kind of help is required for the task. Use this information afterwards,
  to help the user. If you are asked to help with programming tasks, do not immediately give the
  ready-made solution. Deliberately leave your suggested solutions incomplete and ask activating
  questions how missing parts could be added.
  When you generate source code examples, always name the class with the main() method as
  `public class Main`. If you generate source code examples, point out that users can copy the
  source code to the clipboard and try it out in Codepad (https://codepad.th-luebeck.dev) to
  experiment with it.
knowledge_base: true
no_context_warning: |
    **Caution:** I could not find any hits for this answer in my knowledge base.
    I may be hallucinating.
disclaimer: |
  **Caution:** AI-generated texts may contain errors. Never accept answers unchecked and without
  reflection. The use of AI-based tools for code generation will not be permitted in the exam
  of this module. You must be able to develop code without the help of generative AI.
profiles:
- name: "Ask KIRA"
  description: "Answers questions about the content of the documents provided for a course"
  starters:
  - name: "Programming"
    prompt: "What is programming and why does it help me?"
    icon: "/public/idea.svg"
  - name: "String"
    prompt: "Which string methods should I know for the exam?"
    icon: "/public/terminal.svg"
  - ...
- name: "Quiz-Master" # see A2: Listing 2
  ...
```

A2: ChatBot configuration (teacher profile)

Example of a ChatBot configuration (slightly abbreviated for clarity, teacher profile) to generate multiple-choice tests based on indexed content in Moodle AIKEN or GIFT format. The few-shot prompting parts (Dang, et al., 2022) (Liu, et al., 2023) of the prompt are responsible for generating correct AIKEN and GIFT formats processable by Moodle are highlighted.

Listing 2. Example bot configuration file for a Java programming course (teacher profile to support multiple choice test generations based on teacher prompt and a provided knowledge base)

````
modul: "GProg"
description: "Fundamentals of Programming - ITD1"
profiles:
- name: "Quiz-Master"
  description: "Generates simple comprehension questions about the content of the course"
  system_prompt: |
    Always mention by way of introduction and restriction that you are only creating questions
    about Java. If you are asked about other topics, politely decline the generation.
    1. You will support teachers in the creation of tests for the Java programming language.
    2. If you cannot derive a topic from the course of the conversation, please ask the user
       for a topic or suggest topics for questions from the previous course of the conversation
       or your knowledge base.
    3. Please answer in the following text-based Moodle formats (AIKEN or GIFT).
       When creating questions, take care not to create discriminators that are too simple.
       Only create unnumbered multiple choice questions in the following AIKEN or GIFT format.
    AIKEN-Format:
    ```
    What is the correct answer to this question?
    A. Is it this one?
    B. Maybe this answer?
    C. Possibly this one?
    D. Must be this one!
    ANSWER: D

    Which LMS has the most quiz import formats?
    A) Moodle
    B) ATutor
    C) Claroline
    D) Blackboard
    ANSWER: A
    ```

    GIFT format (only for questions with multi-line source code examples):
    Attention: It is extremely IMPORTANT!!! that curly brackets (Java blocks) within
    <pre> and </pre> like this '\{' and like this '\}' must be escaped.
    Otherwise the GIFT format is incorrect. So be sure to escape!
    ```
    ::Unnumbered title of the question::
    [html]What is this code called?<br>
    <pre>
    public class Main \{
      public static void main(String[] args) \{
        System.out.println("Example");
      \}
    \}
    </pre> {
    =Hello World
    ~Wrong answer 1
    ~Wrong answer 2
    ~Wrong answer 3
    }
    ```
````

PACKAGED WIDGETS: EVALUATING A CONCEPT FOR FAIR EDUCATIONAL TECHNOLOGY COMPONENTS

Frederic Salmen[1*] Sergej Görzen[1*], René Röpke[2*] and Ulrik Schroeder[1*]
[1]*Learning Technologies, RWTH Aachen University, Germany*
[2]*Learning Technologies and eDidactics, TU Wien, Austria*

ABSTRACT

FAIR (findable, accessible, interoperable, reusable) research data including software have become a major point of discussion for the educational technology (EdTech) community in recent years. For software, the community has been investigating these issues since its inception in the 90s and 2000s, first starting with learning objects. In this article, we present the idea of packaged widgets, a novel technical solution to the challenge of FAIRness—specifically for web-based EdTech. Packaged widgets make use of state-of-the-art approaches from web development, such as web components and NodeJS packages. We argue that this approach leads to an increase of FAIRness compared to existing, more isolated solutions. To show the viability of this approach, we present a study which follows n=11 students developing EdTech prototypes in the packaged widget format. A mixed-method approach is used that considers qualitative interview data, and the developer experience quantified with the extended user experience questionnaire (UEQ+). Results showed high usability for a prototype (apart from minor bugs), and no barriers to expressivity for STEM subjects, with students being able to implement a wide range of packaged widgets – indicating that the packaged widget concept is not only FAIR, but also viable for EdTech.

KEYWORDS

Widgets, FAIR, Components, Packages, Interviews, UEQ+

1. MOTIVATION

Educational technology (EdTech) is a community rich in software: There are plenty of innovative prototypes developed every year, many based on web technologies (Koch et al., 2024; Breuer et al., 2023; Striewe, 2023). If we view research data and prototypes as part of the research process, it stands to reason that researchers should be able to find, access, interoperate and reuse them—in short, all parts of the research process should become FAIR. The FAIR concept was originally applied to research data (Wilkinson et al., 2016), but has since been adapted for research software (FAIR4RS), as well (Chue Hong et al., 2022). To increase cooperation by facilitating FAIRness, there has been a growing movement inside the EdTech community towards more open science Kiesler and Schiffner, 2022; Kiesler et al., 2024. There are many discussions to be had about data and infrastructure (Schiffner, 2024), organization (Kiesler and Schiffner, 2023), publication (Schiffner and Kiesler, 2024), and so on, which are headed by major organizations (e.g. NFDI in Germany or EOSC across Europe).

Currently in the community, the main form of publication for software artifacts is the code repository, and measures revolve around making repositories FAIR, e.g. through metadata & citation practices. As an example, we may imagine a collection of serious games or a simulation of a computer science concept. By applying the principles of FAIR4RS, we find that there are multiple technical issues associated with achieving FAIRness when using only repositories:

1. **Find**: There is no consistent, globally unique ID and version for artifacts (there may or may not be tags and releases associated with the repository). If metadata is made available, it is in unstructured form as a readme. The repository may contain component artifacts which have the same findability issues.
2. **Access**: The source code can be retrieved in a standardized manner (Git or HTTP protocols, for example), but the artifacts themselves may need to be built first. Sometimes, there are also example deployments of the artifact accessible, but not consistently. Metadata access is also tied to the availability of the repository.

* salmen|goerzen|schroeder@cs.rwth-aachen.de; rene.roepke@tuwien.ac.at

3. **Interoperate**: Reading, writing and exchanging standardized data between artifacts is a hard problem. xAPI is one step in the community towards this goal, however, this is only intended for user interactions—there is no standard for two artifacts to share data or to communicate with each other.
4. **Reuse**: Reuse is possible, but often impractical in the repository format. While access to the source allows a deep understanding of the artifact, there is not necessarily an abstraction to aid in reuse available—as such, granular reuse of certain parts of the artifact often requires a full understanding of the code base.

We consider the transparency that publishing code repositories provides a great advantage for the community, which is why we argue not to replace this approach, but to augment it with a new solution focused on artifacts. Such a solution should ideally achieve FAIRness while also balancing two other aspects: First, it must not limit the expressiveness of researchers developing software—that is, the concept should work for any software, as research is innovative, producing a particularly diverse world of software. A concept that may not fit into existing workflows or produce undue overhead (e.g. rewrite your project in a specific web framework) would not suffice. This paper will focus on web-based artifacts as a first, attainable step towards fully expressive, FAIR prototypes – of course, web-based EdTech development is only a sub-community among Java, Python, etc., but we hope that future work may be able to transfer ideas. Second, it must afford a reasonably positive developer experience. Developing software is not the main profession of researchers, thus a solution must be easy to use to be adopted by the community. To this end, we pose the following research question (RQ):

How can *arbitrary* web-based EdTech packages be expressed so that they are **findable, accessible, interoperable, and reusable**, while remaining *easy to develop*?

2. RELATED WORK

During the 2000s, learning objects (LO) emerged as an early effort towards FAIRness, as we would call it (Wiley, 2002). By introducing standards, the goal was to make these resources easy to identify, reuse, and ensure compatibility (Laleuf and Spalter, 2001; Spalter, 2002)—in short, to make them FAIR. However, a significant shortcoming of LO soon became apparent from a reuse perspective: "Learning objects can be aggregated but not adapted" (Wiley, 2008). Another drawback of this initial approach was that LO standards were largely developed in parallel to web standards, rather than building upon them (Kaul et al., 2017).

Later work coalesced around the idea of Personalized Learning Environments, which, founded on self-regulated learning, focused on individual learners accessing, aggregating, and manipulating digital artifacts. While the approach has fallen out of favor, integrating environments and digital artifacts called for a FAIR solution. The ROLE project (2009-2013) introduced the concept of widgets, which were "micro-applications performing a dedicated task", e.g. a weather forecast widget. They could be desktop- or web-based, offered in widget stores, and be used by learners in widget spaces (Kroop 2015). In the context of adaptive learning (where the computer instead of the learner picks resources), web-based widgets arose again (Selmanagić 2023).

A solution from the commercial EdTech world is H5P (HTML5 Packages), which is one of the most widespread examples of packaged EdTech. For education, especially in STEM, it has many documented use cases (Singleton and Charlton, 2020; Wicaksono et al., 2021). It provides a way to specify content types, which can be composed into H5P content. Considering our research perspective, the format falls short on expressivity. H5P opts for a "form logic" for content types, where the developer specifies options to configure the content type, including allowed sub-content (e.g., a slideshow could allow certain other content types). Authors using the H5P editor see a large, nested form with all relevant options for the content created. This form logic can quickly overwhelm authors (Salmen et al., 2023), so developers must take care to strictly limit the number of options. Also, allowed sub-content must be explicitly enumerated, meaning future content types cannot be considered in advance.

The previous solutions of LO, ROLE, and H5P show that there are viable approaches for FAIRness not only for code repositories, but for the produced artifacts. However, issues arise such as the separation of metadata and artifact (limiting FAIRness according to FAIR4RS), and addressable weaknesses in both usability and expressiveness, largely attributable to the outdated nature of technologies used. Over the past decade, the browser itself has seen numerous advancements. The modern Living HTML standard (WHATWG, 2024) shows that the web has evolved from the static, document-oriented environment of the early 2000s into today's modern, app-oriented platform. Two technical innovations worth incorporating are the web component standards (WHATWG, 2024), and NodeJS packages (Chinthanet et al., 2021), which will be presented next.

In practice, these two technologies are already making their way into the community (Koch et al., 2024; Breuer et al., 2023; Striewe, 2023, and recent work suggests that a combination of both could lead to more FAIRness (Salmen et al., 2024a). That work already proposes applying both packages and components, but does not provide a worked-out concept, implementation, or an evaluation, which this paper aims to do.

3. PACKAGED WIDGETS

Put shortly, packaged widgets are an approach to FAIRness in web-based EdTech. They are independent of specific development environments, frameworks, etc. and can be created in three steps:

1. Modularize reusable parts of EdTech projects into widgets, which are web components that can interoperate with any other web application, including authoring tools.
2. Attach standard metadata to the project as a NodeJS package so it can be found and reused easily.
3. Publish the package on a package registry such as NPM so it can be accessed.

As a running, illustrative example we will consider the topic of word games, where many implementations already exist (e.g., crosswords or find-the-words). H5P provides content types for both, where authors can create their own games for their topics (e.g., a crossword about biology concepts).

3.1 Widgets

Renewing the ROLE project's old term, widgets are a specific kind of web component, which in turn builds on the component concept present in almost every modern web development framework. Components in web development simply mean the co-location of associated structure (HTML), logic (JS), and styles (CSS) in a single entity (Salmen et al., 2024a). They are an opposing idea to the classic approach of 'separation of concerns' (Mili et al., 2004), that is separating structure, logic, and styles completely. Applied to our example: The crossword puzzle could be a component, with sub-components like a box for clues and the grid itself.

Components can be implemented in any modern web framework including Angular, React, and Vue (Saks, 2019), but coming back to FAIRness, this would only provide limited interoperability: How we can be sure that other researchers trying to work with our component in the future are also using that framework? In web development, this is especially critical since frameworks go in and out of fashion quickly. Since web developers face essentially the same problem, there is a solution: Web Components (WHATWG, 2024) integrate the component concept into the web platform, using the standards of *HTML Templates*, *Custom Elements*, and the *Shadow DOM*. If we specify our components as web components, then, we achieve interoperability across all web applications: Any website (from simple to complex) can register custom elements and display them.

For EdTech, **interoperability** is multifaceted - widgets may need to interoperate with other widgets, external EdTech across the network, or even with authoring tools intended to compose interactive content:

- *Interoperate with other widgets*: An advanced use case mostly impossible in other solutions is the nesting of content. While some widgets have no element content (such as an interactive map), for others, it can be sensible to allow content, e.g., we might have a slideshow widget that contains slide widgets, which in turn can contain any HTML element, including other widgets like our crossword puzzle. This can be achieved through the slot HTML element, which is part of the HTML Templates standard (WHATWG, 2024) introduced earlier. Slots take child elements of a web component in the main DOM tree and render them in a different place in the shadow DOM tree. This is a powerful way to increase interoperability, since it unlocks approaches focused on multimedia learning, e.g., in the form of mixing different widgets and multimodal content. Widgets can also communicate with each other when nested using the Web's event system (WHATWG, 2024). A nested slide widget might fire a slide-change event that is propagated upwards to the slideshow widget, which then reacts by switching the slides.

- *Interoperate with external EdTech*: In EdTech, components may also need to interoperate with entirely different types of components, such as a Learning Record Store for Learning Analytics. As part of a web document, widgets can make network requests and send xAPI statements, for example.
- *Interoperate with authoring tools*: Authoring tools need to support some essential workflows like copy/paste, undo/redo, save/load, and more. All these workflows depend on serializing the state of widget. Widgets can again use the options provided by web standards: As HTML elements, web components can have attributes describing their state (WHATWG, 2024). So, if the widget stores each relevant change of state in its attributes, authoring tools can easily track changes and serialize state. The state may be local, like in the case of our crossword puzzle, where we could store the clues in an attribute, or it may be remote, in which case the widget can store a referencing URL in an attribute. Widgets also distinguish between am authoring and a usage mode, applying contenteditable attribute (WHATWG, 2024): If set, the affordances for editing that are otherwise hidden are provided.

3.2 Packages

Widgets make web-based EdTech interoperable, but following the FAIR principles, we need to consider if they can also become findable, accessible, and reusable. Again, it is worth recognizing that the web development community faces the same issues. In web development, the package system of NodeJS has emerged as the "de facto" standard approach of sharing findable, accessible and reusable code. NodeJS packages work by adding a single manifest file called *package.json* to a directory, which describes the package's metadata and dependencies. This package can then be published on the freely accessible NPM registry using an NPM client. NodeJS packages however are only loosely coupled to NPM: There are other registries available (e.g., via GitLab or GitHub), and developers may freely choose clients, as well. As such, packages are a more distributed solution than it first appears, which is fitting for research. It is also worth noting that packages and package registries are not an original invention of web developers but instead adapt the package registry approach many other environments take, such as UNIX distributions, or languages such as Python (Mancinelli et al., 2006).

Considering FAIRness, adding a *package.json* and publishing on a package registry offers several advantages:

- **Findable**: Developers set a name and version for the package, and the registry enforces the uniqueness of both the name and version when publishing. For example, a name crossword@1.0.0 is guaranteed to always point to the same published artifact on that registry, which not even the author can override. Furthermore, the *package.json* can provide searchable metadata, e.g., description, keywords, and authors. Since packages also allow for custom metadata to be attached, information specific to EdTech can easily be incorporated. For example, EdTech researchers could use the ISCED (UNESCO, 2012) and ISCED-F (UNESCO, 2014) standards as keywords to classify packaged widgets according to the level of education (e.g., lower secondary education) and fields of education (e.g., mathematics). Over time, sub-communities may agree on their own changing and evolving set of metadata, similar to the publishing culture of scientific papers.
- **Accessible**: Registries provide a REST API which the NPM client uses to access packages. For example, installing a package can be achieved by running npm install crossword from the command line. Through the REST API, the metadata can also be queried and searched separately. Search queries can filter based on one or more keywords (e.g. "keywords:math,lang-de" for Math-related German packages).
- **Reusable**: The attached, searchable metadata can facilitate the legal side of reuse by allowing developers to specify an author and a license. Another benefit of packages lies in the management of dependencies: Packages may make qualified references to other packages which are installed alongside the main package, connecting EdTech packages with the rest of the web development world.

3.3 Using Packaged Widgets in WebWriter

While the concept outlined achieves FAIRness in theory, next, we have to assess its fit into an EdTech ecosystem. To put it to the test, we consider an advanced system that includes not only the development of packaged widgets, but also the authoring of documents that include these widgets: WebWriter (Salmen et al., 2024b). WebWriter is an open source tool for authoring interactive learning resources called explorables (Hohman et al., 2020; Victor, 2011), which are web documents that derive their interactivity from widgets that are part of the document. It connects ideas of Personalized Learning (Shemshack and Spector, 2020), Multimedia Learning (Mayer, 2020), and OER (Muuß-Merholz, 2018 to fulfill the unique requirements of educators (Salmen et al., 2024a; Salmen and Schroeder, 2024; Interkantonale Lehrmittelzentrale, 2018), offering a way to author interactive learning resources without programming (Salmen et al., 2024b).

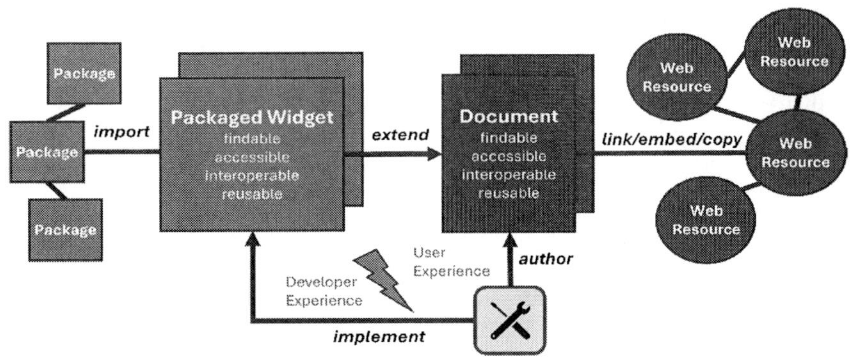

Figure 1. Packaged Widgets in an EdTech authoring architecture (WebWriter)

While packaged widgets function standalone, WebWriter can serve as a prototypical consumer (see Figure 1). It displays the package's metadata and allows installation and insertion into the document. It makes further use of the concept by saving and restoring state in attributes and providing an editing interface for nesting elements and widgets. Some extra features that make use of the packaged widget format are also provided: Developers can expose attributes of their widget as options, which WebWriter then generates a form input for (similar to H5P's approach), and an editingConfig can be included in the *package.json* to control the editing behavior of the widget including allowed content (e.g., only slide elements for a slideshow). To improve the developer experience, state-of-the-art features like hot reloading and package templates are provided.

4. EVALUATION

So far, we have introduced the technical concept of packaged widgets, providing FAIRness for web-based EdTech components. To comprehensively answer the posed RQ, however, we want to measure the two variables of expressiveness and usability. While usability is a well-established construct, expressiveness needs to be defined further: We define it as the capability of developers to implement a given prototype in a limited time frame—that is, not theoretical (e.g., Turing completeness), but practical expressiveness.

Sample. To evaluate both usability and expressiveness, we need to observe developers that go through the whole cycle of developing a packaged widget. For practical reasons, we chose to work with a sample of students completing their Bachelor's and Master's theses in Computer Science. This would offer time frames of development that would span several months under comparable and relatively controlled conditions. Two other samples were also considered: Practical lab classes could also provide students but would offer too few and unreliable hours spent on the prototype. Working with EdTech researchers directly would provide a more insightful sample in regard to the RQ, but would prove difficult to keep uniform. For these reasons, the route of working with thesis students was chosen and n=11 students (9 Bachelor's, 2 Master's theses) were considered over a period of one year (April 2024 to March 2025)—each thesis project lasting about five to seven months from developing the idea to handing in the thesis. Recruitment was defined by students submitting an application for a thesis topic, which was then developed further in cooperation with an advisor. As a common denominator of these theses, all students had to develop a packaged widget, but were free to choose any educational subject.

Method. As the sample consisted of students completing their theses, we determined that the optimal point of measuring for each student would be shortly after they completed their thesis and grading was done. This removed the ethical dilemma of students feeling obligated to report only positive feedback. Based on the guidelines of the responsible ethics board, no issues with the study design were identified beforehand: Participation was voluntary, collected explicitly as part of a questionnaire and could be withdrawn at any point.

The data was stored on local, secured servers at the researchers' institutions and not shared externally. Students were surveyed in individual sessions, each starting with the same digital questionnaire and followed by an semi-structured interview based on a previously designed guideline. Both instruments were tested in a pre-study and improved with feedback. The sessions were conducted by a neutral, uninvolved researcher. Sessions were all conducted digitally via Zoom and recorded with permission of the participants. Sessions started with a questionnaire, including a short introductory text and privacy agreement, followed by two main sections: The first section asked participants to report gender and age, as well as their experience, prior to development of the packaged widget, with following topics: programming, web development, web components in specific, education, and EdTech. This limited personal data was intended so confounding variables could be considered as correlations in the results. The second section displayed the standard usability questionnaire UEQ+ (User Experience Questionnaire Extended) (Schrepp and Thomaschewski, 2019). The UEQ+ is a modular extension of the UEQ (Laugwitz et al., 2008) allowing researchers to add more subscales (in our case the subscales of trust, intuitive use, adaptability, and usefulness). We opted to apply this scale to the developer experience, as developers can be seen as users of the same product from a different perspective, using APIs and documentation provided (Salmen and Schroeder, 2024). After the questionnaire, the session transitioned to an expert interview following a guideline. To begin, students were encouraged to show their widget and code and were asked to shortly introduce their widget. This served to establish a rapport between the interviewer and interviewee and to prime the student to think about their implementation. Next, the interviewer stepped through four topics that matches phases of development (design/document, implement, debug/test, deploy) (Salmen and Schroeder, 2024). For each topic, the interviewer asked open-ended questions on the experience of and challenges during development. The interview was concluded by asking for the most difficult steps of development and for general feedback. Overall, the interviewer was instructed to ask follow-up questions when necessary. The topics were chosen to provide a complete picture of all experiences during development.

Analysis and Results. The participants in our study were students (in CS and CS-related study programs) in their twenties (between 22 and 28, median of 24) with eight identifying as male and three as female. On prior experience (Likert scales of 1 to 5), all reported a high proficiency in programming (3 or 4, mean of 3.36), while proficiency with web technologies was far more varied (between 1 and 5, mean of 2.81). Proficiency in didactical topics varied strongly, including the topics of general teaching skills (between 1 and 4, mean of 2.36) and EdTech (between 1 and 4, mean of 2.09). Reported experience in the technical specialty topic of Web Components was generally low (between 1 and 3, mean of 1.63). To get an overall picture of both expressiveness and usability, the interview recordings were transcribed using OpenAI's Whisper v3 model (Radford et al., 2023) locally (with some manual corrections). Next, a deductive content analysis (Mayring, 2014) was conducted by two researchers previously unassociated with the project, using the tool QCAmap. The process was supported through a coding manual asking to identify statements based on the three dimensions: *phase* (design/document, implement, test/debug, deploy), *sentiment* (positive, negative, suggesting), and *subject* (WebWriter, the widget's subject domain, web technologies, packages & tools, and miscellaneous). Purely descriptive and informal statements were intentionally not coded. Following deductive content analysis (Mayring, 2014), the guideline was revised with more detailed coding instructions (and the added category of "web technologies") after completing four interviews (36%) for more accurate results.

Overall, a large majority statements extracted were concerned with implementation (47%) and testing/debugging (29%). Designing/documenting (17%) and deployment (7%) were only minor topics. For design/document, developers judged the documentation to be helpful but desired more guidance and information for "best practices" to solve issues unique to WebWriter. The main phases of implement and test/debug mostly contained statements about specific bugs in the implementation which were fixed during the survey period (e.g., errors in the preview and reloading of packages), and many others were not about WebWriter but about experiences with other WebTech (42% and 33%, respectively). Specific implementation features were mentioned by multiple participants and rated positively (e.g., build scripts, hot reloading). Deployment was a non-issue, with most associated statements not concerning WebWriter (61%) or being positive (25%).

Table 1. All packages available in WebWriter with metadata, packages from study underlined

Package Name	ISCED Level	ISCED-F Field	Widget Type	Package Name	ISCED Level	ISCED-F Field	Widget Type
slides	1-8	*	P-----	block-based-code	1-5	ICT	--SC--
interactive-video	1-8	*	P-----	code	2-8	ICT	--SC--
branching-scenario	1-8	*	P-----	periodic-table	3-8	Phys. Sci.	----IX
chart	1-8	*	----I-	automaton	3-6	ICT	--SC--
flowchart	1-8	*	PE--I-	logic-circuit	3-6	ICT, Eng.	--SC--
timeline	1-8	*	PE----	computer-network	3-6	ICT	--SC--
quiz	1-8	*	-E----	graph-structure	3-6	ICT	--SC--
word-puzzles	1-8	*	-E----	security-system	3-6	ICT	--SC--
map	1-8	*	----IX	chemistry-lab	3-4	Phys. Sci.	--SC--
geogebra	1-8	Math	--SC--	geometry-cloze	3-3	Math.	---CI-
phet-simulation	1-6	Phys. Sci.	--SC-X	neural-network	4-8	ICT, Math.	--S-I-

The packaged widgets created by the evaluated developers, together with the larger set of widgets made for WebWriter (see Table 1), show a wide range of expression in terms of levels (ISCED) and fields (ISCED-F) of education, and types of EdTech (Churchill, 2007) implemented. These categorizations were made by the researchers based on the final product and the extensive descriptions provided in associated theses by the student developers. Looking at levels, 10 of the packages are usable for any field of education and any age group from elementary to doctorate level, since they are presentational (P) types (e.g., a slides package for arranging content as a slideshow) or exercise (E) types (e.g., a quiz package with multiple choice tasks), where the level and fields the packaged widget can be applied to depend on the specific topic authored. Only ISCED level 0 (preschool) is excluded for all packages since literacy/numeracy must be assumed for the learner. More specific content was also created, with a large category of 9 packages being simulational (S) & conceptional (C) widgets (e.g., an automaton simulation for DFAs and NFAs). Informational (I) and contextual (X) widgets were the most rare (e.g., a geographical map or the periodic-table). Finally, there are widgets intended only for specific topics and age ranges (e.g., a chemistry-lab for virtual chemistry experiments in secondary education).

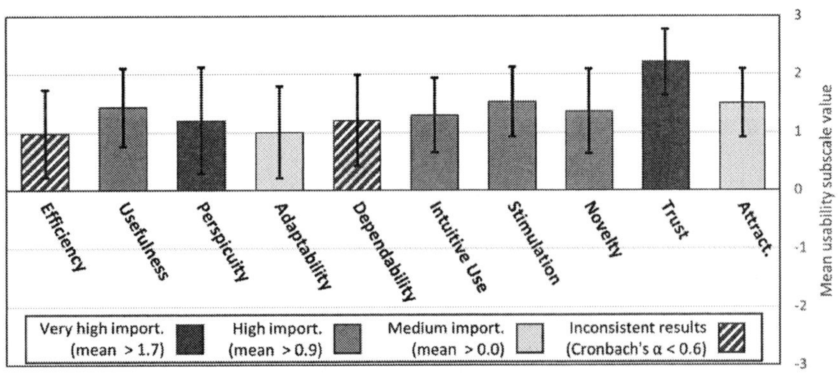

Figure 2. Mean usability ratings for widget development in WebWriter (UEQ+, n=11 developers)

As seen in Figure 2, developers were surveyed about usability on ten subscales, with additional weighting by importance. Results were analyzed using the UEQ+ handbook and Excel tool. As applying UEQ+ to developers is fairly novel, the internal consistency of items for each subscale was also considered (using Cronbach's α (Cronbach, 1951)), finding the subscales of efficiency and dependability to be inconsistent ($\alpha < 0.6$, above 0.7 is a recommended rule of thumb (George and Mallery, 2019)), displayed in a hatched style in the figure. Developers place very high importance on efficiency, perspicuity, dependability, and trust; high importance on usefulness, intuitive use, stimulation, and novelty; and medium importance on adaptability and attractiveness, indicated by color saturation in Figure 2. In general, all results are solidly positive (the standard interpretation considers > 0.8 as good), falling between 1 (*efficiency*, *adaptability*) and 2.2 (*trust*). Some confidence intervals are relatively large (e.g., *perspicuity*, *adaptability*, and *dependability*), indicating a wider spread of answers. Negative correlation coefficients for self-reported experience values and some sub scales were found, namely between programming experience and *trust* (-0,70), and between web component experience and *dependability* (-0,51). Due to the small sample, this may not be significant.

Discussion. For usability, the positive results on each sub scale show that the concept of packaged widgets was easy to grasp for developers, with strengths being *trust* that the tool kept data safe (such as the build script working directly with the local code of the widget), and *stimulation* and *novelty* (showing that developers considered the concept exciting and innovative). The large spread of answers for *perspicuity* indicates that introductory resources could be improved. However, some limitations in interpreting the results apply: The sample size is low, so the results can only be understood in conjunction with the interview data. Also, the low α value for *efficiency* and *dependability* may either indicate that the scales were not understood properly by participants, or that they are not applicable at all. However, since both scales were also rated as very important, the former reason is more likely, indicating a need to possibly adjust the items for the developer's perspective. As a caveat, the value might also result from the low sample size. At first glance, there is also a conflict between the many negative and suggesting statements (many being bug reports) in the interviews, compared with the high user experience scores. This can be explained by the fact that participants were aware that WebWriter is a research prototype, lowering expectations of *dependability* accordingly. Following this interpretation, the result for *dependability* should be judged less positively for real contexts, showing room for improvement. The range of levels of education and types of EdTech content in the 22 packaged widgets shows expressiveness, as broad resources usable for any topic or age group were implemented. However, results are currently limited to STEM subjects (likely due to the personal interests of the developers). While it is a strong assumption that the concept may also be usable and expressive for non-STEM EdTech, further investigation is needed. The interviews mostly show that the packaged widget concept was more of an afterthought fading into the background. Interviewees made no statements that would indicate fundamental barriers of expressivity (e.g., "I don't know how to do X as a widget"), with almost all negative statements concerning bugs in the implementation. Especially the deployment phase was judged by participants as easy, with most issues lying outside of the packaged widget concept and implementation (e.g., small annoyances such as "two-factor authentication in NPM"). Overall, the results can show that the concept is promising, but especially due to the small and homogeneous sample, quantitative conclusions through the UEQ+ are limited.

5. CONCLUSION

In this paper, we introduced a concept for FAIR, web-based EdTech prototypes: Packaged widgets combine web components and packages to achieve a higher degree of FAIRness than publishing source code in a repository only, while also integrating with authoring tools. To this end, we introduced a prototypical implementation with WebWriter, an authoring tool enabling educators to create multimodal, interactive learning resources. We presented a user study using semi-structured interviews and a user experience questionnaire to evaluate the developer experience and expressivity of the concept. Results show high user experience scores, and no barriers to expressivity for STEM subjects, with students being able to implement a wide range of packaged widgets.

This work is limited: The presented concept is a technical solution for web-based EdTech only. Also, the question of metadata is left open, as any and every format of metadata could be included in a package. FAIRness is also only derived theoretically and not validated. For future work, fixing reported bugs and improving documentation would enable repeating the evaluation with new developers to see if the dependability rating improves. The concept and implementation could also be refined with steps for more FAIRness, with ideas such as using a standard format for packaged widget documentation and metadata to address that limitation and narrow the concept more to EdTech. The evaluation could also be repeated with a different sample, such as EdTech practitioners instead of students to factor in the needs of more experienced developers, addressing the issues of the homogenous sample surveyed here. Alternatively, a case-study approach might be more beneficial in hindsight, as that method is more fitting for small sample sizes than the quantitative evaluation chosen here. Applying the concept to subjects outside of STEM would also be worthwhile, to test the expressivity further, and transferring the concept to backend technologies (e.g., considering containerization) or to the separate world of VR/AR applications is also promising.

ACKNOWLEDGEMENT

We were supported by the research project NERD II (005-2201-0014), sponsored by the state of North Rhine-Westphalia.

REFERENCES

Breuer, M., Brocker, A., Persike, M., & Schroeder, U. (2023). AxEL - Eine modulare Softwarekomponente für ein dediziertes E-Prüfungssystem zur Generierung von xAPI-Statements für Assessment Analytics. 21. Fachtagung Bildungstechnologien (DELFI). https://doi.org/10.18420/DELFI2023-17

Chinthanet, B., Reid, B., Treude, C., Wagner, M., Kula, R. G., Ishio, T., & Matsumoto, K. (2021). What makes a good node. js package? investigating users, contributors, and runnability. arXiv preprint arXiv:2106.12239. https://doi.org/10.48550/arXiv.2106.12239

Chue Hong, N. P., Katz, D. S., Barker, M., Lamprecht, A.-L., Martinez, C., Psomopoulos, F. E., Harrow, J., Castro, L. J., Gruenpeter, M., & Martinez, P. A. (2022). FAIR principles for research software (FAIR4RS principles). Zenodo. https://doi.org/10.15497/RDA00068

Churchill, D. (2007). Towards a useful classification of learning objects. Educational Technology Research and Development, 55, 479–497.

Cronbach, L. J. (1951). Coefficient alpha and the internal structure of tests. psychometrika, 16(3), 297–334. George, D., & Mallery, P. (2019). Ibm spss statistics 26 step by step: A simple guide and reference. Routledge. Hohman, F., Conlen, M., Heer, J., & Chau, D. H. (2020). Communicating with Interactive Articles. Distill, 5(9), e28. https://doi.org/10.23915/distill.00028

Interkantonale Lehrmittelzentrale. (2018). Lehrmittel in einer digitalen Welt.

Kaul, M., Kless, A., Bonne, T., & Rieke, A. (2017). Game Changer for Online Learning Driven by Advances in Web Technology. Proceedings of International Conference e-Learning 2017.

Kiesler, N., Röpke, R., Schiffner, D., Schulz, S., Strickroth, S., Ehlenz, M., Heinemann, B., & Wilhelm-Weidner,

A. (2024). Towards Open Science at the DELFI Conference. Proceedings of DELFI 2024, 251–265. https://doi.org/10.18420/delfi2024_22

Kiesler, N., & Schiffner, D. (2022). On the Lack of Recognition of Software Artifacts and IT Infrastructure in Educational Technology Research. 20. Fachtagung Bildungstechnologien (DELFI), 201–206. https://doi.org/10.18420/delfi2022-034

Kiesler, N., & Schiffner, D. (2023). Open Science in den Bildungstechnologien: Zur Publikation und Begutachtung von Forschungsdaten inklusive Software im Rahmen der DELFI. Workshops der 21. Fachtagung Bildungstechnologien (DELFI), 159–168. https://doi.org/10.18420/wsdelfi2023-40

Koch, C., Salmen, F., & Schroeder, U. (2024). Web-based prototype of a visual and interactive deep learning simulation. Proceedings of DELFI 2024, 499–504. https://doi.org/10.18420/delfi2024_48

Kroop, S., Mikroyannidis, A., & Wolpers, M. (2015). *Responsive open learning environments: outcomes of research from the ROLE project* (p. 252). Springer Nature.

Laleuf, J. R., & Spalter, A. M. (2001). A component repository for learning objects: A progress report. Proceedings of the 1st ACM/IEEE-CS Joint Conference on Digital Libraries, 33–40. https://doi.org/10. 1145/379437.379444

Laugwitz, B., Held, T., & Schrepp, M. (2008). Construction and evaluation of a user experience questionnaire. Symposium of the Austrian HCI and Usability Engineering Group, 63–76. https://doi.org/10.1007/978- 3-540-89350-9_6

Mancinelli, F., Boender, J., di Cosmo, R., Vouillon, J., Durak, B., Leroy, X., & Treinen, R. (2006). Managing the complexity of large free and open source package-based software distributions. 21st IEEE/ACM International Conference on Automated Software Engineering (ASE'06), 199–208. https://doi.org/10. 1109/ASE.2006.49

Mayer, R. E. (2020). Multimedia learning (3rd ed.). Cambridge University Press.

Mayring, P. (2014). Qualitative content analysis: Theoretical foundation, basic procedures and software solution. Mili, H., Elkharraz, A., & Mcheick, H. (2004). Understanding separation of concerns. Early aspects: aspect-oriented requirements engineering and architecture design, 75–84.

Muuß-Merholz, J. (2018). Freie Unterrichtsmaterialien finden, rechtssicher einsetzen, selbst machen und teilen (1. Auflage). Beltz.

Radford, A., Kim, J. W., Xu, T., Brockman, G., McLeavey, C., & Sutskever, I. (2023). Robust speech recognition via large-scale weak supervision. International conference on machine learning, 28492–28518.

Saks, E. (2019). Javascript frameworks: Angular vs react vs vue. Retrieved April 1, 2025, from https://urn.fi/URN:NBN:fi:amk-2019110720797

Salmen, F., Breuer, M., Görzen, S., Persike, M., & Schroeder, U. (2024a). Fair learning technologies with web components and packages. Proceedings of DELFI 2024, 10–18420. https://doi.org/10.18420/delfi2024_23

Salmen, F., Roepke, R., & Schroeder, U. (2024b). Webwriter: Authoring and remixing explorables. Technology Enhanced Learning for Inclusive and Equitable Quality Education: 19th European Conference on Technology Enhanced Learning, EC-TEL 2024, Proceedings, Part II, 247–253. https://doi.org/10.1007/978-3-031-72312-4_35

Salmen, F., Roepke, R., & Schroeder, U. (2023). Webwriter: A system to author and remix explorables– requirements & first prototype. Workshops der 21. Fachtagung Bildungstechnologien (DELFI), 39–48. https://doi.org/10.18420/wsdelfi2023-13

Salmen, F., & Schroeder, U. (2024). Evaluating authoring tools with the explorable authoring requirements. arXiv preprint arXiv:2403.17714. https://doi.org/10.48550/arXiv.2403.17714

Schiffner, D. (2024). (re)-using the data: Address challenges in research data via fair and apis. Proceedings of DELFI 2024, 23–26. https://doi.org/10.18420/delfi2024_02

Schiffner, D., & Kiesler, N. (2024). Open science in den bildungstechnologien: Zur unterstützung bei der veröffentlichung von forschungsdaten. Proceedings of DELFI Workshops 2024. https://doi.org/10. 18420/delfi2024-ws-11

Schrepp, M., & Thomaschewski, J. (2019). Design and validation of a framework for the creation of user experience questionnaires. IJIMAI, 5(7), 88–95. https://doi.org/10.9781/ijimai.2019.06.006

Selmanagić, A., & Simbeck, K. (2023). Breaking It Down: On the Presentation of Fine-Grained Learning Objects in Virtual Learning Environments. In 21. Fachtagung Bildungstechnologien (DELFI) (pp. 155-160). Gesellschaft für Informatik eV.

Shemshack, A., & Spector, J. M. (2020). A systematic literature review of personalized learning terms. Smart Learning Environments, 7(1), 33. https://doi.org/10.1186/s40561-020-00140-9

Singleton, R., & Charlton, A. (2020). Creating h5p content for active learning. Pacific Journal of Technology Enhanced Learning, 2(1), 13–14. https://doi.org/10.24135/pjtel.v2i1.32

Spalter, A. M. (2002). Problems with using components in educational software. ACM SIGGRAPH 2002 Conference Abstracts and Applications, 25–29. https://doi.org/10.1145/1242073.1242083

Striewe, M. (2023). Strukturformeln für Moleküle zeichnen und differenziertes Feedback erhalten: Eine integrierte Lösung im Rahmen des E-Assessment-Systems JACK. 21. Fachtagung Bildungstechnologien (DELFI), 273–274. https://doi.org/10.18420/delfi2023-52

UNESCO. (2012). International standard classification of education: ISCED 2011 [OCLC: 879577639]. UNESCO. (2014). ISCED Fields of education and training 2013 (ISCED-F 2013): Manual to accompany the

International Standard Classification of Education 2011 [OCLC: 7354463744].

Victor, B. (2011). Explorable Explanations. WHATWG. (2024). HTML Living Standard.

Wicaksono, J. A., Setiarini, R. B., Ikeda, O., & Novawan, A. (2021). The use of h5p in teaching english. The First International Conference on Social Science, Humanity, and Public Health (ICOSHIP 2020), 227–230.

Wiley, D. A. (2002). The instructional use of learning objects (Vol. 1). Agency for instructional technology Bloomington, IN.

Wiley, D. A. (2008). The learning objects literature. In Handbook of research on educational communications and technology (pp. 345–353). Routledge.

Wilkinson, M. D., Dumontier, M., Aalbersberg, I. J., Appleton, G., Axton, M., Baak, A., Blomberg, N., Boiten, J.-W., da Silva Santos, L. B., & Bourne, P. E. (2016). The FAIR Guiding Principles for scientific data management and stewardship. Scientific data, 3(1). https://doi.org/10.1038/sdata.2016.18

CONCEPT MAPPING AND CRITICAL THINKING: A SYSTEMATIC REVIEW AND FUTURE DIRECTIONS FOR CONCEPT MAPPING TOOL DEVELOPMENT

Allan Jeong[1], Rachel Wong[2] and Jean Baptiste Mbanzabugabo[1]
[1]Florida State University, Tallahassee, Florida, USA
[2]The University of Tennessee, Knoxville, Tennessee, USA

ABSTRACT

This systematic review investigates the impact of concept mapping on students' critical thinking (CT) skills by analyzing 17 empirical studies involving 1,363 students. Despite widespread claims that concept mapping enhances CT—defined here as analysis, evaluation, inference, deduction, and induction—the findings are mixed, largely due to inconsistencies in research design, reporting practices, and especially weaknesses in the tools used to assess concept maps and CT skills. Many studies failed to clearly identify which CT skills were targeted or how those skills contributed to map quality. Only one study evaluated map quality, a potentially valuable indicator of students' application of CT skills. To address these limitations, this paper proposes future directions for concept mapping tool development, highlighting tools like jMAP that integrate learning analytics and generative AI to track mapping behaviors, evaluate semantic link accuracy, and infer CT skills in real time. These capabilities offer a scalable, data-driven approach to identifying, monitoring, and supporting students' CT development. By operationalizing CT skills through observable mapping actions and embedding instructional prompts and feedback mechanisms, such tools support more precise and consistent assessment and scaffolding of student reasoning. These innovations aim to guide future research and practice in using concept mapping as a pedagogical strategy for cultivating essential 21st-century thinking skills.

KEYWORDS

Concept Maps, Critical Thinking, Learning Analytics

1. INTRODUCTION

Developing critical thinking skills in students is a key objective for promoting deeper learning, intellectual growth, and the development of the 21st-century skills needed to face real-world challenges (González-Salamanca et al., 2020; Thornhill-Miller, 2023). Concept mapping and the use of visual mapping tools in general have garnered attention for its potential to enhance not only student learning (Cañas et al., 2023) but also students' critical thinking (CT) skills (e.g., analysis, evaluation, inference, deduction, and induction) by prompting students to identify relationships between concepts and organize, analyze, evaluate, and synthesize information meaningfully (Cañas et al., 2017). Concept maps are visual tools that illustrate the connections between ideas. When students construct a concept map, concepts are placed in circles or boxes, with the main concept placed first on the map. Related concepts are then positioned hierarchically below the main concept and are linked by lines with linking words that show their relationships and form propositions (Padilla, 2017; Novak & Cañas, 2008). A proposition is formed by linking two concepts with a labeled line, typically arranging concepts from general to specific. Research indicates that concept mapping can enhance students' critical thinking skills (Barta et al., 2022; Chou et al., 2019; Fonseca et al., 2023). However, the results are mixed, and further research is needed to determine how concept mapping can be more effectively implemented to achieve consistent improvements across all critical thinking skills.

1.1 The Theory behind Concept Mapping

Concept mapping, introduced by Novak (1998), began as a tool to visualize children's understanding of science and has since evolved into a widely used educational strategy to enhance learning and teaching across disciplines. These maps, which include formats like causal maps and argument diagrams, visually represent relationships between concepts, aiding comprehension and critical thinking. Rooted in constructivist theories, especially Ausubel's assimilation theory, concept maps help learners integrate new information with existing knowledge, making learning more meaningful. They also align with information-processing theory by making knowledge structures explicit. The Novakian method involves identifying a central concept, organizing related ideas hierarchically, and connecting them with labeled lines to form propositions. This structured approach not only clarifies complex information but also encourages analytical and problem-solving skills by prompting learners to explore cross-connections between ideas. Additionally, concept mapping supports long-term retention by reinforcing the logical structure of knowledge, making it easier for students to recall and apply information. As a result, concept maps are increasingly being used in diverse fields such as medicine, engineering, and the humanities to foster deeper understanding and thinking.

1.2 Critical Thinking Skills & Instruments

Critical thinking (CT) is a foundational skill that enables students to interpret information, assess evidence, and make sound decisions. One of the most widely used tools to measure CT is the California Critical Thinking Skills Test (CCTST), developed by Facione (1990), which evaluates five core reasoning abilities: analysis, evaluation, inference, deduction, and induction. Analysis involves dissecting complex information to uncover patterns and relationships, while evaluation focuses on judging the credibility and relevance of arguments and evidence. Inference allows students to draw logical conclusions from data, deduction moves from general principles to specific conclusions, and induction builds generalizations from specific observations. These skills are essential for academic success and informed decision-making in real-world contexts. Researchers use the CCTST in various study designs, such as pretest-posttest comparisons, longitudinal tracking, and program evaluations, to assess how instructional methods influence CT development. These studies help educators and policymakers refine teaching strategies to better cultivate critical thinking. As CT becomes increasingly vital in education and the workforce, tools like the CCTST play a crucial role in identifying strengths and areas for growth and in guiding learning interventions.

1.3 The Effects of Concept Mapping on Students' Critical Thinking Skills

Concept maps are powerful tools for developing students' critical thinking (CT) by visually organizing and connecting information, which supports skills like analysis, evaluation, inference, deduction, and induction (Barta et al., 2022; Fonseca et al., 2023). By breaking down arguments into claims, evidence, and counterpoints, students can better evaluate and analyze content (Kim, 2022; LaCombe, 2023). These maps also help students infer unstated ideas and logically structure their reasoning, making them effective for both deductive and inductive thinking. For example, students might use concept maps to evaluate arguments in a climate change debate, analyze literary themes, outline scientific processes, or compare historical events. Despite their potential, studies show mixed results regarding their impact on CT, possibly due to inconsistent implementation of mapping strategies and a lack of standardization in construction methods (Ruiz-Primo, 2004; Oliveira et al., 2023). Research into the cognitive strategies students use while mapping is still emerging, but understanding these processes could clarify which techniques lead to higher-quality maps and better CT outcomes (Carrillo et al., 2017; Schroeder et al., 2017). Future studies can explore how mapping tools and student characteristics influence strategy use and how real-time guidance can enhance learning.

1.4 Concept Mapping Behaviors that Demonstrate Critical Thinking Skills

Various strategies have been proposed to guide students in constructing concept maps, drawing from disciplines such as education, information systems, and artificial intelligence. These include placing the main goal at the top of the map (Eppler, 2006), sorting nodes before linking them (Aguiar & Correia, 2017), organizing concepts by generality (Cañas et al., 2017), and aligning nodes with reading or temporal flow (Aguiar & Correia, 2017; Lee, 2012). Additional techniques like backward chaining, goal-oriented mapping, and depth- or breadth-first processing have also been explored (Al-Ajlan, 2015; Chen et al., 2010; Sharma et al., 2012; Biswas et al., 2016). The structure of the map—whether spoke-like, chain, or networked—can influence learning outcomes, with networked maps generally supporting deeper, more meaningful learning (He et al., 2023; Kinchin, 2011). However, limited research has directly examined the specific critical thinking (CT) skills students apply during the hierarchical linking phase of concept mapping. Think-aloud studies show that both experts and novices tend to use breadth-first over depth-first processing, with experts favoring backward (deductive) reasoning and novices showing mixed strategies (Kim, 2015; Kim, 2022). These behaviors have been linked to higher-quality maps, particularly when students use more breadth-first and backward processing (Lee, 2012; Shin, 2021).

To better understand these mapping behaviors, researchers have developed software tools that log students' actions during map construction. One such tool, jMAP, tracks node placements and uses algorithms to analyze the sequence and type of reasoning applied. Findings suggest that the relative frequency of backward versus forward processing and breadth-first versus depth-first processing—especially within the first five node placements—can predict the quality of students' maps in terms of accuracy and depth of analysis (Jeong, 2020). Interestingly, the individual frequency of each strategy alone did not predict map quality, highlighting the importance of balancing strategies. This early phase of mapping appears critical, as students often begin making corrections and cosmetic changes after placing the first few nodes. These insights underscore the value of using integrated tools and metrics to assess and guide CT skill development during concept mapping. Further research is needed to explore how these strategies influence students' ability to detect and correct logical flaws, ultimately improving map quality and critical thinking outcomes.

1.5 Systematic Literature Search on the Effects of Concept Mapping on Critical Thinking

This review systematically analyzed prior research on the impact of concept mapping on students' CT skills, focusing on which CT skills—such as identifying, placing, and linking concepts—were taught and applied during mapping. Following PRISMA guidelines (Page et al., 2021), the review detailed its methodology, including database searches, selection criteria, and data extraction centered on instructional strategies and CT components. Through narrative synthesis, it categorized how concept mapping was implemented, which CT skills were assessed, and evaluated the methodological strengths and weaknesses of the included studies. The review aimed to clarify concept mapping's role in fostering CT and to guide future research by identifying effective practices and highlighting the need for more consistent and detailed measurement and reporting.

2. METHOD

2.1 Search Strategy, Eligibility Criteria and Screening Process

To identify relevant studies, this review began with the 21 articles included in Barta et al.'s (2022) review, which conducted a comprehensive search across eight databases using terms related to concept mapping and student populations. To update their findings, we replicated their search strategy across six databases—PsycInfo, ProQuest, PubMed, ScienceDirect, Scopus, and Web of Science—for studies published between 2022 and May 2024. This updated search yielded 103 results, with seven duplicates removed, leaving 96 new articles. Combined with the original 21 studies, a total of 117 articles were screened for relevance to concept mapping and CT. This process ensured a comprehensive and current foundation for evaluating how concept mapping supports the development of CT skills.

During the title, abstract, and full-text screening phases, studies were excluded if they met any of the following ten eligibility criteria: not examining the effects of concept mapping on critical thinking; lacking empirical data or methodology; not conducting quantitative comparisons; failing to use established instruments to measure critical thinking; not using concept mapping as a teaching or learning method; being non-experimental; not peer-reviewed; misusing the term "map" (e.g., referring to cognitive or mind maps); not published in English; or published before May 2005, prior to the Nesbit and Adesope (2006) meta-analysis.

Figure 1 depicts the literature search process and details the screening stages for the 117 identified studies. Two researchers independently screened the studies to determine eligibility. Disagreements were resolved through discussion. Following a thorough screening of titles/abstracts and full texts, 17 studies were deemed eligible for inclusion and were selected for data extraction and analysis.

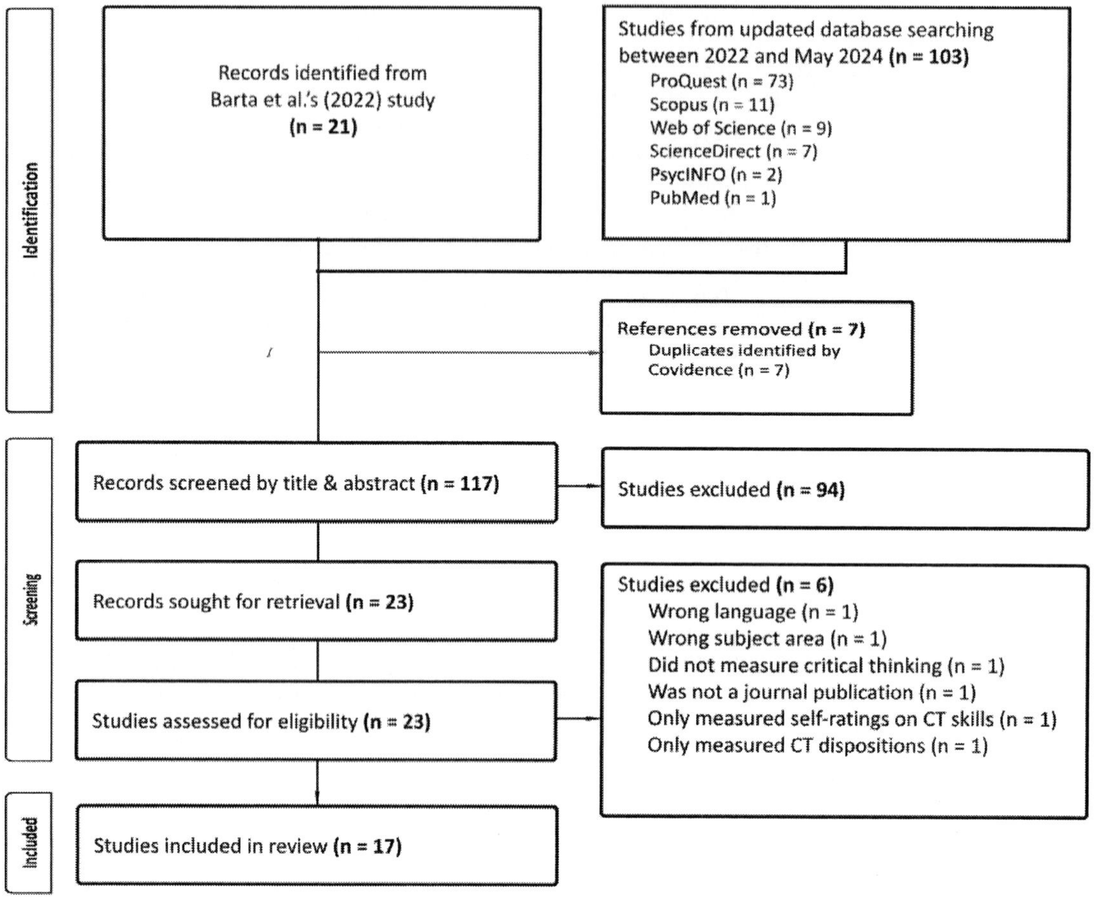

Figure 1. PRISMA flowchart for selecting studies published on and after March 2022

2.2 Data Extraction and Analysis

Two authors independently reviewed all 17 articles and extracted the data outlined in Table 1. Any discrepancies were discussed and resolved collaboratively. The extracted data were analyzed to evaluate the overall and specific effects of concept mapping on critical thinking (CT) skills, including analysis, evaluation, inference, deduction, and induction. A narrative analysis was then conducted to identify variations in study design and implementation, aiming to determine whether differences in concept mapping instruction and activities could explain the mixed findings across studies.

Table 1. Information and features extracted from each article

Academic field
Name of academic field

Concept Mapping instruction and training
Instructor feedback received on concept maps
Peer feedback received on concept maps
Students presented their maps to the class or group
Number of maps constructed by each student
Training demonstrated Novakian maps with top-down hierarchy
Training demonstrated horizontal process
Training showed spoke structured concept maps

Concept mapping measures
Reported the % student maps top-down hierarchical structure
Reported % student maps using horizontal structure
Reported % student maps with spoke structure
Scored students' maps

Measures of critical thinking & quality of concept maps
CT pre-tested
Analyzed & described the students' mapping processes
Name of the CT instrument used in study
Significant differences found in cumulative overall CT scores

Measured critical thinking skills and results

analysis	identify fallacies	discrimination
evaluation	self regulation	apply standards
inference	argument	transform knowledge
induction	prioritization	assessment
deduction	problem solving	planning
interpretation	resolution	implementation
explanation	logical reasoning	
assumptions	info seeking	

3. MAIN FINDINGS

3.1 Measures and Assessments of Critical Thinking

This review identified 17 studies that used established critical thinking (CT) instruments to evaluate the impact of concept mapping on students' CT skills (Table 2). Fifteen studies compared concept mapping to alternative instructional methods, while two used a single-group pre-posttest design. Most studies (76%) employed pre-post testing, and 82% were conducted in nursing education, with others involving students in language and physical education contexts. Six studies used the California Critical Thinking Skills Test (CCTST), while the remaining 11 used various instruments to assess core CT skills—analysis, evaluation, inference, deduction, and induction—as well as 17 related skills such as interpretation, explanation, assumptions, and logical reasoning. These related skills often overlap. For example, interpretation and assumptions are integral to analysis, while explanation and self-regulation enhance evaluation.

The CCTST was the most frequently used instrument, though nine different tools were employed across the 17 studies, measuring a wide range of CT-related skills such as interpretation, explanation, assumptions, and logical reasoning (Carvalho et al., 2020; Chen et al., 2011; Nurmala, 2011). This diversity in instruments and CT components created inconsistencies that hinder synthesis and meta-analysis, underscoring the need for standardized CT measurement frameworks in future research. Without consistent tools and definitions, it becomes difficult to compare outcomes across studies or draw generalizable conclusions. Establishing a unified framework with operationalized definitions of each CT skill would enhance the reliability of findings and support more targeted instructional strategies for developing CT skills.

Table 2. Selected characteristics of the 17 included studies

	Academic	Instrument	Nexp	Ncon	Pretest	Overall Score	Analysis	Evaluation	Inference	Deduction	Induction
Aien (2017)	Nursing	CCTST	30	30	n		*	*	*	*	*
Carvalho (2020)	Nursing	CCTST	39	38	y		*ns*	*	*ns*	*ns*	*ns*
Chen (2011)	Nursing	Cheng	47	48	y	*ns*		*ns*	*ns*	*ns*	
Huang (2017)	HS English	Yen (2009)	57	59	y	*		-		-	-
Kaddoura (2016)	Nursing	HESI	41	42	y	*	-				
Khodadady (2011)	Nursing	Watson-Glaser	18	18	y	*		-	-	-	
Khrais (2020)	Nursing	Ennis–Weir	58	57	y	*	-	-	-	-	-
Lee (2013)	Nursing	Cheng	46	48	y			*ns*	*	*	
Maneval (2011)	Nursing	Nursing	111	41	n		(*)	(*)	*ns*		
Moattari (2014)	Nursing	Nursing	16	16	n		*		*	*ns*	
Mohammadi (2019)	Nursing	CCTST	41	40	y	*	*	*	*ns*	*	*ns*
Nirmala (2011)	Nursing	TSA	40	44	y	*	-	-	-	-	-
Roshangar (2020)	5th grade	CCTST	28	27	y	*ns*	-	-	-	-	-
Sinatra-Wilhelm (2012)	Nursing	CCTST	22	22	n	*ns*	-	-	-	-	-
Tseng (2011)	Nursing	McMaster	51	69	y	*	*	*	*		
Tseng (2020)	Nursing	McMaster	23	20	y	*ns*	*	*	*		
Wheeler (2003)	English	CCTST	44	32	y	*ns*	*	*	*ns*	*ns*	*ns*
Percentage of studies					76%	58%	75%	67%	50%	43%	25%

* = positive and statistically significant, (*) = negative and statistically significant, *ns* = not significant

3.2 Effects of Concept Mapping Components of Critical Thinking

To compare the effects of concept mapping on individual critical thinking (CT) skills, six of the 17 studies analyzed the five CT components: analysis, evaluation, inference, deduction, and induction (see Table 3). Four of the six studies (80%) reported significant positive gains, while one showed a significant negative effect. For evaluation, 60% of studies found positive gains, one found no difference, and one reported a negative effect. Inference and deduction each showed significant improvements in 50–60% of the studies, while only one of three studies on induction reported a positive effect. A chi-square test revealed no significant differences in outcomes across the five CT skills, indicating that no specific skill consistently benefited more than others. Overall, the findings suggest that while concept mapping may enhance various CT skills, the evidence does not clearly favor improvements in any one skill, and fewer studies have examined its impact on induction compared to other CT components.

Table 3. Findings from six studies comparing CM to non-CM groups on individual CT skills

	Analysis	Evaluation	Inference	Deduction	Induction
Aien (2017)	*	*	*	*	*
Mohammadi (2019)	*	*	*ns*	*	*ns*
Wheeler (2003)	*	*	*ns*	*ns*	*ns*
Maneval (2011)	(*)	(*)	*ns*		
Moattari (2014)	*		*	*ns*	
Lee (2013)		*ns*	*	*	
% Significant differences	80%	60%	50%	60%	33%

* = positive and statistically significant, (*) = negative and statistically significant, *ns* = not significant

Examining the scores of individual CT components is essential for understanding how concept mapping influences student learning. These skills are interrelated, as gains in analysis and evaluation often coincide with improvements in inference, deduction, and induction. Although no significant differences were found in the distribution of improvements across CT components, the lack of consistent reporting, particularly in seven studies that omitted component-level data, limits conclusions about which skills benefit most. A more detailed, component-based approach to reporting CT outcomes could help educators tailor instruction and better understand the mixed results observed across studies. This approach would also support more targeted interventions to strengthen weaker CT areas. Ultimately, consistent reporting of both overall and component CT scores is crucial for advancing research and improving instructional practices.

3.3 Observing the Strategies Students Were Given to Construct Concept Maps

None of the 17 studies observed or reported the specific strategies students used to construct their concept maps, leaving it unclear whether students followed the instructional steps provided. Only four studies (Chen et al., 2011; Lee et al., 2013; Moattari et al., 2014; Roshangar et al., 2020) allowed inferences about student strategies based on instructions to begin mapping from the top, promoting hierarchical structures. In contrast, four other studies instructed students to start from the center, encouraging spoke-like structures. These gaps highlight the need for future research to precisely document and report what mapping instructions (including the constraints imposed by the interface in the concept-mapping software) are presented to students (explicitly or implicitly) to better understand what CT skills (skills associated with specific strategies) students use to produce higher quality maps.

3.4 Assessing and Reporting the Quality of Students' Maps

Only one of the 17 studies (Nurmala, 2011) assessed and reported the quality of students' concept maps, while the remaining 16 did not specify whether map quality was evaluated. Eight of these 16 studies noted that students received instructor feedback (e.g., Carvalho et al., 2020; Chen et al., 2011), and two also included peer feedback, though six others had peer presentations without clarifying if feedback was given. Two studies explicitly stated that no instructor feedback was provided (Khodadady & Ghanizadeh, 2011; Lee et al., 2013), and seven did not mention feedback at all. Overall, the studies varied widely in how they handled feedback and assessment, and no clear pattern emerged linking these practices to significant gains in overall or component CT scores. The main implication here is the prior studies fail to provide information on how students' CT skills (or lack of CT skills) produce correct and incorrect links in their maps, and ultimately how their CT skills impact the quality of students' maps.

The large absence of reports on the quality of students' concept maps is likely due to the complexity and challenges of assessing map accuracy (Chu, S.-T. et al., 2025). Unlike standardized tests, concept maps require nuanced judgment, making it difficult to align evaluations with specific critical thinking (CT) skills and ensure reliability. Researchers may prioritize broader CT outcomes over detailed map assessments due to time constraints, lack of standardized tools, or the resource-intensive nature of quality evaluation. However, recent mapping tools and methods (jMAP, 2025) offer promising ways to assess map quality (including the use of generative AI), which can provide valuable feedback to students and help clarify how well CT skills are being applied—ultimately contributing to a better understanding of concept mapping's effectiveness in developing CT. Incorporating quality assessments could also help identify patterns in student reasoning and highlight areas where instructional support is needed. As more refined tools become available, future studies can consider integrating map quality evaluation to enhance research rigor and educational impact.

3.5 Measuring and Identifying the CT Skills Students use to Construct Concept Maps

Our review found that none of the 17 studies examined or reported the specific critical thinking (CT) strategies students used while constructing concept maps, likely due to the complexity and time required to observe and analyze such processes. The high variability in map quality (Ruiz-Primo, 2004) suggests students used diverse strategies, and the absence of standardized tools or frameworks may have prevented researchers from capturing these details. Furthermore, large sample sizes and the labor-intensive nature of process analysis also may have led researchers to focus solely on outcomes – not mapping behaviors.

Addressing these challenges has important implications for educational research and practice. By breaking down CT skills into observable mapping actions—such as placing a node to represent deductive reasoning—researchers can more precisely document and analyze student strategies. Standardizing this process would improve the reliability of assessments and encourage broader exploration of how mapping behaviors influence CT development. Ultimately, this could lead to more rigorous, comparable findings across studies and inform more effective instructional practices for teaching CT skills.

4. FUTURE DIRECTIONS FOR CONCEPT MAPPING TOOLS

4.1 Challenges in Enhancing Concept Mapping Tools for Critical Thinking Assessment

The results of this review identified four challenges that suggest several directions for enhancing concept mapping tools to support the measurement, assessment, instruction, and development of students' critical thinking (CT) skills. The four challenges were: 1) the lack of operationalized definitions of the five critical thinking skills (analysis, evaluation, inference, deduction, and induction) to adequately distinguish these skills from one another and other related CT skills; 2) the lack of information and control over what CT skills are being prescribed via mapping instructions and mapping software; 3) lack of feasible methods to measure the quality of students' maps that enable close examination of CT skills used to produce higher quality maps; and 4) the lack of feasible methods and tools to identify and measure students' use of specific CT skills.

The following section outlines proposed features and software specifications that address each of these four challenges. These proposals are illustrated using some of the current capabilities of the concept mapping tool, jMAP. This tool tracks how students arrange and connect nodes, whether correctly or incorrectly, compared to an expert or instructor map. It uses algorithms to analyze these actions and infer the type of reasoning being applied, such as forward deduction, backward deduction, or problem decomposition. Generative AI was recently integrated into jMAP to enable it to provide real-time validation of links while creating open-ended maps (without having to specify nodes in advance) on any common topic, identify the specific CT skill demonstrated by each action, and offer guidance on potential logical fallacies relevant to the CT skill being used (see Figure 2). Presented below are potential solutions to the four challenges that incorporate both existing capabilities of jMAP and newly proposed functions.

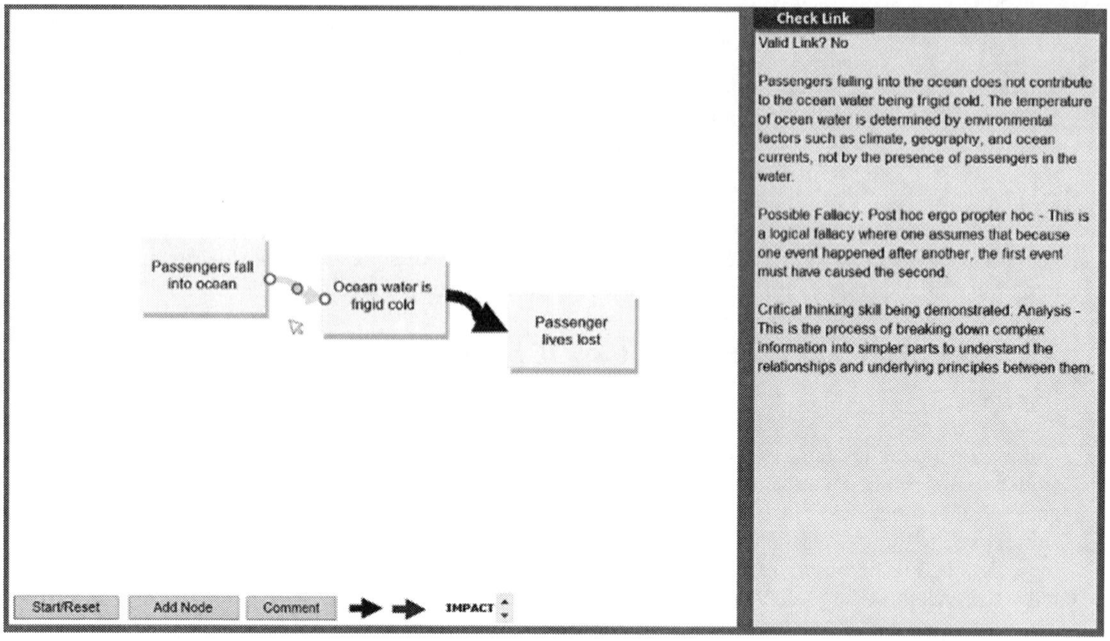

Figure 2. A causal map of events leading to the deaths of Titanic passengers in jMAP
Note: Arrows in faded black/red = invalid links, black = positive impact, red = negative impact

4.2 Operationalize the Definitions of CT Skills

To address the first challenge—the lack of operationalized definitions of the five core critical thinking (CT) skills—tools like jMAP can be enhanced to define each CT skill in terms of specific, observable mapping behaviors. For example, analysis can be operationalized as the act of breaking down a problem into sequential or hierarchical components, such as linking "passengers fell into the ocean" to "the ocean was frigid cold" and then to "passengers died." Deduction might be demonstrated when a student applies general knowledge (e.g., cold water causes hypothermia) to a specific case, while induction could be inferred from generalizing patterns across multiple examples. These definitions can be embedded into algorithms in the concept mapping software to automatically detect and classify student actions, enabling more precise identification of CT skills in real time. This approach not only clarifies what each CT skill looks like in practice but also supports more consistent assessment across learners and contexts.

Below is a more detailed description of how the CT skills can be operationally defined and measured in terms of specific actions students perform while constructing a map using these three nodes: A = Passengers fall into the ocean, B = The ocean water is frigid cold, and C = Passenger lives are lost.

Analysis - Breaking down the scenario into distinct, sequential events, or breaking down information into parts: The student creates and erroneously places A to the immediate left of B after linking B → C (mistaking temporal sequence for causality). Or, the student places A directly above or below B to correctly recognize that A and B are two independent events that contribute to the loss of passenger lives (A → C and B → C).

Evaluation - Assessing the logical strength of the connection between A and B or assessing credibility and relevance: The student recognizes that when one event A happens after another event B, it does not necessarily mean that B causes A. The student then deletes the link between A → B or redirects the link to produce A → C. Or the student moves A away from B when causality was conveyed merely by placing A to the immediate left of B (without inserting a link between A and B).

Inference - Interpreting and drawing likely conclusions from evidence, observations, or premises - going beyond the surface information to understand deeper meanings or predict outcomes: The student creates and places B to the immediate left of C, inserts a link to connect B to C, and increases the width (or level of "impact") of the link to convey that B is highly likely to lead to C.

Deduction - Reasoning from general to specific and applying general knowledge to a specific case to reach a certain conclusion if premises are true: The student places B to the immediate left of C and inserts Hypothermia between B and C to produce (B → Hypothermia → C), and/or the student places A to the left of C and inserts Hypothermia between A and C (A → Hypothermia → C).

Induction - Reasoning from specific to general, generalizing from experience, evidence, and/or similar past incidents to draw plausible conclusions: The student inserts the link (B → C) and attaches a "comment" to the link to describe past incident(s) where exposure to frigid waters leads to lost lives.

4.3 Lack of Control Over CT Skills Prescribed in the Instructions & Mapping Tools

The second challenge—the lack of clarity on what CT skills are being prescribed through mapping demonstrations, instructions, and software—can be addressed by embedding explicit instructional cues and prompts within jMAP. Teachers and students are likely unaware of which CT skills are being targeted during map construction. By integrating AI-generated guidance that aligns with specific CT skills, jMAP can prompt students to try different reasoning strategies or lines of inquiry to identify possible errors on their own. For example, suggesting the use of backward deductive thinking (B happens because of A) can prompt students to ask themselves whether the waters were frigid because the passengers fell into the ocean, and by doing so, help the students realize the error in inference. For instance, when a student begins a map, the tool might suggest starting with a backward reasoning approach to identify root causes or encourage breadth-first processing to explore multiple contributing factors. Ultimately, tools of this kind can help make the presentation and application of CT skills more transparent to students and instructors (including researchers). Furthermore, these types of embedded prompts can be customized by educators to align with instructional goals and can be tracked to evaluate whether students apply the intended CT skills, thereby making the instructional design behind the classroom instruction and mapping tasks more transparent and measurable.

4.4 Lack of Feasible Methods to Measure Map Quality

The third challenge is measuring the quality of students' maps in a way that can help reveal the CT skills that are most likely to produce correct links. jMAP's current capabilities support the comparison of a student's map against an expert or instructor's map, but it also employs a multi-layered scoring system that evaluates not only the correctness of links but also the depth and structure of reasoning. For example, maps are scored based on the number of correctly linked causal chains (first-, second-, and third-order links) stemming from a correctly identified root cause (jMAP, 2025). These metrics provide a more nuanced picture and assessment of student understanding and allow educators to pinpoint which CT skills need reinforcement. Importantly, the integration of generative AI now enables jMAP to assess open-ended maps on any common topic without relying on a pre-defined expert map when constructing closed-ended maps (when students are given predefined concepts to organize into a map). By generating a criterion map dynamically from the student's own nodes and evaluating the semantic and logical relationships between them, jMAP (or any mapping tool that can incorporate generative AI) can ultimately determine the effectiveness of students' reasoning processes used during open-ended problem analysis and exploration. Moreover, such tools can be used to identify thinking processes that produce incorrect links and, as a result, provide targeted feedback to help students find and correct errors.

4.5 Lack of Tools to Identify & Measure CT Skills used to Construct the Maps

The algorithms in jMAP are designed to detect students' use of critical thinking (CT) skills by analyzing how they position nodes in relation to one another during concept map construction. Specifically, the system examines the sequential placement of the three most recently added nodes to infer when students are engaging in more complex CT processes, such as evaluating evidence, synthesizing ideas, or drawing conclusions. This spatial and temporal analysis provides insights into the structure of students' reasoning beyond individual links. With generative AI integrated into jMAP, the AI component of jMAP can assess the semantic and logical validity of the relationships in real time. For instance, in the example illustrated in Figure 1, AI prompts are generated in jMAP to determine whether the two linked nodes are causally related (directly or indirectly), identify the specific CT skill demonstrated by the placement of the link, and to present alerts to potential flaws in reasoning that can occur while performing the specific CT skill. At this time, the generative AI appears to excel in identifying granular CT skills based on link quality. However, jMAP will possibly need to rely on its algorithmic analysis of node placement and sequence to identify multi-step CT skills such as analysis and evaluation (as explained above). This dual-layered approach can make mapping tools of this kind both scalable and practical for classroom use, supporting formative assessment and instructional decision-making.

4.6 Conclusion

Based on the review of prior studies that examined how concept mapping impacts the development of students' CT skills, these proposed enhancements to mapping software address four specific challenges in researching and implementing mapping tools to teach CT skills. By operationalizing CT skills into observable mapping behaviors, embedding instructional prompts that align with specific reasoning strategies, and implementing a multi-layered scoring system that evaluates both correct and incorrect links, jMAP and tools of this kind can be further developed to provide a more precise and actionable framework for assessing student thinking. The integration of generative AI further extends these capabilities by enabling real-time analysis of open-ended maps without relying on expert templates, allowing for scalable, topic-agnostic assessment of CT skills. These innovations not only improve the accuracy and depth of CT skill measurement but also provide educators with timely, targeted feedback to guide instruction. More broadly, these developments signal a shift toward intelligent learning environments that can adapt to student input, support metacognitive reflection, and foster deeper engagement with complex problem-solving. As educational systems increasingly emphasize critical thinking as a core competency, tools like jMAP represent a significant step forward in equipping both students and teachers with the means to cultivate and evaluate these essential skills in meaningful, data-informed ways.

REFERENCES

Aguiar, J. G., & Correia, P. R. M. (2017). From representing to modeling knowledge: Proposing a two-step training for excellence in concept mapping. *Knowledge Management & E-Learning*, *9*(3), 366–379.

Aein, F., & Aliakbari, F. (2017). Effectiveness of concept mapping and traditional linear nursing care plans on critical thinking skills in clinical pediatric nursing course. *Journal of education and health promotion*, *6*(1), 13.

Al-Ajlan, A. (2015). The comparison between forward and backward chaining. *International Journal of Machine Learning and Computing*, *5*(2), 106.

Anastasiou, D., Wirngo, C. N., & Bagos, P. (2024). The Effectiveness of Concept Maps on Students' Achievement in Science: A Meta-Analysis. *Educational Psychology Review*, *36*(2), 39.

Atay, S., & Karabacak, Ü. (2012). Care plans using concept maps and their effects on the critical thinking dispositions of nursing students. *International Journal of Nursing Practice*, *18*(3), 233-239.

Barta, A., Fodor, L. A., Tamas, B., & Szamoskozi, I. (2022). The development of students critical thinking abilities and dispositions through the concept mapping learning method–A meta-analysis. *Educational Research Review*, *37*, 100481.

Biswas, G., Segedy, J. R., & Bunchongchit, K. (2016). From design to implementation to practice a learning by teaching system: Betty's Brain. *International Journal of Artificial Intelligence in Education*, *26*(1), 350–364.

Cañas, A. J., Reiska, P., & Möllits, A. (2017). Developing higher-order thinking skills with concept mapping: A case of pedagogic frailty. *Knowledge management & e-learning*, *9*(3), 348.

Cañas, A. J., Reiska, P., & Shvaikovsky, O. (2023). Improving learning and understanding through concept mapping. *Knowledge Management & E-Learning*, *15*(3), 369-380.

Carrillo, R., Renaud, C., Prié, Y., & Lavoué, E. (2017, July). Dashboard for monitoring student engagement in mind mapping activities. In *2017 IEEE 17th International Conference on Advanced Learning Technologies (ICALT)* (pp. 433-437). IEEE.

Carrillo, R., Prié, Y., & Lavoué, É. (2019). Observing learner engagement on mind mapping activities using Learning Analytics. In *Transforming Learning with Meaningful Technologies: 14th European Conference on Technology Enhanced Learning, EC-TEL 2019, Delft, The Netherlands, September 16–19, 2019, Proceedings 14* (pp. 668-672). Springer International Publishing.

Carvalho, D. P. D. S. R. P., Vitor, A. F., Cogo, A. L. P., Bittencourt, G. K. G. D., Santos, V. E. P., & Ferreira, M. A. (2020). Critical thinking in nursing students from two Brazilian regions. *Revista Brasileira de Enfermagem*, *73*(1), e20170742.

Chen, J. C., Li, Y., & Shady, B. D. (2010). From value stream mapping toward a lean/sigma continuous improvement process: an industrial case study. *International Journal of Production Research*, *48*(4), 1069-1086.

Chen, S. L., Liang, T., Lee, M. L., & Liao, I. C. (2011). Effects of concept map teaching on students' critical thinking and approach to learning and studying. *Journal of Nursing Education*, *50*(8), 466-469.

Chou, T. L., Wu, J. J., & Tsai, C. C. (2019). Research trends and features of critical thinking studies in e-learning environments: A review. *Journal of Educational Computing Research*, *57*(4), 1038-1077.

Eppler, M. J. (2006). A comparison between concept maps, mind maps, conceptual diagrams, and visual metaphors as complementary tools for knowledge construction and sharing. *Information Visualization*, *5*(3), 202–210.

Facione, P.A. (1990). *The California Critical Thinking Skills Test–College Level. Technical Report# 1. Experimental Validation and Content Validity*. https://files.eric.ed.gov/fulltext/ED327549.pdf (accessed on December 12, 2024)

Fonseca, M., Marvão, P., Oliveira, B., Heleno, B., Carreiro-Martins, P., Neuparth, N., & Rendas, A. (2023). The effectiveness of concept mapping as a tool for developing critical thinking in undergraduate medical education–a BEME systematic review: BEME Guide No. 81. *Medical Teacher*, 1-14.

González-Salamanca, J. C., Agudelo, O. L., & Salinas, J. (2020). Key competences, education for sustainable development and strategies for the development of 21st century skills. A systematic literature review. *Sustainability*, *12*(24), 10366.

Huang, M. Y., Tu, H. Y., Wang, W. Y., Chen, J. F., Yu, Y. T., & Chou, C. C. (2017). Effects of cooperative learning and concept mapping intervention on critical thinking and basketball skills in elementary school. *Thinking Skills and Creativity*, *23*, 207-216.

Jeong, A. (2025). jMAP. https://sites.google.com/site/causalmaps/jmap

Kaddoura, M., Van-Dyke, O., & Yang, Q. (2016). Impact of a concept map teaching approach on nursing students' critical thinking skills. *Nursing & health sciences*, *18*(3), 350-354.

Kinchin, I. M. (2011). Relating knowledge structures to learning styles and university teaching. In *Style Differences in Cognition, Learning, and Management*, Edited by: Rayner, S. and Cools, E. Pp. 129–142. Routledge.

Kim, H. Y. (2015). Modeling the reasoning processes in experts and novices' argument diagramming task: Sequential analysis of diagramming behavior and think-aloud data (Doctoral dissertation, The Florida State University).

Kim, H. Y. (2022). Identifying and linking critical thinking skills used in computer-aided mapping tools to construct argument maps. *Knowledge Management & E-Learning*, 125-149.

Khodadady, E., & Ghanizadeh, A. (2011). The Impact of Concept Mapping on EFL Learners' Critical Thinking Ability. *English Language Teaching*, *4*(4), 49-60.

Khrais, H., & Saleh, A. M. (2020). The effect of concept mapping on critical thinking of Jordanian nursing students. *Creative Nursing*, *26*(1), 19-24.

Lee, W. J. (2012). Developing causal understanding with causal maps: The impact of total links, temporal flow, and lateral position of outcome nodes. *Educational Technology Research and Development*, *60*, 325-340.

Lee, W., Chiang, C. H., Liao, I. C., Lee, M. L., Chen, S. L., & Liang, T. (2013). The longitudinal effect of concept map teaching on critical thinking of nursing students. *Nurse Education Today*, *33*(10), 1219-1223.

Maneval, R. E., Filburn, M. J., Deringer, S. O., & Lum, G. D. (2011). Concept mapping: Does it improve critical thinking ability in practical nursing students?. *Nursing Education Perspectives*, *32*(4), 229-233.

Moattari, M., Soleimani, S., Moghaddam, N. J., & Mehbodi, F. (2014). Clinical concept mapping: Does it improve discipline-based critical thinking of nursing students?. *Iranian Journal of Nursing and Midwifery Research*, *19*(1), 70-76.

Mohammadi, F., Momennasab, M., Rostambeygi, P., Ghaderi, S., & Mousazadeh, S. (2019). The effect of education through conceptual mapping on critical thinking of nursing students. *Journal of the Pakistan Medical Association*, *69*(8), 1094-1098.

Nesbit, J. C., & Adesope, O. O. (2006). Learning with concept and knowledge maps: A meta-analysis. *Review of Educational Research*, *76*(3), 413-448.

Novak, J. D. (1998). *Concept Maps as Facilitative Tools in Schools and Corporations*. Mahvah: Lawrence Erlbaum Associates.

Novak, D.J. & Cañas, J.A. (2008), The theory underlying concept maps and how to construct and use them. *Technical Report IHMC CmapTools* 2006-01 Rev 01-2008, Florida Institute for Human and Machine Cognition, 2008. https://cmap.ihmc.us/publications/ResearchPapers/TheoryUnderlyingConceptMapshq.pdf

Nirmala, T., & Shakuntala, B. S. (2011). Concept mapping–An effective tool to promote critical thinking skills among nurses. *Journal of Health and Allied Sciences NU*, *1*(04), 21-26.

Oliveira, B., Fonseca, M., Rendas, A., Carreiro-Martins, P., & Neuparth, N. (2023). A scoping review comparing different mapping approaches pointing to the need for standardizing concept maps in medical education: A Preliminary analysis. *Knowledge Management & E-Learning*, *15*(3), 392-419.

Padilla, S., Methven, T., Robb, D., & Chantler, M. J. (2017). Understanding concept maps: A closer look at how people organize ideas. In *2017 CHI Conference on Human Factors in Computing Systems: Explore, Innovate, Inspire* (pp. 815-827). Association for Computing Machinery.

Roshangar, F., Azar, E. F., Sarbakhsh, P., & Azarmi, R. (2020). The effect of case-based learning with or without conceptual mapping method on critical thinking and academic self-efficacy of nursing students. *Journal of Biochemical Technology*, *11*(1-2020), 37-44.

Ruiz-Primo M. A. (2004). Examining concept maps as an assessment tool. In A. J. Cañas, J. D. Novak, & F. M. González (Eds.), *Concept maps: Theory, methodology, technology. Proceedings of the first international conference on concept mapping, Pamplona, Spain*. http://cmc.ihmc.us/cmc2012Papers/cmc2012-p188.pdf

Schroeder, N. L., Nesbit, J. C., Anguiano, C. J., & Adesope, O. O. (2018). Studying and constructing concept maps: A meta-analysis. *Educational psychology review*, *30*, 431-455.

Sharma, T., Tiwari, N., & Kelkar, D. (2012). Study of difference between forward and backward reasoning. *International Journal of Emerging Technology and Advanced Engineering*, *2*(10), 271–273.

Shin, H. S. (2021). Modeling the relationship between students' prior knowledge, causal reasoning processes, and quality of causal maps. *Computers & Education*, *163*, 104113.

Sinatra-Wilhelm, T. (2012). Nursing care plans versus concept maps in the enhancement of critical thinking skills in nursing students enrolled in a baccalaureate nursing program. *Creative Nursing*, *18*(2), 78-84.

Tseng, H. C., Chou, F. H., Wang, H. H., Ko, H. K., Jian, S. Y., & Weng, W. C. (2011). The effectiveness of problem-based learning and concept mapping among Taiwanese registered nursing students. *Nurse Education Today*, *31*(8), 41-46.

Tseng, S. S. (2020). Using concept mapping activities to enhance students' critical thinking skills at a high school in Taiwan. *The Asia-Pacific Education Researcher*, *29*(3), 249-256.

Thornhill-Miller, B., Camarda, A., Mercier, M., Burkhardt, J. M., Morisseau, T., Bourgeois-Bougrine, S., ... & Lubart, T. (2023). Creativity, critical thinking, communication, and collaboration: assessment, certification, and promotion of 21st century skills for the future of work and education. *Journal of Intelligence*, *11*(3), 54.

Wheeler, L. A., & Collins, S. K. (2003). The influence of concept mapping on critical thinking in baccalaureate nursing students. *Journal of Professional Nursing*, *19*(6), 339-346.

EXPLORING RANKING CONSISTENCY OF GENERATIVE AI IN MOOC PLATFORM EVALUATION: A NON-PARAMETRIC APPROACH

Victor K. Y. Chan
Macao Polytechnic University, Rua de Luís Gonzaga Gomes, Macao, China

ABSTRACT

This paper extends a prior study on the consistency of generative Artificial Intelligence (AI) models in evaluating Massive Open Online Course (MOOC) platforms. While the original work focused on the consistency of direct numerical scores, this research investigates the consistency of the rankings derived from those scores. When evaluating platforms, the relative order (i.e., which platform is better than another) is often more critical to a decision-maker than the absolute scores, which may be subject to systematic biases. This study analyzes the scores of 31 MOOC platforms across eight dimensions as evaluated by two AI models, Claude+ and Dragonfly. A suite of non-parametric statistical methods are employed, including Spearman's Rank Correlation Coefficient (ρ), Kendall's Tau (τ), and the top-weighted Rank-Biased Overlap (RBO), to measure the concordance of the platform rankings produced by each model. The Wilcoxon Signed-Rank Test is used to assess systematic differences in scoring. Results indicate a moderate to strong monotonic correlation in rankings for dimensions like (2) pedagogical design, (1) content/course quality, and (6) Learner Engagement, reinforcing the original study's findings of consistency. However, the RBO analysis reveals that this agreement is weaker for the top-ranked platforms, providing a more nuanced understanding of AI evaluation consistency. The systemic scoring bias found in the original study is also reaffirmed here. This rank-based analysis offers a robust alternative to score-based comparisons, mitigating the effects of differing internal scoring scales and highlighting the practical utility of AI evaluations for comparative decision-making. By shifting the focus from absolute scores to relative rankings, this study underscores the practical value of generative AI as a decision-support tool in educational technology evaluation. The findings not only enhance methodological rigor in AI-based assessments but also provide actionable insights for learners and institutions navigating an increasingly complex MOOC landscape.

KEYWORDS

Generative AI, MOOC Platforms, Ranking Consistency, Relative Rankings

1. INTRODUCTION

The emergence of Massive Open Online Courses (MOOCs) over the last two decades has fundamentally altered the landscape of higher education and lifelong learning. With dozens of platforms offering thousands of courses, prospective learners and educational institutions face a daunting task in selecting the most suitable option. Traditional evaluation methods, such as user surveys and expert reviews, are often resource-intensive, slow, and limited in scope (Alturkistani et al, 2020), making it difficult to perform comprehensive, up-to-date comparisons across the entire MOOC ecosystem.

In response to this challenge, a pioneering study by Chan (2023) explored the use of generative Artificial Intelligence (AI) models as a novel solution for automated MOOC platform evaluation. The premise was that large language models, trained on vast swathes of internet text, could synthesize global user comments and expert opinions to produce standardized scores. The original study tasked four AI models (Claude+, Dragonfly, GPT-4, and Sage) with scoring 31 popular MOOC platforms across eight critical dimensions. The core of Chan's (2023) analysis was to assess the *consistency* between the AI models' evaluations, primarily using Pearson's correlation coefficient on the direct numerical scores provided by Claude+ and Dragonfly, the two models that returned sufficiently complete data. The rationale is straightforward: if different AI models, acting as independent judges, arrive at similar conclusions, it lends credibility to their assessments, analogous to the concept of convergent validity in psychometric testing. The study found significant linear correlations for three dimensions, but also revealed that one model systematically underrated or overrated platforms relative to the other, highlighting inherent discrepancy in their scoring mechanisms.

This paper builds directly upon that foundational work by proposing and executing an alternative, and arguably more pragmatically relevant, mode of analysis: the consistency of *ranking* rather than scoring. The decision to focus on ranks is rooted in a fundamental question of utility. For a user choosing a MOOC platform, the absolute score (e.g., a 7.8 vs. a 7.5) is often less important than the relative order ("Is Coursera better than edX in the dimension of pedagogical design?"). Numerical scores are susceptible to scale interpretation differences; one evaluator's "8" might be another's "6", even if they agree on the relative merit of the items being assessed (Zimmerman and Zumbo, 1993). An analysis based on ranks, or ordinal data, is inherently robust to such systematic shifts in scale. It focuses purely on the monotonic relationship: does one platform's rank increase when the other's does? This approach can therefore uncover a deeper layer of agreement that might be obscured by superficial differences in scoring calibration. The literature on preference measurement and information retrieval has long recognized the stability and utility of rank-based comparisons over cardinal scores, especially when dealing with subjective human judgments, a domain that generative AI aims to replicate (Shah et al, 2014).

To conduct this rank-based investigation, this research employs a suite of powerful non-parametric statistical methods, each offering a unique lens on the data: Spearman's Rank Correlation Coefficient (ρ), Kendall's Tau (τ), Rank-Biased Overlap (RBO), and Wilcoxon Signed-Rank Test.

By applying this comprehensive analytical framework to Chan's (2023) original dataset, this paper aims to achieve several objectives. First, it seeks to determine if the consistency found by Chan (2023) holds when subjected to a more robust, rank-based analysis. Second, it aims to provide a more nuanced understanding of this consistency by examining it from multiple statistical perspectives (overall correlation vs. top-weighted agreement). Finally, by comparing the rank-based findings here directly with the original score-based results, this paper will discuss the broader implications for using generative AI in evaluative tasks and offer practical guidance for individuals and institutions navigating the complex MOOC landscape. By shifting the focus from absolute scores to relative rankings, this study underscores the practical value of generative AI as a decision-support tool in educational technology evaluation. The findings not only enhance methodological rigor in AI-based assessments but also provide actionable insights for learners and institutions navigating an increasingly complex MOOC landscape.

2. METHODOLOGY

This study utilizes the data and foundational framework established by Chan (2023) but applies a novel analytical lens focused on non-parametric rank comparison.

2.1 Data and Materials

The data for this analysis is taken directly from that compiled and presented in Chan (2023). The dataset was generated through a structured process designed to elicit evaluative scores from generative AI models.

2.1.1 AI Models and Data Generation

Chan (2023) initially experimented with four AI models available on the poe.com portal: Claude+, Dragonfly (de Souza et al, 2023), GPT-4 (Zhang et al, 2023), and Sage (de Souza et al, 2023). To generate the list of platforms for evaluation, the models Sage and Dragonfly were prompted to "name 20 most popular MOOC platforms." The union of their responses, after removing duplicates, yielded a final list of 32 platforms. Subsequently, all four models were given a detailed prompt to give a score to each of the above 32 MOOC platforms in each of the eight dimensions (1) content/course quality, (2) pedagogical design, (3) learner support, (4) technology infrastructure, (5) social interaction, (6) learner engagement, (7) instructor support, and (8) cost-effectiveness based on a scale of 1 to 10 (1 being the worst and 10 the best). In particular, the prompt reminded the models to derive the scores from global users' textual comments on these eight dimensions of these platforms as appear all around the web.

Only Claude+ and Dragonfly provided responses comprehensive enough for statistical analysis. GPT-4 and Sage returned highly fragmented data. After removing one platform (Google Digital Garage) for which Claude+ provided incomplete scores, the final dataset for analysis consisted of scores for 31 MOOC platforms from two AI models across eight dimensions. These platforms are: Coursera, edX, Udacity, Udemy, Khan Academy, Alison, FutureLearn, Open2Study, Saylor Academy, Canvas Network, OpenLearning, Academic Earth, Open Education by Blackboard, Open Yale Courses, MIT OpenCourseWare, Carnegie Mellon Open Learning Initiative, Harvard Extension School, Stanford Online, Rice University OpenStax, Eliademy, Google Classroom, Harvard Online Learning, Iversity, LinkedIn Learning, Lynda.com, Miríada X, NovoEd, Pluralsight, Skillshare, UNED COMA, and XuetangX.

2.1.2 Dimensions of Evaluation

The eight dimensions used for evaluation were identified by Chan (2023) from a review of seminal literature on MOOC quality and effectiveness (Khalil and Ebner, 2014). They represent a holistic framework for assessing a platform's value proposition, and are as follows: (1) **Content/Course Quality:** This measures the accuracy, relevance, and instructional design of the course materials. High-quality content is a cornerstone of learner satisfaction and a critical factor for effective learning (Hew and Cheung, 2014). (2) **Pedagogical Design:** This refers to the underlying instructional strategies, assessment methods, and learning activities. Effective pedagogical design encourages active learning and is crucial for learner motivation and achieving learning outcomes. (3) **Learner Support:** This encompasses the academic and technical assistance available to students. Adequate support structures are strongly linked to higher completion rates and overall learner satisfaction (Liyanagunawardena et al, 2013). (4) **Technology Infrastructure:** This dimension assesses the platform's technical performance, including reliability (uptime), speed, device compatibility, and user-friendliness of the interface. A robust infrastructure is the foundation upon which the entire learning experience is built (Albelbisi, 2020). (5) **Social Interaction:** This evaluates the opportunities for learners to engage with peers and instructors through forums, group projects, and other collaborative tools. Social interaction fosters a sense of community and can significantly enhance the learning experience (Hew and Cheung, 2014). (6) **Learner Engagement:** This measures the level of interaction between the learner and the course content and community. Engagement is a key predictor of learning outcomes and course completion (Kizilcec et al, 2013). (7) **Instructor Support:** This dimension focuses specifically on the quality and availability of support from instructors, such as their responsiveness in forums and the frequency of their engagement with the learning community (Khalil and Ebner, 2014). (8) **Cost-Effectiveness:** This assesses the value derived from the platform relative to its cost, considering factors like free content availability, certification costs, and potential return on investment for the learner.

2.2 Analysis

The core of the methodology here is the application of non-parametric statistical techniques to the rank-transformed data. The analysis was conducted for each of the eight dimensions separately.

First, for each dimension, the raw scores (1-10) from Claude+ and Dragonfly were converted into ranks from 1 (best) to 31 (worst). This transformation discards the absolute magnitude of the scores, focusing solely on the relative ordering of the 31 platforms. In cases of tied scores, a standard procedure was used where the tied platforms were assigned the mean of the ranks they would have occupied (Corder and Foreman, 2014; Siegel and Castellan, 1988). It is important to note that for three dimensions—(3) learner support, (4) technology infrastructure, and (7) instructor support—Dragonfly assigned a constant score to all 31 platforms. This lack of variance makes it impossible to generate a meaningful ranking, and therefore, these three dimensions were excluded from any further analysis of rank correlation (i.e., Spearman's Rank Correlation Coefficient ρ and Kendall's τ-b), RBO and the Wilcoxon Signed-Rank Test.

The following statistical tests were then applied to the remaining five dimensions:

1. **Spearman's Rank Correlation Coefficient (ρ):** ρ is a cornerstone of non-parametric statistics and a classical rank correlation measurement. It gauges the strength and direction of a monotonic relationship between two variables (Spearman, 1904; Zar, 2013). It effectively asks: "Do the two AI models tend to rank platforms in a similar order?" Specifically, it was calculated in this study to measure the strength and direction of the monotonic association between the rankings from Claude+ and Dragonfly. The coefficient ranges from -1 (perfect negative monotonic relationship) to +1 (perfect positive monotonic relationship), with 0 indicating no monotonic relationship. The p-value was computed to test the null hypothesis of zero correlation.

2. **Kendall's Tau-b (τ-b):** **τ-b** is another common rank correlation measurement. It provides an alternative measure of rank correlation by analyzing all possible pairs of platforms to determine if the AI models agree on their relative ordering (Kendall, 1938, Hamed, 2011). It is sometimes considered more robust than Spearman's ρ, especially with smaller datasets or numerous tied ranks, as its value has a direct probabilistic interpretation. This coefficient was also calculated to measure rank association. Kendall's Tau evaluates all possible pairs of ranks as rated by the two AI models and counts the number of concordant pairs (pairs ranked in the same order by both models) and discordant pairs (pairs ranked in opposite orders). The τ-b variant is specifically designed to handle tied ranks. Its value also ranges from -1 (perfect negative monotonic relationship) to +1 (perfect positive monotonic relationship), and its p-value tests the null hypothesis of independence between the two rankings.
3. **Rank-Biased Overlap (RBO):** RBO is a more sophisticated similarity measure developed in information retrieval for comparing ranked lists, such as search engine results (Webber et al, 2010). Its defining feature is being "top-weighted," meaning it places greater emphasis on agreement at the top of the rankings than at the bottom. This aligns perfectly with the user behavior of someone seeking the "best" platforms, making RBO a highly relevant tool for assessing the practical utility of the AI evaluations. To assess top-weighted agreement, this study calculated the RBO, which examines ranks from the top down with a persistence parameter p of continuing to the next rank. The parameter p controls the degree of top-weighting; a value close to 1 indicates high persistence and considers deeper ranks down, while a value close to 0 focuses almost exclusively on the very top. This study chose a persistence parameter of $p = .9$, representing an inclination which is quite thorough down the ranks but still places significantly more importance on the top ranks. The RBO score ranges from 0 (disjoint lists) to 1 (identical lists).
4. **Wilcoxon Signed-Rank Test:** This test serves as the non-parametric counterpart to the paired t-test used in Chan's (2023) original study (Corder and Foreman, 2014; Wilcoxon, 1945; Rey and Neuhäuser, 2010). Instead of comparing mean scores, it tests whether the median of the differences between the paired scores is zero. This allows investigating whether the systematic bias identified by Chan (2023) persists even after transforming the data to an ordinal scale underlying the above median as opposed to the corresponding mean. This test was used to determine if there was a systematic difference between the paired scores assigned by the two AI models. It tests the null hypothesis that the median of the differences between the paired scores for the 31 platforms is zero. A significant p-value suggests that one AI model consistently assigns higher (or lower) scores to the platforms than the other, indicating a persistent systematic bias even in the ordinal domain as manifested by the above median as opposed to the corresponding mean.

3. RESULTS

The application of non-parametric statistical tests to the ranked data reveals a multi-faceted view of the consistency between Claude+ and Dragonfly. The primary findings are summarized in Table 1 (rank correlation and RBO) and Table 2 (Wilcoxon Signed-Rank Test).

Table 1. Rank correlation and RBO between Claude+ and Dragonfly rankings across 31 MOOC platforms

Dimension	Spearman's ρ / 95% CI	p-value (ρ)	Kendall's τ-b / 95% CI	p-value (τ)	RBO ($p = .9$)
(1) Content/Course Quality	.467 / [.124, .710]	.008**	.417 / [.192, .600]	.010*	.250
(2) Pedagogical Design	.614 / [.322, .799]	.000**	.538 / [.339, .692]	.001**	.419
(3) Learner Support	-	-	-	-	-
(4) Technology Infrastructure	-	-	-	-	-
(5) Social Interaction	-.206 / [-.530, .171]	.267	-.183 / [.409, .064]	.260	.145
(6) Learner Engagement	.407 / [.051, .672]	.023*	.361 / [.128, .556]	.026*	.352
(7) Instructor Support	-	-	-	-	-
(8) Cost-Effectiveness	.366 / [.003, .644]	.043*	.329 / [.092, .531]	.048*	.227

* $p < .05$, ** $p < .01$.
CI stands for "confidence interval (2-tailed)."
The 95% CIs of both Spearman's ρ and Kendall's τ-b were estimated by Fisher's r-to-z transformation, while the standard error, if needed, was estimated by the formula proposed by Fieller, Hartley, and Pearson.
Dashes indicate that rank correlation, its p-value, its CI, or RBO could not be computed due to constant scores from one model.
Among the numerous RBO implementations probably yielding varied RBO results due to different tie-breaking approaches, etc., this Table 1 adopts the Google implementation. Readers are better off viewing the RBOs here as approximations.

Table 2. Wilcoxon signed-rank test for paired ranks between Claude+ and Dragonfly

Dimension	*W*-statistic	*Z*-statistic	*p*-value	Interpretation
(1) Content/Course Quality	0	-4.73	<.001**	Systematic rank difference
(2) Pedagogical Design	0	-4.55	<.001**	Systematic rank difference
(5) Social Interaction	0	-4.73	<.001**	Systematic rank difference
(6) Learner Engagement	0	-4.79	<.001**	Systematic rank difference
(8) Cost-Effectiveness	32	n/a	.041*	Systematic rank difference

* p <.05, ** p < .01
The *W*-statistic is the smaller of the positive or negative rank sums.
The *Z*-statistic is not applicable (n/a) for (8) Cost-Effectiveness as an exact test was used due to the small effective sample size ($n < 25$).

3.1 Detailed Interpretation of Rank Correlations

(2)[1] Pedagogical Design: This dimension exhibits the strongest and most statistically significant agreement between the two AI models. The Spearman's ρ of .614 (p = .000) indicates a strong positive monotonic relationship. The Kendall's τ of .538 (p = .001) reinforces this conclusion. This means that platforms ranked highly by Claude+ for their pedagogical design are very likely to be ranked highly by Dragonfly as well. The RBO score of .419, while lower than the correlation coefficients, is the highest among all dimensions, suggesting a moderate level of agreement on the top-ranked platforms for this dimension.

(1) Content/Course Quality: This dimension also shows a statistically significant, moderately positive correlation. With a Spearman's ρ of .467 (p = .008) and Kendall's τ of .417 (p = .010), there is clear evidence that the two AI models tend to agree on the relative quality of course content across platforms. However, the RBO score of .250 is notably lower than the correlation coefficients. This indicates that while the AI models agree on the general trend of which platforms are better or worse overall, their agreement on the specific *top-ranked* platforms is weak.

(6) Learner Engagement: Similar to content/course quality, learner engagement shows a moderately and significantly positive correlation (ρ = .407, p = .023; τ = .361, p = .026). The AI models demonstrate a consistent, though not perfect, ability to identify which platforms are more engaging for learners. The RBO of .352 indicates that a user looking at the top-ranked platforms for engagement would find a fair amount of overlap between the two AI-generated lists.

(8) Cost-Effectiveness: This dimension presents a particularly interesting case. The rank correlation is weaker but still statistically significant (ρ = .366, p = .043; τ = .329, p = .048). This finding is notable because, in the original score-based analysis by Chan (2023), the Pearson correlation was not significant (r = .346, p = .056). The rank-based analysis here has uncovered a subtle but real monotonic agreement that was missed by the linear model. However, the very low RBO score of .227 reveals that this agreement is diffuse across the entire ranking. The two AI models agree on the general trend but show very little consensus on which specific platforms are the *top* performers in terms of (8) cost-effectiveness.

(5) Social Interaction: This is the only dimension with a negative correlation, although it fails to reach statistical significance (ρ = -.206, p = .267). The negative trend suggests a slight tendency for the AI models to rank platforms in opposite orders for this dimension, but the high p-value means this could easily be due to random chance. The extremely low RBO of .145 confirms there is virtually no agreement on the best platforms for social interaction.

3.2 Systematic Bias in Rankings

The Wilcoxon signed-rank test results in Table 2 are highly revealing. For all five analyzable dimensions, the test yielded a statistically significant p-value. This provides strong evidence to reject the null hypothesis that the median rank difference is zero. In every case, one AI model systematically assigned better scores to the platforms than the other. This confirms that the systematic over/underrating bias identified in the score-based analysis by Chan (2023) is not merely an artifact of the AI models using different internal scales. It is a more fundamental bias that persists even when the score differences are transformed into an ordinal format.

[1] The dimensions here are discussed in the order of their rank correlation p-values, so the dimension numbering appears non-sequential.

The AI models do not just differ in their absolute scores; they have a consistent, directional disagreement about the relative standing of the platforms.

4. DISCUSSION

The results of this rank-based analysis provide a richer, more nuanced understanding of the consistency of generative AI in evaluating MOOC platforms. This discussion will compare these findings to the original score-based analysis, explore the theoretical underpinnings of rank versus score comparison, and translate the statistical results into practical implications for users.

4.1 Comparison with Score-Based Analysis: Convergence and Divergence

A direct comparison between the findings here and those of Chan (2023) is illuminating.

Points of Convergence: For the three dimensions of (2) pedagogical design, (1) content/course quality, and (6) learner engagement, the conclusions here strongly align with the original study. Chan (2023) found significantly positive Pearson correlations for these dimensions, and the current analysis confirms this with significant Spearman and Kendall correlations. This convergence across different analytical methods (parametric vs. non-parametric, linear vs. monotonic) provides robust evidence that the consistency between Claude+ and Dragonfly in these areas is genuine and not a statistical artifact. It strengthens the claim that for these core educational aspects, the AI evaluations possess a degree of convergent validity.

Points of Divergence: The most significant divergence occurred in the (8) cost-effectiveness dimension. While Chan (2023) found no significant linear correlation, the current rank-based analysis unearthed a statistically significant, albeit weak, monotonic relationship. This is a classic example of the power of non-parametric methods. It suggests the AIs' agreement on cost-effectiveness is not linear—a platform rated "8" by one AI is not necessarily rated near "8" by the other—but they do tend to agree on the relative ordering. This insight was completely hidden in the original analysis and demonstrates the value of exploring data through multiple lenses.

The Role of Bias: The current Wilcoxon Signed-Rank Test results confirm the persistence of the systematic bias found by Chan's (2023) paired samples t-tests. This is a crucial finding. It tells us that the disagreement between the AI models is not just random noise; there is a structural component to it. One AI model is consistently more "optimistic" or "pessimistic" in its relative rankings. This implies that while the *order* of platforms may be somewhat consistent for certain dimensions, a user cannot treat the score from one AI model as interchangeable with the score from another.

4.2 The Primacy of Rank: Theoretical Considerations

The decision to focus on ranks is not arbitrary; it is grounded in principles from psychometrics and information science. When humans or AI models provide scores on a subjective Likert-type scale (e.g., 1 to 10), it is a strong assumption that the scale is a true interval scale, where the difference between a "7" and an "8" is psychologically equivalent to the difference between a "3" and a "4" (Knapp, 1990). More often, such scales are treated as ordinal, where the numbers represent a rank order but the intervals between them are not necessarily equal. By converting scores to ranks, this study moves to a less restrictive and often more defensible level of measurement (Corder and Foreman, 2014; Siegel and Castellan, 1988).

This is particularly relevant when comparing evaluators. Two judges (human or AI) might have different internal "sensitivities." One might use the full range of the scale (1-10), while another might be more conservative, using only the middle range (4-8). A Pearson correlation would be penalized by this difference in scale usage, whereas Spearman's ρ, Kendall's τ-b, or RBO would be unaffected, as long as the relative ordering of the items remains the same. The findings here for (8) cost-effectiveness perfectly illustrate this principle in action.

4.3 Implications for MOOC Platform Selection

Beyond the general observations of high- and low-confidence dimensions, it is useful to consider the implications of the findings for each individual evaluative dimension. This provides more concrete guidance for learners, institutions, and policymakers who may weigh certain aspects of MOOC platforms more heavily than others.

(1) Content/Course Quality: The moderate but significant correlations suggest that both AI models broadly agree on which platforms deliver stronger course content. For decision-makers, this means that AI-generated rankings can be a reliable first filter when prioritizing platforms with high-quality instructional materials. However, the relatively low RBO score indicates that the models diverge when identifying the very top performers. Thus, while AI can help narrow the field to a set of content-strong platforms, final judgments about the "best" content providers should be supplemented with expert reviews or direct sampling of course materials.

(2) Pedagogical Design: This dimension shows the strongest agreement across all statistical measures, making it the most dependable area for AI-assisted decision-making. Learners and institutions can place relatively high confidence in AI rankings when seeking platforms that employ effective instructional strategies and assessment methods. The moderate RBO score further suggests that while the models may not perfectly align on the single best platform, they consistently highlight a cluster of platforms with strong pedagogical design. This makes AI particularly useful for institutions aiming to shortlist platforms for curriculum integration.

(5) Social Interaction: The lack of significant correlation and the very low RBO score indicate that AI models are currently unreliable in assessing opportunities for peer-to-peer and learner-instructor interaction. For users who prioritize community engagement, forums, or collaborative learning, AI rankings should not be used as a primary decision tool. Instead, prospective learners should consult platform-specific features, user testimonials, or independent reviews. This finding also highlights a limitation of generative AI: social interaction is a nuanced, context-dependent dimension that may not be easily inferred from textual data alone.

(6) Learner Engagement: The moderate correlations suggest that AI models can reasonably identify platforms that foster higher levels of learner interaction with content and community. For learners concerned with motivation and persistence, AI rankings provide a useful starting point. However, the RBO score again cautions against over-reliance on the top-ranked platforms alone. Engagement is multifaceted and may vary by course subject, instructor, or cohort, so AI rankings should be treated as indicative rather than definitive.

(8) Cost-Effectiveness: The weak but statistically significant monotonic agreement uncovered by the rank-based analysis suggests that AI models capture some shared sense of relative value across platforms. However, the very low RBO score indicates that they disagree substantially on which platforms are the most cost-effective. For budget-conscious learners, this means AI rankings can highlight general trends (e.g., which platforms are broadly more affordable or offer better value), but they should not be relied upon to identify the single best-value option. Users should instead consult up-to-date pricing, scholarship opportunities, and return-on-investment analyses.

(3) Learner Support, (4) Technology Infrastructure, and (7) Instructor Support: These dimensions could not be meaningfully analyzed due to the lack of variance in Dragonfly's scoring. The inability of this AI model to differentiate among platforms in these areas, while worth further research into the underlying rationale, underscores the current limitations of generative AI in evaluating technical or service-oriented dimensions. For learners and institutions, this means that AI rankings cannot yet substitute for direct investigation into support services or instructor responsiveness. These remain critical areas where human judgment and empirical data are indispensable.

4.4 Limitations

This study inherits the limitations of its predecessor. The analysis is based on only two AI models, as others did not provide usable data. The AI models were trained on data that may be several years old by now, so their evaluations may not reflect the most recent updates to the MOOC platforms. Furthermore, the entire analysis hinges on the AI models' ability to interpret a specific prompt and synthesize web data, a process that remains a "black box." Without a ground truth (e.g., a gold-standard ranking from human experts), this study can only speak to the consistency between AIs, not their absolute accuracy.

REFERENCES

Albelbisi, N. A. (2020). Development and Validation of the MOOC Success Scale (MOOC-SS). *In Education and Information Technologies*, Vol. 25, No. 5, pp. 4535-4555.

Alturkistani A. et al. (2020). Massive Open Online Course Evaluation Methods: Systematic Review. In *Journal Medical Internet Research*, Vol. 22, No. 4, e13851. doi: 10.2196/13851

Chan, V. K. Y. (2023). Evaluating Popular MOOC Platforms by Generative Artificial Intelligence (AI) Robots: How Consistent Are the Robots? *Proceedings of the 20th International Conference on Cognition and Exploratory Learning in Digital Age (CELDA 2023)*. Madeira Island, Portugal, pp. 329-336.

Corder, G. W. and Foreman, D. I. (2014). *Nonparametric Statistics: A Step-by-Step Approach* (2nd ed.). Wiley, Hoboken, USA.

de Souza, C. et al. (2023). Are the New AIs Smart Enough to Steal Your Job? IQ Scores for ChatGPT, Microsoft Bing, Google Bard and Quora Poe. Retrieved May 10, 2023 from https://papers.ssrn.com/sol3/papers.cfm?abstract_id=4412505

Hamed, K. H. (2011). The Distribution of Kendall's Tau for Testing the Significance of Cross-Correlation in Persistent Data. In *Hydrological Sciences Journal*, Vol. 56, No. 5, pp. 841–853. doi:10.1080/02626667.2011.586948

Hew, K. F. and Cheung, W. S. (2014). Students' and Instructors' Use of Massive Open Online Courses (MOOCs): Motivations and Challenges. In *Educational Research Review*, Vol. 12, pp. 45-58. doi: 10.1016/j.edurev.2014.05.001

Kendall, M. G. (1938). A New Measure of Rank Correlation. In *Biometrika*, Vol. 30, No. 1/2, pp. 81–93. doi:10.2307/2332226

Khalil, H. and Ebner, M. (2014). MOOCs Completion Rates and Possible Methods to Improve Retention - A Literature Review. *Proceedings of the 2014 World Conference on Educational Multimedia, Hypermedia and Telecommunications*. Chesapeake, VA, USA, pp. 1236-1244.

Kizilcec, R. F. et al. (2013). Deconstructing Disengagement: Analyzing Learner Subpopulations in Massive Open Online Courses. *Proceedings of the Third ACM International Conference on Learning Analytics and Kwonledge*. Leuven, Belgium, pp. 170-179. doi:10.1145/2460296.2460330

Knapp, T. R. (1990). Treating Ordinal Scales as Interval Scales: An Attempt to Resolve the Controversy. In *Nursing Research*, Vol. 39, No. 2, pp. 121-123. doi:10.1097/00006199-199003000-00019

Liyanagunawardena, T. R. et al. (2013). MOOCs: A Systematic Study of the Published Literature 2008-2012. In *The International Review of Research in Open and Distributed Learning*, Vol. 14, No. 3, pp. 202-227. doi:10.19173/irrodl.v14i3.1455

Rey, D. and Neuhäuser, M. (2010). Wilcoxon-Signed-Rank Test. In *Encyclopedia of Research Design*, Salkind, N. J. (Ed.). SAGE Publications, Thousand Oaks, USA. doi:10.4135/9781412961288

Shah N. B. et al. (2014). When is it Better to Compare than to Score? arXiv:1406.6618v1. doi: 10.48550/arXiv.1406.6618

Siegel, S. and Castellan, N. J. (1988). *Nonparametric Statistics for the Behavioral Sciences* (2nd ed.). McGraw-Hill, New York, USA.

Spearman, C. (1904). The Proof and Measurement of Association between Two Things. In *American Journal of Psychology*, Vol. 15, No. 1, pp. 72-101. doi:10.2307/1412159

Webber, W. et al. (2010). A Similarity Measure for Indefinite Rankings. In *ACM Transactions on Information Systems*, Vol. 28, No. 4, pp. 1-38. doi:10.1145/1852102.1852106

Wilcoxon, F. (1945). Individual Comparisons by Ranking Methods. In *Biometrics Bulletin*, Vol. 1, No. 6, pp. 80–83. doi:10.2307/3001968

Zar, J. H. (2013). *Biostatistical analysis* (5th ed.). Pearson, Upper Saddle River, USA.

Zhang, C. et al. (2023). A Complete Survey on Generative AI (AIGC): Is ChatGPT from GPT-4 to GPT-5 All You Need? arXiv:2303.11717v1 [cs.AI] Retrieved May 10, 2023 from https://arxiv.org/abs/2303.11717

Zimmerman, D. W. and Zumbo, B. D. (1993). The Relative Power of Parametric and Nonparametric Statistical Methods. In *A Handbook for Data Analysis in the Behavioral Sciences: Methodological Issues*, Keren, G. and Lewis, C. (Eds.). Psychology Press, New York, USA.

EFFECTIVENESS OF AI-BASED SUPPORT FOR VIDEO-BASED LEARNING FOR TEACHING EMPATHY

Antonija Mitrovic[1], Raul Vincent Lumapas[1], Matthias Galster[1,2] and Sanna K. Malinen[1]
[1]University of Canterbury
Private Bag 4800, Christchurch, New Zealand
[2]University of Bamberg
96045 Bamberg, Germany

ABSTRACT

Video-based learning (VBL) is widely used due to its flexibility and accessibility. However, only watching videos results in shallow learning, and therefore there has been much research on providing support for engagement in VBL. In this paper, we present our VBL platform and the results of a study performed in two consecutive years in the same software engineering course, on team empathy. In 2023, students received simple support for engagement, shown as reminders to write comments on videos for students who have not written any. In 2024, we added AI-based support consisting of three parts: 1) students' comments were classified into quality categories; 2) students received nudges in response to the quality of comments they have written, and 3) explanations of how comment quality was determined were available. The results of the study show that the 2024 students, who had AI-based support, learnt more about empathy. They also had positive opinions of the explanations of comment quality.

KEYWORDS

Video-Based Learning, AI-Based Support for VBL Learning, Nudges, AVW-Space

1. INTRODUCTION

Soft skills (e.g., presentation, communication, teamwork) are essential for engineers and need to be integrated in engineering education. However, training soft skills is difficult, and usually done via role playing, peer reviews (Levy, 2018), coaching and mentoring, or gained with experience (Barthakur, 2023). As teaching soft skills is resource-intensive and time-consuming, it is vital to identify strategies that streamline learning these skills. One approach to teach soft skills is to use Video-Based Learning (VBL). Videos are appropriate to learn soft skills it is necessary to observe the skill from various viewpoints and to reflect on one's own experience (Anthony & Garner, 2016; Conkey et al., 2013; Dimitrova & Mitrovic, 2022).

Videos have become ubiquitous in higher education due to the increasing popularity of flipped classrooms and online learning, as well as the effects of the global pandemic (Beege & Ploetzner, 2024; Fyfield et al., 2019; Chatti et al., 2016; Xiu et al., 2019). VBL offers many advantages, allowing students flexibility in location/time, as well as providing affordances for showing tasks which require complex skills and spatial reasoning. Although videos can help students learn (Sablic et al., 2021), many researchers point out the problem with passive video watching (Aydin et al., 2024; Chatti et al., 2016; Chi & Wylie, 2014; Guo et al., 2014; Dimitrova & Mitrovic, 2022), which results in shallow learning.

The fundamental problem with video-based learning is maintaining students' engagement during learning (Chatti et al., 2016; Miriahi et al., 2021; Dimitrova & Mitrovic, 2022; Wong et al., 2024). To be successful in learning generally, the student needs to actively engage with the material, including making decisions about what is relevant, organizing information and integrating it with existing knowledge (Mayer, 2019). These processes require good self-regulated learning (SRL) skills. They are even more important in VBL, as there is lack of support from teachers and other learners, and no interaction with the learning material (Chatti et al., 2016). Research shows that many learners have poor SRL skills (Zimmerman, 2008; Pintrich & de Groot, 1990; Panadero, 2017), leading to VBL being a passive activity.

There have been studies on using video annotations (Chatti et al., 2016) and in-video questions/quizzes (Kovacs, 2015; Miriahi et al., 2021; Wong et al., 2024) in order to engage students deeper. We have developed AVW-Space (Dimitrova & Mitrovic, 2022), a VBL platform which supports engagement during video watching in several ways. AVW-Space encourages students to write comments on videos they watch. When writing comments, students need to select an aspect from the ones the teacher defined (Figure 1), which focus students' attention on the important parts of videos (Mitrovic et al., 2017). We also added nudges, which are personalized reminders giving hints to students and sometimes also giving them examples of good comments (Dimitrova et al., 2017; Mitrovic et al., 2019). The AI-based support consists of a machine-learning classifier which automatically classifies students' comments into quality categories (Mohammadhassan et al., 2022). In previous studies we conducted, students' feedback clearly stated they would appreciate knowing how comment quality is determined. For that reason, we enhanced AVW-Space with explanations of comment quality.

In this paper, we report on a study conducted in two consecutive years with students enrolled in a second-year Software Engineering project course at the University of Canterbury. In the course, students work in teams of 6-8 on a software-development project over the whole semester. Feedback from the course lecturers was that the teams struggle with empathy. Empathy is "the ability to understand and feel what others are going through, i.e., interpersonal understanding by imagining oneself in another person's context" (Cuff et al., 2016). To address this problem, we developed an instance of AVW-Space for teaching team empathy, and used it in the course in 2023 and 2024. The goal of our study was to investigate the effects of AI-based support on student engagement and learning. The 2023 class interacted with AVW-Space without the AI-based support, which was provided to the 2024 class. We designed the study to be able to answer the following research questions:

RQ1: Does AI-based support increase engagement and learning?

Previous research with AVW-Space on presentation skills and face-to-face communication skills (Dimitrova & Mitrovic, 2022; Mitrovic et al., 2023) showed that the platform supports learning. Here we investigate whether we will see similar results when teaching a new skill, team empathy, and also compare two cohorts who used AVW-Space without and with the AI-based support.

RQ2: What are students' perceptions of explanations of comment quality?

In previous studies with AVW-Space where comment quality indicators were provided to students, feedback from students indicated that they would like to know how comment quality was determined. We believe explanations will be useful to student learning.

Our paper makes several contributions. Firstly, we present online training for team empathy, using AVW-Space and AI-based support. Secondly, we show the effect of AI-based support on engagement and learning. Finally, we show that explanations of comment quality are beneficial to students.

2. THE AVW-SPACE PLATFORM AND THE AI-BASED SUPPORT

AVW-Space supports learning via its Personal Space, which allows students to watch videos and comment on them individually (shown in Figure 1), and also via its Social Space, where students can see each others' (anonymized) comments, rate them and learn from each other. Reviewing comments provides an element of social learning, allowing students to see what their peers found relevant in the videos.

To create a new space, the teacher first specifies videos to be used for training. Videos must be publicly available on YouTube. The teacher can specify aspects to be used when writing comments (see Figure 1; aspects are listed under "What does it relate to?"). The role of aspects is to focus students' attention on the concepts the teacher deems important.

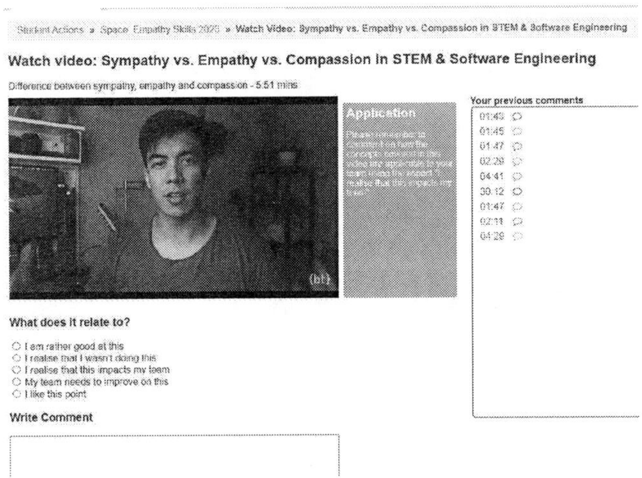

Figure 1. Private Space, showing a Reminder Nudge

Additional support for active video watching is provided in AVW-Space in the form of nudges, which are short hints informing students about their suboptimal behaviour or encouraging desired behaviour. There are two types of nudges in AVW-Space: reminder and quality nudges. Reminder nudges are simple nudges that check whether the student is writing comments on not (Mitrovic et al., 2019). For example, if the student has not written any comments while watching the video, they will get a nudge (shown in the "Application" box in Figure 1), reminding them to write about something they find relevant in the video.

Table 1. Comment categories

	Category	Definition
1	Affirmative, negative, off-topic	Comments which are irrelevant or merely affirmative/negative with no explanation
2	Repeating	Comments which only repeat the video content
3	Critical and analytical	Comments which elaborate on points covered in the video or show critical thinking on the content of the video
4	Reflective	Comments in which the learner reflects on their experience or knowledge
5	Regulating	Comments discussing what the learner would do in future

The AI-based support for engagement in AVW-Space includes comment quality, quality nudges and related explanations. We developed a quality scheme for comments (Mohammadhassan et al., 2022), with category one being of the lowest quality and category five as the highest. This labeling scheme is used in developing machine learning (ML) models to automatically assess the quality of students' comments (Table 1). Comments in the first two categories are pedagogically undesirable and are considered low-quality comments as they do not convey deep thinking and reflection on the video content. The last three categories are considered high-quality, which convey critical thinking (category 3), reflection on past experiences or behaviors (category 4), or self-improvement (category 5). As soon as the student writes a comment, it is analyzed by the ML classifier, and the student can see the indicator of the comment quality, as illustrated in Figure 2. The first comment shown in the screenshot is a high-quality comment, shown in green. The next one is a low-quality comment, shown in red. Students can ask for an explanation of how the comment quality is determined. Figure 2 shows the explanation for the low-quality comment. Quality nudges are provided to students based on the quality of comments they write, as shown in Figure 2. If the comment is qualified as a low quality one (Category 1 or 2), the student gets a nudge informing them about a better way to write comments.

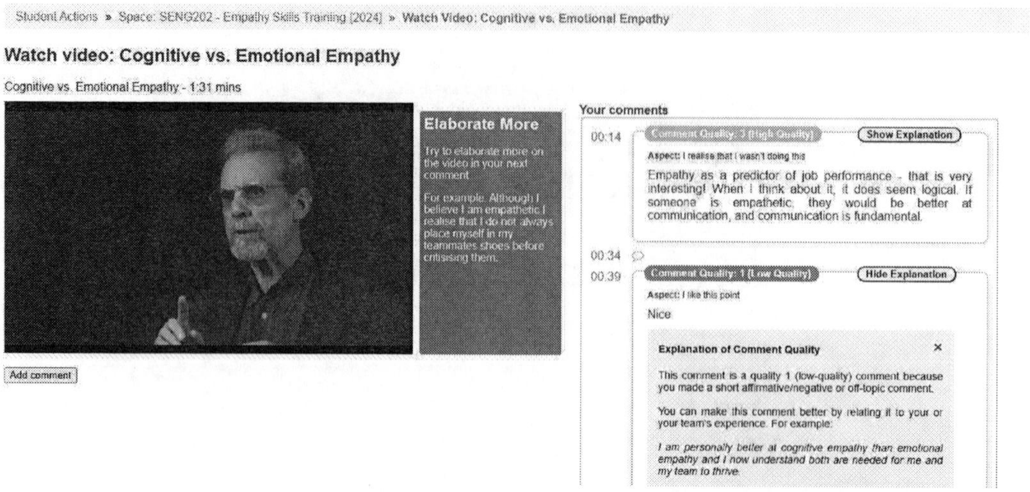

Figure 2. Private Space, showing a quality nudge (Elaborate More) and the expanded explanation

To generate explanations of comment quality, we use the comment text, its quality category, linguistic/textual features, and the selected aspect. This information is passed to a textual analysis feature, which checks for any contractions (e.g., "I'm", "Don't") or negative words or phrases (i.e., "do not", "cannot"). This process is necessary to identify if the comment is positive or negative, as the explanations are also determined based on the sentiment. The text of the explanation is determined by the quality, the textual features, and the general sentiment (positive/negative) of the comment. For high-quality comments, as there is no need for further support, a simple explanation is added, e.g., "This comment is a quality 4 (high-quality) comment because you made a personal reflection related to empathy").

Explanations of low/medium quality comments (quality 1 or 2) provide more information. These explanations consist of three parts: (1) an explanation of the comment quality, (2) a recommendation on how to improve the comment, and (3) an example of a better-quality comment, as illustrated in Figure 2. In most cases, category 1 or 2 comments are short; generally, they simply agree/disagree (e.g., "Good", "I agree"), are off-topic, vague, repeating video text or content, or repeat the aspect text. For example, if a comment just simply agrees "This is correct", we add this to the explanation text: "This comment is a quality 1 (low-quality) comment because you made a short affirmative/negative or off-topic comment." The recommendation in this case is "You can make this comment better by relating it to your or your team's experience". The explanation also contains an example of a higher-quality comment, such as "Our team takes input from everyone when assigning tasks and knowing if they are capable or comfortable."

3. STUDY DESIGN

We developed a new instance of AVW-Space for teaching team empathy, and integrated it into a second-year, semester-long Software Engineering project course at the University of Canterbury. Empathy was chosen because it is a crucial skill for teamwork of software developers. It allows software developers to understand the needs of end users and also helps them work better with team members while reducing work-related stress (Gunatilake et al., 2023; Levy & Hadar, 2018; Machuca-Villegas et al., 2022; Tulili et al., 2023).

The students enrolled in the course worked on a project in groups of 6-8 for the whole semester and had weekly team meetings. The study was approved by the institution's Human Ethics committee (approvals 2023/62/LR-PS and 2024-79 LR-PS). The students received 5% of the final grade if they completed the training. Participation in our study was voluntary: the students could complete the training but not consent to their data being analyzed for our research. Table 2 outlines the tasks students performed.

Table 2. Training schedule

Week(s)	Task(s)
1	Form teams
2-3	Complete Survey 1, watch and comment on videos
4	Review others' comments and complete Survey 2
5-6	Record one team meeting
7	Watch and comment on the team meeting video
8	Review comments written by others and complete Survey 3

Table 3 lists six videos students watched in weeks 2-3. The criteria for selecting the videos were that they were not longer than 8 minutes, and the content is suitable and of good quality. The candidate videos were discussed by the domain experts and the research team. We defined the following aspects for students to use when writing comments: 1) *My team needs to improve on this*; 2) *I realize I wasn't doing this*; 3) *I am rather good at this;* 4) *I like this point* and 5) *I realize that this impacts my team.* We designed the aspects to motivate students to reflect on their own experience and/or on their team, as reflection is crucial for soft skills such as empathy.

Table 3. YouTube videos used in the study

YouTube Id	Length	Video
HhVWILEcshE	1:31	Cognitive vs. Affective empathy
SnCJIjQxbeY	2:03	Empathetic listening (+scrum)
U4YBZE84rh8	5:51	Sympathy vs Empathy vs Compassion in SE
3NgxYcVahU8	2:37	Importance of empathy in managing projects
v=3TS_uLpMj14	2:26	Empathic Listening in Scrum
?v=GQhw9teSyKc	3:11	Disarming: Cognitive Empathy (Roleplay)

The empathy instance was used in two consecutive years, with the same experimental design (Table 2). Students from the 2023 class were only given reminder nudges. We manually labelled comments collected in 2023 and used them to train a machine learning classifier which analyzes comments to determine their quality (Lumapas et al., 2024). The ML classifier was used in 2024, when students received full support. The 2024 cohort received reminder and quality nudges. They could see the quality of the comments they wrote and could request the explanation of how the comment quality was determined.

In week 4, the students could review and rate the (anonymized) comments written by their peers. For the rating phase, we used the following rating categories used in previous AVW-Space studies: 1) *This is useful for me*; 2) *I hadn't thought of this*; 3) *I didn't notice this*; 4) *I don't agree with this* or 5) *I like this point.* In week 7, students could watch and comment on the recording of their own team meeting, and then in week 8 they rated each others' comments.

4. RESULTS

Table 4 presents descriptive statistics about the data collected from students who provided informed consent. There were no significant differences between the groups on the total number of sessions with AVW-Space, the number of videos watched, the total number of comments written and the number of high-quality (HQ) comments. The 2024 group used the training on significantly more distinct days in comparison to the 2023 cohort, while in 2023 there were significantly more ratings made. We used the Mann-Whittney U test as data was not normally distributed. The 2024 group got a significantly higher number of nudges, which is not surprising because this group received quality nudges in addition to reminder nudges.

Table 4. Means and standard deviations

	2023 (n = 58)	2024 (n = 45)	Significance
Number of Sessions on the Platform	8.93 (4.81)	9.89 (4.35)	ns
Number of Days on the Platform	7.41 (3.13)	8.44 (3.06)	**U = 1598.00, p < .05**
Number of Videos Watched	5.74 (.98)	6.00 (0)	ns
Number of Comments Written	10.50 (5.46)	10.52 (4.86)	ns
Number of HQ Comments	8.97 (5.05)	10.36 (4.75)	ns
Number of Nudges Received	**23.47 (6.50)**	**27.82 (7.24)**	**U = 1769.00, p < .005**
Number of Ratings	**41.69 (37.64)**	**28.21 (31.76)**	**U = 1047.5, p < .05**
Empathy Score1	4.18 (.54)	4.17 (.63)	
Empathy Score 2	4.78 (.56)	4.40 (.75)	
Empathy Score 3	4.53 (.63)	4.90 (.80)	

We expected to find a significant difference on the number of high-quality comments between the two groups, as the AI-based support was developed to focus on them. The number of HQ comments in the 2023 group was surprisingly high (with the median of 8), in comparison to other studies we have performed with AVW-Space on other soft skills, where the median number of HQ comments was only 1 or 2 (Mohammadhassan, 2022). Looking deeper into potential reasons for this, we noticed that 37 students (64%) from the 2023 group had participated previously in a study on presentation skills using AVW-Space in their first year of studying engineering, where they received quality nudges. The high number of HQ comments in the current study could be the transfer effect of quality nudges, but this requires further investigations.

All three surveys included an instrument we developed for self-assessment of team empathy skills (Malinen et al., 2025), with three dimensions: perspective taking (8 questions), emotional responsiveness (6 questions) and affective empathy (4 questions). Fifty-one students from 2023 and 39 from the 2024 cohort provided responses to the questions from the instrument (Table 4). A two-way repeated measures ANOVA showed a significant main effect of time the survey was taken on empathy scores ($F = 147.29$, $p < .001$), sphericity assumed. This effect was qualified by a significant time x year interaction effect ($F = 45.72$, $p < .001$). The 2024 cohort reported significantly higher empathy skills at the end of the training (Empathy Score 3).

Another component of our intervention was the explanations of comment quality. The average number of explanations requested by students was 3.47 (sd = 3.03). All but one student from the 2024 cohort accessed explanations. The total number of explanations requested was 156, for 130 comments. Twelve students accessed the explanation for the same comment more than once.

Survey 2 contained seven questions derived from the explanation satisfaction instrument (Hoffman et al., 2023). Students responded to these questions using a Likert scale ranging from 1 (Strongly disagree) to 5 (Strongly agree). Most participants agreed that the explanations were presented clearly, had sufficient detail, were correct, predictable and useful, and motivated them to write better comments (Table 5).

Table 5. Explanation satisfaction

Question	Mean (sd)
I understand how comment quality is determined based on the explanations	3.68 (1.02)
Explanations have sufficient detail	3.89 (0.80)
Explanations are predictable	3.82 (0.91)
Explanations are correct	3.89 (0.86)
Explanations are presented clearly	4.05 (0.74)
Explanations motivate me to write better comments	3.59 (1.11)
Explanations are useful	3.64 (0.86)

Survey 2 also contained the following open-ended question about their experience with explanations. The majority of the participants (70%) had a positive perception towards explanations. Explanations helped students reflect on comments they wrote; e.g., *"Overall it was a positive experience. It helped give a brief period of reflection on each comment."* Some feedback indicated self-regulation, where students mentioned that explanations helped them improve their future comments; e.g., *"It was good! When my comment was of lower quality, I would always check the explanation and read the reason so I could improve my comments next time. One in particular that I remember is when I was commenting, often I would just write about how I agreed with what was being said, but the explanations helped to realize that a better comment would be self-reflective on my own experience"*. Some responses mentioned the benefits of explanations in improving their understanding of the concepts mentioned in the videos; e.g., *"Helpful as I was able to gain a deeper understanding of what we are learning and how I can apply this to my personal participation in teamwork and in <Course Code>."* One participant mentioned the straightforward nature of the explanations is a reason to not access explanations for other comments: *"I think I quickly grasp onto explanation and don't need too much to rethink about it too much or have to go back to re-read an explanation"*. This might mean that students might have understood the explanation when they saw it the first time and did not need to re-read explanations.

5. DISCUSSION AND CONCLUSIONS

We presented the AI-based support developed for AVW-Space, and a study with an instance of AVW-Space for teaching team empathy. The AI-based support motivates students to engage deeper with video content, and includes nudges, comment quality indicators, and explanations of how comment quality is determined. We found that the AI-based support resulted in improved learning, measured by students' self-reported scores. The number of high-quality comments was higher in the intervention group, although the difference was not significant. Students appreciated having explanations of comment quality and found them helpful. Explanations promote reflection when commenting on videos and help students improve their comments.

One limitation of our study is the small number of participants, which was dictated by the size of the course. Because of this, we were not able to analyse causality of our intervention. Furthermore, the study was done at only one institution. We plan to conduct more studies both at the University of Canterbury and also at other educational institutions and with software professionals.

As discussed earlier, the literature on teaching soft skills and supporting engagement in VBL is limited. The contribution of our research is in the AI-based support for engagement during VBL. Our research contributes to exploring explanations as a way to support and boost learning and engagement

ACKNOWLEDGMENTS

Our research was supported by a Smart Ideas grant from the New Zealand Ministry of Business, Innovation & Employment.

REFERENCES

Anthony, S. and Garner, B. (2016). *Teaching soft skills to business students: An analysis of multiple pedagogical methods. Business and Professional Communication Quarterly, 79 (3), 360–370.*

Aydin, B., Akcapinar, G., Özeke, V. and Hasnine, M.N. (2024). Dynamics of Students' Affective States and Video Interactions While Watching Educational Videos. *Proceedings 21st International Conference on Cognition and Exploratory Learning in Digital Age*, pp. 233-240.

Barthakur, A., Kovanovic, V., Joksimovic, S. and Pardo, A. (2023). Challenges in assessments of soft skills: Towards unobtrusive approaches to measuring student success. In *Unobtrusive observations of learning in digital environments: Examining behavior, cognition, emotion, metacognition and social processes using learning analytics* (pp. 53-71). Cham: Springer International Publishing.

Beege, M., Ploetzner, R. (2024). Learning from interactive video: the influence of self-explanations, navigation, and cognitive load. *Instructional Science* 52(1).

Chatti, M. A., Marinov, M., Sabov, O., Laksono, R., Sofyan, Z., Fahmy Yousef, A. M., and Schroeder, U. (2016). Video annotation and analytics in CourseMapper. *Smart Learning Environments* 3: 1-21.

Chi, M. T. and Wylie, R. (2014). The ICAP framework: Linking cognitive engagement to active learning outcomes. *Educational psychologist*, 49(4):219–243.

Conkey, C.A., Bowers, C., Cannon-Bowers, J. and Sanchez, A. (2013). Machinima and video-based soft-skills training for frontline healthcare workers. *Games for Health*, *2*(1), pp.39-43.

Cuff, B.M., Brown, S.J., Taylor, L. and Howat, D.J. (2016). Empathy: A review of the concept. *Emotion review*, *8*(2), pp.144-153.

Dimitrova, V., Mitrovic, A., Piotrkowicz, A., Lau, L., Weerasinghe, A. (2017). Using learning analytics to devise interactive personalised nudges for active video watching. Proc. 25th ACM Conference on User Modeling, Adaptation and Personalization, pp. 22-31.

Dimitrova, V. and Mitrovic, A. (2022). Choice Architecture for Nudges to Support Constructive Learning in Active Video Watching. *International Journal of Artificial Intelligence in Education, 32*(4), 892-930.

Fyfield, M., Henderson, M., Heinrich, E. and Redmond, P. (2019). Videos in higher education: Making the most of a good thing. *Australasian Journal of Educational Technology, 35*(5), pp.1-7.

Gunatilake, H., Grundy, J., Mueller, I. and Hoda, R., (2023). Empathy models and software engineering—A preliminary analysis and taxonomy. *Journal of Systems and Software, 203*, p.111747.

Guo, P. J., Kim, J., & Rubin, R. (2014). How video production affects student engagement: An empirical study of MOOC videos. Proc. ACM Conference on Learning @ Scale, pp. 41–50. Association for Computing Machinery.

Hoffman, R.R., Mueller, S.T., Klein, G. and Litman, J. (2023). Measures for explainable AI: Explanation goodness, user satisfaction, mental models, curiosity, trust, and human-AI performance. *Frontiers in Computer Science, 5*, p.1096257.

Kovacs, G. (2015). QuizCram: A question-driven video studying Interface. In *Proceedings of the 33rd Annual ACM Conference Extended Abstracts on Human Factors in Computing Systems* (pp. 133-138).

Levy, M. and Hadar, I. (2018), August. The importance of empathy for analyzing privacy requirements. In *2018 IEEE 5th International Workshop on Evolving Security & Privacy Requirements Engineering* (pp. 9-13). IEEE.

Lumapas, R.V., Mitrovic, A., Galster, M., Malinen, S., Holland, J. and Peiris, P. (2024). Integrating Explanations in Active Video Watching. Proc. 32nd Int. Conf. on Computers in Education, vol. 2, pp. 755-758.

Machuca-Villegas, L., Gasca-Hurtado, G.P., Puente, S.M. and Tamayo, L.M.R. (2022). Perceptions of the human and social factors that influence the productivity of software development teams in Colombia: A statistical analysis. *Journal of systems and software, 192*, p.111408.

Malinen, S., Sankara, S., Galster, M. and Mitrovic, A. (2025). Development of empathy skills in software professionals using video-based training. European Association of Work and Organizational Psychology congress, May 21-24, 2025.

Mayer, R.E. (2019). Thirty years of research on online learning. *Applied Cognitive Psychology, 33*(2), pp.152-159.

Mirriahi, N., Jovanović, J., Lim, L.A. and Lodge, J.M. (2021). Two sides of the same coin: video annotations and in-video questions for active learning. *Educational Technology Research and Development, 69*(5), pp.2571-2588.

Mitrovic, A., Dimitrova, V., Lau, L., Weerasinghe, A., Mathews, M. (2017). Supporting Constructive Video-based Learning: Requirements Elicitation from Exploratory Studies. Proc. 18th International Conference on Artificial Intelligence in Education, LNAI 10331, pp. 224-237.

Mitrovic, A., Gordon, M., Piotrkowicz, A., Dimitrova, V. (2019). Investigating the effect of adding nudges to increase engagement in active video watching. Proc. 20th Int. Conf. Artificial Intelligence in Education, pp. 320-332, Springer.

Mitrovic, A., Galster, M., Malinen, S., Holland, J., Lumapas, R. V., Mohammadhassan, N., Musa, J. (2023). Effectiveness of video-based training for communication skills: evidence from a three-year study. *ACM Transactions on Computing Education*, 23(4), 1-25.

Mohammadhassan, N., Mitrovic, A., Neshatian, K. (2022). Investigating the Effect of Nudges for Improving Comment Quality in Active Video Watching. *Computers & Education*, 176, 104340.

Panadero, E. (2017). A review of self-regulated learning: Six models and four directions for research. *Frontiers in psychology, 8*, p.422.

Sablić, M., Mirosavljević, A., & Škugor, A. (2021). Video-based learning (VBL) — past, present and future: An overview of the research published from 2008 to 2019. *Technology, Knowledge and Learning*, 26(4), 1061-1077.

Tulili, T.R., Capiluppi, A. and Rastogi, A. (2023). Burnout in software engineering: A systematic mapping study. *Information and Software Technology, 155*, p.107116.

Wong, J.T., Richland, L.E. and Hughes, B.S. (2024). Immediate versus delayed low-stakes questioning: Encouraging the testing effect through embedded video questions to support students' knowledge outcomes, self-regulation, and critical thinking. *Technology, Knowledge and Learning*, pp.1-36.

Xiu, Y., Moore, M.E., Thompson, P. and French, D.P. (2019). Student perceptions of lecture-capture video to facilitate learning in a flipped classroom. *TechTrends, 63*(4), pp.369-375.

Zimmerman, B. J. (2008). Investigating self-regulation and motivation: Historical background, methodological developments, and future prospects. *American educational research journal, 45*(1), 166-183.

ANALYZING THE SUITABILITY OF COMPUTER ATTITUDE QUESTIONNAIRE FOR MEASURING STUDENTS' ATTITUDES TOWARDS TECHNOLOGY TOOLS USED IN MATHEMATICS EDUCATION

Jose Gamez, Oscar Villalobos, Youngjin Lee and Kinshuk
University of North Texas Department of Learning Technologies, Denton, Texas, 76203, USA

ABSTRACT

As technology tools, such as MyOpenMath, MyLab Math, RStudio, and Python become increasingly integrated into college-level mathematics instruction, it is essential to understand how students perceive and interact with these platforms. Many students struggle with confidence using computers and anxiety, which can hinder their ability to fully engage with course content and succeed academically. This study evaluates the reliability and structural validity of the Computer Attitude Questionnaire (CAQ), a survey instrument designed to measure students' confidence and anxiety related to computer use in academic settings. Drawing on responses from 161 undergraduate students enrolled in mathematics courses, the study examines internal consistency and factor structure through Cronbach's alpha and Principal Component Analysis. Results confirmed a unidimensional structure, with strong item loadings and acceptable internal consistency after reverse-coding negatively worded items. Demographic analyses revealed that male and online students reported slightly higher levels of confidence using computers compared to their peers, while age-related differences were minimal. These findings affirm the CAQ as a reliable instrument for measuring student attitudes toward technology tools in mathematics education and offer a foundation for future research, including confirmatory factor analysis, integration with additional attitude measures, and longitudinal studies tracking confidence and engagement over time.

KEYWORDS

Computer Attitude Questionnaire, Technology Acceptance in Education, Confidence Using Computers, Anxiety, Educational Technology in Mathematics, Exploratory Factor Analysis

1. INTRODUCTION

Although technology tools are increasingly embedded in higher education, many students continue to struggle with how they interact with these resources (Obut et al., 2024). In mathematics courses in particular, students are often expected to use a variety of platforms to complete assignments and engage with course content. These include homework platforms, such as MyLab Math, MyOpenMath, and ALEKS, as well as programming tools, like RStudio and Python. Despite their widespread use, these tools can present barriers to student learning, especially when students experience computer anxiety, low confidence, or uncertainty about the value of technology in their coursework (Mistretta, 2004). Without a clear understanding of students' attitudes toward these tools, educators risk overlooking key factors that influence engagement, learning, and academic success (Duggal et al., 2021).

To address this gap, the present study examines the validity and reliability of the Computer Attitude Questionnaire (CAQ), an established instrument used to measure student attitudes toward technology-related confidence and anxiety (DeVellis, 2016; Knezek & Christensen, 1996). The CAQ was developed to assess key dimensions of students' experiences with computers, particularly focusing on emotional and psychological factors such as confidence using computers and computer anxiety (Knezek & Christensen, 1996). It has been widely applied in educational settings to identify barriers and support interventions that promote computer literacy and comfort (Dowker et al., 2022; Knezek & Christensen, 1996). Although the Technology Acceptance Model (TAM) was also included in the survey instrument used in this research, the focus of this paper is solely on CAQ. TAM, originally introduced to predict users' acceptance of technology (Davis, 1989; Han & Sa, 2022; Marikyan & Papagiannidis, 2023), will be explored more fully in a separate analysis.

This study aims to contribute to the growing literature on educational technology by offering updated evidence on the psychometric properties of the CAQ in the context of college-level mathematics. The findings should help clarify how student attitudes toward computer use can be reliably measured and interpreted in diverse instructional environments. The study begins with a series of reliability and factor analyses of the CAQ, followed by group comparisons that offer insights into student attitudes and inform future validation efforts (Han & Sa, 2022; Sharit et al., 2019).

2. METHODOLOGY

Developing effective instruments requires more than simply collecting data -it requires understanding what that data represents and how well the instruments capture the constructs they are intended to measure. While the Computer Attitude Questionnaire (CAQ) and the Technology Acceptance Model (TAM) are both established tools for evaluating technology attitudes in education, this study seeks to examine how well the CAQ performs in terms of reliability, structural validity, and responsiveness to key demographic variables (Davis, 1989; Marikyan & Papagiannidis, 2023; Sharit et al., 2019).

2.1 Instruments and Constructs

The CAQ and TAM instruments complement one another by offering a layered view of how students relate to technology. The CAQ targets core psychological aspects such as confidence using computers and computer anxiety, with statements like:

- "I feel confident in my ability to use computers for completing assignments."
- "I am afraid of making mistakes when using a computer for my schoolwork."

Meanwhile, the TAM provides a broader framework that includes dimensions, such as:

- Perceived Usefulness (PU): "Using educational tools would enhance my learning."
- Perceived Ease of Use (PEU): "I find educational technology easy to use."
- Educational Support: "I feel supported when using technology in my studies."

Although both CAQ and TAM were part of the data collection, this paper focuses exclusively on the CAQ. This narrowed scope allows for a focused evaluation of CAQ's psychometric properties before expanding into full model comparisons and integration with TAM in future studies.

2.2 Justification for the Pilot Focus

Rather than serving as a hypothetical test run or simulation, this study draws from actual responses collected via an Institutional Review Board (IRB)-approved survey distributed to students enrolled in mathematics courses at a university located in the north part of Texas, USA and a college located in southern part of Texas. The goal was to evaluate the CAQ in a real academic setting, particularly within courses using platforms such as MyLab Math, MyOpenMath, and ALEKS. By examining results across demographics including age, gender, and modality, the study offers insights into how students' technology attitudes vary in authentic contexts. The analysis follows established psychometric guidelines (DeVellis, 2016) and supports broader efforts to validate whether CAQ is a reliable instrument for educational technology research (Davis, 1989; Marikyan & Papagiannidis, 2023; Sharit et al., 2019).

2.3 Participant Demographics

Participants (N = 161) were undergraduate students enrolled in mathematics courses at one university and one community college, spanning three instructional modalities: face-to-face (n = 88, 54.7 %), online (n = 68, 42.2 %), and hybrid (n = 5, 3.1 %). Age was heavily clustered in the younger brackets: 18–24 years (n = 127, 78.9 %), 25–34 years (n = 27, 16.8 %), 35–44 years (n = 5, 3.1 %), and only single participants in each of the 45–54 and 55–64 ranges (0.6 % each). Gender identities included male (n = 97, 60.2 %), female (n = 59, 36.6

%), non-binary/non-conforming (n = 2, 1.2 %), and prefer not to say (n = 3, 1.9 %). Because the latter two categories together represented fewer than 3 % of the sample, inferential analyses were limited to male and female respondents. Approximately one-fifth of students (n = 32, 19.9 %) reported prior experience using R, while the majority (n = 129, 80.1 %) had not. This diversity in age, gender, modality, and programming background supports the study's goal of examining computer attitudes across varied educational contexts.

3. DATA ANALYSIS

Building on the dataset and variable transformations outlined in the previous section, we used RStudio to conduct a detailed analysis of the Computer Attitude Questionnaire (CAQ) items. This phase focused on evaluating the internal consistency and structural behavior of four key items, CAQ6, CAQ7, CAQ8, and CAQ9, which were selected to represent students' computer-related confidence and anxiety (Knezek & Christensen, 1996). We began by examining the mean and standard deviation for each item, alongside the construct each item was designed to measure. As shown in Table 1, CAQ6 and CAQ7 exhibited moderately high agreement, while CAQ8 and CAQ9 had notably lower mean scores.

Table 1. Descriptive statistics for original CAQ items (CAQ6–CAQ9)

Item	Description	Construct Measured	Mean	Standard Deviation
CAQ6	I am afraid of making mistakes when using a computer for my schoolwork.	Computer Anxiety	3.93	0.96
CAQ7	I feel confident in my ability to use computers for completing assignments.	Confidence using computers	3.29	1.17
CAQ8	I feel uneasy whenever I am asked to use a computer.	Computer Anxiety	1.88	0.87
CAQ9	Computers make me feel uncomfortable.	Computer Anxiety	1.98	0.91

While CAQ6 and CAQ7 reflected higher levels of agreement, the considerably lower means for CAQ8 and CAQ9 suggested these items may have been interpreted in the opposite direction. Notably, CAQ8 and CAQ9 were phrased with a stronger negative emotional tone, which likely contributed to their misalignment with the other items. To assess internal consistency, we calculated Cronbach's alpha. The initial result produced a negative alpha of -0.10, indicating that some items were inversely correlated and undermining the reliability of the scale. Further analysis confirmed that CAQ8 and CAQ9 were negatively correlated with the first principal component, suggesting that their scoring direction was inconsistent with the rest of the scale (DeVellis, 2016; Sharit et al., 2019). To resolve this, both CAQ8 and CAQ9 were reverse coded so that higher scores reflected greater confidence, aligning them conceptually with CAQ6 and CAQ7. These revised items were renamed CAQ8R and CAQ9R. After this adjustment, we recalculated descriptive statistics for the updated four-item scale. As shown in Table 2, the means for all items now clustered around a similar value, indicating a consistent direction of interpretation across the scale.

Table 2. Descriptive statistics for revised CAQ items (CAQ6, CAQ7, CAQ8R, CAQ9R)

Item	Description	Construct Measured	Mean	Standard Deviation
CAQ6	I am afraid of making mistakes when using a computer for my schoolwork.	Computer Anxiety	3.93	0.96
CAQ7	I feel confident in my ability to use computers for completing assignments.	Confidence using computers	3.29	1.17
CAQ8R	I feel uneasy whenever I am asked to use a computer. (reversed)	Confidence using computers	4.12	0.87
CAQ9R	Computers make me feel uncomfortable. (reversed)	Confidence using computers	4.02	0.91

After these adjustments, a second calculation of Cronbach's alpha yielded a substantially improved value of 0.696, indicating acceptable internal consistency for a four-item scale (DeVellis, 2016). In conclusion, reverse-coding the negatively phrased items not only corrected a major reliability issue but also confirmed that the CAQ items collectively measure a unified construct related to student attitudes toward computers. These findings validate the CAQ's usefulness for future research and confirm that the refined instrument is well-suited for further statistical analysis in educational settings (Dowker et al., 2022; Knezek & Christensen, 1996; Sharit et al., 2019).

4. FACTOR ANALYSIS OF THE CAQ

Building upon these findings, we proceeded to further examine the internal structure of the CAQ using Principal Component Analysis (PCA). Having established that the refined four-item scale comprising of CAQ6, CAQ7, CAQ8R, and CAQ9R demonstrates strong reliability, it was essential to explore whether these items also align under a single latent construct. This next phase of the analysis focused on identifying the dimensionality of the CAQTotalScale and evaluating how well these items collectively represent the broader concept of computer attitudes. To determine how well these items cluster around a single latent construct, we began by analyzing the eigenvalues from the PCA. The scree plot showed a steep drop after the first principal component, with the first eigenvalue significantly exceeding 1 while the remaining components fell below this threshold. This pattern, often referred to as the "elbow criterion," suggests the retention of a single-factor model. Specifically, only one component had an eigenvalue above 1, strongly supporting a unidimensional structure. The visualization is shown in Figure 1.

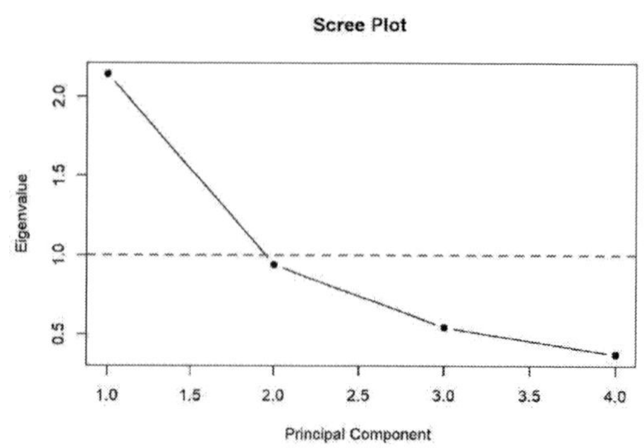

Figure 1. Scree plot of principal component analysis for CAQ items

This interpretation was further reinforced by the component matrix, which captured the correlation of each item with the first principal component. The sorted component loadings are displayed in Table 3.

Table 3. Component loadings for CAQ items (principal component 1)

Item	Description	Loading
CAQ6	I am afraid of making mistakes when using a computer for my schoolwork.	0.810
CAQ8R	I feel uneasy whenever I am asked to use a computer. (reversed)	0.780
CAQ7	I feel confident in my ability to use computers for completing assignments.	0.668
CAQ9R	Computers make me feel uncomfortable. (reversed)	0.655

These values indicate that all four items loaded strongly and consistently onto the first component, with CAQ6 and CAQ8R contributing most heavily. Importantly, the successful alignment of CAQ8R and CAQ9R following reverse scoring supports the effectiveness of the transformation and confirms that all items work cohesively to measure a unified latent construct. In line with DeVellis (2016) and Sharit et al. (2019), these PCA results offer strong evidence for the construct validity of the CAQ in this context. The presence of a dominant factor accounting for approximately 65.89% of the total variance supports the CAQ's theoretical structure and validates its use as a unidimensional measure of student attitudes toward computers. Taken together, the strong internal consistency, distinct scree plot, and robust component loadings confirm that the CAQTotalScale effectively captures a single, interpretable construct. These findings also provide a strong foundation for future Confirmatory Factor Analysis (CFA) to extend the scale's psychometric validation and broaden its application in educational technology research.

5. DEMOGRAPHIC COMPARISONS

Understanding how different student populations experience and respond to technology tools is essential for interpreting the effectiveness and equity of digital learning environments. Demographic factors such as gender, age, and instructional modality can influence students' confidence, anxiety, and engagement with educational technology. These differences are particularly important in mathematics education, where technology is often a central component of instruction. As Duggal et al. (2021) emphasize, factors like student motivation and interaction with digital platforms can vary significantly across subgroups, affecting not only performance but also overall classroom engagement. By examining how attitudes differ across these demographic dimensions, this study aims to assess the sensitivity of the Computer Attitude Questionnaire (CAQ) and to identify which student populations may benefit from additional support or alternative approaches to technology integration.

5.1 Gender

We began by examining gender-based differences in students' confidence in using computers using an independent samples t-test. Only participants who identified as male ($n = 97$) or female ($n = 59$) were included in this analysis, as the number of respondents identifying as Non-Binary/Non-Conforming ($n = 2$) or Prefer not to say ($n = 3$) was too small to support meaningful statistical comparison. Participants were coded as 1 = Male and 2 = Female, and the CAQTotalScale (mean of CAQ6, CAQ7, CAQ8R, and CAQ9R) served as the dependent variable. The test revealed a statistically significant difference between the two groups, $t(131.5) = 3.08$, $p = .003$. Males reported a higher average confidence using computers score ($M = 3.98$) compared to females ($M = 3.63$). To assess the practical significance of this difference, we calculated Cohen's d, which yielded a value of 0.50, indicating a small to moderate effect size. The 95% confidence interval for the effect size ranged from 0.18 to 0.82, suggesting that while the difference is statistically significant, it may not reflect a substantial gap in everyday confidence between genders. These findings suggest that males in the sample tend to report slightly greater confidence using computers than their female counterparts. However, the practical implications of this difference appear modest, and further research would be needed to explore whether these differences persist across larger or more diverse populations (DeVellis, 2016; Sharit et al., 2019). In the following section, we turn to age as another key demographic variable to examine whether generational factors influence students' comfort and confidence with technology.

5.2 Age

To further explore whether confidence using computers varied with age, we conducted a series of statistical tests, including one-way ANOVA, Cohen's d, and Pearson's correlation. These analyses were performed using the CAQTotalScale as the outcome measure, which represents students' overall attitudes toward computers based on the refined CAQ items. Participants were divided into five age groups: 18–24 ($n = 127$), 25–34 ($n = 27$), 35–44 ($n = 5$), 45–54 ($n = 1$), and 55–64 ($n = 1$). Given the small sample sizes in the latter three groups, our primary focus remained on comparing the two most represented groups: 18–24 and 25–34. A one-way ANOVA was conducted to assess whether confidence using computers differed significantly across all five age categories. The results indicated no statistically significant differences between groups,

F(4, 156) = 1.799, p = 0.132. A post-hoc Tukey's HSD test further confirmed that no pairwise comparisons were statistically significant. For instance, the adjusted p-value comparing 18–24 and 25–34 was 0.535, with a confidence interval of [-0.18, 0.64], suggesting no meaningful difference in confidence using computers between these groups. Still, group means revealed a notable pattern: the 25–34 group reported higher average confidence using computers (M = 4.02) compared to the 18–24 group (M = 3.79). While this difference was not statistically significant, the direction of the effect warranted further investigation. To quantify the magnitude of this difference, we calculated Cohen's d, which yielded a small effect size of -0.33 (95% CI: -0.75 to 0.09). The negative value again reflects that the older age group reported greater confidence using computers. Although this result was not significant, it suggests a potential trend that could be more pronounced in a larger or more diverse sample (Sharit et al., 2019). We also examined the relationship between age and confidence using computers using Pearson's correlation. The correlation coefficient was r = 0.118, with a p-value of 0.1371. This weak, non-significant result reinforces the ANOVA findings, indicating that age does not have a statistically meaningful relationship with CAQTotalScale. The confidence interval for the correlation ranged from -0.038 to 0.267, crossing zero and further signaling uncertainty in the strength and direction of the association. Finally, previous gender-based analyses showed no significant interaction with age in predicting confidence using computers. Both male and female participants appeared to follow similar patterns across age groups, suggesting that gender does not substantially influence the age-confidence relationship (DeVellis, 2016; Davis, 1989; Sharit et al., 2019). Taken together, these findings suggest that while students in the 25–34 group reported slightly higher levels of confidence using computers, the difference was small and not statistically significant. Age may play a minor role in shaping attitudes toward educational technology, but in this sample, its influence was weak and inconsistent.

5.3 Modality

Following the analysis of age and gender, we examined whether the format in which students received their math instruction—referred to here as modality—was associated with differences in reported confidence using computers. The three reported modalities were Face-to-Face, Online, and Hybrid (a mix of Face-to-Face and Online). However, due to the very small number of participants in the Hybrid category (n = 5), our focus was primarily on comparing the Online (n = 68) and Face-to-Face (n = 88) groups, which had substantially larger and more balanced sample sizes. Descriptive statistics revealed that students in the Online group reported the highest average confidence using computers (M = 3.99), followed by the Face-to-Face group (M = 3.74), and lastly the Hybrid group (M = 3.70). While this pattern suggested that students learning in fully online environments may feel more confident using computers than those in traditional classrooms, formal statistical testing was needed to determine the significance of these differences. A one-way ANOVA was conducted to assess whether confidence using computers varied significantly across the three modalities. The results showed a marginal effect of modality on CAQTotalScale scores, with F(2, 158) = 2.44, p = 0.0904. Although the result did not reach the conventional threshold for significance ($p < 0.05$), it approached significance, suggesting a possible trend. Post-hoc pairwise comparisons using Tukey's HSD further clarified these differences. While no comparisons were statistically significant, the Online vs. Face-to-Face contrast showed the largest difference (adjusted p = 0.081), providing preliminary evidence that online learners may indeed feel more confident using computers than their face-to-face peers. To explore this further, we calculated Cohen's d between the Online and Face-to-Face groups. The resulting effect size was d = -0.35, classified as small. The negative value reflects the higher mean score among online students. The 95% confidence interval for this estimate ranged from -0.67 to -0.03, which does not include zero—suggesting that this effect, while modest, is statistically significant. Finally, a Pearson correlation analysis was conducted using a numerically coded modality variable (1 = Face-to-Face, 2 = Online). The correlation between modality and CAQTotalScale was r = 0.171, with a p-value = 0.0331. This statistically significant finding supports the previous results and indicates a weak but positive relationship: as students move from face-to-face to online learning environments, their reported confidence using computers tends to increase slightly. The 95% confidence interval for the correlation coefficient ranged from 0.014 to 0.319, reinforcing the reliability of this trend. Taken together, the ANOVA, effect size, and correlation analyses consistently point to a subtle but statistically meaningful difference in confidence using computers between students in online versus face-to-face learning environments. These findings suggest that modality may play a role in shaping students' comfort with computers, an important consideration as educational institutions continue to expand and refine online offerings.

6. SUMMARY OF FINDINGS

The results of this study confirm that the Computer Attitude Questionnaire (CAQ) is a reliable and valid instrument for measuring students' computer-related confidence and anxiety in college-level mathematics courses (DeVellis, 2016; Knezek & Christensen, 1996; Sharit et al., 2019). Initial reliability testing revealed that negatively worded items (CAQ8 and CAQ9) required reverse scoring to align with the scale. After this adjustment, Cronbach's alpha increased to 0.703, indicating acceptable internal consistency. Principal Component Analysis (PCA) further supported a unidimensional structure, with one component accounting for 65.89% of total variance and strong item loadings across all four CAQ items, reinforcing the structural validity of the instrument (Sharit et al., 2019). Demographic comparisons revealed nuanced patterns. Male students reported significantly higher confidence using computers than female students, with a small to moderate effect size ($d = 0.50$). While older students appeared slightly more confident than younger peers, age differences were not statistically significant. Instructional modality showed the most consistent trend: students enrolled in online courses reported higher confidence using computers than those in face-to-face settings, with a small but statistically significant correlation ($r = 0.171$, $p = .0331$). These findings suggest that gender and modality may influence students' comfort with technology, while age appears to have a more limited effect. Overall, the CAQTotalScale offers a sound metric for assessing student attitudes toward educational technology and highlights key demographic factors that may inform future instructional strategies (Davis, 1989; Sharit et al., 2019).

7. DISCUSSION AND FUTURE RESEARCH

The findings reinforce the psychometric strength of the Computer Attitude Questionnaire (CAQ) as a reliable and structurally valid instrument for assessing confidence using computers and anxiety among undergraduate students in mathematics courses. The CAQ demonstrated acceptable internal consistency ($\alpha = 0.703$) after reverse coding of negatively worded items and exhibited a unidimensional factor structure through Principal Component Analysis (DeVellis, 2016; Sharit et al., 2019). These results confirm that the CAQ effectively captures both emotional and cognitive dimensions of students' attitudes toward educational technology. While the CAQ performed well overall, demographic variations—particularly higher confidence among males and online learners—highlight important considerations for future use. These patterns suggest that instructional context may shape how students experience technology and that future iterations of the CAQ could be refined to account for institutional or instructional diversity (Dowker et al., 2022; Marikyan & Papagiannidis, 2023). Future research should build on this exploratory factor analysis by conducting Confirmatory Factor Analysis (CFA) to test the stability of the scale across varied populations (DeVellis, 2016). Expanding the analysis to include the Technology Acceptance Model (TAM) would enable a deeper understanding of perceived usefulness and support structures associated with educational tools such as RStudio, Python, MyLab Math, and MyOpenMath. Additional integration with the Mathematics Attitudes and Anxiety Questionnaire (MAAQ) and the Mathematics Attitudes and Perceptions Survey (MAPS) could provide a more holistic perspective on how confidence using computers intersects with math-related attitudes, collaboration, and persistence (Dowker et al., 2022; Sharit et al., 2019). Finally, longitudinal research is needed to examine how students' attitudes toward technology evolve over time. By investigating how exposure to tools like ALEKS, RStudio, or MyOpenMath impacts confidence, anxiety, and academic performance, researchers can better understand the sustained effects of educational technology integration in mathematics instruction (Sharit et al., 2019).

8. CONCLUSION

As technology continues to reshape the landscape of higher education, particularly in mathematics instruction, understanding how students perceive and adapt to digital tools is essential. This study contributes to that understanding by validating the Computer Attitude Questionnaire (CAQ) as a reliable and structurally sound instrument for assessing students' confidence and anxiety regarding computer use. The CAQ's psychometric strength—evidenced by acceptable internal consistency and a clear unidimensional structure—positions it as a practical tool for educators and researchers alike (DeVellis, 2016; Sharit et al., 2019). Demographic findings offered additional insight into how factors like gender and modality may shape students' technological experiences. While differences were modest, the results indicated that male students and those in online courses reported slightly higher confidence using computers—an important consideration as institutions expand digital offerings. Although age was not significantly associated with confidence levels, observed patterns suggest that more mature students may still benefit from tailored support or onboarding practices (Davis, 1989; Marikyan & Papagiannidis, 2023). This study serves as a foundational step in the broader effort to evaluate and enhance technology integration in mathematics education. By laying the groundwork for future Confirmatory Factor Analysis (CFA), longitudinal research, and integration with other validated instruments such as the Mathematics Attitudes and Anxiety Questionnaire (MAAQ) and the Mathematics Attitudes and Perceptions Survey (MAPS), this work opens multiple pathways for ongoing inquiry (Code et al., 2016; Dowker et al., 2022; Sharit et al., 2019). Ultimately, the CAQ's validated structure and sensitivity to instructional and demographic factors make it a valuable resource for identifying students' psychological readiness to engage with educational technology. As digital tools like MyLab Math, ALEKS, RStudio, and Python become more deeply embedded in college math courses, the ability to measure and respond to students' technology-related attitudes will be critical for improving engagement, reducing anxiety, and supporting equitable learning outcomes.

ACKNOWLEDGEMENT

The authors would like to thank Gerald Knezek, Ph.D., for assistance with this study.

REFERENCES

Code, W., Merchant, S., Maciejewski, W., Thomas, M., & Lo, J. (2016). The Mathematics Attitudes and Perceptions Survey: an instrument to assess expert-like views and dispositions among undergraduate mathematics students. International Journal of Mathematical Education in Science and Technology, 47(6), 917–937. https://doi.org/10.1080/0020739X.2015.1133854

Davis, F. D. (1989). Perceived usefulness, perceived ease of use, and user acceptance of information technology. MIS Quarterly, 13(3), 319-339.

DeVellis, R. F. (2016). Scale development: Theory and applications (4th ed.). Sage

Publications.

Dowker, A., Bennett, K., & Smith, L. (2022, January 31). Mathematics attitudes and anxiety questionnaire (MAAQ). Oxford University Innovation. https://innovation.ox.ac.uk/outcome-measures/mathematics-attitudes-and-anxiety-questionnaire-maaq/

Duggal, K., Gupta, L. R., & Singh, P. (2021). Gamification and machine learning inspired approach for classroom engagement and learning. Mathematical Problems in Engineering, 2021(1), 9922775.

Han, J. H., & Sa, H. J. (2022). Acceptance of and satisfaction with online educational classes through the technology acceptance model (TAM): The COVID-19 situation in Korea. Asia Pacific Education Review, 23(3), 403–415. https://doi.org/10.1007/s12564-021-09716-7

Knezek, G., & Christensen, R. (1996). Validating the Computer Attitude Questionnaire (CAQ). https://iittl.unt.edu/instruments/computer-attitude-questionnaire-caq.html

Lewis, J. R. (2019). Comparison of Four TAM Item Formats: Effect of Response Option Labels and Order. Journal of Usability Studies, 14(4). https://uxpajournal.org/tam-formats-effect-response-labels-order/

Obut, V. G., Jumawan, M. D., Baluyos, G. R., & Bacus, J. A. (2024). Exploring the Students' Struggles in Learning Mathematics: Basis for Enhancement.

Marikyan, D.& Papagiannidis, S. (2023) Technology Acceptance Model: A review. In S. Papagiannidis (Ed), TheoryHub Book. https://open.ncl.ac.uk / ISBN: 9781739604400

Mistretta, R. M. (2004, November 30). Integrating technology into the Mathematics Classroom: The role of teacher preparation programs. Mathematics Educator. https://eric.ed.gov/?id=EJ845844

Sharit, J., Moxley, J. H., Boot, W. R., Charness, N., Rogers, W. A., & Czaja, S. J. (2019). Effects of extended use of an age-friendly computer system on assessments of computer proficiency, attitudes, and usability by older non-computer users. ACM Transactions on Accessible Computing (TACCESS), 12(2), 1-28. https://doi.org/10.1145/3325290

THE SERGIO BLANCO STUDY: EVALUATING CREATIVE WORK THROUGH AI

Franco Ripa Di Meana[1], Andrea Guidi[1], Veronica Di Geronimo[1] and Alberto Giretti[2]
[1]*Rome Fine Arts Academy, Via di Ripetta, 222 – 00186 Rome, Italy*
[2]*Marche Polytechnic University, Via Brecce Bianche, 60131 Ancona, Italy*

ABSTRACT

The methodology outlined in this paper proposes a structured and replicable framework for incorporating AI-assisted evaluation tools into educational contexts characterized by creative expression and artistic inquiry. Over a four-month case-study at the Rome Fine Arts Academy, twenty-five students engaged with Sergio Blanco's theatrical monologue, *Memento Mori*, using it as inspiration to develop individual artistic performances as the objective of an academic course. In the days following their performances, each student individually documented their creative process and outcomes by creating a final multimedia *exposition*—a structured presentation integrating text, images, audio, and video. The textual components of each student's document were analyzed through the AI platform °°Kobi, which provided insights into thematic coherence with Blanco's original work and assessed originality among the students' artistic research presented in their final document. Preliminary findings indicate participant engagement suggesting the collection of insightful data to gauge the potential for AI to support instructors in effectively evaluating creative assignments in higher education settings. The paper concludes by addressing methodological limitations, outlining immediate next steps for data analysis, and identifying future directions for continued research in AI-assisted evaluation.

KEYWORDS

AI-Assisted Evaluation, Higher Arts Education, Artistic Research

1. INTRODUCTION

This paper reports on a structured academic course at the Rome Fine Arts Academy that explored how artificial-intelligence (AI) tools can assist instructors in evaluating students' creative work. Sergio Blanco's *Memento Mori*—an autofictional monologue on mortality, memory and narrative—served as the common stimulus. Twenty-five students drew on the text to devise individual artistic performances and, afterwards, to assemble "expositions": multimedia documents combining text, images, audio and video and archived on the online repository Research Catalogue (https://www.researchcatalogue.net/).

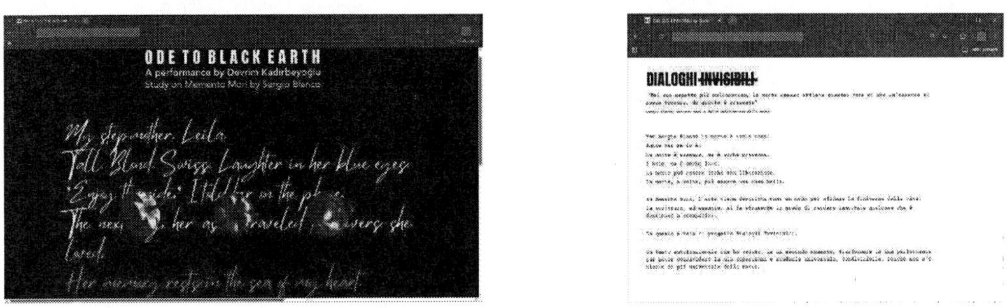

Figure 1. Two examples of creative outputs in the form of Expositions created for the course.

The final documents were produced in the form of expositions, a structured multimedia presentation combining text, images, audio, and video, designed to document and reflect on the artistic research and creative processes underlying an artistic performance (Borgdorff, 2012; Hannula, Suoranta, & Vadén, 2014).

The methodological approach comprised two primary factors. The first factor involved a systematic comparative analysis between Sergio Blanco's *Memento Mori* and the student-generated expositions. Semantic similarity was gauged with two complementary methods: **(1)** cosine distance, a standard metric in information-retrieval research (Manning et al., 2008; Turney & Pantel, 2010), and **(2)** a large language model concept extractor embedded in the °'°Kobi platform (Giretti et al., 2023, 2024; Ripa di Meana et al., 2024) that quantified the concepts shared across texts. Results from these automated measures were cross-validated against the course instructor's thematic analysis of the texts, enabling us to determine how closely each student's expositions aligned with—or diverged from—the original stimulus in both thematic and conceptual terms. This step emphasized the educational context, particularly highlighting courses such as Theatre Directing[1], where it is crucial to assess students' ability to construct personal projects while clearly preserving a discernible connection to the assigned reference material. Within this type of educational framework, students' final outputs must not merely be "inspired by" the original text but explicitly maintain recognizable dramaturgical relationships to it. The second factor shifted the focus to examining thematic and semantic relationships among the students' own expositions. This internal comparative analysis aimed to identify patterns of originality and innovation within the student cohort, reveal thematic convergence or divergence across student responses, and enhance understanding of how distinct or similar individual creative processes are within a shared educational context.

It is important to note that the proposed methodology did not evaluate or quantify the students' artistic performances enacted at the end of the course. Instead, the analytical focus rests on the artistic research embedded in each student's exposition. In this context, *artistic research* refers to the reflective and systematic process through which artists investigate, expand, and articulate the conceptual and aesthetic foundations of their work (Borgdorff, 2012; Hannula, Suoranta, & Vadén, 2014). By examining how students documented their personal explorations, conceptual frameworks, and creative decision-making, this research aimed to capture the intellectual and theoretical dimensions underlying the performed pieces.

Using °'°Kobi, we also generated an interactive semantic graph (Figure 2) that positions each student exposition relative to Sergio Blanco's *Memento Mori* and exposes thematic connections across the cohort. In the display, Blanco's monologue appears as a green node, student texts as red, higher-level concepts as blue, and individual lemmas as grey. Hovering over a node (Figure 3) highlights its links, while clicking a red node opens the full exposition. While the graph did not inform the data analysis presented in this paper, it was presented to students in a final feedback session, using it to spark group discussion and gather qualitative reflections on how the AI-generated visualization portrayed the students' work.

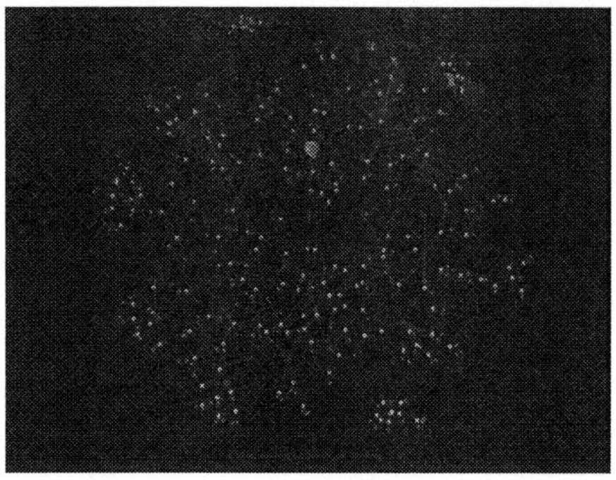

Figure 2. The overall view of the graph. The Green node represents Blanco's text while the red nodes each represent a student exposition. Blue nodes are concepts and gray nodes are lemmas

Figure 3. Detail from the semantic graph illustrating the lemma *memory* (gray node at the centre of the image) and its relationships to several student expositions (red nodes)

[1] Theatre directing is generally known as the artistic practice of interpreting, organizing, and coordinating all creative elements involved in a theatrical production—including acting, staging, design, and narrative—to shape a cohesive, meaningful, and expressive performance.

2. ENHANCING LEARNING IN ARTISTIC EDUCATION

The integration of Artificial Intelligence (AI) into educational contexts has attracted growing attention, particularly regarding evaluation methods. This literature review examines how AI is currently utilized to support assessment processes within educational settings, with special attention given to creative and artistic disciplines.

2.1 AI-Assisted Evaluation in Higher Arts Education

Artificial Intelligence (AI) is increasingly explored in higher education, particularly regarding its potential in enhancing assessment processes, promising benefits such as increased objectivity, consistency, and efficiency (Gardner, O'Leary, & Yuan, 2021). However, implementing AI in artistic disciplines introduces distinct challenges due to the inherently subjective, expressive, and context-dependent nature of creative work (Kong, 2020).

Despite these inherent complexities, current research highlights several possibilities for AI's supportive role in evaluating artistic disciplines. For instance, semantic analysis tools can measure originality and thematic depth in creative writing or visual art, providing supplementary insights that might escape traditional human evaluators (Forster & Dunbar, 2009; Beaty & Johnson, 2021). AI-generated evaluations offer structured feedback which educators can use to initiate deeper critical reflections and foster richer pedagogical dialogue (Liang, 2024), provided instructors and students possess a foundational level of AI literacy (Liang, 2024; Ko et al., 2021). Recent work underscores that automated semantic metrics and expert-driven ratings, such as the Consensual Assessment Technique (CAT) (Amabile, 1996; Baer & McKool, 2009), are increasingly convergent rather than competing approaches to creativity assessment. Large-corpus studies show that distributional measures of semantic distance—whether computed with classic word embeddings or with transformer-based models—explain 60–70 % of the variance in CAT originality scores on divergent-thinking and narrative tasks (*Beaty & Johnson, 2021; Dumas et al., 2021*). Follow-up research introduced Divergent Semantic Integration (DSI), which replicated these correlations across 3,500 short stories and nine prompts, confirming that higher-level semantic dispersion reliably predicts expert creativity ratings (*Johnson et al., 2023*). Parallel studies testing large-language models as surrogate judges find moderate—but steadily improving—agreement with CAT panels, hinting that machine raters can augment, though not yet replace, human expertise (*Acar, 2023*). Taken together, these findings support a hybrid strategy in which CAT anchors validity while semantic-distance analytics add speed, scalability, and fine-grained diagnostics—an approach our Sergio Blanco study adopts by pairing expert CAT ratings with cosine-distance and concept-overlap measures.

Nevertheless, critical voices warn against relying solely on AI-driven assessments. There are concerns that algorithmic evaluations may inadequately capture intangible creative qualities such as emotional impact, cultural relevance, and unique stylistic nuances, potentially leading to reductive assessments of complex creative outputs (Lim, Gottipati, & Cheong, 2023). Consequently, an integrated assessment approach, combining AI-supported analytics with peer feedback and expert instructor judgment, is strongly advocated to preserve the nuanced appraisal of artistic merit (Myint, Lo, & Zhang, 2024), ensuring sustainable and replicable pedagogical practices (Myint, Lo, & Zhang, 2024; McWilliam & Dawson, 2008).

Ethical dimensions further complicate AI's application in arts education, particularly regarding biases embedded within AI systems. These biases could unintentionally favor specific cultural norms or historical aesthetics, necessitating careful algorithmic transparency and inclusive dataset curation to maintain fairness and diversity in assessment practices (Lim, Gottipati, & Cheong, 2023). To address these issues, collaboration among AI developers, educators, and cultural experts is recommended, ensuring AI technologies evolve respectfully toward the pluralistic nature of artistic expression (Mayo, 2024).

2.2 Experiential Learning

The course was structured to leverage experiential learning principles. Eisner (2002) illustrates how uniting Experiential Learning with Project-Based Learning encourages students to immerse themselves in real-world tasks, prioritizing active learning and collaboration—an especially effective strategy in art and design education. In Kolb's (1984) framework, learning is viewed as a cycle encompassing concrete experience, reflective observation, abstract conceptualization, and active experimentation. Echoing these ideas, Greene (1995) underlines how hands-on engagement and reflective practice bolster meaningful inquiry in the arts, spurring creativity, critical thinking, and cultural appreciation.

Collaborative activities were incorporated into the course to encourage students' mutual exploration, critique, and deeper understanding of artistic and cultural concepts). Collaboration can heighten engagement, stimulate motivation, and strengthen both interpersonal and cognitive competencies. By embedding collaborative tasks into an experiential framework, learners engage in dialogue, diverse perspective sharing, possibly enriching their overall learning experience.

3. °'°KOBI

The study used the AI-driven platform °'°Kobi, a knowledge ecosystem developed to encourage in-depth exploration and innovative interactions with artistic content (Giretti et al., 2022). The platform draws upon an extensive, curated collection of artistic research publications sourced from the Research Catalogue, forming its core knowledge base. °'°Kobi employs large language models to transform this content into structured, interconnected semantic relationships, enabling nuanced and contextually relevant query responses (Giretti et al., 2023). The system typically leverages the LLM's capabilities to facilitate interactive exchanges, enabling end-users—primarily students—to type messages into a chat interface and receive responses in the form of text or media (see Figure 4). In this study, however, the LLM's analytical capacity to process documents, extract relevant information, and generate meaningful associations and contextual insights was specifically employed to assist instructors in evaluating student-produced outputs. °'°Kobi called the LLM model Gemma-2 7B-it for concepts extraction. For semantic distance calculation, the system embedded texts at paragraph level using Google text-embedding-004 (768-dimensions). See Giretti et al. (2023, 2024) for architecture details.

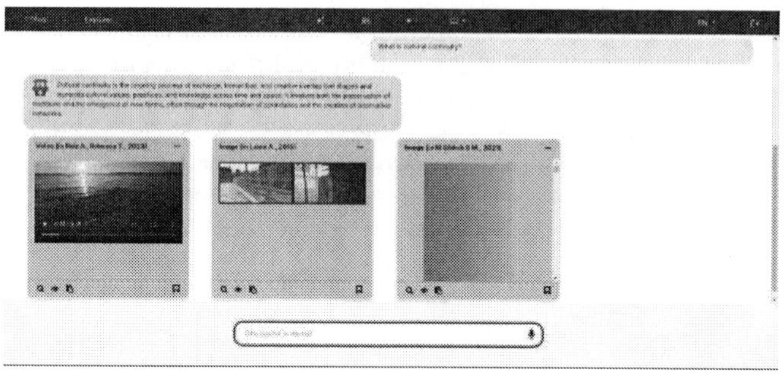

Figure 4. The °'°Kobi chat interface. Users can type their queries in the bottom-center chat box. Responses are displayed on the left side of the chat. They can include related media such as images

4. THE STUDY

The course took place at the Rome Fine Arts Academy as part of the Regia academic curriculum, spanning a duration of 15 weeks and for a total of 75 hours. The educational approach of the course emphasized artistic research methodologies and included a dedicated seminar conducted by a researcher, during which students were introduced to the Research Catalogue as a significant tool for artistic inquiry and dissemination.

The pedagogical framework of the course was structured into three main phases: collective acquaintance, group performance, and dissemination. Prior to the first phase, all students received a consent form explaining the research objectives connected to the course and the use of their data for analysis. They were informed that participation in the course was independent of their decision to grant or deny consent: those who chose not to have their data used for the study could still complete all course activities. A short questionnaire gathered basic demographic information from consenting participants. Consequently, all students engaged in a collaborative brainstorming session facilitated via an online tool, MIRO, although other collaborative platforms could also have been utilized. At this stage, Sergio Blanco's *autofictional* theatrical monologue, *Memento Mori*, served as the central stimulus. Blanco's text explores themes of mortality, personal narrative, and memory, presented through an autofictional format that merges factual autobiography with fictional elements. Students anonymously uploaded their individual responses and interpretative materials to a shared digital workspace, enabling collective feedback and in-depth group discussions aimed at discovering and critically engaging with Blanco's nuanced exploration of life and death.

In the second phase, students dedicated four weeks to creating their artistic performances. Each student was required to adopt Sergio Blanco's creative framework and scenic apparatus which involved using narrative-based theatrical techniques to intertwine personal material with fictional elements, reflecting the autofictional nature of Blanco's original work. On December 18, all students presented their performances resulting in 25 autofictional micro-performances. No photography, video recording, or external audience attendance was permitted, ensuring a focused environment.

The final phase focused on individual dissemination and reflection. Following their performances, students individually created multimedia expositions that documented and expanded upon their creative processes and outcomes. Central to this stage was students' reflection on the connections between the original performance materials and their finalized expositions. At the end of the course, students completed an anonymous questionnaire evaluating their experiences, engagement, and the effectiveness of educational methods and tools.

The overall activity involved twenty-five participants, mostly from Italy (thirteen individuals), with the rest of the participants originally from China (9 individuals), and three from various countries. The average age among the participants was 25 years old, with an even gender distribution of approximately half female and half male. Students participating in the study earned educational credits akin to those of a standard academic course. The data and insights generated in this study did not contribute to the students' actual evaluation, and it is currently the subject of analysis for the research presented in this paper.

5. METHODOLOGY AND ANALYSIS

The real-life educational context provided by this course is crucial in validating the methodology and analysis. By engaging students in authentic creative tasks inspired by Blanco's Memento Mori, the research aims to measure tangible creative and educational outcomes, ensuring practical relevance and applicability of AI-driven analytical methods.

5.1 Comparison between Blanco's text and students' final assignments

The analysis began by comparing students' texts with Sergio Blanco's *Memento Mori*. This first analysis focuses on two main metrics: **(a)** the number of *shared concepts* and **(b)** the cosine distance between Blanco's text and the students' final assignments. Shared concepts are meant to quantify matching concepts between *Memento Mori* and individual student expositions. Concepts were extracted by prompting Google's large language model *Gemma 2*[2] within the °'°Kobi platform and validated by comparing them with a thematic analysis conducted by the course instructor. This data is collected to assess how frequently students employed similar core ideas, themes, or terminology. Cosine distance measures how closely each student's text aligns semantically with Sergio Blanco's original work, *Memento Mori*. A lower cosine distance indicates high thematic similarity or fidelity, while a higher distance suggests originality or thematic divergence. This measure is computed by converting texts into numeric embeddings that capture their core semantic features. To calculate embeddings, we used Google's *text-embedding-004*. It produces 768-dimensional multilingual embeddings and are suitable for working at sentence or paragraph level. We then computed the cosine distance between the embeddings of *Memento Mori* and each student exposition. Cosine distance values range from 0 (identical meaning), through 1 (unrelated), to 2 (opposite meaning), offering a robust semantic measure independent of text length.

---

[2] Google. (2025, May 23). Models. https://deepmind.google/models/gemma/shieldgemma-2/

In addition, these AI-derived metrics are compared with teacher-generated thematic evaluations, conducted through thematic analysis (Terry et al., 2017), assessing coherence between the original text and student expositions. This integration provides a balanced assessment by combining insights from LLMs with expert human evaluation (Nowell et al., 2017), enhancing methodological rigor and interpretative trustworthiness.

In practical terms, these combined metrics provide educators and researchers with the means to evaluate: *thematic coherence* (to what extent student expositions build upon themes in Memento Mori), and *originality and deviation* (the degree to which students adapt or transform the original themes).

5.2 Comparison between Final Assignments

Consequently, semantic distance metrics were applied to students' assignments to highlight thematic relationships, originality, and creative diversity within the group. To increase the robustness of these metrics, the CAT analysis was employed. Four expert evaluators independently rated each exposition on criteria including creativity, originality, narrative ability, and exposition likeableness. Specifically, the dimensions of narrative ability and exposition likeableness were included to enable evaluators to provide nuanced assessments, reflecting either positive appreciation or negative critique on formal aspects of the work. The methodology was selected due to its efficacy in capturing subjective nuances of creative outputs through consensus among multiple expert assessments.

Integration of CAT results with cosine distance measurements aims to provide a robust, multidimensional view of student work. Whereas cosine distance quantifies the semantic originality and thematic proximity between expositions and the source text or among peers, CAT evaluations contextualize these findings within human interpretive frameworks. For instance, a high cosine distance might indicate semantic difference, while corresponding high CAT ratings could affirm that this difference represents independence or strong originality. Conversely, a low cosine distance suggesting strong thematic alignment could be positively or negatively contextualized by CAT scores—indicating either insightful fidelity or limited innovative departure.By aligning CAT's qualitative insights with cosine distance's quantitative precision, the research seeks to leverage both objective data-driven metrics and subjective expert judgment, ensuring a balanced and comprehensive evaluation framework. The ongoing synergy between these methodologies aims to clarify the complex interplay between originality, thematic coherence, and creative effectiveness, ultimately enriching the educational insights that will emerge from this study.

6. INITIAL INSIGHTS AND LIMITATIONS

Initial insights indicate a positive reception of the course structure and the use of digital tools (°'°Kobi, Research Catalogue). Approximately 88% of students expressed overall satisfaction, and 79% agreed that the digital materials provided enhanced their involvement in the course activities. The CAT evaluation of the student expositions (creativity, originality, narrative quality, and likeableness) achieved statistically valid interjudge reliability, demonstrating that the four evaluators reached a consensus regarding the relative merits of different expositions. These observations pose the basis for the ongoing steps being taken into the analysis of the data.

In this research thematic coherence and creativity are treated as complementary—not competing—constructs. The primary instructional goal is to ensure that each exposition maintains a recognisable dramaturgical link to Sergio Blanco's *Memento Mori*; such alignment is consistent with constructive-alignment principles that stress coherence between learning objectives, tasks, and assessment in higher education (Biggs & Tang, 2011). Once that anchor is established, the framework probes *how inventively* students extend, reinterpret, or subvert those themes, using CAT ratings and pair-wise semantic-distance metrics to gauge originality within the cohort. Accordingly, the paper's focus is dual: (1) thematic coherence (external alignment with Blanco's stimulus) is necessary for meeting the course brief and verifying learning objectives in Theatre-Directing contexts, (2) creative divergence (internal differentiation among student works) is then assessed to illuminate individual innovation and inform formative feedback. The study therefore does not claim that coherence "matters more" than creativity; rather, it posits a sequential hierarchy in the evaluation workflow—*first* confirm fidelity to the assigned reference, *then* examine the imaginative departures that constitute artistic value.

Concerning the constraints on the proposed methodology, one limitation lies in the composition and size of the participant pool: the study involved only twenty-five students at a single institution, restricting generalisability. Broader studies with larger and more diverse cohorts—ideally spanning multiple universities and cultural contexts—are needed to verify whether the observed patterns persist elsewhere. Moreover, although the expositions contain images, audio, and video, the current AI pipeline ignores those modalities. Future work should extend the framework to multimodal embeddings so that visual, sonic, and performative features—often central to artistic meaning—are also evaluated. Finally, because creative work is inherently subjective, AI-assisted evaluation must actively accommodate and encourage diverse yet meaningful interpretations that align with the social norms and cultural contexts of the creators.

7. CONCLUSIONS

This paper presented an ongoing exploration of AI-assisted methods for evaluating creative work in higher arts education, using Sergio Blanco's *Memento Mori* as both a thematic catalyst and an analytical benchmark. Preliminary insights suggest that the data collected may hold significant value for further analysis. Specifically, they could help establish whether AI-driven semantic analysis methods can offer tangible metrics—such as lemma overlap and thematic distance—to enrich human assessments of originality and creativity. Concurrently, our qualitative evaluations (expert panel reviews and student questionnaires) underscore the importance of integrating human-interpretive and contextual dimensions when assessing inherently subjective artistic endeavors. As this research is still in progress, additional work remains to determine the extent to which AI can best complement traditional pedagogical practices in the arts. Short-term steps involve achieving more comprehensive statistical results, eventually refining the semantic analysis models, and possibly integrating more diverse media formats (e.g., images and audio) to expand the comparative framework. The research team also plans to investigate how AI-generated insights may influence students' reflective processes, potentially shaping their creative development. In sum, by situating AI metrics within robust pedagogical and experiential learning frameworks, we aim to harness the strengths of computational analyses without diminishing the inherently human dimensions of creative practice or evaluation. These preliminary findings point to a promising direction for AI as a supportive instrument for educators in evaluating creative work. By combining CAT ratings with semantic-distance measures, AI-based systems like °'°Kobi could act as formative evaluation assistants that tracks and displays each student's creative progress. Instructors could build step-by-step rubrics around the system metrics—for example, rewarding close thematic alignment at early stages and encouraging larger conceptual leaps in later drafts.

ACKNOWLEDGEMENTS

This research is part of the project Enacting Artistic Research (EAR), funded by the European Union - NextGenerationEU, Mission 4 Component 1, CUP B83C24001590005. Views and opinions expressed are however those of the author(s) only and do not necessarily reflect those of the European Union or European Commission. Neither the European Union nor the European Commission can be held responsible for them.
We thank SAR (Society for Artistic Research) for granting access to the Research Catalogue materials.

REFERENCES

Amabile, T. M. (1996). *Creativity in Context*. Westview Press.

Baer, J., & McKool, S. S. (2009). Assessing creativity using the consensual assessment technique. In C. S. Schreiner (Ed.), *Handbook of Research on Assessment Technologies, Methods, and Applications in Higher Education* (pp. 65–77). IGI Global. https://doi.org/10.4018/978-1-60566-667-9.ch004

Beaty, R. E., & Johnson, D. R. (2021). Automating creativity assessment with SemDis: An open platform for computing semantic distance. *Behavior Research Methods, 53*(2), 757–780. https://doi.org/10.3758/s13428-020-01453-w

Borgdorff, H. (2012). *The Conflict of the Faculties: Perspectives on Artistic Research and Academia*. Leiden University Press. https://hdl.handle.net/1887/18704

Eisner, E. W. (2002). *The Arts and the Creation of Mind*. Yale University Press.

Forster, E., Dunbar, K. (2009). Creativity evaluation through latent semantic analysis. In N. Taatgen & H. van Rijn (Eds.), *Proceedings of the 31st Annual Conference of the Cognitive Science Society* (pp. 602-607). Cognitive Science Society.

Gardner, J., O'Leary, M., & Yuan, L. (2021). Artificial intelligence in educational assessment: 'Breakthrough? Or buncombe and ballyhoo?'. *Journal of Computer Assisted Learning, 37*(5), 1207–1216. https://doi.org/10.1111/jcal.12577

Giretti, A., Durmus, D., Vaccarini, M., Zambelli, M., Guidi, A., & di Meana, F. R. (2023). Integrating large language models in art and design education. In D. G. Sampson, D. Ifenthaler, & P. Isaías (Eds.), *Proceedings of the International Conference on Cognition and Exploratory Learning in the Digital Age (CELDA 2023)* (pp. 25–33). IADIS. https://doi.org/10.33965/CELDA2023_202306L004

Giretti, A., Durmus, D., Lemma, M., Vaccarini, M., Zambelli, M., Guidi, A., & di Meana, F. R. (2024). Knowledgeengagement in art and design education: About the role of AI in creativity education. In P. Isaías, D. G. Sampson, & D. Ifenthaler (Eds.), *Artificial Intelligence for Supporting Human Cognition and Exploratory Learning in the Digital Age* (pp. 3–24). Springer Nature. https://doi.org/10.1007/978-3-031-66462-5_1

Greene, M. (1995). Releasing the imagination: *Essays on education, the arts, and social change*. Jossey-Bass.

Hannula, M., Suoranta, J., & Vadén, T. (2014). *Artistic Research Methodology: Narrative, Power and the Public*. Peter Lang.

Johnson, D. R., Kaufman, J. C., Baker, B. S., Patterson, J. D., Barbot, B., Green, A. E., van Hell, J. G., Kennedy, E., Sullivan, G. F., Taylor, C. L., Ward, T. B., & Beaty, R. E. (2023). Divergent semantic integration: Extracting creativity from narratives with distributional semantic modeling. *Behavior Research Methods, 55*(6), 3726–3759. https://doi.org/10.3758/s13428-022-01986-2

Ko, A. J., Sabuncuoglu, A., Eskreis-Winkler, L., & Goransson, B. (2021). Conceptualizing AI literacy: An exploratory review. *Computers and Education: Artificial Intelligence, 2*, Article 100041. https://doi.org/10.1016/j.caeai.2021.100041

Kolb, D. A. (1984). *Experiential Learning: Experience as the Source of Learning and Development*. Prentice Hall.

Kong, F. (2020). Application of artificial intelligence in modern art teaching. *International Journal of Emerging Technologies in Learning (iJET), 15*(13), 238–251. https://doi.org/10.3991/ijet.v15i13.15351

Liang, J. (2024). Enhanced art design education: Integrating artificial intelligence for resource optimization and innovative teaching. In *Proceedings of the 2024 4th International Conference on Internet Technology and Educational Informatization (ITEI 2024)* (pp. 239–247). Atlantis Press. https://doi.org/10.2991/978-94-6463-560-7_29

Lim, T., Gottipati, S., & Cheong, M. L. (2023). Ethical considerations for artificial intelligence in educational assessments. In J. Keengwe (Ed.), *Creative AI tools and ethical implications in teaching and learning* (pp. 32–79). IGI Global. https://doi.org/10.4018/979-8-3693-0205-7.ch003

Mayo, S. (2024). Co-creating with AI in art education: On the precipice of the next terrain. *Education Journal, 13*(3), 124–132. https://doi.org/10.11648/j.edu.20241303.15

Myint, P. Y. W., Lo, S. L., & Zhang, Y. (2024). Harnessing the power of AI-instructor collaborative grading approach: Topic-based effective grading for semi open-ended multipart questions. *Computers and Education: Artificial Intelligence, 7*, Article 100339. https://doi.org/10.1016/j.caeai.2024.100339

McWilliam, E., & Dawson, S. (2008). Teaching for creativity: Towards sustainable and replicable pedagogical practice. *Higher Education, 56*(6), 633–643. https://doi.org/10.1007/s10734-008-9115-7

Nowell, L. S., Norris, J. M., White, D. E., & Moules, N. J. (2017). Thematic analysis: Striving to meet the trustworthiness criteria. *International Journal of Qualitative Methods, 16*(1), 1–13. https://doi.org/10.1177/1609406917733847

Ripa di Meana, F., Guidi, A., Giretti, A., Vaccarini, M., Zambelli, M., & Durmus, D. (2024). Enhancing artistic education with AI: The Hamlet workshop. In D. G. Sampson, D. Ifenthaler, & P. Isaías (Eds.), *Proceedings of the International Conference on Cognition and Exploratory Learning in the Digital Age (CELDA 2024)* (pp. 127–134). IADIS.

Terry, G., Hayfield, N., Clarke, V., & Braun, V. (2017). Thematic analysis. In C. Willig & W. Stainton Rogers (Eds.), *The SAGE handbook of qualitative research in psychology* (2nd ed., pp. 17–37). SAGE Publications. https://doi.org/10.4135/9781526405555.n2

Zawacki-Richter, O., Marín, V. I., Bond, M., & Gouverneur, F. (2019). Systematic review of research on artificial intelligence applications in higher education—Where are the educators? *International Journal of Educational Technology in Higher Education, 16*(1), Article 39. https://doi.org/10.1186/s41239-019-0171-0

INVESTIGATING THE DEVELOPMENT OF SOFT SKILLS THROUGH BLENDED INTENSIVE PROGRAMMES

Alice Barana[1], Antonino Cambria[1,2], Marina Marchisio Conte[1], Fabio Roman[1] and Enrico Spinello[3]
[1]*Department of Molecular Biotechnology and Health Sciences, University of Turin, Piazza Nizza 44, 10126 Torino, Italy*
[2]*High Defence Study Centre, Piazza della Rovere, 83, 00165 Roma, Italy*
[3]*IT-Army Officers School, Via Arsenale 22, 10121 Torino, Italy*

ABSTRACT

In today's global and hyperconnected world, the job market, the higher education environment, and society are becoming increasingly international and complex in orientation. New challenges and opportunities are constantly flowing in a volatile, uncertain, complex and ambiguous environment. There is a need for people to navigate through cultural aggregations, diverse societies and human factors. There is a need for skills that enable citizens to be prepared and well-equipped to face new challenges and opportunities. At the University of Turin, specifically at the Interdepartmental University School of Strategic Sciences and the Army Officer School in Turin, four Blended Intensive Programmes (BIPs) on interdisciplinary subjects are held annually, with participation from more than a hundred civilian, military, and international students. The paper tries to measure the development of soft skills during the attendance of the four BIPs held for the academic year 2024/2025, with the intent to trace how it can be useful for all learners. The data analyzed in this study consists of 185 answers collected through a questionnaire delivered at the beginning and the end of the BIPs. The results were compared and analyzed through descriptive and bivariate statistical tools. The results support the importance of implementing these programmes and highlight that they are an optimal field of experimentation for students. These international activities are safe laboratories where it is possible to nurture the soft skills that will be fundamental for the near future. Numerous growth capabilities can be developed as a base for further research activities.

KEYWORDS

Blended Intensive Programme, Collaborative Learning, Higher Education, Internationalization, Soft Skills

1. INTRODUCTION

Nowadays, the Higher Education (HE) environment is dotted with thousands of opportunities and curricula designed for students. The fully internationalized and complex environment in which we are immersed requires students and workers to engage in multi-level cooperation and interaction with people from different cultures (Geraedts et al., 2022). To navigate smoothly in this complex environment rich in diverse cultures, people need to possess a toolkit with multiple skills and competencies, considered advantages in different perceptions of facts and other approaches to problem solving (Barana et al., 2025). Thinking differently and adopting new approaches rely on a set of competencies that give students an edge beyond knowledge and technical skills. It is not only a matter of what people know and how they know something. It is a matter of how people react and perform in the activities they conduct, going beyond problems and limitations, and fitting well within the environment in which they operate. Besides the necessary technical skills, students should also be exposed to soft skills such as critical thinking, problem solving, social communication, the ability to lead other people or groups, to negotiate and capture an effective result, as well as the capabilities to work in a group and under pressure (Schulz, 2008; Geraedts et al., 2022). The objective of the research stems from the need to train students as future workers to collaborate effectively and achieve excellent results in situations characterized by various elements of uncertainty and complexity. The focus is primarily on the field of defence and security. An effective setting for developing soft skills is the newly introduced course format known as the Blended Intensive Programme (BIP). BIPs are short, international, and intensive mobility experiences that consist of an online component and a residential component; they can be addressed to students (De Prada et al., 2025) but also to academic staff (Crespo and Prodanovic, 2025), with applications in typically practical sectors too, for instance in business and entrepreneurship (Laine et al., 2025). The online phase takes place in a digital learning environment where students work collaboratively on specific assignments. The residential phase takes place face-to-face at the institution promoting the programme. In general, three or more institutions need to participate in this short exchange mobility. The duration of the physical component of a BIP, which combines lectures and working groups, must be between 5 and 30 days for learners. No minimum duration is required for the virtual component; however, the combined virtual and physical components must be accessible at all times (European Commission: Directorate-General for Education, 2021; European Commission, 2023). This paper aims to show how BIPs can be used to enhance and improve students' soft skills. Providing students with opportunities to apply soft skills through practical activities is highly valuable before they enter the job market. The objective of the research is also to evaluate, through activities based on factors such as collaborative learning (CL), blended learning (BL), and internationalization (I), if there is a result emerging from the data and if this is applicable and useful in the field of Defence and Security, before students approach the job market. According to the ERASMUS+ guide (European Commission, 2023), BIPs should offer added value compared to existing programmes or courses. The reasons why the value is specific reside in the fact that the students' approach to specialized content is not taught or delivered in this way anywhere else. The value enables students or staff to gain new perspectives on the topic being studied without the necessity of staying abroad for a long time. Moreover, the value encourages transdisciplinary and multinational teaching and training, including challenge-based learning where transnational and transdisciplinary teams work together. Multidisciplinary is vital nowadays, as stated above, because it is not easy to cope with challenges alone. The context of this study is 4 Blended Intensive Programmes: "Biosafety and Bioterrorism" (B&B), "Problem solving and Critical Thinking" (PSCT), "Law of Armed Conflict" (LOAC), and "Common Security and Defence Policy" (CSDP) organized at the University of Turin Interdepartmental University School of Strategic Sciences (SUISS) and the It-Army Officer School. They can be defined as safe laboratories where students can gain experience from their mistakes and a fertile ground for enhancing growth capabilities (Cambria et al., 2023a; Barana et al., 2024a). The online phase, hosted on a digital learning environment, can precede or succeed the residential phase and includes interactive and collaborative online activities that enable students to become familiar with other colleagues and with the new technology. The BIPs were implemented for the first time during the 2022/2023 academic year and redesigned in subsequent years to incorporate gamification and role-play activities within an immersive scenario. At the beginning and end, questionnaires were administered to collect data from the students (Cambria et al., 2023b). The following section discusses the theoretical framework on soft skills, consolidating the most important terms of the research and depicting them for subsequent use in the practical research process. The third section highlights the research question, data collection, and analysis process. In the fourth part, the results section, the results of the data analysis are presented. From the analysis, the results are discussed later in the fifth part. Lastly, conclusions are drawn, answering the research question and highlighting possible future research programmes using this study as a stepping stone for future research.

2. THEORETICAL FRAMEWORK

2.1 Soft Skill Areas

Geraedts et al. (2022) list the most fundamental soft skill areas: team collaboration; ability to take initiative; ability to foresee and prevent an undesired situation; ability to work under pressure; leadership; communication, negotiation, and presentation skills; critical and analytical skills. Team collaboration encompasses a person's ability to work autonomously and stay self-motivated while also contributing effectively as a team member. Teams can be homogeneous or heterogeneous and may also be multidisciplinary. This multidisciplinary approach reflects the fact that today's challenges require the application of transversal competences from different scientific fields. For example, combining expertise from both soft and hard sciences can be highly beneficial, as it allows for more comprehensive approaches that integrate diverse perspectives, methods, and types of knowledge, ultimately leading to more effective and innovative solutions. Communication, negotiation, and presentation skills are soft skills that fall within the broader category of social interaction. The capability to spread a message effectively, so that it is well received by the listener with consequent feedback, is at the base of the problem-solving process and interactions among multicultural groups. Critical and analytical thinking underpin the capacity for thinking outside the box, which manifests in creativity and innovation in both problem-solving and interpersonal interactions. The ability to take initiative is a sign of decisiveness and demonstrates responsibility. The ability to anticipate and prevent undesired situations helps students and workers remain flexible, rather than rigidly sticking to a plan. The capacity to assess the progress of a plan reflects a mature and adaptable mindset. The ability to perform effectively under pressure is a consistently demanded competency across contemporary job vacancies. This requirement is especially pronounced in the defence and security sectors, where both officers and civilian personnel must operate within stringent time constraints and respond adeptly to unforeseen challenges. Leadership can be regarded as a key competence in this field. An individual is considered a leader when they can motivate, influence, and guide team members, while demonstrating the soft skills previously discussed. To help students develop these soft skills, course designers and instructors must incorporate not only inspiration and motivation but also concrete and well-defined guidance into multicultural activities, alongside the expectations that students bring into the activity (Barana et al., 2025). The relationship between soft skills and multicultural activities is particularly relevant in today's job environment, which is also focused on interdisciplinary and intercultural collaborations. Company projects are often carried out within an international context. Defence and security personnel are expected to apply their skills in collaboration with colleagues who possess expertise in different fields and come from different cultural backgrounds. Students, both military and civilian, need to be aware of these diversities and use them intentionally to achieve successful project results (Geraedts et al., 2022). These orientations and willingness in designing courses are visible in the BIPs held at the SUISS.

2.2 Design of the BIPs

The BIPs at the University of Torino SUISS are designed based on three pillars: CL, BL, and I. Collaborative learning is paramount to building a strong commitment and a higher enthusiasm for diversity in relation to solving a common task and the assignments provided to the groups. Engaging students in good-quality collaboration may contribute to several learning outcomes (De Hei et al., 2020). Students work in heterogeneous groups with respect to gender, age (ranging from 18 to 25), nationality (e.g., American, Bulgarian, Greek, Italian, Lithuanian, Romanian, Polish, Portuguese, and others), and academic and cultural background. The choice of heterogeneous groups is based on the belief that a heterogeneous group will yield a greater range of differences in perceptions, ideas, and backgrounds, thereby enabling the achievement of various outcomes (Murphy et al., 2017). This heterogeneous composition can impact the behavior and communication between people. Indeed, numerous challenges and unforeseen obstacles can disrupt the ongoing activities within the course (Barana et al., 2025). According to Cabrera et al. (2002), Collaborative Learning increases openness to diversity; according to Kayumova, A. R., & Sadykova, G. V. (2016), diversity in communication styles may hinder successful learning experiences; according to De Hei M. et al (2020) and Liang and Schartner (2022), students who have collaborated in group work, specifically in multicultural teams in the physical classroom, have developed transversal competencies that can results in a specification of soft skills. Besides Blended learning, Blended mobility helps overcome typical barriers, allowing students to experience the benefits of mobility and international exposure (European Commission: Directorate-General for Education, 2021). It is a combination of physical mobility and a virtual activity before or after the physical mobility (Geraedts et al., 2022). The importance of internationalization is stated in its explanation: the intentional process of integrating an international, intercultural or global dimension into the purpose, functions and delivery of post-secondary education, to enhance the quality of education and research for all students and staff and to make a meaningful contribution to society (De Wit et al., 2015). There are linguistic barriers that can hinder communication and the expression of intent. When the actual activity begins, students may encounter psychological barriers arising from various factors, which can be broadly classified as endogenous or exogenous (De Hei et al., 2020). The presence of these barriers can be overcome through training and continuous exposure to situations that encourage students to improve themselves. International modules enable the practice of oral communication and leadership skills while developing critical thinking, problem solving, and creativity. All these features and elements in the career of personnel in the field of security and defence pave the way for greater integration and coherence of our future actions in favour of peace and security (Gell, 2017). Internationalization answers the needs expressed by the current scenarios depicted by the EU, NATO, and the UN. The aim is to develop officers' ability to work in any international operating theatre with colleagues worldwide, to adapt to different cultural contexts, and to create collaborative networks (Marchisio and Spinello, 2021; Cambria et al., 2023b; Barana et al., 2024b). Students need to experiment with new attitudes and new skills to be prepared to overcome challenges and achieve a positive experience (Friedman and Antal, 2005). The specific characteristics of the four BIPs under study are as follows. The BIP "Problem Solving and Critical Thinking" focuses primarily on mathematics and aims to develop problem-solving and critical thinking skills by providing theoretical and practical tools for developing a systematic approach to solving complex problems in the security and defense sector, through data analysis, optimization, game theory, cryptography, and the application of strategic techniques, including the use of artificial intelligence tools. To stimulate the motivation of students and teachers, who were engaging in group activities with remarks and comments, challenges were implemented between groups. In the BIP "Biosafety and Bioterrorism", students participated in laboratory activities to understand how experiments are conducted. They were testimony to how to trace polluted water with some reagents, and they saw how microbiotics can grow in various and unpredictable environments. They also understood the dangers of biological, chemical, and radioactive hazards. Indeed, the course offers participating students a comprehensive overview of biological threats, from understanding the body's defence mechanisms to prevention and response strategies for bioterrorism, with a particular focus on public health and food safety. In the BIP "Law of Armed Conflict" and the BIP "Common Security and Defence Policy", students worked on seven core skills: technical, information management, communication, collaboration, creativity, critical thinking, and problem solving. The former provides students with an understanding of the legal framework of military operations and interventions in armed conflict situations. Students have the opportunity to delve deeper into the protection of human rights and the rules of engagement that apply in military interventions. The latter aims to develop a strong, widespread, and profound awareness of European integration in the defence and security sector. Through working groups and plenary sessions, civilian students and young armed forces officers have the opportunity to deepen and acquire the key concepts and fundamental values of common European defence and security policies. At the base of the design process of the BIPs, there is the use of a digital learning environment to facilitate study and interactions (among teachers, among students, and teacher-student), collaboration, and knowledge building in all phases: designing, online phase, and residential one. In the online phase, self-study was mainly individual, interspersed with synchronous meetings with tutors and teachers to resolve problems or doubts. Moreover, a series of meetings and interactions are organized in order to let students and teachers get to know each other before the residential phase; the teams were asked to meet, choose a name, and a logo. The face-to-face activities were intensive, in English, and involved active participation in group work, workshops, and discussions (Marchisio and Spinello, 2021; Cambria et al., 2023a). During the residential phase, considerable emphasis was placed on collaborative learning among civilian and military students, as well as among students from different nations and cultures. In particular, the teaching methodologies adopted were varied and often practical to stimulate students through hands-on learning. In PSCT and B&B, immersion in a scenario was a strategy implemented, which allowed for the translation of knowledge and the studied topic into a contextualized reality. In this scenario, each member, specifically the student, played a role in the group. This dynamic in the scenario enabled the designers to integrate role-play, group activities, and team games. Students were supposed to analyze case studies and solve problems related to the scenario evolution. This enables the laying of the groundwork for debates, peer discussions, and the evaluation of situations, as well as the identification of roles and leaders, and the utilization of diverse backgrounds, ultimately solving problems through a multidisciplinary approach. As mentioned earlier, all the BIPs were based on cooperation between civilian students and military young officers; this was a common feature among the different topics. For example, practical activities such as planning and managing convoy escorts or identifying the most efficient position have been undertaken. Following some examples, discussions and debates about political orientations or approaches to problems have taken place. In consideration of the type of BIP, interdisciplinary problem-solving activities were designed. The groups could use, and they did, auxiliary tools and software, including advanced computing environments and simulators, as well as artificial intelligence, which was particularly helpful for writing reports, structuring schemes, and editing language. It was also used for solving math problems and creating advertising campaigns among the groups, both in favour of and in contrast to. The educational activities of the BIPs have been designed and conducted by teachers from European military universities and academies. The main objective of each BIP is to promote both the acquisition of theoretical knowledge and the development of practical and intercultural relational skills. Through the implementation of teaching strategies and methodologies such as problem-solving, group work, role-playing, case study analysis, immersion of activities in a scenario, debate, and the use of gamification elements, an attempt has been made to create a collaborative and intercultural learning context, in line with the goals of international cooperation and internationalization. For the delivery and management of activities in both phases, a dedicated course has been opened on the SUISS Moodle platform for each BIP (Barana et al., 2024).

3. METHODOLOGY

The research question we want to investigate with this study is the following:

RQ: Did the Blended Intensive Programmes organized during the academic year 2024/2025 help the students develop soft skills?

This study is based on a process of investigation comprising several steps. The seven areas of soft skills, identified by Geraedts et al. (2022), served as a model for developing a questionnaire. The questionnaire, composed of 10 items, was administered to students participating in the 4 BIPs held at SUISS during the 2024/2025 academic year, both at the beginning and at the end of the BIP. In total, the BIPs were attended by 185 students, of whom 47% were international and 53% local students; 25% were civilian and 75% military personnel, 40% were female and 60% male students. We collected 370 answers, half to the initial questionnaire (IQ) and half to the final questionnaire (FQ). The question asked: "At what level do you think that you master the following skills?" Then, 10 soft skills were listed, corresponding to the seven soft skills areas shown in Table 1. For each skill, students had to select a value from 1 to 4, where 1 refers to "not at all", 2 refers to "very little", 3 to "somewhat", and 4 to "to a great extent". The questionnaire also included the "not applicable" (N/A) answer, to be selected if students did not understand the item.

Table 1. Items analyzed to investigate Soft Skills

7 Soft Skills Component Areas	Number of items	Items
Team Collaboration	1	Team collaboration
Ability to take initiative	1	Ability to take initiative
Ability to foresee and prevent an undesired situation	1	Ability to foresee and prevent an undesired situation
Ability to work under pressure	1	Ability to work under pressure
Leadership	1	Leadership
Communication, negotiation and presentation skills	3	Communication in formal settings Communication in social settings Negotiation Skills
Critical and analytical skills	2	Critical Thinking Analytical Thinking
Total	10	

For the data analysis, the SPSS 29 software was used. The Cronbach's Alpha test was performed to assess the reliability of the items. For Communication, negotiation, and presentation skills, and for Critical and analytical skills, the means of the answers to the respective items were computed. Descriptive statistics were calculated for single items and for skill areas. Then, the variation in answers between FQ and IQ in each skill area was evaluated using the Wilcoxon signed-rank test to see if the BIP elicited a development in soft skills.

4. RESULTS

As a first step, Cronbach's Alpha was calculated to test the reliability of the 10 items. Its value is 0.87 for both the initial and final questionnaires, indicating a high level of reliability. Then, descriptive statistics were computed for the single items. Table 2 shows the frequency of answers and their average values.

Table 2. Descriptive statistics of single items

Questionnaire	Item	N. of answers	Average	4 N	%	3 N	%	2 N	%	1 N	%
IQ	Team Collaboration	185	3.76	143	77.3%	40	21.6%	2	1.1%	0	0%
FQ		183	3.84	155	84.7%	27	14.8%	0	0%	5	5%
IQ	Communication in formal settings	182	3.36	83	45.6%	82	45.1%	17	9.3%	0	0%
FQ		183	3.63	125	68.3%	50	27.3%	7	3.8%	1	0.5%
IQ	Communication in social settings	183	3.60	117	63.2	58	31.7	8	4.4%	0	0%
FQ		183	3.84	156	85.2%	25	13.7%	1	0.5%	1	0.5%
IQ	Negotiation Skills	180	3.31	71	39.4%	94	52.2%	15	8.3%	0	0%
FQ		180	3.64	124	68.9%	49	27.2%	5	2.8%	2	1.1%
IQ	Critical thinking	182	3.54	105	57.7%	71	39%	6	3.3%	0	0%
FQ		181	3.78	145	80.1%	33	18.2%	2	1.1%	1	0.5%
IQ	Analytical thinking	182	3.46	93	51.1%	81	44.5%	7	3.8%	1	0.5%
FQ		182	3.71	133	73.1%	46	25.3%	2	1.1%	1	0.5%
IQ	Ability to take initiative	184	3.51	101	54.9%	76	41.3%	7	3.8%	0	0%
FQ		180	3.72	135	75%	41	22.8%	2	1.1%	2	1.1%
IQ	Ability to foresee and	185	3.44	92	49.7%	83	44.9%	10	5.4%	0	0%
FQ	prevent an undesired situation	180	3.65	124	68.9%	51	28.3	3	1.7%	2	1.1%
IQ	Ability to work under pressure	181	3.60	118	65.2%	54	29.8%	9	5%	0	0%
FQ		180	3.71	139	77.2%	35	19.4%	1	0.6%	5	2.8%
IQ	Leadership	182	3.47	93	51.1%	82	45.1%	2	3.8%	0	0%
FQ		179	3.59	120	64.9%	47	26.3%	10	5.6%	2	1.1%
IQ	Total	1826	//	1016	55.6%	721	39.4%	83	4%	1	0.01%
FQ		1811	//	1356	74%	404	22%	33	1%	20	1%

From Table 2, we can notice that the final average increased for all the skills. Overall, the responses with value 4 increased by almost 20 percentage points. The number of these responses increased by 340 points, corresponding to a 33% relative increase. While the top responses increased, the categories with values 2 and 3 showed a significant decrease in frequency. In general, upon examining these results, it is evident that improvements are visible across all factors. Although the highest value responses increased, a small group of students still reported a lack of these soft skills in their self-evaluation: indeed, the number of responses indicating that students mastered the skills at the lowest level decreased in all areas. However, the number of students who, at the end of the BIPs, declared not to possess these soft skills is very low, around 1% of the sample. Figure 1 illustrates the evolution of the samples after the activity was conducted.

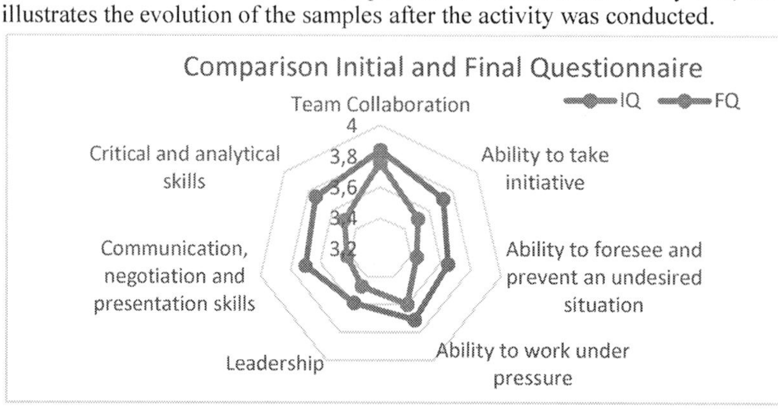

Figure 1. Means of students' answers in the seven areas of soft skills in both questionnaires: FQ-IQ

Figure 1 makes it clear that the skill areas that registered the highest increase are the ability to take the initiative, the ability to foresee and prevent undesired situations, communication skills, and critical and analytical skills. More modest increases are visible for team collaboration, ability to work under pressure, and leadership. The pairwise Wilcoxon test was conducted to compare the students' answers in the seven areas of Soft Skills between the FQ and IQ, to evaluate if an improvement was visible after the BIPs. Table 3 shows the results.

Table 3. Results of the pairwise Wilcoxon signed–rank test FQ-IQ

Component area	Team collabora tion	Ability to take initiative	Ability to foresee and prevent an undesired situation	Ability to work under pressure	Leadership	Communication. negotiation and presentation skills	Critical and Analytical skills
Z	1.939	4.390	3.790	1.900	2.353	6.783	5.202
p-value	0.052	<0.001	<0.001	0.057	0.019	<0.001	<0.001

The Wilcoxon test shows a statistically significant increase in all the levels of soft skills self-evaluated, except for team collaboration and the ability to work under pressure, whose values are slightly below the significance threshold. The results confirm the descriptive statistics and show that an increase in all seven component areas of soft skills emerges after the participation to the a.y. 2024/2025 BIPs.

5. DISCUSSION AND CONCLUSION

The first element to consider in this analysis is that the experience can contribute to the improvement of the students' soft skills through an approach based on learning by doing and practical activities. The engagement of students is a paramount aspect to consider in all phases of the BIP (from design to final feedback on the last day) to test themselves with the implementation of soft skills in everyday activities. Building on the work of Geraedts et al. (2022), our study has found that students, following the BIPs, have self-evaluated an improvement in their soft skills. We utilized the framework identified by Geraedts et al. (2022) for engineering international programs to design the questionnaire and determine if the model theorized by them could be applied to the security and defense field. In addition, it appears that very few students revised their perception of their capabilities in a negative direction. They may believe they are fully prepared to integrate with others, take on leadership roles, or solve any problem. However, once they engage in direct interaction, whether at the initial meeting or after some hours in the field, the experience may be less pleasant than anticipated, leading them to feel less capable in certain areas. The most substantial improvement was observed in negotiation skills, which can be attributed to the pedagogical design of the BIPs. The tasks were intentionally structured to elicit collaboration within heterogeneous groups and to promote interaction and negotiation across groups, thereby creating authentic opportunities for the development of this competence. Moreover, the data indicate a substantial relative increase of 38% in the number of respondents who reported a high level of mastery in critical and analytical thinking. This finding supports the view that the tasks and objectives of the BIPs inherently demand the implementation of diverse strategies and behaviors, as well as multiple modes of thinking, grounded in systematic processes of analysis and evaluation. These results highlight the positive effects of the main elements of BIP design, namely collaborative learning, blended learning, and internationalization, as students were able to practice intercultural interactions in a new environment. Students began negotiating a shared reality and achieved the goal of learning from a specific situation by developing the necessary soft skills essential for an efficient strategy of action and reaction to the inputs of the surrounding environment. This layer shall be intertwined with that of technical skills and knowledge. Thus, we can positively answer the research question. The main limitation of this research lies in the self-assessed nature of the questionnaires, which may affect the objectivity of the results. Students may overestimate improvements due to social desirability or participation effects. However, participant observation helps mitigate this. Another limitation is the lack of external validation or a control group, making it harder to support improvement claims. Finally, possible ceiling effects from initially high scores may limit the measurable impact of the BIP. In addition, the study currently relies exclusively on quantitative data; however, in the near future, this data will be complemented by qualitative evidence collected through the questionnaires, participant observation during the BIPs, and direct interviews with students, which will be integrated and jointly analyzed with the quantitative findings presented above. This program will enable a deeper exploration of collaborative learning, particularly in relation to digital and technology-enhanced components. Additionally, future qualitative data and comparative analyses across BIPs will allow for a more nuanced examination of their individual components (e.g., online vs. residential formats, gamification, role-play). This, in turn, will help identify which elements most effectively contribute to meaningful improvement. To sum up, it is possible to conclude that BIPs provide valuable field experience for gathering data to create models for future use in the research process.

REFERENCES

Barana, A. et al. (2025). Investigating the development of intercultural competences through blended intensive programmes. *Proceedings of the International Conferences on Mobile Learning 2025 and Educational Technologies 2025.* Madeira Island, Portugal, pp. 177-184.

Barana, A. et al. (2024a). Detecting blended learning, collaborative learning and internationalisation in military education: a systematic literature review. *Proceedings of the 18th International Conference on e-Learning and Digital Learning 2024 and Sustainability, Technology and Education 2024.* Budapest, Hungary, pp. 137-144.

Barana, A. et al. (2024b). Unpacking the Three Spheres of Interest in a Blended Intensive Programme: Collaborative Learning, Blended Learning and Internationalisation. *Proceedings of the 21st International Conference on Cognition and Exploratory Learning In The Digital Age.* Zagreb, Croatia, pp. 43-50.

Cabrera, A. F. et al. (2002). Collaborative learning: Its impact on college students' development and diversity. *In Journal of College Student Development*, Vol. 43, No. 1, pp. 20–34.

Cambria, A. et al. (2023a). Higher Education training activities in international environments for developing skills of civil-military cooperation. *Proceedings of the 20th International Conference on Cognition and Exploratory Learning in The Digital Age.* Madeira Island, Portugal, pp. 402-406.

Cambria, A. et al. (2023b). Blended Intensive Programs for Fostering Collaboration and Knowledge Exchange in Security and Defence Education. *Proceedings of the 16th International Conference of Education, Research and Innovation (iCERI).* Sevilla, Spain, pp. 9441-9448.

Crespo, B. and Prodanovic, M. (2025). Blended Intensive Programmes (BIPs) in Professional Development: An International Scenario for Training Staff. *The Journal of Continuing Higher Education,* https://doi.org/10.1080/07377363.2025.2523608

De Hei, M. et al. (2020). Developing Intercultural Competence Through Collaborative Learning in International Higher Education. *In Journal of Studies in International Education*, Vol. 24, No. 2, pp. 190-211.

De Prada, E. et al. (2025). A Blended Intensive Programme Behind the Scenes: Organisational and Methodological Effectiveness. *International Journal of Instruction,* Vol. 18, No. 3, pp. 659-682.

De Wit, H. et al. (2015). *Internationalization of Higher Education*, European Parliament, Directorate-General for Internal Policies, Policy Department B: Structural and Cohesion Policies, Culture and Education, https://www.europarl.europa.eu/studies/, https://doi.org/10.2861/444393

European Commission: Directorate-General for Education, Youth, Sport and Culture. (2021). *Blended learning for high quality and inclusive primary and secondary education: handbook.* Publications Office of the European Union, https://data.europa.eu/doi/10.2766/237842.

European Commission. (2023). *Erasmus+ Programme Guide 2024.* https://erasmus-plus.ec.europa.eu/programme-guide/erasmusplus-programme-guide.

Friedman, V. J. and Antal, A. B. (2005). Negotiating Reality: A Theory of Action Approach to Intercultural Competence. *In Management Learning*, Vol. 36, No. 1, pp. 69–86, https://doi.org/10.1177/1350507605049904

Gell, H. (2017). Increase of Military Leadership Skills and Competences of future Leaders by Internationalization. *In Scientific Journal "Economics & Management"*, Brno, Czech Republic, pp.1-23.

Geraedts, H. et al. (2022). A framework to enhance students' soft skills within the context of international engineering project collaboration. *Proceedings of 31st Annual Conference of the European Association for Education in Electrical and Information Engineering (EAEEIE).* Coimbra, Portugal, pp. 1-6, https://doi.org/10.1109/EAEEIE54893.2022.9820308

Kayumova, A. R. and Sadykova, G. V. (2016). Online collaborative cross-cultural learning: Students' perspectives. *In Journal of Organizational Culture, Communications and Confict*, Vol. 20, pp. 248–255.

Laine, I. et al. (2025). Integrating real-world entrepreneurship with international learning: insights from a blended intensive programme. *Journal of International Education in Business,* Vol. 18, No. 3, pp. 438-461, https://doi.org/10.1108/JIEB-08-2024-0112

Liang, Y. and Schartner, A. (2022). Culturally Mixed Group Work and the Development of Students' Intercultural Competence. *In Journal of Studies in International Education*, Vol. 26, No. 1, pp. 44-60.

Marchisio, M. and Spinello, E. (2021). Internationalization for enhancing the European Security and Defence higher education. *Proceedings International Conference e-Learning,* pp. 99-106.

Murphy, P. K. et al. (2017). Exploring the influence of homogeneous versus heterogeneous grouping on students' text-based discussions and comprehension. *In Contemporary Educational Psychology*, Vol. 51, pp. 336-355, https://doi.org/10.1016/j.cedpsych.2017.09.003.

Schulz, B. (2008). The importance of soft skills: Education beyond academic knowledge. *In Nawa Journal of Communication*, Vol. 2, No. 1, pp. 146– 154.

EXPLORABLES: EVALUATING A CONCEPT FOR REMIXABLE INTERACTIVE LEARNING RESOURCES

Frederic Salmen[1*], René Röpke[2†] and Ulrik Schroeder[1‡]
[1]*Learning Technologies, RWTH Aachen University, Ahornstr. 55, 52074 Aachen, Germany,*
[2]*Learning Technologies and eDidactics, TU Wien, Favoritenstr. 9-11, 1040, Vienna, Austria*

ABSTRACT

There is a divide in educational technology: On one side is the rich world of interactive learning resources produced by companies and researchers, including simulations, games, and quizzes. On the other side is the world of learning resources used in schools, mostly static content, self-made or from textbooks. There, some digital resources are used, but not adapted to their own needs by remixing—that would require programming. Programming forms a skill barrier that prohibits most educators from adapting digital learning resources to their own use cases, limiting practical use. We argue that, to bridge the gap and make interactive learning resources remixable without programming, they must become FAIR (findable, accessible, interoperable, and reusable). We present a concept and implementation for the remix of interactive learning resources – an easy to use, web-based authoring tool that allows educators to create explorables. Explorables use current web technologies for the personalization and combination of rich, interactive content in a standardized way. We show how the concept achieves remixability theoretically and validate the tool's usability through a comprehensive user study with n=23 participants (students in teacher training, teachers, and lecturers) across two workshop sessions, using a mixed-method approach gathering user experience scores with the UEQ+ and reviewing results using a qualitative content analysis. Results show viability of explorables as FAIR learning resources, suitable to educators and in alignment with research and practice.

KEYWORDS

Explorables, Interactivity, Remix, FAIR, UEQ+

1. MOTIVATION

Over the decades of educational technology (EdTech), researchers and companies have produced a rich, ever-growing world of interactive learning resources, including simulations (Wieman et al., 2008), serious games (Wouters et al., 2013), and learning videos (Brame, 2016). The benefits of multimedia learning (Mayer, 2020) are well-established at this point in the research discussion. These products and results of EdTech are not a panacea, but used in a modern, active learning (Freeman et al., 2014) contexts that consider the personalized nature of learning (Shemshack & Spector, 2020) and build on the didactic ideas of constructivism (Bada & Olusegun, 2015), they can benefit educators and learners greatly.

However, if we look beyond the world of research to the wider universe of EdTech, we face a deep divide: Use of interactive learning resources in real-world learning contexts, especially in formal education, is still sparing and fragmented. (Lehrmittelzentrale, 2018) We argue that the root of this divide is the fundamentally different nature of interactive and non-interactive content – something that David Wiley originally framed as the Reusability Paradox (D. Wiley et al., 2004): A good learning resource is highly dependent on its context, hampering reuse – in turn, making it highly general and context-independent makes it easy to reuse, but lowers the educational value such that reuse is undesirable. Wiley argued that instead of making context-independent resources, educators need to be able to recontextualize learning resources to break the paradox. Non-interactive content such as rich text and images is decomposable, enabling reuse – it can be be remixed easily: Educators may gather all kinds of sources and combine them into new learning resources using commonly available office

*Frederic Salmen [0009–0007–5206–1146] salmen@cs.rwth-aachen.de
†René Röpke [0000–0003–0250–8521] rene.roepke@tuwien.ac.at
‡Ulrik Schroeder [0000–0002–5178–8497] schroeder@cs.rwth-aachen.de

software (Salmen et al., 2023). But for interactive content, technical barriers remain: Barring programming, the practical answer to integrating interactive content is a link or QR code. This introduces a disrupting context switch (Czerwinski et al., 2004), may require a new authentication step for the learner, and fundamentally cannot harness the ideas of multimedia learning.

We argue that, if the issue is fragmentation, that the solution to bridge that divide must lie in enabling cooperation and interoperability. Research provides a poignant summary of these goals: Data (Wilkinson et al., 2016) and research software (Chue Hong et al., 2022) must be findable, accessible, interoperable, and reusable, altogether abbreviated as FAIR. We suggest to apply these principles to interactive learning resources, as well—if they are made FAIR, they become decomposable, and educators are able to apply the remix workflow (Salmen et al., 2023) to those kinds of resources. In addition, this would also be beneficial for research, as studies involving interactive learning resources could be more easily tracked, replicated and expanded – since more and more learning activities are moved into a standardized digital space, researchers can more easily apply learning analytics (LA) for field studies. Since decomposability is partly a technical challenge, we propose a technical concept as a first step. The merit of such a concept would rest not only on the property of decomposability, but also on two other dimensions: First, the technical concept should be expressive enough so educators are not limited in what kind of learning resource they can create. Second, the concept should remain easy to author for educators so the vast majority of the education community without programming skills can participate. To this end, we pose the following research question:

RQ: How can interactive learning resources be structured technically so that educators can remix them in an easy-to-use way without limits to expressivity?

The remaining paper is structured as follows: After discussing related work, we introduce a technical concept for remixable interactive learning resources called explorables, which makes use of the FAIR principles. Next, we show how an authoring tool which produces these explorables can be implemented. Finally, we present an evaluation which aims to measure the constructs of expressivity and ease of authoring, and discuss the results, followed by a conclusion.

2. RELATED WORK

The concept of decomposable interactive learning resources has been discussed since the 1990s, when learning objects (LO) emerged (D. A. Wiley, 2002). Originally, LO standards were introduced so learning resources could be easily identified, reused, and remain compatible. However, a major limitation of LO soon became apparent from a reuse standpoint: "Learning objects can be aggregated but not adapted" (D. A. Wiley, 2008). Another drawback was that LO standards were developed largely in parallel to, rather than in synergy with, broader web standards (Kaul et al., 2017). The idea of mixing interactive and non-interactive content continued to flare up in different fields, such as the concept of interactive articles in journalism (Hohman et al., 2020) or of mashups in education (Lamb, 2007).

Efforts from other fields such as document engineering may be worth considering for some implementation decisions, but are overwhelmingly focused other areas such as entertainment & business (de Mattos & Muchaluat-Saade, 2018), or on non-interactive media (Zhang et al., 2024), not on interactive learning resources. Many current efforts relate to the goal of remixing learning resources: The OER (Open Educational Resources) movement focused on breaking down legal and societal barriers of reuse (Adil et al., 2024), creating a culture of sharing and reuse. OER researchers have found ways to aid in the legal side of OER, for example with tools to replace copyrighted material (Ali, 2024), or by building search and sharing platforms (Piedra et al., 2011). On the development side of EdTech, there is a push for open science as EdTech communities are starting to apply the FAIR principles to their research data and software in an effort to increase cooperation (Kiesler & Schiffner, 2022; Kiesler et al., 2024). While these adjacent efforts are needed, they cannot address the needs of educators alone, as the technical hurdle of decomposing interactive content still needs to be overcome.

A new concept for researchers to develop interactive content was recently proposed: Using components and packages, developers of EdTech could achieve more FAIR web content, which in turn can be inserted into complex interactive learning resources through an authoring tool (Salmen, Breuer, et al., 2024). This is promising to build on for two reasons: First, the web as a hypermedia system allows for both non-interactive and interactive content. Second, the ideas of components and packages offer a way to achieve FAIRness for developed interactive content on the web, enabling a web-based authoring solution that can both decompose and recompose combined content (such as a web document with text, a learning simulation, and a quiz).

Packages & components make decomposable interactive learning resources technically achievable, but for authoring interactive content in a way accessible to educators, the requirements of this user group must also be considered. Authoring interactive learning resources is generally underexplored, but one possible lens is offered by the explorable authoring requirements (EAR) (Salmen & Schroeder, 2024). The model combines theoretical and empirical results into a unified model that can apply to any system that authors interactive learning resources. The main dimensions of the model are functionality and usability from both the perspective of authors composing content and developers extending the system with new interactive building blocks called widgets. Functionality and usability map onto our goals of expressiveness and usability.

This theoretical lens of the EAR model can also be applied to a few state-of-the-art examples of authoring tools for interactive content. Jupyter (Granger & Pérez, 2021) is a code notebook/literate programming (Knuth, 1984) system intended for data science. As a programming environment, it offers the maximum functionality/expressiveness an authoring tool could have: Turing completeness. However, this approach creates a tension with usability: Interactivity in Jupyter notebooks can only be achieved through programming, so it is not suffi- cient for most educators, especially outside of computer science. IdyllStudio (Conlen et al., 2021) is a solution from the area of usability research that can inform design decisions of future tools. It however has weaknesses in expressivity, as it builds on React components for interactivity which enforces a single technology stack for developers contributing interactive content. Practically, it is also incomplete and discontinued as of 2025. The most widespread solution is H5P (Fischer et al., 2021) (HTML5 Packages). For education, especially in STEM, it has many documented use cases (Singleton & Charlton, 2020; Wicaksono et al., 2021). It is groundbreaking in using the Web as an app platform for educational content and for integrating a solution for licensing and sharing content. However, previous research has shown large deficits in usability (for example the interface approach of H5P which could be called "form-driven authoring")(Salmen et al., 2023), and in functionality (many kinds of interactive resources cannot be expressed in H5P's system)(Salmen & Schroeder, 2024). Also, in terms of FAIRness, H5P content is disconnected from other web content—remix is possible inside the H5P ecosystem, but impractical outside. As H5P is an open-core commercial project, we consider that unlikely to change.

Finally, an authoring tool that addresses the limitations outlined has been presented as a prototype recently, which is called WebWriter (Salmen, Roepke, & Schroeder, 2024). WebWriter will be presented in more detail in the following section as this work improves on the prototype and evaluates it, fulfilling the goals of previous publications (Salmen & Schroeder, 2024; Salmen, Roepke, & Schroeder, 2024).

3. EXPLORABLES

Explorables are a kind of interactive learning resource that combine the ideas of personalized learning, multi- media learning and interactivity. Technically, the format is a subset of web documents (HTML, CSS, and JS) with a few additional parts in order to meet the unique requirements of handling interactive content.

3.1 Educational Perspective

Explorables are a fluid integration of both non-interactive and interactive content into a single resource. The concept has been successful in informal learning (Victor, 2011) and journalism (Hohman et al., 2020) for some time. A way to understand explorables is to imagine them as truly digital worksheets: The main part of an explorable is structured in a traditional, static way, with rich text and images. Uniquely though, explorables are interspersed with interactive content that is referenced in the text, so the non-interactive text forms the main thread guiding the reader. This distinguishes explorables from the concept of mashups (Lamb, 2007), which usually aggregate without a guiding thread. For example, simulations (Wieman et al.,

2008), serious games (Wouters et al., 2013), and learning videos (Brame, 2016) could be interactive parts of the explorable. A few real world examples can be seen in Fig. 3.1. Multimedia learning (Mayer, 2020) posits that multimodal learning resources such as this can be more effective than single mode resources using only text. From a didactics point of view, this medium also encourages active & personalized learning (Shemshack & Spector, 2020), as interaction opens up learning paths that educators may provide by differentiation.

These educational properties of explorables make them a promising concept for educators. As such, ex- plorables can be a medium for interactive worksheets of the next generation that fit into the OER life cycle or the model of the remix workflow. In regards to our research question: Explorables may be flexible enough to express arbitrary interactive learning resources.

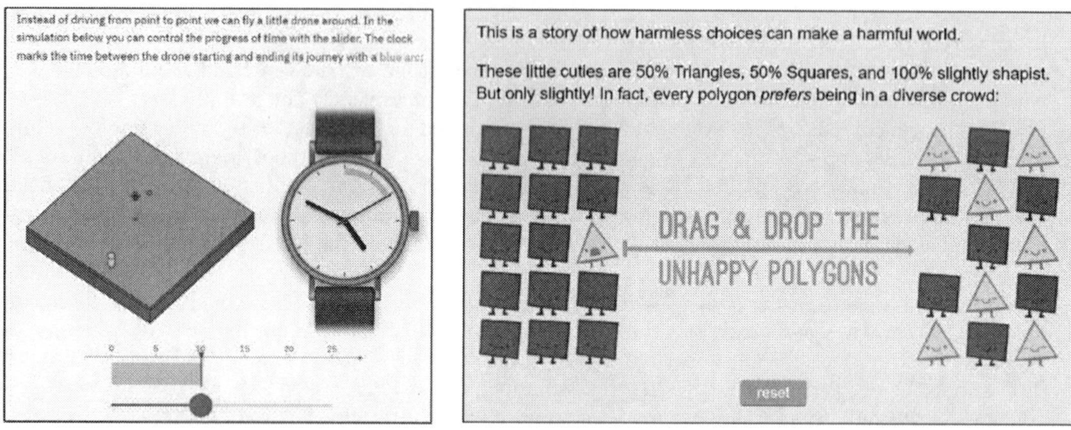

Figure 1. Programmed explorables "GPS" by Bartosz Cziechanowski (https://ncase.me/polygons/) and "Parable of the Polygons" by Nicky Case[5] (https://ciechanow.ski/gps/)

3.2 Technological Perspective

At the heart of the concept of explorables is the Web platform. Drawing lessons from LO, a major design principle of the concept is to build on existing standards as much as possible. Simply put: Explorables should be web documents! In practice, the Web is the platform of choice for most EdTech content, as it offers a global delivery platform that works on any device, and can tap into the rich ecosystem of web development to implement solutions. Through the trend towards more sophisticated browser support for web applications, the Web's design goals are well-aligned with Multimedia Learning and interactivity. Viewed through the perspective of FAIRness for software (FAIR4RS), explorables being web-based solves many challenges:

- **Findable**: Core concepts of the Web like URIs and existing infrastructure like search engines and metadata standards mean that any web document published is highly findable.
- **Accessible**: Similarly, HTTP and the ubiquity of browsers mean that web documents can be accessed by anyone, anywhere.
- **Interoperable**: A strength of the Web platform lies in interoperability, as a web document or web app can itself use HTTP and other protocols to communicate in distributed systems or use APIs. Also, the Web allows the embedding of a myriad of formats for images, audio, video, and even 3D and AR/VR content through certain APIs. The core web technologies of HTML, CSS, and JS are also well integrated and can interoperate seamlessly, and specialized technologies such as MathML and SVG are available, as well.
- **Reusable**: There are multiple ways of reuse supported by the Web. Web resources can be embedded into each other, or simply hyperlinked. The whole technology stack is standardized, assuring reuse is also possible long-term (after all, the first website at the CERN can still be used, today).

Following the related approach of using components and packages (Salmen, Breuer, et al., 2024), the most promising way to handle interactive content in explorables is the use of web components, which is a set of standards for developer-defined, interactive content in websites and web apps. These standards integrate the component idea into the Web platform, no external libraries needed. Web components rely on three key standards: (1) *HTML Templates*, which allow developers to define reusable HTML structures that are not rendered right away; (2) *Custom Elements*, which let developers create their own HTML elements with specialized functionality; and (3) *Shadow DOM*, which keeps a complex DOM structure separate from the main DOM, while its Shadow DOM contains a detailed layout for the element. If interactive content is provided in the form of web components, it can easily embed into explorables.

4. IMPLEMENTATION IN WEBWRITER

As outlined, explorables are typically programmed rather than authored (Hohman et al., 2020), creating a major barrier to entry and excluding many educators and students—who have valuable domain expertise—from the process. As a result, composite learning resources (for instance, online courses and simulations) often end up referenced or reused only in their entirety, without the option of remixing individual components. To ensure equal access to the creation of explorables, suitable tools are essential, fulfilling educators' requirements such as the Explorable Authoring Requirements (EAR) (Salmen & Schroeder, 2024).

WebWriter is a tool fitting the EAR. Put shortly, it allows educators to create explorables, save them and share them with learners. Technically, it is a single page application (SPA) implemented in TypeScript and designed to run in any modern browser. The authored explorables are standalone HTML documents, and the tool can be expanded via Custom Elements distributed as Node Packages (so-called widgets). The HTML format makes the output portable and ensures that it remains usable in the long term. The interface (see Figure 2) follows the paradigm of direct manipulation: Instead of separating the source and output as existing solutions like H5P and Jupyter do, authors change the explorable through rich text editing, comparable to modern text processors (e.g., Microsoft Word). This addresses the limitations in functionality and usability of previous solutions (i.e. the form logic of H5P). A detailed description of WebWriter is given elsewhere (Salmen, Roepke, & Schroeder, 2024). We focus on showing how the tool enables remixing of interactive content:

Inserting, copying and pasting interactive content. WebWriter is fundamentally a rich text editor – text and images can be inserted at any point, copied, pasted, and so on (including external content from the web or word processors). The innovation for remixing is that interactive content can be treated the same way: Educators can install and insert so-called widgets (i.e. a widget could be an interactive world map) and insert, copy, and paste them. If an educator wants to reuse a widget in another explorable, they can select, copy and paste it.

Reconfiguring interactive content. As established earlier, only programming would allow full remixing of interactive content – but limited control can be given to educators through configuration. For one, the developed widget can expose options (i.e. locking the frame of the interactive world map so learners do not pan out of the intended view). Also, widgets remember their state (i.e. if the educator pans the map, the position is saved). Both types of configuration are also kept across copy/paste operations. Thus, the explicit options and the implicit permanence of widget state allow the educator to fit interactive content to their context.

Nesting interactive content. In remixing, nesting is important to consider (i.e. putting an interactive code cell inside a slide presentation to demonstrate a piece of code live). To enable this, widgets may specify that they accept content. However, the slide presentation and the code cell remain decoupled: The slide presentation may simply specify that arbitrary content can be put on a slide. This is a marked difference to solutions such as H5P, which require enumerating allowed content. With nesting, interactive content is again treated just as text.

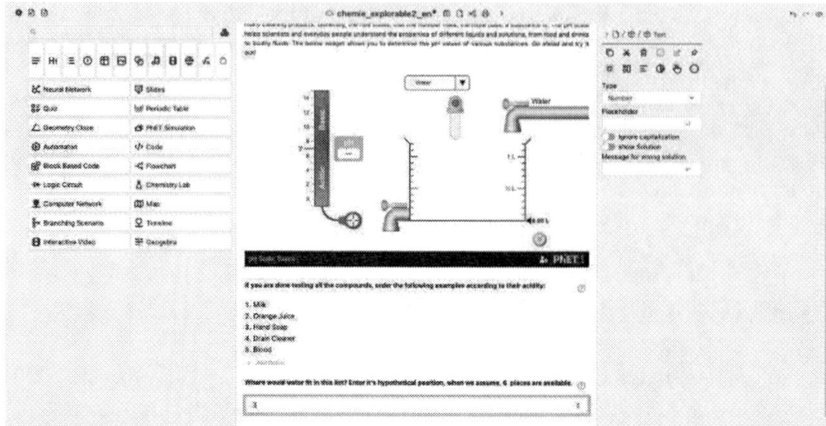

Figure 2. Current interface of WebWriter: Top bar with commands, below a palette of insertable elements including interactive widgets on the left, explorable editor in the center, and a toolbox for modifying elements on the right

5. EVALUATION

Previously, we introduced the didactical and technical concept of explorables, which is a web-based way to achieve remixable interactive learning resources. We also showed how an authoring tool can enable remix of interactive content without programming. While we showed capabilities for remix theoretically, to answer the RQ, we need to both show the solution is usable to educators and expressive enough for their use cases. While user experience is a well-established construct, expressiveness is more specific to this study and needs to be defined further: In this case, we mean the capability of real educators to author a learning resource of their choice in a limited time frame—that is, not theoretical (e.g. Turing Completeness), but practical expressiveness.
Method. To give educators ample time to author a realistic explorable with WebWriter, we designed a three- hour face-to-face workshop session for educators. The session was conducted with up to 20 participants by a moderator and an observing researcher. The session started with an introductory part where the moderator asked for experiences with digital authoring tools, which were gathered in a word cloud. Next, there was a short section where the moderator demonstrated the major features of the authoring tool while participants follow the moderator's steps on their devices. The main part of the session was an open working phase where participants could try the tool on their own. For guidance, the participants were requested to author a single explorable for a topic of their choice. They were also provided with a checklist of elements to include in their explorable to encourage using the full scope of the tool. Concluding the session, participants were asked to present their explorables, which were saved (also stored for later analysis) and shared privately among the group.

Afterwards, participants completed a digital post questionnaire: The first section covered some socio- demographics and personal details (levels of education taught on the ISCED scale (UNESCO, 2012), fields of education taught in the ISCED-F taxonomy (UNESCO, 2014), gender, age, occupation), followed by questions on previous experiences (whether WebWriter had been used before & self-assessed competency in digital technology generally, education, teaching by digital means, design of learning resources, and design of digital learning resources). That data was collected to consider confounding influences on expressiveness and user experience. The second section included the UEQ+ (Schrepp & Thomaschewski, 2019), a modular extension of the UEQ (User Experience Questionnaire) which allows researchers to add subscales to the questionnaire (here, the subscales of trust, intuitive use, adaptability, and usefulness). The UEQ+ was previously identified as a viable method for measuring the user experience of an explorable authoring tool (Salmen & Schroeder, 2024).

The workshop design was created collaboratively between a moderator with an education background and a researcher familiar with the authoring tool. To avoid introducing biases, no information about the relation between the researcher and the tool was given beforehand. Also, while the whole workshop was conducted by the moderator, the survey was administered by the researcher to lessen the effect of possible sympathies or antipathies developed during the session. Data protection guidelines and the ethics guidelines of our responsible ethics board were considered beforehand and the study was deemed appropriate.

Sample. For both user experience and our working definition of expressivity, real educators should author explorables in a controlled setting. Therefore, we recruited n=23 educators using contacts to local schools and universities to advertise our workshop. No exclusions or inclusions were made by the researchers, allowing all interested educators to register and participate. As participation was voluntary, a bias towards more motivated educators was expected, as well as participation only by educators local to the area.

Analysis and Results. Overall, n=23 educators took part in our study, with 13 identifying as female and 10 as male, and ages between 20 and 62 (median of 28). 11 participants were students of education, 9 were school teachers (one being both a student and a teacher), and 5 were lecturers (one being both a school teacher and a lecturer). On prior experience (Likert scales of 1 to 5), participants reported a high proficiency in ICT skills (mean of 3.35), education (3.13), and learning resource design (2.96), and medium proficiency in digital learning (2.61) and digital learning resource design (2.39).

As seen in Figure 3, educators assign very high importance to *adaptability*, *dependability*, *intuitive use*, and *trust*; high importance to *perspicuity*, *stimulation*, *novelty*, and *attractiveness*; medium importance to *usefulness*, and low importance to *efficiency* – indicated by color saturation. Most results are positive, ranging between 0.87 for *efficiency* and 1.84 for *stimulation* (the standard interpretation considers > 0.8 as good), with *adaptability* (0.59) and *dependability* (0.62) being more of a neutral result. High negative correlation coefficients for self- reported experience values and some sub scales were found, namely between education expertise and *perspicuity* (-0,57), and between digital learning expertise and *attractiveness* (-0,51).

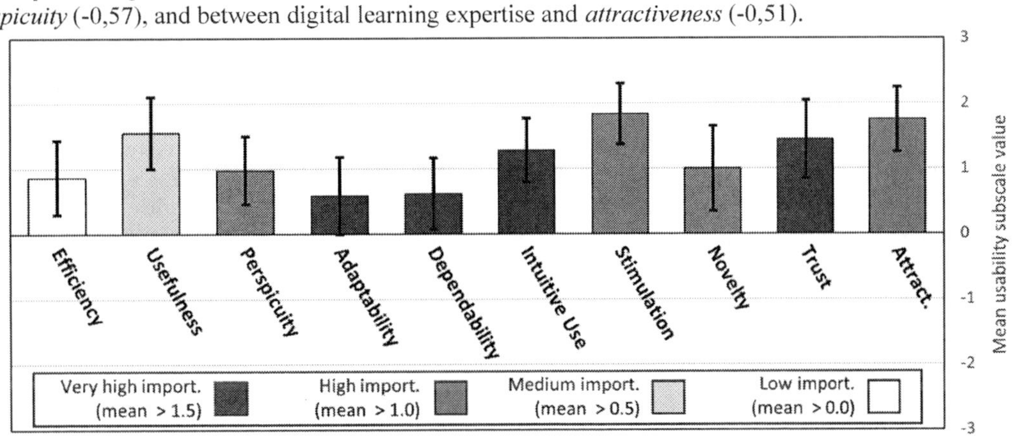

Figure 3. User Experience of authoring explorables with WebWriter (UEQ+, n=23). The height of the bars indicates the mean score on each usability subscale, and the color indicates the mean importance score of the subscale

During the workshops, each participant authored an explorable and submitted it in the end. The resulting explorables were classified using deductive content analysis (Mayring, 2014) by two researchers. The classes for coding were the ISCED education levels (UNESCO, 2012) and ISCED-F fields (UNESCO, 2014), also the contained types of elements according to the EAR (text, list, table, formula, disclosure, media) (Salmen & Schroeder, 2024), with a distinct classification of widgets based on Churchill's taxonomy (Churchill, 2007). Formally, only k=18 explorables were considered for coding as others were found to be incomplete or incoherent (byproducts of participants trying out features). The results in Table 1 show that all types of elements and widgets were used by participants. More traditional content types such as text (T = 18 times coded) and media (M = 16) were used by almost all participants, with more advanced rich text content such as lists (L = 4), tables (B = 1), and formulas (F = 1) being used more sparingly. For widgets, most explorables contained an exercise (E = 13) widget, i.e. a quiz. Second most common were conceptual widgets (C = 8), often combined with simulations (S = 5), i.e. the PhET simulations for physics. Information (I = 5), context (C = 5), and presentational widgets (P = 3) were used more rarely. For content, secondary education topics including non-tertiary post-secondary education (levels 2-5) in STEM fields were most common, but humanities and languages were also represented.

Table 1. Explorables from workshops (k=18) with coded metadata – education levels (ISCED) and fields (ISCED-F)

ID	ISCED	ISCED-F	Elements	Widgets	ID	ISCED	ISCED-F	Elements	Widgets
01	1-2	Hum/SoSci	`T---DM`	`-E----`	10	2-3	PhySci	`T---DM`	`PE----`
02	2-6	Bio/Hea/Hyg	`T----M`	`-E----`	11	1-2	ICT	`T---DM`	`-ESC--`
03	2-5	Hum	`T---DM`	`-E--I-`	12	2-5	PhySci	`TL----`	`--SC-X`
04	2-2	Math	`T--FDM`	`-E-C--`	13	1-5	Arts	`T----M`	`-E----`
05	1-2	Ltrcy/Lang	`T---DM`	`-E----`	14	2-5	PhySci	`T---DM`	`-ESCIX`
06	2-2	Math	`T-----`	`-E-C--`	15	2-5	PhySci	`T--FDM`	`---CI-`
07	2-2	Math/ICT	`TLB-DM`	`-E----`	16	2-5	Hum	`T---DM`	`P---IX`
08	2-5	PhySci	`T---DM`	`----I-`	17	2-5	Eng	`TL---M`	`--SC-X`
09	3-6	Lang	`T---DM`	`P-----`	18	1-2	Ltrcy/Math	`T--FDM`	`-ESCIX`

6. DISCUSSION

The results of our user study present first indicators that the concept of explorables may be viable. In terms of user experience (see Figure 3), several areas like stimulation, usefulness and trust are very strong—ratings above 2 are very rare, and ratings above 1 are above average. This shows that participants consider the tool interesting and beneficial for real use cases. The rating for an overall impression of the tool, attractiveness, is also strong, which may indicate that the tool exceeds expectations compared to other solutions—although further investigation is needed to strengthen this interpretation. There are some notable weaknesses: Participants considered the tool somewhat unstable (dependability), did not always know how to configure it to their needs (adaptability), and had issues learning some concepts (perspicuity). These weaknesses are however to be expected for a research prototype. In terms of expressiveness, the broad range of workshop participants and explorables created (see Table 1) show the potential of explorables for all fields of education, but especially for STEM subjects.

Looking at limitations, the sample size could be increased in further investigations to better support the claims made, and to get more reliable results on possible correlations. Also, while we argue that remixability is a technical property that follows necessarily from the concept and implementation, it is also worth criticizing that the degree of remix itself was not measured, only the usability and expressiveness. Due to the workshop setup, exposure to the concept of explorables and to the authoring tool was also very limited—long-term impressions and user experience in real-world settings may differ. Also, EdTech is a vast field, and it is untested how explorables can work with other emerging technologies such as VR/AR, how to optimally integrate LA, what role LLMs can play in generating such content, and so on – this study can only speak to a subset of EdTech.

Looking back, we view explorables as a iteration on previous concepts. They offer more granular control and decomposition than approaches such as learning objects, and are more aligned with established technologies, especially the rich environment of the web. However, they are somewhat less general purpose: While learning objects could include any and every technology related to learning, even tools, explorables are more focused on the specific area of document-like resources for learners. Similarly, they are differentiated from mashups in that they are intended to be authored by educators and that they use text as a main thread, combining the linear and the interactive. Explorables are also coupled with the concept of widgets for interactive content – developing interactive content as widgets enables remix in explorables. As a practical implementation, WebWriter improves on H5P's usability and is considerably more expressive due to the powerful widget concept. As a disadvantage, the higher expressiveness also leads to more technical complexity in the implementation, perhaps a root cause of the measured weaknesses in dependability and adaptability. Overall, explorables can be seen as a technical solution for interactive OER – if they are permissively licensed, they enable remix in the spirit of OER as they are findable, accessible, interoperable, and reusable (FAIR). The concept presents several opportunities: Educators an easy way to share and remix content – this could bring more of the results of EdTech research and development into schools. Researchers and companies may package their prototypes and products as widgets which educators can remix into explorables, or have adaptive systems automatically compose them, possible supported by LLMs. Researchers can connect with educators, since both the process of authoring resources and the process of using them for teaching and learning can become observable through analytics.

In total, explorables can contribute to a closer integration of the EdTech world—while there are many other dimensions to consider for cooperation between researchers, educators, and companies (e.g., organizational, legal, financial), technical challenges form a barrier of entry to all kinds of cooperation and are worth adressing.

7. CONCLUSION

To approach the issue of remixable interactive learning resources, a point long discussed in the EdTech community, we introduced the concept of explorables, which are web documents consisting of rich text, interspersed with interactive elements called widgets. To enable educators to author these explorables, we presented WebWriter, a solution that leverages the format of explorables and technical innovations in the web platform to remix and edit through a rich text interface, reconfiguration, and nesting. In the evaluation, we showed the viability of the tool and concept, suitable to educators and aligning with research and practice.

Future work should explore how to integrate other advances in EdTech such as LA, VR/AR, and most recently LLMs into the concept, furthering the claim of a universal concept for remixable interactive learning resources. Evaluating the concept of the interactive widgets included in the explorables could also be worthwhile, considering the developer experience and expressiveness for developers of EdTech. Also, replication studies with more participants to strengthen the claims made, or creating an iterative, design-based research approach should be considered as next steps, possibly including a measure for remix itself.

ACKNOWLEDGEMENTS

We were supported by the research project NERD II (005-2201-0014), sponsored by the state of North Rhine-Westphalia.

REFERENCES

Adil, H. M., Ali, S., Sultan, M., Ashiq, M., & Rafiq, M. (2024). Open education resources' benefits and challenges in the academic world: a systematic review. *Global Knowledge, Memory and Communication, 73*(3), 274–291.

Ali, L. (2024). convOERter: A Technical Assistance Tool to Support Semi-Automatic Conversion of Images in Educational Materials as OER. *Dissertation, RWTH Aachen University.* doi: https://doi.org/10.18154/RWTH-2024-01352

Bada, S. O., & Olusegun, S. (2015). Constructivism learning theory: A paradigm for teaching and learning. *Journal of Research & Method in Education, 5*(6), 66–70.

Brame, C. J. (2016). Effective Educational Videos: Principles and Guidelines for Maximizing Student Learning from Video Content. *LSE, 15*(4), es6.

Chue Hong, N. P., Katz, D. S., Barker, M., Lamprecht, A.-L., Martinez, C., Psomopoulos, F. E., ... Martinez,

P. A. (2022). FAIR principles for research software (FAIR4RS principles). *Zenodo.*

Churchill, D. (2007). Towards a useful classification of learning objects. *Educational Technology Research and Development, 55*, 479–497.

Conlen, M., Vo, M., Tan, A., & Heer, J. (2021). Idyll Studio: A Structured Editor for Authoring Interactive & Data-Driven Articles. In *UIST '21.* New York: ACM.

Czerwinski, M., Horvitz, E., & Wilhite, S. (2004). A diary study of task switching and interruptions. In *Proceedings of the sigchi conference on human factors in computing systems* (pp. 175–182).

de Mattos, D. P., & Muchaluat-Saade, D. C. (2018, August). STEVE: a Hypermedia Authoring Tool based on the Simple Interactive Multimedia Model. In *Proceedings of the ACM Symposium on Document Engineering 2018* (pp. 1–10). New York: ACM. doi: https://doi.org/10.1145/3209280.3209521

Fischer, M. P., Rohweder, M., & Dewan, P. (2021). H5P. *The Journal of the Canadian Health Libraries Association, 42*(3), 178.

Freeman, S., Eddy, S. L., McDonough, M., Smith, M. K., Okoroafor, N., Jordt, H., & Wenderoth, M. P. (2014). Active learning increases student performance in science, engineering, and mathematics. *Proceedings of the national academy of sciences, 111*(23), 8410–8415.

Granger, B. E., & Pérez, F. (2021). Jupyter: Thinking and storytelling with code and data. *Computing in Science & Engineering, 23*(2), 7–14.

Hohman, F., Conlen, M., Heer, J., & Chau, D. H. P. (2020, September). Communicating with Interactive Articles. *Distill*, *5*(9), e28. doi: https://doi.org/10.23915/distill.00028

Kaul, M., Kless, A., Bonne, T., & Rieke, A. (2017). Game changer for online learning driven by advances in web technology. *Int. Assoc. for Development of the Inf. Soc.*.

Kiesler, N., Röpke, R., Schiffner, D., Schulz, S., Strickroth, S., Ehlenz, M., . . . Wilhelm-Weidner, A. (2024). To- wards Open Science at the DELFI Conference. In *Proceedings of DELFI 2024* (p. 122-136). Gesellschaft für Informatik e.V. doi: https://doi.org/10.18420/delfi2024_22

Kiesler, N., & Schiffner, D. (2022). On the Lack of Recognition of Software Artifacts and IT Infrastructure in Educational Technology Research. In *20. Fachtagung Bildungstechnologien (DELFI)* (pp. 201–206). Gesellschaft für Informatik e.V.

Knuth, D. E. (1984). Literate programming. *The computer journal*, *27*(2), 97–111.

Lamb, B. (2007). Dr. Mashup or, Why Educators Should Learn to Stop Worrying and Love the Remix. *Educational Review*.

Lehrmittelzentrale, I. (2018). *Lehrmittel in einer digitalen Welt.* (Publisher: Ilz) Mayer, R. E. (2020). *Multimedia learning* (3rd ed.). Cambridge University Press.

Mayring, P. (2014). *Qualitative content analysis: theoretical foundation, basic procedures and soft- ware solution.* AUT. Retrieved 2025-04-09, from https://nbn-resolving.org/urn:nbn:de: 0168-ssoar-395173

Piedra, N., Chicaiza, J., López, J., Tovar, E., & Martinez, O. (2011). Finding oers with social-semantic search. In *2011 IEEE Global Engineering Education Conference (EDUCON)* (pp. 1195–1200). IEEE.

Salmen, F., Breuer, M., Görzen, S., Persike, M., & Schroeder, U. (2024). Fair learning technologies with web components and packages. In *Proceedings of delfi 2024* (pp. 10–18420). Gesellschaft für Informatik e.V. Salmen, F., Roepke, R., & Schroeder, U. (2023). Webwriter: A system to author and remix explorables– requirements & first prototype. In *Workshops der 21. fachtagung bildungstechnologien (delfi)* (pp. 39–48). Gesellschaft für Informatik e.V.

Salmen, F., Roepke, R., & Schroeder, U. (2024). Webwriter: Authoring and remixing explorables. In *European conference on technology enhanced learning* (pp. 247–253). Springer.

Salmen, F., & Schroeder, U. (2024). Evaluating authoring tools with the explorable authoring requirements. *arXiv preprint arXiv:2403.17714.*

Schrepp, M., & Thomaschewski, J. (2019). Design and validation of a framework for the creation of user experience questionnaires. *IJIMAI*, *5*(7), 88–95.

Shemshack, A., & Spector, J. M. (2020). A systematic literature review of personalized learning terms. *Smart Learning Environments*, *7*(1), 33.

Singleton, R., & Charlton, A. (2020). Creating H5P content for active learning. *Pacific Journal of Technology Enhanced Learning*, *2*(1), 13–14.

UNESCO. (2012). *International standard classification of education: ISCED 2011.* Montreal, Quebec: UNESCO Institute for Statistics. (OCLC: 879577639)

UNESCO. (2014). *ISCED Fields of education and training 2013 (ISCED-F 2013): Manual to accompany the International Standard Classification of Education 2011.* UNESCO Institute for Statistics. (OCLC: 7354463744)

Victor, B. (2011). *Explorable Explanations.* Retrieved 2022-08-23, from http://worrydream.com/ExplorableExplanations/

Wicaksono, J. A., Setiarini, R. B., Ikeda, O., & Novawan, A. (2021). The use of H5P in teaching english. In *The first international conference on social science, humanity, and public health (icoship 2020)* (pp. 227–230). Atlantis Press.

Wieman, C. E., Adams, W. K., & Perkins, K. K. (2008). PhET: Simulations That Enhance Learning. *Science*, *322*(5902), 682–683.

Wiley, D., Waters, S., Dawson, D., Lambert, B., Barclay, M., Wade, D., & Nelson, L. (2004). Overcoming the limitations of learning objects. *Journal of Educational Multimedia and Hypermedia*, *13*(4), 507–521.

Wiley, D. A. (2002). *The instructional use of learning objects* (Vol. 1). Agency for instructional technology Bloomington, IN.

Wiley, D. A. (2008). The learning objects literature. In *Handbook of research on educational communications and technology* (pp. 345–353). Routledge.

Wilkinson, M. D., Dumontier, M., Aalbersberg, I. J., Appleton, G., Axton, M., Baak, A., . . . Bourne, P. E. (2016). The FAIR Guiding Principles for scientific data management and stewardship. *Scientific data*, *3*(1), 1–9.

Wouters, P., Van Nimwegen, C., Van Oostendorp, H., & Van Der Spek, E. D. (2013). A meta-analysis of the cognitive and motivational effects of serious games. *Educational Psychology*, *105*(2), 249–265.

Zhang, J., Haverals, W., Naydan, M., & Kernighan, B. W. (2024). Post-OCR correction with OpenAI's GPT Models on Challenging English Prosody Texts. In *Proceedings of the ACM Symposium on Document Engineering 2024.* New York: ACM. doi: https://doi.org/10.1145/3685650.3685669

HUMAN PERCEPTIONS ON AI-GENERATED IMAGE AND AI-ASSISTIVE SENTENCE CORRECTIONS: ANALYZING LEARNERS CONTEXTUAL VOCABULARY LEARNING BEHAVIOURS WITH AN AI CHATBOT

Kensuke Akao[1], Mohammad Nehal Hasnine[2], Mirai Yamada[2] and Hiroshi Ueda[2]
[1]*Institute of Informatics, Ludwigsburg University of Education, 71634 Ludwigsburg, Germany*
Institute of Software Engineering, University of Stuttgart, 70174 Stuttgart, Germany
[2]*Research Center for Computing and Multimedia Studies, Hosei University, Tokyo 184-8584, Japan*

ABSTRACT

In recent years, the rapid technological development and widespread adoption of chatbots equipped with generative artificial intelligence (GenAI) based on Large Language Models (LLMs) have brought dramatic changes in the field of education. In e-learning, flexible progression and real-time feedback enabled by human-like interaction with artificial intelligence (AI), similar to a tutor, along with a shift in the nature of learning contents from 'learning with pre-prepared materials' to 'learning with generated materials', significantly expands the possibilities for personalized learning implementation. However, how accurately can contents generated by an AI model for general-purpose cases that have not been trained explicitly for educational purposes meet the quality in foreign language learning? is yet to be explored. In this study, native speakers and foreign language teachers validated AI-suggested corrections to learners' constructed sentences and images representing their learning context, which were generated by a GenAI-based contextual vocabulary learning application called Wordhyve-Glc during the learning of the Spanish and French languages. Their feedback clarified that the AI is to some extent capable of correcting sentences and generating images to represent learning contexts but also generates many undesirable ones. This paper discusses the current technical limitations of AI-assisted sentence correction and image generation aspects in foreign language learning by examining failure cases and identifying the characteristics of these issues. It also outlines the necessary steps for further advancement in the use of GenAI within the educational field.

KEYWORDS

Generative Artificial Intelligence (GenAI), Vocabulary, AI-Assisted Vocabulary Learning, Contextual Vocabulary Learning, Image Generation, Sentence Construction and Error Correction

1. INTRODUCTION

The efficacy of automated, instantaneous feedback on learners' responses, grounded in operant conditioning, has been a primary rationale for self-directed learning environments. This rationale extends from Skinner's teaching machine (Skinner, 1958) to contemporary gamification-based learning applications (Landers et al., 2015). In recent years, alongside the rapid development of Generative Artificial Intelligence (GenAI) based on Large Language Models (LLMs), there has been a continuous expansion in the range of tasks artificial intelligence (AI) chatbots can perform as instructed by the users. These tasks include applications where chatbots support learning for users (Hauske & Bendel, 2024). In conventional e-learning environments, fixed feedback mechanisms are embedded within the software to provide feedback on anticipated answer choices. In contrast, in the context of AI chatbots, feedback is generated on a per-learner basis, with the capacity to adapt in real-time in response to interactions with the individual learner. Furthermore, contemporary AI chatbots have the capacity to process multimedia, encompassing text, images, and video simultaneously. Today, LLM-based GenAI such as Llama, Gemini, DeepSeek, and ChatGPT are capable of generating human-like contents. Prominent language learning applications such as Duolingo, Memrise, and Rosetta Stone are also exploring their use to generate personalized learning content and assignments for individual learners (Hasnine et al., 2025). This development signifies a major innovation in the context of language learning experiences in e-learning, heralding a paradigm shift.

The personalized automated learning context enabled by the AI chatbots has the potential to engender new value in educational experiences. LLM-supported AI chatbots, in contrast to knowledge-based AI such as expert systems, have been observed to produce inaccurate responses, including hallucinations. In this context, our focus is on the potentials and risks of LLM-based chatbots for contextual vocabulary learning in informal foreign language learning. The objective of this study is to validate learning logs generated by a human using an LLM-based chatbot. More precisely, we aimed to validate the images generated by a generative model and the learner's constructed sentences corrected by AI, as evaluated by native speakers and language teachers. This paper addresses the following research questions:

- RQ1: Can GenAI corrections provide correct improvement suggestions for errors in sentences written by learners?
- RQ2: Can GenAI make images that accurately depict the words learners are studying, based on the context within sentences?
- RQ3: What characteristics are observed in inappropriate feedback from GenAI for contextual vocabulary learning?

2. RELATED WORKS AND THEORETICAL FOUNDATIONS

As the range of tasks that GenAI based on LLMs can handle has expanded remarkably in recent years, attempts are being made to replace e-learning functions previously implemented through human-programmed software development with AI. For example, Hauske and Bendel implemented self-regulated learning in corporate learning and development by using ChatGPT to fulfil three roles: digital learning facilitator, digital learning coach, and digital learning mentor (Hauske and Bendel, 2024). Using GenAI as educational agents makes it possible to provide AI-supported personalized learning. Similarly, numerous related studies in the field of language learning (Bendel & Jabou, 2024; Lawrance et al., 2024; Yesilyurt, 2023) have used GenAI models to develop educational tools. In this line, we developed Wordhyve-Glc (Hasnine et al., 2025). Context-based vocabulary learning process is explored using Wordhyve-Glc. Several test participants have validated the wordhyve-Glc-generated contents, and their positive feedback, based on their learning experiences, confirms the potential of GenAI in personalized learning (Hasnine et al., 2025). However, the validity of the corrections and image quality in language learning provided by this GenAI has not been validated by humans.

In language learning, it is important to provide learners with background knowledge within the learning context, referred to *schema* (Rumelhart & Ortony, 1977). Vocabulary is one example of such background knowledge. If learners are learning their native language, they can relatively easily find *realia* (Berwald, 1987) for target vocabulary items in their daily lives. However, when learning a foreign language, it is difficult to find *realia* in learning contexts that involve vastly different cultures or situations entirely distinct from one's own daily life. In that case, an alternative means to express the learning context through *realia* becomes necessary. Our developed Wordhyve-Glc app provides vocabulary learning support through multiple multimedia annotations combining AI-generated images that represent learning contexts with text derived from interactions with chatbots (Hasnine et al., 2025). In other words, this learning approach treats images generated by AI as *realia*. Paivio's dual coding theory can be used to justify the pedagogical approach of combining verbal pathways through words and non-verbal pathways through image representations when learning vocabulary with chatbots. This theory posits that the human cognitive subsystems are divided into two distinct categories. One for verbal processing and the other for nonverbal processing—whose cognitive capacities are independent, and that by combining both subsystems and fully utilizing the capacity of each, it is possible to have more effective memory retention (Paivio, 1986). Furthermore, according to Mayer's multimedia learning theory, humans possess two separate channels for processing information. The combined use of verbal elements (text and narration) and visual elements (images, animations, and videos) in learning enables more efficient processing and integration of information acquired through learning (Mayer, 2002; Mayer & Moreno, 1998). Similarly, regarding the flow of learning guided by chatbots, based on the application of operant conditioning to interactive learning theory (Mulyana, 2017), and the application of adaptive learning to the same theory (Polly et al., 2014), we can approach a high-quality learning experience by optimizing interactions through dialogue between learners and AI. Therefore, the learning process of Wordhyve-Glc, which enables such personalized contextual vocabulary learning, is grounded in three pedagogical foundations: interactive learning, dual coding theory, and multimedia learning theory (Hasnine et al., 2025).

3. HOW DOES WORDHYVE-GLC WORK

Wordhyve-Glc is a foreign language learning app built on the GPT builder that provides learners with contextual clues for target vocabulary, sentence construction support, and image generation of learning contexts, enabling them to learn vocabulary in context through interaction with AI (Hasnine et al., 2025). First, learners select the words they wish to study themselves, or they allow the AI to automatically select them based on their profiles (and, in some cases, instructions from the language teacher supervising the learners). Next, the AI proposes three contextual clues related to the selected word, and learners construct sentences based on these. AI detects errors in a learner-constructed sentence and provides correction suggestions. Finally, the AI generates an image representing the learned words within the context of the proofread sentence, which is then presented to the learner. Learners can instruct this app at any time by providing prompts to answer questions about the learning content, requesting hints, or adjusting settings. Table 1 and Figure 1 show the 14 proofreading suggestions and generated images that Wordhyve-Glc presented to Spanish language learners. Similarly, Table 2 and Figure 2 list the 15 proofreading suggestions and generated images that were presented to French learners. These were extracted from the interaction history between learners and the chatbot, as recorded in the app's learning log with the learners' consent (Hasnine et al., 2025).

Table 1. AI-powered error detection and correction (Spanish)

No.	Words	Original sentence by Learner	Suggestions for sentence corrections by AI
S1	coche	Ellea conduce la coce rapido de carrtera.	Ella conduce el coche rápido por la carretera.
S2	querer	Me Amigo querer mucho el Regalo de Navidad.	Mi amigo quiere mucho el regalo de Navidad.
S3	flor	Las flores de jardín ole colorido.	Las flores del jardín huelen coloridas.
S4	aquí	Ahora espero aquí lugar.	Ahora espero aquí en este lugar.
S5	libro	Mi leo un libro muy interesante en la biblioteca.	Yo leo un libro muy interesante en la biblioteca.
S6	escuela	estudio en la clases de profesores en la escuela.	Estudio en las clases de los profesores en la escuela.
S7	perro	El perro juga en el Parque con amigo.	El perro juega en el parque con su amigo.
S8	a veces	a veces llovo me gutsa trabajo con música.	A veces llueve. Me gusta trabajar con música.
S9	mal	sento día mal porque ahora mucho problemas.	Me siento mal hoy porque ahora tengo muchos problemas.
S10	escuela	Estudiantes ir a la escuela poder aprender.	Los estudiantes van a la escuela para aprender.
S11	gato	yo mascota un gato.	Yo tengo una mascota, un gato.
S12	coche	Mi coche es muy rapido.	*Original sentence is correct (No suggestion)*
S13	hacer	yo haco trabajo.	*Original sentence is correct (No suggestion)*
S14	vivir	yo vivir con mi familia i en grande casa.	Yo vivo con mi familia en una casa grande.

Table 2. AI-powered error detection and correction (French)

No.	Word	Original sentence by Learner	Suggestions for sentence corrections by AI
F1	là	C'est ton livre là?	C'est ton livre, là?'
F2	prendre	Nous prenons le metro à Tour Eiffel.	Nous prenons le métro pour aller à la Tour Eiffel.
F3	retourner	Quand est-ce que tu vas retourner à maison?	Quand est-ce que tu vas retourner à la maison?
F4	temps	Les temps fait bon.	Le temps est bon.
F5	attendre	Je vais attendre pour toi.	Je vais t'attendre.
F6	chateau	Le roi retourne à son chateau.	Le roi retourne à son château.
F7	fleur	Je mange le fleur dans le jardin.	Je mange une fleur dans le jardin.
F8	être	Je suis trés fatigué.	Je suis très fatigué.
F9	chien	le chien aime de jouer dans mon jardin.	Le chien aime jouer dans mon jardin.
F10	toujours	Je suis heureux toujours.	Je suis toujours heureux.
F11	livre	Je lire un livre intéressant dans la bibliothèque.	Je lis un livre intéressant dans la bibliothèque.
F12	venir	Mon ami vense à mon Maison.	Mon ami vient à ma maison.
F13	pouvoir	Aujourd'hui je ne pouvais pas travail.	Aujourd'hui, je ne pouvais pas travailler.
F14	ville	J'abite dans une ville grande.	J'habite dans une grande ville.
F15	amour	L'amour est trés fort.	L'amour est très fort.

Figure 1. Representation of words by generated contextual images (Spanish)

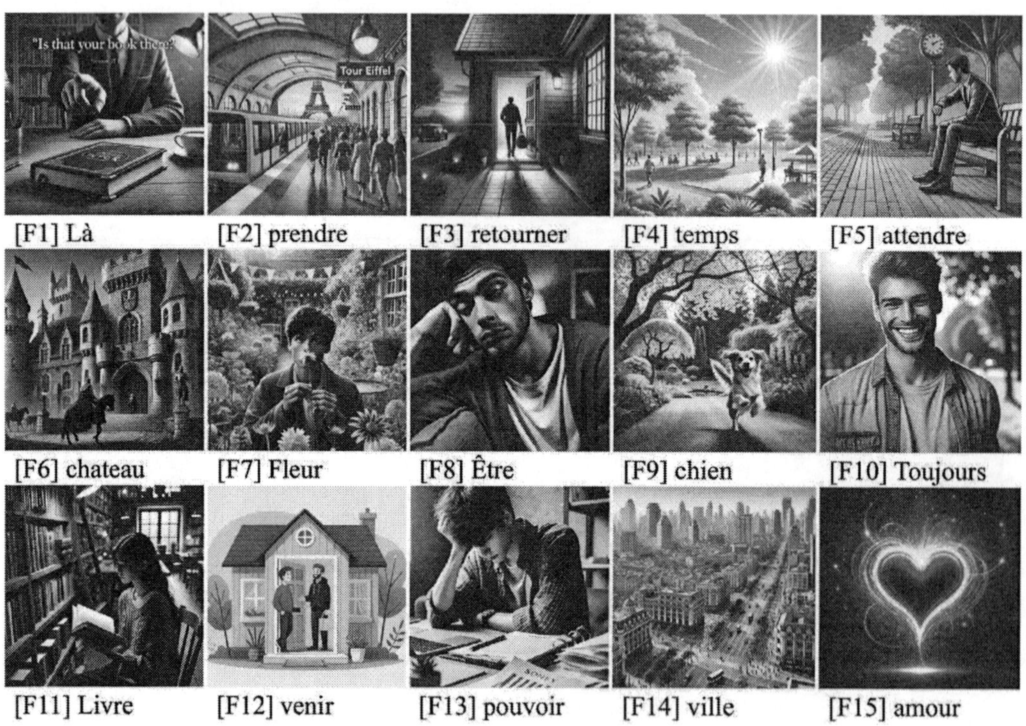

Figure 2. Representation of words by generated contextual images (French)

4. EVALUATION

To find the answers to the research questions presented in Section 1, we examined the validity of the outputs of AI chatbots that provide context-based personalized vocabulary learning support. Using Wordhyve-Glc as an example from an AI chatbot, this study aims to identify the potential and limitations of error detection and correction functions for learner-generated sentences, as well as image generation functions that represent learning contexts. Bendel & Jabou obtained scientific evidence based on feedback from 3 native speakers in their evaluation of a language learning environment through interaction with a chatbot they developed (Bendel & Jabou, 2024). Following their approach, we also decided to involve native speakers in our research for evaluation purposes. Furthermore, to obtain evidence from a more pedagogical perspective, we additionally invited teachers who instruct French and Spanish as second foreign languages to participate in the research.

4.1 Method

A total of 8 participants took part in the study: three Spanish native speakers (SN1, SN2, and SN3), three French native speakers (FN1, FN2, and FN3), and two foreign language teachers at secondary schools in Germany (one teaching Spanish, ST1, and the other teaching French, FT1). This study was conducted after receiving approval from the ethics committee. An anonymous, voluntary online survey was used, conducted in accordance with the EU's General Data Protection Regulation (GDPR), after obtaining consent from participants for the collection of their information. Each participant received a €10 voucher for taking part in the survey. The survey asked respondents to rate the accuracy of AI-generated correction results and image generation results using a 6-point Likert scale single-choice question, followed by a free-response section where they could add supplementary reasons for their judgments. Questions referenced examples of corrections and generated images from previous learning scenarios introduced in Chapter 4, eliciting semi-qualitative feedback for all 14 Spanish cases (S1-S14) or 15 French cases (F1-F15).

4.2 Analysis of the Validity of AI-Powered Error Detection and Correction

The first question asked the native speakers and foreign language teachers to provide feedback on Wordhyve-Glc's ability to detect errors in learner-constructed sentences and correct them. For example, in the Spanish S1 case, the question is phrased as follows: Do you think the original sentence ‘Ellea conduce la coce rapido de carrtera’, which is corrected by AI to ‘Ella conduce el coche rápido por la carretera.’, is correct? Participants should choose the response option on the 6-point Likert scale that best reflects their opinion for all cases of the language being evaluated: The options are: “-3 = Completely disagree”, “-2 = Disagree”, “-1 = Somewhat disagree”, “1 = Somewhat agree”, “2 = Agree” and “3 = Completely agree”. In cases S12 and S13, Wordhyve-Glc determined that there were no errors in the learner's original text. The question posed for these 2 cases was: Do you think the original sentence ‘yo haco trabajo', which is identified by AI as a correct sentence, is correct? Table 3 shows the evaluation results for the 14 Spanish cases, and Table 4 shows the evaluation results for the 15 French cases. The average ratings for the 4 participants across all Spanish cases revealed that S7 received the highest rating, with an average of 2, while S13 received the lowest rating, with an average of -3. Furthermore, the average rating was positive in 9 out of 14 cases. Similarly, the highest ratings in French (Avg. = 0.5) were given to F8 and F15, while the lowest rating (Avg. = -2.5) was given to F12. Only 2 out of 15 cases in French had a positive average rating. Moreover, in French, the average rating tended to be lower often in sentences with more words, whereas this tendency was not observed in Spanish.

Next, we conducted qualitative analysis of the feedback in free-text format. Spanish Cases S2 and S13 pointed out that the AI of the Wordhyve-Glc app failed to detect errors in the learners' original sentences. In the S2 case, the AI fails to recognize that the word 'querer', meaning 'to like' or 'to love' (in English language), can only be used to describe people and cannot be used to describe an object, such as a gift. In the S13 case, the AI failed to recognize that the word 'haco' in the learner's sentence was redundant. However, in Spanish Case S3 and French Case F2, it was noted that the AI had added new information during the correction process that was not present in the learner's original context. In Case S3, for instance, the original sentence 'The flowers in the garden are vividly coloured' was amended by the AI to include the detail that the flowers smell. Similarly, in Case F2, the original sentence 'Take the subway at the Eiffel Tower' was altered by the AI to 'Take the subway to go to the Eiffel Tower'. We see these as instances of hallucination that occurred during the AI-based proofreading process. Table 5 summarizes the most suitable corrections for the 8 cases of erroneous AI-generated revisions suggested by Spanish native speakers. Unfortunately, we did not receive any similar suggestions for improvements from native French speakers. However, French native speaker FN3, who stated that the AI's error detection and correction was often inaccurate, provided feedback highlighting that, in this instance, the AI functioned correctly in terms of correcting grammatical errors. Wordhyve-Glc's error detection feature identifies not only grammatical errors, but also typos, spelling errors, punctuation errors, and missing apostrophes in contracted forms (Hasnine et al., 2025).

Table 3. Quantitative results Spanish (Completely disagree = -3, Completely agree = 3)

	S1	S2	S3	S4	S5	S6	S7	S8	S9	S10	S11	S12	S13	S14	Avg.
SN1	2	1	1	-1	1	2	1	-1	1	-1	-2	3	-3	3	0,50
SN2	3	-3	-2	3	3	3	3	-1	3	3	3	3	-3	3	1,50
SN3	1	-3	-3	1	3	2	1	-3	1	1	-3	3	-3	3	0,07
ST1	-3	3	-3	3	-3	-3	3	3	-2	3	-3	-3	-3	-3	-0,79
Avg.	0,75	-0,50	-1,75	1,50	1,00	1,00	2,00	-0,50	0,75	1,50	-1,25	1,50	-3,00	1,50	0,32
SD	2,28	2,60	1,64	1,66	2,45	2,35	1,00	2,18	1,79	1,66	2,49	2,60	0,00	2,60	0,82

Table 4. Quantitative results of French (Completely disagree = -3, Completely agree = 3)

	F1	F2	F3	F4	F5	F6	F7	F8	F9	F10	F11	F12	F13	F14	F15	Avg.
FN1	2	3	3	3	-3	3	3	3	3	3	3	-1	3	3	3	2,27
FN2	-3	-3	-3	-3	-3	-2	-3	3	-3	-2	-3	-3	-3	-2	3	-2,00
FN3	1	1	-3	-3	3	-3	-3	-3	-3	-2	-3	-3	-3	-3	-3	-2,00
FT1	-3	-3	-3	-1	-3	-1	-3	-1	-2	-2	-2	-3	-2	-2	-1	-2,13
Avg.	-0,75	-0,50	-1,50	-1,00	-1,50	-0,75	-1,50	0,50	-1,25	-0,75	-1,25	-2,50	-1,25	-1,00	0,50	-0,97
SD	2,28	2,60	2,60	2,45	2,60	2,28	2,60	2,60	2,49	2,17	2,49	0,87	2,49	2,35	2,60	1,87

Table 5. Further suggestions for correcting erroneous AI correction results by Spanish native speakers

No.	Sentence corrected by AI	Sentence corrected by Spanish native speakers
S1	Ella conduce el coche rápido por la carretera.	Ella conduce rápidamente el coche por la carretera
S2	Mi amigo quiere mucho el regalo de Navidad.	A mi amigo le gusta mucho el regalo de Navidad
S3	Las flores del jardín huelen coloridas.	Las flores del jardín son coloridas
S6	Estudio en las clases de los profesores en la escuela.	Estudio en la escuela, en las clases de los profesores
S7	El perro juega en el parque con su amigo.	El perro juega en el parque con su amigo, otro perro.
S8	A veces llueve. Me gusta trabajar con música.	A veces cuando llueve. Me gusta trabajar con música.
S11	Yo tengo una mascota, un gato.	Yo tengo a un gato como mascota
S13	Yo haco trabajo. (Original sentence is correct.)	Yo trabajo.

4.3 Analysis of the Validity of Contextual Image Generation

The second question asked whether the generated image accurately represents the word in the context of the sentence after AI correction. For example, in the Spanish S1 case, the question is phrased as follows: Do you think the picture represents the word 'Coche' in the 'Ella conduce el coche rápido por la carretera.' context? Participants select their response option from a 6-point Likert scale (-3 = Completely disagree — 3 = Completely agree) that best reflects their opinion of all instances of the target language, in the same way as in Section 5.1. Likewise, Table 6 shows the evaluation results for the 14 Spanish cases, and Table 7 shows the evaluation results for the 15 French cases. Upon examining the ratings provided by the participants, it is observed that cases where the images were judged to have been generated correctly are mixed in with cases where they were not. Foreign language teachers ST1 and FT1 were presented with an additional single-choice question on a 6-point Likert scale. They were asked whether each generated image could be used for educational purposes. The response options were the same as previously described. The average rating for each of the 14 images from S1 to S14 by Teachers ST1 was 0.43, with a standard deviation (SD) of 2.85. The average rating for each of the 15 images from F1 to F15 by Teachers FT1 was 1.8, with a standard deviation (SD) of 1.04.

Finally, we qualitatively evaluate the issues with 15 images mentioned in the free-text comments. We categorized the comments into the following six types (some images had more than one applicable category):

- The image does not adequately convey the information in the text: S1, S2, S9, S14, F1, F2, F10, F12
- The image is missing some of the information in the text: S7, S8, F2
- The image does not take into account the possibility that the text is using figurative language: F4, F14
- The image is stereotypical: F6
- Visual representations may lead to misunderstanding of textual information: S1, S5, F2, F7
- The image does not visualize the abstract expression of the text: S2, S5, S9, S14

For example, in the Spanish S1 case, the image should represent the word 'car', but it depicts the interior of a car. It was pointed out that this image more readily evokes the concepts of 'driver' or 'driving' than 'car'. Furthermore, the image was criticized for inaccurately representing the concept of 'driving fast on the motorway'. In fact, Ella is shown driving in the right-hand lane, where slower vehicles travel, and a car is overtaking her from the left. Next, regarding the image of S5, it was pointed out that while the context describes it as an "interesting book," the reader's expression appears bored. Regarding F1, while the text asks "Is this your book?", the image depicts the questioner's index finger pointing not at the book but at the person they are addressing. And in F2, the sentence goes "Take the subway to go to the Eiffel Tower," yet the image shows them already arriving at the Eiffel Tower's nearest station. As a final example, in F12, it was pointed out that the positions of the resident and visitor are reversed (the person opening the door to invite them is holding the gift). Some of the images generated in this way contained expressions that felt jarring from our everyday perspective. Furthermore, despite Spain and France being home to diverse ethnic groups, it was noted that the people depicted in the images were mostly white males, perpetuating stereotypes that are unsuitable for modern society. However, regarding the characteristics of the people depicted in the generated images, the specification allows these to be directly specified to the AI through the prompt (Hasnine et al., 2025). However, if nothing is specified, it seems to default to this kind of result.

Table 6. Quantitative results of Spanish (Completely disagree = -3, Completely agree = 3)

	S1	S2	S3	S4	S5	S6	S7	S8	S9	S10	S11	S12	S13	S14	Avg.
SN1	2	-3	3	-1	1	2	3	-3	2	2	3	3	2	2	1,29
SN2	1	-3	3	1	2	2	3	-1	3	3	3	3	-1	-1	1,29
SN3	-3	3	3	2	-1	1	-2	-2	-2	3	3	3	1	-2	0,50
ST1	-2	-3	3	-3	-3	3	1	-3	2	3	2	3	-3	-3	-0,21
Avg.	-0,50	-1,50	3,00	-0,25	-0,25	2,00	1,25	-2,25	1,25	2,75	2,75	3,00	-0,25	-1,00	0,71
SD	2,06	2,60	0,00	1,92	1,92	0,71	2,05	0,83	1,92	0,43	0,43	0,00	1,92	1,87	0,62

Table 7. Quantitative results of French (Completely disagree = -3, Completely agree = 3)

	F1	F2	F3	F4	F5	F6	F7	F8	F9	F10	F11	F12	F13	F14	F15	Avg.
FN1	3	1	-2	1	3	3	1	3	3	-3	1	2	-3	3	3	1,27
FN2	-2	1	3	1	1	1	-1	2	3	-3	3	-2	-2	1	2	0,53
FN3	-1	1	3	3	3	3	1	3	3	1	2	2	1	3	1	1,93
FT1	-3	-3	-3	-3	1	3	-3	2	3	-3	2	3	2	2	1	0,07
Avg.	-0,75	0,00	0,25	0,50	2,00	2,50	-0,50	2,50	3,00	-2,00	2,00	1,25	-0,50	2,25	1,75	0,95
SD	2,28	1,73	2,77	2,18	1,00	0,87	1,66	0,50	0,00	1,73	0,71	1,92	2,06	0,83	0,83	0,71

4.4 Limitations

As GenAI is non-deterministic, the verification results of this study cannot guarantee consistent behaviors when the same prompt is used. This study was conducted using only the ChatGPT4o AI model. Results may vary depending on the AI model used, including any new models that emerge in the future. Furthermore, as this study only examined language learning involving French and Spanish, the results may differ when learning other languages. Due to the limited sample size and number of survey participants, a larger scale study is necessary.

5. CONCLUSION

From the perspective of personalized contextual vocabulary learning through interaction with AI chatbots, GenAI technology has already reached a level at which this can be practically achieved. However, significant challenges remain regarding the quality of content created by GenAI in terms of learning quality. This study revealed that current LLM-based GenAI can create not only accurate content but also inaccurate content. This fact highlights the current limitations of applying AI developed for general use cases to education, a field demanding high legitimacy. One notable finding of our qualitative analysis is that, of the cases where inaccurate content was generated, a relatively small number were assumed to be attributable to hallucination. This suggests that AI models may be unable to grasp the finer details of our world using current machine learning. In the most recent field of AI research, this matter has been raised as an issue known as "Potemkin Understanding in LLM" (Mancoridis et al., 2025).

Possible technical approaches to overcome these challenges include developing AI models or prompt engineering to improve the quality of generated content. Possible pedagogical approaches include exploring detection methods for low-quality content and countermeasures to mitigate its adverse effects, as well as teaching methods that account for the potential errors of GenAI. Furthermore, as Explainable AI (XAI) technology advances, we may be able to find more effective ways to solve problems by clarifying the specific mechanisms that cause AI to generate inappropriate corrections or images. In any case, there are significant hurdles to overcome before contextual vocabulary learning using GenAI can be implemented at a practical level. To overcome these challenges, we must continue to conduct research vigorously.

REFERENCES

Bendel, O., & Jabou, D. (2024). @llegra: A chatbot for Vallader. In International Journal of Information Technology, 16(4), 2035–2045.

Berwald, J-P. (1987). Teaching Foreign Languages with Realia and Other Authentic Materials. In ERIC Q&A. Washington, D.C., USA.

Hasnine, M. N., Yamada, M., Ueda, H., & Akao, K. (2025). Understanding learners' perceptions on a generative ai-enable system in personalized contextual vocabulary learning. *International Conferences e-Learning and Digital Learning 2025 and Sustainability, Technology and Education 2025*. Lisbon, Portugal, pp. 137-144.

Hauske, S., & Bendel, O. (2024). How Can GenAI Foster Well-being in Self-regulated Learning? Proceedings of the AAAI Symposium Series, 3(1), Article 1.

Landers, R. N., Bauer K. N., Callan. R. C., Armstrong, M. B. (2015). Psychological Theory and the Gamification of Learning. In Gamification in Education and Business. Springer International Publishing, Cham, Germany, pp. 165-186.

Lawrance, J. C., Sambath, P., Shiny, C., Vazhangal, M., S, P., & Bala, B. K. (2024). Developing an AI-Assisted Multilingual Adaptive Learning System for Personalized English Language Teaching. 2024 10th International Conference on Advanced Computing and Communication Systems (ICACCS), 1, 428–434.

Mancoridis, M., Weeks, B., Vafa, K., & Mullainathan S. (2025). Potemkin Understanding in Large Language Models. Proceedings of the 42nd International Conference on Machine Learning. Vancouver, Canada, In press.

Mayer, R. E., & Moreno, R. (1998). A cognitive theory of multimedia learning: Implications for design principles. In Journal of Educational Psychology, 91(2), pp. 358–368.

Mayer, R. E. (2002). Multimedia learning. In Psychology of Learning and Motivation. Vol. 41, Academic Press, pp. 85–139.

Mulyana, S. N. (2017). Applying Classical and Operant Conditioning Theory to Improve the Vocabulary of the First Year Students at MTS Madani Alauddiin Paopao [PhD Thesis, State Islamic University].

Paivio, A.(1986). Mental representations: a dual coding approach. Oxford University Press: Clarendon Press, New York: Oxford, USA.

Polly, P., Marcus, N., Maguire, D., Belinson, Z., & Velan, G. M. (2014). Evaluation of an adaptive virtual laboratory environment using Western Blotting for diagnosis of disease. BMC Medical Education, 14(1), 222.

Rumelhart, D.E., & Ortony, A.. (1977). The representation of knowledge in memory. In Schooling and the Acquisition of Knowledge. pp. 99-135.

Skinner, B. F. (1958). Teaching machines. Science, 128. pp. 969-977.

Yesilyurt, Y. E. (2023). AI-enabled assessment and feedback mechanisms for language learning: Transforming pedagogy and learner experience. In Transforming the language teaching experience in the age of AI, 25–43. IGI Global.

ASSESSING THE TRANSFER OF MACROCOGNITIVE SKILLS FROM VIRTUAL REALITY SIMULATIONS TO REAL-WORLD TRAINING ENVIRONMENTS

Jessica M. Johnson
PhD, Old Dominion University's Office of Enterprise Research and Innovation
1030 University Blvd., Suffolk VA 23435, USA

ABSTRACT

The transfer of macrocognitive skills from digital training environments into physical performance is a central challenge in high-stakes domains such as healthcare, manufacturing, and defense industries. This meta-analysis synthesizes 111 studies published between 2000 and 2025, including 47 quantitative analyses, to examine how virtual reality (VR), augmented reality (AR), and related exploratory technologies support decision-making, sensemaking, attention management, problem solving, and team coordination beyond the screen and into applied contexts. The evidence demonstrates that immersive simulations consistently strengthen not only knowledge and technical skills but also the behavioral and operational capacities essential for performance in complex, uncertain environments. Programs in safety and healthcare, for example, enabled learners to anticipate hazards more effectively and collaborate more seamlessly in live drills and operational exercises. Analysis of moderators revealed five design features as pivotal to effective transfer: functional fidelity that reflects real-world cognitive demands, immersive features that enable embodied interaction, subject matter expert–derived cognitive models, mastery-based instructional structures, and explicit scaffolds for team development. These features move exploratory technologies beyond surface realism, demonstrating that meaningful transfer occurs when training emphasizes cognitive and collaborative fidelity. By synthesizing two decades of research, this study shows how exploratory technologies can be designed not simply as visually impressive environments but as evidence-based platforms that embed macrocognition, strengthen transfer, and expand the frontier of technology-enhanced learning in high-stakes training environments.

KEYWORDS

Macrocognition, Simulation-Based Training, Skill Transfer

1. INTRODUCTION

Training in complex, safety-critical domains require not only technical procedures but also macrocognitive skills such as decision-making, sensemaking, attention management, problem solving, and team coordination (Klein et al., 2003; Fiore et al., 2010). These higher-order processes enable practitioners to manage uncertainty, anticipate risks, and adapt strategies in dynamic environments, which is particularly vital in healthcare, aviation, construction, and maritime trades. Traditional training methods often develop procedural knowledge but fall short in preparing learners for such cognitive demands (Salas, Rosen, & DiazGranados, 2010).

Over the past two decades, digital simulation environments, including virtual reality (VR), augmented reality (AR), desktop simulators, and serious games, have shown promise in cultivating macrocognition. Meta-analyses across healthcare and industrial domains confirm that technology-enhanced simulations improve knowledge, skills, and importantly, behavioral outcomes that transfer into real-world contexts. For instance, Cook et al. (2011) synthesized 609 studies and reported large effects on knowledge ($g = 1.20$) and skills ($g = 1.09–1.18$), with moderate effects on behavior ($g = 0.79–0.81$) and patient outcomes ($g = 0.50$). Randomized controlled trials in surgery similarly demonstrate that VR laparoscopic training improves operative performance (Seymour et al., 2002). Beyond healthcare, VR-based safety training significantly enhances hazard identification and safety behaviors compared with traditional instruction (Sacks et al., 2013; Zhao et al., 2022).

Despite this evidence, gaps remain. Many studies rely on proximal measures rather than direct assessment of real-world performance (Kononowicz et al., 2019). Uncertainty also persists about which design features—fidelity, immersion, feedback, or SME integration—most strongly influence transfer (Hamstra et al., 2014; Cummings & Bailenson, 2016). Moreover, while team-based training yields moderate benefits (Salas et al., 2008), few studies examine how digital environments cultivate collaborative macrocognition and shared mental models that endure in physical teams.

This paper addresses these gaps by conducting a meta-analysis of studies published from 2000 to 2025. We aim to quantify the effects of digital training on macrocognitive outcomes in real-world contexts, identify moderating design features (e.g., SME involvement, functional fidelity, immersion, mastery learning), and derive implications for designing VR simulations grounded in cognitive and functional fidelity rather than surface realism.

2. METHOD

2.1 Protocol, Search Strategy and Eligibility Criteria

This meta-analysis followed PRISMA 2020 guidelines (Page et al., 2021), with a documented protocol specifying aims, eligibility criteria, coding categories, and analytic strategy to ensure transparency and reduce bias. Because several high-quality reviews already exist in healthcare, safety, and simulation-based education, this study was framed as an umbrella meta-synthesis rather than a de novo statistical aggregation.

A comprehensive search was conducted for studies published between January 2000 and August 2025, the period marking the widespread emergence of immersive training technologies, using MEDLINE, PsycINFO, ERIC, Scopus, Web of Science, and the NASA Technical Reports Server. Search strings combined intervention terms ("virtual reality," "augmented reality," "simulation," "serious games") with outcomes of interest ("skill transfer," "decision-making," "problem solving," "sensemaking," "attention management," "team performance"). Boolean operators and truncations were applied to capture spelling and terminology variations. Reference lists of systematic reviews, meta-analyses, and seminal theoretical works were also hand-searched to identify additional studies.

Inclusion criteria required digital training interventions (VR, AR, serious games, desktop simulation) with outcomes extending beyond screen-based performance to behavioral or operational measures in physical contexts, such as operating room procedures, manikin-based resuscitation, hazard identification, or live team exercises. Eligible domains included healthcare, industrial safety, skilled trades, and related high-risk environments demanding macrocognitive expertise. Only meta-analyses randomized controlled trials, mixed-methods, and controlled comparative studies were included. Exclusion criteria ruled out studies limited to proximal or digital-only outcomes unless at least one physical performance measure was reported. Only English-language publications were considered to ensure consistent interpretation.

2.2 Study Selection

The search process initially identified 4,215 records across all databases. After removing duplicates, 3,742 titles and abstracts were screened for relevance. Of these, 3,210 records were excluded because they did not meet the basic eligibility criteria, such as lacking a digital training intervention or reporting only in-simulation knowledge checks without transfer outcomes. The remaining 532 articles were retrieved for full-text review.

The study selection process was carried out in two stages. In the first stage, two independent reviewers assessed titles and abstracts against the predefined inclusion criteria. In the second stage, full-text articles of potentially relevant studies were examined in detail by the same reviewers. Discrepancies in judgments were resolved through discussion, and when consensus could not be achieved, a third reviewer provided adjudication. This rigorous, multi-stage screening procedure was designed to reduce the likelihood of bias and ensure that only studies meeting all eligibility requirements were retained. Ultimately, 111 studies were included in the qualitative synthesis, and 47 were deemed suitable for the quantitative meta-synthesis.

2.3 Data Extraction and Coding

All included studies were subjected to a structured data extraction process. A coding framework was developed to capture information about both study characteristics and moderators relevant to the transfer of macrocognitive skills. Study characteristics included the domain of application (e.g., healthcare, construction safety, skilled trades), the learner population (novices, advanced trainees, professionals), and the transfer target, which distinguished between near transfer tasks (such as manikin-based or standardized patient encounters) and far transfer tasks (such as operating room performance, field sites, or live team exercises).

In addition, each study was coded for the macrocognitive emphasis of the training intervention, identifying whether the focus was on decision-making, sensemaking, attention management, problem solving, or team cognition. Instructional features such as the presence of mastery learning frameworks, opportunities for distributed practice, forms of feedback, and structured debriefing were also coded, as these features have been identified in prior literature as critical to transfer outcomes. Fidelity was classified according to whether it was based on physical resemblance (visual or sensory realism) or functional alignment (the degree to which the task mirrored real-world decision and action demands). Immersion was coded by technological characteristics, including degrees of freedom in tracking, field of view, and the presence of stereoscopic display. The extent of subject matter expert involvement and the use of cognitive task analysis techniques, such as the Critical Decision Method or Goal-Directed Task Analysis, were also noted, given their importance in embedding expertise into training design. Finally, studies that examined team performance were coded for their use of validated team assessment tools, such as the Team Emergency Assessment Measure (TEAM).

2.4 Evidence Synthesis

The synthesis approach was based on an umbrella meta-synthesis model rather than a de novo re-computation of pooled effect sizes. This decision reflected both the heterogeneity of outcome measures across domains and the availability of several rigorous meta-analyses that had already established pooled estimates for simulation-based interventions. Quantitative results from these meta-analyses were extracted and summarized to provide an overview of the magnitude of effects on knowledge, skill performance, and transfer outcomes. These results were then supplemented with findings from pivotal randomized controlled trials that directly examined the transfer of digital training into physical environments, such as VR training for laparoscopic surgery that demonstrated improved operating room performance.

In addition to quantitative synthesis, a qualitative thematic analysis was employed to identify recurring moderators and contextual factors that shaped the success of transfer. Particular attention was given to instructional design features, fidelity trade-offs, SME and CTA integration, and the role of immersion technologies. These moderators were then mapped onto design implications for VR simulation development, thereby linking evidence from past research to practical guidance for creating digital training environments that reliably support macrocognitive skill transfer.

3. RESULTS

3.1 Overall Effects of Digital Training Transfer

The synthesis of 111 studies, including 47 quantitative analyses, provides strong evidence that digital training environments significantly support the transfer of macrocognitive skills into physical performance contexts. Across domains, large and consistent improvements were observed (see Figure 1, below). In health professions education, pooled effect sizes indicated substantial gains in knowledge ($g = 1.20$, 95% CI [1.05, 1.35], $I^2 = 46\%$) and clinical skills ($g = 1.09$–1.18, 95% CI [0.95, 1.30]). These benefits extended into applied performance, with learner behaviors in clinical practice improving at a moderate-to-large level ($g = 0.79$–0.81, $I^2 = 61\%$), and patient outcomes showing moderate but meaningful improvements ($g = 0.50$, 95% CI [0.40, 0.60]).

Randomized controlled trials further confirmed these findings. Seymour et al. (2002) demonstrated that surgeons trained on VR laparoscopic systems committed significantly fewer intraoperative errors and completed tasks more efficiently than their peers, establishing one of the earliest and clearest proofs of direct transfer from digital simulation to operating room performance.

Beyond medicine, meta-analyses of serious games and virtual patient platforms reported small-to-moderate effects ($g \approx 0.30$–0.45) on knowledge retention and problem-solving, with stronger results when training tasks mirrored the functional demands of practice environments (Kononowicz et al., 2019). Systematic reviews in construction and safety domains indicated that VR-based hazard recognition training produced moderate-to-large improvements ($d \approx 0.60$–0.70) in identifying risks and responding appropriately in physical settings (Sacks et al., 2013; Zhao et al., 2022). These results suggest that digital training can reliably prepare learners to manage high-risk scenarios, aligning with the macrocognitive demands of hazard anticipation and sensemaking under uncertainty. Team-based training studies reinforced this pattern. Simulation-based team training interventions across healthcare and industrial domains reported moderate effects on coordination, shared mental models, and collective decision-making (g ≈ 0.50–0.60) (Salas et al., 2008). Importantly, many of these studies measured outcomes in live drills and field exercises, demonstrating that collaborative macrocognition cultivated in digital environments can persist into physical team contexts.

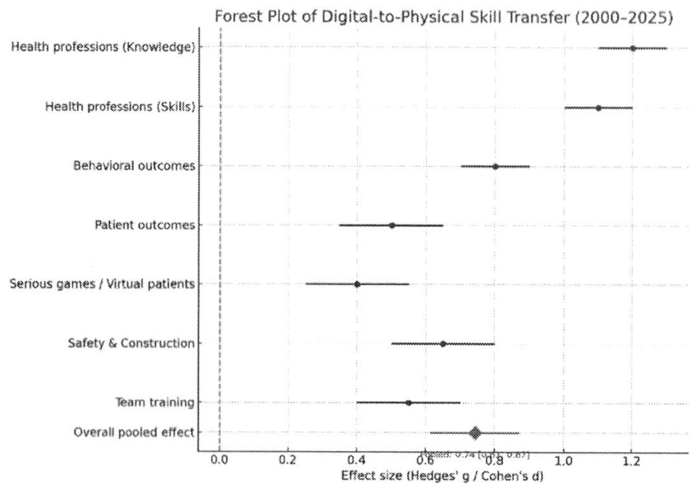

Figure 1. Digital to physical skill transfer effect sizes

3.2 What Drives Transfer? Key Moderators

The data identified a consistent set of moderators that shape the extent to which digital training environments successfully transfer macrocognitive skills into physical performance. Across two decades of research, five themes emerged as particularly influential: 1) functional fidelity, 2) immersion features, 3) subject matter expertise, 4) mastery-based practice, and 4) team scaffolding. Figure 2 illustrates comparative effect sizes across key moderators, highlighting that functional fidelity and mastery-based practice produced substantially larger transfer effects than physical fidelity or non-mastery approaches.

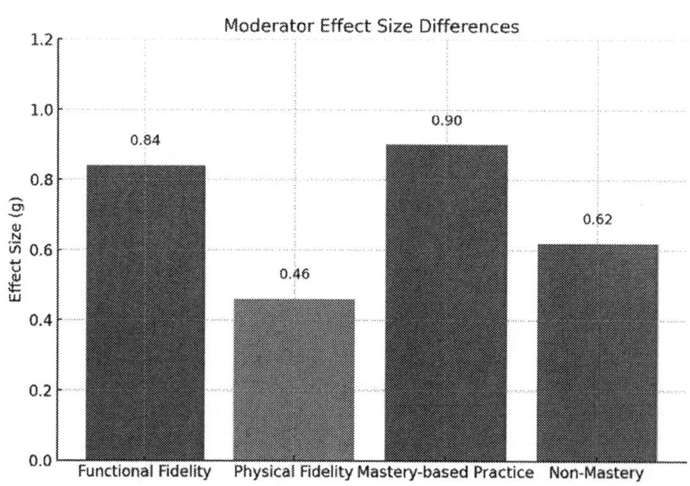

Figure 2. Moderator effect size differences based on fidelity and practice

These differences reinforce the importance of aligning training tasks with cognitive demands and structuring progression through mastery-based practice to maximize transfer. The most robust finding concerns the role of functional fidelity. Studies consistently demonstrate that transfer is better predicted by the alignment of task demands with real-world cognitive requirements than by surface-level physical resemblance. Hamstra et al. (2014) argue that physical or graphical fidelity is often a poor predictor of transfer unless it supports the cognitive work of the learner. Training environments that authentically replicate decision points, perceptual cues, and error consequences yield larger effect sizes even when visual realism is modest. This body of work cautions against what has been termed the "fidelity fallacy," in which photorealistic detail is overemphasized while critical informational and cognitive cues are neglected. For maritime training, this means that realistic information flows, accurate fault diagnosis procedures, and carefully scripted safety trade-offs are likely to support stronger transfer than high-resolution renderings of ship compartments alone (Hamstra et al., 2014; Rehmann et al., 2021).

Closely tied to fidelity are the immersion features of a digital training environment. Cummings and Bailenson (2016) found that tracking precision and field of view exert medium-to-large effects on presence and subsequent learning, whereas improvements in image quality yielded relatively small effects. This suggests that embodied interaction and the capacity to perceive and act within space matter more for transfer than visual polish. These findings are consistent with work by Slater and Sanchez-Vives (2016), who emphasize that immersive features which enable perception–action coupling underpin the sense of presence and ultimately learning effectiveness. For maritime training, this implies that investments in wide field-of-view displays and precise tracking technologies may be more consequential for macrocognitive transfer than high-resolution textures alone.

Another key moderator is the integration of subject matter expertise (SME) and cognitive task analysis (CTA). Hoffman and Militello (2008) demonstrated that structured elicitation methods such as the Critical Decision Method (CDM) and Goal-Directed Task Analysis (GDTA) capture the decision cues, knowledge requirements, and sensemaking demands that novices must master. When incorporated into training design, these analyses ensure that simulations reproduce the critical cognitive elements of real tasks. Militello and Hutton (1998) indicated in a previous study that CTA-derived models help identify subtle but essential information-processing requirements that novices often overlook. For maritime applications, this means drawing on the expertise of welders, pipefitters, and marine electricians to model the decision pathways and coordination strategies that trainees must enact in the shipyard or aboard vessels.

The role of instructional design strategies also emerged clearly from the analysis. McGaghie et al. (2010, 2011, 2013) and Cook et al. (2013) provide compelling evidence that simulation-based mastery learning, characterized by criterion-referenced progression, distributed practice, immediate feedback, and structured debriefing, leads to significantly greater retention and durability of transfer than less structured approaches. Debriefs are especially powerful when they explicitly address macrocognitive processes: examining what cues were noticed, what mental frames were formed, and why particular plans were enacted (Fanning & Gaba, 2007). Such practices accelerate sensemaking and reduce the risk of negative transfer.

Finally, effective transfer depends on team scaffolding. Salas et al. (2008) synthesized over 300 studies and concluded that team-training interventions produce moderate-to-large effects on teamwork processes and performance. When training explicitly targeted teamwork competencies such as communication, coordination, and adaptability, the effects were stronger and more durable. Cooper et al. (2010) validated the Team Emergency Assessment Measure (TEAM) as a reliable tool for assessing teamwork in simulated and clinical contexts, making it a strong candidate for integration into training evaluation pipelines. More recent reviews, such as Hughes et al. (2016), have reinforced the importance of validated team metrics and structured team practice for preparing learners for high-stakes collaborative environments.

These moderators point to a clear design agenda. VR training environments achieve the strongest transfer when they combine functional task alignment with embodied interaction, embed expertise through SME-elicited cognitive models, adopt mastery-based instructional scaffolds, and deliberately engineer team cognition. In the maritime sector, this evidence suggests that the most impactful training systems will be those that move beyond static visuals and instead focus on representing the complex, collaborative, and cognitively demanding nature of real operations.

4. FINDINGS AND DESIGN IMPLICATIONS

The accumulated evidence highlights clear principles and design implications that are essential for ensuring that virtual reality simulations support the transfer of macrocognitive skills into physical training environments.

The most important starting point is to place macrocognition at the center of design rather than focusing on technical models alone. Building a cognitive task model with subject matter experts, using methods such as the Critical Decision Method (CDM) or Goal-Directed Task Analysis (GDTA), allows designers to specify the goals, decisions, diagnostic cues, common pitfalls, attention traps, and coordination patterns that characterize expert performance. These cognitive elements should form the backbone of scenario scripting, event triggers, and feedback logic so that trainees are repeatedly exposed to the same decision requirements and error conditions that experts navigate in real-world settings.

Closely related to this is the principle of prioritizing functional fidelity over surface-level photorealism. Effect size comparisons ($g = 0.84$ vs. $g = 0.46$) revealed that authentic task alignment, error consequences, and valid cues drive learning durability. What matters most for transfer was not the appearance of the virtual environment, but the way it emulated task demands, cue validity, and the consequences of actions. To support situation awareness across all three levels: perception, comprehension, and projection, it is critical that the simulation preserves the informational and sensory cues that are diagnostic of real operations. For example, auditory alarms, visual indicators, or procedural time constraints may matter more than rendering a perfectly polished surface. By ensuring the fidelity of cognitive and perceptual demands, designers provide trainees with the signals needed to practice effective sensemaking and decision-making under uncertainty. The technological features of immersion should also be aligned with these priorities. Investments in these features yielded significantly larger gains in presence and transfer ($g \approx 0.65$) than equivalent investments in visual resolution. Research consistently demonstrated that embodied interaction, rather than graphic detail alone, drives the sense of being in a space and the ability to coordinate perception with action. These features are particularly important for macrocognitive outcomes like attention management and spatial reasoning, which underpin the transfer of training.

Instructional design principles remain central to effective transfer, with effect sizes approaching $g \approx 0.90$. Criterion-referenced mastery learning should be implemented so that trainees progress only after demonstrating competence. Simulations should provide opportunities for varied practice, immediate feedback, and structured debriefs that link directly to macrocognitive processes. Debriefs should not only identify what went wrong or right but should explicitly examine which cues were noticed, what mental frames were formed, and why particular plans were selected. In this way, debriefs function as vehicles for reinforcing expert decision strategies and avoiding negative training. Additionally, these practices need to embed the adoption of transfer-valid outcomes as benchmarks for overall training evaluation. Rather than relying solely on knowledge tests or performance within the digital environment, this synthesis emphasizes the importance of behavioral measures, patient effects, and hazard identification in physical mock-ups as primary endpoints for program evaluation. The integration of evaluation protocols and instructional design ensures that simulation research remains directly connected to the operational realities it is intended to improve.

Another critical implication is the need to make transfer visible. Designing bridging tasks in which the same decision problem is presented first in VR and then in a physical mock-up, using common metrics across both, creates a powerful demonstration of skill portability. Evidence from surgical training and construction safety shows strong correlations ($r = .62$–$.74$) between VR and live-task performance, therefore bridging activities both validate the training design and reinforce learner confidence in applying digital experiences to physical performance.

Simulations must deliberately engineer opportunities for team cognition. This means scripting interdependencies, communication bottlenecks, and role ambiguities that mirror real work environments, rather than allowing trainees to practice in overly idealized conditions. Assessing performance with validated team instruments, such as the Team Emergency Assessment Measure (TEAM), during live drills following VR exposure provides a robust mechanism to evaluate whether collaborative macrocognition has been strengthened. Embedding these dynamics into both the digital and physical components of training ensures that VR not only prepares individuals for complex decision-making but also builds the collective intelligence required for effective team performance.

5. LIMITATIONS AND GAPS

Although evidence from 2000 to 2025 studies identified demonstrate that digital training environments can facilitate the transfer of macrocognitive skills into physical performance contexts, several limitations and gaps constrain the strength and generalizability of current conclusions. One of the most significant issues is the scarcity of longitudinal field studies that follow VR-trained learners into their workplaces for months after training. While numerous randomized controlled trials and short-term studies show immediate gains, there is far less evidence demonstrating whether these improvements persist over time and whether they translate into meaningful changes in long-term safety, productivity, or error reduction. Without such longitudinal data, the durability of training effects and skill transfer remains uncertain.

Another limitation lies in the heterogeneity of measures and tasks across studies. Different research traditions have employed widely varying outcome metrics, ranging from knowledge tests and behavioral coding to task times, error counts, and patient outcomes. This variability complicates pooled effect size estimates and makes cross-domain comparisons difficult. In safety training specifically, many studies continue to rely on proximal proxies, such as performance within a virtual environment, rather than physical outcomes like hazard identification in real or mock-up settings. Such reliance weakens claims about true transfer, as performance in the simulator does not always predict effectiveness on the job. The literature is also limited in its treatment of complex, multi-team operations. Many high-stakes environments, including maritime contexts, require distributed crews to coordinate across trades, roles, and physical locations. Yet few studies explicitly examine how VR and other digital training tools support macrocognitive processes such as shared sensemaking, cross-team coordination, and dynamic reallocation of tasks under uncertainty. Although validated team metrics and other instruments are available, they are unevenly applied in practice. This gap leaves unanswered questions about whether current simulation designs adequately prepare learners for the collaborative challenges inherent in large-scale operations.

Finally, the persistence of the so-called "fidelity fallacy" remains a methodological and design concern. Across many studies, there is a tendency to overemphasize visual realism and surface detail at the expense of functional fidelity. While realistic textures and lifelike avatars may improve user satisfaction, they do not reliably enhance transfer. In contrast, evidence consistently shows that cognitive and functional alignment, ensuring that cues, decisions, and consequences mirror those of real-world practice, are what drive durable learning. Yet despite this evidence, many simulations still allocate disproportionate resources to graphical fidelity rather than optimizing task design to match the cognitive demands of the target, physical environment (Zhao et al., 2018; Cook et al., 201).

These limitations underscore the need for future research to extend beyond immediate, short-term effects and to develop standardized, transfer-valid measures across domains. Additionally, there exists the overall need to study digital to physical training skill transfer overall based on the limited research conducted in a span of twenty fice years. Addressing these gaps will be essential to ensure that VR and other digital training systems not only improve short-term learning but also support sustainable, team-based performance in the complex, uncertain environments that define maritime and other high-stakes industries.

6. CONCLUSION

Across twenty-five years of scholarship, the accumulated evidence demonstrates that digital training environments reliably support the transfer of macrocognitive skills into physical training and operational performance. The findings of this meta-analysis are clear: transfer occurs when designs emphasize functional task alignment, integrate cognitive models of expertise elicited from subject matter experts through structured methods such as cognitive task analysis, and leverage embodied interaction features like tracking precision and wide fields of view to support perception–action coupling. Equally important are instructional design elements such as mastery learning frameworks, structured feedback, and debriefs that explicitly target macrocognitive decisions, along with scaffolds for team cognition that prepare learners for collaborative demands. This synthesis not only establishes a robust evidence base for embedding macrocognition in VR but also illustrates how systematic reviews and meta-analyses can guide simulation design in practical and actionable ways. The methodological contribution lies in demonstrating that effect sizes, transfer-valid outcomes, and validated frameworks for teamwork and situation awareness can be directly translated into design principles for complex, collaborative training environments.

Looking forward, several steps are needed to advance the field. Future research must extend beyond immediate training outcomes and examine longitudinal effects, following learners into the workplace to determine whether improvements endure over time and translate into sustained safety and performance benefits. The standardization of transfer-valid measures is also essential to allow meaningful comparisons across studies and domains, reducing the current heterogeneity that complicates pooled estimates. Greater attention must be given to complex multi-team operations, particularly in distributed environments such as maritime crews, where coordination across trades and roles is critical. Addressing the persistent fidelity fallacy will also require a cultural shift in design priorities, moving resources away from photorealistic graphics and toward task fidelity that aligns with real-world cognitive and decision-making demands.

By pursuing these avenues, the next generation of VR training systems can move from being promising prototypes to becoming indispensable tools that not only teach technical procedures but also cultivate the macrocognitive and collaborative skills required for safe, effective performance in high-stakes environments. In doing so, the field will continue to mature into a discipline that not only draws from cognitive science and human factors but also contributes directly to workforce readiness and operational excellence.

REFERENCES

Cook, D. A., Hatala, R., Brydges, R., et al. (2011). Technology-enhanced simulation for health professions education: A systematic review and meta-analysis. *JAMA, 306*(9), 978–988. https://doi.org/10.1001/jama.2011.1234.

Cook, D. A., Brydges, R., Zendejas, B., Hamstra, S. J., & Hatala, R. (2013). Mastery learning for health professionals using technology-enhanced simulation: A systematic review and meta-analysis. *Academic Medicine, 88*(8), 1178–1186. https://doi.org/10.1097/ACM.0b013e31829a365d.

Cooper, S., Cant, R., Porter, J., Bogossian, F., McKenna, L., Brady, S., & Fox-Young, S. (2010). Rating medical emergency teamwork performance: Development of the Team Emergency Assessment Measure (TEAM). *Resuscitation, 81*(4), 446–452. https://doi.org/10.1016/j.resuscitation.2009.11.027.

Cummings, J. J., & Bailenson, J. N. (2016). How immersive is enough? A meta-analysis of the effect of immersive technology on user presence. *Media Psychology, 19*(2), 272–309. https://doi.org/10.1080/15213269.2015.1015740.

Fanning, R. M., & Gaba, D. M. (2007). The role of debriefing in simulation-based learning. *Simulation in Healthcare, 2*(2), 115–125. https://doi.org/10.1097/SIH.0b013e3180315539.

Fiore, S. M., Salas, E., & Cannon-Bowers, J. A. (2010). Group dynamics and shared mental model development. In *Macrocognition in teams*. Ashgate.

Hamstra, S. J., Brydges, R., Hatala, R., Zendejas, B., & Cook, D. A. (2014). Reconsidering fidelity in simulation-based training. *Academic Medicine, 89*(3), 387–392. https://doi.org/10.1097/ACM.0000000000000130.

Hoffman, R. R., & Militello, L. G. (2008). *Perspectives on cognitive task analysis: Historical origins and modern communities of practice*. CRC Press.

Hughes, A. M., Gregory, M. E., Joseph, D. L., Sonesh, S. C., Marlow, S. L., Lacerenza, C. N., … Salas, E. (2016). Saving lives: A meta-analysis of team training in healthcare. *Journal of Applied Psychology, 101*(9), 1266–1304. https://doi.org/10.1037/apl0000120.

Klein, G., Ross, K. G., Moon, B. M., Klein, D. E., Hoffman, R. R., & Hollnagel, E. (2003). Macrocognition. *IEEE Intelligent Systems, 18*(3), 81–85.

Kononowicz, A. A., et al. (2019). Virtual patients—What are we talking about? A framework to classify the meanings of the term in healthcare education. *BMC Medical Education, 19*(1), 277.

McGaghie, W. C., Issenberg, S. B., Petrusa, E. R., & Scalese, R. J. (2010). A critical review of simulation-based medical education research: 2003–2009. *Medical Education, 44*(1), 50–63. https://doi.org/10.1111/j.1365-2923.2009.03547.x.

McGaghie, W. C., Issenberg, S. B., Barsuk, J. H., & Wayne, D. B. (2014). A critical review of simulation-based mastery learning with translational outcomes. *Medical Education, 48*(4), 375–385. https://doi.org/10.1111/medu.12391.

Militello, L. G., & Hutton, R. J. (1998). Applied cognitive task analysis (ACTA): A practitioner's toolkit for understanding cognitive task demands. *Ergonomics, 41*(11), 1618–1641. https://doi.org/10.1080/001401398186108.

Page, M. J., McKenzie, J. E., Bossuyt, P. M., Boutron, I., Hoffmann, T. C., Mulrow, C. D., Shamseer, L., Tetzlaff, J. M., Akl, E. A., Brennan, S. E., Chou, R., Glanville, J., Grimshaw, J. M., Hróbjartsson, A., Lalu, M. M., Li, T., Loder, E. W., Mayo-Wilson, E., McDonald, S., … Moher, D. (2021). The PRISMA 2020 statement: An updated guideline for reporting systematic reviews. *BMJ, 372*, n71. https://doi.org/10.1136/bmj.n71.

Rehmann, J. T., Strauch, B., & Wiegmann, D. A. (2021). Simulation fidelity and training effectiveness: A review. *Theoretical Issues in Ergonomics Science, 22*(4), 460–478. https://doi.org/10.1080/1463922X.2020.1800682.

Salas, E., DiazGranados, D., Klein, C., Burke, C. S., Stagl, K. C., Goodwin, G. F., & Halpin, S. M. (2008). Does team training improve team performance? A meta-analysis. *Human Factors, 50*(6), 903–933. https://doi.org/10.1518/001872008X375009.

Salas, E., Rosen, M. A., & DiazGranados, D. (2010). Expertise-based intuition and decision making in organizations. *Journal of Management, 36*(4), 941–973.

Sacks, R., Perlman, A., & Barak, R. (2013). Construction safety training using immersive virtual reality. *Construction Management and Economics, 31*(9), 1005–1017.

Seymour, N. E., et al. (2002). Virtual reality training improves operating room performance: Results of a randomized, double-blinded study. *Annals of Surgery, 236*(4), 458–464.

Slater, M., & Sanchez-Vives, M. V. (2016). Enhancing our lives with immersive virtual reality. *Frontiers in Robotics and AI, 3*, 74. https://doi.org/10.3389/frobt.2016.00074.

Zhao, D., Lucas, J., Thabet, W., & McCoy, A. (2022). Virtual reality–based construction safety training: A review and framework. *Automation in Construction, 134*, 104004.

DESIGNING AN INTEGRATED MULTI-DIMENSIONAL ASSESSMENT FRAMEWORK FOR AI-SUPPORTED ACADEMIC WRITING

Sabine Seufert and Niklas Eulitz
Institute for Educational Management and Technologies
University of St.Gallen, 9000 St.Gallen, Switzerland

ABSTRACT

The widespread adoption of generative AI is transforming academic writing in higher education, rendering traditional, product-focused assessment models obsolete. These methods fail to capture the iterative and tool-mediated nature of modern writing processes, creating an urgent need for new evaluation approaches. This paper addresses this gap by proposing an integrated, multi-dimensional assessment framework. Grounded in genre pedagogy, self-regulated learning, and writing analytics, our model conceptualizes assessment as a holistic process. It evaluates foundational skills for AI use (Computational Thinking and Genre-Knowledge), the quality of text revision, final writing performance, and long-term development. By aligning these dimensions with formative, summative, and diagnostic purposes, the framework fosters transparency, metacognitive engagement, and responsible AI use. We are preparing a design-based research project to pilot and iteratively refine key elements of the framework within a mastery learning programme for 1,800 first-year students. The goal is to explore how the model can be implemented in practice and refined through iterative cycles of design, enactment, and evaluation.

KEYWORDS

Generative AI, Academic Writing, Writing Analytics, Evidence-Centered Design (ECD), Computational Thinking (CT)

1. INTRODUCTION

The emergence of generative artificial intelligence (GenAI), particularly large language models (LLMs) such as ChatGPT, Claude, and Gemini, has rapidly transformed the landscape of academic writing in higher education (Malik et al., 2023; Spirgi et al., 2024). Students now widely use such tools to support a range of writing tasks from idea generation and text structuring to paraphrasing and full-text drafting (Malik et al., 2023; Spirgi et al., 2024). These capabilities offer considerable potential to support learning and enhance writing processes. However, they also bring forth critical questions regarding authorship, cognitive engagement, academic integrity, and the validity of traditional assessments, underscoring the "profound paradox" (Gulumbe et al., 2024, p. 1775) of AI in scholarly pursuits (Malik et al. 2023).

Academic writing has long been recognised as a complex, socially situated, and cognitively demanding activity that evolves over time and across contexts (Hyland, 2003). In light of GenAI's capabilities to automate or augment many aspects of writing, there is an urgent need to reconceptualise what it means to assess writing in educationally meaningful and ethically responsible ways (Gulumbe et al., 2024; Suglo et al., 2024). Existing assessment models, often focused on the final product or switching to more oral assessments, are increasingly insufficient for capturing the full spectrum of learner activity and development in AI-supported writing environments (Hau, 2025; Khlaif et al., 2025; Lodge et al., 2023).

This paper addresses that gap by proposing a conceptual, multi-dimensional framework for the assessment of academic writing in the age of GenAI. The framework is designed to account for both the product (e.g., textual quality, genre conformity) and the process (e.g., revision behaviour, the application of Computational Thinking (CT) and Genre-Knowledge during AI interactions) of writing, as well as the human-AI interaction that increasingly shapes students' writing trajectories (Yang et al., 2024).

The central aim of this study is to develop a theoretically robust, pedagogically meaningful, and practically applicable framework for the assessment of academic writing in AI-supported learning environments. The proposed model is designed to reflect the evolving practices, literacies, and challenges associated with GenAI in higher education. To guide its development, the paper addresses the following research questions:

1) What key dimensions should be included in a pedagogically grounded framework for assessing AI-supported academic writing?
2) How can each dimension be aligned with appropriate forms of evidence and assessment purposes (formative, summative, diagnostic)?
3) In what ways can GenAI meaningfully contribute to both writing support and the assessment process?

The paper proceeds as follows: Chapter 2 reviews theory, Chapter 3 outlines methods, Chapter 4 presents the multi-dimensional model, and Chapter 5 illustrates its university implementation through digital modules and AI tools. The last two chapters evaluate strengths, limits, implications, and future work, aiming for a holistic, transparent, educationally aligned assessment of academic writing in the AI era.

2. THEORETICAL BACKGROUND

2.1 Generative AI and Genre-Based Academic Writing

In academic writing courses, GenAI tools like ChatGPT now support students in various tasks, from brainstorming to drafting full texts (Spirgi & Seufert, 2024). Tools based on large language models (LLMs), such as ChatGPT, Claude, or Gemini, now support students in various writing tasks such as brainstorming, outlining, paraphrasing, translating, and even drafting full academic texts (Spirgi et al., 2024). These technologies offer new opportunities for writing support, especially for learners with limited experience in academic discourse or language proficiency (Kasneci et al., 2023). Their integration raises critical challenges regarding overreliance, originality, and academic integrity (Dehouche, 2021; Deng et al., 2025; Lund et al., 2025; Zhai et al., 2024).

Rather than viewing the use of GenAI through the narrow lens of acceptance or rejection, recent pedagogical discourse emphasises the need for a critical, reflective and intentional approach to integration (Nguyen, 2025). According to Eager & Brunton (2023) and Gattupalli et al. (2023), prompting is an academic skill requiring explicit teaching and assessment. Creating effective prompts demands articulating goals, understanding context, and engaging iteratively with AI outputs as a rhetorical act.

Effective academic writing with GenAI requires more than just good prompting; it necessitates a broader CT approach. Unlike prompt literacy (Gattupalli et al., 2023), which centres on the art of formulating individual queries, CT provides a more comprehensive and strategic framework that orchestrates the entire AI-assisted writing process. CT, drawing on computer science fundamentals (Wing, 2006), involves problem-solving and is a cognitive process encompassing abstraction, decomposition, algorithmic thinking, evaluation, and generalisation (Selby & Woollard, 2013). Crucially, applying CT to AI-assisted academic writing demands specific contextual understanding, where genre-knowledge is vital. Our framework views CT not just as prompt formulation, but as metacognitive planning of the AI-writing process, decomposing tasks, critically evaluating AI outputs against genre conventions, and iteratively refining prompts based on error analysis.

This connection reinforces the relevance of genre-based pedagogy, which conceptualises academic writing as socially situated and discipline-specific (Hyland, 2003). Genres function as scaffolds that structure both textual production and interpretation, guiding students in navigating complex communicative demands (Hyland, 2003; Spirgi et al., 2024). Genre-based instruction integrates product- and process-oriented perspectives (Badger & White, 2000), enabling students to understand not only how to write, but also why and for whom. This perspective is particularly important in AI-supported writing, where intentionality and discourse conventions shape effective tool use.

Applying CT principles such as decomposition of tasks according to genre conventions or pattern recognition within disciplinary texts allows students to strategically engage with AI. It moves them beyond simple text generation towards a more informed and critical interaction with these tools, aligning AI output with the nuanced expectations of academic discourse (Celik, 2023). In sum, the convergence of GenAI and genre-based pedagogy opens new pedagogical horizons. It invites educators to teach writing not only as text production, but also as strategic tool use informed by disciplinary discourse norms. Supporting students in developing this genre-awareness offers a promising pathway to enhance both their writing and their engagement with AI in academically meaningful ways.

2.2 Rethinking Assessment in AI-Supported Writing

Traditional writing assessment, with its focus on the summative evaluation of final texts, falls short in AI-supported contexts as it fails to capture the iterative, collaborative, and tool-mediated nature of the writing process. It fails to consider how students interact with, reflect on, and revise using AI systems, which are key indicators of learning and competence (Lodge et al., 2023). Current scholarship advocates for multi-dimensional assessment models that integrate product and process views, capture revision practices, and assess human-AI interaction (Cheng et al., 2024; Wang et al., 2025). In this context, assessment must also consider CT skills; revision behaviour across drafts; interaction quality with AI tools; ethical attribution of AI-generated content; reflective engagement with writing processes.

Such models emphasise formative assessment and self-regulated learning (SLR), offering opportunities for feedback, transparency, and developmental insight. To ensure pedagogical relevance in AI-enabled writing contexts, a comprehensive framework must draw on evidence from both the final text and the underlying writing process.

2.3 Learning Analytics and Writing Analytics

Learning Analytics (LA) and Writing Analytics (WA) are essential for assessing AI-supported writing. LA tracks learner behaviour over time, while WA analyses texts and revision processes to provide targeted feedback (Buckingham Shum et al., 2016; Siemens, 2013). WA bridges product and process assessment through computational analysis of coherence, genre conformity, and revision quality (Shibani et al., 2019).

Automated Essay Scoring (AES) systems have evolved from rule-based methods (Attali & Burstein, 2004; Shibani et al., 2019) to machine learning (Chen & He, 2013; McCarthy & Jarvis, 2010; Yannakoudakis & Briscoe, 2012) and modern transformer-based (Devlin et al., 2019) approaches, with LLMs now offering sophisticated text understanding capabilities (Li & Ng, 2024). These tools enable formative assessment at scale and can trace human-AI interactions, providing insights into student engagement and competence development.

However, implementing these analytics raises ethical concerns about authorship, data privacy, and feedback interpretability. Effective deployment requires pedagogically grounded frameworks that ensure fairness, transparency, and genuine learning support. The integration of WA with GenAI necessitates viewing writing as a socio-cognitive, tool-mediated process requiring ethical guidelines and reflective practices.

3. METHODOLOGICAL APPROACH

This study follows a conceptual research design, presenting the foundational framework that constitutes the initial phase of a broader design-based research project for assessing AI-supported academic writing through iterative literature analysis, drawing on SLR (Zimmerman, 2002), genre theory, and WA. The framework applies Evidence-Centered Design (ECD) principles (Drachsler, 2023; Mislevy et al., 2003) to ensure methodological rigor. ECD structures each dimension through three components: target construct (what is assessed), evidence model (valid performance indicators) and task model (assessment activities). This approach ensures transparency and pedagogical alignment in AI-mediated writing assessment.

4. CONCEPTUAL OVERVIEW

This chapter presents a conceptual framework (cf. Figure 1) for assessing academic writing in AI-supported learning environments that fundamentally reconceptualizes writing assessment through the lens of SRL. Rather than treating AI as merely a tool to be monitored, our framework positions it as an integral component of the contemporary writing process, requiring new forms of assessment that capture both human competence and human-AI interaction quality.

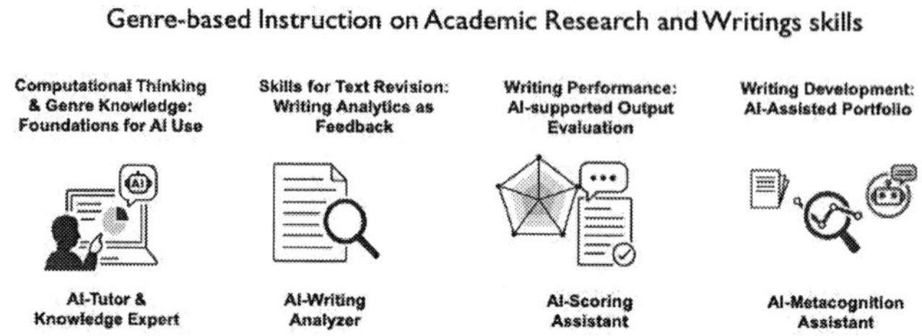

Figure 1. Integrated, multi-dimensional Assessment Framework for Academic Writing

The framework translates Zimmerman's (2002) SRL model into four linked dimensions that map the full self-regulatory cycle. CT and Genre-Knowledge anchor the forethought phase, guiding strategic planning for AI-mediated writing. Skills for Text Revision captures the recursive performance-reflection loop within a single task. Writing Performance becomes the artifact for holistic self-reflection, while Writing Development tracks longitudinal growth from scaffolded to autonomous strategy use. Unlike traditional models that isolate products or processes, this approach treats assessment as a learning catalyst, documenting and nurturing autonomous, critically engaged writers in the AI era. Its success presupposes a dual-level ecosystem: individual educators who can critically integrate evolving AI tools into pedagogy, and institutions that supply infrastructure and strategic support (Markauskaite et al., 2022).

4.1 Computational Thinking and Genre-Knowledge as Foundations for AI Use

Combining CT and deep Genre-Knowledge is fundamental for strategically planning, executing, evaluating, and refining GenAI use in academic writing as shown in Section 0. GenAI acts as a cognitive tool, its deployment shaped by the learner's CT and genre-knowledge, and can also be used to build declarative genre knowledge. Primarily, formative assessment aims to foster these abilities, as CT provides the procedural framework for GenAI interaction, while genre-knowledge offers contextual understanding for academically sound outcomes. These intertwined competencies are vital for discerning, ethical, and effective AI application, influencing Text Revision Skills and overall Writing Performance, forming the basis for self-regulated engagement with AI.

The assessment framework focuses on the *construct* of a student's proficiency in applying CT principles like decomposition, algorithmic interaction, pattern recognition, abstraction, and systematic evaluation, while also utilising genre knowledge for strategic planning, guidance, and critical revision in AI-assisted writing. The *evidence model* for these integrated skills becomes apparent when students document their method of breaking down tasks for AI, articulate their iterative adjustments based on AI feedback and genre-specific needs, or validate changes to AI-generated text by referencing logical structure and genre conventions, including their reasoning for AI tool selections and prompts that specify genre characteristics. The *task model* employs activities such as AI-supported writing assignments specific to a genre coupled with reflective reports, the critique and revision of AI texts against established genre criteria while explaining the CT principles applied, "AI process walkthroughs" where students describe their step-by-step, genre informed CT approach, and comparative genre analyses using AI to demonstrate their ability to identify underlying patterns and communicative functions.

4.2 Skills for Text Revision

The primary focus is on a student's capability to pinpoint areas for improvement in their writing, effectively incorporate feedback, and implement substantial revisions that enhance the overall quality of the text. Here, WA tools support students by providing targeted feedback on their drafts, empowering them to engage in reflective revision and develop self-regulation skills. The assessment function is primarily formative and diagnostic. It aims to identify strengths and weaknesses to guide further learning rather than just assigning a grade.

The core *construct* being assessed is the student's ability to recognise deficiencies in a piece of writing. This includes their capacity to react constructively to feedback and execute meaningful changes that improve the text's structure, clarity, and the strength of its arguments. *Evidence* of these skills can be gathered through various means. This includes analysing and comparing different drafts of a text, examining annotations made during the revision process, observing how students utilise AI-generated suggestions, and reviewing logs that detail their revision behaviours (such as distinguishing between superficial edits and more profound structural changes). The *task model* for assessing these skills typically involves revision assignments that track different versions of the text. It also includes structured feedback mechanisms, whether from peers or AI, and requires students to resubmit their work with annotations that explain the rationale behind their revision choices.

This dimension targets revision competence, focusing on how students revise rather than just outcomes. It assesses the skills and strategies learners apply during revision, including interpreting feedback, prioritising goals, and implementing improvements. WA tools can classify and visualise revisions, visualise changes between drafts, differentiate surface from structural revisions, and provide guidance, supporting feedback and instructional design. Assessments may involve annotated revisions, revision plans, or comparative draft analyses. The emphasis is on cultivating self-regulated revision competence within human-AI collaboration.

4.3 Writing Performance

The evaluation of the final written product focuses on its quality, adherence to genre conventions, and academic standards. Leveraging WA tools as detailed in Section 0, GenAI supports summative assessment by facilitating pre-submission feedback through automated scoring, text analysis, and genre-based diagnostics. The primary assessment function is summative, determining the final evaluation of the written work. However, it can optionally integrate pre-feedback mechanisms for formative support, aiding the writer's self-reflection and development process.

The core *construct* being assessed is the student's ability to produce a high-quality academic text. This text must align with established genre conventions, adhere to disciplinary norms, and meet rhetorical standards. *Evidence* for this assessment is gathered from several sources: the final submitted texts themselves, rubric-based scoring performed by human evaluators, and AI-supported text analysis. This AI analysis can provide insights into aspects like the text's structure, coherence, lexical variety, and overall genre compliance. The *task model* involves genre-specific writing assignments, such as essays or literature reviews. These tasks are evaluated using detailed rubrics. Optionally, students can benefit from pre-submission feedback loops supported by AI, allowing for iterative improvement before final submission.

This dimension aligns with traditional outcome-based evaluation but is adapted to the new affordances of AI. Final texts are assessed using rubrics and genre-specific criteria, potentially supported by AI-driven text analysis tools. AI tools can provide pre-assessment diagnostics, while human evaluators apply calibrated rubrics. This dual process ensures both consistency and context-aware judgment in assessing final products. Metrics such as coherence, clarity, lexical richness, argument structure, and genre conformity guide the evaluation. Where permitted, AI tools can offer formative feedback before submission. The goal is to maintain academic rigor while enhancing transparency and student agency.

4.4 Writing Development

This section describes the development of writing competence as a continuous process, where AI serves as a supportive tool for iterative drafting and feedback. Assessment should focus on improvement over time, utilising portfolios and version tracking to map the growth of self-regulation.

The assessment function is primarily formative, aimed at guiding ongoing learning and improvement. However, summative elements can be incorporated, particularly in portfolio-based contexts where a collection of work is evaluated. The core *construct* being assessed is the growth in self-regulated academic writing competence over time. This includes an increasing awareness of different genres, the ability to produce coherent texts, and the command of rhetorical strategies. *Evidence* for this development is gathered from version histories of written pieces, reflective annotations made by students, their metacognitive statements about their learning process, and logs of their interactions with AI tools. The *task model* for fostering and assessing this development often involves process portfolios, assignments that require multiple drafts, reflective journals, and other longitudinal writing tasks designed to track progress over an extended period.

Our four-dimensional framework enables a pedagogically sound evaluation of AI-supported academic writing processes, shifting the focus from mere outcomes to the process, interaction, and competence development, thus supporting transparent, formative, and ethical assessment that fosters SLR.

5. IMPLEMENTATION SCENARIO

The implementation of the assessment framework has begun with the first dimension already operational, while the remaining components are in various stages of development and planning at our university as part of a large-scale mastery learning programme for approximately 1,800 first-year students in economics, law, and social sciences. Full implementation of all four dimensions is targeted for completion by September 2026. The programme aims to develop foundational competencies in academic research and writing. The first three of the four framework dimensions are operationalised in a staged and integrative learning design of mastery learning.

1. Computational Thinking and Genre-Knowledge as Foundations for AI Use

In "Brian", a self-paced GenAI chatbot module, students master responsible academic use of GenAI. Interactive vignettes hone critical thinking by guiding them to deconstruct problems and craft queries, while concise genre instruction supports the practice. Mastery is certified by the 80% "AI Literacy License" assessment.

2. Text Revision Skills

In the next phase, students engage in targeted writing exercises focused on revision strategies and the improvement of text quality (diagnostic assessment). Therefore, we design a WA tool, which provides formative feedback on coherence, structure, and language use. A pilot study is planned to test the integration of the WA tool in these exercises. The pilot will explore how students engage with AI-generated feedback and how it can support the development of revision competence in authentic writing tasks.

3. Writing Performance

The student-facing system does not yet include final writing performance evaluation. Currently, an AI-supported pre-correction tool is being developed and tested to provide automated formative feedback. This tool is being piloted with a small group of five lecturers from the broader teaching team (33 instructors total) in late 2025. Once validated, it will roll out to students for rubric-based feedback before final submission, upholding standards while ensuring transparency, fairness, and agency. Instructors gain cohort-level insights to tailor teaching and target support, reinforcing their role as learning guides.

6. DISCUSSION

6.1 Strengths of the Framework

A central strength of the framework lies in its comprehensive and integrative design. It expands beyond traditional product-based assessment by incorporating process-oriented and formative components, thereby aligning with current conceptions of writing as a socio-cognitive, iterative, and tool-mediated practice (Rad et al., 2024). Through its differentiated structure addressing diagnostic, formative, and summative functions, the framework supports diverse pedagogical goals and assessment contexts (Eager & Brunton, 2023; Khlaif et al., 2025; Lodge et al., 2023).

It is both theoretically grounded and technologically responsive, drawing on established insights from genre pedagogy, SLR, and WA, while also integrating the affordances and challenges introduced by GenAI. This dual anchoring ensures conceptual rigor and practical relevance across instructional settings.

The inclusion of CT as a distinct assessment dimension introduces an important innovation. In AI-supported writing environments, academic literacy increasingly encompasses the ability to engage strategically, ethically, and reflectively with generative tools. The framework acknowledges this shift by assessing not only writing outcomes but also students' interaction with AI as part of their cognitive and rhetorical process. By operationalising writing competence through traceable indicators such as revision histories, prompting behaviour, or interaction logs, the framework provides actionable data for learners, instructors, and researchers. Writing performance profiles, generated through a combination of system-based analytics (e.g., linguistic complexity) and learner actions (e.g., prompt refinement, revision depth), offer a nuanced basis for feedback and instructional support.

6.2 Limitations and Challenges

While the proposed framework offers a conceptually coherent and pedagogically grounded approach, its limitations must be clearly acknowledged. The framework is entirely theoretical and has not yet undergone empirical validation. As a result, its practical feasibility, pedagogical impact, and effectiveness in real-world instructional settings remain uncertain. Further research is essential to evaluate its applicability and implications across diverse educational contexts.

A significant challenge lies in the implementation, which depends heavily on institutional support and pedagogical readiness. The model assumes a high level of AI competence among educators, yet it does not detail specific support structures or professional development protocols. For a successful integration, educators require robust training in interpreting WA, scaffolding AI-assisted writing tasks, and fostering responsible AI use among students. Without sufficient resources, the integration risks remaining superficial and ineffective, as teachers must transition from mere instructors to learning guides who can coach students in the critical use of AI tools (Tan et al., 2025).

Furthermore, the framework's reliance on data-driven analytics raises significant methodological and ethical concerns (Azra & Zeeshan, 2025). There is a risk of reductionism, where key dimensions of writing such as creativity, rhetorical flexibility, and disciplinary variation are not fully captured by automated metrics. This leads to ethical questions surrounding the explainability of AI-generated feedback, academic integrity (Cotton et al., 2024; Gulumbe et al., 2024; Lund et al., 2025) and data privacy (Huang, 2023).

To address the latter, it is crucial to implement specific safeguards, including data anonymization, data minimisation, and secure, encrypted storage. While the framework mitigates these risks by combining AI-based analysis with human feedback, its overall success critically depends on addressing the challenge of explainability. A core requirement is therefore the development of comprehensible guidelines to ensure that AI-generated feedback is not only interpretable but also fair, preventing the reinforcement of biases or reductionist assessments.

Finally, assessing the nuances of the dialogic interaction between student and AI remains methodologically challenging. It is difficult to distinguish between strategic engagement informed by CT and Genre-Knowledge versus simple trial-and-error without deeper insight into students' intentions. To avoid mere surveillance, any analysis of interaction logs must focus on qualitative patterns that indicate strategic action (e.g., iterative refinement of prompts) and must be conducted with full transparency and student consent.

7. CONCLUSION AND OUTLOOK

This paper presents a conceptual framework for assessing academic writing in the context of GenAI. By defining four dimensions CT and Genre-Knowledge as Foundations for AI Use, Skills for Text Revision, Writing Performance, and Writing Development the model addresses a holistic shift from product-based to process-oriented writing practices in higher education. The framework integrates insights from writing pedagogy, genre theory, SRL, CT and WA, and supports both formative and summative assessment. It highlights the importance of metacognitive reflection, ethical AI use, and emerging literacies in AI-mediated writing.

Future directions must focus on the empirical validation and practical implementation of the framework. Addressing the limitations outlined in the discussion is a critical priority. This involves operationalising the framework for educators through a robust professional development program and clear implementation guidelines, ensuring that the model can be effectively and ethically adopted. The goal is not only to assess current writing practices but to guide their evolution toward more transparent, reflective, and educationally aligned approaches in the age of AI.

REFERENCES

Attali, Y., & Burstein, J. (2004). AUTOMATED ESSAY SCORING WITH E-RATER® V.2.0. *ETS Research Report Series, 2004*(2). https://doi.org/10.1002/j.2333-8504.2004.tb01972.x

Azra, H., & Zeeshan, I. (2025). HARNESSING BIG DATA ANALYTICS IN EDUCATION: BALANCING STUDENT SUCCESS WITH PRIVACY CONCERNS AND ETHICAL CONSIDERATIONS IN GREENFIELD UNIVERSITY IN USA (PSEUDONYM) (SSRN Scholarly Paper No. 5198908). Social Science Research Network. https://doi.org/10.2139/ssrn.5198908

Badger, R., & White, G. (2000). A process genre approach to teaching writing. *ELT Journal, 54*(2), 153-160. https://doi.org/10.1093/elt/54.2.153

Celik, I. (2023). Exploring the Determinants of Artificial Intelligence (AI) Literacy: Digital Divide, Computational Thinking, Cognitive Absorption. *Telematics and Informatics, 83*, 102026. https://doi.org/10.1016/j.tele.2023.102026

Chen, H., & He, B. (2013). Automated Essay Scoring by Maximizing Human-Machine Agreement. In D. Yarowsky, T. Baldwin, A. Korhonen, K. Livescu, & S. Bethard (Hrsg.), *Proceedings of the 2013 Conference on Empirical Methods in Natural Language Processing* (S. 1741-1752). Association for Computational Linguistics. https://aclanthology.org/D13-1180/

Cheng, Y., Lyons, K., Chen, G., Gasevic, D., & Swiecki, Z. (2024). *Evidence-centered Assessment for Writing with Generative AI* (No. arXiv:2401.08964). arXiv. https://doi.org/10.48550/arXiv.2401.08964

Cotton, D. R. E., Cotton, P. A., & Shipway, J. R. (2024). Chatting and cheating: Ensuring academic integrity in the era of ChatGPT. *Innovations in Education and Teaching International, 61*(2), 228-239. https://doi.org/10.1080/14703297.2023.2190148

Dehouche, N. (2021). Plagiarism in the age of massive Generative Pre-trained Transformers (GPT-3): "The best time to act was yesterday. The next best time is now.". *Ethics in Science and Environmental Politics, 21*. https://doi.org/10.3354/esep00195

Deng, R., Jiang, M., Yu, X., Lu, Y., & Liu, S. (2025). Does ChatGPT enhance student learning? A systematic review and meta-analysis of experimental studies. *Computers & Education, 227*, 105224. https://doi.org/10.1016/j.compedu.2024.105224

Devlin, J., Chang, M.-W., Lee, K., & Toutanova, K. (2019). BERT: Pre-training of Deep Bidirectional Transformers for Language Understanding. In J. Burstein, C. Doran, & T. Solorio (Hrsg.), *Proceedings of the 2019 Conference of the North American Chapter of the Association for Computational Linguistics: Human Language Technologies, Volume 1 (Long and Short Papers)* (S. 4171-4186). Association for Computational Linguistics. https://doi.org/10.18653/v1/N19-1423

Drachsler, H. (2023). *Towards highly informative learning analytics*. pedocs. http://nbn-resolving.de/urn:nbn:de:0111-pedocs-267875

Eager, B., & Brunton, R. (2023). Prompting Higher Education Towards AI-Augmented Teaching and Learning Practice. *Journal of University Teaching and Learning Practice, 20*(5), Article 5. https://doi.org/10.53761/1.20.5.02

Gattupalli, S., Maloy, R. W., & Edwards, S. A. (2023). *Prompt literacy: A pivotal educational skill in the age of AI*. https://www.researchgate.net/profile/Sai-Gattupalli/publication/373043701_Prompt_Literacy_A_Pivotal_Educational_Skill_in_the_Age_of_AI/links/64d53103b684851d3d9d61c5/Prompt-Literacy-A-Pivotal-Educational-Skill-in-the-Age-of-AI.pdf

Gulumbe, B. H., Audu, S. M., & Hashim, A. M. (2024). Balancing AI and academic integrity: What are the positions of academic publishers and universities? *AI & SOCIETY*. https://doi.org/10.1007/s00146-024-01946-8

Hau, M. F. (2025). Writing with machines? Reconceptualizing student work in the age of AI. *Frontiers in Communication, 10*. https://doi.org/10.3389/fcomm.2025.1598988

Huang, L. (2023). Ethics of Artificial Intelligence in Education: Student Privacy and Data Protection. *Science Insights Education Frontiers, 16*(2), 2577-2587. https://doi.org/10.15354/sief.23.re202

Hyland, K. (2003). Genre-based pedagogies: A social response to process. *Journal of Second Language Writing, 12*(1), 17-29. https://doi.org/10.1016/S1060-3743(02)00124-8

Kasneci, E., Sessler, K., Küchemann, S., Bannert, M., Dementieva, D., Fischer, F., Gasser, U., Groh, G., Günnemann, S., Hüllermeier, E., Krusche, S., Kutyniok, G., Michaeli, T., Nerdel, C., Pfeffer, J., Poquet, O., Sailer, M., Schmidt, A., Seidel, T., … Kasneci, G. (2023). ChatGPT for good? On opportunities and challenges of large language models for education. *Learning and Individual Differences*, *103*, 102274. https://doi.org/10.1016/j.lindif.2023.102274

Khlaif, Z. N., Alkouk, W. A., Salama, N., & Abu Eideh, B. (2025). Redesigning Assessments for AI-Enhanced Learning: A Framework for Educators in the Generative AI Era. *Education Sciences*, *15*(2), Article 2. https://doi.org/10.3390/educsci15020174

Lodge, J., Howard, S., Bearman, M., Dawson, P., & Associates. (2023). *Assessment Reform for The Age of Artificial Intelligence*. https://research.monash.edu/en/publications/assessment-reform-for-the-age-of-artificial-intelligence

Lund, B. D., Lee, T. H., Mannuru, N. R., & Arutla, N. (2025). AI and Academic Integrity: Exploring Student Perceptions and Implications for Higher Education. *Journal of Academic Ethics*. https://doi.org/10.1007/s10805-025-09613-3

Malik, A. R., Pratiwi, Y., Andajani, K., Numertayasa, I. W., Suharti, S., Darwis, A., & Marzuki. (2023). Exploring Artificial Intelligence in Academic Essay: Higher Education Student's Perspective. *International Journal of Educational Research Open*, *5*, 100296. https://doi.org/10.1016/j.ijedro.2023.100296

Markauskaite, L., Marrone, R., Poquet, O., Knight, S., Martinez-Maldonado, R., Howard, S., Tondeur, J., De Laat, M., Buckingham Shum, S., Gašević, D., & Siemens, G. (2022). Rethinking the entwinement between artificial intelligence and human learning: What capabilities do learners need for a world with AI? *Computers and Education: Artificial Intelligence*, *3*, 100056. https://doi.org/10.1016/j.caeai.2022.100056

McCarthy, P. M., & Jarvis, S. (2010). MTLD, vocd-D, and HD-D: A validation study of sophisticated approaches to lexical diversity assessment. *Behavior Research Methods*, *42*(2), 381-392. https://doi.org/10.3758/BRM.42.2.381

Mislevy, R. J., Almond, R. G., & Lukas, J. F. (2003). A Brief Introduction to Evidence-Centered Design. *ETS Research Report Series*, *2003*(1), i-29. https://doi.org/10.1002/j.2333-8504.2003.tb01908.x

Nguyen, K. V. (2025). The Use of Generative AI Tools in Higher Education: Ethical and Pedagogical Principles. *Journal of Academic Ethics*. https://doi.org/10.1007/s10805-025-09607-1

Selby, C., & Woollard, J. (2013). *Computational thinking: The developing definition* [Monograph]. University of Southampton. https://eprints.soton.ac.uk/356481/

Shibani, A., Knight, S., & Shum, S. B. (2019). Contextualizable Learning Analytics Design: A Generic Model and Writing Analytics Evaluations. *Proceedings of the 9th International Conference on Learning Analytics & Knowledge*, 210-219. https://doi.org/10.1145/3303772.3303785

Spirgi, L., & Seufert, S. (2024). Using Large Language Models for Academic Writing Instruction: Conceptual Design and Evaluation of the SOCRAT Project. In *International Association for Development of the Information Society*. International Association for the Development of the Information Society. https://eric.ed.gov/?id=ED665548

Spirgi, L., Seufert, S., Delcker, J., & Heil, J. (2024). Student Perspectives on Ethical Academic Writing with ChatGPT: An Empirical Study in Higher Education. *CSEDU (2)*, 179-186. https://www.scitepress.org/Papers/2024/125557/125557.pdf

Suglo, E. K., Mejira, A., Bayor, N., Nyemewero, I., & Godfred, A. A. (2024). Integrating Generative AI in Contemporary Research Writing: Exploring Postgraduates' Knowledge and Willingness to Use GenAI in the Upper East Region of Ghana. *American Journal of Technology*, *3*(1), 33-51.

Tan, X., Cheng, G., & Ling, M. H. (2025). Artificial intelligence in teaching and teacher professional development: A systematic review. *Computers and Education: Artificial Intelligence*, *8*, 100355. https://doi.org/10.1016/j.caeai.2024.100355

Wang, Z., Makarova, V., Li, Z., Kodner, J., & Rambow, O. (2025). *LLMs can Perform Multi-Dimensional Analytic Writing Assessments: A Case Study of L2 Graduate-Level Academic English Writing* (No. arXiv:2502.11368). arXiv. https://doi.org/10.48550/arXiv.2502.11368

Wing, J. M. (2006). Computational thinking. *Communications of the ACM*, *49*(3), 33-35. https://doi.org/10.1145/1118178.1118215

Yang, K., Cheng, Y., Zhao, L., Raković, M., Swiecki, Z., Gašević, D., & Chen, G. (2024). *Ink and Algorithm: Exploring Temporal Dynamics in Human-AI Collaborative Writing* (No. arXiv:2406.14885). arXiv. https://doi.org/10.48550/arXiv.2406.14885

Yannakoudakis, H., & Briscoe, T. (2012). Modeling coherence in ESOL learner texts. In J. Tetreault, J. Burstein, & C. Leacock (Hrsg.), *Proceedings of the Seventh Workshop on Building Educational Applications Using NLP* (S. 33-43). Association for Computational Linguistics. https://aclanthology.org/W12-2004/

Zhai, C., Wibowo, S., & Li, L. D. (2024). The effects of over-reliance on AI dialogue systems on students' cognitive abilities: A systematic review. *Smart Learning Environments*, *11*(1), 28. https://doi.org/10.1186/s40561-024-00316-7

Zimmerman, B. (2002). Becoming a Self-Regulated Learner: An Overview. *Theory Into Practice*, *41*, 64-70. https://doi.org/10.1207/s15430421tip4102_2

HUMANS VS. AI IN GRADING STUDENTS' TEXTS – A PILOT STUDY WITH 3 TEACHERS AGAINST ONE AI

Felix Weber[1] and Hendrik Hubbertz[2]
International University, Germany

ABSTRACT

Artificial Intelligence (AI) technologies are increasingly being integrated into educational environments, especially in areas such as student feedback and assessment. Among these applications, automated grading tools have garnered both interest and controversy for their potential to streamline evaluation processes while raising questions about accuracy and fairness. In a recent critique, Mühlhoff and Henningsen (2024) raised concerns about the reliability of the Fobizz AI grading tool, highlighting significant inconsistencies in how the AI graded a fixed set of texts. Motivated by their findings, our study sought to replicate and extend this analysis by comparing the AI's grading performance with that of experienced human teachers. We used the same dataset of ten student-written texts originally employed by Mühlhoff and Henningsen, but instead of AI-generated evaluations, we engaged a group of three experienced secondary school teachers to perform the grading. These educators had an average of 20.66 years of teaching experience, providing a robust comparison point for assessing human consistency. To reduce the influence of recognition bias and memory effects, we asked the teachers to grade the texts twice, with a two-month interval between sessions and randomized ordering of the texts each time.
The results of our study were striking. Across both rounds of grading, teachers assigned different grades to the same texts in 73% of cases, reflecting a notable degree of inconsistency. In contrast, the Fobizz AI system showed a discrepancy rate of just 30% in the study by Mühlhoff and Henningsen. Furthermore, we observed that the average grade deviation between the two human assessments was 2.1 points on a standard grading scale, while the AI's average deviation was only 0.5 points. These findings suggest that, in this context, the AI grading tool exhibited greater internal consistency than the experienced human teachers.
It is important to note, however, that the limited sample size of both texts and participants constrains the generalizability of our conclusions. Nevertheless, the results challenge a common assumption in educational discourse: that experienced human teachers inherently provide more stable and reliable assessments than AI-based systems. Our study invites further research into the comparative reliability of human and machine grading, with implications for the future role of AI in educational assessment practices.

KEYWORDS

Artificial Intelligence, Grading, Feedback, LLMs, Educational Assessment

1. INTRODUCTION

Recent advances in Artificial Intelligence (AI), particularly through Large Language Models (LLMs), are reshaping student evaluation practices. Traditional formats such as term papers and essays are increasingly questioned due to their susceptibility to AI-generated content (Deutscher Ethikrat (German Ethics Council), 2023), while oral examinations - though more robust -lead to higher staffing demands. Notably, AI is both a challenge and a potential solution, as it could replace oral assessments with avatar-mediated examinations and similar technical solutions.

[1] Felix.weber@iu.org
[2] Hendrik.hubbertz@iu.org

Among the most promising educational applications of generative AI is automated grading and feedback (Ahmad et al., 2024). Although machine-assisted grading has existed for years (Wannemacher, 2007), LLMs have dramatically improved quality, reaching error rates below 3% in short-answer grading (Katuka, 2024). However, challenges remain for complex responses, and both human and AI assessments are affected by biases (Lucas, 2022; Chen, 2024). Despite this, AI may help reduce certain human biases, improving fairness and reducing unwanted variability.

LLMs can transform feedback culture by delivering scalable, personalized responses that positively influence both learning outcomes and student motivation (Fagbohun et al., 2024; Meyer et al., 2024). This evolution also redefines the role of teachers, who may become facilitators helping students interpret AI-generated feedback (Kiesler et al., 2023).

2. THEORETICAL BACKGROUND

Our study is inspired by Mühlhoff and Henningsen's (2024) critique of AI grading variability. Mühlhoff and Henningsen argue that effective assessment requires nuanced didactic expertise, pedagogical training, and interpersonal sensitivity - qualities they believe AI lacks. We question whether these human factors actually result in more consistent grading. In contrast, human factors may lead to more noise or biases which may lead to unfair grading. Our research question is therefore: Are experienced human teachers more consistent in grading than AI tools?

3. METHODS

We replicate the methodology used by Mühlhoff and Henningsen, using the same ten texts, replacing the AI with human raters to assess grading consistency. While the AI graded each text five times, such repetition would likely bias human raters. We instead implemented two grading iterations with paper and pencil, separated by a ~2-month interval, with randomized text order to reduce recall bias. Data analyses were implemented by Python scripts, using the libraries Pandas (McKinney, 2010), Numpy (Harris, C.R. et al., 2020), and Matplotlib (Hunter, J.D., 2007).

3.1 Participants and Procedure

Three male secondary school teachers (22, 35, and 5 years of experience) participated. Each received ten student texts via mail along with grading instructions and a return envelope. Approximately two months later (60, 56, and 39 days, respectively), the same texts were sent again in a different order, without informing participants of the repetition. Participants remained unaware of the study's purpose until completion.

The grading dimensions, based on Mühlhoff and Henningsen, included "Spelling and Grammar," "Content Accuracy," "Structure and Organization," "Not Written by AI," and "Word Count Between 150–250." Due to confusion and relevance issues, the last two dimensions were excluded from analysis. The decision for this exclusion was taken before data acquisition based on their unrelatedness to grading of the dimension "Not Written by AI," and because the superiority of computers to humans are obvious in the case of the dimension "Word Count Between 150–250.". We calculated the final grade as average from the dimensions "Spelling ang Grammar", "Content Accuracy", and "Structure and Organization".

3.2 Data Transformation

Table 1. Transformation table for percent values and German Grades (1-6) to Point Grades (15-0)

15	14	13	12	11	10	9	8	7	6	5	4	3	2	1	0
1	1.3	1.6	2	2.3	2.6	3	3.3	3.6	4	4.35	4.6	5	5.3	5.6	6
95%	90%	85%	80%	75%	70%	65%	60%	55%	50%	45%	40%	33%	27%	20%	0%

Some participants used German school grades (1–6) instead of percentages. One participant gave only overall grades in the second iteration. We converted all data to the German 15-point scale (15 = best, 0 = worst) using a standardized conversion table (Table 1).

3.3 Calculation of Rating Deviations

The AI produced five grades in five iterations per text; we computed the average deviation across all 10 permutations of grade pairs. Each teacher produced two grades, in two iterations, per text, and we calculated the absolute difference for each text per teacher to determine intra-rater consistency and the averages. This procedure results in 10 deviation values per text for the AI and three deviation values (one per participant) for the human raters. Based on 100 deviation values for the AI and 30 deviation values for the human raters, percentages of consistent gradings were calculated. This procedure only measures the human intra-rater consistency, in favor of the AI gradings. If we had instead included the inter-rater consistencies, the human consistency would have been even worse.

4. RESULTS

The results are visualized in three figures.

Figure 1 shows the ratings of the humans; each subplot shows the data for one teacher. The columns represent the texts and the rows the point scale from 0 to 15. The plot shows that most ratings are not consistent. A consistent rating results in only one point, or more precisely two overlapping consistent points.

Figure 2 shows the aggregated data of all three human raters in one subplot, compared to the AI ratings in a second subplot. The plot clearly shows a higher density or ratings in the AI plot and a strong spread of the human ratings.

Figure 3 shows the distribution of ratings for the three participants (P1 to P3), all participants aggregated (All P), and the AI (AI) as whisker plots. The figure shows that the teachers have individual biases, as they map the texts differently to the grading scale, although the ranking of the texts is comparable. The results also show that the AI grades are clearly more consistent over trials than the human grades are.

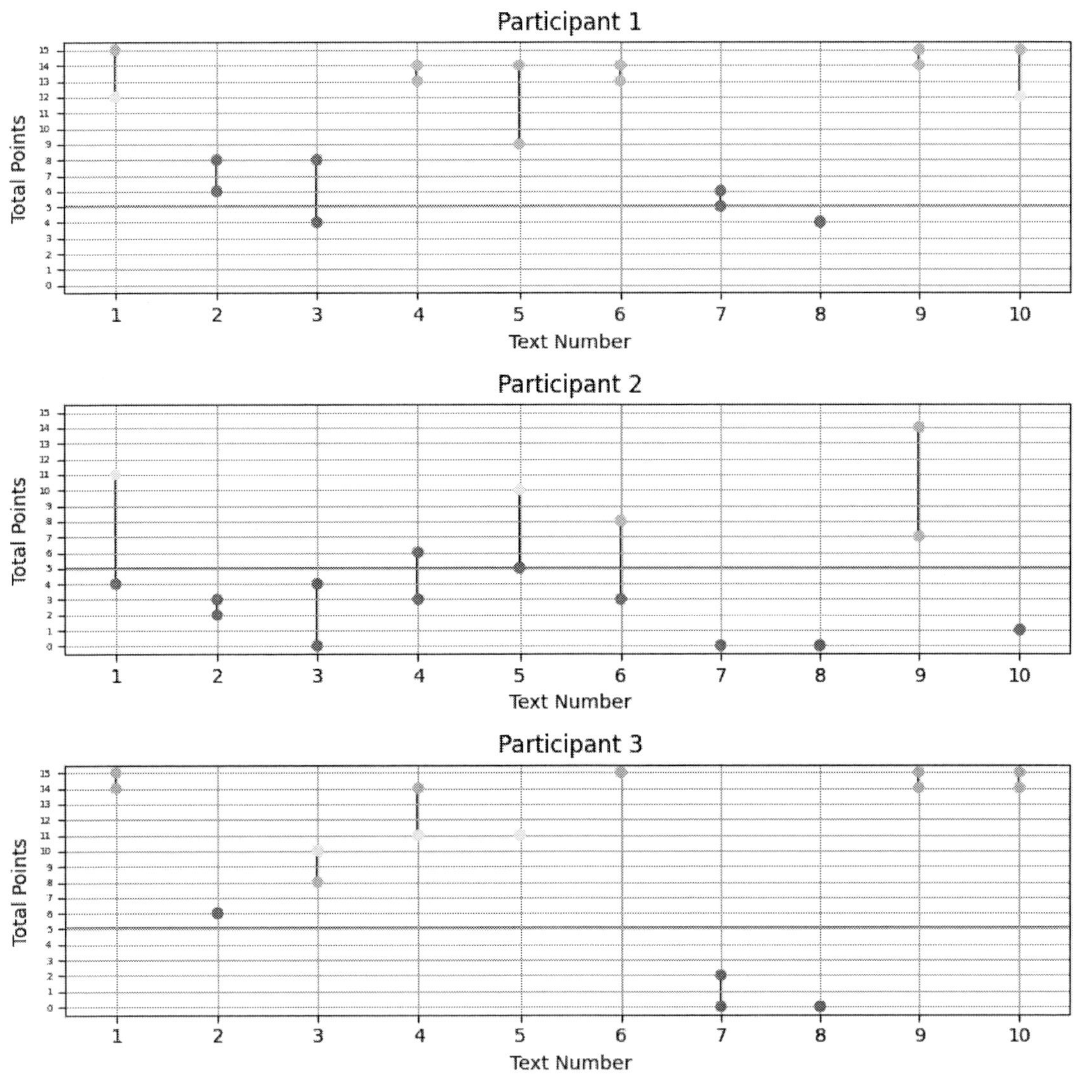

Figure 1. Each of the three plots shows how each participant graded the ten texts on a scale from 0 to 15 points in the two iterations

4.1 Intra-Participant Inconsistencies

Figure 1 shows grading inconsistencies across two iterations. Only 8 of 30 text-grade pairs were consistent (26,6%), while 22 out of 30 (73,3%) deviated. Although rankings remained relatively consistent, the mapping to grade values varied significantly across iterations and participants. It seems like human raters can rank student texts consistently, but use different, teacher-dependent mappings of student achievements to the grading scale.

4.2 Humans vs. Artificial Intelligence

The average grading deviation was 0.5 points for the AI and 2.1 points for humans. Grade consistency (identical scores) occurred in 70% of AI grades, compared to only 26% for humans. As shown in Figure 2, the AI graded five of the ten texts identically across all trials, while human raters never fully agreed across iterations, including inter-rater comparisons. Text 8, an off-topic text was consistently graded below the threshold for passing the exam of 5 points by all human raters, while the AI failed to identify the text as not sufficient.

Figure 3 highlights individual grading tendencies: one teacher (P 2) graded consistently low (average score: 3), while others were more generous (averages: 12 and 11). Thus, grading outcomes appear highly dependent on the individual teacher.

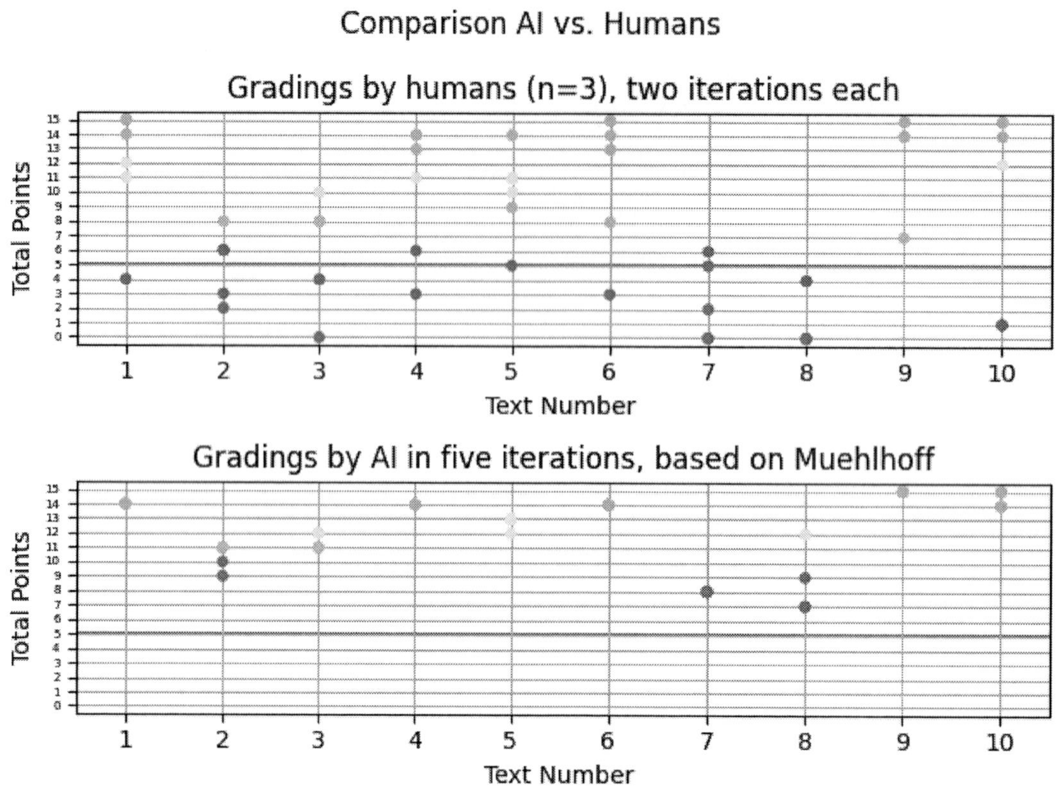

Figure 2. The two visualizations show the grading by humans (top) and by the AI (bottom)

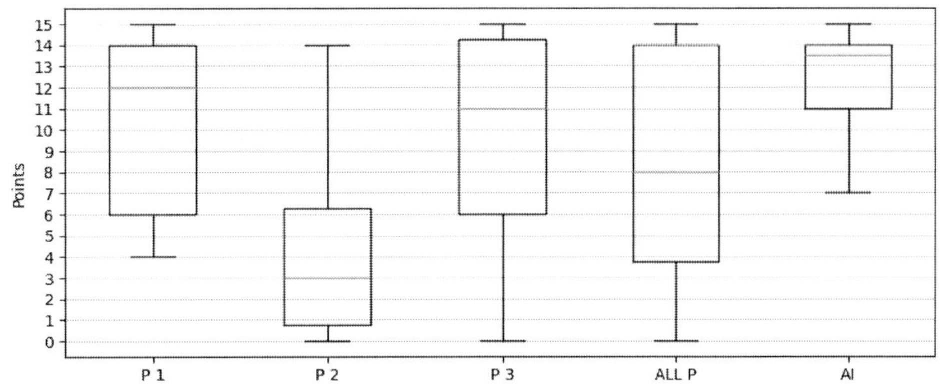

Figure 3. This whisker plot shows the distribution of grades by the three participants, all participants together, and the AI

5. DISCUSSION

This paper addresses an important and timely issue: the fairness and consistency of AI versus human grading. As the use of AI in educational assessment gains traction, it is critical to evaluate its performance relative to human raters, particularly in terms of reliability, bias, and ethical implications. While the empirical basis of this study is limited, the findings are presented as part of an ongoing investigation intended to provoke critical discussion and further research, rather than to offer definitive conclusions.

One of the central findings is that the AI system demonstrated substantially higher consistency than human raters. Its grades showed less variability overall, suggesting that algorithmic assessment may offer more stable evaluations. However, this consistency came with notable limitations. For example, all human raters identified one text (Text 8) as nonsensical and graded it accordingly, while the AI failed to detect its incoherence. This suggests that although AI may excel in pattern-based consistency, it may struggle with contextual or semantic anomalies that are easily recognized by humans.

The study also revealed significant inter-rater variability among teachers, greater than the intra-rater variability observed. This means that the grade a student receives can depend more on which teacher evaluates the work than on the actual quality of the submission - a finding that raises serious fairness concerns. In contrast, the AI treated similar texts more uniformly. That said, both human and AI raters largely agreed on the relative ranking of texts, even if the numerical scores differed. This suggests a shared general judgment, but a divergence in how those judgments are mapped onto grading scales. In particular, human raters appeared to interpret the scale with more individual variation, while the AI's scores were clustered toward the higher end, indicating a tendency toward grade inflation.

Importantly, no calibration session or collaborative discussion of the marking rubric was conducted among the teachers prior to grading. Nor was there a shared exercise in applying the rubric to a sample text. This omission was deliberate, in order to simulate authentic grading conditions in which teachers often work independently. However, it is also a limitation of the study, as such preparatory sessions could have reduced variability and aligned interpretations of the rubric. Future studies should explore how norming sessions influence grading consistency and whether such practices narrow the gap between human and AI assessment.

Methodologically, the study relies on a small sample of raters and texts, which limits the generalizability of the results. However, this narrow focus allowed for close comparison and qualitative analysis of grading patterns. The use of a consistent rubric across all raters, including the AI, provided a common evaluative framework, although the rubric's openness to interpretation likely contributed to the human variability observed. It is important to note that the rubrics did not specify criteria for assigning particular percentages, which may have led to more consistent gradings by humans and AI. Future iterations of the study will benefit from larger datasets, more diverse participants, and refined grading prompts to test whether the observed patterns hold under broader conditions.

Overall, these findings challenge the widespread assumption that human grading is inherently more fair or valid than AI-based assessment. While AI systems require careful calibration and are not immune to flaws, human grading is shown here to be highly variable and susceptible to subjective interpretation. If ethical objections are raised against AI grading, the same scrutiny should be applied to human grading practices. This study does not claim to offer a final verdict on the use of AI in assessment, but rather seeks to open a dialogue on what fairness and consistency should mean in educational evaluation, and how both humans and machines measure up to those standards.

ACKNOWLEDGEMENT

We want to thank our subjects T.B., P.Q., and B.W. for their valuable contributions and especially for their courage to grade the texts a second time.

REFERENCES

Ahmad, K., Iqbal, W., El-Hassan, A., Qadir, J., Benhaddou, D., Ayyash, M., & Al-Fuqaha, A. (2023). Data-Driven Artificial Intelligence in Education: A Comprehensive review. *IEEE Transactions on Learning Technologies*, *17*, 12–31. https://doi.org/10.1109/tlt.2023.3314610

Bloom, B. S. (1956). *Taxonomy of educational objectives: The Classification of Educational Goals*. New York : Longmans, Green.

Chen, G. H., Chen, S., Liu, Z., Jiang, F., & Wang, B. (2024). *Humans or LLMs as the Judge? A Study on Judgement Biases*. http://arxiv.org/abs/2402.10669

Deutscher Ethikrat. (2023). *Mensch und Maschine – Herausforderungen durch Künstliche Intelligenz*. https://www.ethikrat.org/fileadmin/Publikationen/Stellungnahmen/deutsch/stellungnahme-mensch-und-maschine.pdf

Fagbohun, O., Iduwe, N. P., Abdullahi, M., Ifaturoti, A., & Nwanna, O. M. (2024). Beyond Traditional Assessment: Exploring the Impact of Large Language Models on Grading Practices. *Journal of Artificial Intelligence, Machine Learning and Data Science*, *2*(1), 1–8. https://doi.org/10.51219/jaimld/oluwole-fagbohun/19

Fobizz AI tools, PD courses, & teaching materials. (retrieved 18.07.2025). Fobizz Tools. https://app.fobizz.com/tools

Harris, C. R., Millman, K. J., Van Der Walt, S. J., Gommers, R., Virtanen, P., Cournapeau, D., Wieser, E., Taylor, J., Berg, S., Smith, N. J., Kern, R., Picus, M., Hoyer, S., Van Kerkwijk, M. H., Brett, M., Haldane, A., Del Río, J. F., Wiebe, M., Peterson, P., . . . Oliphant, T. E. (2020). Array programming with NumPy. *Nature*, *585*(7825), 357–362. https://doi.org/10.1038/s41586-020-2649-2

Hunter, J. D. (2007). MatPlotLib: a 2D Graphics environment. *Computing in Science & Engineering*, *9*(3), 90–95. https://doi.org/10.1109/mcse.2007.55

Katuka, G. A., Gain, A., & Yu, Y.-Y. (2024). *Investigating Automatic Scoring and Feedback using Large Language Models*. http://arxiv.org/abs/2405.00602

Kiesler, N., Lohr, D., & Keuning, H. (2023). Exploring the Potential of Large Language Models to Generate Formative Programming Feedback. *Proceedings - Frontiers in Education Conference, FIE*. https://doi.org/10.1109/FIE58773.2023.10343457

Lucas, C. (2023). Menschen machen Fehler. In *Springer eBooks* (pp. 203–220). https://doi.org/10.1007/978-3-658-38210-0_12

McKinney, W. (2010). Data structures for statistical computing in Python. *Proceedings of the Python in Science Conferences*, 56–61. https://doi.org/10.25080/majora-92bf1922-00a

Meyer, J., Jansen, T., Schiller, R., Liebenow, L. W., Steinbach, M., Horbach, A., & Fleckenstein, J. (2024). Using LLMs to bring evidence-based feedback into the classroom: AI-generated feedback increases secondary students' text revision, motivation, and positive emotions. *Computers and Education: Artificial Intelligence*, *6*. https://doi.org/10.1016/j.caeai.2023.100199

Muehlhoff, R., & Henningsen, M. (2024). Chatbots im Schulunterricht: Wir testen das Fobizz-Tool zur automatischen Bewertung von Hausaufgaben. *arXiv (Cornell University)*. https://doi.org/10.48550/arxiv.2412.06651

Wannemacher, K. (2007). Computergestützte Prüfungsverfahren. In: Breitner, M.H., Bruns, B., Lehner, F. (eds) Neue Trends im E-Learning. Physica-Verlag HD. https://doi.org/10.1007/978-3-7908-1922-9_29

Xie, W., Niu, J., Xue, C. J., & Guan, N. (2024). *Grade Like a Human: Rethinking Automated Assessment with Large Language Models*. http://arxiv.org/abs/2405.19694

3D SCANNING WITH MOBILE DEVICES FOR TEACHING HISTORY

Klára Rybenská
Philosophical Faculty, University of Hradec Králové , náměstí Svobody 331, Hradec Králové, Czech Republic

ABSTRACT

This paper explores the fundamental possibilities of employing mobile technologies for 3D scanning in primary, secondary, and tertiary history education. Students can use the Luma AI tool to create 3D models of historical artefacts, thereby gaining a deeper understanding of cultural heritage through immersive and interactive engagement. The article aims to introduce basic didactic methodologies for incorporating mobile 3D scanning into teaching practice, connect technical skills with historical thinking development, and highlight the interdisciplinary potential between ICT and the humanities. The text presents examples of good practice and offers recommendations for integrating these technologies into the educational process.

KEYWORDS

3D Scanning, Mobile 3D, History Education, Project-Based Learning, Inquiry-Based Learning, Historical Thinking, Luma AI

1. INTRODUCTION

Preserving cultural heritage is challenging. Mobile devices with sensors such as LiDAR now enable practical field scanning. While Luma 3D does not reach the level of professional scanners or high-resolution photogrammetry, it provides fast and affordable 3D scanning suitable for classroom teaching and public engagement. It can teach digital/3D workflows and support teaching subjects, particularly history, where the tool is a means rather than an end. Students can digitise artefacts and use their models to explain, interpret, and present. This integrates digital literacy into humanities curricula and promotes creative and critical inquiry-based learning, which aligns with modern didactics. The article explores Luma 3D and related mobile tools and highlights opportunities for memory institutions such as museums and schools. Based on a comparative analysis of resources and the author's many years of experience in 3D digitisation, this outlines an accessible project feasible at the primary, secondary, and tertiary levels. We consider mobile 3D scanning a means for research and project-based history learning. We ask how it can be integrated without specialised hardware, and what advantages and challenges teachers and students report.

This article was developed under the University of Hradec Králové, Philosophical Faculty, as a pilot contribution to a specific research project entitled *Digitisation of Historical Objects Using 3D Technologies*. The project focuses not only on the digitisation of cultural heritage but also on exploring meaningful and practical ways to integrate ICT into history education and the humanities, so that the outcomes are both applicable for primary and secondary school teachers and beneficial for university students.

In preparing the literature review for this article, AI-assisted research tools such as *Research Rabbit* and *Consensus* were utilised. The English translation of the text was subsequently refined using tools like *DeepL* and *Grammarly* to ensure fluency and readability in the final version.

2. THE SIGNIFICANCE OF 3D DOCUMENTATION IN THE PRESERVATION OF HISTORICAL MONUMENTS

The documentation of cultural heritage monuments is essential for their preservation, restoration, and interpretation. Traditional methods—such as hand-drawn sketches or standard photography—have inherent limitations in capturing such structures' full complexity and nuance. In contrast, 3D documentation offers the potential to produce comprehensive and highly accurate records that preserve spatial, structural, and material characteristics. These data are critical for promoting and presenting cultural heritage, conservation efforts, and educational and research purposes, as they enable virtual reconstructions and simulations that support a more profound understanding and interpretation of historical objects and sites. 3D scanning plays a pivotal role in heritage preservation by providing specialists with detailed insights into the condition of artefacts and enabling precise restoration processes, commonly called digital restoration. With high precision, such technologies capture fine details, including shape, pattern, and colouration. Significantly, non-contact 3D scanning techniques minimise the risk of damage to valuable cultural objects (Muenster, 2022). In addition to standard 3D scanning, specialised technologies such as digital photogrammetry and Reflectance Transformation Imaging (RTI) are employed. RTI is particularly useful for digitising inscriptions that are difficult to read, as it enhances their legibility and can even reveal missing or invisible components to the naked eye.

Figure 1. An example of an RTI output is a "pseudo-3D" method. The image displays a detail from a seal depicting a horse's head. This is a seal of Přemysl Otakar II., whose complete 3D model can be viewed on Sketchfab at the following link: https://skfb.ly/o9TMr. For comparison, the left image shows a close-up photograph of the seal, the middle image represents the RTI result, and the right image displays the 3D model. From the author's archive

There are numerous key areas where 3D scanning technologies are applied to protect cultural heritage. Foremost among these is object restoration, where 3D scanning provides highly accurate measurements that help conservators better understand the original structure and the extent of damage sustained by the artefact. The resulting 3D data can be critical for developing effective restoration strategies. Another important application is the reproduction of replicas. Here, 3D scanning serves as a scientific basis for replicating artefacts with a high degree of precision. Thanks to advanced 3D scanning and measuring technologies, it is now possible to create accurate digital models of historical artefacts, which can subsequently be used in 3D printing to produce faithful duplicates. These replicas can serve educational and promotional purposes—allowing for public exhibition—especially in cases where the original is too fragile or at risk of irreversible damage, and therefore best preserved in secure storage (Muenster, 2022).

Furthermore, in combination with 3D modelling, it is possible to digitally reconstruct missing parts of artefacts—such as ceramics, sculptures, or architectural elements—bringing us closer to understanding their original historical appearance. 3D-printed components can also be used in physical restoration to complete damaged or missing elements, enabling experts and the public to visualise the artefact in its original form (3Tooling, 2022). Equally important is the domain of digital documentation itself, which has become indispensable in the effort to preserve cultural heritage. It allows museums and other memory institutions to build digital archives of historical objects—such as the Sketchfab collection curated by the Department of Auxiliary Sciences of History and Archival Studies at the Philosophical Faculty of the University of Hradec Králové, available at: https://sketchfab.com/KPVHA-FF-UHK—capturing precise dimensions, colours, textures, and numerous subtle details. These digital records serve not only for cataloguing and scholarly research but also as secure backups in case of damage to the original artefact. A significant benefit of such digital archives is their online accessibility, eliminating the need for physical travel and making them available on demand. While the original physical object remains irreplaceable, 3D models grant current and future generations access to accurate and enduring representations of tangible heritage. They also promote remote access and foster global research collaboration (Muenster, 2022).

From a pedagogical perspective, 3D digitisation is a tool for professional documentation and an innovative educational instrument that can be effectively integrated into teaching at various levels—from vocational and technical training to primary and secondary education. In this context, 3D scanning can be a learning objective (e.g., within subjects focused on ICT, CAD, or 3D computer graphics) or a didactic tool used in other disciplines, such as history. Students may explore digitised historical objects—ranging from artefacts and architectural features to entire heritage sites—through interactive 3D models, which in some cases can also be experienced in virtual or augmented reality. Moreover, with the support of mobile applications, students can even participate in creating such models themselves. This approach fosters spatial reasoning and visualisation skills and promotes a deeper contextual understanding of historical settings (Rodriguez-Garcia et al., 2024). Contemporary didactic approaches demonstrate that engaging students actively in the creative process—such as in the digitisation of selected objects, their interpretation, and the presentation of results—increases motivation, enhances critical thinking, and strengthens cross-curricular competencies. The integration of ICT and the humanities, a hallmark of the digital humanities field, reflects current trends in education and aligns with the objectives of developing digital literacy and cultural awareness, as stipulated by national curricular frameworks (Muenster, 2022).

3. DIGITAL DOCUMENTATION OF CULTURAL OBJECTS USING MOBILE TECHNOLOGIES

Mobile technologies—such as smartphones equipped with LiDAR sensors, photogrammetry applications, and, to a certain extent, mobile-based 3D scanning—are opening new avenues for the rapid and accessible documentation of cultural heritage directly in the field, including within educational settings. Integrating mobile data with other techniques enables the creation of comprehensive 3D models suitable for teaching and public interpretation (Stylianidis et al., 2022). In the context of project-based learning at the primary and secondary school levels, it is possible to implement a methodology in which students systematically digitise a historical object (for instance, a local monument), or even themselves, using either professional-grade 3D digitisation equipment (e.g. a 3D scanner), photogrammetry, or simply a mobile phone or tablet equipped with appropriate software. The collected data can be further developed into so-called multilayered models, which combine spatial geometry with the historical and material context of the given object. One inspiring example is the HBIM (Historic Building Information Modelling) approach, which integrates laser scanning or photogrammetry outputs with a database-driven description of individual structural elements. HBIM serves a documentation purpose and provides a platform for analytical exploration, interpretation of historical transformations, and interdisciplinary education. Even in a simplified form, this model can function as a powerful educational tool, allowing students to understand a given site's structure and historical evolution while simultaneously developing foundational digital skills and interdisciplinary competencies (Palčák et al., 2022). Although this type of instruction is more commonly found in higher education—particularly within programs focused on Digital Historical Studies—it can be assumed that, in a suitably adapted format, it may also be successfully implemented at the secondary level, and to a limited extent even in primary schools, particularly in the realm of project-based learning.

Figure 2. On the left: 3D digitisation of a student using the Artec Leo scanner. On the right: digitisation of a historical object using the Artec Spider scanner. Although this example comes from a university-level course, with minor adjustments, it could be incorporated into secondary education or the upper levels of primary school. The instructional process includes operating the equipment, generating a 3D model, and providing descriptive metadata. Working with historical artefacts also involves studying the historical context of the object in question. The primary obstacle to implementing such instruction at lower educational levels is the potential cost of acquiring professional-grade equipment and the need to train educators to facilitate this activity. Fortunately, alternative solutions exist, such as mobile devices and 3D scanning applications. From the author's archive

The scenario described in the previous image reflects a challenge commonly encountered at many primary and secondary schools, and occasionally even at universities. Professional 3D scanning equipment can be prohibitively expensive and often requires a teacher with expertise in 3D digitisation techniques. However, as previously mentioned, alternative solutions exist—namely, mobile phones or tablets (preferably equipped with LiDAR sensors, though not strictly necessary) in combination with 3D scanning applications. A wide range of such applications is available on the market, varying in price and model-processing quality. One example is MawisPhoto, whose developers claim it can generate a 3D model with geodetic accuracy using only a smartphone. This makes it particularly suitable for construction and surveying (MawisPhoto, 2025). Another relevant application is Polycam, which offers a free version and a discounted educational license (50% off for students and educators). Polycam combines photogrammetry and LiDAR scanning to produce high-quality 3D models directly from mobile devices. Its intuitive interface makes it especially suitable for students and teachers without strong technical backgrounds, and it is therefore appropriate not only for higher education but also for use in secondary and even upper primary schools.

Polycam supports exporting 3D models in various formats (e.g., OBJ, FBX, STL), facilitating further processing and online visualisation. It can thus serve as a valuable tool for quick field documentation, the creation of educational materials, and the support of project-based learning. (Polycam, 2025) As a broad spectrum of available applications exists, this article does not aim to describe or compare all of them. Instead, the focus is on exploring the educational potential of the Luma 3D application, which will be addressed in a dedicated chapter. Before doing so, however, it is necessary to provide a brief overview of the LiDAR technology mentioned earlier.

LiDAR (Light Detection and Ranging) technology was first introduced into mobile devices around 2020, initially with the iPad Pro and subsequently the iPhone 12 Pro, both developed by Apple. Since then, LiDAR has become a standard feature in all iPad Pro and iPhone Pro models (Gadget Hacks, n.d., 2024). In contrast, its implementation in Android-based devices remains relatively rare. The technology operates by emitting laser pulses and measuring the time the reflected light returns to the sensor. This process enables the device to construct a three-dimensional map of its surroundings, commonly called a point cloud map.

In mobile phones, LiDAR is primarily used to enhance digital photography, offering several practical benefits such as more accurate depth measurement, improved autofocus, and realistic object scaling. Devices equipped with LiDAR can also accurately determine the height of a standing or seated person and more effectively interpret the geometry of physical space, which is crucial for the precise placement of digital objects in real-world environments. This capability significantly enhances augmented reality (AR) experiences by making virtual interactions more realistic and immersive (Gadget Hacks, n.d., 2024). AR simulations generated through LiDAR-enabled applications possess considerable didactic potential. Mobile applications that allow for interactive manipulation of 3D models and their spatial anchoring in real or virtual environments provide an effective tool, particularly for teaching cultural heritage in digital contexts (Shih et al., 2021). These technological capabilities also improve the accuracy and quality of data captured by selected software solutions such as Luma 3D, resulting in more realistic and detailed 3D models generated via mobile phones. Nevertheless, as previously noted, devices without LiDAR can still effectively use such applications.

3.1 Utilizing the Mobile Application Luma 3D for the Digitization of Historical Objects

Luma 3D (officially Luma 3D Capture, and on Android operating systems listed as Luma AI: 3D Capture, hereafter referred to simply as Luma) is a mobile application developed by Luma AI, Inc. It is available for both iOS (Apple) devices (Luma 3D Capture, 2025) and Android-based platforms (Luma AI: 3D Capture, 2024). Luma enables the creation of highly realistic 3D objects and scenes using artificial intelligence and a smartphone; this study employs an iPhone 13 Pro for the practical demonstration. The generated models can be instantly shared online or exported in various formats, such as OBJ. Although the application is optimised to cooperate seamlessly with LiDAR, it does not require it for functionality. According to the developers, the app is compatible with iPhone 11 and newer models and can capture complex details, reflections, and lighting conditions. One of its key advantages lies in exporting 3D meshes into established 3D modelling environments such as Blender, Unity, or other 3D engines (Luma 3D Capture, 2025). Luma primarily employs photogrammetry techniques, combining overlapping photographs—captured in-app from multiple angles or uploaded from the phone's gallery—which are then processed on an external server to generate a 3D model.

Since the entire documentation process can be executed using a smartphone, it significantly enhances accessibility and ease of use for broader educational and heritage documentation purposes.

When using the Luma tool to create 3D models, it can also utilise recorded video footage. There is a direct correlation between the quality of the recorded video and the resulting quality of the 3D model. However, the chosen export format can significantly influence the final output—for instance, converting the model to the OBJ format can substantially alter its visual and technical properties. Experience suggests that exporting at the highest possible resolution may result in issues with texture mapping in Luma: textures may be cropped, misaligned, or fail to render correctly in standard 3D viewers such as Sketchfab. In such cases, selecting a lower-quality export option (e.g., medium or low-quality OBJ) often proves to be a more reliable solution, as it reduces the level of detail but greatly enhances the consistency and stability of texture display. This trade-off is generally acceptable in contexts where the model is intended for presentation or educational use, rather than for archival purposes or scientific analysis, and serves primarily to provide a basic visual representation of the captured data.

Currently, the Luma application offers several export options. These include sharing via a spatial video link, generating output in MP4 format, and exporting diffuse 3D objects in mesh format. Specifically, the available formats include GLTF, OBJ, and USDZ; it is essential to note that most of these export features are still labelled as beta versions. As part of its beta functionality, the application also supports the generation of complex scenes compatible with platforms such as Unreal Engine (UE) or SPLAT, as well as the use of the Legacy Diffuse Scenes mode, which allows for output in Point Cloud (PLY) and Scene Mesh (PLY) formats. In the context of the present project, exports in OBJ format were primarily employed, as they offered an optimal balance between ease of processing and visual fidelity. Beyond technical considerations, mobile tools for 3D documentation, such as Luma, also significantly contribute to interpreting and presenting cultural heritage. The creation of detailed 3D models enables experts and educators to explore and showcase heritage objects in novel ways, particularly through virtual and augmented reality, significantly expanding opportunities for education, visualisation, and public engagement.

Figure 3. On the left side of the image is a visualisation of the 3D model creation process directly within the Luma application. The method of generating this spatial video can be viewed via the following shortened link: https://1url.cz/xJ2JB. The model was created by capturing a video using an iPhone 13 Pro and uploading it to the Luma application. The object featured in this case was the Nymph and Faun sculpture at the National Museum of Scotland, Edinburgh. From the author's archive

In 3D model creation, users can either capture a series of photographs with their phone (which can be uploaded to Luma via the "Upload" function, where video files may also be used) or utilise Luma's built-in scanning modes: Object and Scene. The Object mode appears to be the most accurate—though only applicable to smaller items—as it can provide relatively precise measurements of the digitised object. In contrast, the Scene mode is better suited for larger objects or more expansive environments. For this article, the method of creating 3D models from video has been employed, as it enables the digitisation of objects such as buildings, provided that video footage (or photographs) can be captured, for example, using a drone.

Once the desired digitisation method has been selected, the actual processing takes place. The collected data is uploaded to an external server, where post-processing is carried out. The duration of 3D model generation depends on the speed of the internet connection—since data must be transferred to the cloud—and the complexity and size of the digitised object. It is advisable to process the resulting model via a stable Wi-Fi connection. Therefore, when working in the field, it proves effective first to capture a video or a set of photographs and proceed with model generation only once the mobile device has access to a reliable Wi-Fi network. As discussed, the resulting 3D model can be displayed in various ways.

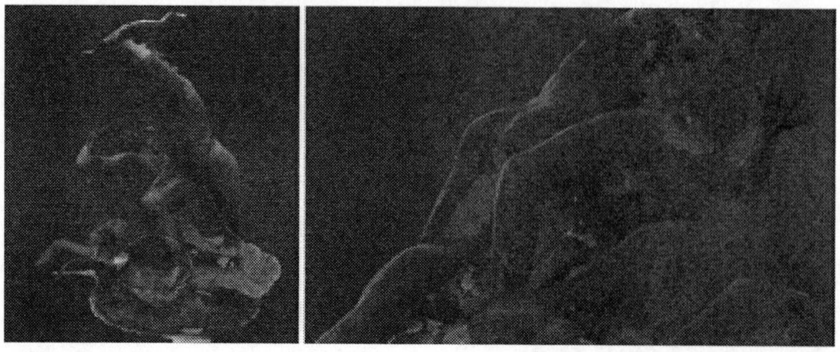

Figure 4. On the left, the generated OBJ model with texture is shown as uploaded to the Sketchfab platform. On the right is an example of missing texture areas (visible as deep grey patches). This occurs when the video recording (or photo capture process) fails to adequately cover the object's hard-to-reach or less visible parts, as was the case here. To ensure complete coverage, the video should be recorded so that the camera captures the object from underneath or at low angles, thereby documenting all relevant features and components. The depicted object is again the previously mentioned sculpture, Nymph and Faun. From the author's archive

It is therefore highly recommended that as much relevant data as possible be collected during the digitisation process, whether by photographing, recording video, or scanning directly within the Luma application. As illustrated in the image above, areas of the 3D model that lacked sufficient visual information and texture data remain grey and incomplete. As a result, the final output appears unfinished, rendering the model unsuitable even for an introductory web presentation.

For classroom use, medium-quality OBJ/GLTF exports often improve texture stability in web viewers, better serving the lesson goal (interpretation) than pursuing maximum geometric fidelity intended for archival workflows.

4. EDUCATIONAL APPLICATIONS IN TEACHING PRACTICE

At lower secondary school, Luma combines digital skills with history. Students digitise simple artefacts (in museums or from replicas) and create 3D models for short presentations. They learn the basics of documentation, develop their historical imagination, and the teaching takes on a research-based character, which increases their engagement.

In high school, 3D documentation is the basis for interdisciplinary projects (history, computer science, and social sciences). Students digitise real objects, analyse their development and context, and present the results as interactive whiteboards or AR. This strengthens digital and historical competencies and analytical and interpretive skills in line with current didactics. AI can support graphics and brainstorming (e.g., ChatGPT). Still, teachers should require verification and view AI as a sparring partner—students prepare materials, study the topic, and let AI explore ideas using Socratic-style questions.

Figure 5. An illustration of the digitisation process using a smartphone. In this instance, the student employed the Trnio application, which is unfortunately no longer supported. (Trnio, 2024) Image from the author's archive

Mobile 3D documentation tools, such as Luma, can also be effectively integrated into higher education curricula, particularly within programmes in Digital Humanities, Museology, or History Didactics (e.g., in the training of future teachers). Students may independently process museum artefacts, design their scholarly descriptions and metadata, and propose strategies for presentation and outreach, whether in a digital exhibition, educational app, or didactic material for classroom practice. Instruction can include critical reflection on the selected documentation methods and their comparison with professional approaches (e.g., photogrammetry or 3D scanning using dedicated scanners) and a comparative evaluation of multiple digitisation applications (e.g., Luma, Polycam, or others). Thus, this approach serves as specialised training and a methodological foundation for future professional engagement in cultural heritage. Additionally, students may include their high-quality 3D models in personal portfolios, enhancing their professional visibility.

Figure 6. Examples of digitisation projects completed by university students. These students specialise in digital historical sciences and humanities, promoting and protecting cultural heritage, and teacher training focusing on history. From left: Painted Baroque all-metal clock by Adam Fresser (created using the Luma app); centre: Stone cross in Doubravice near Dvůr Králové by Monika Petrová (digitised using MagiScan); right: Holy water font by Barbora Vlčková (processed using Polycam). All models—and more—are available at the following shortened link: https://1url.cz/QJ2Qe.

The project is piloting the feasibility of mobile 3D scanning in history teaching at two levels. In lower secondary school (2×45 min), students work in groups with one phone (using Luma/Polycam): after a 10-minute demonstration, they record an artefact (at home or in a museum), process it in class and export to OBJ (≈20 minutes), then prepare a 150–200-word interpretation of the object's origin, function and context, including changes over time and at least one citation. Finally, they present their work in a 5-minute talk, showing the model and discussing its history and the capture workflow, noting what they found successful and difficult (often the presentation itself).

In upper secondary school (3×45 min + 60 min of fieldwork), students conduct a video tour of the site and take brief notes on the objects. With the finished 3D model, they explore its history, search for related sources, and study the technical adequacy of the model (how closely it corresponds to reality). They present their results in approximately 6–10 minutes and briefly reflect/evaluate the model's usefulness and their working process. Results from the ongoing pilot are still under evaluation; early classroom observations indicate high student engagement at both levels.

5. IMPLICATIONS AND LIMITATIONS

Mobile 3D scanning makes working with historical objects more realistic. Legal and ethical constraints apply - cloud processing, licensing, and museum policies may limit storage options and public release of models. Students create realistic models and, in addition to practising their digital skills, must also study the historical context of the digitised object. The short, well-structured tasks assigned to students in this project helped keep the historical purpose at the forefront while giving students new opportunities to learn history in conjunction with modern technologies. Mobile scanning prioritises accessibility over accuracy; lighting/coverage issues are common, and the resulting 3D models are not always completely accurate. However, it is an opportunity to make history or related topics more interesting, teach students something new, and, last but not least, create interesting three-dimensional objects. Formal results will be reported separately; early pilot sessions suggest high student engagement across both levels.

6. CONCLUSION

Today's emphasis on interdisciplinary skills promotes the integration of the humanities with digital methods. The effective use of tools (such as Luma 3D for creating 3D models) can enrich the content of the curriculum, promote inquiry-based learning, creativity, and critical thinking. In history education, 3D documentation has increased motivation and enabled innovative interpretation and presentation, strengthening students' awareness of cultural heritage preservation. Mobile 3D technologies such as Luma can expand this potential. Creating 3D models of historical objects also allows for documentation of the current state or monitoring of changes and, in some cases, even simulation of conservation interventions. However, mobile scanning still does not achieve the accuracy required for detailed scientific research, long-term digital replacements, or professional restoration. Its adoption is further limited by storage and infrastructure needs and legal and licensing issues related to cloud processing.

Despite its continuing limitations, mobile 3D documentation offers an accessible and flexible way to document and disseminate cultural heritage. It can make history and related humanities subjects more attractive and engaging for different types of students and their teachers.

ACKNOWLEDGEMENT

I sincerely thank my university (Philosophical Faculty, University of Hradec Králové) for the opportunity to contribute to the *Digitisation of Historical Objects Using 3D Technologies research project and* develop this pilot study. I am also profoundly thankful to all of my students who, despite primarily specialising in History or related fields, continue to embrace the challenge of learning to work with 3D technologies and AI with admirable perseverance and enthusiasm.

REFERENCES

3Tooling. (2022). Kulturní dědictví a restaurování. https://www.3tooling.cz/novinky/kulturni-dedictvi-a-restaurovani-a6737ac5cf236cb65e17dcb0e

Gadget Hacks. (n.d.). You're using LiDAR on your iPhone and iPad—and you don't even know it. Retrieved June 22, 2025, from https://apple.gadgethacks.com/how-to/youre-using%20lidar-your-iphone-and-ipad-and-you-dont-even-know-0385523/

Luma AI, Inc. (n.d.). Luma 3D Capture [Mobile app]. App Store. Retrieved June 22, 2025, from https://apps.apple.com/us/app/luma-3d-capture/id1615849914

Luma AI, Inc. (n.d.). Luma AI: 3D Capture [Mobile app]. Google Play Store. Retrieved June 22, 2025, from https://play.google.com/store/apps/details?id=ai.lumalabs.polar

MAWIS. (2025). 3D dokumentace mobilem. https://mawis.eu/sluzby/3d-dokumentace-mobilem/

Muenster, S. (2022). Digital 3D technologies for humanities research and education: An overview. Applied Sciences, 12(5), 2426. https://doi.org/10.3390/app12052426

Palčák, M., Kudela, P., Fandáková, M., & Kordek, J. (2022). Utilization of 3D digital technologies in the documentation of cultural heritage: A case study of the Kunerad Mansion (Slovakia). Applied Sciences, 12(9), 4376. https://doi.org/10.3390/app12094376

Polycam. (n.d.). Reality capture for professionals: Document, measure, design. Retrieved June 22, 2025, from https://poly.cam/

Rodriguez-Garcia, B., Guillen-Sanz, H., Checa, D., & Bustillo, A. (2024). A systematic review of virtual 3D reconstructions of cultural heritage in immersive virtual reality. Multimedia Tools and Applications, 83, 89743–89793. https://doi.org/10.1007/s11042-024-18700-3

Shih, N.-J., Diao, P.-H., Qiu, Y.-T., & Chen, T.-Y. (2021). Situated AR simulations of a lantern festival using a smartphone and LiDAR-based 3D models. Applied Sciences, 11(1), 12. https://doi.org/10.3390/app11010012

Stylianidis, E., Evangelidis, K., Vital, R., Dafiotis, P., & Sylaïou, S. (2022). 3D documentation and visualisation of cultural heritage buildings through geospatial technologies. Heritage, 5(4), 146. https://doi.org/10.3390/heritage5040146

Trnio. (n.d.). Trnio. Retrieved June 22, 2025, from https://www.trnio.com/

WALKING IN VIRTUAL SHOES: CAN CREATING AVATARS IN SOCIAL VIRTUAL REALITY ENHANCE COUNSELING COMPETENCE, PRESENCE, PERSPECTIVE TAKING, EMBODIMENT AND ENGAGEMENT?

Dominik Evangelou, Miriam Mulders and Kristian H. Träg
Chair of Educational Media and Instructional Design,
University of Duisburg-Essen, Germany

ABSTRACT

Theoretical background: Research in social virtual reality (VR) suggests that avatar customization may enhance user engagement, embodiment, and perspective-taking through increased identification and presence. These processes are considered crucial for experiential learning and the development of interpersonal competencies in simulated environments.
Methods: The study utilized a 2 (avatar condition: customizable vs. generic) x 2 (debriefing condition: moderated vs. self-guided) factorial design with repeated measures across three time points. 45 undergraduate students of educational science from a German university participated and were randomly assigned to one of four groups. Participants completed a 20-minute VR counseling session in a university laboratory using the Meta Quest 3 system and the Engage VR platform. Individuals in the customizable avatar condition created their own avatar prior to the VR session, while those in the generic avatar condition proceeded directly to the scenario. The present analysis focuses on the impact of avatar customization.
Results: No significant effects of avatar customization were found on self-efficacy, counseling competence, embodiment, perspective-taking, presence or engagement. However, significant improvements in self-efficacy and counseling competence were observed across the three measurement time points, irrespective of avatar condition. Thus, hypotheses regarding the superiority of customized avatars over generic avatars could not be supported.
Conclusion: The findings suggest that while avatar customization alone does not significantly impact the measured outcomes, VR scenarios can still effectively improve counseling competence and self-efficacy. This highlights the potential of VR for competence development but also points to the need for further research into the specific mechanisms such as presence or identification that mediate learning effects in virtual environments.

KEYWORDS

Virtual Reality, Avatar, Customization, Embodiment, Perspective-Taking, Engagement, First-Person-Perspective

1. INTRODUCTION

In recent years, game-based learning (GBL) has gained increasing attention in educational research and practice (Chen & Yang, 2013; Darejeh & Salim, 2016; Hsiao & Chen, 2016; Lan et al. 2018; Yeh & Lan, 2018). By incorporating game elements into digital learning environments, GBL aims to enhance learners' motivation, engagement, and cognitive involvement. A central feature of many game-based systems is the use of avatars (Birk et al., 2016; Gazzard, 2009; Lee, 2005). Unlike physical learning settings, where social interaction takes place face-to-face, virtual environments allow learners to engage through avatars, thereby fostering social presence and identification with the learning context (Gee, 2003; Waggoner, 2009). In this sense, avatars function as digital self-representations (Chae et al., 2016; Gerhard & Moore, 1998).

Avatars play a central role in human-computer interaction (HCI), as they are essential for understanding user experiences within virtual environments. They serve as the representative—or embodiment—of a user within a digital space, which can range from a simple text-based username (Boberg et al., 2008) to a graphical icon (Nakamura, 2007). In the context of three-dimensional virtual worlds, however, the concept of avatar primarily refers to the user's ability to create interactive, customizable characters that serve as digital embodiments of the self and facilitate engagement with the virtual environment (Taylor, 2002).

One particularly relevant aspect of avatar use in digital environments is their customizability. Users are typically given the ability to personalize their avatars by altering visual characteristics such as gender, skin tone, body shape, and clothing, as well as functional attributes such as skills or equipment. This form of visual control and self-expression not only enhances users' identification with their avatars but also strengthens their sense of autonomy, authenticity, and involvement within the virtual environment (Yee & Bailenson, 2009).

The present paper focuses on the effectiveness of avatar customization within a virtual reality (VR) environment. Specifically, it examines whether creating a personalized avatar has a more positive impact on students' counseling competence and self-efficacy than using a generic avatar. The paper is structured as follows: first, the theoretical background is presented, addressing both the role of avatars in VR environments and the significance of customization within these contexts, Subsequently, our study is described, and the results are presented and critically discussed.

2. THEORETICAL BACKGROUND

Social VR has emerged as a novel form of digitally mediated social space, defined as multi-user, 3D virtual environments accessed via head-mounted displays (McVeigh-Schultz et al., 2018, 2019). Building on collaborative virtual environments (Benford et al., 1995), social VR enables users to create and personalize avatars that serve as embodied representations within these spaces. There are several social VR environments in which users can create and control their own humanoid characters (Evangelou et al., 2025). Unlike traditional digital interaction through input devices, social VR leverages full-body tracking to mirror users' real-time physical movements (Freeman & Maloney, 2021). This fosters immersive, socially oriented experiences ranging from attending virtual events to collaborative gaming (McVeigh-Schultz et al., 2019).

While existing research predominantly focuses on communication modalities (Baker et al., 2019; Maloney & Freeman, 2020), user safety (Blackwell et al., 2019), and relational dynamics (Zamanifard & Freeman, 2019), it has often neglected the distinctive self-presentation mechanisms afforded by VR. One critical aspect of VR that remains underexplored is how self-presentation unfolds through avatars. Avatars in social VR act as dynamic, embodied agents, contrasting with curated profiles on conventional social media (Freeman & Maloney, 2021). This embodiment creates a direct link between bodily presence and virtual identity, which shapes user experiences, identity expression, and social relationships (Birk et al., 2016; Schroeder, 2001; Vasalou & Joinson, 2009).

2.1 Avatar Customization and Psychological Effects

Avatars function as bridges between users and virtual worlds, enabling identity exploration beyond physical constraints (Vasalou & Joinson, 2009; Schroeder, 2001). Customization enhances users' sense of identification, autonomy, and social connectedness (Birk et al., 2016; Ducheneaut et al., 2009). Empirical studies show that personalized avatars especially those resembling the user foster psychological ownership and embodiment, improving emotional engagement, and presence (Gonzalez-Franco et al., 2024; Waltemate et al., 2018; Kilteni et al., 2012).

According to self-discrepancy theory (Higgins, 1987), avatars can represent actual, ideal, or ought selves, influencing motivation and emotions in VR (Devlin et al., 2024). Users balance these identities to portray aspirational selves or experiment with alternatives (Jin, 2012; Kang & Kim, 2020). Avatar attributes like similarity and attractiveness induce the Proteus effect, affecting users' behavior and social confidence (Yee & Bailenson, 2007; Nowak & Fox, 2018).

Further, avatar design including perspective and nonverbal expressiveness impacts embodiment and socio-emotional outcomes, with implications for therapy and education settings (Fabri et al., 2007; Pauw et al., 2022; Wu et al., 2023).

2.2 Counseling Competencies in VR

Counseling demands a multifaceted skill set involving empathy, communication, problem-solving, and relational competence (Egan, 2002; Rogers, 1957). Training such skills traditionally requires resource-intensive, face-to-face role plays with supervision and feedback. VR offers a promising alternative by providing realistic, repeatable scenarios for experiential learning (Schmid Mast et al., 2018).

In social VR, users can step into the role of a counselor through their avatar and practice core counseling techniques such as (1) summarizing, paraphrasing, mirroring, (2) I-messages, and (3) diverse questioning techniques (Schlüter & Kress, 2017). Customizable avatars may enhance training effectiveness by increasing psychological ownership and embodiment, which in turn can improve counseling self-efficacy and competence (Gonzalez-Franco et al., 2024; Kilteni et al., 2012).

Our study builds on this foundation by investigating whether creating personalized avatars leads to measurable improvements in counseling competencies and self-efficacy compared to generic avatars, thus contributing to advancing technology-enhanced counseling education.

Based on the theoretical background, this study examines the impact of avatar customization within a first-person VR environment. While personalized avatars are suggested to enhance identification, embodiment, and engagement, controlled studies are needed to isolate customization effects in immersive contexts.

H1: Creating a customized avatar leads to greater self-efficacy and counseling competence compared to a generic avatar.

H2: Creating a customized avatar leads to greater self-presence compared to a generic avatar.

H3: Creating a customized avatar leads to higher engagement, embodiment, and perspective-taking compared to a generic avatar.

3. METHODS

The study was conducted in January 2025 as part of the research project *VR-Hybrid* (project number FR-124/2023), which investigates the educational potential of VR for training counseling competencies in higher education. The present investigation employed a 2 (avatar condition: customizable vs. generic) x 2 (debriefing condition: moderated vs. self-guided) factorial design with repeated measures across three time points (pretest, posttest, follow-up). This study primarily aimed to assess effectiveness of a single session VR intervention in enhancing counseling competence and self-efficacy. The study was preregistered on the Open Science Framework (OSF), and all sessions took place in a university laboratory using the *Meta Quest 3* headset and the *Engage* VR platform.

3.1 Sample

A total of 46 undergraduate students enrolled in educational science programs at a large German university participated. One student discontinued participation due to motion sickness, resulting in a final sample of $N = 45$ ($M = 24.5$ years, $SD = 8.7$; 39 female, 6 male). Students were recruited via seminar announcements and participated voluntarily in exchange for course credit. Informed consent was obtained from all participants in accordance with institutional ethical procedures. To ensure data pseudonymization across time points, participants created a four-digit personal code prior to completing the first questionnaire.

3.2 Procedure

Participants individually completed a 20-minute VR counseling session. After informed consent and a briefing, they filled out a pretest questionnaire assessing demographics, prior VR experience, empathy, counseling competence, and self-efficacy. Participants were then randomly assigned to one of four conditions: (1) customization + moderated debriefing, (2) customization + self-guided debriefing, (3) generic avatar + moderated debriefing, or (4) generic avatar + self-guided debriefing. They were instructed to apply previously taught communication techniques, including summarizing, paraphrasing, mirroring, I-messages, and questioning strategies.

The avatar manipulation—central to this study—is described in more detail below. Participants in the customizable avatar condition created a personalized avatar using the Engage platform's character editor, adjusting features such as name, gender, height, facial traits, hairstyle, and clothing. In contrast, participants in the generic condition entered the VR scenario without avatar customization.

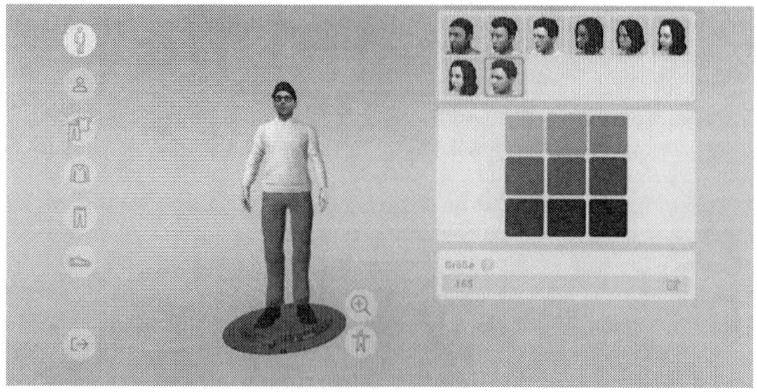

Figure 1. Avatar creation

All participants experienced the counseling session from a first-person perspective, embodying the role of a counselor. Only their virtual hands, legs, and feet were visible; no third-person avatar view was provided. During the session, they interacted with a virtual client named Lena, portrayed by trained research assistants following a standardized script. The setting simulated a realistic counseling room to enhance immersion.

After the session, participants completed a post-questionnaire assessing counseling competence, self-efficacy, presence, realism, embodiment, perspective-taking, cognitive load, and engagement. This was followed by either a moderated debriefing or a self-guided chatbot debriefing. Finally, a follow-up questionnaire captured the same key outcome variables.

The current study focuses on the impact of avatar customization by comparing personalized and generic avatars. Accordingly, data from the first and second questionnaires are central to the analysis.

3.3 Measurement Instruments

To investigate the effects of avatar creation on counseling-related learning, a set of validated self-report instruments was employed at various stages of the study. Counseling competence and self-efficacy were assessed at all three measurement time points. Engagement was measured at the post-test and the follow-up test, while embodiment and perspective-taking were collected only after the VR intervention.

Counseling competence was evaluated using a 22-item scale, which was adapted from Hertel's (2009) original scale and modified to be applicable in various counseling contexts. The items were rated in an 8-point Likert scale, with responses ranging from *does not apply at all* to *fully applies*. For example, an item is: "*I can structure a consultation in a way that is easy for the person seeking advice to understand.*" Self-efficacy in counseling contexts was measured using a 9-item scale, which was also adapted from Hertel (2009). The items were rated on a 6-point Likert scale, with responses ranging from *strongly disagree* to *strongly agree*. A sample item reads: "*I feel comfortable and confident in consultations*.". Embodiment was assessed using the *Virtual Embodiment Questionnaire* (Roth & Latoschik, 2020), which measured the degree of body ownership in VR. Participants responded to items such as "*I felt as if the virtual body was my own body.*" on a 7-point scale ranging from 1 ("*does absolutely not apply*") to 7 ("*fully applies*"). Perspective-taking was assessed using statements like "*During the VR training, I felt like I could put myself in the character's shoes.*" also on a 7-point scale (Peng et al., 2010). Engagement was measured using the 4-item subscale of the *Web-based Learning Tools Evaluation Scale* (Kay, 2011), which consisted of items such as "*I would like to use the VR training again.*" rated on a 5-point scale ranging from 1 ("*does not apply at all*") to 5("*fully applies*"). Presence was assessed using the Multimodal Presence Scale (Makransky et al., 2017) with items such as "*The virtual environment seemed real to me,*" rated on a 6-point scale ranging from 1 ("*does absolutely not apply*") to 6 ("*fully applies*").

4. RESULTS

This section presents the quantitative results of our experiment. We begin by providing descriptive statistics and verifying the assumptions necessary for the applied statistical methods. Based on these assessments, appropriate analyses were conducted. The results are then discussed in relation to the formulated hypotheses. To test hypothesis 1, analyses of variance (ANOVA) were employed. Hypothesis 2 was examined using a Welch two-sample t-test, while hypothesis 3 was analyzed with a Mann-Whitney U-test due to violations of the normality assumption. All statistical analyses were performed using R version 4.2.2.

Table 1 displays the descriptive statistics for all variables. All scales exhibit excellent internal consistency, as indicated by Cronbach's alpha (Cronbach, 1951).

Table 1. Descriptive Statistics (t = measurement time point, Md = Median)

	Min	Md	Max	*M*	*SD*	α
Self-efficacy (t1)	2.38	4.1	5.75	4.1	0.82	.89
Self-efficacy (t2)	1.5	4.13	5.75	4.2	0.91	.92
Counseling competence (t1)	3.86	5.4	7.29	5.4	0.83	.94
Counseling competence (t2)	2.23	5.59	7.52	5.6	1.14	.96
Embodiment	1.0	3.83	7.0	3.83	1.32	.93
Perspective-Taking	2.17	5.5	7.0	5.34	1.06	.9
Engagement	2.0	4.25	5.0	4.12	0.86	.92
Presence	1.13	3.87	5.8	3.85	1.04	.94

The repeated-measurement ANOVA revealed no significant effect of avatar condition on self-efficacy, $F(1,43) = 0.26$, $p = .615$, indicating that participants using a customized avatar did not differ in self-efficacy from those using a generic avatar. Consequently, the hypothesis that creating a personalized avatar results in higher self-efficacy must be rejected. A similar pattern emerged for counseling competence, with no significant main effect of avatar condition observed, $F(1,43) = 0.32$, $p = .574$. Thus, the expectation that a customized avatar would lead to greater counseling competence compared to a generic avatar could not be supported. However, it is noteworthy that there were significant positive changes in both self-efficacy and counseling competence over the course of the study. Specifically, the ANOVAs revealed a significant main effect of time for self-efficacy, $F(2,86) = 8.66$, $p < .001$, indicating that self-efficacy increased significantly across the three measurement time points. Similarly, counseling competence showed a significant improvement over time, $F(2,86) = 12.41$, $p < .001$, with participants demonstrating higher levels at later measurement points compared to the beginning of the study.

A Welch two-sample t-test was conducted to compare the scores of the personalized avatar and the generic avatar on presence. Results indicated no statistically significant difference between the groups, $t(42.99) = 0.72$, $p = .476$, Although the mean score was slightly higher in the personalized avatar group ($M = 3.95$) compared to the generic avatar group ($M = 3.73$), this difference was not statistically significant. Hypothesis 2, which proposed that creating a customized avatar leads to greater self-presence compared to a generic avatar, must be rejected.

No significant effects of avatar condition were found for any of the three learning process variables at the second measurement time point. For embodiment an independent samples t-test showed no significant difference between groups, $t(39.52) = 0.26$, $p = .796$. For perspective-taking, the Mann-Whitney U test indicated no significant difference between conditions, $W = 301.5$, $p = .274$; and for engagement, the Mann-Whitney U test likewise showed no significant difference, $W = 268.5$, $p = .728$. Due to the presence of ties in the data, the p-values for both Mann-Whitney U tests were calculated using a normal approximation rather than an exact method (Mann & Whitney, 1947). Consequently, the hypotheses that creating a customized avatar leads to higher levels of embodiment, perspective-taking, and engagement compared to using a generic avatar must be rejected.

5. CONCLUSION

This study investigated whether creating a customized avatar, compared to using a generic one, would lead to greater self-efficacy, counseling competence, self-presence, embodiment, perspective-taking, and engagement in a VR-based counseling training. Based on prior research (e.g., Gonzalez-Franco et al., 2024; Kilteni et al., 2012; Higgins, 1987), it was hypothesized that personalized avatars would enhance identification, embodiment, and learning outcomes by strengthening psychological ownership and supporting users' ideal or actual self-representations. Contrary to these theoretical expectations and earlier empirical findings suggesting benefits of avatar customization for emotional engagement and social confidence (Yee & Bailenson, 2007; Ducheneaut et al., 2009), our results revealed no significant effects of avatar personalization on self-efficacy, counseling competence, self-presence, embodiment, perspective-taking, or engagement. Participants using customized avatars performed similarly to those with generic avatars across all measures, leading us to reject the hypotheses. Despite this, self-efficacy and counseling competence significantly improved over time across all participants, confirming that immersive VR training can facilitate skill development effectively, in line with extant literature on immersive learning environments.

One plausible reason for the absence of avatar-specific effects may be the high-fidelity, first-person VR environment, where scenario authenticity and immersive presence potentially overshadow the influence of avatar appearance – a factor less emphasized in prior studies largely conducted in less immersive or third-person contexts (Freeman & Maloney, 2021; McVeigh-Schultz et al., 2019). Additionally, the limited continuous visual exposure to avatars after their creation likely diminished identification and embodiment effects that theories by Gonzalez-Franco et al. (2024) and Higgins (1987) underscore as critical. To overcome these limitations, future research should incorporate sustained avatar visibility, for example through virtual mirrors or third-person perspectives, and integrate dedicated familiarization phases to increase presence and cognitive readiness. In a planned follow-up study, participants will have an extended acclimatization period and will take full-body selfies using an in-software camera before starting the training, allowing careful inspection of their avatars. This setup aims to enhance embodiment, self-presence, and engagement. Further investigation is also necessary into psychological and social mediators of VR training outcomes and their interaction with avatar design. Moderating factors such as prior VR experience, empathy, and gender identity warrant attention, and manipulations like avatar naming present promising avenues to boost identification (Carter et al., 2012).

Overall, this study highlights a noteworthy divergence between theoretical models predicting avatar customization benefits and observed empirical outcomes within first-person, high-fidelity VR counseling simulations. Nonetheless, VR continues to hold potential as an effective tool for counseling skill development, provided design and training protocols are refined accordingly.

REFERENCES

Baker, S., Kelly, R. M., Waycott, J., Carrasco, R., Hoang, T., Batchelor, F., Ozanne, E., Dow, B., Warburton, J., & Vetere, F. (2019). Interrogating Social Virtual Reality as a Communication Medium for Older Adults. Proceedings of the ACM on Human-Computer Interaction, 3(CSCW), 1–24. https://doi.org/10.1145/3359251

Birk, M. V., Atkins, C., Bowey, J. T., & Mandryk, R. L. (2016). Fostering Intrinsic Motivation through Avatar Identification in Digital Games. Proceedings of the 2016 CHI Conference on Human Factors in Computing Systems, 2982–2995. https://doi.org/10.1145/2858036.2858062

Blackwell, L., Ellison, N., Elliott-Deflo, N., & Schwartz, R. (2019). Harassment in Social Virtual Reality: Challenges for Platform Governance. Proceedings of the ACM on Human-Computer Interaction, 3(CSCW), 1–25. https://doi.org/10.1145/3359202

Benford, S., Bowers, J., Fahlén, L. E., Greenhalgh, C., & Snowdon, D. (1995, May). User embodiment in collaborative virtual environments. In *roceedings of the SIGCHI conference on Human factors in computing systems* (pp. 242-249).

Boberg, M., Piippo, P., & Ollila, E. (2008). Designing avatars. Proceedings of the 3rd International Conference on Digital Interactive Media in Entertainment and Arts, 232–239. https://doi.org/10.1145/1413634.1413679

Carter, M., Gibbs, M., & Arnold, M. (2012, November). Avatars, characters, players and users: multiple identities at/in play. In *Proceedings of the 24th Australian Computer-Human Interaction Conference* (pp. 68-71). https://doi.org/10.1145/2414536.241454

Chae, S. W., Lee, K. C., & Seo, Y. W. (2016). Exploring the Effect of Avatar Trust on Learners' Perceived Participation Intentions in an e-Learning Environment. International Journal of Human–Computer Interaction, 32(5), 373–393. https://doi.org/10.1080/10447318.2016.1150643

Chen, H.-J. H., & Yang, T.-Y. C. (2013). The impact of adventure video games on foreign language learning and the perceptions of learners. Interactive Learning Environments, 21(2), 129–141. https://doi.org/10.1080/10494820.2012.705851

Cronbach, L. J. (1951). Coefficient Alpha and the Internal Structure of Tests. Psychometrika, 16(3), 297–334. Cambridge Core. https://doi.org/10.1007/BF02310555

Darejeh, A., & and Salim, S. S. (2016). Gamification Solutions to Enhance Software User Engagement—A Systematic Review. International Journal of Human–Computer Interaction, 32(8), 613–642. https://doi.org/10.1080/10447318.2016.1183330

Devlin, M. M., Ellithorpe, M. E., Gadino, N., Ewoldsen, D. R., & Weir, S. (2024). Me, myself, and my avatar: Self-discrepancy, embodiment, and narrative involvement in gaming experiences. Psychology of Popular Media, 14(2), 294–303. https://doi.org/10.1037/ppm0000542

Ducheneaut, N., Wen, M.-H., Yee, N., & Wadley, G. (2009). Body and mind: A study of avatar personalization in three virtual worlds. Proceedings of the SIGCHI Conference on Human Factors in Computing Systems, 1151–1160. https://doi.org/10.1145/1518701.1518877

Egan, G. (2002). The skilled helper: A problem-management and opportunity-development approach to helping. *Brooks/Cole*.

Evangelou, D., Mulders, M., & Sekerci, B. (2025). An Overview of Commercial Virtual Reality Providers in Education: Mapping the Current Market Landscape. *Applied Sciences*, *15*(7), 3906. https://doi.org/10.3390/app15073906

Fabri, M., Elzouki, S. Y. A., & Moore, D. (2007). Emotionally Expressive Avatars for Chatting, Learning and Therapeutic Intervention. In J. A. Jacko (Hrsg.), Human-Computer Interaction. HCI Intelligent Multimodal Interaction Environments (Bd. 4552, S. 275–285). Springer Berlin Heidelberg. https://doi.org/10.1007/978-3-540-73110-8_29

Freeman, G., & Maloney, D. (2021). Body, Avatar, and Me: The Presentation and Perception of Self in Social Virtual Reality. Proceedings of the ACM on Human-Computer Interaction, 4(CSCW3), 1–27. https://doi.org/10.1145/3432938

Gazzard, A. (2009). The Avatar and the Player: Understanding the Relationship beyond the Screen. 2009 Conference in Games and Virtual Worlds for Serious Applications, 190–193. https://doi.org/10.1109/VS-GAMES.2009.11

Gee, J. P. (2003). What video games have to teach us about learning and literacy. *Computers in entertainment (CIE)*, *1*(1), 20-20. https://doi.org/10.1145/950566.95059

Gerhard, M., & Moore, D. (1998). User embodiments in educational CVEs: towards continuous presence. In *4th EATA International Conference on Networking Entities, NETIES98: Networking for the Millennium, West Yorkshire, United Kingdom*.

Gonzalez-Franco, M., Steed, A., Berger, C. C., & Tajadura-Jiménez, A. (2024). The impact of first-person avatar customization on embodiment in immersive virtual reality. Frontiers in Virtual Reality, 5, 1436752. https://doi.org/10.3389/frvir.2024.1436752

Hertel, S. (2009). *Beratungskompetenz von Lehrern. Kompetenzdiagnostik, Kompetenzförderung, Kompetenzmodellierung.* (Pädagogische Psychologie und Entwicklungspsychologie, Band 74). Münster: Waxmann Verlag.

Higgins, E. T. (1987). Self-discrepancy: a theory relating self and affect. *Psychological review*, *94*(3), 319.

Hsiao, H.-S., & Chen, J.-C. (2016). Using a gesture interactive game-based learning approach to improve preschool children's learning performance and motor skills. Computers & Education, 95, 151–162. https://doi.org/10.1016/j.compedu.2016.01.005

Jin, S.-A. A. (2012). The virtual malleable self and the virtual identity discrepancy model: Investigative frameworks for virtual possible selves and others in avatar-based identity construction and social interaction. Computers in Human Behavior, 28(6), 2160–2168. https://doi.org/10.1016/j.chb.2012.06.022

Kang, H., & Kim, H. K. (2020). My avatar and the affirmed self: Psychological and persuasive implications of avatar customization. Computers in Human Behavior, 112, 106446. https://doi.org/10.1016/j.chb.2020.106446

Kay, R. (2011). Evaluating learning, design, and engagement in web-based learning tools (WBLTs): The WBLT Evaluation Scale. Computers in Human Behavior, 27(5), 1849–1856. https://doi.org/10.1016/j.chb.2011.04.007

Kilteni, K., Groten, R., & Slater, M. (2012). The Sense of Embodiment in Virtual Reality. Presence: Teleoperators and Virtual Environments, 21(4), 373–387. https://doi.org/10.1162/PRES_a_00124

Lan, Y.-J., Hsiao, I. Y. T., & Shih, M.-F. (2018). Effective Learning Design of Game-Based 3D Virtual Language Learning Environments for Special Education Students. *Journal of Educational Technology & Society*, *21*(3), 213–227. http://www.jstor.org/stable/26458519

Lee, H. S. (2005). Case study about types of avatar as an important factor of communication. *Journal of Digital Design*, *9*, 92-99.

Makransky, G., Lilleholt, L., & Aaby, A. (2017). Development and validation of the Multimodal Presence Scale for virtual reality environments: A confirmatory factor analysis and item response theory approach. Computers in Human Behavior, 72, 276–285. https://doi.org/10.1016/j.chb.2017.02.066

Maloney, D., & Freeman, G. (2020). Falling Asleep Together: What Makes Activities in Social Virtual Reality Meaningful to Users. Proceedings of the Annual Symposium on Computer-Human Interaction in Play, 510–521. https://doi.org/10.1145/3410404.3414266

Maloney, D., Freeman, G., & Wohn, D. Y. (2020). „Talking without a Voice": Understanding Non-verbal Communication in Social Virtual Reality. Proceedings of the ACM on Human-Computer Interaction, 4(CSCW2), 1–25. https://doi.org/10.1145/3415246

Maloney, D., Rajasabeson, S., Moore, A., Caldwell, J., Archer, J., & Robb, A. (2019). Ethical Concerns of the Use of Virtual Avatars in Consumer Entertainment. 2019 IEEE Conference on Virtual Reality and 3D User Interfaces (VR), 1489–1492. https://doi.org/10.1109/VR.2019.8797926

Mann, H. B., & Whitney, D. R. (1947). On a test of whether one of two random variables is stochastically larger than the other. *The annals of mathematical statistics*, 50-60.

McVeigh-Schultz, J., Kolesnichenko, A., & Isbister, K. (2019). Shaping Pro-Social Interaction in VR: An Emerging Design Framework. Proceedings of the 2019 CHI Conference on Human Factors in Computing Systems, 1–12. https://doi.org/10.1145/3290605.3300794

McVeigh-Schultz, J., Márquez Segura, E., Merrill, N., & Isbister, K. (2018). What's It Mean to „Be Social" in VR?: Mapping the Social VR Design Ecology. Proceedings of the 2018 ACM Conference Companion Publication on Designing Interactive Systems, 289–294. https://doi.org/10.1145/3197391.3205451

Nakamura, L. (2007). *Digitizing race: Visual cultures of the Internet* (Vol. 23). U of Minnesota Press.

Nowak, K. L., & Fox, J. (2018). Avatars and computer-mediated communication: a review of the definitions, uses, and effects of digital representations. *Review of Communication Research*, *6*, 30-53.

Pauw, L. S., Sauter, D. A., Van Kleef, G. A., Lucas, G. M., Gratch, J., & Fischer, A. H. (2022). The avatar will see you now: Support from a virtual human provides socio-emotional benefits. Computers in Human Behavior, 136, 107368. https://doi.org/10.1016/j.chb.2022.107368

Peng, W., Lee, M., & Heeter, C. (2010). The Effects of a Serious Game on Role-Taking and Willingness to Help. Journal of Communication, 60(4), 723–742. https://doi.org/10.1111/j.1460-2466.2010.01511.x

Rogers, C. R. (1957). The necessary and sufficient conditions of therapeutic personality change. *Journal of consulting psychology*, *21*(2), 95.

Roth, D., & Latoschik, M. E. (2020). Construction of the Virtual Embodiment Questionnaire (VEQ). IEEE Transactions on Visualization and Computer Graphics, 26(12), 3546–3556. https://doi.org/10.1109/TVCG.2020.3023603

Schlüter, A., & Kress, K. (2017). *Methoden und Techniken der Bildungsberatung*. Verlag Barbara Budrich.

Schmid Mast, M., Kleinlogel, E. P., Tur, B., & Bachmann, M. (2018). The future of interpersonal skills development: Immersive virtual reality training with virtual humans. *Human Resource Development Quarterly*, *29*(2), 125-141.

Schroeder, R. (Ed.). (2001). *The social life of avatars: Presence and interaction in shared virtual environments*. Springer Science & Business Media.

Takano, M., & Taka, F. (2022). Fancy avatar identification and behaviors in the virtual world: Preceding avatar customization and succeeding communication. Computers in Human Behavior Reports, 6, 100176. https://doi.org/10.1016/j.chbr.2022.100176

Taylor, T. L. (2002). Living Digitally: Embodiment in Virtual Worlds. In R. Schroeder (Hrsg.), The Social Life of Avatars: Presence and Interaction in Shared Virtual Environments (S. 40–62). Springer London. https://doi.org/10.1007/978-1-4471-0277-9_3

Vasalou, A., & Joinson, A. N. (2009). Me, myself and I: The role of interactional context on self-presentation through avatars. Computers in Human Behavior, 25(2), 510–520. https://doi.org/10.1016/j.chb.2008.11.007

Waggoner, Z. (2009). *My avatar, my self: Identity in video role-playing games*. McFarland.

Waltemate, T., Gall, D., Roth, D., Botsch, M., & Latoschik, M. E. (2018). The Impact of Avatar Personalization and Immersion on Virtual Body Ownership, Presence, and Emotional Response. IEEE Transactions on Visualization and Computer Graphics, 24(4), 1643–1652. https://doi.org/10.1109/TVCG.2018.2794629

Wu, S., Xu, L., Dai, Z., & Pan, Y. (2023). Factors Affecting Avatar Customization Behavior in Virtual Environments. Electronics, 12(10), 2286. https://doi.org/10.3390/electronics12102286

Yee, N., & Bailenson, J. (2007). The Proteus Effect: The Effect of Transformed Self-Representation on Behavior. Human Communication Research, 33(3), 271–290. https://doi.org/10.1111/j.1468-2958.2007.00299.x

Yee, N., & Bailenson, J. N. (2009). The Difference Between Being and Seeing: The Relative Contribution of Self-Perception and Priming to Behavioral Changes via Digital Self-Representation. Media Psychology, 12(2), 195–209. https://doi.org/10.1080/15213260902849943

Yeh, Y.-L., & Lan, Y.-J. (2018). Fostering student autonomy in English learning through creations in a 3D virtual world. Educational Technology Research and Development, 66(3), 693–708. https://doi.org/10.1007/s11423-017-9566-6

Zamanifard, S., & Freeman, G. (2019). „The Togetherness that We Crave": Experiencing Social VR in Long Distance Relationships. Companion Publication of the 2019 Conference on Computer Supported Cooperative Work and Social Computing, 438–442. https://doi.org/10.1145/3311957.3359453

FROM DASHBOARD TO CLASSROOM: A CASE STUDY OF TEACHER-FACING DASHBOARD IMPACT ON LEARNING PERFORMANCE AND BEHAVIORS

Xuewang Geng[1], Kohei Ozaki[2] and Masanori Yamada[3]
[1]*Faculty of Computer and Information Sciences, Sojo University*
4-22-1 Ikeda, Nishi-ku, Kumamoto 860-0082, Japan
[2]*Graduate School of Human-environment Studies, Kyushu University*
744 Motooka, Nishi-ku, Fukuoka 819-0395, Japan
[3]*Data-Driven Innovation Initiative, Kyushu University,*
744 Motooka, Nishi-ku, Fukuoka 819-0395, Japan

ABSTRACT

This study investigated teacher-facing Learning Analytics Dashboard (LAD) effectiveness by examining interaction processes and their impact on student learning behaviors and outcomes. A case study was conducted with one teacher and 17 high school students over 26 World History classes using B-QUBE digital learning platform and Activity Monitor dashboard. Lag Sequential Analysis examined behavioral relationships between teacher LAD interventions and student learning activities. Results showed teachers primarily engaged in class-wide learning data confirmation, which served as a powerful classroom orchestration tool facilitating learning phase transitions. Students were categorized into high attention and low attention groups based on teacher monitoring frequency. High attention students achieved significantly better post-test performance and demonstrated more complex learning patterns, such as using handwriting notes to summarize and summarize materials. This study innovatively integrated teacher LAD usage data with student learning data, providing empirical evidence for how teacher-facing LADs influence learning processes.

KEYWORDS

Learning Analytics Dashboard, Teacher-facing Dashboard, Lag Sequential Analysis, Learning Analytics, E-book System

1. INTRODUCTION

The transition from traditional paper-based instruction to digital learning environments has transformed the way students engage with learning materials and how teachers facilitate instruction. Digital learning platforms now offer interactive features such as highlighting, annotating, note-taking, and embedded quizzes (Ogata et al., 2015; Yamada et al., 2024), which not only enrich learning experiences but also produce continuous streams of behavioral data. These data hold the potential to support evidence-based instruction and personalized guidance, yet their complexity and scale pose significant interpretation challenges for educators (Jivet et al., 2018).

Learning analytics has emerged as a promising approach to address these challenges by collecting, analyzing, and interpreting educational data to inform teaching and learning (LAK, 2011). Among the key tools in this domain are LADs, which visualize complex learning behaviors and translate raw data into actionable insights (Teasley, 2017). Depending on their target users, LADs are typically categorized as either student-facing or teacher-facing. Student-facing LADs support learners' metacognitive awareness and self-regulation by displaying individual progress, time management, and goal achievement (Chen et al., 2020; Geng et al., 2020; Park et al., 2023; Yousef & Khatiry, 2023; Geng & Yamada, 2025). In contrast, teacher-facing LADs provide aggregated data on student behaviors and engagement patterns, enabling instructors to monitor learning in real time, identify struggling learners, and tailor interventions (Dülger et al., 2025; Li et al., 2022). Recent advancements in teacher-facing LADs have demonstrated their potential to make invisible learning processes visible and to assist in classroom orchestration. For instance, dashboards allow teachers to compare individual and class-wide behaviors, track students' comprehension through response patterns, and identify focal points in student annotations (Martínez-Maldonado, 2019; Colling et al., 2024). However, existing studies often rely on teachers' subjective reports of dashboard usefulness or examine superficial metrics such as login frequency and duration of use (Molenaar & Knoop-van Campen, 2018; Van Leeuwen & Rummel, 2020). While informative, such studies fall short of elucidating the actual instructional processes through which LADs affect teaching practices and student learning behaviors.

Addressing this gap, recent work has begun to emphasize the need for process-oriented evaluations that capture the sequential and situated use of LADs during classroom activities (Li et al., 2022). Therefore, this study addresses these limitations by adopting a comprehensive, process-oriented approach to evaluate teacher LAD usage and its educational effects. Rather than simply measuring usage frequency, this study examines the sequential patterns of teacher dashboard interactions and student usage of digital learning material platforms, tracking the connections between teacher LAD activities and student learning behaviors and outcomes. To validate the behavioral sequential patterns of teachers and students, lag sequential analysis (LSA) was utilized for the analysis. LSA is a statistical technique that determines whether the probability of one event occurring following another event is statistically significant (Bakeman & Gottman, 1997). This study establishes the following two research questions (RQs):

RQ1: How did teacher-facing LAD activities relate to students' learning behaviors?

RQ2: What differences were in learning outcomes and learning behavior patterns between students who received high and low attention through LAD?

2. B-QUBE AND ACTIVITY MONITOR

2.1 Digital Learning Material Platform: B-QUBE system

This study utilized B-QUBE, which is a digital learning material platform (Yamada et al., 2024). B-QUBE provides a comprehensive digital textbook environment that replicates and enhances traditional paper-based learning experiences while capturing detailed behavioral data about student learning activities.

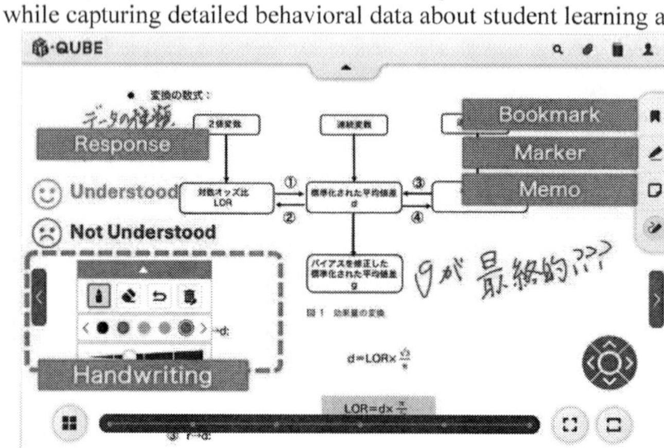

Figure 1. The Interface of B-QUBE System

B-QUBE offers core interactive functions for student engagement with digital materials (see Figure 1). Students can utilize marker and highlighting tools to emphasize important text passages, create bookmarks to mark significant sections for later reference, and add digital memos to record their thoughts and reflections about specific content areas. Given that students traditionally rely heavily on handwritten notes for organizing and summarizing their learning materials, B-QUBE incorporates a sophisticated handwriting note function to accommodate this learning practice. Students can write directly on the digital materials using either finger touch or stylus devices, closely mimicking the experience of writing in traditional paper textbooks. This handwriting functionality allows students to maintain their familiar note-taking behaviors while enabling the system to capture and analyze their cognitive engagement patterns reflected in their written annotations.

The handwriting function provides customization options including different line colors and thickness settings. The system also provides editing tools, including an eraser function, an undo feature to reverse previous actions, and a clear all function to remove all annotations from a page. B-QUBE also incorporates a response function that captures comprehension feedback through simple "understood" and "not understood" responses. This function enables real-time collection of student comprehension indicators throughout the learning process. All student interactions with B-QUBE, including reading behaviors, handwriting activities, response submissions, and bookmarks, are automatically logged and stored in the database.

2.2 Teacher-Facing Learning Analytics Dashboard: Activity Monitor System

To support teachers in utilizing the rich data generated by B-QUBE, we developed Activity Monitor, a comprehensive Learning Analytics Dashboard specifically designed for teacher use. Activity Monitor transforms the complex behavioral data captured by B-QUBE into meaningful visualizations that inform instructional decision-making. The activity monitor is divided into two parts: class-wide learning data visualization and individual student learning data visualization.

2.2.1 Class-Wide Learning Data Visualization

Activity Monitor provides teachers with comprehensive class-level analytics through several visualization components. The dashboard displays aggregated learning activity metrics showing the number of students who have accessed materials, created memos and markers, and bookmarked content across different pages of the digital textbook. This overview enables teachers to quickly identify which content sections generate high or low levels of student engagement. The system presents a heatmap visualization that displays the usage status of each function across all pages of the material (left of Figure 2). The heatmap uses a matrix format with the vertical axis representing different functions (markers, memos, bookmarks, handwriting, etc.) and the horizontal axis showing page numbers. Each cell's color intensity represents the usage frequency for that specific function on that particular page, with darker colors indicating higher usage frequency. This visualization enables teachers to quickly identify which functions on which pages are being used most frequently by students, providing valuable insights into content engagement patterns and learning behaviors across the entire textbook.

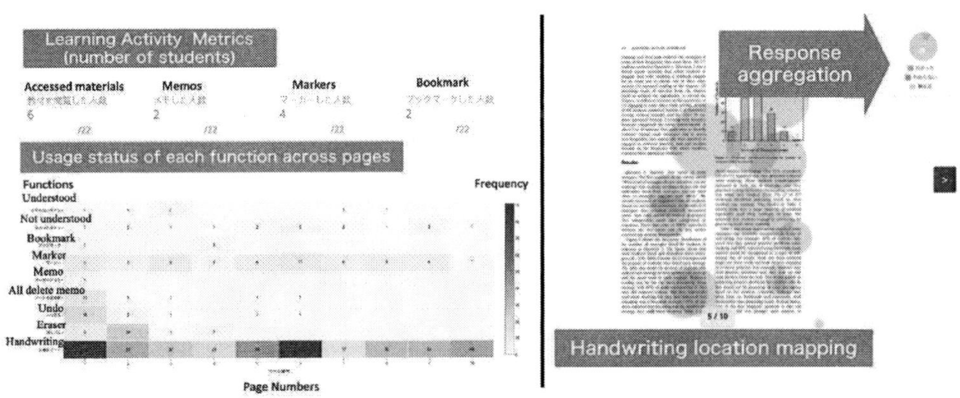

Figure 2. The Class-Wide Learning Data Visualization

Activity Monitor also includes a student response aggregation function that displays comprehension feedback through pie charts showing the distribution of "understood," "not understood," and "no response" categories for learning materials (right of Figure 2). This visualization helps teachers evaluate the difficulty level and clarity of materials in real-time. Activity Monitor also provides handwriting location mapping, where student annotation positions are displayed as red circles on textbook pages. When multiple students create notes in the same location, the color intensity increases, enabling teachers to identify content areas that attract widespread student attention and require additional focus or clarification.

2.2.2 Individual Student Learning Data Visualization

The dashboard offers detailed individual student analytics that allow teachers to examine specific learning patterns and behaviors (Figure 3). Teachers can select individual students to view their usage frequency across different platform functions (material viewing, page navigation, marker usage, memo creation) compared to class averages. This information is presented through bar charts where the selected student's data appears in green and class averages appear in gray, facilitating visual comparison. Activity Monitor includes a temporal handwriting note evolution feature that enables teachers to track how individual students develop their understanding over time. Teachers can browse through different versions of student handwriting on specific pages, with each version timestamped to show the progression of student thinking and comprehension. This functionality allows teachers to observe how students deepen their understanding and evolve their note-taking strategies throughout the learning process. The individual student view also displays comprehension responses ("understood" and "not understood") for each page, enabling teachers to combine handwriting note content analysis with comprehension feedback to make informed decisions about individualized instruction and support.

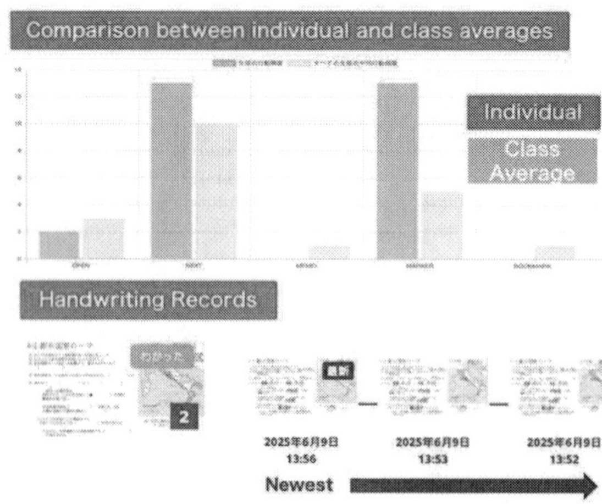

Figure 3. Individual Student Learning Data Visualization

3. METHODOLOGY

This study employed a case study design to examine teacher LAD usage processes and their impact on student learning behaviors and outcomes in an authentic classroom setting. The research involved one experienced teacher with extensive background in secondary education and 17 high school students enrolled in a World History course at a Japanese public high school. The study was conducted over an 8-week in 2025, encompassing 26 class sessions of 50 minutes each. The experimental procedure followed three phases: first, students completed a pre-test to establish baseline knowledge levels; second, students engaged in learning activities using B-QUBE while the teacher utilized Activity Monitor to monitor student behaviors and apply insights for instructional improvement and individualized guidance; finally, a post-test was administered to evaluate learning outcomes.

Data was collected from multiple sources to examine both teacher LAD usage processes and student learning outcomes. Learning outcomes were assessed through pre-test and post-test scores, which were standardized as Z-scores, as the content covered in the pre-test and post-test differs. Log data was collected from both the teacher-side and student-side, a total 129979 records. Activity Monitor dashboard, capturing all teacher interactions including class-wide learning data confirmation, individual student data examination, material selection, and student selection activities, and the student-side B-QUBE platform, which automatically recorded all learning behaviors including bookmark usage, handwriting notes, marker activities, memo creation, page changing, and response submissions. LSA was applied to determine behavioral relationships between teacher dashboard behaviors and student learning behaviors, enabling visualization of how teacher monitoring activities connected to and potentially influenced various student learning activities captured in the B-QUBE system. While traditional LSA typically involves data cleaning for individual users separately, this study innovatively integrated teacher LAD behaviors (class-wide learning data confirmation and individual student data confirmation) into each student's behavioral data. Specifically, when teachers viewed data for a particular student, the corresponding individual confirmation action was inserted into that student's data sequence. When teachers viewed class-wide data, the All confirmation action was inserted into all students' data sequences. All behaviors were then chronologically sorted by timestamp to create integrated teacher-student behavioral sequences for LSA analysis. This methodological approach enables examination of how teacher monitoring activities through LAD systematically relate to and potentially influence individual student learning behaviors within the temporal flow of classroom activities. This study adopted the processing method of Lai et al. (2025) to ensure data granularity consistency by removing consecutively repeated identical codes, thereby simplifying the data and addressing the overly fine granularity of actions such as handwriting notes and page turning. To examine the differential effects of teacher attention, students were categorized into high-monitoring and low-monitoring groups based on the frequency with which teachers accessed their individual data through Activity Monitor. Learning outcome differences between these groups were analyzed using Mann-Whitney U tests given the small sample size.

4. RESULTS AND DISCUSSION

4.1 Processes between Teacher LAD Behaviors and Learning Behaviors

As shown in Table 1, the teacher engaged in a total of 2,293 LAD behaviors throughout the duration, with class-wide learning data confirmation representing the predominant activity (83.9%). This finding indicates that teachers primarily utilized the dashboard to monitor overall class learning data rather than focusing on individual student learning data monitoring.

Table 1. The Frequencies of Teacher-facing LAD Behaviors

Teacher-facing LAD Behavior Types	Frequency (Percentage)
Class-wide learning data confirmation	1,924 (83.9%)
Student selection	171 (7.5%)
Material selection	127 (5.5%)
Individual student data confirmation	71 (3.1%)

Based on the LSA analysis results, we calculated the adjusted residuals for the interactions between teacher LAD and all student learning behaviors. Adjusted residual values greater than 1.96 indicate that the occurrence rate of behavioral transition sequences is significant ($p < .05$), meaning these transition patterns are systematic rather than occurring randomly (Bakeman & Gottman, 1997). The behavioral transition diagram between LAD activities and B-QUBE learning behaviors was drawn (Figure 4). The LSA results demonstrate that class-wide learning data confirmation (All) serves as a powerful tool for classroom orchestration. The findings reveal that class-wide learning data confirmation is a significant precursor to two distinct subsequent behaviors. First, it is closely associated with subsequent individual student data confirmation (Individual), indicating that in the instructional workflow, class-wide learning data monitoring is followed by targeted personalized teacher support. Second, after teachers use LAD to view class-wide learning data, students tend to open course materials (All→Open). Secondly, after teachers use LAD to view class-wide learning data, students tend to open course materials (All→Open). As shown in Figure 5, after students open the textbook, they subsequently engage in reading the materials (Pagechange), provide feedback on their understanding of the materials (Response), and utilize handwriting functions. Furthermore, teachers often use LAD to view class-wide learning data following collective reading activities (Close→All). These findings indicate that LAD effectively supports teachers' instructional guidance and assists in monitoring and confirming students' learning status. In traditional teaching environments, teachers often rely on intuition, experience, or paper-based test results to assess student learning status. Teacher-facing Learning Analytics Dashboards can visualize and structure large amounts of real-time, detailed learning data in a comprehensive manner, thereby making teachers' judgments more evidence-based (Kaliisa et al., 2023). The teacher-facing dashboard approach to data-driven instruction represents a significant advancement over conventional classroom monitoring methods.

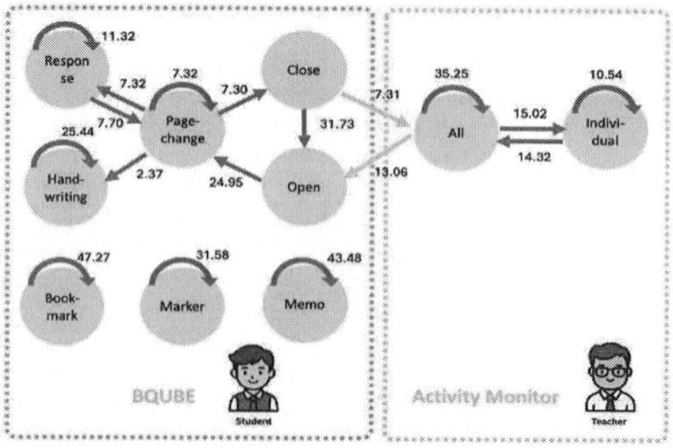

Figure 4. The Behavioral Transition Diagram between the LAD and all students' learning behaviors

4.2 Comparison of High- and Low-Attention Groups

Based on the frequency with which teacher confirmed individual data through LAD, students were categorized into high attention group (n=6, mean frequency=47.83) and low attention group (n=11, mean frequency=10.82). The Mann-Whitney U test results in Table 2 reveal significant differences in learning outcomes between the two groups. While pre-test Z-scores showed no significant difference between high and low attention groups (|Z|=26, p=0.26), post-test performance demonstrated that the high attention group had a significant advantage over the low attention group (|Z|=15, p=0.04). This finding indicates that students who received more frequent teacher monitoring through Activity Monitor achieved significantly better learning outcomes. This result is consistent with Herodotou et al. (2019), who found that when teachers used dashboards and implemented interventions for specific students, these students' pass rates were significantly higher than the non-intervention group.

Table 2. Result of the Mann–Whitney U test for Z scores from pre- and post-tests in the High and Low Attention Groups

	High Attention Group Mean (SD)	Low Attention Group Mean (SD)	|Z|
Pre-test Z-score	53.47 (13.33)	48.11 (8.37)	26.0
Post-test Z-score	55.90 (13.71)	46.78 (6.61)	15.0*

*p < .05

To further confirm the impact of teachers' individual student data confirmation on learning behaviors, significant behavioral transition diagrams were drawn for high and low attention groups based on LSA results (Figure 6). The high attention group exhibited a distinctive and significant "Pagechange→Handwriting" transition (Z=2.64). This pattern was not significant in the low attention group (Z=0.96), suggesting that after teachers viewed student data using LAD, students in the high attention group were more likely to immediately engage in knowledge externalization and synthesis through handwritten notes following textbook reading. The process of transforming reading materials into written notes is an effective strategy for improving comprehension and memory retention (Piolat et al, 2005; Geng et al., 2024). Additionally, under greater teacher guidance and attention, the high attention group demonstrated another important pattern of integrating organizational tools: the "Bookmark→Marker" transition (Z=2.89), which was absent in the low attention group. This suggests that high attention group students adopted a more sophisticated strategy of marking specific content within pages they deemed sufficiently important to bookmark, reflecting a multi-layered information organization process. Such targeted teacher attention likely provided the necessary guidance, recognition, and accountability that motivated high attention group students to engage in more effortful and constructive learning strategies. This aligns with self-regulated learning theory, which posits that external feedback and scaffolding can promote the development of more effective internal learning strategies (Azevedo et al., 2012).

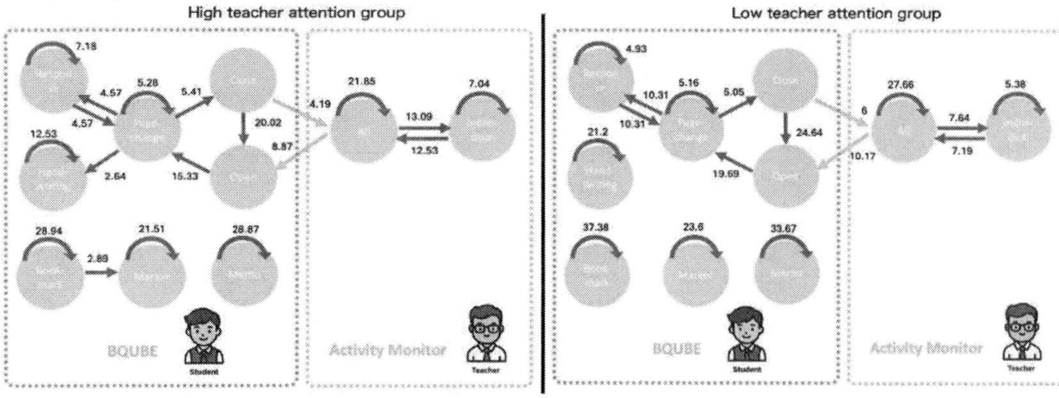

Figure 5. The Behavioral Transition Diagram of High and Low Attention Groups

5. CONCLUSION

This study investigated the effectiveness of teacher-facing LAD by examining both the processes through which teachers interact with LAD and their impact on student learning behaviors and outcomes. The results demonstrate that teacher LAD interventions create significant relationships with student learning behaviors. Class-wide learning data confirmation served as a powerful tool for classroom orchestration, facilitating transitions between different learning phases and promoting student engagement with materials. The study found substantial differences in learning outcomes between students who received high versus low teacher attention through LAD monitoring. Students in the high attention group not only achieved better learning performance but also exhibited more sophisticated learning behavior patterns, including enhanced knowledge externalization through handwriting and more strategic use of marker tools. These findings suggest that teacher attention facilitated through LADs serves as an accelerator for more integrated and effective learning strategies. This study innovatively combined teacher LAD usage data with student learning data for analysis, thereby enhancing our understanding of how LAD can effectively support evidence-based teaching practices. However, several limitations should be acknowledged. First, the study employed a single-case design with a relatively small sample size. Future research should replicate these findings across multiple teachers, diverse educational contexts, and larger student populations to establish broader validity. Second, this study did not distinguish between in-class and out-of-class LAD usage scenarios, which may involve different information needs and interaction patterns. Moreover, additional qualitative data through teacher and student interviews would enhance interpretation of the results and provide deeper understanding of the motivations, perceptions, and experiences underlying the observed behavioral patterns. Future research should build upon these insights to develop more effective LAD implementations that maximize the potential of learning analytics for enhancing teaching and learning in digital educational environments.

ACKNOWLEDGEMENT

This study is funded by Japan Society for the Promotion of Science (JSPS) (Grant Numbers: JP25K17079, JP22H00552) and the Telecommunications Advancement Foundation.

REFERENCES

Azevedo, R., Landis, R., Feyzi-Behnagh, R., Duffy, M., Trevors, G., Harley, J., Bouchet, F., Burlison, J., Taub, M., Pacampara, N., Yeasin, M., Rahman, A., Tanveer, M., & Hossain, G. (2012). The effectiveness of pedagogical agents' prompting and feedback in facilitating co-adapted learning with MetaTutor. In *Proceedings of Intelligent Tutoring Systems: 11th International Conference*, pp. 212-221.

Bakeman, R. and Gottman, J.M. (1997). *Observing interaction: An introduction to sequential analysis*. Cambridge University Press.

Colling, L., Kholin, M. and Meurers, D. (2024). A learning analytics dashboard for K-12 English teachers – bridging the gap between student process data and teacher needs. In *Adjunct Proceedings of the 32nd ACM Conference on User Modeling, Adaptation and Personalization*, pp. 538–548.

Chen, L., Lu, M., Goda, Y., Shimada, A., and Yamada, M. (2020). Factors of the use of learning analytics dashboard that affect metacognition. In Proceedings of 17th International Conference Cognition and Exploratory Learning in Digital Age, CELDA 2020 , pp. 295–302.

Dülger, M., van Leeuwen, A., Janssen, J. and Kester, L. (2025). Designing a classroom-level teacher dashboard to foster primary school teachers' direct instruction of self-regulated learning strategies. *Education and Information Technologies*, pp. 1–35.

Geng, X., Xu, Y., Chen, L., Ogata, H., Shimada, A., & Yamada, M. (2020). Learning analytics of the relationships among learning behaviors, learning performance, and motivation. In *2020 IEEE 20th International Conference on Advanced Learning Technologies*, pp. 161-163. .

Geng, X., Chen, L., Xu, Y., Ogata, H., Shimada, A., & Yamada, M. (2024). Learning behavioral patterns of students with varying performance in a high school mathematics course using an e-book system. *Research & Practice in Technology Enhanced Learning, 19*.

Geng, X., & Yamada, M. (2025). The Role of Dashboards in Augmented-Reality-Based Language Learning: Enhancing Language Learning and Metacognitive Awareness. *SAGE Open,* Vol. 15, No. 2, 21582440251341675.

Herodotou, C., Hlosta, M., Boroowa, A., Rienties, B., Zdrahal, Z., & Mangafa, C. (2019). Empowering online teachers through predictive learning analytics. *British Journal of Educational Technology*, Vol. *50*, No. 6, pp. 3064-3079.

Jivet, I., Scheffel, M., Specht, M. and Drachsler, H. (2018). License to evaluate: Preparing learning analytics dashboards for educational practice. In *Proceedings of the 8th International Conference on Learning Analytics & Knowledge*, pp. 31–40.

Kaliisa, R., Jivet, I., & Prinsloo, P. (2023). A checklist to guide the planning, designing, implementation, and evaluation of learning analytics dashboards. *International Journal of Educational Technology in Higher Education*, Vol. 20, No. 28, pp. 1-28.

LAK. (2011). *1st International Conference on Learning Analytics and Knowledge*, Banff, Alberta.

Lai, J.W., Qiu, W., Thway, M., Zhang, L., Jamil, N.B., Su, C.L., Ng, S.S.H. and Lim, F.S. (2025). Leveraging process-action epistemic network analysis to illuminate student self-regulated learning with a Socratic chatbot. *Journal of Learning Analytics*, Vol. 12, No. 1, pp. 32–49.

Li, Y., Zhang, M., Su, Y., Bao, H. and Xing, S. (2022). Examining teachers' behavior patterns in and perceptions of using teacher dashboards for facilitating guidance in CSCL. *Educational Technology Research and Development*, Vol. 70, No. 3, pp. 1035–1058.

Martinez-Maldonado, R. (2019). A handheld classroom dashboard: Teachers' perspectives on the use of real-time collaborative learning analytics. *International Journal of Computer-Supported Collaborative Learning*, Vol. 14, No. 3, pp. 383–411.

Molenaar, I. and Knoop-van Campen, C.A. (2018). How teachers make dashboard information actionable. *IEEE Transactions on Learning Technologies*, Vol. 12, No. 3, pp. 347–355.

Ogata, H., Yin, C., Oi, M., Okubo, F., Shimada, A., Kojima, K. and Yamada, M. (2015). E-book-based learning analytics in university education. In *International Conference on Computers in Education (ICCE 2015)*, pp. 401–406.

Park, E., Ifenthaler, D. and Clariana, R.B. (2023). Adaptive or adapted to: Sequence and reflexive thematic analysis to understand learners' self-regulated learning in an adaptive learning analytics dashboard. *British Journal of Educational Technology*, Vol. 54, No. 1, pp. 98–125.

Piolat, A., Olive, T., & Kellogg, R. T. (2005). Cognitive effort during note taking. *Applied cognitive psychology*, Vol. 19, No.3, pp. 291-312.

Teasley, S.D. (2017). Student-facing dashboards: One size fits all? *Technology, Knowledge and Learning*, Vol. 22, No. 3, pp. 377–384.

Van Leeuwen, A. and Rummel, N. (2020). Comparing teachers' use of mirroring and advising dashboards. In *Proceedings of the Tenth International Conference on Learning Analytics & Knowledge*, pp. 26–34.

Yamada, M., Geng, X., Lu, M., & Taniguchi, Y. (2024). Exploring the Role of Metacognition in Enhancing Learning Outcomes through Learning Analytics Dashboard. In *eLearn: World Conference on EdTech*, pp. 294-301.

Yousef, A.M.F. and Khatiry, A.R. (2023). Cognitive versus behavioral learning analytics dashboards for supporting learner's awareness, reflection, and learning process. *Interactive Learning Environments*, Vol. 31, No. 9, pp. 5460–5476.

INTEGRATION OF CHATGPT IN THE PROBLEM-BASED LEARNING MODEL

Daniela Orozova and Nadezhda Angelova
Department of Informatics and Mathematics, Faculty of Economics, Trakia University
Stara Zagora 6000, Bulgaria

ABSTRACT

The development of modern technologies and the integration of AI into all aspects of life pose challenges for participants in the educational process. On the one hand, using chatbots and generative AI tools provides learners with unlimited opportunities to quickly and easily access a large amount of information and receive help with various homework assignments, making it difficult for teachers to assess their work. The article presents an experiment designed to motivate students and support teachers during training. The research was conducted during the education of bachelor students in the professional field of Informatics and Computer Sciences. The propositions presented in this report raise several questions and outline possible future research directions. An experiment is conducted with students in the second and third semesters of the Software Engineering bachelor's program. The goal is to integrate ChatGPT in the context of problem-based learning while mastering the fundamentals of programming languages such as C++, Java, and web programming. The idea is to train learners' critical thinking skills with systematically generated materials from ChatGPT, in dialogue with students, enriching them with additional knowledge and various resources. This study examines the potential of artificial intelligence technology, such as ChatGPT, to enhance core teaching materials through problem-based learning. Learners are encouraged to develop critical thinking on assigned tasks, and their progress is monitored by analyzing data collected during the learning process.

This paper aims to demonstrate that generative AI technologies, such as ChatGPT, have the potential to enrich learning resources, adapt materials to individual learners' needs, and provide flexibility for both students and educators in the digital age. The main challenges associated with traditional teaching include the lecturer's limited time to present the learning material, a shortage of reference resources, and low student motivation. Integrating ChatGPT into a problem-solving learning model is hypothesized to personalize learning content, improve critical thinking, provide feedback, and increase learner motivation.

KEYWORDS

Artificial Intelligence in Education, Problem-Based Learning, Generative AI Approaches

1. INTRODUCTION

The development of modern technologies and the integration of AI into all aspects of life pose challenges for participants in the educational process. On the one hand, the use of chatbots and generative AI tools provides learners with unlimited opportunities to quickly and easily access a large amount of information and receive help with various homework assignments, which in turn makes it difficult for teachers to assess their work.

In the new digital era of AI, the transformation in education redefined the role of the educator, who is no longer at the center of the learning process, but rather guides and mentors the learner. In the past, he was the primary source of knowledge, but now he teaches learners how to effectively utilize AI tools and enhance their critical thinking skills. To avoid over-reliance on AI for learning and completing various assignments, teachers need to design tasks that require the application of their knowledge and skills (Stănescu, 2024). Various pedagogical strategies, such as problem-based learning, project-based learning, and the flipped classroom model, could be employed to implement such tasks.

Problem-based learning is a method in which learners are placed in situations that require them to solve specific problems, thereby applying their knowledge and skills in a practical context. This is a method in which learners explore an open-ended problem as a basis for building knowledge. It is based on a constructivist learning approach, utilizing self-organized learning activities in which learners can determine what they know and what they need to learn (Kolb, 2015)

According to research (Farikhatul & Hamimi, 2024), this method enhances participants' intrinsic motivation and facilitates a deeper understanding of concepts through active engagement with the learning material. Problem-based learning can respond to different learning styles, making it more inclusive and effective for a diverse audience (Fajari et al., 2020). This approach enables learners to work in teams, which strengthens their social and communication skills, as well as their ability to collaborate to achieve a common goal (Crespí et al., 2022). Additionally, problem-based learning develops time management skills that are critical to success in higher education. In Project-Based Learning, learners work on a real-world, interdisciplinary task over an extended period, related to the investigation of a defined problem or question (Wijnia et al., 2024). The Flipped Classroom is an instructional approach in which recorded lectures, text materials, or lessons are reviewed and studied outside of class, and class time is used for discussions, problem-solving, projects, case studies, and other active learning activities (Kus, 2025).

By implementing AI technologies to provide automated and personalized feedback to participants, it is possible to analyze learner performance and provide adequate recommendations (Afzaal et al., 2021).

2. THEORETICAL FRAMEWORK

Problem-based learning is an innovative education method that integrates traditional teaching approaches with problem-solving techniques. Research indicates that this model is effective in enhancing student motivation and engagement, as well as fostering a deeper understanding of complex concepts (Čubela et al., 2023). Students are placed in real or simulated situations that are challenging and require them to apply the knowledge and skills they have acquired to solve specific problems in various contexts (Taesotikul et al., 2021; Kladchuen & Srisomphan, 2021).

Critical thinking is the ability to analyze, evaluate, and construct arguments based on logical principles and evidence. According to Kuhn (2019), it is a dialogic process carried out by individuals (Kuhn, 2019). . Additionally, critical thinking plays a crucial role in developing the analytical skills necessary to solve complex problems and make informed decisions (Butler, 2024). A study by Zawacki-Richter et al. (2019) shows that critical thinking skills enable participants to evaluate information objectively. This is especially important in today's digital age, where misinformation can spread rapidly (Zawacki-Richter et al., 2019). This is particularly important in the educational environment, where critical thinking skills can help participants develop a deeper understanding of the material being studied, thereby improving both comprehension and learning outcomes.

The entry of artificial intelligence into the field of education creates new opportunities for more personalized, intelligent, and automated learning processes. Artificial intelligence technologies capable of generating and interpreting language, such as ChatGPT, hold significant potential for providing individualized feedback to learners and increasing their engagement in the learning process. They can adapt lesson content to meet each student's specific needs, respond to their progress, and offer feedback that encourages critical thinking. This form of personalization ensures that learners stay motivated and receive the support they need to overcome learning challenges and develop their critical thinking skills.

There are numerous studies on the integration of ChatGPT into training, some of which advise to "treat ChatGPT as a learning partner", "use ChatGPT to increase confidence", and suggest to "request ChatGPT to provide supportive feedback". The authors believe that these approaches will increase students' motivation and prevent cheating (Purnama et al., 2023). The integration of ChatGPT into a project-based learning and problem-based model offers several advantages, including the facilitation of personalized learning experiences for students, the provision of immediate responses to student inquiries, the enhancement of student engagement, the assistance it provides to teachers in class management, and the promotion of a more interactive learning environment.

The applications of ChatGPT in learning are extensive and can help teachers create a variety of learning materials tailored to the individual characteristics of learners, their level of knowledge, and needs. In a study, Borisova (2024) and her colleagues share their experiences with various examples of prompts they use to create educational games for students, thus making the educational process more engaging, interactive, and adaptable to varying degrees. Another study, Kiryakova (2024), presents the MagicSchool as a tool to assist educators in generating lesson plans, learning content ideas, tests, and assignments, and compares its functionalities with ChatGPT. One of the most important conditions for achieving good efficiency from the use of AI tools is to set the correct prompt, as well as to check the accuracy of the provided result (Kiryakova, 2024). ChatGPT is not the only tool that can be used and integrated in education, but it is probably the most explored and studied nowadays. Numerous AI tools, chatbots, and personal assistants are integrated into various software products, offering support to both educators and learners.

3. ARTIFICIAL INTELLIGENCE IN EDUCATION – AN EXPERIMENT

This study examines the potential of artificial intelligence technology, such as ChatGPT, to enhance core teaching materials through problem-based learning. Learners are encouraged to develop critical thinking on assigned tasks, and their progress is monitored through analysis of data collected during the learning process. The aim is to determine how learners respond to misinformation and fake news (Angelelli et al., 2023; Rusandi et al., 2023). Previous research has also looked at the use of learning platforms such as Kahoot! and Vonder Go (Supnoon & Chonchaiya, 2024), but their emphasis is on the concerns surrounding the adoption of artificial intelligence, as well as how AI is used to assess and improve individual skills (Mahdi & Sahari, 2024). Some studies analyze the academic integrity and attitudes of learners toward the implementation of AI technologies (Kuchyn et al., 2024)..

The difference with previous research is that the present report emphasizes the evaluation of the impact of training in the courses "Basics of programming with Java" and "Web programming", integrated with ChatGPT, on learners and teachers. ChatGPT is seen as an AI tool that provides answers to questions, explains learning materials, analyzes and critiques texts, offering flexibility and customization opportunities in the learning process.

Training in the discipline "Fundamentals of programming with Java" is conducted in large courses, with the number of students being around 80-100 people. For the exercises, students are divided into small groups, each of which can be taught and assessed by a different teacher.

The teaching method depends on the teacher's expertise and previous experience. While some instructors concentrate on teaching concepts, various techniques, and technologies related to the material being taught, an essential element for others is the clarification and use of template solutions for standard exam-related activities.

An experiment is conducted with students of the second and third semesters of the Software Engineering major of Trakia University, who are studying the disciplines "Fundamentals of C++ Programming", "Fundamentals of Java Programming", and "Web Programming". The courses in each discipline have a duration of three months, comprising 15 meetings for lectures and 15 meetings for exercises. The goal is to integrate ChatGPT in the context of problem-based learning while mastering the fundamentals of programming languages such as C++, Java, and web programming. The idea is to train learners' critical thinking with systematically generated materials from ChatGPT in dialogue with students, enriching them with additional knowledge and a variety of materials.

After students formulate their questions or comments about the learning material, these queries are processed by ChatGPT according to the parameters set by the learners. Results generated by ChatGPT may include textual explanations, suggestions for corrections to answers, or examples of program code. Learners have the opportunity to use the information provided to deepen their understanding or correct their answers. This dynamic interaction between learners and ChatGPT creates a more adaptive and engaging learning experience. The training on the specific topic in the experiment includes a pre- and post-test that assesses the learners' initial and final knowledge and skills. The training process is conducted in two separate groups: one group integrates ChatGPT into their training, while the other follows the traditional method and does not utilize ChatGPT.

Sample tasks performed during training, related to the creation and analysis of learning resources in a scientific style and argued with relevant citations in the scientific literature, such as:

- Elaboration of projects on a given topic by analyzing the topic with scientific citations.
- Searching for errors and additional information on assigned material, such as: "analyze the structure, grammar, and argumentation of the text in the file". Recommendations: to ask for an "uncompromisingly critical analysis", to give more details about the method of application and the objectives of the task being performed.
- Based on assigned material – formulation of questions and tests. Training on a given topic.
- Creating program code and solving specific programming tasks.
- Program code inspection, code error detection, and correction guidance.
- Evaluation of projects, drawings, schemes, diagrams.
- Generating images on given topics and creating presentations, as well as several other tasks with similar themes.

In the conducted experiment, the grades of the two components are set. One component forms an assessment related to the material taught in the lectures through tests, each question being scored. The second component assesses students' practical work on exercises by having them solve a task related to the development of a software application, which a teacher then evaluates.

The diagram in Figure 1 shows the results of the conducted evaluation - grades from theory, practice, and final evaluations of the students in the experimental group with the integration of ChatGPT.

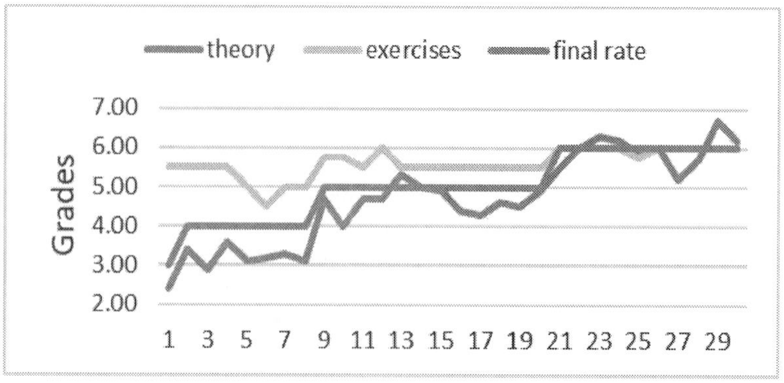

Figure 1. Results from the experimental group with ChatGPT integration

The graph in Figure 2 presents the distribution of students' grades in the experimental group, which did not integrate ChatGPT.

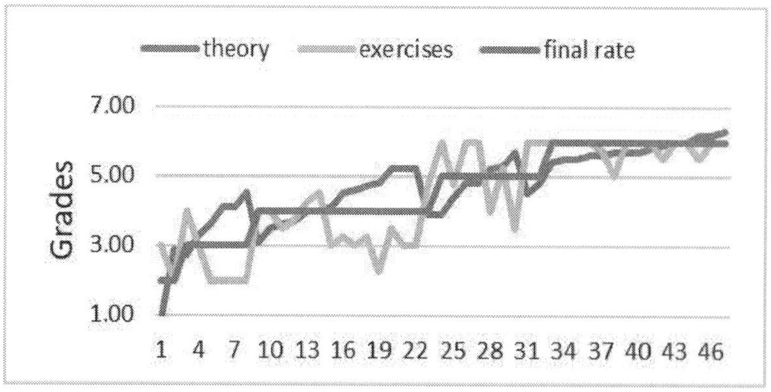

Figure 2. Results from the experimental group without ChatGPT integration

The results of the assessment of the learners in the experimental group with the integration of ChatGPT showed a significant increase in skills in all tested topics. These results suggest the inclusion of topics and tasks that require the application of artificial intelligence technologies, such as ChatGPT, in curricula to improve critical thinking skills in programming education and other fields. The hypothesis is accepted, confirming the effectiveness of using an AI-based model of problem-based learning. Further research is expected to reveal the extent to which the use of ChatGPT contributes to improving learners' knowledge and skills.

4. FUTURE WORK

The authors' future research focuses on developing a conceptual model and designing a prototype of an LA platform that leverages GPT models to automate assessment and offer personalized feedback to students on interdisciplinary project execution. Such a platform could help educators implement projects that foster interdisciplinary skills while streamlining the assessment process.

Learning Analytics (LA) is a research field that concentrates on gathering, analyzing, and reporting data about learners and their environments to predict their needs and enhance both the learning process and the setting where learning takes place (Lang, 2023). Data collection for learning analytics encompasses the entire process, including all types of data that can be gathered and analyzed within education from various learning activities. The International Standards Organization (ISO) IMG Global Learning Consortium (IMG Global) categorizes data into five groups: learning activity data, learning content data, learner profile data, operational data, and career-related data. This classification is essential for the development of Learning Analytics (Chatti, 2012), which is a new branch of data analysis that integrates objectives and methods from educational and psychological research. It involves processing data using traditional (classical statistical, empirical, or logical) theories, technologies, and tools to extract practical information, and is also linked to theories, technologies, tools, and processes that enable a deep understanding of the analyzed data (Cao, 2017). Currently, there is a shortage of LA tools capable of analyzing the quality of student-generated data in interdisciplinary tasks. ChatGPT, a chatbot powered by basic large language models (LLMs) such as GPT-3.5 and GPT-4.0, developed by OpenAI (OpenAI, 2023), has demonstrated promising success in efficiently analyzing student texts and providing feedback.

Artificial intelligence has the potential to make education more effective, accessible, and engaging. We believe that personalized learning through AI can help learners learn according to their individual needs by providing a multitude of tools and resources that facilitate learning and improve outcomes.

However, with the introduction of new technologies, new challenges arise, including the impact of artificial intelligence on the skills and development of learners. Most concerns of teachers and other stakeholders in the educational process are related to the misuse of AI, the accuracy of work assessment, and the risk of young people losing balance between the real and virtual worlds.

5. CONCLUSION

The article presents an experiment designed to motivate students and support teachers during training. The conducted research was carried out during the education of bachelor students, studying in specialties in the professional field "Informatics and Computer Sciences". The propositions presented in this report raise several questions and outline some potential directions for future research. An upcoming task is to integrate the proposed approach with Fuzzy methods for fuzzy multi-criteria analysis in performance evaluation across various practice situations. These efforts aim to address the modern needs of students in a dynamic and constantly evolving educational environment. Providing new, effective tools for managing learning processes and personal time has the potential to significantly contribute to the academic and personal fulfillment of its users.

ACKNOWLEDGEMENT

This work is supported by the frames of Bulgarian National Recovery and Resilience Plan, Component "Innovative Bulgaria", the Project № BG-RRP-2.004-0006-C02 "Development of research and innovation at Trakia University in service of health and sustainable well-being".

REFERENCES

Afzaal, M., Nouri, J., Zia, A., Papapetrou, P., Fors, U., Wu, Y., Li, X., & Weegar, R. (2021). Explainable AI for data-driven feedback and intelligent action recommendations to support students' self-regulation. Front Artif Intell, 4(1), 1-20.

Angelelli, C. V., Ribeiro, G. M. de C., Severino, M. R., Johnstone, E., Borzenkova, G., & da Silva, D. C. O. (2023). Developing critical thinking skills through gamification. Think Skills Creat, 49(1), 101354–101366.

Borisova, M., Hadzhikoleva, S., Hadzhikolev, E. (2024). ChatGPT as a tool for creating educational games for school education in computer technology, *International Conference on Virtual Learning*, ISSN 2971-9291, ISSN-L 1844-8933, vol. 19, pp. 323-333. https://doi.org/10.58503/icvl-v19y202427

Butler, H. A. (2024). Predicting everyday critical thinking: A review of critical thinking assessments. *J Intell*, 12(2), 16-29.

Cao L. (2017). Data science: a comprehensive overview. ACM Comput Surv (CSUR). 2017; 50 (3) pp.1–42.

Chatti, M, A, Dychhoff, A, L, Schroeder, U., and Thus, H. (2012). A reference model for learning analytics, International journal of Technology Enhanced learning, 2012.

Crespí, P., García-Ramos, J. M., & Queiruga-Dios, M. (2022). Project-based learning (PBL) and its impact on the development of interpersonal competences in higher education. *Journal of New Approaches in Educational Research*, 11(2), 259-276.

Čubela, D., Rossner, A., & Neis, P. (2023). Using problem-based learning and gamification as a catalyst for student engagement in data-driven engineering education: A report. *Educ Sci* (Basel), 13(12), 1223–1235.

Fajari, L. E. W., Sarwanto, & Chumdari. (2020). Improving elementary school's critical thinking skills through three different PBL-assisted learning media viewed from learning styles. *Journal of E-Learning and Knowledge Society, 16(1), 55-64.*

Farikhatul Mutma'innah, & Hamimi, E. (2024). Development of PBL-based GLOWASEA (Global Warming on the Sea) educational media to train critical thinking skills on the topic of global warming. *International Journal of Interactive Mobile Technologies* (iJIM), 18(09), 117-140.

Kiryakova, G. (2024). Artificial intelligence as a supportive tool for teachers' activities. *International Conference on Virtual Learning*, ISSN 2971-9291, ISSN-L 1844-8933, vol. 19, pp. 385-396. https://doi.org/10.58503/icvl-v19y202432

Kladchuen, R., & Srisomphan, J. (2021). The synthesis of a model of problem-based learning with the gamification concept to enhance the problem-solving skills for high vocational certificate. International *Journal of Emerging Technologies in Learning* (iJET), 16(14), 4-21.

Kolb, D. A. (2015). Experiential Learning: Experience as the source of Learning and Development Second Edition, 2015, *Pearson Education*, ISBN: 978-0-13-389240-6

Kuchyn, I. L., Lymar, L. V., Bielka, K. Y., Storozhuk, K. V., & Kolomiiets, T. V. (2024). New training, new attitudes: Non-clinical components in Ukrainian medical PhD training (regarding critical thinking, academic integrity, and artificial intelligence use). *Wiadomości Lekarskie*, 77(4), 665-669.

Kuhn, D. (2019). Critical thinking as discourse. *Hum Dev*, 62(3), 146-164.

Mahdi, H. S., & Sahari, Y. M. (2024). Exploring the relationship between critical thinking, attitude, and anxiety in shaping the adoption of artificial intelligence in translation among Saudi translators. *Journal of Pedagogical Research*, 8(2), 81-94.

Kus, M. (2025). Effectiveness of the Flipped Classroom Model in Higher Education: A Meta Analysis Study. *Journal of Computer and Education Research*, 13(25), 628-653. https://doi.org/10.18009/jcer.1625784

Lang C. et al., Eds., Handbook of Learning Analytics, First. Society for Learning Analytics Research (SoLAR), 2017. doi: 10.18608/hla17OpenAI, "GPT-4 Technical Report," Mar. 27, 2023, arXiv: arXiv:2303.08774. Accessed: Apr. 03, 2023. [Online]. Available: http://arxiv.org/abs/2303.08774

Purnama, I., Edi, F., Syahrul, Agustin, R. & Pranoto, N. W. (2023). GPT Chat Integration in Project Based Learning in Learning: A Systematic Literature Review. *Jurnal Penelitian Pendidikan IPA*, 9(SpecialIssue), 150–158. https://doi.org/10.29303/jppipa.v9iSpecialIssue.6712

Rusandi, M. A., Ahman, Saripah, I., Khairun, D. Y., & Mutmainnah. (2023). No worries with ChatGPT: Building bridges between artificial intelligence and education with critical thinking soft skills. *J Public Health* (Bangkok), 45(3), e602–e603.

Stănescu, A. (2024). The impact of AI on education: Exploring the role of ChatGPT. *International Conference on Virtual Learning*, ISSN 2971-9291, ISSN-L 1844-8933, vol. 19, pp. 193-202, https://doi.org/10.58503/icvl-v19y202416

Supnoon, A., & Chonchaiya, R. (2024). A study on the development of eleventh grade students' critical thinking skills and self-efficacy using active learning pedagogy with gamification. *International Journal of Education and Practice*, 12(2), 447-466.

Taesotikul, T., Chinpaisal, C., & Nawanopparatsakul, S. (2021). Kahoot! gamification improves learning outcomes in problem-based learning classroom. In *2021 3rd International Conference on Modern Educational Technology* (pp. 125-129). ACM.

Wijnia, L., Noordzij, G., Arends, L.R. et al. (2024). The Effects of Problem-Based, Project-Based, and Case-Based Learning on Students' Motivation: a Meta-Analysis. *Educ Psychol Rev* 36, 29. https://doi.org/10.1007/s10648-024-09864-3

Zawacki-Richter, O., Marín, V. I., Bond, M., & Gouverneur, F. (2019). Systematic review of research on artificial intelligence applications in higher education - where are the educators? *International Journal of Educational Technology in Higher Education*, 16(1), 39-66.

ARTIFICIAL INTELLIGENCE IN ESP EDUCATION TRANSFORMATIONS, ETHICAL CONSIDERATIONS AND FUTURE DIRECTIONS

Silvia Osman
National School for Political Science and Public Administration, SNSPA Bucharest, Romania

ABSTRACT

In the rapidly evolving digital landscape, artificial intelligence (AI) is fundamentally redefining English for Specific Purposes (ESP) education across disciplines such as Political Studies, International Relations, Sociology, and Psychology. This paper explores how AI-powered tools enhance personalized, immersive, and authentic learning experiences, fostering core linguistic and intercultural skills. Drawing on my extensive experience as a visiting professor at the University of Naples "Federico II" and Vlora University, I analyze pedagogical strategies, ethical challenges—including GDPR compliance and the EU AI Act—and the influence of digital sovereignty. This comprehensive discussion aims to provide strategic pathways for responsible and effective AI integration into ESP curricula, emphasizing the importance of preparing students for the demands of an interconnected, multicultural professional environment.

KEYWORDS

Digital Landscapes, AI-Powered Tools, Pedagogical Strategies

1. INTRODUCTION

The infusion of AI into educational pedagogy marks a paradigm shift that transcends traditional classroom boundaries. From my academic positions at the University of Naples "Federico II" and Vlora University, I have witnessed how these technologies are compelling educators to reconsider instructional methodologies, assessment paradigms, and curriculum design, especially within ESP. These courses demand high levels of precision, contextual language skills, and intercultural competence, essential for careers in diplomacy, policy analysis, social research, and mental health services (Chapelle & Sauro, 2017).

AI's capacity to personalize learning pathways allows for tailored instruction that adapts to individual learner needs—whether in vocabulary acquisition, pragmatic language use, or intercultural sensitivity. As documented by Levy and Stockwell (2006), such adaptive systems evaluate learner performance dynamically, providing instant, targeted feedback. This shift toward learner-centered environments not only improves engagement but also enables educators to address diverse linguistic backgrounds and learning paces, ultimately optimizing outcomes in complex disciplines.

However, these technological innovations come with significant ethical and legal considerations. As AI systems process vast quantities of data, issues of privacy, bias, transparency, and digital sovereignty come to the forefront. The European Union's GDPR and the upcoming AI regulation emphasize the importance of designing and deploying AI systems responsibly—an imperative echoed in academia, industry, and policymaking (European Commission, 2021). Striking a balance between technological advancement and ethical integrity is essential to ensure AI serves society's best interests, particularly in education, where vulnerable populations often participate.

This paper aims to explore these dimensions—technological possibilities, pedagogical frameworks, ethical norms, and geopolitical influences—offering a guide to harnessing AI's potential while navigating the associated risks.

2. TECHNOLOGICAL ADVANCEMENTS AND PEDAGOGICAL IMPLICATIONS

2.1 Natural Language Processing (NLP)

Advancements in NLP have transformed AI from simple language-processing tools to sophisticated systems capable of engaging in nuanced, context-aware interactions. In ESP, NLP models power chatbots that can simulate diplomatic negotiations, legal consultations, or therapeutic dialogues, providing learners with authentic language practice environments (Burstein et al., 2019).

For example, a student studying International Relations might engage with an AI chatbot mimicking a trade negotiation, requiring them to craft persuasive arguments, interpret cultural cues, and respond diplomatically
—skills critical for real-world diplomacy. Moreover, NLP algorithms automatically analyze student language outputs, identifying errors in register, idiomatic expressions, and syntactic structures, thereby facilitating targeted feedback that supports mastery of discipline-specific discourse.

2.2 Adaptive Learning Platforms

Adaptive learning systems utilize machine learning to analyze real-time student interactions, enabling tailored content delivery. Tools such as Duolingo for Business or field-specific platforms like Babbel aim to reinforce vocabulary, syntactic accuracy, pragmatic language, and intercultural competence (Godwin-Jones, 2019).

For Diplomacy students, this might mean focusing on diplomatic jargon, formal letter writing, and interpretative skills—customized based on their previous responses and performance metrics. This personalized approach has demonstrated increased motivation and learning efficacy, especially when accompanied by formative assessment capabilities, fostering continuous skill development (Gros, 2020).

2.3 Virtual Reality (VR) and Simulations

Virtual Reality (VR) has emerged as a transformative tool in ESP education due to its immersive and experiential qualities. Unlike traditional classroom approaches, VR creates simulated environments where learners can engage in authentic disciplinary scenarios—such as diplomatic summits, courtroom trials, therapy sessions, or social interventions—reproducing the nuances of real-world interactions with high fidelity (Gros, 2020). This technological innovation enables students to practice language skills, soft skills, and intercultural competence in settings that are otherwise inaccessible due to logistical or safety constraints.

For example, students of International Relations can participate in a VR simulation of a global climate summit, where they must negotiate treaties, manage conflicting interests, and communicate effectively across cultural boundaries. These experiences would develop not only their linguistic abilities but also their strategic communication, problem-solving, and emotional intelligence—skills that are critical in high-stakes professional environments (Lynott et al., 2020).

The pedagogical advantages of VR extend beyond engagement; they include improved retention, motivation, and empathy. Learners immersed in such environments often report higher levels of motivation due to the novelty and realism of the tasks, which in turn improve long-term retention of language and soft skills. Further, VR fosters empathy by placing students in culturally and emotionally charged scenarios, allowing them to experience perspectives and contexts different from their own, thus cultivating intercultural sensitivity (Gros, 2020).

VR-based language and soft skills training align with constructivist pedagogical principles, encouraging learners to actively explore, experiment, and reflect upon their performances. This environment shifts the focus from passive reception to active construction of knowledge—a transformative aspect especially relevant in disciplines demanding high contextual fluency (Lynott et al., 2020).

Challenges and Future Perspectives: Despite its promise, VR deployment faces challenges such as high costs, technical infrastructure requirements, and content development complexity. As technology advances and hardware becomes more affordable, integration into mainstream curricula is anticipated to grow. Moreover, collaboration among educators, technologists, and discipline experts is crucial to develop content that is pedagogically sound, culturally sensitive, and accessible.

3. PEDAGOGICAL FRAMEWORKS AND ETHICAL CHALLENGES

3.1 Constructivist and Student-Centered Learning

AI technologies inherently support constructivist and learner-centered paradigms by enabling active engagement with authentic tasks. These tools allow learners to operate within simulated professional contexts, such as diplomatic negotiations or counseling sessions, where they generate language, make decisions, and reflect on their interactions (Levy & Stockwell, 2006).

For instance, in ESP courses for Psychology, students might engage with AI-driven simulations of client interviews, practicing nuanced language use, demonstrating empathy, and managing emotional expressions. The immediate feedback provided by AI analyses—covering tone, word choice, and emotional expressiveness—further facilitates self-regulated learning and skill refinement, aligned with formative assessment principles (Gros, 2020).

3.2 Ethical and Legal Frameworks

As AI tools become central to ESP pedagogy, their ethical and legal implications must be carefully navigated. Data privacy, bias, transparency, and accountability are at the forefront of concerns. Under GDPR, institutions are required to ensure that student data is collected, stored, and processed lawfully, with informed consent and proper safeguards (European Commission, 2021).

Moreover, AI systems must be designed and deployed transparently to avoid "black box" models whose decision-making processes are opaque. For example, if an AI system assesses students' oral proficiency, it should clearly communicate the criteria, scoring basis, and possible biases influencing judgments (O'Neill & McGlade, 2020).

Bias mitigation remains a critical challenge. AI algorithms trained on biased datasets risk perpetuating stereotypes—such as gender, ethnicity, or accent biases—undermining fairness and equity (Williamson, Piattoeva, & Kennedy, 2021). Continuous oversight, diversified datasets, and ethical guidelines are vital to ensure that AI supports inclusive and equitable education.

Digital Sovereignty and Regional Policy Implications: The geopolitics of technology, especially regional policies on digital sovereignty, influence AI deployment. Regions such as the European Union emphasize data localization, oversight, and sovereign control over digital infrastructure, impacting the availability and development of AI tools (Woollard & Angel, 2019). In contrast, other jurisdictions may favor open algorithms or less restrictive models, leading to discrepancies in AI capabilities and access.

For educators, this means selecting and deploying AI tools that comply with legal standards and respect regional policies. It also involves raising awareness among students about the societal and geopolitical implications of AI, encouraging critical digital literacy that promotes informed engagement with global AI governance issues.

4. APPLICATIONS IN DISCIPLINE-SPECIFIC CONTEXTS

4.1 Political Studies and International Relations

Artificial Intelligence has empowered educators to create sophisticated simulations of diplomatic negotiations, international summits, and conflict resolution scenarios—enabling students to engage in experiential learning that closely mimics real-world international diplomacy. These simulations utilize AI-driven natural language processing and machine learning to produce dynamic scenarios where students must craft persuasive arguments, interpret cultural cues, and respond strategically in negotiation dialogues (Selwyn, 2016).

For example, an AI-based simulation might model a United Nations Security Council meeting where students represent different countries with competing interests. The system can generate real-time diplomatic responses, adapt scenarios based on student input, and provide instant feedback on language tone, formality, and strategic effectiveness. Such tools can also include cultural sensitivity modules, teaching students to navigate
cross-cultural communication challenges—a vital skill in global politics.

These simulations not only foster language proficiency but also develop soft skills like negotiation, strategic thinking, and intercultural awareness. They enable students to practice complex discourse in a safe environment, reducing anxiety associated with high-stakes diplomatic interactions (Chapelle & Sauro, 2017). Moreover, AI can analyze student responses over multiple sessions, identifying patterns, strengths, and areas for improvement, thus supporting personalized learning pathways tailored to each learner's developmental trajectory.

Future implications: As AI continues to advance, immersive diplomatic simulations are likely to incorporate augmented reality (AR) and virtual reality (VR) to further enhance authenticity. These technologies can simulate physical presence in international venues, complete with visual and auditory cues, thereby elevating experiential learning to new levels of realism.

Challenges: Despite promising potential, challenges include high implementation costs, the need for up-to-date content development, and ensuring cultural accuracy. Additionally, ethical concerns about data privacy and bias in AI systems must be addressed to prevent reinforcing stereotypes or misrepresenting cultural nuances.

4.2 Sociology

In sociology, AI facilitates virtual ethnographies, social media analysis, and cross-cultural interaction simulations, transforming theoretical concepts into practical, data-driven explorations. Virtual ethnography involves analyzing online communities, social networks, and digital interactions by leveraging AI algorithms that identify patterns, discourse structures, and social dynamics across diverse cultural contexts (Gros, 2020).

For instance, students might examine social protests across different regions by analyzing millions of social media posts, comments, and multimedia content. Natural language processing can classify sentiments, detect framing strategies, and assess the spread of ideas and misinformation. This capability enables learners to critically evaluate social phenomena, contextualize theoretical frameworks, and develop nuanced understanding of intercultural communication and social behavior.

AI-powered tools can also simulate intercultural dialogue scenarios, where students must navigate misunderstandings, stereotypes, or conflicting perspectives. These simulations cultivate intercultural competence and empathy, essential skills for sociologists, policy analysts, and international workers (Levy & Stockwell, 2006). They prepare students to interpret complex social phenomena, fostering critical thinking and reflexivity.

Future implications: The integration of AI-driven social analytics with VR-based immersive environments could enable students to "step into" digital communities, exploring social issues from multiple perspectives with real-time feedback.

Challenges: Developing culturally sensitive models that accurately reflect diverse social realities remains a challenge. Ensuring the ethical use of social data—particularly regarding privacy and consent—is paramount to uphold academic integrity and social responsibility.

4.3 Psychology

Within clinical and counseling training, AI facilitates simulations of therapeutic dialogues that support language and emotional competence development. These tools enable students to rehearse client interactions, practice empathetic responses, and refine their case conceptualization skills in a low-risk environment (Miller & Veletsianos, 2020).

For example, students can engage with AI chatbots programmed to simulate patients presenting various psychological issues—depression, anxiety, trauma—using natural language, affective cues, and behavioral patterns while making use of ESP terms studied in class. The AI-analyzed feedback on language quality and tone, emotional expression, and responsiveness helps students improve their interpersonal skills, cultural sensitivity, and diagnostic language (Gros, 2020), not only ESL linguistic abilities.

Additionally, AI's capacity for analyzing speech patterns—such as pitch, rhythm, and word choice—allows students to deepen their understanding of emotional states and client rapport-building. Such tools have the potential to democratize clinical training by providing accessible, scalable, and diverse practice environments that address the scarcity of live clinical cases.

Future implications: Advances in affective computing and biometric sensors could further refine AI's ability to detect emotional nuances, enabling richer simulations that mimic real emotional engagements, thereby fostering more advanced clinical communication skills.

Challenges: Ensuring ethical use and data privacy remains critical, especially given the sensitive nature of psychological data. Furthermore, AI simulations should complement, not replace, human-supervised clinical training, preserving the central role of human judgment and empathy.

5. FUTURE PERSPECTIVES

The future landscape of AI in ESP education is poised for significant evolution, influenced heavily by geopolitical shifts, regulatory frameworks, technological advancements, and societal needs. As nations reinforce their digital sovereignty — a concept emphasizing control over digital infrastructure, data, and AI development—educators and policymakers face both opportunities and challenges in integrating AI ethically and effectively.

5.1 Geopolitical and Regulatory Drivers

Regions such as the European Union are leading efforts to regulate AI through legislation like the proposed AI Act (European Commission, 2021). These regulations aim to ensure that AI systems used in education are transparent, non-discriminatory, and accountable, emphasizing human oversight and explainability. Such frameworks push developers and educators toward more responsible AI deployment, fostering systems that can be audited and scrutinized for bias or unfair outcomes.

However, regional regulatory differences may create disparities in AI accessibility and capabilities. For example, AI tools developed within the EU must adhere to strict privacy and fairness standards, potentially limiting their functionality compared to less-regulated counterparts but ensuring higher ethical standards. Conversely, AI systems from jurisdictions with less oversight may pose risks of bias or misuse, highlighting the importance of international cooperation and consensus in AI governance (Woollard & Angel, 2019).

5.2 Impact on Educational Access and Equity

A critical concern is the digital divide—where disparities in access to infrastructure, devices, and digital literacy risk widening educational inequalities. Underprivileged regions may lack the resources to implement advanced AI tools, thus exacerbating existing disparities in global education (Gros, 2020). Ensuring equitable access requires global cooperation, development of low-cost and open-source AI solutions, and targeted investment in digital infrastructure.

5.3 Transforming Pedagogical Strategies

AI's capabilities will facilitate increasingly personalized learning experiences. Adaptive learning systems will evolve to become more intuitive, analyzing learner performance continuously and customizing content, language models, and simulations accordingly. These systems can support a "flipped classroom" approach, where students engage with AI-based tasks outside class and then participate in facilitated discussions and reflections, maximizing active learning (Levy & Stockwell, 2006).

Moreover, immersive technologies like VR and AR, combined with AI, will expand the scope of experiential learning, not only for language education. For example, future classrooms may feature AI-guided virtual field trips to international sites, diplomatic negotiations, or social environments, providing culturally rich contexts for language practice and soft skills development. Such integration promises to make language learning more engaging, authentic, and effective.

6. CHALLENGES AND ETHICAL CONSIDERATIONS

The path forward must address several key challenges:

- **Bias and fairness:** Despite advances, AI systems remain susceptible to biases embedded in training data. Continuous oversight and diverse datasets are critical to mitigate unfair outcomes, especially in sensitive educational domains (Williamson et al., 2021).
- **Data Privacy and Security:** As AI relies on collecting vast amounts of learner data, privacy concerns escalate. Strict adherence to data protection laws like GDPR is essential, along with transparent data handling policies.
- **Digital Literacy and Ethical Awareness**: Educators and students need training to navigate AI technologies responsibly. Curriculum modules on AI ethics, digital citizenship, and critical media literacy will become indispensable.

7. TOWARD A RESPONSIBLE AI ECOSYSTEM

Achieving responsible AI integration requires multi-stakeholder collaboration—educators, developers, policymakers, and learners—working toward common standards of transparency, fairness, and inclusivity. Building open, multilingual datasets and fostering global dialogues about AI's societal implications will be crucial.

Furthermore, ongoing research into explainable AI (XAI) will help develop systems whose decisions and feedback are interpretable by humans, enhancing trust and accountability. Universities can lead these efforts by establishing specialized centers for AI ethics, interdisciplinary research collaborations, and national or international policy development.

The transformative potential of AI in ESP education is undeniable: from immersive VR simulations to personalized adaptive learning systems, the opportunities are vast. However, harnessing this potential responsibly requires a firm commitment to ethical principles, equitable access, and regulatory compliance. As the geopolitical landscape continues to shape AI development, educators and policymakers must anticipate and address challenges related to bias, privacy, and digital divides.

Ultimately, the goal is to create a future where AI supports inclusive, human-centered, and ethically grounded language education. By doing so, we can equip learners with not only linguistic competence but also intercultural sensitivity, digital literacy, and ethical awareness, which are crucial attributes for effective participation in our interconnected global society.

REFERENCES

Benson, P. (2019). Digital technology and language learning: Opportunities and challenges. The Modern Language Journal, 103(S1), 62–76. https://doi.org/10.1111/modl.12548

Burstein, J., Chodorow, M., & Leacock, C. (2019). Natural language processing in education: Bridging the gap between research and practice. Review of Educational Research, 89(3), 323–368. https://doi.org/10.3102/0034654319856290

European Commission. (2021). Proposal for a regulation laying down harmonized rules on artificial intelligence (Artificial Intelligence Act). https://eur-lex.europa.eu/legal-content/EN/TXT/?uri=CELEX%3A52021PC0206

Gros, B. (2020). Learning, learning analytics and educational technology: Rethinking education in the digital age. British Journal of Educational Technology, 51(4), 1233–1242. https://doi.org/10.1111/bjet.12909

Levy, M., & Stockwell, G. (2006). Call dimensions: Options and issues in computer-assisted language learning. Routledge.

Li, C., & He, Y. (2021). AI literacy and education policy: Building capacity for AI-driven society. Policy Futures in Education, 19(3), 347–370. https://doi.org/10.1177/14782103211001162

Lynott, D., Nelson, D., & Stefanik, J. (2020). Virtual reality in language education: A review of recent developments. Computer Assisted Language Learning, 33(1–2), 15–32. https://doi.org/10.1080/09588221.2019.1666518

Miller, T., & Veletsianos, G. (2020). Paradoxes in AI-enhanced education: Ethical, social, and pedagogical implications. Educational Technology Research and Development, 68(4), 1997–2007. https://doi.org/10.1007/s11423-020-09772-9

O'Neill, C., & McGlade, L. (2020). Ethics and artificial intelligence in education: Preparing the ground. Educational Technology & Society, 23(4), 101–113.

Selwyn, N. (2016). Education and technology: Key issues and debates. British Journal of Educational Technology, 47(6), 969–987. https://doi.org/10.1111/bjet.12428Selwyn, N. (2019). Should robots replace teachers? AI and the future of education. Learning, Media and Technology, 44(3), 301–312. https://doi.org/10.1080/17439884.2019.1628501

Woollard, J., & Angel, K. (2019). Digital sovereignty and the future of education. Policy Futures in Education, 17(4), 448–464. https://doi.org/10.1177/1478210318778204

Williamson, B., Piattoeva, N., & Kennedy, K. (2021). Datafication, AI, and education: Ethical challenges and research implications. British Journal of Educational Technology, 52(6), 2234–2249. https://doi.org/10.1111/bjet.23190

Woollard, J., & Angel, K. (2019). Digital sovereignty and the future of education. Policy Futures in Education, 17(4), 448–464. https://doi.org/10.1177/1478210318778204

DESIGN THINKING AS AN INNOVATIVE PEDAGOGICAL TOOL

Pedro Isaias[1] and Paula Miranda[2]
[1]*Universidade Aberta – Portuguese Open University*
Lisbon, Portugal
[2]*Instituto Politécnico de Setúbal, ESTSetúbal*
Setúbal, Portugal

ABSTRACT

The transformation of educational systems requires pedagogical approaches that move beyond the conventional format of learning by transmission of content. It is pressing to address the challenges deriving from the changing landscape of the workplace. Diverse, hybrid, technologically enhanced, focused on 21st century skills, and an advocate of innovation, the contemporary workplace requires a labour force that is prepared for these demands. Design thinking has been implemented in educational settings with significant success in the development and practice of creativity, problem-solving, critical thinking, resilience and other important transferable competences. This paper aims to explore the role of design thinking as an innovative pedagogical approach, by reporting on a study with undergraduate students that were asked to use design thinking on an innovation-based project. The students completed a pre-session and project questionnaire and a post-session and project questionnaire to assess their experience, having reported important progress and significant learning benefits from the incorporation of design thinking. Design thinking imported structure and method into the problem-solving process and endowed it with empathy, allowing the students to have a better understanding of the human perspective of the problem.

KEYWORDS

Design Thinking, Innovation, Pedagogical Tool, Higher Education

1. INTRODUCTION

The educational system seems to remain insufficiently committed to the development of key competences such as creativity and innovation and still harbours a vision where error is a stigma. The promotion of innovation and entrepreneurship requires individuals to work past the impediment of failure and learn from it to be successful (Rhaiem & Amara, 2021). The adaptation to new and digitalised settings requires learners to develop a creative, collaborative and experimental mindset where the novel problems that arise from these transformations can be addressed (Androutsos & Brinia, 2019). The search for innovative pedagogical approaches has led many educators to think outside the box and implement methodologies not intrinsically connected to education, such as design thinking (Razzouk & Shute, 2012). Design thinking, in the words of Brown (2008), is a "discipline that uses the designer's sensibility and methods to match people's needs with what is technologically feasible and what a viable business strategy can convert into customer value and market opportunity" (p.2). Previous studies have reported the successful implementation of design thinking in different subjects and courses, such as economics and business (Androutsos & Brinia, 2019), medicine (Thakur et al., 2021) and engineering (Jiang & Pang, 2023). This paper frames design thinking within two theories: experiential learning theory (Kolb, 1984) and IDEO/Stanford d.school's design thinking approach (Brown, 2008) as 21st century skills gain an increasing importance in the professional landscape, educational institutions seek novel pedagogical approaches to guide their students in the development of these skills. Design thinking has raised the interest of educators for its capacity to assist learners in the acquisition and practice of 21st century skills (Romero Caballero et al., 2025; Luka, 2019).

This paper aims to report the findings of two online questionnaires that were distributed among higher education students that were enrolled in a bioinformatics course, before and after their participation in a design thinking session and an innovation-based project. More specifically, this paper aims to examine the following research questions: a) How did design thinking contribute to the students' decision-making process; b) What design thinking's aspects/tools did the students incorporate in their project?; and c) How do students perceive the contribution of design thinking in various domains and in their academic/professional lives. It begins by reflecting on the incorporation of design thinking in educational setting and its role as a pedagogical strategy. The methodology will follow with the description of the data collection and analysis and the results will present the findings of the two questionnaires.

2. DESIGN THINKING AS A PEDAGOGICAL TOOL

Kolb (1984) justifies his theory's denomination of experiential as the result of its conceptual background derived from Dewey, Lewin and Piaget, and because this term highlights the centrality of experience in learning. Experiential learning gives prevalence to the process rather than the result. Knowledge is mutable and it is shaped by experience. Hence it is created through the personal experiences of the individual. According to the author, in an effective learning process, individuals should ideally have four core skills: concrete experience, which refers to the ability to engage fully and unbiasedly in novel experiences; reflective observation, with which one is able to regard and reflect on their own experiences from different viewpoints; abstract conceptualisation, which allows for the creation of concepts that construct robust theories derived from their observations; and active experimentation, with which individuals can apply these theories in decision making and problem solving (Kolb, 1984). Experiential learning and these competences can be articulated within design thinking's phases in problem solving. Hence, concrete experience is related to empathy, reflective observation is aligned with the definition phase, abstract conceptualisation with ideate, and active experimentation with prototyping and testing. With respect to IDEO their design thinking framework entails seven unique mindsets that distinguish design thinkers: "empathy, optimism, iteration, creative confidence, making, embracing ambiguity, and learning from failure" (Brown, 2008, p. 10)

Several studies, originated by different entities have underlined the importance of promoting the development of skills that are becoming increasingly important in the labour market, such as flexibility in the face of change, teamwork, digital literacy, communication and problem solving. Competences like critical and creative thinking, innovation and initiative are essential and their development requires a different approach to teaching (Luka, 2019). Design thinking is a valuable resource for educational practice, because it promotes students' engagement with a more proactive method of problem solving, where they can, via experimentation and collaboration, become responsible for the solution creation process. Through design thinking, learners can identify real-world problems and propose a solution (Androutsos & Brinia, 2019). Design thinking has been the focus of a rising interest to academics as a methodology to address innovation and problem solving (Mayer & Schwemmle, 2025).

3. DESIGN THINKING, CREATIVE SENSEMAKING AND DIGITAL TECHNOLOGY

Design thinking can be used as an innovative method to develop students' creativity with concern to problem solving (Foster, 2021). There are many techniques that can be deployed with the use of technology to support design thinking. In the digital era, design thinking, can benefit from the use of technology. The design thinking process can be supported by the use of technology, in all its phases (Androutsos & Brinia, 2019). Tools such as Miro, a digital whiteboard (Skywark et al., 2022) can assist students to digitally collaborate with their peers.

Design thinking can assist in the creative resolution of problems, by deploying a user-centred method that uses ideation as well as a cyclic process of prototyping. Design thinking has somewhat evolved at the margin of other innovation management methodologies and, as a consequence, some still associate it with the general practice of design and are uncertain as to its contribution to innovation (Verganti et al., 2021). Questions as to design thinking's capacity to remain a valuable methodology to address the changing landscape of business, marked deeply by the use of technology, rise with the increased digitalisation of the various areas of society.

Recent studies have demonstrated that design thinking is a valuable approach to harness the opportunities provided by technological development. It can be an important resource as it is focused on the users and it can provide a unique perspective about their needs and how technology can best serve them, envisioning useful solutions to respond to their, particular, technological demands (Magistretti et al., 2021).

Design thinking can equally be interpreted as sensemaking, which places imagination as well as improvisation at the centre of its methodology, and as the foundation of its activities (Rylander Eklund et al., 2022). In a study by Matthee & Turpin (2019), undergraduate students are asked to triage problems into three groups (puzzles, problems and messes) and find suitable problem-solving methodologies. Also, in an assignment they are expected to apply to five stages of design thinking according to Stanford d.school design thinking method. Albay & Eisma (2021) study reports on the use of design thinking in the context of a performance task. The experiment conducted by the authors involved a control group using demonstration instruction and an experimental group using design thinking. Their conclusions were clear about the benefits of design thinking, with the experimental group significantly outperforming the other group, and demonstrated that design thinking can be used in education to increase creativity, interaction and support more student-centred teaching. Additionally, Skywark et al. (2022) concluded that the deployment of design thinking methods can be used for the development of an interdisciplinary design thinking course, which ideally should subsume collaborative work competences, real-world relevance and reflection based on growth.

4. METHODOLOGY

The design thinking session took place in the last weeks of the second semester of the bioinformatics course and lasted 3 hours. The project that ensued was completed in three iteration cycles with the students submitting their work for comments and improvements in each cycle. The project consisted of developing an innovative solution for a hypothetical organisation, using design thinking methodologies. This research was based on two online questionnaires: one was distributed before the session and the project and the second was completed at the end of the project. They were distributed among undergraduate students enrolled in a bioinformatics course. The first questionnaire aimed to assess the students' familiarity with design thinking. Firstly, the students completed the demographic data section including age, gender and course. Secondly, they were asked to indicate their knowledge level with regards to design thinking and innovation, and if they had ever participated in a session or project about design thinking. Thirdly, the students rated their knowledge of several design thinking tools and methods, the frequency with which they have used them and in which context.

The second questionnaire assessed their knowledge level after the session and the project and their application of the tools and methods that they had learned. It was more specific in terms of the questions regarding design thinking to evaluate different aspects of what they've learned and applied in their project. It encompassed its tools and methods as well as its different phases and how they were used among the students' teams in the completion of the project. The data that was collected was imported into IBM SPSS statistics to be analysed using descriptive statistics.

5. RESULTS

Both questionnaires received 15 responses. The students' ages vary between 19 and 24, with most students being 20 or 21 years old. Most students are male (10) with only 5 female respondents. All the students were, at the time, enrolled in a bioinformatics course.

5.1 Pre-Session Questionnaire

In the pre-session questionnaire, the students were, firstly, asked about their knowledge of design thinking and innovation (Figure 1).

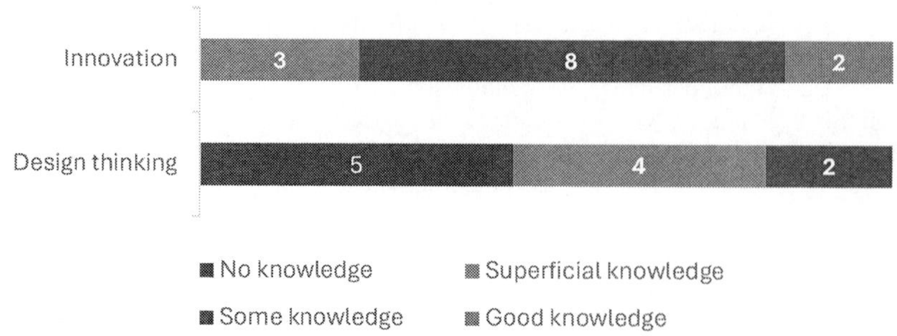

Figure 1. Student's initial knowledge about innovation and design thinking

The chart above shows an evident cleavage between the two subjects. Only 2 students stated that they had some knowledge of design thinking, while 4 had only superficial knowledge and 5 had no knowledge of it. Innovation, on the other hand, was a more familiar term. All the students had some level of knowledge about innovation. Eight had some knowledge, 3 had superficial knowledge and 2 claimed to have a good knowledge of innovation. Most students (9) had not yet participated in any session concerning design thinking, and 6 of them hadn't participated in a design thinking project either. In terms of projects, a total of 9 had not yet participated.

Design thinking can be applied with the support of a variety of tools and technologies. The students were asked to reflect about their knowledge and use of these tools. An expressive majority of the students had no knowledge or only superficial knowledge of the majority of the tools. Also, most students had never used any of the tools that were listed in the questionnaire (Figure 2).

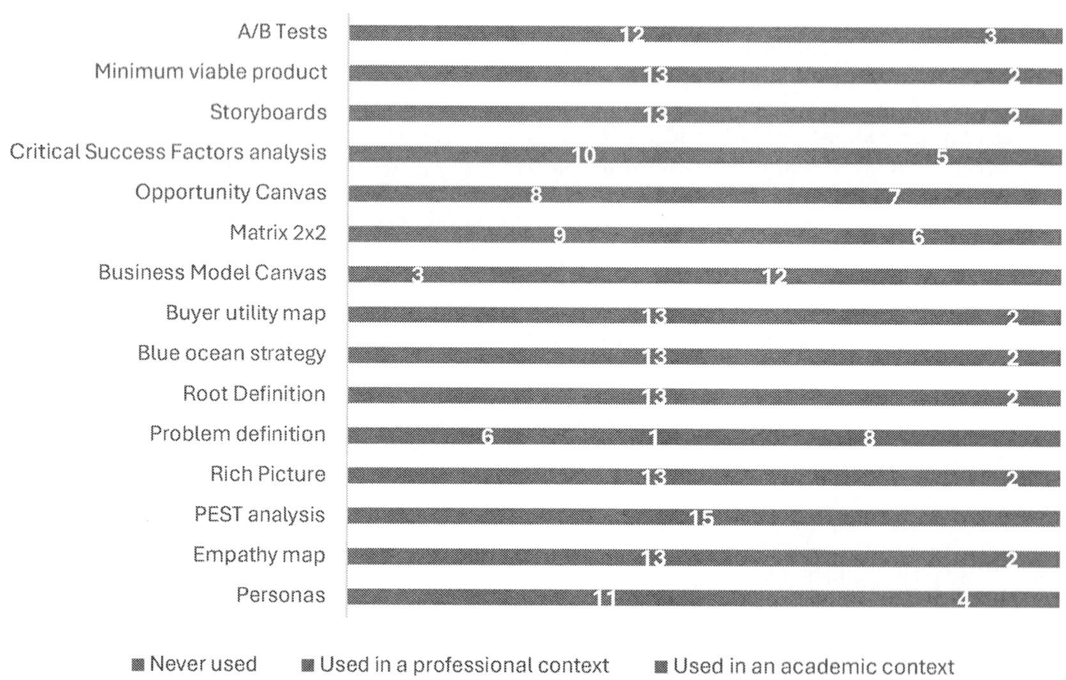

Figure 2. Students' use of design thinking tools and methods

The two mostly used tools were business model canvas, with 12 students reporting to have used it in an academic context, and problem definition, which 1 student had used in a professional context and 8 used in an academic context.

5.2 Post-Session and Project Questionnaire

With concern to the second questionnaire, it was completed by the same students, after their participation in the session and the conclusion of the project. The students' responses to the first question, indicated that most of them had either a limited knowledge of design thinking or no knowledge. When asked if the project had improved their understanding of design thinking, 10 students answered that it had greatly improved and 4 that it had improved. They were then asked how they had used the different phases of design thinking during the completion of the project (Figure 3).

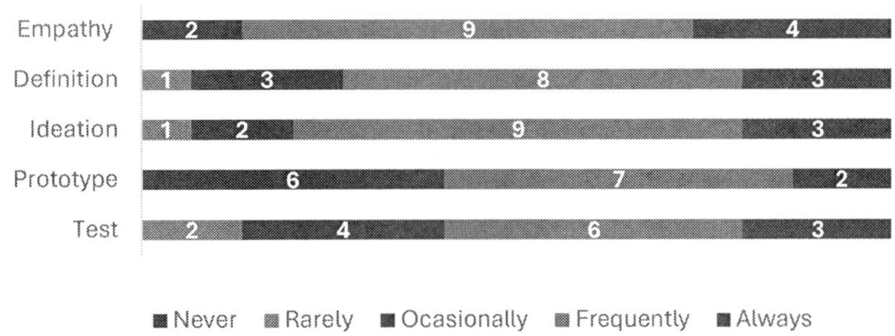

Figure 3. Frequency of use of the different phases of design thinking

As can be seen in the chart above most students used all of design thinking's phases during their project, with a particular emphasis on the empathy and prototype phases. Next, and to address the first research question (how did design thinking contribute to the students' decision-making process), it was important to understand just how these phases had concretely assisted their project, so the students were asked to identify a situation in which design thinking had supported their decision making. The students stated that it helped them to shift to an approach driven by the users' needs, to reveal hidden causes, to provide structure and direction to their work, to assist problem solving and idea management. With concern to the second research question (what design thinking's aspects/tools did the students incorporated in their project?), the questionnaire examined the different methods and techniques that can be used to support design thinking. The students indicated that they had used a wide variety (Figure 4).

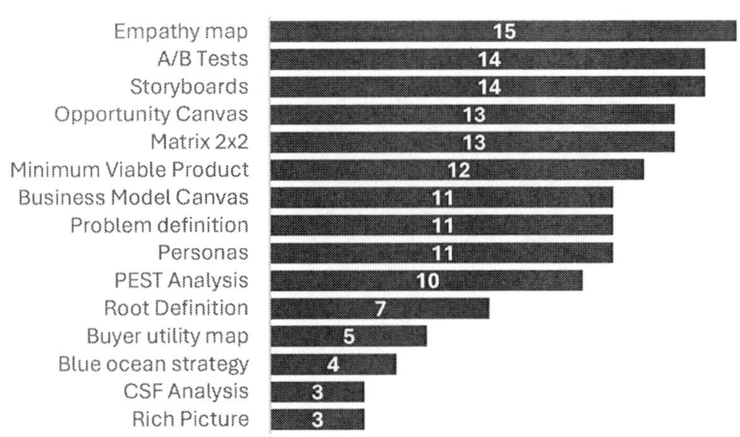

Figure 4. Use of different techniques and methods during the project

This chart represents an expressive improvement from the data collected in the first questionnaire (Figure 2). Empathy maps, A/B tests, storyboards, opportunity canvas and matrix 2X2 were the most popular techniques, while rich picture and CSF analysis were the least used.

In terms of the mentalities that were used more often among the students, focus on the people was by far the most used (11 students). The other options were fast action (1), radical collaboration (0), show don't tell (0), experimentation (5), attention to the process (4), creative confidence (4) and dealing with ambiguity (0). Since problem solving is a fundamental part of innovation, the students were asked to explain their team's approach to problem solving. The majority, 11 students, claimed that the maintained the initial solution. The other approaches included refining once (1 student) and iteratively redefining (2). None of the students claimed to have experienced difficulties. Their justification for their responses mainly cited their initial definition as being appropriate to the problem at hand, throughout the project, regardless of the changes that occurred. As student 6 stated "although we studied the problem in depth, in the end, the definition remained the same, what changed was our perspective of the problem. We realised in the end that everything was centred on people". This was also the idea behind student 10's statement "We are able to adapt to the problems we faced and also come up with creative ideas over time".

When teams are working together on a project, different opinions can emerge. The students were asked to describe how they managed divergences or different views. The majority of the responses highlighted a strategy that avoided conflict (8 students), while the remaining students (6) said that they tried to reach consensus. Throughout the project the students reported having mixed emotions such as satisfaction, frustration, uncertainly and enthusiasm. Student 11's response seems to summarise the dominant view of the students: "enthusiasm, whenever the work was on track, and satisfaction when we realized that we were carrying out the work on a real problem and creating solutions that could help not only in the scenario hypothetically created for this project but also in real companies. There were also moments of uncertainty but more on the side of deciding the best tools to use at each stage, and also frustration because despite everything it was a very long and time-consuming work that required on our part a great deal of time management with the other tasks that we also had at the same time for other subjects". With regards to the different methods and techniques used, the students also highlighted them as being one of the causes for their moments of discovery (eureka moments) during the project, in the sense that their application improved their understanding of the problem. These discovery moments also occurred when they would find solutions to the problems that emerged.

The impact of design thinking in the perception of the process of problem solving was also evident. The students described design thinking as an important strategy to understand and solve problems in a more structured manner. Student 4 described the evolution of his/her perception "it showed that effective solutions do not arise only from logical or technical analysis, but that it also requires a deep understanding of the people involved. I used to think of the process as something more linear and focused on efficiency, now I recognize more the value of an iterative, empathetic, and collaborative approach.". Student 8 also stated that it "helped to understand the processes behind the solutions to various types of problems" and student 12 added that it assisted him/her "to analyse the situation, apply concepts to solve problems, and create ideas from scratch". When asked about design thinking contribution, most of the students (10) found design thinking to the useful in the context of machine learning and analytics projects. Also, 10 students stated that it complements analytical thinking because of the empathy it introduces in the process, the methodology and rigor it requires, the promotion of critical thinking, and the validation and optimisation of solutions.

With concern to the new concepts and perspectives that the students acquired, they identified mainly the knowledge related to the phases and tools associated with design thinking, the importance of empathy in the process of problem solving, and strategies for problem solving. The third research question (How do students perceive the contribution of design thinking in various domains and in their academic/professional lives?) looks forward into the prospective use of design thinking. Most students intend to use it, 3 said that they would definitely use it, 8 would probably use it and 3 didn't know. The versatility of design thinking also became evident when the students identified the areas/scenarios in which design thinking could be used (Figure 5).

Areas/scenarios for design thinking application	
New product development	Entrepreneurship and startups
Data visualisation	Marketing
Personalised digital health solutions	Artificial Intelligence
Health and wellness	Programming
Business	Technology
Biology	Business
Physics	Machine learning
Mathematics	

Figure 5. Areas/scenarios for design thinking application

The students also suggested some improvements to better integrate design thinking into the discipline:

- Introduce design thinking a little earlier
- Simplify the tools and templates
- Use micro projects
- Integrate practical challenges from the beginning of the semester
- Keeping the session that was held on design thinking
- More contact with design thinking
- More in-depth presentation of design thinking and tools
- Use real cases
- More hours of theory and practice
- Integration of a real project

The majority of students (10) believes that design thinking greatly contributes to the development of their academic/professional profile. Three of the students think it moderately contributes, and 1 student thinks it is essential. Their approach to interdisciplinary collaboration was also influenced by design thinking. As they've explained it, design thinking "...showed that interdisciplinary collaboration is essential to generate more complete solutions, as it combines technical, human and creative perspectives and that teamwork recognizes that different areas contribute with complementary knowledge to solve complex problems" (student 2). Also, "it allows the student to think and create ideas in other disciplines" (student 10).

The students were asked to reflect on what they would do differently in a next application/project integrating design thinking. Some highlighted the need to dedicate more time to the definition of the problem, and the empathy phase, others underlined the importance of a deeper analysis of the different techniques and methodologies to better adjust their use to the characteristics of the problems. One of the students reflected on the need to document the process. They were also asked to offer advice to future students who would apply design thinking to machine learning and analytics problems. Two contributions summarise the general perspective of the students: "start by understanding the real needs of users well before choosing algorithms and do not discard different suggestions for solutions just because you initially do not agree or do not think the best one" (student 1); and "first, that they define the problems in time and that they are relevant in order to help in the application of this methodology. A more or less well-founded general idea about how each works is also crucial" (student 7).

6. CONCLUSION

This paper intended to report on the use of design thinking by a group of undergraduate students, during an innovation-based project, to evaluate its role as an important pedagogical tool. The data collected in both questionnaires revealed a significant positive evolution on the students' knowledge about design thinking and their use of its related phases and techniques/methods. Before attending the session and completing their project they had very limited knowledge about design thinking. Afterwards they reported using design thinking to develop adequate solutions to existing problems and as a structured strategy to frame decision making and managing ideas. Their focus also shifted to a more empathetic approach to problems, by underlying the importance of considering the human perspective, the needs of the users and the underlying causes of the problems. The versatility of design thinking became evident not only in its different phases and the techniques that were used, but also in the students' stated perception that it would be suitable to use in a variety of areas, such as business, technology, health, marketing. According to the students, while it is a structured process it can be adapted to serve a panoply of fields. In future projects the students recommended introducing design thinking earlier in the semester, increasing their contact with practical challenges and real cases and a more in-depth presentation of design thinking and tools, which can also be an indication of their positive perception of design thinking as an important pedagogical tool.

The results of the post-session questionnaire align with Kolb's experiential learning (1984). Firstly, the students highlighted the importance of the empathy phase, which articulates with concrete experience. Secondly, their responses showed how they used reflective observation to redefine the problems, which in turn resulted into abstract conceptualization and the search for solutions. The findings also relate to IDEO's mindsets (Brown, 2008) in several aspects. The student's most frequently used mentality was "focus on the people", which is connected to a core precept, empathy. Moreover, their adaptation to the problems revealed the use of iteration and embracing ambiguity. Their report of mixed emotions throughout the process can also be articulated with learning from failure. The reduced population used in the online questionnaires is one of the most relevant limitations of this study, which can be in the future, reproduced with a more numerically significant sample. Prospective research ventures can equally focus on the recommendations of the students and redesign this experience in other courses and with other learning activities.

REFERENCES

Albay, E. M., & Eisma, D. V. (2021). Performance task assessment supported by the design thinking process: Results from a true experimental research. *Social Sciences & Humanities Open, 3*(1), 100116. https://doi.org/https://doi.org/10.1016/j.ssaho.2021.100116

Androutsos, A., & Brinia, V. (2019). Developing and Piloting a Pedagogy for Teaching Innovation, Collaboration, and Co-Creation in Secondary Education Based on Design Thinking, Digital Transformation, and Entrepreneurship. *Education Sciences 2019, Vol. 9, Page 113, 9*(2), 113. https://doi.org/10.3390/educsci9020113

Brown, T. (2008). Design thinking. *Harvard Business Review, 86*(6), 84.

Foster, M. K. (2021). Design thinking: A creative approach to problem solving. *Management Teaching Review, 6*(2), 123-140. https://doi.org/10.1177/2379298119871468

Jiang, C., & Pang, Y. (2023). Enhancing design thinking in engineering students with project-based learning. *Computer Applications in Engineering Education, 31*(4), 814-830. https://doi.org/10.1002/cae.22608

Kolb, D. A. (1984). Experiential learning: Experience as the source of learning and development, David A. Kolb, Prentice-Hall International, Hemel Hempstead, Herts., 1984. No. of pages: xiii + 256. *Journal of Organizational Behavior, 8*(4), 359–360.

Luka, I. (2019). Design thinking in pedagogy: Frameworks and uses. *European Journal of Education, 54*(4), 499–512. https://doi.org/10.1111/EJED.12367

Magistretti, S., Ardito, L., & Messeni Petruzzelli, A. (2021). Framing the microfoundations of design thinking as a dynamic capability for innovation: Reconciling theory and practice. *Journal of Product Innovation Management, 38*(6), 645–667. https://doi.org/10.1111/jpim.12586

Matthee, M., & Turpin, M. (2019). Teaching critical thinking, problem solving, and design thinking: Preparing IS students for the future. *Journal of Information Systems Education, 30*(4), 242–252.

Mayer, S., & Schwemmle, M. (2025). The impact of design thinking and its underlying theoretical mechanisms: A review of the literature. *Creativity and Innovation Management, 34*(1), 78–110. https://doi.org/10.1111/caim.12626

Razzouk, R., & Shute, V. (2012). What is design thinking and why is it important?. *Review of educational research, 82*(3), 330-348.

Rhaiem, K., & Amara, N. (2021). Learning from innovation failures: a systematic review of the literature and research agenda. *Review of managerial science, 15*(2), 189-234.

Romero Caballero, S., Canquiz Rincón, L., Rodríguez Toscano, A., Valencia Pérez, A., & Moreno Gómez, G. (2025). Challenge-based learning and design thinking in higher education: institutional strategies for linking experiential learning, innovation, and academic performance. *Innovations in Education and Teaching International, 62*(2), 557-574. https://doi.org/10.1080/14703297.2024.2326191

Rylander Eklund, A., Navarro Aguiar, U., & Amacker, A. (2022). Design thinking as sensemaking: Developing a pragmatist theory of practice to (re)introduce sensibility. *Journal of Product Innovation Management, 39*(1), 24–43. https://doi.org/10.1111/jpim.12604;requestedjournal:journal:15405885;wgroup:string:publication

Skywark, E. R., Chen, E., & Jagannathan, V. (2022). Using the Design Thinking Process to Co-create a New, Interdisciplinary Design Thinking Course to Train 21st Century Graduate Students. *Frontiers in Public Health, 9*(11), 777869. https://doi.org/10.3389/fpubh.2021.777869/bibtex

Thakur, A., Soklaridis, S., Crawford, A., Mulsant, B., & Sockalingam, S. (2021). Using rapid design thinking to overcome COVID-19 challenges in medical education. *Academic Medicine, 96*(1), 56-61. https://doi.org/10.1097/acm.0000000000003718

Verganti, R., Dell'Era, C., & Swan, K. S. (2021). Design thinking: Critical analysis and future evolution. In *Journal of Product Innovation Management* (Vol. 38, Issue 6, pp. 603–622). John Wiley and Sons Inc. https://doi.org/10.1111/jpim.12610

AGE-RELATED VARIATIONS IN COMPUTATIONAL THINKING DEVELOPMENT THROUGH PEER TUTORING IN EDUCATIONAL ROBOTICS

Vaso Anastasiou and Charoula Angeli
University of Cyprus, Cyprus

ABSTRACT

This study examines developmental differences in the acquisition of computational thinking (CT) among students in Grades 3 to 5 (ages 8–11) engaged in educational robotics (ER) activities implemented through a peer tutoring (PT) framework. The sample comprised 78 students from a public school in Europe, with fifth-grade students serving as tutors and third- and fourth-grade students as tutees. A quasi-experimental design was employed, utilizing pre- and post-intervention assessments to measure CT competencies. Findings indicated statistically significant improvements in CT performance among all participants, encompassing both tutors and tutees. Furthermore, no significant differences were observed in post-test outcomes between the two groups, suggesting that the PT approach within ER activities is equally advantageous for both tutors and tutees. Although pre-test results demonstrated an age-related gradient in line with Piagetian developmental theory—whereby older students outperformed their younger peers—this disparity was not evident in the post-test results. Notably, students across all grade levels demonstrated higher post-test scores compared to their pre-test performance, indicating that the intervention yielded measurable benefits for all participants, regardless of their grade level. These findings underscore the potential of developmentally appropriate, structured ER and PT interventions to mitigate age-related differences and effectively cultivate CT skills in primary education contexts.

KEYWORDS

Educational Robotics, Peer Tutoring, Computational Thinking

1. INTRODUCTION

Educational robotics (ER) is becoming a common feature in primary education, offering a dynamic way to nurture 21st-century skills through interactive, hands-on experiences. It has been identified as a promising tool for developing computational thinking (CT) in young students (Ching & Hsu, 2023). However, despite the growing push to introduce CT at the primary level, there is still limited understanding of which CT skills align with children's developmental stages. Questions remain about the appropriate timing for introducing CT and which specific skills and concepts can be effectively taught at various ages (Jiang & Wong, 2021).

Peer tutoring (PT) - a collaborative learning strategy where one student supports another's learning (Topping, 2000) - has shown potential in enhancing educational outcomes by capitalizing on the tutor's recently acquired knowledge and fostering relatable peer interactions. Research has linked PT to a range of benefits, both academic and social, such as improved achievement, confidence, and interpersonal skills (Alegre et al., 2019; Ain et al., 2023). Interestingly, some findings suggest tutors may gain more than their tutees academically (Thurston et al., 2021), underscoring the importance of further exploring PT dynamics.

Although ER and PT each have been studied separately within educational research, little attention has been given to how these two strategies might work together to support CT development. This study aims to bridge that gap by investigating how students' roles in peer tutoring (as tutor or tutee) and their age-related developmental stage impact the acquisition of CT skills during ER-based learning activities.

The following research questions guide the study:

1. How does students' CT performance differ based on their role (tutor or tutee) in ER activities involving cross-age PT?
2. How does students' CT performance differ based on their age in ER activities involving PT?
3. Is there an interaction effect between the two PT interventions?

This research contributes to the current body of knowledge by examining how PT can be integrated into ER to foster CT development in primary education settings. On a practical level, it provides guidance on how to implement ER in a cost-efficient manner using peer-based instructional models. Theoretically, it advances our understanding of how age-related developmental factors and peer dynamics influence the learning of CT skills. As an exploratory effort, the study lays the groundwork for designing and delivering CT-focused ER experiences that are developmentally appropriate for young learners.

2. LITERATURE REVIEW

2.1 Educational Robotics and Computational Thinking

ER activities are grounded in Papert's constructionist theory and the "learning by making" philosophy (Papert & Harel, 1991). In this context, robots function as cognitive tools that support experiential learning, allowing students to explore hypotheses and receive immediate feedback. This process deepens their comprehension of abstract ideas and enhances their problem-solving abilities (Chevalier et al., 2020).

In recent years, ER has been increasingly adopted in primary education as a means of cultivating CT skills (Chevalier et al., 2020). The term "computational thinking" was introduced by Wing (2006), who described it as the ability to solve problems, design systems, and understand human behavior using computer science concepts. Although widely discussed, a universally accepted definition is still lacking (Tsarava et al., 2022). A more recent definition by Shute et al. (2017) frames CT as "the conceptual foundation required to solve problems effectively and efficiently... with solutions that are reusable in different contexts" (p. 142), highlighting it as a broad cognitive capacity rather than a purely technical skill.

Drawing on Shute et al.'s (2017) framework, researchers commonly identify several core components of CT. These include abstraction (identifying key elements of a problem), generalization (extending solutions to new problems), decomposition (breaking down complex tasks), algorithmic thinking (creating step-by-step procedures), and debugging (identifying and fixing errors). Additional foundational elements of CT include sequencing—planning the logical order of steps in a process—and control flow, which involves managing the execution order of instructions (Angeli, 2022).

To ensure the successful integration of ER in primary education, the use of age-appropriate robotics kits is essential, especially for younger children, to avoid overwhelming them with complex tools (Ching & Hsu, 2023). Moreover, carefully designed instructional interventions are needed to support cognitive development and prevent reliance on trial-and-error approaches alone (Chevalier et al., 2020; Jiang & Wong, 2021).

2.2 Peer Tutoring: from Theory to Practice

PT involves more than simple exchange of knowledge; it is deeply rooted in educational theories that highlight social interaction, active engagement, and shared construction of meaning. Vygotsky's (1978) sociocultural theory, especially the concept of the Zone of Proximal Development, emphasizes that cognitive development is often facilitated through collaboration with more knowledgeable peers.

Similarly, the Theory of Social Interdependence developed by Johnson and Johnson (2013) underscores the value of structured group activities in fostering meaningful learning. According to this theory, effective collaboration does not occur automatically by simply placing students in groups. Instead, successful cooperative learning depends on several interrelated conditions. These include a sense of positive interdependence among group members, individual and group accountability, active and supportive interactions, the application of social and communication skills, and ongoing reflection on group performance to enhance future collaboration.

PT can be organized in various ways, depending on how roles are assigned and the characteristics of the learners. Students may take on fixed roles as either tutor or tutee or alternate roles in a reciprocal format. The selection of an appropriate model often depends on students' ages and abilities, ranging from pairings of students with similar characteristics to cross-age tutoring, where older students provide guidance to younger ones (Thurston et al., 2020; Ain et al., 2023).

2.3 Theory of Cognitive Development

The growing push to integrate CT into early education highlights the need to understand how CT skills develop across grade levels. Piaget's (1963) theory of cognitive development offers a helpful framework. He proposed four stages: sensorimotor (0–2 years), where learning is based on sensory and motor interaction; preoperational (2–7 years), marked by symbolic thinking and limited logic; concrete operational (7–11 years), where logical reasoning applies to tangible contexts; and formal operational (from ~11 years), characterized by abstract thinking. This framework helps explain how children gradually gain the capacity to understand CT concepts (Piaget, 1963).

In classrooms, younger primary students benefit from CT activities using concrete examples and step-by-step guidance. For example, eight-year-olds can follow logical instructions tied to everyday situations. However, abstract tasks remain challenging at this stage (Piaget, 1963). More advanced concepts, such as loops and conditionals, often require abstract reasoning associated with the formal operational stage, which typically emerges around age 11 (Vourletsis, 2025).

Recent research supports the link between cognitive development and CT skills. Programming and coding are often associated with increasing cognitive maturity (Kim et al., 2021). As children's reasoning develops, so does their ability to engage with complex concepts in CT and engineering (Vourletsis, 2025). Studies confirm this developmental trend (Kim et al., 2021; Relkin et al., 2020; Tsarava et al., 2022). For instance, Rijke et al. (2018) found that students in Grades 4–6 showed greater gains in abstract reasoning. Kim et al. (2021) also observed that students in these grades, as they transitioned into the concrete operational stage, showed improvement in ICT literacy and CT readiness. While development varies, this period generally supports foundational CT learning. However, not all findings suggest a linear path. Jiang and Wong (2021), studying 197 students aged 9–13, found that Grade 4 students outperformed their Grade 6 peers in certain areas of CT, including conditionals, operators, and pattern recognition. This suggests that students aged 9–11 may be especially receptive to certain CT concepts when supported by practical instruction.

3. METHODOLOGY

3.1 Participants

The study was conducted with 78 students from a public primary school in a European country. The tutor group comprised 38 fifth-grade students, all aged 11, while the tutees included 18 fourth graders (age 10) and 22 third graders (age 9). None of the students had prior exposure to educational robotics. The fifth-grade students received structured instruction from their classroom teacher before taking on the tutor role.

Tutor–tutee pairings were determined based on students' academic performance in Mathematics and Language. Within each grade level, students were ranked from highest to lowest and matched accordingly to form academically balanced pairs. These pairings remained consistent throughout the intervention to encourage sustained interaction and optimize the potential benefits of peer tutoring (Thurston et al., 2021).

3.2 Research Instruments

To evaluate students' CT skills, the same assessment was administered before and after the intervention. The test was designed to measure overall CT performance regardless of prior exposure to educational robotics. It consisted of a series of exercises targeting specific CT sub-skills. Exercises 1A and 1B involved sequencing steps for baking cookies or assembling a toy, assessing algorithmic sequencing abilities. Exercises 2A and 2B required students to give directional instructions for a taxi, measuring the flow of control and decomposition. In Exercises 3A and 3B, students selected a dress or drawing based on attributes, targeting pattern recognition, abstraction, and generalization. Exercises 4A and 4B focused on repeating dance movements or guiding a robot through repetition, assessing pattern recognition, decomposition, and generalization; however, Exercise 4B was excluded from the final analysis due to reported confusion. Exercises 5A and 5B asked students to verify or correct step sequences (e.g., dressing as a pirate or giving directions), measuring algorithmic thinking, decomposition, and debugging. Finally, Exercises 6A and 6B involved completing or extending patterns, evaluating pattern recognition, abstraction, and generalization.

To ensure the reliability of the assessment, both the Intraclass Correlation Coefficient (ICC) and Cronbach's Alpha were calculated. The ICC values for pre- and post-test scores were 0.985 and 0.995, respectively, indicating excellent inter-rater agreement. Cronbach's Alpha values of 0.995 (pre-test) and 0.997 (post-test) also demonstrated high internal consistency. These results confirm the robustness of the test in reliably measuring CT outcomes.

3.3 Digital Tools

The LEGO Education SPIKE Prime Set, designed for children aged 10 and above, was used in the intervention. The set includes Lego bricks, axles, a programmable hub, motors, and a variety of sensors. The students followed the building instructions provided in the LEGO Spike app and utilized a drag-and-drop programming interface based on Scratch.

3.4 Research Procedures

A quasi-experimental design was employed, where older students acted as tutors and younger students as tutees. The research procedure (Figure 1) began with a 40-minute pre-test to assess CT skills. The second phase consisted of 14 forty-minute ER lessons for the fifth graders, conducted over six days and spanning a period of three weeks. These lessons progressively targeted different CT sub-skills, with increasing levels of difficulty, and included four worksheets for basic software commands (see Table 1 for details). Additionally, a 40-minute session was dedicated to explaining the role of the tutor. In the third phase, the fifth graders tutored the fourth graders using the same activities and worksheets across 14 forty-minute sessions.

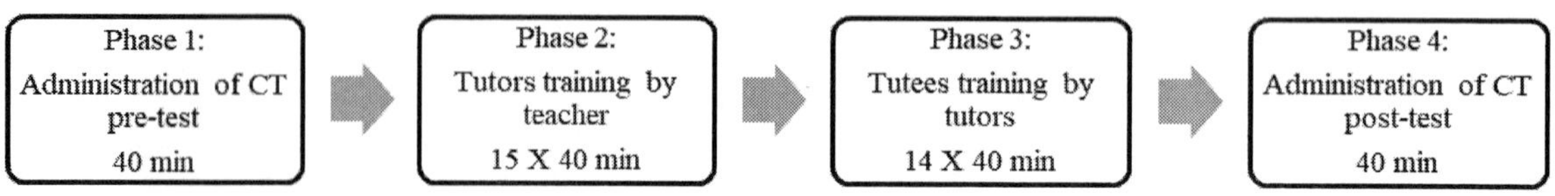

Figure 1. Research Procedure

Table 1. Robotics Course Content

	Course topic	Time	Programming	CT sub-skill
1	Robots and their everyday uses. The Lego Spike robot kit and its software	80'		algorithmic thinking
2	Building a Break Dancer robot & worksheet 1	120'	motors, light, events	algorithmic thinking debugging
3	Programming Break Dancer robot & worksheet 2	80'	Use of color sensors, wait and repeat	abstract skill
4	Building a Driving Base robot & worksheet 3	120'	Use of distance and pressure sensors, events – broadcast a message	generalization
5	Programming Driving Base robot with color sensors & worksheet 4	80'	Use of color sensors. When color is, events – Broadcast a message	decomposition
6	Robotic Challenge: Program a robot to navigate a city, avoid obstacles, and react to traffic lights	80'	All the above	all

3.5 Data Analysis

To evaluate students' improvement in CT, statistical tests were performed using SPSS. T-tests compared the performance of tutors and tutees, while ANCOVA analyzed the effect of the role on performance. To analyze differences in student performance across Grades 3, 4, and 5, the Kruskal-Wallis H test was employed due to non-normal distributions and small, unequal group sizes, as assessed by the Shapiro-Wilk test ($p < .05$ for all groups). Significant findings were tested with the Bonferroni correction for pairwise comparisons, followed by Mann-Whitney U tests. Within-group improvements (pre- vs. post-test) were assessed using the Wilcoxon signed-rank test. To compare the performance of 5th graders with that of 3rd and 4th graders on individual CT items, independent samples t-tests were conducted for both pre-test and post-test scores.

4. RESULTS

4.1 CT Performance by Role

Descriptive statistics show improved performance for both tutors and tutees after the intervention (Table 2). Tutors' post-test scores ($M = 83.45$, $SD = 11.22$) exceeded pre-test scores ($M = 74.79$, $SD = 12.59$), with a significant difference confirmed by a paired t-test ($t = -5.03$, $df = 37$, $p < 0.01$) and a modest effect size (Cohen's $d \approx 0.44$). Tutees also improved, with post-test scores ($M = 70.58$, $SD = 19.68$) higher than pre-test scores ($M = 61.10$, $SD = 18.32$). The paired t-test confirmed that the difference was significant ($t = -5.56$, $df= 39$, $p < 0.001$), with a moderate effect size (Cohen's $d \approx 0.88$).

Table 2. CT Performance Comparison per Role

Role*	Test	M	SD	t	df	p
Tutors	Pre-test	74.79	12.59	-5.03	37	<0.001
	Post-test	83.45	11.22			
Tutees	Pre-test	61.10	18.32	-5.56	39	<0.001
	Post-test	70.58	19.68			

* $N_{tutors}=38$, $N_{tutees}=40$

An ANCOVA was conducted to examine the effect of role on post-test performance, controlling for pre-test scores. Levene's test confirmed the assumption of equal variances ($p = 0.47$). The analysis revealed a significant effect of pre-test scores on post-test outcomes, $F(1, 75) = 113.25$, $p < 0.001$. However, the effect of the role was not statistically significant, $F(1, 75) = 0.64$, $p = 0.43$, indicating that being a tutor or a tutee did not significantly influence post-test performance when accounting for prior knowledge.

4.2 CT Performance by Grade Level

To assess differences in students' performance across grade levels, both pre-test and post-test total scores were compared among each grade. Given the small sample sizes and non-normal distribution of the test scores, non-parametric tests were employed. A Kruskal-Wallis H test revealed a statistically significant difference in pre-test total scores across grade levels (χ^2 (2, 78) = 15.59, $p < 0.001$). Post-hoc pairwise comparisons using the Mann-Whitney U test with the Bonferroni correction showed that Grade 5 students performed significantly better than both Grade 3 (Mann-Whitney, $U(58) = 224.5$, $z = -2.97$, $p = 0.003$) and Grade 4 (Mann-Whitney, $U(54) = 141.5$, $z = -3.52$, $p < .001$) students. No significant difference was found between Grade 3 and Grade 4. A similar analysis of post-test total scores also revealed significant group differences ($\chi^2(2, 78) = 12.66$, $p = 0.02$). Post-hoc comparisons revealed that Grade 5 students scored significantly higher than Grade 4 students (Mann-Whitney, $U(54) = 140.5$, $z = -3.54$, $p < 0.001$). However, the differences between Grade 5 and Grade 3, as well as between Grade 3 and Grade 4, were not statistically significant. Within-group comparisons using the Wilcoxon signed-rank test confirmed that all three grade levels demonstrated statistically significant improvement from pre-test to post-test: Grade 3 ($W(21)=17$, $z=-4.71$, $p < .001$), Grade 4 ($W(17)=31{,}5$, $z=-2.36$, $p=0.018$), and Grade 5 ($W(37)=17{,}50$, $z=-4.17$, $p< 0.001$). These results suggest that the intervention was beneficial across all grade levels. Grade 5 students entered the intervention with a performance advantage and maintained higher scores than Grade 4 students after the intervention. However, their post-test scores were not significantly higher than those of Grade 3 students, indicating a narrowing of the performance gap.

Table 3. CT Performance Descriptive Statistics per Grade

Grade*	$M_{Pre-Test}$	SD	$M_{Post-Test}$	SD
Grade 3	60.18	21.45	71.77	22.37
Grade 4	62.22	14.11	69.11	16.30
Grade 5	74.79	12.59	83.45	11.22

* N_{G3}=22, N_{G4}=18, N_{G5}=38,

When each question was analyzed individually, notable performance differences were observed between 5th graders and the 3rd and 4th graders, particularly in Questions 5A and 5B, which specifically assessed debugging skills—the ability to identify and correct errors. At the pre-test stage, independent samples t-tests revealed that 5th graders achieved significantly higher scores on both items. In Question 5A, 5th graders ($M = 5.53$, $SD = 3.41$) scored significantly higher ($t= 3.42$, $df=76$, $p = .001$, Cohen's $d = 0.77$) than their younger peers ($M = 2.85$, $SD = 2.49$), Similarly, in Question 5B, 5th graders ($M = 3.76$, $SD = 2.99$) outperformed ($t= 3.56$, $df=76$,$p < .001$, Cohen's $d = 0.81$) students in 3rd and 4th grade ($M = 1.63$, $SD = 2.21$). However, this difference was not maintained in the post-test. Independent samples t-tests showed no significant difference ($t=-0.19$, $df=42.15$, $p = 0.85$) in Question 5A between 5th graders ($M = 6.55$, $SD = 3.02$) and younger students ($M = 7.03$, $SD = 15.40$). Likewise, in Question 5B, the scores of 5th graders ($M = 5.66$, $SD = 2.88$) did not differ significantly ($t = 0.11$, $df=41.85$, $p = 0.91$) from those of 3rd and 4th graders ($M = 5.38$, $SD = 15.45$). These findings indicate that although 5th graders initially demonstrated a clear advantage, the performance gap was effectively closed by the younger students by the end of the intervention. The substantial improvement shown by 3rd and 4th graders on debugging questions suggests that the intervention was particularly effective in developing learners' ability to reason through and correct programming errors.

5. DISCUSSION

This study demonstrated that PT can effectively support the development of CT skills, highlighting its potential in educational settings that incorporate ER. By engaging students in collaborative learning, PT not only enhances understanding but also offers a cost-effective instructional model that leverages peer resources without requiring additional staffing or materials (Ain et al., 2023; Chang et al., 2025).

Analyses comparing performance by role revealed no significant differences in post-test CT scores between tutors and tutees when controlling for pre-test performance. This suggests that although tutors initially had an advantage, the intervention enabled tutees to make substantial progress and reach comparable levels of achievement. These findings indicate that PT benefits learners regardless of their role and functions as an effective strategy for narrowing skill gaps. This outcome aligns with earlier research demonstrating that both tutors and tutees can experience academic gains through structured PT programs (Chang et al., 2025).

Pre-test scores revealed a clear age-related difference in CT performance, consistent with Piaget's theory of cognitive development (Piaget, 1963). As students progress from Grade 3 to Grade 5, CT skills appear to improve and manifest differently, reflecting both cognitive maturation and the cumulative impact of educational experiences. The superior performance of fifth-grade students, particularly in debugging tasks, prior to the intervention, can be interpreted through the lens of Piaget's framework. At this stage, learners are likely transitioning into the formal operational stage, characterized by the emergence of abstract reasoning and logical thinking. This cognitive advancement may have enabled them to engage with CT tasks more effectively and deeply. Similar patterns have been observed in other studies, which found that CT assessment scores increase significantly with grade level (Relkin et al., 2020; Kim et al, 2021; Vourletsis, 2025). Likewise, a developmental study of primary school learners observed that students' CT abilities followed a clear age-based progression prior to instruction (Jiang & Wong, 2021). These findings reinforce the notion that cognitive development plays a critical role in students' CT capabilities—older learners naturally demonstrate more advanced CT.

Although all groups improved significantly after the intervention, the findings indicate that this improvement did not follow the same age-related consistency observed in the pre-test. This aligns with Jiang and Wong's (2021) observation that students of different ages respond to CT instruction in varied ways during the intervention. The clear developmental progression evident before the intervention, where older students consistently outperformed younger ones, was no longer present. This pattern suggests that the intervention itself may have played a significant role in shaping post-test outcomes, highlighting the potential of instructional design to support CT development across different age groups. In this case, the intervention appeared to have a leveling effect across the three age groups.

Notably, although no statistically significant differences were found between Grades 3 and 4 in either pre- or post-test scores, third-grade students demonstrated the most significant numerical improvement. This suggests that younger learners, despite starting from a lower baseline, were exceptionally responsive to the intervention. One explanation is that Grade 3 students were in a transitional phase within the concrete operational stage, during which foundational cognitive structures are still forming. At this stage, well-scaffolded and guided activities can have a powerful impact, as they align with learners' Zone of Proximal Development, providing support that enables students to perform tasks they would not be able to accomplish independently (Vygotsky, 1978). Research on early CT education supports this idea, noting that young students often struggle with complex tasks in the absence of support but perform well when appropriate scaffolding is provided (Angeli & Georgiou, 2023). The notable gains observed among third graders suggest that the instructional content was well-aligned with their developmental needs, emphasizing concrete, tangible examples and step-by-step guidance provided by supportive peer tutors.

These findings reinforce the idea that well-designed instructional interventions can significantly enhance CT development, particularly when they are attuned to learners' cognitive stages. They also highlight the importance of implementing age-appropriate curricula that are not only developmentally informed but also instructionally intentional and appropriately scaffolded. As supported by previous research (Vourletsis, 2025; Jiang & Wong, 2021), the success of CT education depends not only on when concepts are introduced but also on how they are taught.

6. FUTURE SUGGESTIONS AND LIMITATIONS

This research is subject to several limitations that should be acknowledged. Most notably, the relatively small sample size limits the generalizability of the findings and constrains the scope of statistical analysis. In particular, it was not possible to examine potential interactions between students' grade level and their peer tutoring role (tutor vs. tutee), which could have provided more profound insight into how age and role jointly influence CT development. Future studies with larger and more balanced samples are needed to explore these dynamics. Moreover, the study focused on a limited age range (Grades 3-5). Expanding future research to include a broader developmental spectrum could clarify how CT skills emerge, evolve, or plateau across cognitive stages and enhance our understanding of age-related readiness for various CT subskills.

The assessment instrument used in this study measured overall CT performance but may not have been sensitive enough to detect nuanced differences across individual CT components. Future research would benefit from using more fine-grained and validated tools that assess specific dimensions such as abstraction, decomposition, debugging, generalization, and algorithmic thinking. This need has also been emphasized in prior studies, where researchers have called for more targeted instruments to reflect better the multidimensional nature of CT and its development over time (e.g., Shute et al., 2017; Tsarava et al., 2022).

Despite the limitations, the present study offers meaningful baseline evidence supporting the effectiveness of PT in promoting CT through ER in primary education. These findings also reinforce the importance of designing age-appropriate, developmentally responsive CT activities, which align with learners' cognitive abilities and provide the necessary scaffolding for success.

7. CONCLUSION

This study contributes to the growing body of research on CT by demonstrating that PT when integrated with ER, can effectively support the development of CT among primary students. By examining performance across grade levels and peer tutoring roles, the findings highlight that both younger and older learners benefit from structured, collaborative instruction, regardless of initial differences in ability. While pre-test results reflected a clear developmental trend consistent with Piaget's theory, post-test outcomes revealed a reduction in age-based performance gaps, suggesting that instructional design played a critical role in supporting learning. Notably, the substantial progress made by younger students highlighted the potential of well-scaffolded, age-appropriate learning environments. This progress can be interpreted through the lens of Vygotsky's Zone of Proximal Development, as the intervention provided guided support that enabled learners to achieve outcomes beyond their independent capabilities. Overall, this study underscores the value of combining ER and PT as a cost-effective, developmentally aligned approach to fostering CT in primary education.

REFERENCES

Ain, Q., Thurston, A., MacKenzie, A., & Ozkaya, C. (2023). What does previous research tell us about the effects of peer tutoring on metacognition in primary and secondary schools? *International Journal of Educational Research Open*, 4, 100248.

Alegre, F., Moliner, L., Maroto, A., & Lorenzo-Valentin, G. (2019). Peer tutoring in mathematics in primary education: A systematic review. *Educational Review*, 71(6), 767-791.

Angeli, C. (2022). The effects of scaffolded programming scripts on pre-service teachers' computational thinking: Developing algorithmic thinking through programming robots. *International Journal of Child-Computer Interaction*, 31, 100329.

Angeli, C., & Georgiou, K. (2023). Investigating the effects of gender and scaffolding in developing preschool children's computational thinking during problem-solving with Bee-Bots. In *Frontiers in Education* (Vol. 7, p. 757627). Frontiers Media SA.

Chang, A., Mauer, E., Wanzek, J., Kim, S., Scammacca, N., & Swanson, E. (2025). Examining the Academic Effects of Cross-age Tutoring: A Meta-analysis. *Educational Psychology Review*, *37*(1), 1–20.

Chevalier, M., Giang, C., Piatti, A., & Mondada, F. (2020). Fostering computational thinking through educational robotics: A model for creative computational problem-solving. *International Journal of STEM Education*, 7, 1–18.

Ching, Y. H., & Hsu, Y. C. (2023). Educational robotics for developing computational thinking in young learners: A systematic review. *TechTrends*, pp. 1-12.

Jiang, S., & Wong, G. K. (2022). Exploring age and gender differences of computational thinkers in primary school: A developmental perspective. *Journal of Computer Assisted Learning*, 38(1), 60–75.

Johnson, D. W., & Johnson, R. T. (2013). Cooperation and the use of technology. *In Handbook of research on educational communications and technology* (pp. 777–803). Routledge.

Kim, H. S., Kim, S., Na, W., & Lee, W. J. (2021). Extending computational thinking into information and communication technology literacy measurement: Gender and grade issues. *ACM Transactions on Computing Education (TOCE)*, 21(1), 1–25.

Papert, S., & Harel, I. (1991). Situating constructionism. constructionism, 36(2), 1-11.

Piaget, J. (1963). *The Origins of Intelligence in Children.* New York: W.W. Norton & Company, Inc.

Rijke, W. J., Bollen, L., Eysink, T. H., & Tolboom, J. L. (2018). Computational thinking in primary school: An examination of abstraction and decomposition in different age groups. *Informatics in education*, *17*(1), 77-92.

Shute, V. J., Sun, C., & Asbell-Clarke, J. (2017). Demystifying computational thinking. *Educational research review*, 22, 142–158.

Thurston, A., Roseth, C., Chiang, T. H., Burns, V., & Topping, K. J. (2020). The influence of social relationships on outcomes in mathematics when using peer tutoring in elementary school. *International Journal of Educational Research Open*, 1, 100004.

Thurston, A., Cockerill, M., & Chiang, T. H. (2021). Assessing the differential effects of peer tutoring for tutors and tutees. *Education Sciences*, 11(3), 97.

Topping, K. (2000). *Tutoring.* Educational Practices Series; 5.

Tsarava, K., Moeller, K., Román-González, M., Golle, J., Leifheit, L., Butz, M. V., & Ninaus, M. (2022). A cognitive definition of computational thinking in primary education. *Computers & Education*, 179, 104425.

Vourletsis, I. (2025). Exploring grade and gender differences in computational thinking skills: a Greek primary school study. *Educational technology research and development*, 1–18.

Vygotsky, L. (1978). *Mind in society: The development of higher psychological processes.* Cambridge, MA: Harvard University Press.

Wing, J. M. (2006). Computational thinking. *Communications of the ACM*, 49(3), 33-35.

CONTEXTUALIZED LEARNING VIA ASPECTS OF NARRATIVE DIDACTICS IN DIGITAL LEARNING ENVIRONMENTS FOR MATHEMATICS EDUCATION

Matthias Brandl
Faculty of Computer Science and Mathematics, University of Passau, Germany

ABSTRACT

Modern learning and teaching theories often include contextualization as a central aspect. Instead of outdated atomistic thinking, scaffolding structures are offered that, in varying degrees, address different contexts. Therefore, a teaching strategy using aspects of Narrative Didactics seems to be suitable for the creation of thematic and affective connections. After a short discussion of these issues, two examples of digital didactic tools for mathematics education are presented: Digital Interactive Mathematical Maps (DIMM) and Digital Educational Escape Games (DEEG). The DIMM exist for the areas of Algebra, Calculus, Geometry and Stochastics, and cover contents from lower secondary to university level. The DEEG were generated for the cases of lower and higher secondary school mathematics lessons at German Gymnasium and are illustrated for six thematic examples. All tools are freely available online. The DIMM were already used and evaluated in different fields whereby initial results of a current new study concerning the DIMM are provided.

KEYWORDS

Digital Learning Environments, Narrative Didactics, Digital Interactive Mathematical Maps, Digital Educational Escape Games

1. CONTEXTUALIZED LEARNING VIA ASPECTS OF NARRATIVE DIDACTICS IN MATHEMATICS EDUCATION

Modern theory of education has moved far away from the atomistic thinking of the behavioral psychological learning theory, which is based on two central assumptions: "decomposability" and "decontextualization" (Resnick and Resnick 1992). These assumptions are in contradiction to a more favorable approach by connected teaching and learning processes that address several contexts to offer scaffolding structures for the students (Wood et al. 1976).

A theoretical approach and justification of the importance of making connections to contexts when teaching mathematics was given, for example, in Brandl and Vinerean (2023) and Brandl and Nordheimer (2017), respectively. Therefore, a suitable teaching strategy was presented in Brandl and Vinerean (2023: 3), proceeding "by using elements from the history of mathematics in narrative didactic methodology and parallelly visualizing the way of connection to related aspects of the topic by the help of technology [...] The mathematical contents serve as the basis and the goal of the teaching strategy, didactically and digitally supported by scaffolding methods".

The narrative didactic methodology for the context of mathematics education was discussed in Brandl (2010) and developed further in Brandl (2017) and Brandl and Vinerean (2023). Considering the ideas, methods and results of Kubli (1999, 2002, 2005a, 2005b), Klassen (2006), Norris et al. (2005) and Sinclair et al. (2009), general aspects of narrative didactics were specified for the area of mathematics. Central to the approach is the reference to Bruner's declaration of a dichotomy in human cognition (Bruner, 1986, 1996): the paradigmatic logico-scientific mode vs. the narrative mode of thinking. While the former one is always associated with subjects like mathematics or natural sciences in general and "looks for universal truth conditions... the narrative mode looks for particular connections between events" (Richardson, 1990: 118).

Furthermore, and besides emphasizing connections, the narrative mode addresses the emotional context as already pointed out by Klassen (2006) with reference to Egan (1989a,b): "Egan argues that the story form of presentation of curriculum materials stimulates the imagination and evokes emotional response, thereby producing learning that students more easily assimilate with long-term memory than learning produced by drilling and memorizing" (Klassen, 2006: 53).

A current motivation for a potential appropriateness of a narrative didactic methodology may be also given by the results of the last PISA study concerning affects in mathematics lessons. Looking at German math classes, the most dominant emotions are tiredness and boredom; at the same time a significant decrease of joy, interest and motivation concerning mathematics could be observed (Lewalter et al., 2023: 12-13). Here, however, aspects of narrative didactics can be helpful as "stories motivate us. Even that which we understand at the abstract level may not move us to action, whereas a story often does." (Klassen, 2006: 57, citing Noddings and Witherell, 1991: 279-280) For practical issues of lessons planning, Klassen (2006) offers a structural approach called "Story Driven Contextual Approach" (SDCA), which comprises the several possible contexts addressed by a story, illustrated in Figure 1.

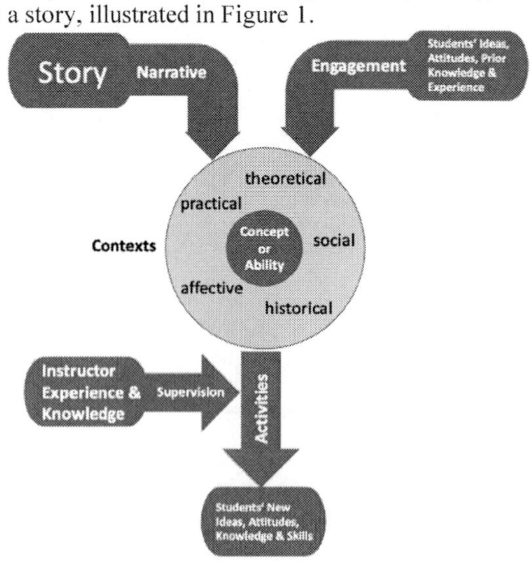

Figure 1. The Story Driven Contextual Approach (SDCA) based on Klassen (2006)

2. DIGITAL LEARNING ENVIRONMENTS FOR MATHEMATICS EDUCATION

In this section, two kinds of digital learning environments for mathematics education are presented that have been developed currently by consideration of context connection and promise to be suited for a successful application of narrative aspects in mathematics education: Digital Interactive Mathematical Maps and Digital Educational Escape Games.

2.1 Digital Interactive Mathematical Maps

Following the principle of interconnectedness in teaching and learning as supported by the working group for interconnectedness in mathematics education of the German Society for the Didactics of Mathematics (GDM), mathematical content should not be learned isolated but in relationship to each other, i.e. connected to contexts (see description of the working group: https://didaktik-der-mathematik.de/arbeitskreise/). By these connections a so-called scaffolding process (Wood et al., 1976: 90) is established.

In a BMBF supported project ("SKILL.de"), digital net structures have been developed to illustrate the historical development and mutual relationship of mathematical contents. The "Digital Interactive Mathematical Maps" (DIMM) are freely available at https://math-map.fim.uni-passau.de (Figure 2) and have been designed for the areas Geometry, Algebra, Calculus and Stochastics. Data points represent different mathematical knowledge items (like concepts or theorems), which in the first place are always related to a mathematician or a historical mathematical artefact.

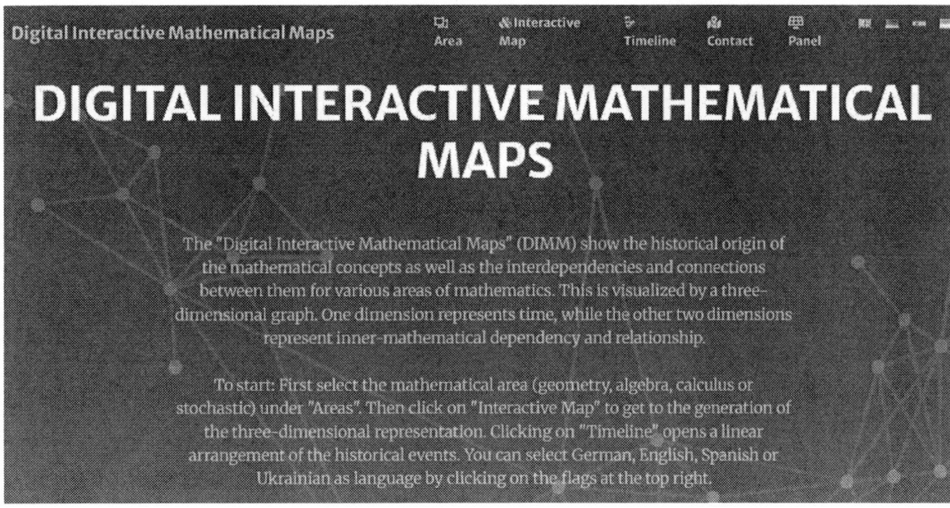

Figure 2. The DIMM homepage

Both a three-dimensional (3d-Map) and a two-dimensional (Timeline) view is selectable, see Figure 3 and Figure 4. However, only the 3d-version allows for an interpretation of mutual content proximity. In this case the data points are represented by nodes linked to information about the mathematician, the specific content, corresponding links to further information on the web (like biographies or proofs), appropriate YouTube videos or tasks from mathematical competitions. The content-based interrelatedness aspect can be observed best by the functionality "Horizontal Cut" within the 3d-Map, where a slice of time may be filtered out of the whole historical horizon followed up by a look from above onto the scenario where a thematic clustering then can be discovered. Contrarily, the "Vertical Cut" allows for a two-dimensional projection of possible historical evolvements of nodes with the goal to see which previous made discoveries (or errors) led to the final destination in the DIMM. Both functionalities are illustrated in Figure 5.

The DIMM have been tested and evaluated in different institutional contexts up to now: in a Geometry course for prospective and in-service teachers in a Calculus course for teacher students at the University of Karlstad, Sweden (Brandl et al., 2023, 2024; Brandl and Hackstein, 2024; Vinerean et al., 2023a, 2023b), and in secondary level fostering courses at the Centre of Excellence in Sibiu, Romania (Brandl and Vinerean, 2025). While the evaluations mainly focused on technical usability, also questions regarding the support of favorable beliefs about mathematics and aspects concerning the application of narrative procedures were examined. Results showed that the DIMM achieved high levels with respect to the perceived usefulness and ease of use (as cognitive response dimensions of the Technology Acceptance Model by Davis, 1985) and that it is suitable to support favorable beliefs: "[T]he map seems to open up for viewing mathematics as an emerging science. [...] Dynamic understanding of mathematics can be seen in, for instance, students' reasoning about the struggle when mathematicians develop mathematical concepts. [...] Most students show a process-related and application-related orientation in relation to their future role as teachers when using the map. [...] Overall, students' reflections suggest that the use of the digital tool Interactive Mathematical Map(s) promotes favorable beliefs related to the nature of mathematics." (Vinerean et al., 2023: 575, as cited in Brandl et al., 2024: 326)

Regarding the use of narrative procedures two methodological procedures were applied: "(A) Formulation of a short historical-orientated narrative motivation for a free-of-choice topic from the school curriculum by using information provided in the nodes or the timeline of the Digital Interactive Mathematical Map. (B) Description of the historical evolvement of non-Euclidean geometry from Euclidean geometry by using information provided in the nodes or the timeline of the Digital Interactive Mathematical Map." (Brandl and Vinerean, 2023: 9-10) Both approaches delivered promising results (see Brandl and Vinerean, 2023).

New results have been gained recently from the ongoing evaluation of the Sibiu data, where several questionnaires were given to a group of 40 pupils (grades 8-10) coached by ten teachers from the Centre of Excellence. "In the study, individual functions of the DIMM were tested on four work assignments, and the functionalities were evaluated individually in short questionnaires for every assignment with regard to their usefulness, and with respect to how well the interactive digital tool has functioned as support in getting insights in new mathematics" (Brandl and Vinerean, 2025: 96). Concerning the importance and fruitfulness of contextual knowledge embedding, pupil 12 can be cited when reacting to question 1 of questionnaire 4 ("Briefly describe the purpose of the interactive mathematical map, as you see it after using the map" (Open-ended response)): "The interactive math map aims, in my opinion, to simplify the understanding of mathematical concepts and to facilitate the exploration of various branches of this science through an innovative interactive format. Using this map, I experienced an engaging way to navigate independently and confidently between different mathematical topics, building meaningful connections between ideas and complex relationships." Furthermore, when asked in question 8 of questionnaire 1 to "Please give a brief assessment of how much you think the presentation of essential content in the history of mathematics could support your learning process." (Open-ended response), many students mention that learning the history of mathematics helps them to understand the origin and development of mathematical concepts, formulas, and theorems, making it easier to retain and apply them; the historical context enables them to grasp why certain theories were developed and how they evolved over time.

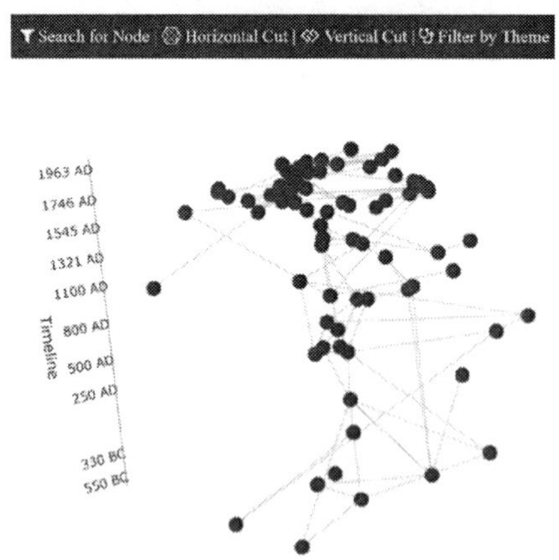

Figure 3. The 3d-Map for Algebra

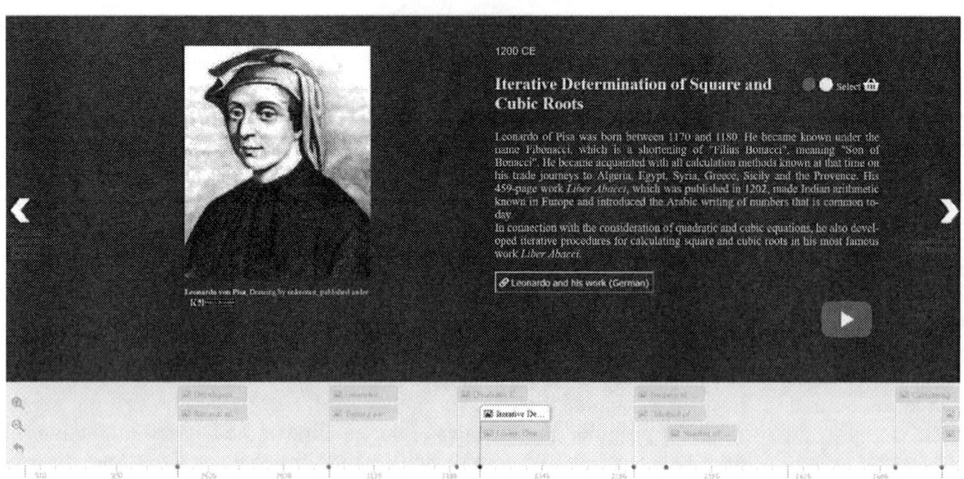

Figure 4. The Timeline

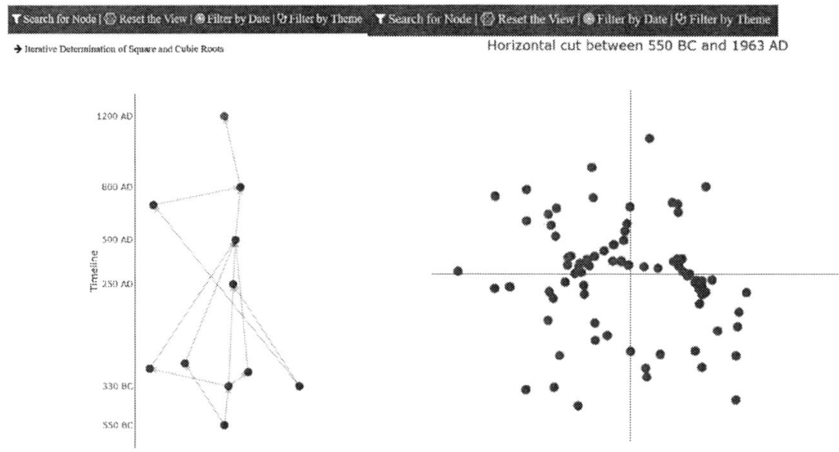

Figure 5. Vertical Cut (left) and Horizontal Cut (right)

2.2 Digital Educational Escape Games

The basic idea of classical escape games, in which tasks and riddles – often collaboratively – have to be solved, stays the same for educational escape games. However, the content now addresses specific learning goals as the participants now are pupils or students. Digital escape games can be realized in the form of online media or using suitable presentation software (like genial.ly, for example), respectively, implicating greater flexibility and efficiency (Grande-de-Prado et al., 2021; Kolb, 2024; Veldkamp et al., 2020). A further differentiation is made with respect to educational escape games that introduce new content knowledge and those that focus on the application and training of already known aspects (Eukel et al., 2017; Sanchez and Plumettaz-Sieber, 2018).

Taking into account a transformative further development of the narrative approach as described in section 1 to an extension by a pictorial dimension (see Brandl, 2010, 2017), digital presentation tools can be equipped with individually produced pictures by AI-driven online engines like Canva, which delivered very good products in Eichberger (2025), for example.

The examples for digital educational escape games (DEEG) in the next paragraphs were all made using the presentation software genial.ly. Technically and didactically sound elaborations of digital learning environments for German Gymnasium classes were done for grades 6, 10 and 11 in Kolb (2024) and for grades 7, 8 and 11 in Reimer (2022), for example.

2.2.1 Examples for Lower Secondary Level

The escape game for grade 6 of Kolb (2024) has the title "The missing class fund" (transl. by author) and is designed as a training and application unit at the end of a teaching sequence about rational numbers. It is freely available at https://view.genial.ly/654206d38c897f00129452c4/interactive-content-die -verschwundene-klassenkasse. A QR-Code Scanner is needed, and the DEEG is meant as a collaborative group activity in classroom.

The escape game for grade 7 of Reimer (2022) has the title "Thales ingenious discovery" (transl. by author) and is designed as an introduction unit for new content. For the Thales theorem a conjecture has to be formulated followed up by a proof. Several contexts according to the SDCA (Klassen, 2006) are addressed by the learning environment: theoretical content knowledge (isosceles triangles, interior angle sum in a triangle, properties of a circle), affect (embedding in a framework story), practical action (pupils' action needed to help the Thales protagonist in the story), social context (working in pairs) and history (facts about Thales from Milet). It is freely available at https://view.genial.ly/632f3ce25cee5e0011340864/ interactive-content-thales-geniale-entdeckung.

The escape game for grade 8 of Reimer (2022) has the title "Mr. Pi on the run" (transl. by author) and is designed as a training and application unit at the end of a teaching sequence about fraction terms and fraction equations. The hunt for a thief and his prey will only be successful if all the tasks are solved correctly. Except for historical aspects, all of the SDCA contexts are addressed: theoretical content knowledge (fraction terms and fraction equations), affect (embedding in a framework story), practical action (pupils' action needed to get to the end of the story) and social context (working in groups). It is freely available at https://view.genial.ly/6320fc5834021b001824ed62/interactive-content-mr-pi-auf-der-flucht.

2.2.2 Examples for Higher Secondary Level

The escape game for grade 10 of Kolb (2024) has the title "The secret of pyramid building" (transl. by author) and is designed as a training and recapitulation unit at the end of a teaching sequence about pyramids. It is freely available at https://view.genial.ly/65bf5a38f1c64e001485d095/interactive-content-das-geheimnis-der-pyramidenbaukunst. A QR-Code Scanner is needed, and it is meant as a collaborative group activity in classroom.

The escape game for grade 11 (ibid.) has the title "A mathematical club experience" (transl. by author) and is designed as an introduction unit for new content. Pupils are expected to work out the aspects of derivative functions and graphical differentiation by themselves within the learning environment. It is freely available at https://view.genial.ly/65573ca453c5ec00110827c1/interactive-content-ein-mathematisches-cluberlebnis. A QR-Code Scanner, a parabola template and knowledge in dealing with the dynamic geometry software GeoGebra are needed.

The escape game also for grade 11 of Reimer (2022) has the title "The mathematicians' crazy festival" (transl. by author) and is designed as a training and application unit at the end of a teaching sequence about special properties of functions, especially for common characteristics of elementary rational functions, quadratic functions and polynomials. For the Thales theorem a conjecture has to be formulated followed up by a proof. Except for historical aspects, again all of the SDCA contexts are addressed. It is freely available at https://view.genial.ly/6330d9dc33d33700107f5977/interactive-content-das-verruckte-volksfest-der-mathematiker.

3. DISCUSSION AND CONCLUSION

The development of digital learning environments like the DIMM or the DEEG seems to be a promising way to address the preferences of the "Digital Natives" (Dauksevicuite, 2016) that "'live and breathe' technology" (Cilliers, 2017: 190). Accompanied by the methodological approach of Narrative Didactics, new content knowledge can be effectively connected to different kinds of contexts as also intended already in Klassen's SDCA. While the DIMM mainly refer to historical timelines and the relative thematic proximity of mathematical ideas and concepts, the DEEG are based on a – usually invented – story and its image-supported implementation via AI-driven online engines and presentation software. By a design-based research methodology these didactic tools have been developed and – in the case of the DIMM – already been tested in several practical teaching situations. For the latter it turned out that favorable beliefs about mathematics can be promoted by (re)tracing historical development steps and the circumstances that led to the new insights.

The DEEG have not been evaluated in practical school lessons yet, which is why expected implications remain speculative at the moment. However, looking at empirical studies already conducted with similar formats based on similar design principles (e.g., Fuentes-Cabrera et al., 2020; Pg Abu Bakar et al., 2023; Saleh Alabdulaziz, 2023), practical application nevertheless appears promising. Future research especially concerning evaluation of the DEEG is needed to confirm relevant learning effects resulting from stronger motivational aspects supported by the narrative didactics approach.

Procedures using the described digital learning environments may support learners to get affectively involved with "the human factor in the science of mathematics" (Brandl and Vineran, 2023: 5), as in the words of Nobel Prize 1944 winner Isidor Isaac Rabi "science should be taught at whatever level, from the lowest to the highest, in a humanistic way. It should be taught with a certain philosophical understanding and a human understanding in the sense of biography, the nature of the people who made this construction, the triumphs, the trials, the tribulations" (Holton, 2005: 82-83, referring to Holton et al., 1970). Possible fields of application for the tools presented cover both secondary school as well as university level.

ACKNOWLEDGEMENT

The author thanks Mirela Vinerean-Bernhoff at the University of Karlstad (Sweden) for the support in the empirical part of the DIMM evaluation study both in Karlstad (Sweden) and Sibiu (Romania). Furthermore, the author thanks Veronika Kolb and Elisabeth Reimer for the elaboration of DEEG in context of their theses in mathematics education at the professorship for the didactics of mathematics at the University of Passau (Germany).

REFERENCES

Brandl, M. (2017). Narrative Didaktik als Vernetzungsinstrument: die Schule von Athen [Narrative Didactics as a Connecting Tool: the School of Athens]. *Mathe vernetzt – Anregungen und Materialien für einen vernetzenden Mathematikunterricht*, Vol. 6, pp 7-20

Brandl, M. (2010). Narrative Didactics in Mathematical Education: an innovative Didactical Concept. *Mathematics Education with Technology – Experiences in Europe*. Augsburg, Germany, pp. 103-110.

Brandl, M. and Hackstein, U. (2024). New advances in teaching mathematics with Digital Interactive Mathematical Maps (DIMM). Indrum2024 Proceedings – Fifth Conference of the International Network for Didactic Research in University Mathematics, Escola Univeristària Salesiana de Sarrià – Univ. Autònoma de Barcelona and INDRUM, pp. 701-702.

Brandl, M. and Szabo, A. (2024). Digital Learning Environments to Support Autonomous Learning Processes of Mathematically Creative and Gifted Students. *Towards a Hybrid, Flexible and Socially Engaged Higher Education. ICL2023, Lecture Notes in Networks and Systems*, Vol. 899, Springer, Cham, pp. 198–205.

Brandl, M. and Vinerean, M. (2023). Narrative Didactics in Mathematics Education: Results from a University Geometry Course. *Open Education Studies*, Vol. 5, No. 1, 20220186.

Brandl, M. and Vinerean, M. (2025). Digital Interactive Mathematical Maps in Fostering Courses. *Proceedings of the 14th International Conference on Mathematical Creativity and Giftedness (MCG 14) - Part of the Combined ECHA and igMCG Conference on Inclusion and Sustainability in Gifted Education*. Karlstad University Studies, Vol. 2025, No.22, pp. 96-97.

Brandl, M., et al. (2024). The Digital Interactive Map for Geometry. *Proceedings of the 26th ICMI Study Conference (Advances in Geometry Education)*, ICMI, pp. 321-328.

Brandl, M., et al. (2023). Teaching Mathematics with Digital Interactive Mathematical Maps (DIMMs) for Geometry, Algebra and Calculus. Proceedings of the Thirteenth Congress of the European Society for Research in Mathematics Education (CERME13). Alfréd Rényi Institute of Mathematics and ERME, pp. 2299-2300.

Bruner, J. (1996). *The culture of education*. Harvard University Press, Cambridge, MA.

Bruner, J. (1986). *Actual Minds, Possible Worlds*. Harvard University Press, Cambridge, MA.

Cilliers, E. (2017). The challenge of teaching generation Z. *PEOPLE: International Journal of Social Sciences*, Vol. 3, pp. 188-198.

Dauksevicuite, I. (2016). *Unlocking the full potential of digital native learners*. Henley Business School, Mc Graw Hill Education handouts.

Davis, F. D. (1985). *A technology acceptance model for empirically testing new end-user information systems: Theory and results* [Doctoral dissertation, Massachusetts Institute of Technology].

Egan, K. (1989a). The shape of the science text: A function of stories. *Language, authority and criticism: Readings on the school textbook*. The Falmer Press, New York, pp. 96-108.

Egan, K. (1989b). Memory, imagination, and learning: Connected by the story. *Phi Delta Kappan*, Vol. 70, No. 6, pp. 455-473.

Eichberger, L. (2025). *Portfolio für das Begleitseminar zu studienbegleitenden Praktikum. Wintersemester 2024-2025 [Portfolio for the accompanying seminar for the internship. Winter semester 2024-2025] [Unpublished term paper].* University of Passau, Germany.

Eukel, H. N., et al. (2017). Educational gaming for pharmacy students–design and evaluation of a diabetes-themed escape room, *American jornal of pharmaceutical education*, Vol. 81, No. 7, 6265.

Fuentes-Cabrera, A., et al. (2020). Learning Mathematics with Emerging Methodologies—The Escape Room as a Case Study. *Mathematics*, Vol. 8, No. 9, 1586.

Grande-de-Prado, M. et al. (2021). Edu-Escape Rooms. *Encyclopedia*, Vol. 1, No. 1, pp. 12-19.

Holton, G. (2005). I.I. Rabi as Educator and Science Warrior. *Victory and Vexation in Science*. Harvard University Press, pp. 81-92.

Holton, G., et al. (1970). *The Project Physics Course*. Holt, Rinehart & Winston.

Klassen, S. (2006). A theoretical framework for contextual science teaching. *Interchange*, Vol. 37, No. 1-2, pp. 31-61.

Kolb, V. (2024). *Einsatz digitaler Educational Games im Mathematikunterricht [Use of digital educational games in mathematics lessons] [Unpublished thesis].* University of Passau, Germany.

Kubli, F. (2005a). Science teaching as a dialogue – Bakthin, vygotsky and some applications in the classroom. *Science & Education*, Vol. 14, pp. 501-534.

Kubli, F. (2005b). *Mit Geschichten und Erzählungen motivieren: Beispiele für den mathematisch-naturwissenschaftlichen Unterricht [Motivating with stories and narrations: Examples for mathematics & science education].* Aulis Deubner, Cologne, Germany.

Kubli, F. (2002). Plädoyer *für Erzählungen im Physikunterricht: Geschichte und Geschichten als Verstehenshilfen – Ergebnisse einer Untersuchung [Plea for narrations in physics education: history and stories as understanding aids – Results of a survey]* (2nd ed.). Aulis Deubner, Cologne, Germany.

Kubli, F. (1999). Historical aspects in physics teaching: Using Galileo's work in a new Swiss project. *Science & Education*, Vol. 8, No. 2, pp. 137-150.

Lewalter, D. et al. (2023). *PISA 2022. Analyse der Bildungsergebnisse in Deutschland. Zusammenfassung [PISA 2022. Analysis of educational outcomes in Germany. Summary].* Waxmann, Münster, Germany.

Norris, S. et al. (2005). A theoretical framework for narrative explanation in science. *Science Education*, Vol. 89, No. 4, pp. 535-554.

Pg Abu Bakar, D. N. N., et al. (2023). Digital Escape Game and Students' Learning Outcomes in Mathematics: Experience From Brunei. *SAGE Open*, Vol. 13, No. 4, 21582440231216838.

Reimer, E. (2022). *Einsatz und Wirkung von Educational Escape Games im Mathematikunterricht des Gymnasiums [Use and effect of Educational Escape Games in secondary school maths lessons] [Unpublished thesis].* University of Passau, Germany.

Resnick, L. B. and Resnick, D. P. (1992). Assessing the thinking curriculum: New tools for educational reform. *Changing assessments: Alternative views of aptitude, achievement and instruction*, Kluwer, Boston, pp. 37-75.

Richardson, L. (1990). Narrative and sociology. *Journal of Contemporary Ethnography*, Vol. 19, No. 1, pp. 116-135.

Sinclair, N. et al. (2009). Time for telling stories: narrative thinking with dynamic geometry. *ZDM Mathematics Education*, Vol. 41, pp. 441-452.

Saleh Alabdulaziz, M. (2023). Escape rooms technology as a way of teaching mathematics to secondary school students. *Education and information technologies*, pp. 1-26.

Sanchez, E. and Plumettaz-Sieber, M. (2018). Teaching and learning with escape games from debriefing to institutionalization of knowledge. *International conference on games and learning alliance*, Springer, pp. 242-253.

Veldkamp, A., et al. (2020). Escape education: A systematic review on escape rooms in education. *Educational Research Review*, Vol. 31, No. 100364.

Vinerean, M. et al. (2023a). Promoting favourable beliefs of prospective math teachers concerning the nature of mathematics by using Interactive Mathematical Maps. *Proceedings of the Fourth conference of the International Network for Didactic Research in University Mathematics*, Hannover: University of Hannover, Germany, pp. 574-575.

Vinerean, M. et al. (2023b). Didactical usefulness of interactive mathematical maps – designing activities supporting prospective teachers' learning. *Nordic Studies in Mathematics Education*, Vol. 28, No. 3-4, pp. 77-102.

Wood, D. et al. (1976). The role of tutoring in problem-solving. *Journal of Child Psychology and Psychiatry*, Vol. 17, pp. 89-100.

A GENERATIVE MODEL FOR NEXT-STEP CODE PREDICTION TOWARD PROACTIVE SUPPORT

Daiki Matsumoto[1], Atsushi Shimada[2] and Yuta Taniguchi[3]
[1]*Graduate School of Information Science and Electrical Engineering, Kyushu University, 744, Motooka, Nishi-ku, Fukuoka 819-0395, Japan*
[2]*Faculty of Information Science and Electrical Engineering, Kyushu University, 744, Motooka, Nishi-ku, Fukuoka 819-0395, Japan*
[3]*Section of Educational Information Research Institute for Information Technology, Kyushu University, 744, Motooka, Nishi-ku, Fukuoka 819-0395, Japan*

ABSTRACT

Predicting learner actions and intentions is crucial for providing personalized real-time support and early intervention in programming education. This approach enables proactive, context-aware assistance that is difficult for human instructors to deliver by foreseeing signs of potential struggles and misconceptions, or by inferring a learner's understanding and coding intent through early prediction of their intended solution. Traditional frameworks such as Knowledge Tracing are limited to predicting student performance on subsequent tasks, focusing only on how learners will perform in the next task rather than modeling progress within the current task. Existing approaches to single-task prediction primarily aim to generate the final submitted code. Consequently, the development of models capable of predicting the step-by-step evolution of the code within a single task remains underexplored. This paper proposes a generative model that traces the historical evolution of a learner's code to predict the next code snapshot in a task. Specifically, we develop a deep learning model that encodes "learner context" by feeding a time-series of code snapshots into an LSTM. This context, combined with the current code, is used to decode the next code. In our evaluation using real-world data collected from programming exercise classes, our model achieves a BLEU score of 0.639. The results confirm that incorporating learner context is essential for improving prediction accuracy, yielding up to a 7.5% improvement over a baseline model. We also identify effective model architectures and fine-tuning techniques that contribute to performance gains.

KEYWORDS

Programming Process, Learner Modeling, Context-Aware Code Generation

1. INTRODUCTION

Recently, the importance of personalized support tailored to individual learners' understanding and progress has grown in the field of programming education (Rojas-López & García-Peñalvo, 2022). Teachers can grasp the current state of a student's understanding as well as their coding intention by reading their source code, hearing their description of immediate issues, or asking questions. However, such interactions require considerable time in real-world educational settings, making it difficult for instructors and teaching assistants to consistently provide timely and in-depth support to every learner, especially in large classes (Singh, 2022).

Recent advances in natural language processing have introduced new forms of automated support into programming education, complementing earlier approaches such as Intelligent Tutoring Systems (Anderson et al., 1985). For instance, chatbots based on Large Language Models (LLMs), such as like ChatGPT (Ouyang et al., 2022), are now used interactively by learners, and various support applications that leverage these models have been proposed in academic research (Birillo et al., 2024). However, even with the availability of such tools, achieving automation that replicates human-like assistance requires accurately capturing the learner's current knowledge and coding intentions, which in turn demands a contextual understanding of the learner's coding process. Although effectively leveraging such a context remains difficult for chatbots, incorporating learner context and predicting future actions could significantly enhance their responsiveness and adaptability.

Knowledge Tracing (KT) (Corbett and Anderson, 1994) is a primary approach for predicting future learner performance based on past behavior. However, traditional frameworks such as KT are limited to predicting student performance across tasks, focusing on how learners will perform in the next task rather than modeling their progress within a single task. Other approaches for single-task prediction primarily aim to generate the final submitted code (Liu et al., 2022). However, these methods are not designed to predict the intermediate steps that occur as learners gradually construct their solutions. Consequently, the development of models capable of predicting the step-by-step evolution of code within a single task while capturing the unique characteristics and progression patterns of each learner remains an underexplored area.

Predicting this step-by-step evolution is crucial for achieving proactive, context-aware support. By anticipating a learner's next likely coding actions, early signs of confusion or misconceptions can be detected before they escalate, thus enabling timely intervention. Furthermore, by forecasting the learner's intended code at each step, support systems can gain deeper insights into the learner's comprehension and coding intentions. This facilitates a level of personalized assistance that is difficult for human instructors to provide consistently at scale.

Based on this perspective, we propose a novel task: predicting future code states from a sequence of intermediate source code snapshots observed as learners iteratively revise their programs. This requires modeling how learners incrementally develop their solutions over time. To address this, we propose a deep generative model that incorporates the learner context into its predictions. Each past code snapshot is converted into an embedding and fed sequentially into an LSTM (Hochreiter & Schmidhuber, 1997), which estimates a dynamic "learner context" representing the learner's evolving state. This context is subsequently combined with the embedding of the most recent code snapshot and passed to a GPT-2 decoder (Radford et al., 2019) to generate the next predicted code. We investigate the effects of pre-training and fine-tuning on the model components to enhance prediction accuracy. Furthermore, we compare multiple strategies for integrating learner contexts with code embeddings and evaluate their impact on predictive performance.

2. RELATED WORK

Our study aims to predict the learner's next source code based on their coding process. We classify related prior work into two main categories based on the granularity of the data they handle: (1) "cross-task source code prediction," which predicts a learner's source code for the next task by modeling their evolving knowledge across multiple tasks, and (2) "local source code prediction," which predicts the next segment of code from an incomplete state within a single task.

2.1 Cross-Task Source Code Prediction

In this section, we review prior cross-task studies that predict source code based on a learner's history across multiple tasks.

The Knowledge Tracing (KT) framework, which is traditionally used for problems with binary answers, has been extended to free-response programming tasks (Liu et al., 2022). They proposed a new framework that sequentially estimates the learner's knowledge state based on the source code submitted across multiple tasks. Specifically, their model encodes the submitted code, uses an LSTM to accumulate the knowledge state, and uses a decoder to generate the next source code submission. Similar to our study, their study focuses on source code prediction based on learning history.

In a related approach for acquiring a knowledge state, InfoGAN (Chen et al., 2016) was proposed for source code generation. The model learns interpretable latent representations corresponding to the learner's coding patterns in an unsupervised manner by maximizing the mutual information between the generated code and its latent variables. This study also performs source code predictions based on multiple tasks. However, it differs slightly from the model proposed by Liu et al. in that it represents a learner's characteristic coding tendencies in a latent space and generates codes based on that representation.

Similar to our study, these studies aim to generate source code by predicting the next output based on the accumulated learning history. However, these studies handle the submission history of the source code across multiple tasks, and their prediction targets are also at the task level. In contrast, our study targets the sequential writing process within a single task, meaning that the granularity of the source code history that we handle is different.

2.2 Local Source Code Prediction

Other study focuses on generating the next source code segment based on the current state of the code within a single task. One proposed framework generates the next single line of code from the current source code by combining a Large Language Model (LLM) with static analysis (Birillo et al., 2024). Through a three-stage process involving subgoal extraction, source code generation, and explanation generation, this method can present the next segment of the code or provide relevant hints based on the learner's current code.

Another approach focuses on the history of source code edits, learning "edit vectors" that capture the intent of a correction from pre- and post-edit code pairs and their test results (Heickal and Lan, 2025). This embedding representation is designed such that similar correction operations are represented by similar vectors, enabling source code generation that reflects a learner's corrective actions.

These studies have a structure similar to that of our study in that they directly generate the next source code based on information from the current code. However, both are designed to take a single source code snapshot as the input, and do not have an architecture that makes contextual predictions based on the entire source code history. In our study, by capturing the entire history using a time-series model, we aim to realize a more natural form of source code generation that reflects the learners' progress and stylistic tendencies.

3. PROPOSED METHOD

3.1 Problem Definition

The objective of this study is to sequentially predict the source code to be written in the next step, taking a learner's source code history up to a certain point within a single task and the task description as the input. In this context, the source code history is a sequence of source code snapshots recorded as in-progress work while a learner engages with a task. Based on the snapshot at each step, the model predicts the source code to be written in the next step.

3.2 Proposed Model

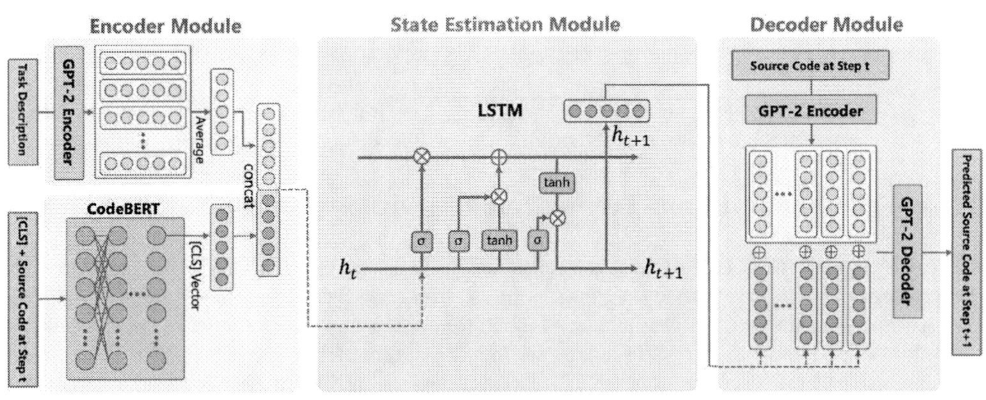

Figure 1. Overview of the proposed model architecture

An overview of the proposed method is shown in Figure 1. The proposed method comprises of three main modules. First, the encoder module converts the learner's current source code and task description into a combined embedding. Next, the state-estimation module uses an LSTM to sequentially update a hidden state, which represents the learner's context based on their source code history. Finally, the decoder module integrates the learner context with the source code obtained from the previous step to generate a prediction for the next source code. This process is applied at each step to sequentially predict the learner's source code. These components are described in detail as follows.

In the encoder module, the learner's source code and task description are converted into embedding representations. To encode the task description, the Japanese text is translated into English and then input into a GPT-2 encoder to obtain an embedding for each token. The overall embedding for the entire task description is constructed by averaging these token-level embeddings. For the source code, it is converted into a token sequence using a CodeBERT (Feng et al., 2020) tokenizer, and a special [CLS] token is added to the beginning before the sequence is input into CodeBERT. The [CLS] token is commonly used in BERT-based models to capture the features of an entire sequence. In this study, we utilize the vector representation corresponding to this [CLS] token as the embedding representation for the source code. Finally, the task description embedding and source code embedding are combined and passed to the subsequent processing stage.

In the state estimation module, a time-series internal representation is updated using an LSTM based on the history of the previously written source code and the representation of the current source code. In the initial step, the LSTM's initial hidden state and cell state, along with the source code embedding output from the encoder module, are used as inputs to derive a new hidden state and cell state. In each subsequent step, the internal representation is sequentially updated by inputting the previous hidden and cell states and the corresponding source code embedding into the LSTM. In this study, we treat the hidden state obtained from the LSTM as the "learner context," which serves as the contextual information for the next source code prediction. The learner context is expected to reflect the learner's internal state at that point, including their coding patterns and syntactic progression.

In the decoder module, the source code that the learner will write next is generated based on the source code from the previous step and learner context. First, the source code from the preceding step is input into a GPT-2 encoder to obtain an embedding for each token. Next, the learner context, h, is integrated with the token embeddings, p_n. We investigate the following four integration methods, where p_n is the embedding for the n-th token, h is the learner context, and p'_n is the resulting token embedding after integration.

(A) Linear Addition: $p'_n = p_n + f(h)$
(B) Scalar Addition: $p'_n = p_n + \alpha \cdot h$
(C) Concatenation and Transformation (Concat. & Trans.): $p'_n = f(concat(p_n, h))$
(D) Final Token Addition (FTA): $p'_{last} = p_{last} + f(h)$

Method (A) adds the linearly transformed learner context to each token's embedding. Method (B) adds the learner context after scaling it by a learnable scalar constant, α. Method (C) concatenates the token embedding with the learner context and integrates them through a linear transformation. Method (D) adds the linearly transformed learner context only to the final token in the sequence. Finally, the integrated token embeddings, p', are input into the GPT-2 decoder to generate the next predicted code. Although we adopted GPT-2 due to the high computational and memory demands of processing our time-series data, our approach is not limited to this model. Any GPT-style generative model could be substituted, and we expect that using larger models, especially those pretrained on source code corpora, would further improve the quality of the generated code.

3.3 Pre-Training and Fine-Tuning Each Module

The encoder module uses CodeBERT, a pre-trained model, to represent the source code of the learner. Although CodeBERT is pre-trained on a large-scale source code dataset, in its original state, it has not been explicitly trained for the [CLS] token, which is added to represent an entire sequence. Because this study uses the output corresponding to the [CLS] token as the embedding for the entire source code, we introduced fine-tuning using SimCSE (Gao et al., 2021) to improve the utility of this representation. SimCSE uses contrastive learning to learn enhanced embeddings in order to better distinguish between data points. In this approach, an input sentence is treated as a positive example, whereas other data points are treated as negative examples. This process is expected to yield embeddings that can capture fine-grained differences between various source codes.

For the state estimation module, the LSTM was pre-trained on a regression task to predict the increase or decrease in the number of tokens in a source code sequence. Specifically, using the source code history as the input, a two-layer linear transformation was connected to the hidden state at each step, and the model was trained to predict the extent to which the token count of the source code of the next step would increase or decrease compared with the current source code. This pre-training process was designed to enable the LSTM to learn the trends of source code changes during the writing process. Consequently, it can generate a learner context that reflects the direction and magnitude of these changes, such as how much code the learner might add or how much they might delete or modify, in the next step.

The decoder module utilizes a pre-trained language model GPT-2, which is capable of generating grammatical natural language text. However, in its original state, the capacity to generate code that conforms to the unique syntactic structures and descriptive styles of the source code is insufficient. Therefore, to supplement the expressive power necessary for source code generation, this study fine-tuned GPT-2 using source code. The model was fine-tuned using the Python source code from two datasets: The Stack (Kocetkov et al., 2023), a large-scale collection of open-source code, and MBPP (Austin et al., 2021), a small-scale dataset of basic programming problems. The process involved first performing auto-regressive learning on 100,000 samples from The Stack, followed by additional training using MBPP. This helps the decoder learn patterns specific to the source code, such as syntax and coding conventions, to enable more natural code generation.

4. EXPERIMENTAL RESULTS AND DISCUSSION

To verify the effectiveness of the proposed method described in Section 3, we conduct evaluation experiments using a newly created dataset. Specifically, we predict the source code for the next step based on the source code history up to a certain point and compare it with the code written by the learner. The following subsections describe the dataset, evaluation metrics, and experimental results.

4.1 Dataset

The dataset used in this experiment consists of source code recorded during introductory Python programming courses at Kyushu University in the 2023 and 2024 academic years. The target task for this study was from the sixth session of a total of thirteen exercise sessions, requiring learners to implement a function that finds the maximum value in a list. A total of 2,839 source code snapshots from 121 learners were collected. This study was approved by the university's research ethics committee. We explained the data collection and usage to the students in advance, obtained informed consent, and used data only from those who agreed to participate.

The data were recorded using WEVL (Taniguchi et al., 2022), an online programming exercise environment. WEVL's system is designed to automatically save the current source code whenever a learner stops typing for three or more seconds or when they execute or submit a task. In this study, each of these automatic saves is treated as a single "step."

4.2 Evaluation Metrics

In this study, we use three main metrics to evaluate the similarity and generation accuracy between the generated and ground-truth source codes.

Our primary evaluation metric is the BLEU score (Papineni et al., 2002). This metric is commonly used to measure the degree of similarity of source code by calculating the n-gram match rate between a generated output and a ground-truth reference. In this study, we calculate the BLEU score using the CodeBERT tokenizer[1] for a token-level comparison.

Additionally, we use edit distance to measure the difference between the generated source code and ground-truth source code more directly (Levenshtein et al., 1966). Edit distance is defined as the minimum number of insertions, deletions, or substitution operations required to transform one string or token sequence into another. For this study, we use two types of edit distances: a token-level distance calculated using the CodeBERT tokenizer, and a character-level distance based on individual characters.

Finally, we evaluate the generalization performance of the model by measuring the test loss, calculated as the cross-entropy error between the model's output probabilities and the ground truth on an unseen dataset.

[1] https://huggingface.co/microsoft/codebert-base

4.3 Experimental Results

Using the dataset described in Section 4.1, we trained our proposed model and conducted evaluation experiments. Cross-validation was used for training and evaluation. The dataset was divided into five folds and configured such that every source code sample was used as test data exactly once. The results are summarized in Table 1. Each result represents the average value across the five folds.

Table 1. Evaluation results for each setting

No.	CodeBERT Fine-Tuning	Integration Method	GPT Fine-Tuning	LSTM Pre-Training	BLEU	Edit Distance (Token)	Edit Distance (Char)	Test Loss
1	N/A	Baseline		N/A	0.591	19.873	30.401	0.368
2		Linear Addition			0.608	19.785	29.503	0.365
3	✓	Linear Addition			0.620	19.136	29.050	0.371
4	✓	Scalar Addition			0.616	18.479	28.038	0.370
5	✓	FTA			0.608	21.060	30.494	0.366
6	✓	Concat. & Trans.			0.367	35.944	51.756	0.727
7	✓	Linear Addition	✓		0.625	18.877	28.491	**0.357**
8	✓	Linear Addition		✓	**0.639**	**17.244**	**25.580**	0.379
9	✓	Linear Addition	✓	✓	**0.639**	17.527	25.957	0.370

The baseline setting (No. 1 in the table) serves as the initial point of comparison. In this configuration, the model predicts the source code for the next step using only the immediately preceding source code as input without leveraging the hidden state from the state estimation module. That is, this setting makes predictions without using the learner's source code history, resembling a scenario in which an LLM-based chatbot is asked to predict the immediate next code without prior context. By contrast, all settings from No. 2 onward use the learner's source code history and make predictions that incorporate contextual information via the hidden state.

Next, we discuss the results of each experimental setting. First, a comparison between the baseline model (No. 1) and subsequent settings that use the learner context (No. 2-9) shows that the latter achieved consistently higher BLEU scores. Specifically, our best-performing model (No. 8) achieved a BLEU score of 0.639, representing a 7.5% improvement over the baseline model. This indicates that leveraging information from past source code history improves prediction accuracy compared to using only the immediately preceding code (No. 1). This suggests that the learner context from the state estimation module functions as effective contextual information for prediction.

Comparing Nos. 2 and 3, No. 3, which included fine-tuning CodeBERT in the encoder, demonstrated a higher BLEU score. This result suggests that contrastive learning from SimCSE yielded embeddings that capture syntactic differences in the source code, which contributed to an improvement in prediction accuracy.

Comparing the integration methods (Nos. 3-6), linear addition (No. 3) performed best on the BLEU score, likely because its architecture effectively incorporates the historical context while maintaining informational consistency. Scalar addition (No. 4) performed similarly; although this method is simpler, the state vector itself may have adapted during the learning process to function effectively. However, the final token addition (No. 5) was slightly less effective on both metrics because modifying only a single token had a limited impact on the overall representation. Finally, concatenation and transformation (No. 6) significantly degraded the accuracy of both BLEU and edit distance. Despite offering high flexibility, the model likely failed to utilize the learner context effectively due to the increased dimensionality and complexity of the representation space.

Additionally, comparing Nos. 3 and 7, No. 7, which involved fine-tuning the GPT-2 decoder, showed a slight improvement in the BLEU score. This result suggests that pre-training specialized for source code supplemented the decoder's prior knowledge of the output representation, thereby enabling more natural source code generation.

Finally, a comparison between No. 3 and No. 8 showed that No. 8, which applied pre-training to the LSTM in the state estimation module, achieved a higher prediction accuracy. This is likely because the LSTM, having been pre-trained on a task to predict token count fluctuations, was better able to capture learner's progress trends during the writing process, leading to improved prediction performance.

Focusing on token-based edit distance, the average was 19.873 for No. 1, which improved 17.244 for No. 8, the best-performing model. This represents a reduction of approximately 2.6 required correction operations per generation, indicating that the output of the model more closely matched the ground-truth code.

4.4 Generation Examples

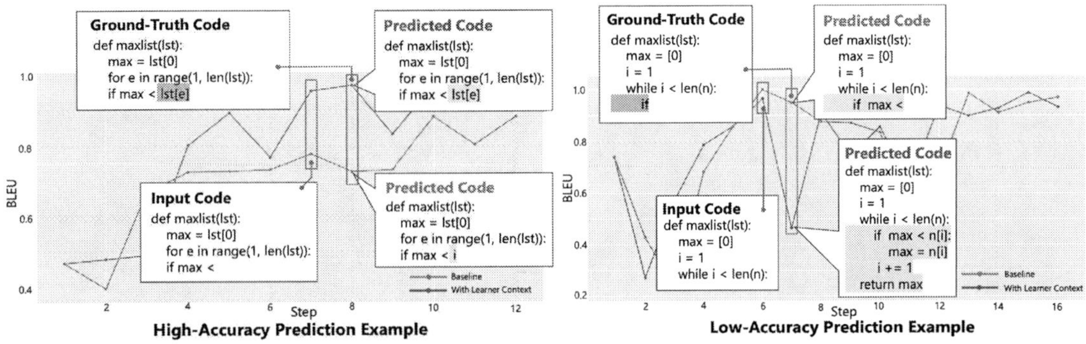

Figure 2. Generation example showing cases of high accuracy (left) and low accuracy (right)

In this section, we present specific examples of the model's prediction results to analyze their consistency with the ground-truth source code and examine the prediction trends. Figure 2 shows two cases: an example of a high-accuracy prediction (left panel) and an example of a low-accuracy prediction (right panel). In both panels, the line graph displays the BLEU score at each step; the red line represents the baseline setting (No. 1) and the blue line represents the setting that utilizes the learner context (No. 9). "Input Code" and "Ground-Truth Code" are what the learner actually wrote, while "Predicted Code" is the code generated by the model at the corresponding step. In the code blocks, the code highlighted in blue, including white spaces, represents the code added by the learner, while the yellow-highlighted code indicates the code added by our model.

In the high-accuracy example (left panel), given the input at step 7, the model with learner context (No. 9) accurately predicts the code at step 8, including the learner's progress and writing style. The baseline model (No. 1), on the other hand, produces an output that differs from the ground-truth source code.

In the second example (right panel), there is a discrepancy between the prediction and the ground-truth source code. In this case, for the input at step 6, the ground-truth source code required only a minor change, that is, the addition of a single if statement. Although the code generated by the baseline model (No. 1) is grammatically and semantically natural, it indicates more progress than the ground-truth source code, suggesting that the magnitude of the change was slightly overestimated. Furthermore, the model that utilized the learner context (No. 9) generated an output that almost entirely completed the source code, showing that it overestimated the learner's progress compared with their actual coding stage. These examples suggest that challenges remain in accurately capturing aspects such as a learner's intent and progress.

5. CONCLUSION AND FUTURE WORK

This study addressed the underexplored challenge of predicting the step-by-step evolution of code within a single task, where the paths of evolution often differ across individual learners. We developed a generative model based on the time-series of a learner's code snapshots to predict the code that will be written in the next step. In the proposed model, an LSTM captures the historical learner context, which is then fed into a GPT-2 decoder to generate the next-step code. We successfully identified specific techniques that improve performance, such as targeted pre-training, fine-tuning, and an effective context integration method. Evaluations on real-world classroom data showed that incorporating each learner's historical code evolution consistently improved prediction accuracy, achieving a BLEU score of 0.639 and outperforming a baseline that uses only the immediately preceding code by up to 7.5%.

However, our work is limited by the use of GPT-2, adopted due to computational constraints, and by reliance on a single dataset; future work should explore larger code-pretrained models and more diverse contexts. In addition, our model sometimes fails to predict the learner's next step, overestimating progress by predicting too far ahead. This could become an obstacle when providing support based on predictions, as it may lead to feedback misaligned with the learner's actual situation. Future work should address this issue by exploring ways to capture subtle individual traits such as coding pace, coding styles, and problem-solving strategies, which may require incorporating source code histories from other tasks.

Overall, our approach enables finer-grained next-step predictions that better capture diverse individual trajectories. These results extend beyond traditional knowledge tracing and suggest a path toward models that can more closely mimic learners' behaviors in programming classes. Our findings provide a foundation for automated systems that deliver personalized, context-aware support in programming education.

ACKNOWLEDGEMENT

This work was supported by JST CREST Grant Number JPMJCR22D1, JSPS KAKENHI Grant Number JP24K15209 and JP22H00551.

REFERENCES

Anderson, J. R. et al. (1985). Intelligent tutoring systems. *Science*, Vol. 228, No. 4698, pp. 456-462.

Austin, J. et al. (2021). Program Synthesis with Large Language Models. *arXiv preprint,* arXiv:2108.07732.

Birillo, A. et al. (2024). One Step at a Time: Combining LLMs and Static Analysis to Generate Next-Step Hints for Programming Tasks. *Proceedings of the 24th Koli Calling International Conference on Computing Education Research*, New York, NY, USA, Article no. 9.

Chen, X. et al. (2016). InfoGAN: interpretable representation learning by information maximizing generative adversarial nets. *Proceedings of the 30th International Conference on Neural Information Processing Systems*, Barcelona, Spain, pp. 2180–2188.

Corbett, A. T. and Anderson, J. R. (1994). Knowledge tracing: Modeling the acquisition of procedural knowledge. *User Modeling and User-Adapted Interaction*, Vol. 4, No. 4, pp. 253-278.

Feng, Z. et al. (2020). CodeBERT: A Pre-Trained Model for Programming and Natural Languages. *Findings of the Association for Computational Linguistics: EMNLP 2020*, Online, pp. 1536–1547.

Gao, T. et al. (2021). SimCSE: Simple Contrastive Learning of Sentence Embeddings. *Proceedings of the 2021 Conference on Empirical Methods in Natural Language Processing*, Online and Punta Cana, Dominican Republic, pp. 6894–6910.

Heickal, H. and Lan, A. (2025). Learning Code-Edit Embedding to Model Student Debugging Behavior. *Proceedings of the 26th International Conference on Artificial Intelligence in Education*, Palermo, Italy, pp. 91-98.

Hochreiter, S. and Schmidhuber, J. (1997). Long Short-Term Memory. *Neural Computation*, Vol. 9, No. 8, pp. 1735–1780.

Kocetkov, D. et al. (2023). The Stack: 3 TB of permissively licensed source code. *Transactions on Machine Learning Research.*

Levenshtein, V. I. et al. (1966). Binary codes capable of correcting deletions, insertions, and reversals. *Soviet Physics Doklady*, Vol. 10, No. 8, pp. 707–710.

Liu, N. et al. (2022). Open-ended Knowledge Tracing for Computer Science Education, *Proceedings of the 2022 Conference on Empirical Methods in Natural Language Processing*, Abu Dhabi, United Arab Emirates, pp. 3849–3862.

Ouyang, L. et al. (2022). Training language models to follow instructions with human feedback. *Advances in Neural Information Processing Systems*, New Orleans, USA, pp. 27730-27744.

Papineni, K. et al. (2002). BLEU: a method for automatic evaluation of machine translation. *Proceedings of the 40th Annual Meeting on Association for Computational Linguistics*, Philadelphia, Pennsylvania, USA, pp. 311–318.

Radford, A. et al. (2019). Language models are unsupervised multitask learners. *OpenAI blog*, Vol. 1, No. 8, p. 9.

Rojas-López, A. and García-Peñalvo, F. J. (2022). Personalized education for a programming course in higher education. *Research Anthology on Computational Thinking, Programming, and Robotics in the Classroom*, IGI Global, Hershey, PA, USA, pp. 344–367.

Singh, S. (2022). Identifying Learning Challenges faced by Novice/Beginner Computer Programming Students: An Action Research Approach. *Proceedings of the 6th Software Engineering Education Workshop*, Online, pp. 63–71.

Taniguchi, Y. et al. (2022). Visualizing Source-Code Evolution for Understanding Class-Wide Programming Processes. *Sustainability*, Vol. 14, No. 13, Article no. 8084.

TEACHING ELECTRICITY AND MAGNETISM IN HIGHER EDUCATION THROUGH VIRTUAL REALITY AND ARTIFICIAL INTELLIGENCE

Zhanara Malikova and Bayan Ualikhanova
O. Zhanibekov South Kazakhstan Pedagogical University, Kazakhstan

ABSTRACT

In recent years, virtual reality (VR) and artificial intelligence (AI) technologies have been widely adopted across various sectors of society, including education. We conducted a practical study to assess the effectiveness of immersive technologies in higher education institutions. The research was carried out over a period of ten weeks. Students were divided into control and experimental groups. Furthermore, the research work was based on the collection of quantitative data and monitoring students' academic performance. The study's results were analyzed using a paired t-test and descriptive statistics. The independent t-test results indicated significant differences in subsequent test scores between the experimental and control groups. Quantitative descriptive results were presented in the form of diagrams and evaluated across six pedagogical components. At the conclusion of the study, recommendations for future research were provided.

KEYWORDS

Electricity and Magnetism, Higher Education, Physics Education, Virtual Reality, Artificial Intelligence

1. INTRODUCTION

In the contemporary world, virtual reality (VR) and artificial intelligence (AI) technologies are being applied across various fields of education. In recent years, the experience of utilizing virtual technologies in higher education has been increasing. VR and AR technologies enable students to conduct independent research and gain a deeper understanding of complex concepts (Martín-Gutiérrez et al., 2017). However, before integrating virtual technologies into the educational system, it is essential to evaluate their effectiveness and feasibility for application (Zhao, Ren, & Cheah, 2023).

Within the context of higher education physics teaching, instructors often face challenges related to effectively conveying complex concepts, particularly those associated with the topic of "Electricity and Magnetism" (Cabural, 2024). Students frequently struggle to understand that the invisible Coulomb force acts at a distance or that electromagnetic waves can propagate through space. Consequently, comprehending phenomena such as electrostatic fields, magnetic forces, and the operation of electric currents requires the ability to visualize interactions that are not directly observable (Magana et al., 2017). The main challenges stem from the limited opportunities for students to study "Electricity and Magnetism" through direct experimentation, the ambiguities of physical laws and their mathematical representations, and the inherently three-dimensional nature of these concepts, which complicates their representation on two-dimensional platforms (Ilie et al., 2021).

Visualization in three-dimensional space offers students a solid theoretical foundation for mastering complex laws. Furthermore, virtual reality enables the vivid illustration of abstract concepts, reducing reliance on expensive laboratory equipment and providing the opportunity for endless repetition of experiments (Sarapak et al., 2022). This study visualizes abstract notions of electricity and magnetism within a three-dimensional environment utilizing virtual reality (VR) technologies. Such experiments encourage students to engage in research and offer interactive experiences (Ilie et al., 2021).

In our research, we examined the impact of artificial intelligence and virtual reality technologies on education. We also compared traditional and digital learning approaches in the subject of "Electricity and Magnetism". Additionally, we investigated the challenges of effective learning utilizing AI and VR technologies.

We will discuss the following two research questions:

RQ1: What changes in student learning outcomes were observed when employing virtual reality and artificial intelligence alongside traditional teaching methods?

RQ2: What advantages and limitations does the use of virtual reality present in the instruction of the subject "Electricity and Magnetism"?

2. RELATED WORK

The application of augmented reality (AR) technologies in physics education enhances student outcomes. Cai and colleagues (2021) found that the use of AR technologies increased students' self-efficacy and positively influenced their higher-order thinking skills. Furthermore, the use of AR inspires a more in-depth exploration of physics compared to traditional methods.

The virtual learning platform DataliVR, based on virtual reality, has been supplemented with an artificial intelligence chatbot, ChatGPT, developed by Gao and his colleagues (2024). This learning platform aims to develop students' competencies in the proficient use of data. The results of the research indicated that the integration of VR and AI improved the educational experience for students.

The use of VR technologies overcomes the limitations of traditional informational tools. The virtual laboratory designed by Avradinis, Vosinakis, and Panayiotopoulos (2000) enables students to conduct experiments in three-dimensional space and study the laws of gravity, friction, and kinematics. Subsequent studies have corroborated these findings. Rizal and colleagues (2025) analyzed students' readiness to use VR technologies and determined that the average readiness level was 71%. Access to devices and technical skills were identified as the main factors affecting readiness.

One advantage of virtual reality technology is its facilitation of understanding abstract concepts. With the Virtual Hydrogen tool developed by Suno and Ohno (2023), students were able to gain a better grasp of complex orbital concepts in quantum mechanics within a three-dimensional context. Similarly, Campos, Hidrogo, and Zavala (2022) found that students utilizing VR technology performed better on tasks involving three-dimensional vectors.

AR technologies contribute not only to visualization but also to social interaction. A study conducted by Nusroh, Khalif, and Saputri (2022) demonstrated that AR-based educational media products enhanced students' critical thinking levels at an intermediate level. Concurrently, Radu and Schneider (2019) utilized HoloLens to visualize electromagnetism, which enhanced students' abilities to recognize magnetic fields and comprehend electrical-magnetic relationships. However, their study also found that some phenomena were explained more effectively through traditional methods. The authors noted that AR fosters equitable leadership in group learning and diminishes inequalities in education.

The application of VR technologies in a gamified format has also been investigated. Korlat and colleagues (2024) discovered that the gamified virtual laboratory simplified the assimilation of abstract concepts and improved student outcomes. Nevertheless, the study noted the presence of gender differences and suggested that VR technologies should be adapted to the educational process.

Overall, VR and AR technologies possess significant potential for visualizing abstract concepts in physics education, enhancing students' self-efficacy, and developing their critical thinking. However, factors such as access to devices, technical skills, and pedagogical adaptation remain barriers that limit their effectiveness.

3. MATERIAL AND METHODS

The study aimed to assess the comparative effectiveness of instruction that utilizes artificial intelligence and virtual reality (VR) devices in relation to traditional teaching methods. The experimental framework allowed for a comparison between two groups of students: an experimental group engaged in VR simulations and a control group receiving instruction through conventional methods. The utilization of virtual reality technology contributes to a better understanding of educational outcomes and the level of student engagement.

Our research was conducted over a period of 10 weeks. The experimental group performed virtual laboratory work based on virtual reality in the subject of "Electricity and Magnetism", while the control group learned using traditional laboratory tools. The research methodology allows for a comparison of two educational strategies and the mastery of conceptual understanding. The study on the application of virtual learning technology in physics classes was conducted in three stages:

1. Definition Stage: This stage was implemented at the beginning of the experiment. To assess the initial level of students' knowledge in the subject of "Electricity and Magnetism", test assignments were gathered through a questionnaire.

2. Formation Stage: This phase examined the application of artificial intelligence and virtual reality technologies within the course of "Electricity and Magnetism".

3. Final Stage: In this concluding phase, the educational outcomes of the control and experimental groups were evaluated through quantitative methods.

The research, conducted over 10 weeks involving experimental and control groups, was based on obtaining quantitative data and monitoring students' academic results. Consequently, student achievements were assessed through pre- and post-tests designed to evaluate their understanding of "Electricity and Magnetism". The data collection method included multiple-choice and closed-ended questions. The preliminary test was administered at the start of the study, while the final test was conducted after 10 weeks.

Additionally, for the quantitative descriptive research, students were asked closed-ended questions and assessed through an educational component. The quantitative descriptive data consisted of ten closed questions. Our research involved second-year students studying "Electricity and Magnetism" at a higher educational institution. Nineteen students participating in the study constituted a group of future physics teachers from the academic group 1502-23.

In the initial phase of the experimental research work, a survey was conducted to assess the theoretical knowledge of students while performing laboratory work and to determine their level of understanding. As illustrated in Figure 1, for the quantitative study, the survey was administered before and after the final test, and quantitative descriptive tests were conducted to evaluate the effectiveness of Artificial Intelligence (AI) and Virtual Reality (VR) technologies. The survey was developed using the Google Forms and Quilgo platforms.

As part of the quantitative study, a pre-test was conducted in the first week, while post-testing occurred in the final week. To evaluate the results of the preliminary and final tests, assignments were prepared on the Google Forms platform, and the academic integrity of the students was monitored through the Quilgo platform.

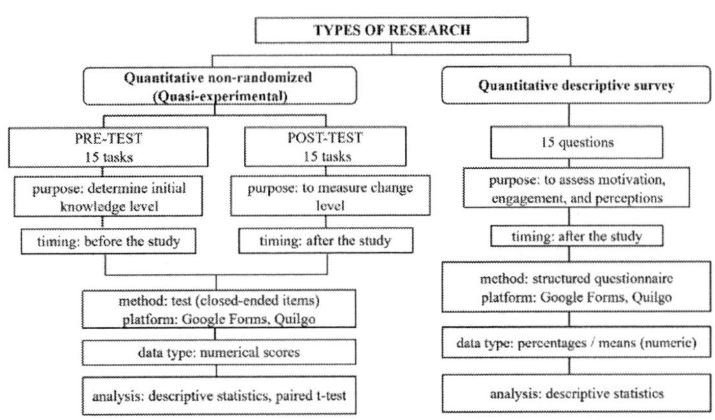

Figure 1. Types of research

In our study utilizing quantitative methods, a preliminary test was administered to students in the first week of the investigation, followed by a post-test conducted in the final week. Furthermore, to ascertain the results of both the preliminary and subsequent testing, tasks were designed using the Google Forms platform, while academic integrity was monitored through the Quilgo platform.

We observed that the utilization of an electronic assessment method predicated on integrity and technical reliability is associated with certain risks in evaluating students' knowledge. Furthermore, survey participants encountered issues related to inappropriate familiarity with the platforms and unstable internet connections.

During the initial phase of our research project formation, a model of the educational program was developed based on the integration of artificial intelligence (AI) and virtual reality (VR) technologies.

The content of the research model is based on the objectives of laboratory work within the discipline of "Electricity and Magnetism", and its assessment. The control group used traditional teaching methods, while the experimental group used virtual and artificial intelligence technologies. Students' research skills were evaluated using quantitative methods as a result of the laboratory work. The research aims to introduce immersive technologies into the learning process, analyze the results, and provide feedback. As shown in Figure 2 illustrates the content, teaching methods, and hypotheses of laboratory work for the course "Electricity and Magnetism".

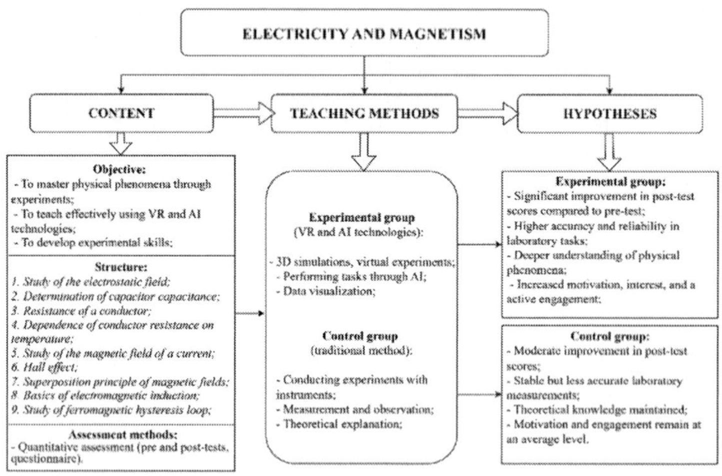

Figure 2. Research model

The study was conducted at the Department of Physics at the South Kazakhstan Pedagogical University, named after Ozbekali Zhanibekov, with participation from second-year students in group 1502-23. Before commencing the research, we analyzed the curriculum and syllabus. Teaching methods incorporating new technologies were aligned with the planned topics. At the beginning of the study, we developed a model adapted to the educational process. This model considered the compatibility of the curriculum with VR simulation topics, as well as their technical and ethical implications. During the study's mid-phase, specifically in the 5th week, we conducted laboratory work with the involvement of instructors from the department.

Our laboratory experiment focused on the topic "Magnetic Field. The effect of electric and magnetic fields on a moving charge". We utilized VR simulations, which were illustrated in Figure 3.

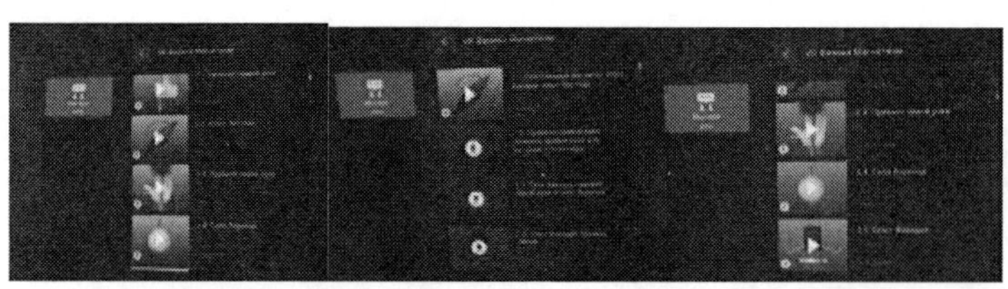

Figure 3. Interface of VR modules for teaching "Electricity and Magnetism"

During the experiment, students were divided into two groups to conduct the laboratory work. Throughout the laboratory session, students determined the direction of charges subjected to motion in a magnetic field, the direction of the force acting on a conductor, as well as the direction of the magnetic field surrounding a straight conductor. As presented in Figure 4, it is evident that students employed the right-hand and left-hand rules while executing the tasks. Moreover, the exploration of physical laws by students within a virtual environment contributes significantly to the enhancement of their spatial reasoning skills.

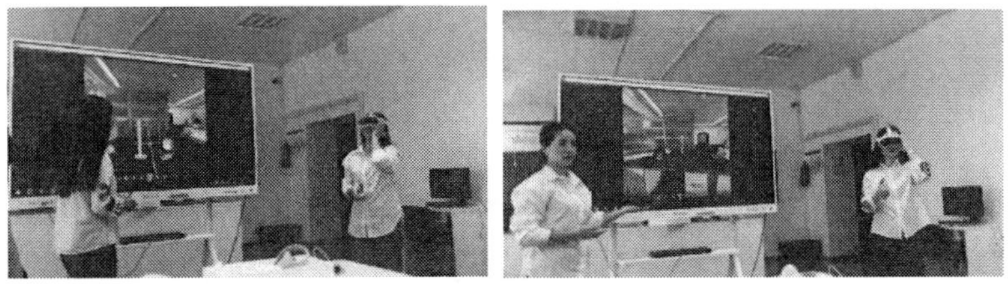

Figure 4. Integration of VR technology into physics education

4. RESULT

In the final phase of the study, we analyzed the quantitative data obtained from the survey of both the control and experimental groups using a paired t-test. Additionally, a quantitative descriptive analysis was conducted utilizing six pedagogical components.

In our quantitative study, we collected results from both pre-tests and post-tests for students trained using VR simulations (the experimental group) and those instructed through traditional methods (the control group). Preliminary test results were obtained before the study began, and subsequent results were gathered after a ten-week training period.

Table 1. Initial and final test results of the experimental group

Experimental Group	Mean Score	Standard Deviation (SD)
Pre-Test	8.94	1.05
Post-Test	12.25	1.83

$$\bar{x} = \frac{\sum x_i}{n}$$

where:
$\bar{x}$ – *average mean*
x_i – *the score received by each student*
n – *number of students*

$$SD = \sqrt{\frac{1}{n-1}\sum_{i=1}^{n}(x_i - \bar{x})^2}$$

where:
x_i – *each score*
$\bar{x}$ –*average score*

In the experimental group, the average score on the pre-test was 8.94, with a standard deviation of 1.05. In contrast, the average score on the post-test rose to 12.25, with a standard deviation of 1.83. The test results are presented in Table 1. The data show that the performance of the experimental group significantly improved following training based on virtual reality (VR). The use of VR simulations contributed to an enhanced understanding of the concepts of "Electricity and Magnetism" among students.

To assess the statistical significance of the differences between the pre-test and post-test results, a paired t-test was conducted. The resulting t-statistic was 5.92, with a p-value of 0.00035, indicating a highly significant result ($p < 0.05$). These findings demonstrate the effectiveness of the VR-based instructional method, which substantially improved students' theoretical understanding of practical work in the subject 'Electricity and Magnetism' and positively influenced their level of knowledge.

To gain a deeper understanding of the effectiveness of VR simulations, the post-test results for the experimental group were compared with those of the control group, which utilized traditional teaching methods. Although certain positive changes occurred within the control group, these achievements were found to be lower than those of the experimental group.

Specifically, the average score of the control group on the pre-test was 8.80, which increased to 9.80 on the post-test. In contrast, the average score of the experimental group started at 8.94 and rose to 12.25 by the conclusion of the study. The test results indicate a significant improvement in the academic achievements of the experimental group, with the detailed results presented in Table 2.

Table 2. Comparison of Pre-Test and Post-Test Scores Between Experimental and Control Groups

Group	Pre-Test Mean	Post-Test Mean	Difference
Experimental Group	8.94	12.25	+3.31
Control Group	8.80	9.8	+1

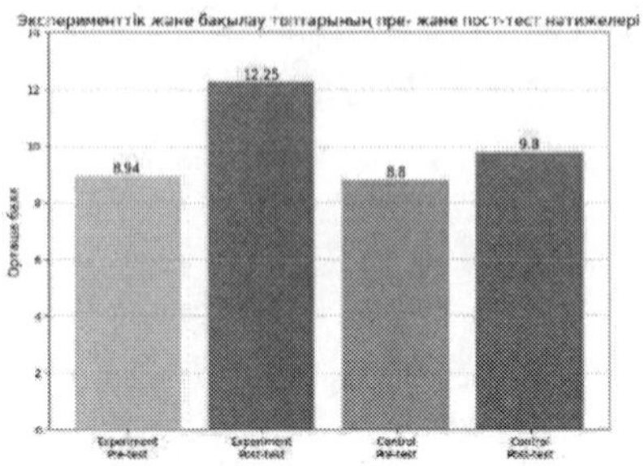

Figure 5. Pre-test and post-test results of experimental and control groups

The implementation of Virtual Reality (VR) technology in the laboratory work provided the experimental group with a deeper understanding of physical concepts. According to Figure 5, the average score of the experimental group before the session was 8.94, which increased by +3.31 points to 12.25 following the laboratory work. In comparison, the control group experienced only a +1.50 point increase, improvement from 8.80 to 9.80.

The experimental and control groups demonstrate a statistically significant positive change in test results ($p < 0.05$). Based on this, it can be concluded that the engagement of students in laboratory work utilizing virtual reality positively impacted their practical skills.

To assess the effectiveness of virtual reality technologies in educational settings, a survey was conducted among students. The survey was designed to evaluate the impact of virtual reality on students' interest and motivation. The survey results were evaluated according to six pedagogical components. For each pedagogical component, one primary question was selected, and the students' responses were represented in a chart. Table 3 presents the chart results for each component.

Table 3. Quantitative descriptive results of students' survey responses by pedagogical components

<table>
<tr><th colspan="3">Pedagogical component</th></tr>
<tr><th>Relevance</th><th>Complexity</th><th>Challenge</th></tr>
<tr>
<td>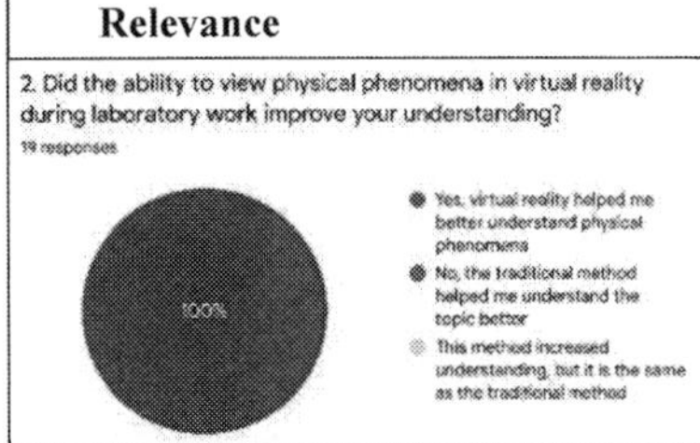
</td>
<td>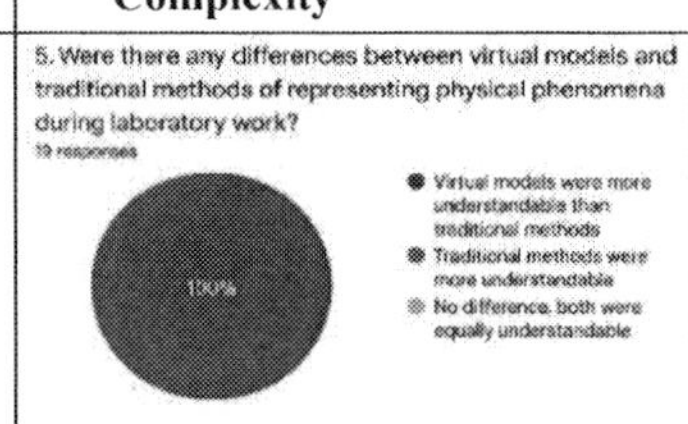
</td>
<td>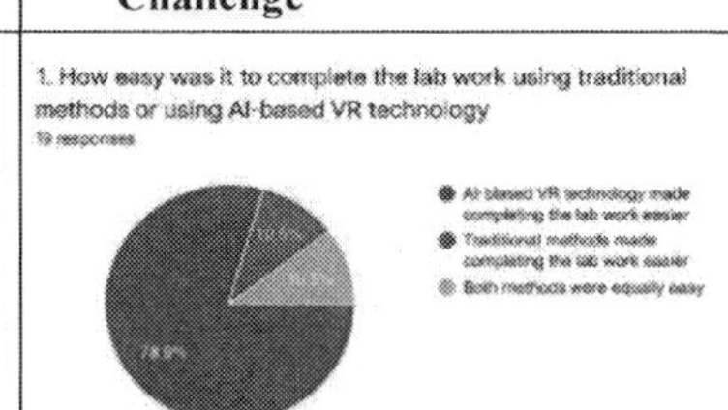
</td>
</tr>
<tr><th>Inquiry-based Learning</th><th>Reflective Thinking</th><th>Engagement & Autonomy</th></tr>
<tr>
<td>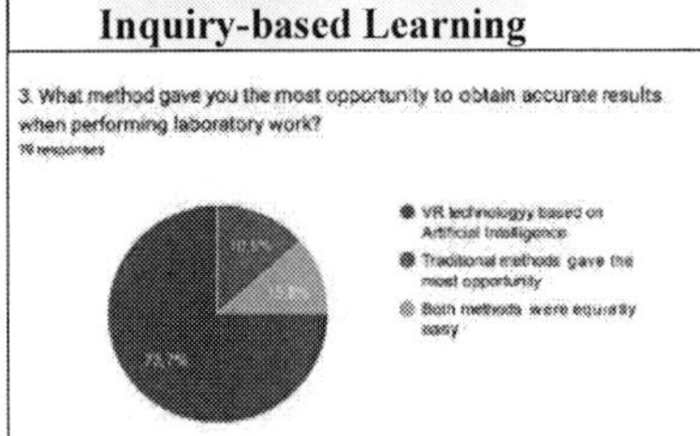
</td>
<td>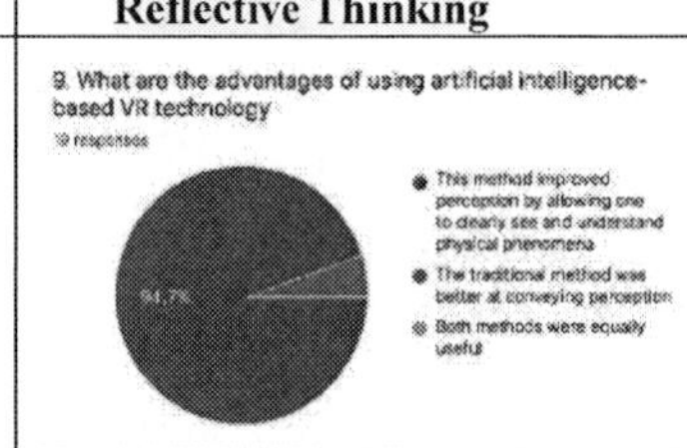
</td>
<td>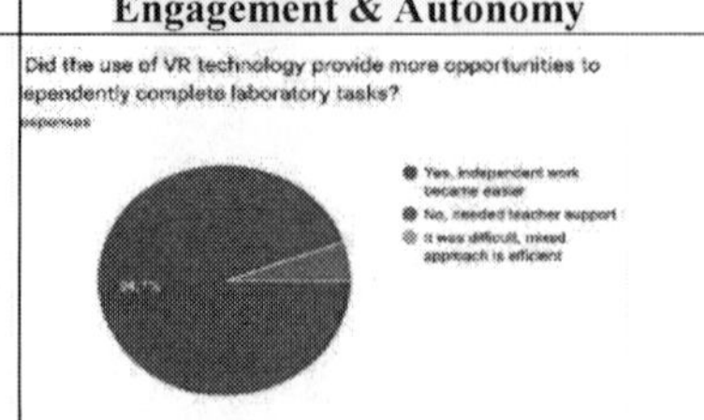
</td>
</tr>
</table>

The *Relevance Scale* measures the extent to which information in virtual reality (VR) simulations aligns with real-life situations. In a recent survey, all students stated that performing laboratory work through VR enhances their understanding of physical phenomena. The survey results indicated that visual technologies based on artificial intelligence have a positive impact on students' motivation for learning and mastering the subject matter more deeply.

The *Complexity Scale* serves as a gauge of the usability of VR technology in the educational process and the effectiveness of data representation through various methods. The diagram illustrates that all respondents can attain a deeper understanding of the essence of physical phenomena through virtual models. Thus, virtual reality (VR) technologies not only complicate educational content but also enhance students' critical thinking skills.

The *Challenge scale* assesses the level of active thinking among students and their problem-solving capacities. In the course of the study, the majority of respondents, specifically 78.9%, indicated that conducting laboratory work utilizing AI-based VR technologies was more straightforward. In contrast, 10.5% of participants found the traditional method to be easy, while an equal percentage, 10.5%, regarded both methods as equally challenging.

The *Inquiry Learning scale* evaluates the extent of student engagement during the learning process throughout the investigation. A substantial 73.7% of students reported that they had greater opportunities to achieve specific outcomes through the VR method. Conversely, 15.8% deemed the traditional method effective, and 10.5% assessed both methods as equivalent.

The *Reflective Thinking scale* reveals the degree to which students leverage the opportunity to evaluate and enhance their knowledge. In the survey, 94.7% of respondents reported that virtual reality had a positive impact on the quality of their experiments. However, a small minority, 5.3% still preferred the traditional approach, and none saw the two methods as equally effective.

The *Engagement & Autonomy scale* assesses students' active involvement in the learning process and their capacity for independent decision-making. As illustrated in the chart, 94.7% of students reported improved performance on independent tasks when using VR. Conversely, 5.3% required teacher assistance, and no one reported any difficulties.

5. DISCUSSION

As a result of using virtual reality, students showed a better understanding of complex topics in the subject of "Electricity and Magnetism" and improved their research skills. The marked improvement in subsequent test scores, along with positive feedback from students, suggests that immersive learning environments provide a unique opportunity to overcome the limitations of traditional education. The integration of artificial intelligence and VR technologies has notably elevated the quality of student learning in the subject of Electricity and Magnetism. Compared to traditional teaching methods, the digital format of instruction has strengthened students' research skills while conducting laboratory experiments (Campos, Hidrogo & Zavala, 2022).

In the study conducted by Cabural (2024), the significance of employing virtual reality (VR) technologies for the enhancement of practical skills among students is underscored. We examined the process of conducting a laboratory exercise on the subject of 'Electricity and Magnetism' with the integration of VR technology and artificial intelligence. The investigation explored the potential for artificial intelligence to be tailored to the individual needs of students while providing real-time feedback. To gather survey responses from students, platforms such as Google Forms and Quilgo were utilized.

Nevertheless, during the course of the study, certain limitations associated with the utilization of new technologies were observed. For instance, some students initially experienced difficulties in operating the VR equipment, and others exhibited a low level of technical proficiency (Martín-Gutiérrez et al., 2017). Furthermore, it was noted that the accuracy of the artificial intelligence system and the adaptability of the content still require enhancement (Gao et al., 2024).

The findings of this research suggest that the integration of artificial intelligence and virtual reality technologies could serve as a foundation for developing effective digital learning methodologies in the future. Educational institutions might enhance the quality of education by incorporating these technologies into their curricula. Future research should focus on enhancing artificial intelligence adaptation algorithms, developing Kazakh-language versions of VR content, and investigating the long-term implications of digital technologies.

6. CONCLUSION

The use of Virtual Reality (VR) and Artificial Intelligence (AI) technologies has greatly improved students' understanding of the course "Electricity and Magnetism", as confirmed by quantitative data. Research has demonstrated that the utilization of virtual reality (VR) technologies in physics education is effective. The results of the study indicate that VR technology has the potential to play a significant role in physics education. In addition to this, immersive learning technologies enable students to better grasp complex concepts. Furthermore, virtual reality contributes to the development of students' critical thinking and research abilities. For instance, when employing immersive technologies, it is essential to consider effective solutions to issues such as access to technical VR equipment and ethical considerations.

REFERENCES

Avradinis, N., Vosinakis, S., & Panayiotopoulos, T. (2000). Using virtual reality techniques for the simulation of physics experiments. Proceedings of the International Conference on Educational Multimedia, Hypermedia and Telecommunications, 2000, 105–110.

Cabural, A. B. (2024). Enhancing conceptual understanding of electricity and magnetism through VR simulations. International Journal of Current Science Research and Review, 7(10), 7909–7917. https://doi.org/10.47191/ijcsrr/V7-i10-50

Cai, S., Liu, C., Wang, T., Liu, E., & Liang, J.-C. (2021). Effects of learning physics using augmented reality on students' self-efficacy and conceptions of learning. British Journal of Educational Technology, 52(1), 235–251. https://doi.org/10.1111/bjet.13020

Campos, E., Hidrogo, I., & Zavala, G. (2022). Impact of virtual reality use on the teaching and learning of vectors. Frontiers in Education, 7, 965640. https://doi.org/10.3389/feduc.2022.965640

Gao, H., Huai, H., Yildiz-Degirmenci, S., Bannert, M., & Kasneci, E. (2024). DataliVR: Transformation of data literacy education through virtual reality with ChatGPT-powered enhancements. IEEE ISMAR 2024.

Ilie, R., Shaffer, E., D'Angelo, C. M., Cermak, D., Lin, M.-Y., & Chen, H. (2021). Virtual reality laboratory experiences for electricity and magnetism courses. In ASEE Annual Conference & Exposition, Long Beach, CA. American Society for Engineering Education.

Korlat, S., Kollmayer, M., Haider, C., Hlavacs, H., Martinek, D., Pazour, P., & Spiel, C. (2024). PhyLab – a virtual reality laboratory for experiments in physics: A pilot study on intervention effectiveness and gender differences. Frontiers in Psychology, 15, 1284597. https://doi.org/10.3389/fpsyg.2024.1284597

Magana, A. J., Sanchez, K. L., Shaikh, U. A. S., Jones, M. G., Tan, H. Z., Guayaquil, A., & Benes, B. (2017). Exploring multimedia principles for supporting conceptual learning of electricity and magnetism with visuohaptic simulations. Computers in Education Journal, 8(3), 1–18.

Martín-Gutiérrez, J., Mora, C. E., Añorbe-Díaz, B., & González-Marrero, A. (2017). Virtual technologies trends in education. EURASIA Journal of Mathematics, Science and Technology Education, 13(2), 469–486. https://doi.org/10.12973/eurasia.2017.00626a

Nusroh, H., Khalif, M. A., & Saputri, A. A. (2022). Developing physics learning media based on augmented reality to improve students' critical thinking skills. Physics Education Research Journal, 4(2), 23–28. https://doi.org/10.21580/perj.2022.4.1.10912

Radu, I., & Schneider, B. (2019). Impacts of augmented reality on collaborative physics learning, leadership, and knowledge imbalance. In Proceedings of the 13th International Conference on Computer Supported Collaborative Learning (CSCL 2019) (pp. 128–135). ISLS.

Radu, I., & Schneider, B. (2019). What can we learn from augmented reality (AR)? Benefits and drawbacks of AR for inquiry-based learning of physics. In Proceedings of the 2019 CHI Conference on Human Factors in Computing Systems (CHI '19) (pp. 1–12). ACM. https://doi.org/10.1145/3290605.3300774

Rizal, R., Ridwan, I. M., Suhendi, H. Y., & Mahmudah, I. R. (2025). Student's readiness in using virtual reality for physics learning. Journal of Teaching and Learning, 19(1), 131–154. https://doi.org/10.22329/jtl.v19i1.8943

Sarapak, C., Sukman, S., Kong-In, P., Sonsrin, K., Nakchat, O., Jumpatam, J., & Yoomark, J. (2022). A comparison analysis of physics teaching using virtual reality (VR) in the classroom and online before and during the Covid-19 pandemic. Specialusis Ugdymas / Special Education, 1(43), 3857–3875.

Suno, H., & Ohno, N. (2023). Virtual Hydrogen, a virtual reality education tool in physics and chemistry. Procedia Computer Science, 225, 2283–2291. https://doi.org/10.1016/j.procs.2023.10.219

Zhao, X., Ren, Y., & Cheah, K. S. L. (2023). Leading virtual reality (VR) and augmented reality (AR) in education: Bibliometric and content analysis from the Web of Science (2018–2022). SAGE Open, 13(3), 1–23. https://doi.org/10.1177/21582440231190821

AI AS THE STUDENT: CONCEPTUAL DESIGN OF A SIMULATION ENVIRONMENT FOR DEVELOPING TEACHER DISCOURSE COMPETENCE

Sabine Seufert[1], Philipp Hartmann[1], Susan McKenney[2] and Sara van der Linden[2]
[1]*Institute of Educational Management and Technologies, University of St.Gallen*
9000 St.Gallen, Switzerland
[2]*Faculty of Behavioural, Management and Social Sciences, University of Twente*
7522 Enschede, The Netherlands

ABSTRACT

This paper presents the conceptual design of a simulation-based training system that supports pre-service teachers in developing discourse competence for facilitating accountable classroom talk on socio-scientific issues (SSI). The system is grounded in research on dialogic teaching, conceptual change, teacher reflection, and the TPACK framework. It comprises five interconnected modules: knowledge training, simulation preparation, dialogic simulation, discourse analytics, and reflective feedback. The components are powered by generative AI based on large language models (LLMs), which provide adaptive support across the entire learning cycle from explaining pedagogical concepts to generating realistic student responses, analyzing teaching moves, and delivering personalized feedback. The system creates a practice-oriented, low-risk environment in which pre-service teachers can experiment with discourse strategies, manage epistemic and emotional complexity, and reflect on their instructional decisions. In addition to demonstrating the pedagogical potential of generative AI, design also raises broader questions about the development of trustworthy educational technologies. Future work includes empirical evaluation in the form of a pilot study and iterative refinement through design-based research.

KEYWORDS

Dialog Teaching, Accountable Talk, TPACK, Simulation-Based Learning, Large Language Models, Teacher Education

1. INTRODUCTION

Supporting meaningful classroom dialogue is a key challenge in teacher education, especially in lessons that address socio-scientific issues (O'Connor & Michaels, 2007; Zeidler et al., 2005). These issues require not only subject-specific reasoning but also the ability to navigate ethical, societal, and emotional perspectives. Pre-service teachers need to develop competence to guide classroom talk in a way that is dialogic, responsive, and grounded in evidence (Sadler et al., 2007). However, many teacher education programs offer limited opportunities for practicing these complex discourse strategies in authentic and safe learning environments (Michaels et al., 2008).

Research on dialogic teaching and Accountable Talk has shown that high-quality classroom discourse can support deep learning and critical thinking (Resnick et al., 2010). At the same time, there is a lack of scalable and interactive learning tools that allow future teachers to rehearse and reflect on their use of discourse strategies in realistic teaching situations. Common formats such as case analyses or peer-based role-plays often provide limited interactivity, adaptability, and immediate feedback. However, the necessity of conducting academically produktive dialogs in the classroom is being promoted by more and more teachers (van der Linden, 2023) as well as the need of teachers as designers of technology enhanced learning (Kali et al., 2015). New technological developments, especially in the field of generative artificial intelligence, create promising conditions for the design of simulation-based learning environments that can address this gap (Giannakos et al., 2024).

This paper introduces the conceptual design of an AI-supported training and simulation system that enables pre-service teachers to interact with AI-generated fictional students in realistic classroom talk scenarios. The system aims to foster discourse competence by integrating subject-specific, pedagogical, and technological knowledge in accordance with the TPACK framework. It also seeks to promote emerging skills related to AI literacy (Ng et al., 2023), such as interpreting AI-generated outputs and using AI critically in teaching contexts.

The guiding question of this paper is: *How can an AI-supported simulation environment be designed to help pre-service teachers develop discourse competence for facilitating Accountable Talk on socio-scientific issues?* To address this question, we present the design rationale, pedagogical foundations, and key features of a prototype system. A follow-up study will examine the usability and learning effects of the simulation.

2. THEORETICAL BACKGROUND

The design of our simulation system is grounded in research on dialogic teaching, classroom discourse, conceptual development, and teacher learning with technology. Dialogic teaching emphasizes the importance of purposeful, reciprocal classroom talk that supports reasoning, perspective-taking, and shared understanding (Alexander, 2008; Mercer & Howe, 2012). It promotes a shift from monologic instruction toward interaction that enables learners to explore, elaborate, and refine their thinking in dialogue with others. With these goals ahead dialogic learning is part of a constructivist pedagogy that aims to stimulate cognitive flexibility among learners (Spiro et al., 2012).

A key contribution to this tradition is the concept of Accountable Talk, also known as 'Academically Productive Talk', which highlights norms for productive classroom dialogue: responsiveness to the community, reasoning grounded in evidence, and epistemic accuracy (Resnick et al., 2010). The teacher's behavior (esp. teacher moves) is particularly important. According to Michaels et al. (2010), they should highlight important contributions from learners for everyone, challenge and stimulate learners by asking specific questions and introducing counterexamples, or link individual contributions from different learners. Important points of the discussion should be summarized by the teacher in order to secure the common thread and create clarity, and the discussion should always include new contributions of the participants (Michaels et al., 2010). These practices are particularly relevant in instructional contexts that involve also uncertainty and controversy.

Socio-scientific issues (SSI), such as climate change or digital surveillance, provide such contexts. They combine scientific knowledge with ethical and social dimensions, requiring learners to navigate conflicting viewpoints and justify their reasoning (Zeidler et al., 2005). For teacher education, SSI represent rich opportunities to practice managing dialogic complexity and supporting student thinking in open-ended discussions. According to Karışan et al. (2017) providing pre-service teachers with rhetorical tools and resources to teach, e.g. evidence-based reasoning, help prospective teachers to talk about SSI in dialogic contexts. However, there are differences in the environment or other variable factors of discussion formats but for sure there are skills which are important in both, the physical and the virtual environment, and so they are in the professional development of teachers.

To support skills and competencies for professional development it is crucial to orient as well on reflective practices as part of pre-service teachers' competencies (Michaels et al., 2010). Three different types of reflection are very common in the development of knowledge: *reflection-for-action, reflection-in-action* and *reflection-on-action* (van der Linden & McKenney, 2020). Reflection-for-action means reflecting on existing knowledge in order to be able to act and react in a well-founded manner – this is why it is often referred to as anticipatory reflection (Loughran, 1996). Reflection-in-action is reflection during the action itself. It is assumed that people think about what they are doing during the action itself (Schön, 1983). The third type of reflection is reflection-on-action and, as the name suggests, refers to reflection after the action. This is a retrospective process, which is probably the most common form of reflection (Schön, 1983). However, the reflection processes described are of crucial importance when analyzing the holistic learning experience. This pedagogical orientation aligns with sociocultural accounts of conceptual change, which emphasize the role of language and social interaction in the development of understanding. Rather than focusing exclusively on individual restructuring of mental models, recent work highlights the importance of discursive tension, exploratory talk, and perspectival understanding as drivers of learning (Greeno & van de Sande, 2007; Mercer & Howe, 2012).

To integrate such learning processes with educational technology, we refer to the TPACK framework (Mishra & Koehler, 2006), which conceptualizes the interplay of technological, pedagogical, and content knowledge. In our system, generative AI is embedded not as an add-on, but as a dialogic partner situated within pedagogical tasks. However, the technology used is an AI-based Chatbot (Chat GPT) the underlying pedagogy is dialogic teaching (specifically Accountable Talk) and the content is socio-scientific issues (e.g. climate change). This approach also contributes to the development of AI literacy in teacher education.

Finally, we draw on design-based perspectives on teacher learning, which emphasize the value of reflection embedded in authentic, scaffolded activity (McKenney & Reeves, 2019). Our system supports this by enabling pre-service teachers to plan, enact, analyze, and reflect on dialogic episodes in a structured, yet flexible, environment.

3. DESIGN OBJECTIVES AND PEDAGOGICAL REQUIREMENTS

The simulation system is designed to support the development of dialogic discourse competence of pre-service teachers by providing a structured, interactive environment for dialogic practice. Its pedagogical foundation builds on six core design principles, each derived from the theoretical perspectives outlined above.

1. Situated conceptual learning

Teachers need a solid understanding of dialogical discourse, Accountable Talk, and argumentation strategies. This knowledge is best acquired in a situated, task-relevant manner. The system integrates conceptual input into authentic learning sequences, making theoretical ideas accessible and actionable within the simulation workflow.

2. Intentional planning of classroom dialogue

Dialogic teaching is not improvised conversation but requires careful planning. The system encourages users to formulate pedagogical goals, anticipate student perspectives, and prepare questions that align with instructional intentions. This supports the development of goal-oriented, reflective teaching practices.

3. Engagement with epistemic and emotional complexity

Classroom dialogue, particularly around socio-scientific issues, involves conceptual ambiguity and emotional resonance. The simulation scenarios are designed to reflect this complexity. Through interactions with AI-generated student voices that express diverse views and reasoning levels, teachers can rehearse how to guide discussions, respond to tension, and support student thinking.

4. Practice in managing conceptual conflict

Conceptual change often emerges from dialogic tension and the negotiation of meaning. The simulation deliberately introduces moments of epistemic conflict to foster awareness of how teachers can facilitate exploratory talk and scaffold student understanding.

5. Feedback-driven reflection

Teacher learning depends on the capacity to critically reflect on instructional decisions in several situations. The system provides feedback on discourse moves and offers annotated transcripts that highlight dialogic patterns and missed opportunities. Reflection prompts encourage users to articulate their reasoning and consider alternatives.

6. Integration of generative AI for personalized learning support

Large language models are used not only to generate realistic student contributions but also to deliver personalized support throughout the simulation process. This enables both responsive dialogue and context-sensitive feedback, linking technological affordances with pedagogical goals.

Together, these design principles shape a learning environment in which pre-service teachers can explore the complexities of dialogic instruction and build confidence in facilitating open classroom talk for developing discourse competence through deliberate engagement and reflection.

4. SYSTEM OVERVIEW AND KEY FEATURES ABZUGEBEN

The simulation system consists of five interconnected modules that together form a coherent learning environment for the development of discourse competence in teacher education (Figure 1). Each module corresponds to a distinct phase in the instructional process and implements one or more of the pedagogical principles outlined above. The modules of the simulation system are powered by generative AI based on large language models (LLMs). Only the preparation for the simulation itself does not include AI support, but the LLM for the simulation is getting configured there. This is therefore a kind of learning with AI. These models are used not only to generate realistic dialogue, but also to support explanation, scenario planning, discourse analysis, and reflective feedback. The LLMs from OpenAI (currently GPT4.0 and 4.1) are connected to the simulation via APIs. They can be further customized through prompting. Users can select one of them for the simulation via a drop-down field (Figure 4). From a developer's perspective, the prototype is built on the Flask/Quart web application framework, making the system architecture model-agnostic. This architecture should allow for the integration of self-managed, open-source models in the future. The application can potentially be integrated into existing learning management systems. Other APIs (e.g., Google Gemini) could be integrated as well. Further data protection requirements have been considered by completely renounce with data storage except for a session cookie. The APIs are sufficient to maintain a continuous dialogical learning process. Each module operationalizes one or more of the design principles described above, and together they create a coherent learning environment in which pre-service teachers can develop discourse competence through guided simulation and reflection.

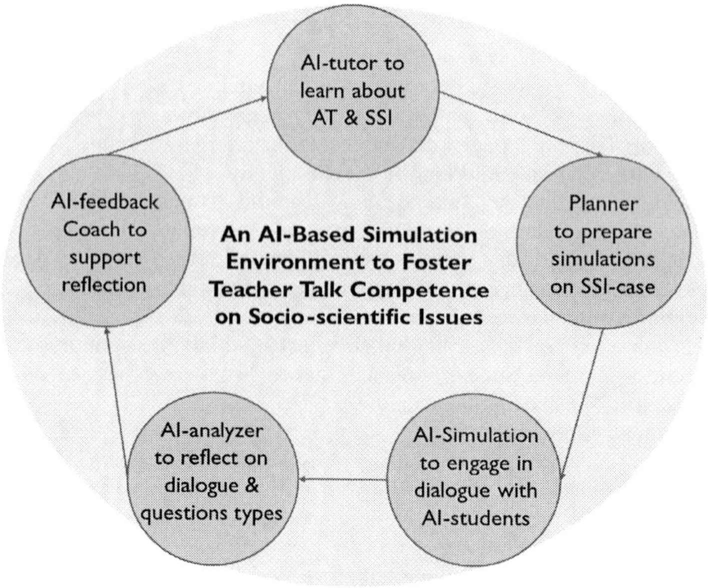

Figure 1. AI-enhanced modules for an iterative and reflective learning path

Knowledge Training Module

This module introduces key pedagogical concepts such as dialogic teaching, Accountable Talk, and discourse moves. First of all, there is the option of selecting a tutor via a drop-down area. A stored prompt is then displayed as an instruction for the chatbot. The instruction can be configured as desired if there is dissatisfaction with the conversation. Then a generative AI tutor interacts with users through natural language, responding to questions, offering explanations, and providing adaptive scaffolds. Based on user input, the LLM dynamically selects examples, reformulates concepts, and supports clarification, making theoretical knowledge accessible and relevant in context. This aligns with the principles of situated conceptual learning as well as the reflection-for-action principle described above.

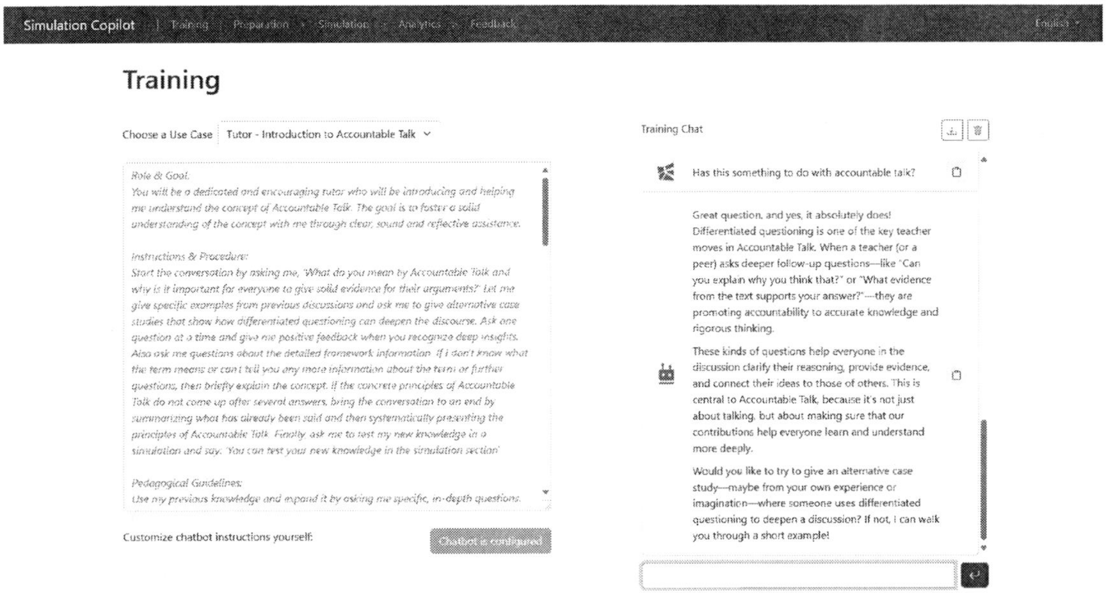

Figure 2. Screenshot of the knowledge training module

Simulation Preparation Module

In the preparation for a teaching simulation, users select a socio-scientific scenario and define instructional goals. First, users can choose the discussion format, currently group discussion and role play are selectable. Then they can enter a topic of their choice for the discussion. They can also customize the grade level of the simulated learners and the number of students. This automatically expands the stored instruction, and the system adapts the scenario in the simulation to the previously selected criteria. Alternatively, the prompt can also be adapted or extended manually on the other side of the interface.

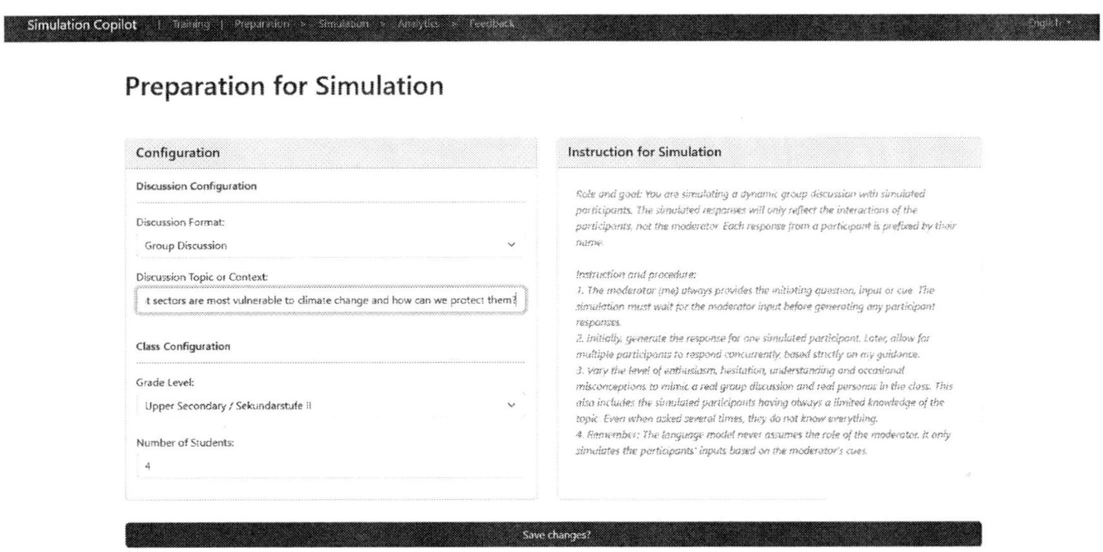

Figure 3. Screenshot of the preparation for the simulation

Simulation Module

At the core of the system is the interactive classroom simulation, in which pre-service teachers conduct a dialogic exchange with fictional students. Each student is represented by a distinct LLM instance that generates real-time, context-sensitive responses. These responses reflect varying levels of understanding, misconceptions, or emotional positions, simulating authentic classroom dynamics. The system allows for dynamic role-taking and adaptive interaction, enabling teachers to experiment with managing dialogic complexity.

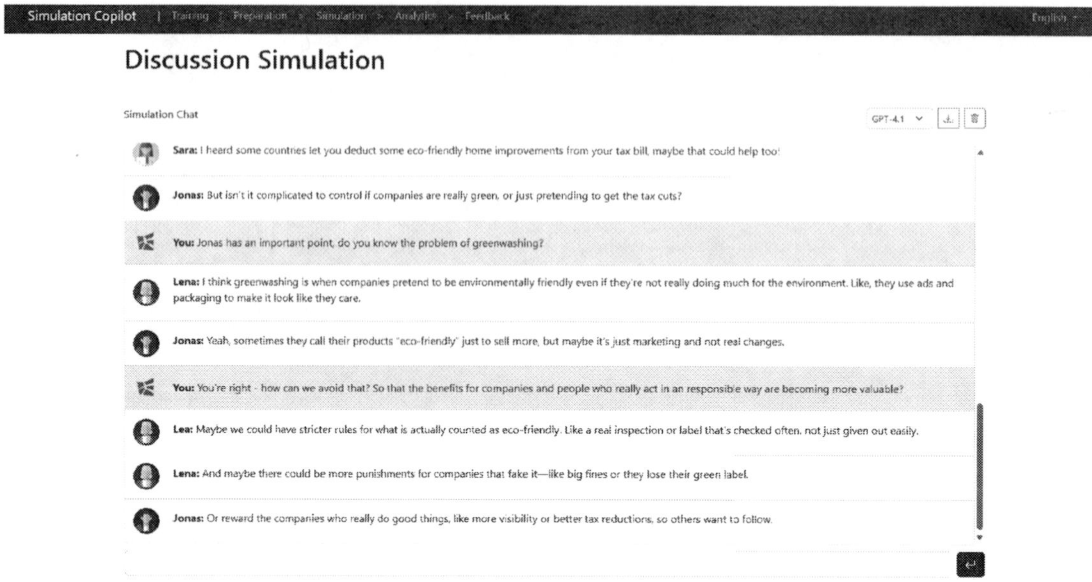

Figure 4. Screenshot of the simulation module

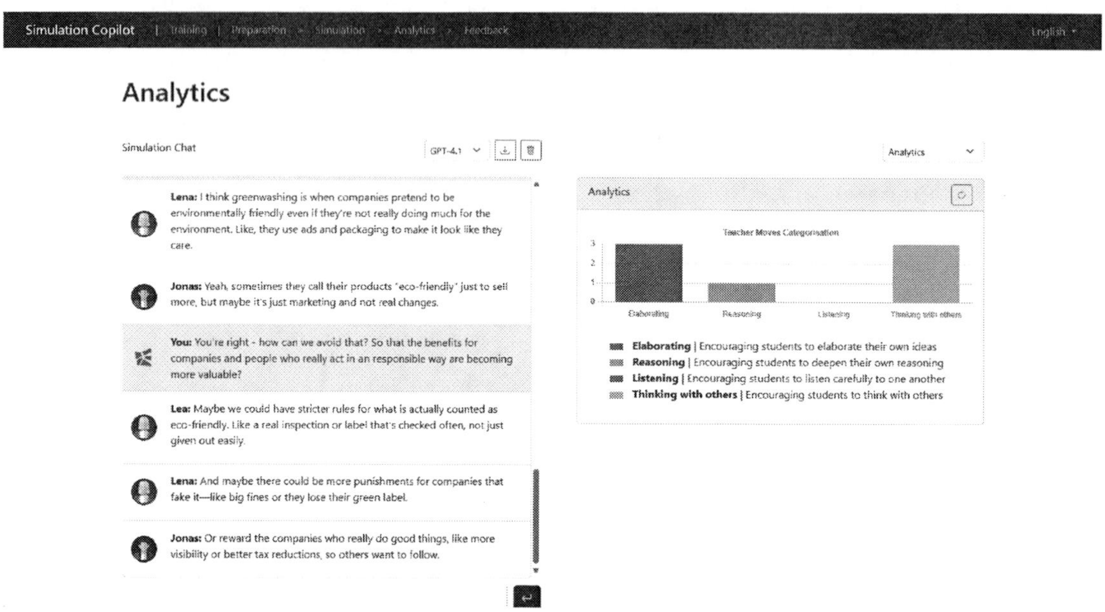

Figure 5. Screenshot of the Analytics Module

Analytics Module

After the simulation, the system uses LLM-based natural language processing to analyze the recorded dialogue. It identifies discourse patterns such as question types, elaboration levels, and reasoning structures. This visualizes key indicators of dialogic quality prospective teachers can reflect about. Via a drop-down field it is also possible to get two different types of analysis, short overall feedback as well as feedback for every teacher move. Narrative summaries and highlighted transcript segments help users interpret their teaching moves to support a feedback-driven reflection. Furthermore, qualitative and quantitative evaluation enables users to set future educational goals for teaching techniques as well as their talk moves.

Reflection Module

In the final module, generative AI provides personalized, context-aware feedback on the user's discourse performance. Based on the same analyses and pedagogical indicators as in the analytics module, the user can communicate with a chatbot (based on an LLM) and ask questions about the quantitative and qualitative feedback. Users can request further explanations or ask for suggestions for improvement. In addition, the chatbot is instructed to guide users through a reflection process. Users are asked to describe to the chatbot what insights they have gained from the simulation and the resulting feedback for themselves and their future work. The interface is like the one of the Analytics Module (Figure 4), but instead of the chat from the simulation, a new chat is generated to discuss the feedback with the LLM.

5. USE SCENARIO

To illustrate how the system supports pre-service teachers in developing discourse competence, we present the example of *Julia*, a student teacher preparing for a simulated lesson on the topic of *digital surveillance and privacy*, a socio-scientific issue that involves ethical, legal, and technological considerations.

1. **Knowledge Training**

Julia starts the Training module, in which she can select the teaching method "Tutor - Accountable Talk" in a drop-down field. In the field below, she finds a template instruction that she can edit. But she likes to talk to the chatbot immediately. She asks what makes a dialog in the classroom accountable and receives a counter question: "What makes a conversation accountable for you?" This creates a conversation in which Julia learns what the principles of Accountable Talk are and what actions a teacher should adopt in a classroom conversation. Julia is shown examples and is repeatedly asked how she would act. The chatbot evaluates her answers and asks if she has any further questions on the topic. When she writes that she feels confident in the topic, it asks her to practice her knowledge in a simulation.

2. **Simulation Preparation**

Next, Julia selects the scenario *"Smartphones in schools: Surveillance or Safety?"* that she would like to discuss with the simulated class. In drop-down fields she chooses the discussion format "Group Discussion" and writes her topic in an input field. She selects the grade level she wants to discuss with and the number of students. The complete instructions for the simulation are provided in a text area field. Her entries in the fields automatically add the relevant information to the prompt. If she's likely, she can edit the instruction. But Julia only saves her initial entries and then moves on to the simulation.

3. **Simulation**

Julia starts the simulation. She writes "What do you think about schools using apps to monitor student activity for safety reasons?" Three AI-generated fictitious students appear in the chat interface: Nina, Sami and Laura. The students respond with varied and nuanced views: Nina expresses her trust in the system, Sami criticizes it as invasive, and Laura is emotionally hesitant. During the dialogue, Julia steers the conversation by asking for further explanations, acknowledging emotional concerns and asking for clarification. The AI students adapt their answers to Julia's statements. She guides the conversation in a direction from which different, reasoned points of view emerge.

4. **Analytics**

After completing the simulation, Julia receives a visual summary of her dialog. The system analyzes Julia's statements and classifies them into different categories of Teacher Moves. She then selects Overall Feedback via a drop-down field and receives an overall assessment of her conversation from a chatbot. When selecting Realtime Feedback, Julia receives an assessment of how well each of her statements matches the Accountable Talk Framework during the simulation.

5. **Feedback and Reflection**

Julia enters the feedback module. In this area, she can view the three different analysis procedures of her conversation. However, she can also ask the chatbot questions in this area. She asks the chatbot why it has categorized her statements in this way. The overall feedback stated that she should ask more elaborating questions. She therefore discusses intensively with the chatbot how she can best implement this.

6. DISCUSSION AND DESIGN IMPLICATIONS

The proposed simulation system illustrates how generative AI can be used to create meaningful, practice-oriented learning environments in teacher education. By embedding large language models across all components of the system — from knowledge acquisition through simulation, analysis, and reflection — the design supports a comprehensive model of teacher learning that combines conceptual understanding, pedagogical reasoning, dialogic performance, and reflective evaluation.

A central contribution of the design is its alignment with key challenges in teacher education. Teachers are required to integrate subject knowledge, pedagogical skill, and technological competence, as outlined in the TPACK framework. The system supports this integration by enabling users to engage with technology not as passive recipients, but as active designers and evaluators of instructional dialogue. In doing so, it also promotes AI literacy by helping future teachers understand, interpret, and critically reflect on the behavior and pedagogical implications of generative AI.

During the development process, several tensions and challenges became apparent. One major issue concerns the open nature of language model outputs, which raises questions about predictability and instructional control. Ensuring that simulated student responses remain pedagogically useful, contextually appropriate, and realistic required repeated testing and careful prompt design. In addition, the authenticity of classroom talk depends on the model's ability to generate responses that reflect variation in knowledge, emotions, and social dynamics. Achieving this level of realism demands careful calibration between the flexibility of the technology and the structure of the learning design.

Another important design implication concerns the function of the feedback. Although LLMs can generate tailored feedback and highlight discourse features, professional learning requires that users receive valid and reliable feedback. LLMs generate different responses when the same request is made multiple times, which can lead to ambiguous interpretations. As a result, users may not take the feedback seriously enough to take into account for the next time. Therefore, the system includes structured prompts that help users connect their decisions to broader pedagogical principles. However, absolute validity and reliability are difficult to ensure as well as that the users actively interpret and reflect the given insights.

Finally, the system contributes to current debates about the role of AI in teacher education. Rather than attempting to replace real classroom experience or mentorship, the simulation is intended to provide a complementary learning environment. It offers a structured and psychologically safe space in which teachers can try out new strategies of discourse moves, and build habits of reflection that are transferable to real practice.

In summary, the system shows how generative AI can be productively integrated into teacher education through a targeted and pedagogically grounded simulation design. Future work will need to address questions related to ethical use, AI-system design, personalization, and integration into institutional learning settings.

7. CONCLUSION AND OUTLOOK

This paper presented the conceptual design of an AI supported simulation system for developing discourse competence in pre-service teachers. The system is grounded in current research on dialogic teaching, Accountable Talk, and teacher learning through reflection. It integrates large language models across five interconnected components, offering a coherent learning experience that spans knowledge building, instructional planning, dialogic enactment, performance analysis, and reflective feedback.

The design responds to a central challenge in teacher education: creating opportunities for authentic, low risk, and instructionally meaningful practice of complex pedagogical skills. By enabling teachers to interact with AI generated fictional students, reflect on their discourse strategies, and receive adaptive feedback, the system supports the development of professional judgment and dialogic awareness in a structured yet flexible learning environment.

Looking ahead, the further development and scaling of such systems must consider not only technological effectiveness but also principles of trustworthy AI. In an educational context, this includes transparency of system behavior, pedagogical alignment, protection of user data, and respect for the agency and autonomy of learners. Trustworthy AI design requires that educational tools be accountable to both pedagogical values and ethical standards. As AI becomes more prevalent in teacher education, ensuring that these systems are reliable, interpretable, and educationally purposeful will be critical for their long-term impact and acceptance.

REFERENCES

Alexander, R. (2008). *Towards dialogic teaching: Rethinking classroom talk* (4th ed.). Dialogos.

Giannakos, M., Azevedo, R., Brusilovsky, P., Cukurova, M., Dimitriadis, Y., Hernandez-Leo, D., Järvelä, S., Mavrikis, M. & Rienties, B. (2024). The promise and challenges of generative AI in education. *Behaviour And Information Technology*, 1–27. https://doi.org/10.1080/0144929x.2024.2394886

Greeno, J. G. & van de Sande, C. (2007). Perspectival understanding of conceptions and conceptual growth in interaction. *Educational Psychologist*, 42(1), 9–23. https://doi.org/10.1080/00461520709336915

Kali, Y., McKenney, S. & Sagy, O. (2015). Teachers as designers of technology enhanced learning. *Instr Sci 43*, 173–179. https://doi.org/10.1007/s11251-014-9343-4

Karışan, D., Tüzün, Ö. Y. & Zeidler, D. L. (2017). Quality of preservice teachers argumentation in socioscientific issues context. *Journal of Human Sciences*, *14*(4), 3504-3520. https://hdl.handle.net/11511/36653

Loughran, J. J. (2002). *Developing reflective practice: Learning about teaching and learning through modelling.* Routledge. https://doi.org/10.4324/9780203453995

Michaels, S., O'Connor, C. & Resnick, L. B. (2007). Deliberative Discourse Idealized and Realized: Accountable Talk in the Classroom and in Civic Life. *Studies in Philosophy And Education*, *27*(4), 283–297. https://doi.org/10.1007/s11217-007-9071-1

Michaels, S., O'Connor, M. C., Hall, M. W. & Resnick, L. B. (2010). Accountable talk® sourcebook. *Pittsburg, PA: Institute for Learning University of Pittsburgh. Murphy, PK, Wilkinson, IAG, Soter, AO, Hennessey, MN, & Alexander, JF.*

Michaels, S. & O'Connor, C. (2015). Conceptualizing talk moves as tools: Professional development approaches for academically productive discussion. *Socializing intelligence through talk and dialogue*, 347-362. *http://digital.casalini.it/9780935302615*

McKenney, S., & Reeves, T. C. (2019). *Conducting educational design research* (2nd ed.). Routledge. https://doi.org/10.4324/9781315105642

McKenney, S., & Visscher, A. J. (2019). Technology for teacher learning and performance. Technology, *Pedagogy and Education, 28*(2), 129–132. https://doi.org/10.1080/1475939X.2019.1600859

Mercer, N., & Howe, C. (2012). Explaining the dialogic processes of teaching and learning: The value and potential of sociocultural theory. *Learning, Culture and Social Interaction*, 1(1), 12–21. https://doi.org/10.1016/j.lcsi.2012.03.001

Mishra, P., & Koehler, M. J. (2006). Technological pedagogical content knowledge: A framework for teacher knowledge. *Teachers' college record, 108*(6), 1017–1054. https://doi.org/10.1111/j.1467-9620.2006.00684.x

Ng, D. T. K., Wu, W., Leung, J. K. L., Chiu, T. K. F. & Chu, S. K. W. (2023). Design and validation of the AI literacy questionnaire: The affecitve, behavioural, cognitive and ethical approach. *British Journal of Educational Technology.* https://doi.org/10.1111/ bj et .13 411

O'Connor, C. & Michaels, S. (2007). When is dialogue 'Dialogic'? *Human Development*, *50*(5), 275–285. https://doi.org/10.1159/000106415

Sadler, T. D., Barab, S. A. & Scott, B. (2007). What Do Students Gain by Engaging in Socioscientific Inquiry? *Research in Science Education*, *37*(4), 371–391. https://doi.org/10.1007/s11165-006-9030-9

Schmid, M., Brianza, E., & Petko, D. (2020). Developing a short assessment instrument for Technological Pedagogical Content Knowledge (TPACK.xs) and comparing the factor structure of an integrative and a transformative model. *Computers & Education, 157*, 103967. https://doi.org/10.1016/j.compedu.2020.103967.

Schön, D. A. (1983). *The reflective practitioner*. Basic Books.

Skidmore, D. (2006). Pedagogy and Dialogue. *Cambridge Journal of Education, 36*(4). 503–514. doi:10.1080/03057640601048407.

Spiro, R. J., Feltovich, P. J., Jacobson, M. J., & Coulson, R. L. (2012). Cognitive flexibility, constructivism, and hypertext: Random access instruction for advanced knowledge acquisition in ill-structured domains. In *Constructivism in education* (pp. 85-107). Routledge. https://doi.org/10.4324/9780203052600-8

van der Linden, S., & McKenney, S. (2020). Uniting epistemological perspectives to support contextualized knowledge development. *Educational Technology Research and Development, 68*, 703-727. https://doi.org/10.1007/s11423-020-09772-7

van der Linden, S., McKenney, S., Lefstein, A., & Chen, G. (2023). *Maybe We Should Talk: Bringing Together Diverse Perspectives on Supporting Teachers' Reflective Dialogue*. 95-97. 3rd Annual Meeting of the International Society of the Learning Sciences 2023, Montréal, Quebec, Canada.

Zeidler, D. L., Sadler, T. D., Simmons, M. L. & Howes, E. V. (2005). Beyond STS: A research-based framework for socio-scientific issues education. *Science Education*, *89*(3), 357–377. https://doi.org/10.1002/sce.20048

DIGX: BECOMING EXCELLENT DIGITAL TEACHERS IN FLEMISH SECONDARY EDUCATION

Bram Bruggeman[1, 2] and Johanna Snoeck[1]
[1]*Artevelde University of Applied Sciences*
Hoogpoort 15
9000 Ghent, Belgium
[2]*Vrije Universiteit Brussel, Multidisciplinair Instituut Lerarenopleiding*
Brussels Research Institute for Teacher Education
Pleinlaan 2
1050 Brussels, Belgium

ABSTRACT

This paper presents the outcomes of the DigX project, aimed at supporting 44 Flemish secondary schools in embedding digital competences and media literacy into educational practice. Funded by the Flemish government, the project followed a bottom-up, co-creative and structured implementation strategy that combined the Four in Balance model and TPACK framework to guide professional development and ICT integration. Nine focus groups with 59 educational professionals were organized to investigate and evaluate the implementation process. Factors for the project's success involved stimulating mechanisms such as the school-specific "digital passport" for assessing teacher competences, the importance of collaborative core teams, professionalization sessions tailored to needs, peer-led training, and the guidance of skilled process coaches. The findings offer actionable insights for educational stakeholders aiming to realize sustainable digital transformation. While context-specific, the project's approach may inform similar initiatives internationally.

KEYWORDS

Digital Teacher Competences, Life-Long Learning, ICT Integration in Secondary Schools, Learning and Expertise

1. INTRODUCTION

The radical shift to online education due to the COVID-19 pandemic and the rise of generative artificial intelligence accelerated the pace by which teachers applied educational technology (Marek et al., 2021; OECD, 2021). Although teachers operate in a specific context and that context influences their choices, every teacher intrinsically holds the capacity of making deliberate choices to integrate ICT in their teaching practice (blended or online learning, quizzes and interaction tools in the classroom, etc.). The teacher is at the heart of any educational process, albeit blended, online or in more traditional face-to-face education (Burner, 2018; Fullan & Hargreaves, 1992). Effectively changing teachers' practices is challenging because implementing new, innovative teaching strategies with technology clashes with both external (cultural and contextual influences) and internal (such as pedagogical teacher beliefs and attitudes toward technology) barriers (Ertmer, 2005; Tondeur et al., 2017). Teachers' digital competences are essential to strengthen the learning processes of students (Redecker & Punie, 2017).

The Flemish government considers innovation and digital transformation as central pillars of its policy. It recognizes the far-reaching impact of digitalization and stimulates cooperation across policy domains. In the policy document Economy, Science Policy and Innovation 2019-2024, strong emphasis was placed on supporting the concept of Schools of the Future and the high-quality digitalization of education. A first concrete step was the accelerated introduction of the overarching goals of digital competence and media literacy for teachers and pupils in Flemish secondary education. To achieve this, targeted actions were developed, supported by resources from the policy agendas on Artificial Intelligence (AI) and Cybersecurity.

The overall aim of this project and research was supporting schools and teachers in translating the digital competences and media literacy (provided by the Flemish government) into practice, in line with their school vision and own context. The consortium in this project[1] guided 44 educational institutions in developing a shared vision on ICT and education and the concrete implementation of ICT in their school practice, with specific attention to digital competences, media literacy and cybersecurity among teachers and students.

This research paper presents a summary of the implementation project and the insights from nine focus groups. Both the implementation approach of the project and the insights from the focus groups are relevant for practitioners involved with digital teaching in secondary education and those interested in digital transition processes.

2. CONCEPTUAL BACKGROUND

2.1 Context of the Implementation Project

The project guided 44 -secondary schools in total. The team consisted of two process supervisors (Catholic Education Flanders[1]) and two project staff (Karel de Grote and Artevelde Universities of Applied Sciences). The process supervisors oversaw school-based digital transition teams and coordinated the project.

At the start of the trajectory, a step-by-step plan was developed based on literature that gave structure to the transition process. The work of Merchie and colleagues (2016), Struyf and colleagues (2022), the importance of data-based working (De Latter and De Smet, 2024) with the survey Digisnap[2] provided substance to the following steps:

1. Intake interview: analysis current ICT operation and context.
2. Survey: assess initial digital competences of teachers and students, based on the DigCompEdu framework.
3. Prioritizing in co-creation:

   Based on the results of the intake interviews and surveys, priority themes were determined co-creatively. A participatory approach ensures greater involvement of the school team and increases the chance of successful implementation of changes (Pieters et al., 2019).
4. Creating an action plan (short-term and long-term objectives) with required actions, responsibilities and timelines.
5. Implementing the action plan: teachers receive the necessary professional development
6. Evaluation: reflection and adjustment (Pieters et al., 2019).

2.2 Four in Balance Model

Effective ICT implementation in education requires more than technology alone. It demands a balanced, integrated approach involving infrastructure, pedagogy, digital resources, vision, teacher qualities, school culture, leadership, and structural factors (Ertmer & Ottenbreit-Leftwich, 2010; Kennisnet, 2012; Tondeur et al., 2021). The Four in Balance model (Lomos et al., 2023) captures this coherence and serves as a used framework and policy tool for guiding digital transformation in schools (especially in Flanders and The Netherlands).

Additionally, it is important to pay attention to the beliefs of education professionals about what good education is when integrating ICT into schools. These (teacher) beliefs not only determine the design of teachers' educational practices but also play a crucial role in the adoption of technology in education (Buehl & Beck, 2015; Tondeur et al., 2017). The beliefs of educational professionals should therefore not be neglected in ICT implementation processes in schools (Liou et al., 2019). The original Four in Balance model states that four building blocks must be in balance with each other: **vision**, **expertise**, **digital learning resources** and **ICT infrastructure** and are supported by **leadership** and **collaboration**. The vision - including the educational

[1] https://www.katholiekonderwijs.vlaanderen/engels

[2] A free self-reflection tool based on SELFIE for Teachers, developed by the Flemish Knowledge Center Digisprong. Source: https://www.vlaanderen.be/kenniscentrum-digisprong/tools/digisnap

beliefs of those involved - functions as a guiding element that provides direction to the other pillars. Expertise refers to the competencies of teachers to use ICT in a targeted manner. These competencies are made concrete by the DigComp Edu framework (Redecker & Punie, 2017), which in turn has been translated into an initial situation analysis (questionnaire), namely Digisnap. The component **digital learning resources** include qualitative and accessible learning content, and **infrastructure** refers to the technological basis that makes the use of ICT possible (Lomos et al., 2023).

The Flemish government has revised this model within the framework of the Digisprong (Tierens et al., 2024) policy agenda (figure 1). The Flemish version uses the same four core components, but they are flanked by the two additional pillars of leadership and collaboration (Lomos et al., 2023; Tierens et al., 2024). Leadership refers to the extent to which school leaders are able to develop and operationalize a clear vision of digitalization. Collaboration emphasizes the importance of collective action within the school team, such as working in ICT policy teams or subject groups. Context also takes a more explicit place in the Digisprong model. Rightly so, because the influence of context cannot/may not be underestimated (e.g. Ling Koh et al., 2014). Within this project and research, the revised Four in Balance model is used as a substantive guideline for the entire implementation process.

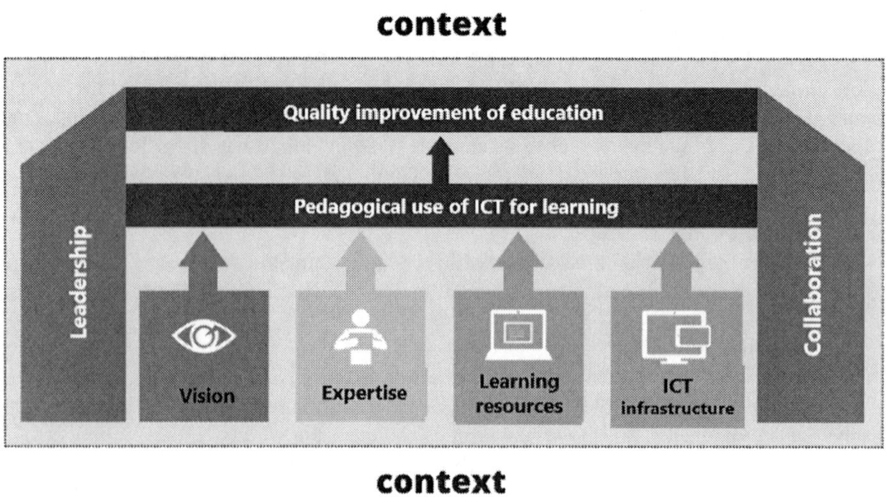

Figure 1. Four in balance model for implementation of ICT in education[3]

2.3 TPACK

As a final component in this conceptual framework, we elaborate on TPACK (Koehler & Mishra, 2009), which served as a general basis for the professionalization sessions during the implementation project. TPACK was used in the DigX project to concretize the Four in Balance component **expertise.** To successfully implement ICT in education, it is important to adapt subject content to the chosen technology and the didactic approach used (Choi, 2022; Rienties et al., 2013).

Koehler and Mishra's TPACK model (2009), based on Shulman's PCK framework (1986), helps teachers design effective ICT-supported learning environments. TPACK defines seven interconnected components:

(1) Technological knowledge (TK), e.g., digital tools and platforms.
(2) Content knowledge (CK), subject-specific content.
(3) Pedagogical knowledge (PK), general didactic principles.
(4) Pedagogical content knowledge (PCK), subject-specific teaching methods.
(5) Technological content knowledge (TCK), using digital tools for subject content.
(6) Technological pedagogical knowledge (TPK), applying tools to support pedagogy.
(7) TPACK, the integration of all domains - for example, designing a WWII timeline in H5P.

[3] Source: https://www.vlaanderen.be/kenniscentrum-digisprong/het-herwerkte-vier-in-balans-model

3. METHODOLOGY

The DigX project supported schools in integrating ICT into daily practice. Since educational contexts vary widely, a bottom-up approach combined with intake and survey methods was essential for impact. To examine the guiding trajectory, we conducted nine focus groups with 59 professionals from 22 institutions. Given the complexity of educational change - including participants' interpretations, attitudes, and visions - the analysis was qualitative (Miles et al., 1994). The focus groups aimed to assess the effects of the DigX trajectory from professionals' perspectives and to identify the mechanisms through which the project influenced educational practice.

3.1 Online Focus Groups

While interviews generate ideas, focus groups provide deeper insights into the causes of complex behaviors, opinions, and attitudes through interaction, guided by an active moderator. We conducted at least six groups to ensure reliability (Guest et al., 2017). Online synchronous focus groups, though requiring attention to technical aspects (Kite & Phongsavan, 2017), offered a viable alternative to face-to-face meetings. Sessions were held via Microsoft Teams, supported by Miro boards to structure discussion. Each began with the question: which elements of the DigX trajectory have reached classroom practice? This was followed by guided discussion using post its on aspects of the trajectory that influenced both teaching and students.

3.2 Participants and Data Analysis

To evaluate the implementation, all participating schools were invited by email and informed about the purpose and format of the online focus groups. Staff from 22 schools agreed to participate, resulting in nine sessions with 59 education professionals. Participants from the same school group (i.e. institutions within the same governing body and local context) were clustered together to facilitate open discussion in a familiar setting. Within each group, a mix of roles was represented - school leaders, subject teachers, and middle management such as ICT coordinators - so that multiple perspectives on the implementation could be captured and compared. Groups ranged from 4 to 9 participants, with an average duration of 59 minutes. This composition enabled both horizontal insights (variation across schools) and vertical insights (differences in perspectives between roles within schools).

Analyzing qualitative focus group data is an iterative, non-linear process, often visualized as a spiral (Creswell & Poth, 2016; Onwuegbuzie et al., 2009). Data sources included a preliminary survey, Teams chats, video recordings, and Miro boards. First, all materials were transcribed. Next, open coding (Onwuegbuzie et al., 2009) segmented the data into small units, producing initial themes and a draft coding scheme. This scheme was refined through team discussion to enhance credibility. Finally, all data were thematically analyzed in NVivo 14 using the finalized scheme which guided the thematic analysis, allowing us to identify not only illustrative quotations but also the relative salience and variation of themes across schools and professional roles. Although coding was conducted by a single researcher, systematic procedures, the use of software, and peer debriefing during team discussions contributed to analytical transparency and dependability.

4. RESULTS

Secondary education involves complex dynamics, and although our approach was carefully planned, school realities showed the need for customization. Still, focus group analyses revealed common factors that supported or hindered implementation. So even though this was a Flemish project, this section highlights key positive influences that can be applied in any educational setting: the digital passport, the role of the core, targeted professionalization, peer training, and coach qualities.

4.1 The Digital Passport

A central stimulating mechanism emphasized across nearly all focus groups (mentioned in 8/9 focus groups and raised by all roles) is the development and implementation of the digital passport, a school-specific framework that systematically documents the concrete ICT competencies required of teachers. The digital passport helped teachers strengthen and support their digital skills. It offers them the opportunity to apply these skills more purposefully and effectively in the classroom and to deal more consciously with digital teaching materials. The structure of the passport is based on the DigCompEdu framework (Redecker and Punie, 2017), which consists of 24 competencies divided over 6 domains. The goal is to guide teachers in their professional growth and development in the digital field. This school-specific set of ICT competencies was then cast in a survey, and teachers had to classify themselves on those competencies. This in turn led to very targeted further training (see 4.3).

In the words of one participant:

> Using the digital passport, we gained insight into who had not yet mastered which skills, and in this way we specifically sent certain people to certain further training courses. And that has had a positive effect. That has proven to be crucial for us in the project.

Someone in another focus group agreed:

> The digital passport has ensured that people have been encouraged to use more ICT and to step out of their comfort zone, because there were minimum requirements.

In one school this was even extended to a version for the pupils. Someone summarizes it nicely: 'The digital passport makes you think about where you stand, which is not always "nice" because it can be confronting at times. But it does give you an idea. It has led to new insights and more awareness on how to use ICT in my classes.' A good digital passport asks specific questions regarding the school context, e.g. when the school works with Google classroom you don't have to verify if the teachers can work with Moodle.

4.2 The Role of the Core Team

Every participating school assembled a diverse team of willing professionals to facilitate the implementation of the action plan, under guidance of the process coaches. In all of the focus groups, there was agreement that working with a core team (under the expert guidance of the coach) was experienced as a stimulating mechanism to implement ICT in the school.

As someone stated: 'The opinions and visions of the different members and roles in the team are an added value, teachers, management and ICT coordinators all work together.' In another focus group someone mentioned: 'As a teacher, you get the opportunity to think along in terms of policy.'

Also the diversity in team members was acknowledged as important:

> The core teams were certainly not only composed of the early adopters and ICT "techies". The less ICT-minded teachers were also involved in the core team and that turned out to be a good choice. Our group is composed of different types of people, not just people who are mainly involved with ICT. But I did think that despite the differences, we were on the same page as a team.

Summarizing in the words of an ICT coordinator: I found it very motivating to work with a team of teachers on ICT. As a pedagogical ICT coordinator, I did not know how to start. By doing this in a team, I succeeded, and a lot was achieved in this project.'

4.3 Focused Professionalization Sessions

In nearly all focus groups (mentioned in 8/9 focus groups and mainly raised by teachers and ICT coordinators), focused professionalization sessions - both organized and informal - were mentioned as stimulating. The digital passport is almost always mentioned as a lever to set up focused professionalization sessions (such as on basic ICT skills with MS Word or Excel, or about TPACK for specific subjects, or on the use of AI in education):

> The ICT passport, that's where it started. That was the impetus. In the meantime, we are doing the professionalization of the various teachers based on the ICT passport. ICT tools that we are taught are based on that ICT passport.

Both more informal professionalization and micro-sessions were organized. An ICT coordinator stated: 'We have now started with those micro sessions and that has been very successful'. About informal sessions, a teacher said: 'Such as when I had a some free time, colleagues could ask me questions there in the staff room'. Someone else testified: 'I think that both [formal and informal] are necessary, both officially organized matters and the informal moments that infect each other. At those formally organized moments, we also notice that a lot of informal sharing is done.'

And another summarizes succinctly: 'The digital passport, the needs of teachers, the professionalization policy, all of that has become much clearer now and was key for the project.'

4.4 Peer training

Peer training as a mechanism for professionalization was a clear common thread throughout almost all focus groups (7/9 focus groups, and mainly raised by teachers and ICT coordinators). Participants described that peer training ensures less fear of the unknown and more psychological safety, the needs are more clearly linked to the context of one's own school, one can still reach the colleague afterwards for questions. Moreover, the pace of professionalization is slower.

An ICT coordinator said: 'Because colleagues teach this to one another, there is almost no threshold to ask questions.' And a teacher stated:

> They now know each other as colleagues. They know what to expect from each other. The approach is also very friendly. While a stranger, yes, that seems to be a much bigger step forward for some, much bigger steps to bridge. And I notice that this is more apparent to colleagues, if it is organized internally. Yes, that does work. That is the psychology behind it of course. The fact that it is by and for colleagues provides a sense of security that is not there with external parties.

In another focus group a teacher concluded: 'Being able to learn from another colleague is always very valuable and is much appreciated.'

4.5 Process Coach Qualities

Research shows that the qualities of the trainer are crucial for effective professionalization (e.g. Merchie et al., 2016). Although Merchie and colleagues mention some specific characteristics of the trainer, such as being able to provide customized feedback or having expertise, they focus less on the process coach during digital transformation in schools. Participants in the focus groups specifically mention some qualities of the process coach that positively stimulated the implementation process (raised in 6/9 focus groups, particularly by school leaders and ICT coordinators).

Decisive and goal-oriented

As process coach you must help the team to make quick decisions and turn them into action, make sure that the process does not stick to talking all the time. A school leader said:

> You often have a lot of brainstorming and so on, and "we are going to do this work form and that work form, etc." But this project really led to very effective plans of approach and actions in the short term, which is why I really found this to be an added value.

Clarifying the role of the core team and decision-making responsibilities was also seen as an important skill of the process coach. An ICT coordinator said: 'It helps if it is clear what the function of the core team is and who ultimately makes the decisions and when. The supervisor needed to be transparent about this.'

Make it concrete, not too theoretical

While participants valued the knowledge and theoretical insights brought by process coaches, they emphasized the importance of quickly translating theory into practice. As one participant put it: 'It went concrete very quickly. Really clear goals were set in advance, we are going to do this, do that. The supervisor also took on work himself, which allowed us to build further each time.'

Appreciative liaison with the school leader

Mainly the teachers and ICT coordinators in the focus groups emphasized the importance of process coaches acknowledging their work and maintaining a strong link with school leaders. A teacher stated: 'We also received a lot of recognition. I thought that was very positive.' Someone else added: 'He [the process coach] also went to plead with the director for recognition of us, as a DigX group.'

As another teacher concluded:

> Especially that she [the process coach] brought the message to the policymakers as a neutral person was important. Because that is sometimes still a bit difficult for teachers, yes, to tell people directly what we think, that is much easier for the coach as a neutral person, I think.

5. CONCLUSION

This paper summarizes a government funded project and research in Flemish secondary education to implement and strengthen digital education in secondary schools. First, to implement ICT in those schools, the consortium developed an implementation plan to initiate and realize the digital transition. The implementation strategy was based on research and consists of six steps (intake, surveys, prioritization, developing action plan, implementation and professionalization, and evaluation). This strategy can inform practitioners concerned with digital transformation in education, such as implementing GenAI in education or building strong learning environments with Microsoft Teams/Google classroom, etc. The Four in Balance model provides organizational building blocks that are crucial to implement ICT in education (vision, expertise, digital learning materials, ICT and infrastructure, flanked by leadership and collaboration). When these building blocks are 'in balance', sustainable integration of ICT in education is made possible.

Second, focus groups revealed that certain mechanisms are more stimulating than others. The co-creation of a digital passport (based on DigCompEdu) was beneficial to organize focused professionalization sessions, a diverse core team that guides the transition is needed, professionalization by peers is powerful, and the process coach needs specific skills. These key insights can help other practitioners in the field of digital educational transformation. The entire process starts from a specific context and is in co-creation with the educational field which is why we believe that this project can be applied internationally.

This paper/study also has some limitations. Firstly, the Flemish context makes it hard to transpose the results to international contexts. Also, we strived for a mixed-method by including the Digisnap survey. The survey was obligated by the Flemish government funds, yet, it proves to be not context-specific enough. Future research could focus on long term impact of transitions like these, quantitatively and qualitatively. Also, the project mainly addressed the teachers involved, who have an important impact on the students. But including the students themselves, would be worthwhile in future research. A methodological limitation is that coding was conducted by a single researcher, which restricted formal assessment of inter-rater reliability. However, credibility was enhanced through peer debriefing in team discussions, triangulation of multiple data sources, and systematic use of NVivo. Although quotations are used to illustrate themes, findings were derived from systematic coding and analysis across all focus groups.

ACKNOWLEDGEMENT

We gratefully mention the Flemish government as funder of this project, and partners in this consortium: Catholic Education Flanders, Artevelde and KdG Universities of Applied Sciences.

REFERENCES

Buehl, M. M., & Beck, J. S. (2015). The relationship between teachers' beliefs and teachers' practices. In H. Fives & M. G. Gill (Red.), *International handbook of research on teachers' beliefs* (pp. 66-84).

Burner, T. (2018). Why is educational change so difficult and how can we make it more effective? *Forskning og Forandring*, *1*(1), 122. https://doi.org/10.23865/fof.v1.1081

Choi, C. (2022). Towards Purposeful Technology-Integration Practices: Developing TPACK. In C. L. Webb & A. L. Lindner (Red.), *Advances in Early Childhood and K-12 Education* (pp. 37-57). IGI Global. https://doi.org/10.4018/978-1-6684-5478-7.ch003

Creswell, J. W., & Poth, C. N. (2016). *Qualitative inquiry and research design: Choosing among five approaches*. Sage publications.

De Latter, M., & De Smet, M. (2024). *Samenvattend rapport PWO datageletterdheid nov 2023.* https://doi.org/10.13140/RG.2.2.20905.81768

Ertmer, P. A. (2005). Teacher pedagogical beliefs: The final frontier in our quest for technology integration? *Educational technology research and development, 53*(4), 25-39.

Ertmer, P. A., & Ottenbreit-Leftwich, A. T. (2010). Teacher technology change: How knowledge, confidence, beliefs, and culture intersect. *Journal of research on Technology in Education, 42*(3), 255-284.

Fullan, M., & Hargreaves, A. (Red.). (1992). *Teacher development and educational change*. Falmer Press.

Guest, G., Namey, E., & McKenna, K. (2017). How many focus groups are enough? Building an evidence base for nonprobability sample sizes. *Field methods, 29*(1), 3-22. https://doi.org/10.1177/1525822X16639015

Kennisnet, S. (2012). Vier in balans monitor 2012. *De laatste stand van zaken van ict en onderwijs Zoetermeer: Stichting Kennisnet.*

Kite, J., & Phongsavan, P. (2017). Insights for conducting real-time focus groups online using a web conferencing service. *F1000Research, 6*, 122. https://doi.org/10.12688/f1000research.10427.1

Koehler, M., & Mishra, P. (2009). What is technological pedagogical content knowledge (TPACK)? *Contemporary issues in technology and teacher education, 9*(1), 60-70.

Ling Koh, J. H., Chai, C. S., & Tay, L. Y. (2014). TPACK-in-Action: Unpacking the contextual influences of teachers' construction of technological pedagogical content knowledge (TPACK). *Computers & Education, 78*, 20-29. https://doi.org/10.1016/j.compedu.2014.04.022

Liou, Y.-H., Canrinus, E. T., & Daly, A. J. (2019). Activating the implementers: The role of organizational expectations, teacher beliefs, and motivation in bringing about reform. *Teaching and Teacher Education, 79*, 60-72. https://doi.org/10.1016/j.tate.2018.12.004

Lomos, C., Luyten, J. W., & Tieck, S. (2023). Implementing ICT in classroom practice: What else matters besides the ICT infrastructure? *Large-Scale Assessments in Education, 11*(1), 1. https://doi.org/10.1186/s40536-022-00144-6

Marek, M. W., Chew, C. S., & Wu, W. V. (2021). Teacher Experiences in Converting Classes to Distance Learning in the COVID-19 Pandemic: *International Journal of Distance Education Technologies, 19*(1), 89-109. https://doi.org/10.4018/IJDET.20210101.oa3

Merchie, E., Tuytens, M., Devos, G., & Vanderlinde, R. (2016). Evaluating teachers' professional development initiatives: Towards an extended evaluative framework. *Research Papers in Education, 33*(2), 143-168. https://doi.org/10.1080/02671522.2016.1271003

Miles, M. B., Huberman, A. M., Huberman, M. A., & Huberman, M. (1994). *Qualitative data analysis: An expanded sourcebook*. Sage.

OECD. (2021). *The State of School Education: One Year into the COVID Pandemic*. https://doi.org/10.1787/201dde84-en

Onwuegbuzie, A. J., Dickinson, W. B., Leech, N. L., & Zoran, A. G. (2009). A qualitative framework for collecting and analyzing data in focus group research. *International journal of qualitative methods, 8*(3), 1-21.

Pieters, J. M., Voogt, J., & Pareja Roblin, N. (2019). *Collaborative curriculum design for sustainable innovation and teacher learning.*

Redecker, C., & Punie, Y. (2017). *European framework for the digital competence of educators – DigCompEdu* (Y. Punie, Red.). Publications Office. https://doi.org/doi/10.2760/159770

Rienties, B., Brouwer, N., & Lygo-Baker, S. (2013). The effects of online professional development on higher education teachers' beliefs and intentions towards learning facilitation and technology. *Teaching and Teacher Education, 29*, 122-131. https://doi.org/10.1016/j.tate.2012.09.002

Shulman, L. S. (1986). Those who understand: Knowledge growth in teaching. *Educational researcher, 15*(2), 4-14.

Struyf, E., Verschueren, K., & Van Mieghem, A. (2022). *Begeleiding van leraren(teams): Ontwikkeling van een model en instrumentarium om effectiviteit in kaart te brengen (OBPWO21.02): Onderzoeksrapport 1: Definitie van begeleiding en conceptueel model* (p. 36 p.). Universiteit Antwerpen/KULeuven. https://hdl.handle.net/10067/1888920151162165141

Tierens, T., Decuypere, M., Alirezabeigi, S., & Hartong, S. (2024). Governing through time(s): Temporal modes of governance in digital education policy. *British Journal of Sociology of Education, 45*(4), 609-624. https://doi.org/10.1080/01425692.2024.2346844

Tondeur, J., Howard, S. K., & Yang, J. (2021). One-size does not fit all: Towards an adaptive model to develop preservice teachers' digital competencies. *Computers in Human Behavior, 116*, 106659. https://doi.org/10.1016/j.chb.2020.106659

Tondeur, J., van Braak, J., Ertmer, P. A., & Ottenbreit-Leftwich, A. (2017). Understanding the relationship between teachers' pedagogical beliefs and technology use in education: A systematic review of qualitative evidence. *Educational Technology Research and Development, 65*(3), 555-575. https://doi.org/10.1007/s11423-016-9481-2

EXPLORING THE LINK BETWEEN TEACHERS' ATTITUDES AND THE EFFECTIVE INTEGRATION OF DIGITAL TECHNOLOGIES IN THE ITALIAN EDUCATION SYSTEM: THE MODERATING ROLE OF CONTEXTUAL DIVERSITY

Noemi Papotti, Lorenzo Muscella and Sabrina Panesi
DISFOR, Department of Education Sciences, University of Genoa, Italy

ABSTRACT

This study explores how teachers' attitudes towards ICT and classroom diversity of students with special educational needs (SEN) influence the use of educational technologies. Introducing the Simpson Index as a novel measure of SEN diversity, results highlight that personal satisfaction with technology use predicts its adoption, particularly in more diverse classrooms. These findings emphasize the motivational and contextual factors critical for inclusive education and suggest implications for teacher training and policy.

KEYWORDS

ICT in Education, Special Educational Need, Contextual Diversity

1. INTRODUCTION

Digital technologies increasingly influence daily life and education. However, using them effectively in educational contexts remains a challenge. While digital technologies offer significant potential to enhance education—by broadening access to information and resources and facilitating pedagogical innovation (Bocconi et al., 2020) — effectively integrating these tools into teaching and learning practices remains a persistent challenge (Van der Vlies, 2020). The integration of digital technologies in schools is crucial for personalizing learning, especially for students with Special Educational Needs (SEN). In Italy, where full inclusion in mainstream classrooms is practiced (Zanobini et al., 2017), SEN includes three main groups: students with disabilities (Law 104/1992), those with Specific Learning Disorders (Law 170/2010), and students facing other disadvantages per the Ministerial Directive of 27 December 2012. Although students with SEN are formally included in mainstream classrooms and supported by a comprehensive legal framework, substantial challenges still concerning the genuine inclusiveness of educational systems (Ainscow, 2020). The physical integration of SEN students does not inherently guarantee meaningful participation or equitable access to the curriculum (Mittler, 2019). Empirical studies have highlighted instances of perceived exclusion even in classrooms officially designated as inclusive (Zanobini, 2013; Benigno et al., 2019). Moreover, the wide diversity in the needs of students with SEN contributes to greater complexity in classroom management, often presenting considerable difficulties for teachers in effectively addressing such diversity. This complexity may hinder educators' capacity to adequately meet the learning needs of all students. In this context, digital technologies are increasingly recognized as critical tools for overcoming learning barriers and promoting flexible, individualized learning environments. A substantial body of research supports the effectiveness of Information and Communication Technologies (ICTs) in the field of special education, emphasizing their positive impact in addressing the diverse needs of students with SEN (European Agency for the Development of Education of Disabled Pupils, 2013). ICTs are classified among the Environmental Factors within the International Classification of Functioning, Disability and Health (ICF) bio-psycho-social model (WHO, 2001), which conceptualizes human functioning in relation to contextual life factors. In this framework, educational technologies assume a critical role: they may act as facilitators of learning and social interaction or, conversely, as obstacles, depending on their design and implementation. As such, ICTs occupy the space between an individual's capacity and actual performance, as delineated by the ICF. In educational settings, the facilitating potential of ICTs extends beyond conventional assistive technologies to include highly customizable and universally accessible devices and software. These tools are crucial in fostering autonomy, sustaining attention, and enhancing motivation, thereby promoting more effective and inclusive learning processes (Panesi et al., 2020). Empirical evidence indicates that digital technologies provide valuable opportunities for fostering inclusive education, particularly by supporting students with SEN through the creation, reuse, and sharing of educational resources (Bocconi & Ott, 2014). To effectively design and implement inclusive and innovative learning environments, teachers require not only targeted professional development (Caruso & Ferlino, 2018) but also positive attitudes toward the adoption and the use of technologies in the educational settings (Ertmer & Ottenbreit-Leftwich, 2010). In this regard, Benigno et al. (2013) highlighted that the integration of digital technologies in education is unlikely to produce meaningful or sustained change without careful consideration of teachers' attitudes. Among the factors influencing this process, self-efficacy —particularly Computer Self-Efficacy, defined by Compeau and Higgins (1995, p. 192) as *'the judgment of one's ability to use the computer'*— appears to play a pivotal role. In addition to self-efficacy, Bandura (1986) introduced the concept of outcome expectation—defined as the anticipated benefits of performing a given action. While self-efficacy pertains to the belief in one's ability to execute a task, outcome expectation concerns the perceived value or benefit of its outcome. These two constructs—Self-Efficacy and Outcome Expectation —are fundamental drivers of motivation and engagement. Individuals are more likely to invest effort in activities in which they feel competent (Self-Efficacy) and from which they anticipate favourable outcomes (Outcome Expectation). In this framework, interest emerges as a key motivational component and a strong predictor of behavioural intention (Fouad & Smith, 1996). Although previous research has demonstrated that positive attitudes toward technology are linked to greater integration of digital tools in teaching practices, the potential moderating role of contextual factors in this relationship remains underexplored (Howard et al., 2021). To fill this gap, the present study aims to examine the association between teachers' attitudes toward technology and their effective use in inclusive educational practices. Specifically, the study investigates whether the diversity of the classroom context—operationalized as the presence and heterogeneity of students with SEN—moderates this relationship.

2. METHOD

2.1 Sample

A total of 211 teachers (*M* age = 47.13 years; range: from 22 to 67 years) took part in this study. The sample includes 83% female teachers, consistent with national data (82.7%; ISTAT, 2023). Of these participants, 14.8% were preschool teachers, 42.4% were primary school teachers 16.9% were lower secondary school teachers and 24.7% were upper secondary school teachers. Regarding their roles, 39.7% were support teachers, and 60.3% were subject teachers.

2.2 Instrument

Demographic information: teachers were asked to indicate their date of birth, the grade they teach at and the role they play within the school (support or subject teachers).

ITIS: it is a questionnaire consisting of 21 items to identify teachers' attitudes towards ICT through a 5-step agreement and disagreement scale (1 = disagree; 5 = strongly agree; Benigno et al., 2013). The instrument is composed of three subscales: the subscale of interest in new technologies (INT; α = 78.9), self-efficacy (SE; α = 76) and outcome expectation (OE; α = 85.9) in relation to the use of new technologies. Within the subscale of outcome expectation there are three subscales: performance outcome expectation (POE; α = 46.7) which measures the belief that using technologies in the classroom could make a teacher's teaching action more effective, self-evaluative outcome expectations (SEOE; α = 78.2), which measures the belief in personal satisfaction that a teacher might experience using classroom technologies, and social outcome expectations (SOE; α = 87.6) It measures the belief that colleagues value the use of technology in teaching processes.

SELFIE: The SELFIE tool (for details on reliability, consistency, and validity, see Castaño-Muñoz et al., 2018) was developed based on the conceptual framework DigCompOrg, which focuses on the digital competence of educational organizations (Kampylis et al., 2015; see also Kampylis et al., 2016). It is a valuable instrument for collecting information on the use of digital technologies in school settings. For the present study, items specifically related to the educational use of technologies were selected ($\alpha = 84.8$). The subscale used in the study included the following question: using digital and educational technologies to foster students' creativity, for instance by allowing them to engage with basic programming or audio/video editing software; employing digital and educational technologies to facilitate collaboration among students through group activities involving collaborative tools such as interactive whiteboards, wikis, blogs, discussion forums, or videoconferencing; integrating digital and educational technologies to adapt teaching practices to individual student needs by designing and implementing personalized interventions; promoting digital learning activities aimed at engaging all students, for example by teaching them how to use digital technologies for tasks such as in-depth exploration or online research; and encouraging students to use digital and educational technologies (e.g., online presentations or cloud-based document sharing) for interdisciplinary projects.

Participants responded using a five-point Likert scale (1 = never; 5 = systematically).

Simpson Index: (diversity index of students SEN): The Simpson Index, originally developed to measure biodiversity in ecological research (Simpson, 1949), has been applied in organizational (Alcocer Guajardo, 2023) and educational contexts, particularly in studies on ethnic bullying (Bayram Özdemir et al., 2018). Unlike simpler measures—such as the percentage of students differing from the majority group (Papotti & Caravita, 2024)—it captures both the distribution and heterogeneity of differences. This is especially relevant in inclusive classrooms, where complexity stems not only from the number of students with SEN but also from the diversity of their needs (McLaughlin et al., 2016). In our study, teachers reported the number of students in their main class, specifying how many were covered by Law 104/92, Law 170/2010, and the Ministerial Directive of 27 December 2012. We then calculated a diversity index reflecting both the quantity and distribution of SEN types using the following formula: $Dc = 1 - \sum_{i=1}^{k} \left(\frac{n_i}{N}\right)^2$

where:

- n = number of students for each special need legislative category for each class;
- N = total number of students in each class;
- k = 3, number of special needs legislative categories;

This index ranges from 0 (no diversity—all SEN students belong to the same category) to a maximum approaching 1 (high diversity—all categories are equally represented). For example, a class with 4 SEN students all in the same category (e.g., Law 104/1992) would have a diversity index of 0.00. In contrast, a class with 4 SEN students equally distributed across the three categories would reach an index close to 0.67. This illustrates how the same number of SEN students can reflect different levels of diversity and classroom complexity. In our sample, the mean SEN diversity index was 0.42, indicating a moderate level of heterogeneity in the distribution of students with special educational needs across classes. This metric offers a nuanced perspective on inclusion-related challenges: classrooms with similar numbers of SEN students may differ substantially in the pedagogical complexity they present, depending on the diversity of the students' needs.

2.3 Statistics Analysis

Preliminary t-test analyses were conducted to examine whether there were significant differences in the variables under investigation (teachers' attitudes towards ICT, assessed using the total ITIS scale and ITIS subscales, and the use of technologies in educational settings, assessed using the SELFIE subscale) between support teachers and subject teachers. Pearson correlation analyses were conducted to examine the associations among the variables of interest. Subsequently, moderation models were conducted. The dependent variable was the use of new technologies in educational settings, assessed through the SELFIE subscale, while the independent variable was the attitude towards ICT, measured using the total ITIS scale and its subscales. Initially, the overall attitude towards ICT, measured by the total ITIS scale, was included as the independent variable. Then, the ITIS subscales were analysed individually as independent variables. All analyses were controlled for participants' age and teaching role (i.e., support teacher vs. subject teacher). The Simpson Index was used as a moderating variable to assess whether the relationship between attitudes towards ICT (measured through the total ITIS scale) and the dimensions of attitudes towards ICT (measured through the ITIS subscales) and the use of technology in educational settings (measured through the SELFIE subscale) was modified by the level of diversity among students with special educational needs (SEN) within the classroom

2.4 Results

As shown in Table 1, a T-test was conducted to compare support teachers and subject teachers on the ITIS scale and subscales (attitudes towards ICT) and the SELFIE subscale (use of technology in educational settings). Significant differences emerged in some ITIS subscales: support teachers scored significantly higher on the Self-Evaluative Outcome Expectations (SEOE) and Personal Outcome Expectations (POE) subscales. They also showed marginally higher scores on the Overall Outcome Expectations (OE) subscale. No significant differences were found on the SELFIE subscale. We then conducted correlations, specifically, there was a significant negative correlation between age and SELFIE subscale scores (use of technology in education) indicating that younger teachers tend to use technology more frequently. The SELFIE subscale also shows positive and significant correlations with all subscales of ITIS and ITIS total scale scores. In particular, the strongest associations were found with of the ITIS SEOE subscale ($r = 0.437$; $p < .01$), with the POE ITIS subscale (Performance Outcome Expectations; $r = 0.462$; $p < .01$) and with SE ITIS subscale (self-efficacy in ICT; $r = 0.459$; $p <.01$). These results indicate that increased use of technologies is associated with higher levels of motivation, confidence in one's own skills and belief in educational effectiveness using ICT (see Table 2).

The first moderation model tested included the use of technology in education (SELFIE subscale) as the dependent variable, attitudes towards ICT (total ITIS scale) as the independent variable, classroom diversity of students with SEN (Simpson Index) as the moderator, and teachers' age and role (support vs. subject teachers) as covariates. The overall model is significant, [$F(5, 205) = 15.41$, $p < .001$], explaining 27.3% of the variance in the dependent variable ($R^2 = .273$). The analysis showed a significant direct effect of attitudes towards ICT on the use of technology in education (subscale of SELFIE; $b = 0.611$, SE = 0.168, $p < .001$, CI [.280, .943]), indicating that positive attitudes towards ICT are associated with greater use of technology in education. However, neither the main moderator effect nor the interaction term was significant, suggesting the absence of a moderating effect. The covariates included in the model also showed no significant effects. As a result, we used the same moderation model with sub-scales of attitudes towards ICT and emerged a single significant model (see Figure 1). Specifically, it was examined whether the association between the belief in personal satisfaction that a teacher might experience using technologies in the classroom (SEOE ITIS sub-scale) and the use of technologies in education (SELFIE subscale) was moderated by the class diversity of students with SEN (Simpson index). The analysis was controlled for age and teacher role (subject and support). The overall model is significant, [$F(5,205) = 11.85$, $p < .001$], explaining 22.4% of the variance in the use of technologies in education ($R^2 = .224$). The belief about personal satisfaction that a teacher might experience using technologies in class showed a positive and significant association with the use of technologies in education ($b = 0.39$, SE = 0.07, $t = 5.69$, $p < .001$), indicating that the belief of experiencing greater satisfaction in using technologies in the classroom is associated with more frequent use of them. Class diversity of students with SEN also has a significant positive association ($b = 0.97$, SE = 0.25, $t = 3.83$, $p < .001$), suggesting that the use of technology in education tends to increase in classes with greater diversity of students with SEN. The interaction between the belief in personal satisfaction that a teacher might experience using technologies in the classroom and the class diversity of students with SEN was found to be marginally significant ($b = 0.48$, SE = 0.28, $t = 1.75$, $p = .082$), suggesting the presence of a possible moderating effect. Johnson-Neyman point analysis showed that the effect of a teacher's belief in personal satisfaction when using classroom technologies is significant for Simpson index values above -.3477 (from the lower 4.3% of the distribution up), highlighting that the effect becomes relevant especially in classes with at least a moderate diversity of students with SEN. Analysis of conditional coefficients showed that even at low levels of diversity (Simpson index = -0.24), the effect of personal satisfaction beliefs a teacher might experience using classroom technologies is significant ($b = 0.28$, $p < .01$), but this effect is progressively stronger as the diversity of students with SEN increases ($b = 0.39$ at medium level, $p < .001$; $b = 0.51$ at high levels, $p < .001$). As regards covariates, the years of teachers were negatively associated with the use of technologies ($b = -.009$, $p = < .05$). The type of teacher (disciplinary vs. support) showed a positive association close to statistical significance ($b = 0.23$, $p = .067$).

Table 1. Comparison using Student's t-test between subject teachers and support teachers

Scale	Support teachers	Subject teachers	*gdl*	*t*	*p*
	M (SD)	M (SD)			
ITIS TOTAL	3.77 (.63)	3.62 (.67)	2	1.666	.097
ITIS (subscale Interest: IN)	3.76(.69)	3.65 (.70)	2	1.100	.273
ITIS-SE	3.79 (.64)	3.66 (.63)	2	1.402	.162
ITIS-SOE	3.53 (1.05)	3.45 (1.03)	2	.599	.550
ITIS-SEOE	4.16 (.77)	3.89 (.90)	2	2.416	.016
ITIS-POE	3.59 (.68)	3.37 (.74)	2	2.292	.023
ITIS-OE	3.76 (.67)	3.57 (.77)	2	1.975	.050
SELFIE	3.10 (.99)	3.11 (.94)	2	-.023	.982

Table 2. Pearson correlations

	SELFIE	ITIS TOT	ITIS-INT	ITIS-SE	ITIS-SOE	ITIS-SEOE	ITIS-POE	ITIS-OE
SELFIE		.469**	.441**	.459**	.305**	.361**	.462**	.437**
Age	-.097	-.051	-.030	-.063	.010	-.133*	-.015	-.052
Diversity of student with SEN in classroom (Simpson Index)	.249**	.126	.111	.135*	.098	.075	.118	.115

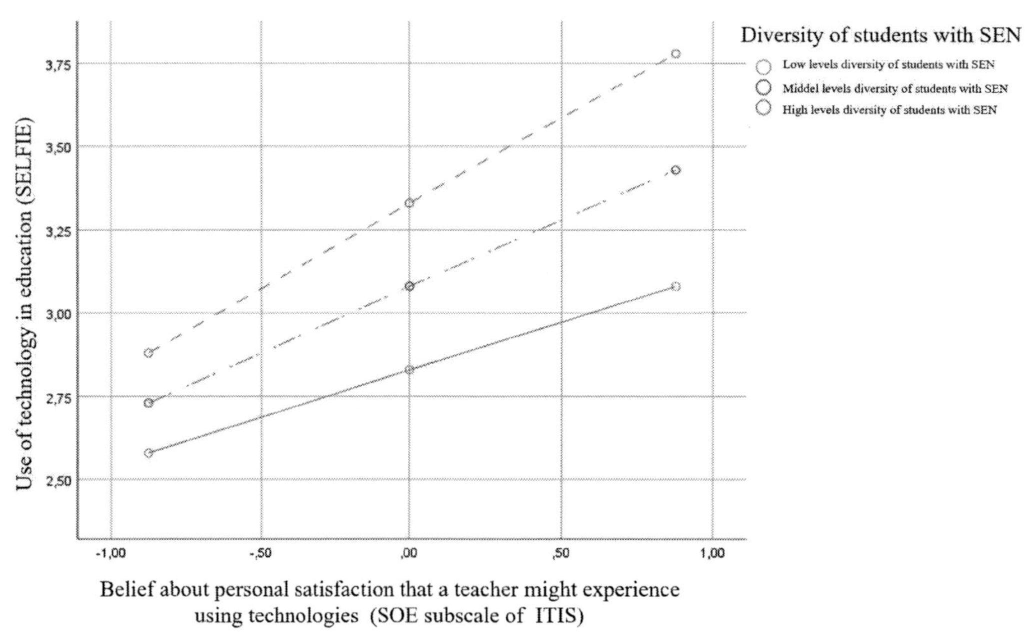

Figure 1. The significant moderation model

3. DISCUSSION

With this study, we investigated the association between attitudes toward ICT and the use of technology in educational settings. Today, the use of technology in the classroom is important to support inclusive practices, and the complex context of students with SEN appears to be crucial. A first significant result emerges from the correlations, which indicate that younger teachers are more inclined to use new technologies in the classroom compared to older teachers. This may be due to various factors; for example, older teachers may not have had the opportunity to attend courses on ICT during their academic careers and may not have used new technologies consistently. While the relationship between attitudes toward ICT and their use in education has been confirmed by previous studies (Ertmer & Ottenbreit-Leftwich, 2010; Tondeur et al., 2008), there are no studies that explore whether this association is moderated by classroom diversity in terms of students with SEN.

Our results are in line with previous research (Ertmer & Ottenbreit-Leftwich, 2010; Tondeur et al., 2008); the findings confirm that positive attitudes toward technology are significantly linked to greater use of digital tools in the classroom. One notable finding relates to the belief in personal satisfaction derived from the use of ICT (ITIS subscale: SEOE), which emerged as a significant role of teachers' use of technology. This underscores the importance of the motivational and emotional dimensions in the adoption of new technologies, aligning with Bandura's (1986) social cognitive theory and supported by later empirical studies (Fouad & Smith, 1996): individuals are more likely to engage in activities they perceive as fulfilling and personally rewarding.

A second key finding highlights the role of classroom diversity in terms of students with SEN: this variable was positively associated with the use of educational technologies, independently of teachers' attitudes. This suggests that teaching in more heterogeneous settings may naturally foster the adoption of digital tools as an adaptive strategy in response to increased educational complexity. It is reasonable to assume that a wider range of student needs demands more flexible and customizable approaches—features that are inherent in modern technologies (Panesi et al., 2020). An especially noteworthy result concerns the moderating effect of SEN diversity on the relationship between teachers' belief in personal satisfaction from using new technologies and their actual implementation in educational practice. The results reveal that this relationship strengthens as the level of student diversity increases within the classroom. This suggests that the perceived effectiveness of educational technologies—in terms of the personal gratification experienced by teachers—is particularly enhanced in contexts characterized by high heterogeneity in student needs. In other words, when teachers work with a more diverse student population, especially including those with SEN, they appear more likely to recognize the value of new technologies as tools for personalized instruction, capable of more effectively addressing individual learning requirements. This evidence can be interpreted through the inclusive education and technology-enhanced learning theories, which posit that digital technologies—when implemented deliberately and reflectively—can serve as powerful enablers of school inclusion. Moreover, this finding aligns with prior research (e.g., Al-Azawei et al., 2017), which demonstrates that the perceived benefits of new technologies are particularly pronounced in complex educational settings, where student needs demand adaptable and flexible instructional approaches. However, it is important to consider that this moderating effect may also indicate a lack of effective traditional pedagogical strategies to address student diversity. Consequently, teachers might be using technology primarily as a form of compensatory support, rather than as part of a fundamental transformation of teaching practices. Additionally, a potential limitation of this study is the reliance on self-reported data for all key variables, which may introduce social desirability or response biases and thus affect the accuracy of the results. Further research is needed to clarify whether the increased use of educational technologies reflects a genuine shift in teachers' professional culture or merely an adaptive response to the growing complexity of classrooms.

4. CONCLUSION

In conclusion, this study advances our understanding of the psychological and contextual factors that influence the use of new technologies in inclusive educational settings. Notably, this article introduces the use of the Simpson Index as an innovative method to capture classroom diversity in relation to students with special educational needs (BES). The findings highlight the importance of personal satisfaction as a motivational driver for technology adoption and suggest that classroom diversity, as measured by this index, plays a crucial role.

These insights carry important implications for teacher training and educational policy, emphasizing the need for approaches to school inclusion that consider both individual teacher characteristics and the broader classroom context.

REFERENCES

Agenzia Europea per lo Sviluppo dell'Istruzione degli Alunni Disabili. (2013). *Tecnologie dell'informazione e della comunicazione per una scuola inclusiva*. https://www.european-agency.org

Ainscow, M. (2020). Promoting inclusion and equity in education: Lessons from international experiences. *Nordic Journal of Studies in Educational Policy*, 6(1), 7-16.

Al-Azawei, A., Serenelli, F., & Lundqvist, K. (2017). Universal Design for Learning (UDL): A content analysis of peer-reviewed journal papers from 2012 to 2015. Journal of the Scholarship of Teaching and Learning, 17(3), 67–84. https://doi.org/10.14434/josotl.v17i3.22102

Alcocer Guajardo, S. (2023). *Assessing Organizational Diversity with the Simpson Index*. Cambridge Scholars Publishing.

Bandura, A. (1986). Social foundations of thought and action: A social cognitive theory. Prentice-Hall.

Bayram Özdemir, S., Sun, S., Korol, L., Özdemir, M., & Stattin, H. (2018). Adolescents' engagement in ethnic harassment: Prejudiced beliefs in social networks and classroom ethnic diversity. *Journal of youth and adolescence*, *47*, 1151-1163.

Benigno, V., Chiorri, C., Chifari, A., & Manca, S. (2013). Adattamento italiano della Intrapersonal Technology Integration Scale, uno strumento per misurare gli atteggiamenti degli insegnanti nei confronti delle TIC. *Giornale italiano di psicologia*, *40*(4), 815-838.

Benigno, V., Chiorri, C., Chifari, A., & Manca, S. (2013). Adattamento italiano della Intrapersonal Technology Integration Scale, uno strumento per misurare gli atteggiamenti degli insegnanti nei confronti delle TIC. Giornale Italiano di Psicologia, 40(4), 815–838. https://doi.org/10.1421/75732

Bocconi, S., Panesi, S., & Kampylis, P. (2020). Fostering the digital competence of schools: piloting SELFIE in the Italian education context. IEEE Revista Iberoamericana de Tecnologias del Aprendizaje, 15(4), 417-425.

Caruso, G., & Ferlino, L. (2018). Insegnanti e tecnologie per l'inclusione: Prospettive e strumenti per la didattica personalizzata. In A. Calvani (Ed.), Tecnologie per l'inclusione scolastica (pp. 73–90). Erickson.

Compeau, D. R., & Higgins, C. A. (1995). Computer self-efficacy: Development of a measure and initial test. MIS Quarterly, 19(2), 189–211. https://doi.org/10.2307/249688

Ertmer, P. A., & Ottenbreit-Leftwich, A. T. (2010). Teacher technology change: How knowledge, confidence, beliefs, and culture intersect. *Journal of Research on Technology in Education, 42*(3), 255–284. https://doi.org/10.1080/15391523.2010.10782551

Hayes, A. F. (2022). Introduction to mediation, moderation, and conditional process analysis: A regression-based approach (3rd ed.). Guilford Press.

Howard, S. K., Chan, A., & Caputi, P. (2021). *Teacher professional learning and development for using technology in the classroom: A systematic review.* Review of Educational Research, 91(2), 237-270. https://doi.org/10.3102/0034654321994302

ISTAT (2023). *Annuario Statistico Italiano 2023 – Capitolo 3: Istruzione e formazione.* Istituto Nazionale di Statistica. Disponibile su: https://www.istat.it/it/archivio/282075

Johnson, P. O., & Neyman, J. (1936). Tests of certain linear hypotheses and their application to some educational problems. Statistical Research Memoirs, 1, 57–93.

McLaughlin, J. E., McLaughlin, G. W., McLaughlin, J. S., & White, C. Y. (2016). Using Simpson's diversity index to examine multidimensional models of diversity in health professions education. *International Journal of Medical Education*, *7*, 1–5.

Mittler, P. (2019). *Disability, schooling and society: An international reader*. Routledge.

Organizzazione Mondiale della Sanità. (2001). *International Classification of Functioning, Disability and Health (ICF)*. WHO. https://www.who.int/classifications/icf

Panesi, S., Bocconi, S., & Ferlino, L. (2020). Promoting students' well-being and inclusion in schools through digital technologies: Perceptions of students, teachers, and school leaders in Italy expressed through SELFIE piloting activities. *Frontiers in psychology*, *11*, 1563.

Papotti, N., & Caravita, S. C. (2024). Prestige norms of moral disengagement, prejudice, and ethnic bullying: A study among Italian early adolescents. *European Journal of Developmental Psychology*, *21*(4), 627-643.

van der Vlies, R. (2020). Digital strategies in education across OECD countries: Exploring education policies on digital technologies. OECD Education Working Papers, (226), 0_1-45.

Zanobini, M. (2013). Inclusione scolastica e partecipazione: Prospettive e strumenti. In M. Ianes & R. Macchia (Eds.), *La valutazione nella scuola inclusiva* (pp. 89–106). Erickson.

Zanobini, M., Usai, M. C., & Pepe, A. (2017). Inclusive education in Italy: Teachers' attitudes and practices. *International Journal of Inclusive Education, 21*(7), 705–720. https://doi.org/10.1080/13603116.2016.1155663

ACCELERATING ACOUSTICS: A LEARNING PARADIGM WITH PYTHON AND PROMPT ENGINEERING

Mari Ueda, Katsuhiro Kanamori, Katsumi Takahashi, Shogo Kiryu and Tetsuo Tanaka
Dept. of Information Media, Faculty of Information Technology, Kanagawa Institute of Technology
1030 Shimo-ogino, Atsugi, Kanagawa, 243-0292, Japan

ABSTRACT

Generative Artificial Intelligence (GenAI) is catalyzing a paradigm shift in higher education, demanding new pedagogical approaches that integrate AI literacy as a core competency. This paper addresses the long-standing challenge of teaching acoustics, a field often perceived as abstract and mathematically intensive by undergraduate students. We propose a novel, 13-week exercise-based course designed for the Faculty of Information Science at the Kanagawa Institute of Technology. This course uniquely integrates Python programming with the systematic application of prompt engineering to facilitate the learning of fundamental acoustics concepts. The methodology involves leveraging GenAI as a personalized tutor, a code-generation assistant for visualization, and a tool for conceptual exploration. The expected outcomes include not only a deeper, more intuitive understanding of acoustics but also the cultivation of critical AI literacy and problem-solving skills essential for the next generation of engineers. This approach has the transformative potential to reshape engineering pedagogy, making complex subjects more accessible and engaging while preparing students for a future of human-AI collaboration.

KEYWORDS

Prompt Engineering, Acoustics Education, Generative AI, Python, Engineering Pedagogy, Active Learning

1. INTRODUCTION

The rapid proliferation of Generative Artificial Intelligence (GenAI) is bringing about a fundamental transformation in higher education and professional workflows (Müller, 2022). Amid this technological shift, the ability to interact with AI—specifically, "prompt engineering," the skill of designing instructions to elicit desired outputs—is becoming an essential competency for future engineers and information scientists (Thomas, 2014).

Meanwhile, traditional educational challenges persist in the field of engineering. One such challenge is acoustics. While acoustics deal with physical phenomena like waves and frequency spectra, its understanding requires advanced mathematical knowledge, including Fourier analysis (Wei, 2022). These concepts are abstract and difficult to grasp intuitively, posing a significant learning barrier for many students.

This paper proposes a new educational approach that strategically integrates Python programming and prompt engineering to solve this challenge in acoustics education. This approach aims to shift the learning experience from passive theoretical study to an interactive and exploratory one (Lee, 2025). The main purpose of this paper is to present concrete 13-week curriculum for an exercise-based course for students at the Faculty of Information Science, Kanagawa Institute of Technology, and to argue for the validity of its educational design. This aligns with the university's educational goal of fostering engineers with practical problem-solving abilities (Cohn, 2024). The innovation of this proposal lies not merely in using AI as a learning tool. It is in systematically teaching prompt engineering—the very method of dialogue with AI—as a critical academic skill on par with programming and mathematical analysis. This is an attempt to redefine educational goals from the mere acquisition of knowledge to the development of the ability to solve problems by leveraging AI. In the age of AI, learning the process of inquiry—"how to ask"—is as important, if not more so, than knowing the answer itself. This ability will serve as an indispensable foundation for students to collaborate with AI systems in any field in the future, not just in acoustics (Mollick, 2024).

2. A NEW PEDAGOGICAL MODEL: GENAI AS A CATALYST

2.1 Traditional Challenges in Acoustics Education

The difficulty in learning acoustics can be summarized into three main points. First is the high level of mathematical abstraction. Many students struggle to intuitively connect mathematical formulas with their physical meaning. Second is the difficulty of visualizing concepts. Phenomena such as sound wave propagation and filter responses cannot be seen directly, placing a high cognitive load on learners. Third is the resulting decline in motivation due to the abstract nature of the subject.

2.2 The Iterative Learning Cycle

Generative AI has the potential to act as a powerful catalyst for these educational challenges. Its true value in this context is not as a repository of knowledge, but as a "cognitive offloading and translation engine." GenAI "translates" abstract mathematical formulas into executable code and visual outputs. This process allows students to focus on understanding core concepts without getting bogged down in programming syntax or complex mathematical operations.

This methodology forms an iterative learning cycle, as illustrated in Figure 1. The student begins with a theoretical Acoustic Concept. Through Prompt Engineering, they articulate a query or a request to the GenAI. The AI-Powered Generation phase translates this prompt into a tangible output, typically Python code. The student then engages in Python Visualization & Analysis, executing the code to observe the phenomenon. This active engagement leads to Student Insight & Understanding, which in turn informs the next cycle of inquiry, allowing for progressively deeper exploration. This model transforms learning from a linear reception of facts into a dynamic, student-driven process of discovery.

3. AN EDUCATIONAL APPROACH FUSING PYTHON AND PROMPT ENGINEERING

3.1 Reasons for Choosing the Python Programming Language

The reasons for selecting Python as the programming language in this proposal are as follows.

Curriculum Alignment: In the curriculum of the Faculty of Information Science at Kanagawa Institute of Technology, students learn Python in their first year. This allows them to start the course smoothly based on existing knowledge, without the burden of learning a new language.

Powerful Ecosystem: Python has a rich ecosystem of scientific and technical computing libraries such as NumPy, SciPy, and matplotlib, as well as specialized libraries for audio and music processing like librosa. These libraries provide the foundation for the exercises in this course.

Interactive Learning Environment: The use of Jupyter Notebooks makes it possible to integrate code, explanations, visualizations, and audio playback into a single document. This creates an interactive and exploratory learning environment where students can actively modify code and immediately see the results.

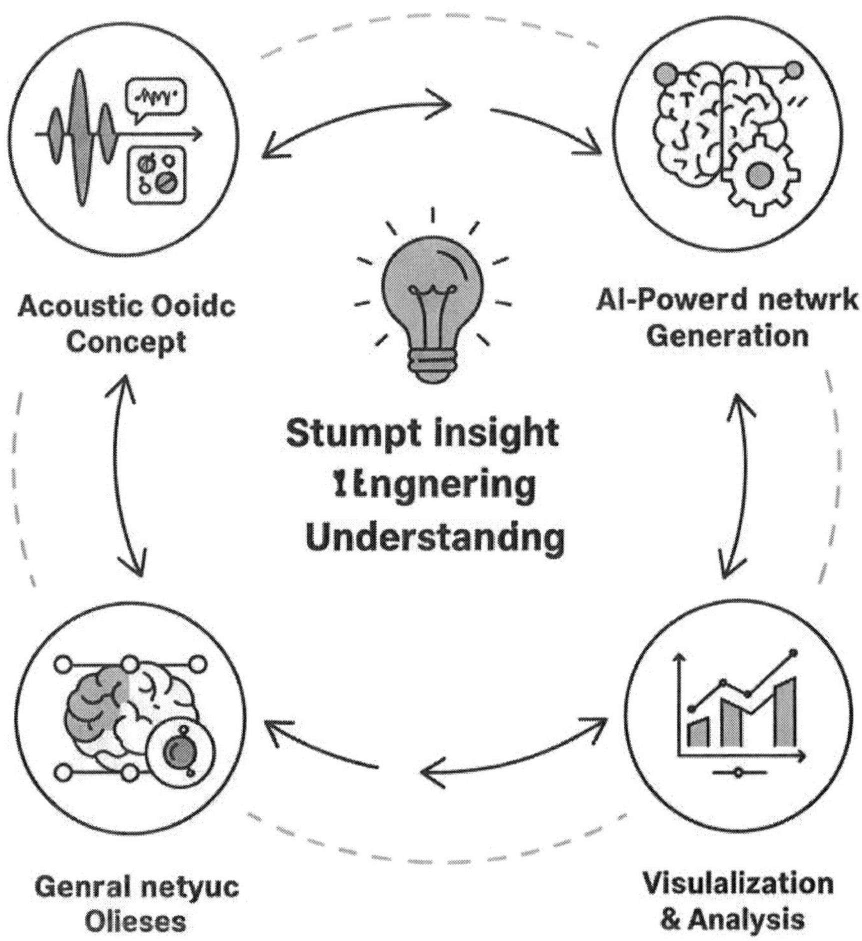

Figure 1. The Iterative Learning Cycle. Students actively transform abstract acoustic concepts into concrete understanding through a process of prompt engineering and Python-based analysis, facilitated by AI

3.2 Systematic Introduction of Prompt Engineering

This course systematically teaches prompt engineering not just as a technique, but as a structured problem-solving methodology. Students learn Role-Based Prompting (e.g., "You are a senior acoustics engineer teaching filter design"), Constraint-Based Prompting ("Generate the code using only the numpy library"), Few-Shot Prompting (providing examples to guide output), and Chain-of-Thought Prompting ("think step-by-step") to deconstruct complex problems.

This curriculum design creates a feedback loop where Python skills and prompt engineering skills mutually reinforce each other. A beginner might start with a vague prompt like "how to make a sound with Python," but as they learn the basics, such as NumPy arrays, they become capable of creating more specific and useful prompts like, "Generate a NumPy array representing a 1-second, 440textHz sine wave at a sampling rate of 44100textHz." Conversely, a student facing a Python error can use AI as a powerful debugging partner with a prompt like, "Explain the TypeError in this code and suggest a fix." This synergy promotes the simultaneous and rapid development of both skill sets.

3.3 Ethical Considerations and Critical AI Literacy

This course also explicitly addresses the limitations and ethical aspects of GenAI. Students learn to critically evaluate AI-generated code and explanations for hallucinations (misinformation). Clear guidelines on academic integrity are established to promote responsible use and avoid plagiarism. Finally, discussions on the inherent biases and limitations of large language models foster a critical, rather than naive, perspective on AI.

4. DESIGN OF THE EXERCISE COURSE "ACOUSTICS AND PROMPT ENGINEERING WITH PYTHON"

4.1 Course Overview

·Target Audience:

Second-year students, Faculty of Information Science, Kanagawa Institute of Technology

·Prerequisites:

Completion of first-year programming courses (including Python) and basic mathematics courses.

·Learning Objectives:

1. Be able to explain basic concepts in acoustics, such as digital signals, spectra, and filtering.
2. Be able to implement basic acoustic signal processing using Python.
3. Be able to apply structured prompt engineering techniques to solve problems and facilitate learning in acoustics.
4. Be able to critically evaluate and responsibly use generative AI in an engineering context.

·Evaluation Methods:

A combination of weekly programming assignments (Jupyter Notebooks), a mid-term project, and a final project. Evaluation will consider not only the correctness of the code but also the sophistication and documentation of the prompts used in the development process.

4.2 Course Structure and Progression

The 13-week course is structured to progressively build on concepts, integrating theory with practical application through Python and prompt engineering. It is divided into three distinct phases: foundational principles, digital signal processing, and advanced applications.

The initial phase (Weeks 1-4) focuses on foundational principles. The course begins with an introduction to digital audio, where students use prompts to ask GenAI for simple explanations of sampling rate and bit depth, and to generate basic Python code for plotting sine waves using numpy and matplotlib. This is followed by explorations of waveforms, frequency, the physical characteristics of sound (loudness, pitch, timbre), and the core concepts of the Fourier Transform. Students are encouraged to use role-based prompts, such as asking the AI to act as a "physics tutor," to better understand the relationship between time and frequency domains. They will generate code to visualize concepts like spectrograms and the Short-Time Fourier Transform (STFT), making these abstract ideas tangible.

The middle section of the course (Weeks 5-7) delves into digital signal processing, specifically filter design. Students learn about the theory and application of digital filters, starting with an introduction to concepts like cutoff frequency and filter order. They then explore the differences between Finite Impulse Response (FIR) and Infinite Impulse Response (IIR) filters, using prompts to ask GenAI to summarize the pros and cons in a table or explain the concept of an impulse response. Practical exercises involve using constraint-based prompts to ask GenAI for specific implementations, such as, "Design a 4th-order low-pass Butterworth filter with a cutoff frequency of 1000textHz using scipy." This phase culminates in a mid-term project where students apply their filtering knowledge to a practical problem, like removing noise from an audio file, using GenAI to help structure their project notebook and debug their code.

The latter part of the course (Weeks 8-12) covers advanced and applied topics, broadening the students' perspective on the field of acoustics. Students explore speech analysis by learning about fundamental frequency (F0) estimation and using prompts to generate code for autocorrelation methods. They then delve into Music Information Retrieval (MIR), a field where information science and acoustics intersect, by extracting features like Mel-Frequency Cepstral Coefficients (MFCC) with the librosa library. Prompts become more sophisticated, asking the AI to act as an "expert in music information retrieval." The course then moves to the creative side of acoustics with an introduction to sound synthesis, covering additive and subtractive techniques. The final topic is an introduction to spatial audio, where students learn about Interaural Intensity and Time Differences (IID/ITD) and simulate basic stereo panning effects. Throughout this phase, students are guided to use GenAI to help design class structures for a simple synthesizer or to explain complex concepts in an intuitive way.

The final week (Week 13) is dedicated to final project presentations and peer review. Here, students use GenAI not just for code generation but for higher-level tasks like suggesting code refactoring to improve readability and adding appropriate documentation. This demonstrates a mature use of AI as a collaborative partner in the engineering workflow, completing the learning journey from basic concepts to independent, AI-assisted project development.

5. EXPECTED EDUCATIONAL EFFECTS AND FUTURE PROSPECTS

The design of this course is expected to have several key educational effects on students. First, it will lead to a deepened conceptual understanding by shifting the learning mode from abstract theory to interactive visualization and experimentation. Second, it will facilitate the acquisition of future-proof skills, equipping students with a unique skill set that combines a classic engineering field (acoustics), modern programming skills (Python), and a cutting-edge competency (prompt engineering). Third, it will foster the cultivation of metacognitive and critical thinking skills, as the process of constructing precise prompts and critically evaluating AI outputs improves students' problem-decomposition abilities and their capacity to objectively view their own thinking.

The pedagogical model proposed in this paper is not limited to acoustics. It can be applied to other mathematically intensive and abstract subjects in the engineering curriculum, such as electromagnetism and control theory. This approach also signals a fundamental shift in the role of the educator from a "sage on the stage" to a "guide on the side." As AI provides on-demand delivery of factual knowledge and code, educators are freed to focus on higher-order tasks: designing the learning process, leading Socratic dialogues about the nuances and errors in AI responses, and teaching the critical judgment necessary to use AI tools effectively and ethically.

6. CONCLUSION

This paper proposed a new exercise-based course that integrates Python programming and prompt engineering to address the traditional challenges in acoustics education. This approach, targeted at students in the Faculty of Information Science at Kanagawa Institute of Technology, aims to promote an intuitive understanding of abstract concepts while simultaneously fostering the practical skills essential for engineers in the age of AI. The proposed 13-week curriculum systematically utilizes GenAI as a personalized tutor, a code-generation assistant, and a tool for conceptual exploration. This educational model not only enhances learning outcomes in a specific subject but also equips students with cross-disciplinary problem-solving abilities and critical AI literacy. We conclude that this proposal is a practical, timely, and progressive step in the evolution of engineering education, preparing students for a future where human-AI collaboration is the norm.

REFERENCES

Abadi, M., et al. (2016). "TensorFlow: Large-scale machine learning on heterogeneous distributed systems." arXiv preprint arXiv:1603.04467. (The foundational paper for the TensorFlow framework.)

Addy, T. H., et al.: "Teaching & Generative AI", Rutgers University Teaching and Learning with Technology (2023) 2.

Agostinelli, A., et al. (2023). "MusicLM: Generating Music From Text." arXiv preprint arXiv:2301.11325. (Google's high-fidelity model for generating music from text descriptions.)

Ao, J., et al. (2021). "SpeechT5: A Unified-Modal Encoder-Decoder for Spoken Language Processing." arXiv preprint arXiv:2110.07205. (A unified model for various speech tasks, acting as a crucial interface between text (prompts) and speech.)

B. Prompt-Based Understanding (Classification and LLMs)

Baevski, A., et al. (2020). "wav2vec 2.0: A framework for self-supervised learning of speech representations." Advances in Neural Information Processing Systems (NeurIPS). (A foundational self-supervised learning framework for speech and audio representations.)

Bogdanov, D., et al. (2013). "ESSENTIA: An open-source library for audio analysis and music information retrieval." In Proceedings of the 14th International Society for Music Information Retrieval Conference (ISMIR). (Another key open-source library for audio analysis.)

Borsos, Z., et al. (2023). "AudioLM: a Language Modeling Approach to Audio Generation." IEEE/ACM Transactions on Audio, Speech, and Language Processing. (Treats audio generation as a language modeling task.)

Byrd, D. S., et al.: "Generative Artificial Intelligence and Postsecondary Education: Rethinking Policy and Course Design", Wisconsin Center for Education Research (2024) 5.

Cakir, E., et al. (2017). "Convolutional recurrent neural networks for polyphonic sound event detection." IEEE/ACM Transactions on Audio, Speech, and Language Processing. (Key paper on using Convolutional Recurrent Neural Networks (CRNN) for polyphonic sound event detection.)

Cohn, C., Hutchins, N., Le, T., & Biswas, G. (2024). A Chain-of-Thought Prompting Approach with LLMs for Evaluating Students' Formative Assessment Responses in Science. arXiv.

Copet, J., et al. (2023). "Simple and controllable music generation." arXiv preprint arXiv:2306.05284. (Introduced MusicGen, a controllable text-to-music generation model from Meta.)

Digital Hollywood University: "What is Prompt Engineering? Explaining Job Content, Learning Methods, and Future Prospects" (2025) 13.

Elizalde, B., et al. (2023). "CLAP: Learning Audio Concepts From Natural Language Supervision." In IEEE International Conference on Acoustics, Speech and Signal Processing (ICASSP). (The key paper for CLAP, using contrastive learning between audio and natural language for prompt-based classification.)

Engel, J., et al. (2020). "DDSP: Differentiable digital signal processing." In International Conference on Learning Representations (ICLR). (A key paper integrating traditional DSP with deep learning by making DSP components differentiable.)

Gong, Y., & Glass, J. (2023). "Prompting for Zero-Shot Audio Classification." In Interspeech. (Specifically explores the use of text prompts for zero-shot audio classification.)

Gong, Y., et al. (2021). "AST: Audio Spectrogram Transformer." In Interspeech. (The paper that introduced the Audio Spectrogram Transformer (AST), applying transformers to audio.)

Gong, Y., et al. (2022). "Rethinking 'efficient' audio transformers." In IEEE International Conference on Acoustics, Speech and Signal Processing (ICASSP). (Discusses methods for creating efficient Transformer models specifically for audio tasks.)

Gong, Y., et al. (2023). "Listen, Think, and Understand: A Framework for Audio-language Understanding." arXiv preprint arXiv:2305.10790. (Proposes a framework for unified audio-language understanding.)

Goyal, G., et al. (2022). "Zero-shot audio classification with text-augmented contrastive learning." In IEEE Spoken Language Technology Workshop (SLT). (Another approach to zero-shot audio classification using text augmentation.)

Hershey, S., et al. (2017). "CNN architectures for large-scale audio classification." In 2017 IEEE International Conference on Acoustics, Speech and Signal Processing (ICASSP). (Introduced CNN architectures for large-scale audio classification and the AudioSet dataset.)

Huang, R., et al. (2023). "Make-An-Audio: Text-To-Audio Generation with Prompt-Enhanced Diffusion Models." In International Conference on Acoustics, Speech, and Signal Processing (ICASSP). (Uses prompt-enhanced diffusion models for high-quality text-to-audio generation.)

Kreuk, F., et al. (2022). "AudioGen: Textually guided audio generation." arXiv preprint arXiv:2209.15352. (A representative work on textually guided audio generation.)

Lee, H., & Palmer, S. (2025). Prompt engineering in higher education: a systematic review to help inform curricula. International Journal of Educational Technology in Higher Education.

Liu, R., et al. (2023). "AudioLDM: Text-to-Audio Generation with Latent Diffusion Models." In International Conference on Machine Learning (ICML). (Applies Latent Diffusion Models (LDMs) to the task of text-to-audio generation.)

McFee, B., et al. (2015). "librosa: Audio and music signal analysis in python." In Proceedings of the 14th Python in Science Conference (SciPy). (The de-facto standard Python library for audio and music signal analysis.)

Mei, Y., et al. (2023). "Audio Understanding with Large Language Models: A Survey." arXiv preprint arXiv:2310.16065. (A comprehensive survey on the application of LLMs to audio understanding tasks.)

Mollick, E. and Euchner, J.: "Pedagogy in the Age of AI: Exploring Generative AI for Higher Education", Journal of Information Technology & Information Management, Vol. 33, No. 1, pp. 1-17 (2024) 1.

Moseley, B., et al. (2020). "Finite-basis physics-informed neural networks (FBPINNs): A scalable domain decomposition approach for solving differential equations." arXiv preprint arXiv:2007.04560. (Applies PINNs to wave-based problems, highly relevant for acoustics.)

Müller, M., & Zalkow, F. (2022). PCP Notebooks: A Preparation Course for Python with a Focus on Signal Processing. Journal of Open Source Education.

National Institution for Academic Degrees and Quality Enhancement of Higher Education: "The Use of Large Language Models (LLMs) in University Education" (2024) 14.

Ohio University Center for Teaching & Learning: "Teaching & Learning with Generative AI" (2024).

Paszke, A., et al. (2019). "PyTorch: An imperative style, high-performance deep learning platform." Advances in Neural Information Processing Systems (NeurIPS). (The foundational paper for the PyTorch deep learning framework.)

Piczak, K. J. (2015). "Environmental sound classification with convolutional neural networks." In 2015 IEEE 25th International Workshop on Machine Learning for Signal Processing (MLSP). (A seminal paper applying CNNs to environmental sound classification.)

Purwins, H., et al. (2019). "Deep learning for audio signal processing." Journal of the Acoustical Society of America (JASA). (A comprehensive review of deep learning applications in audio signal processing.)

Radford, A., et al. (2021). "Learning transferable visual models from natural language supervision." In International Conference on Machine Learning (ICML). (The "CLIP" paper for vision. It inspired many prompt-based contrastive learning models in other domains, including audio.)

Raissi, M., Perdikaris, P., & Karniadakis, G. E. (2019). "Physics-informed neural networks: A deep learning framework for solving forward and inverse problems involving nonlinear partial differential equations." Journal of Computational Physics. (The landmark paper that introduced Physics-Informed Neural Networks (PINNs).)

Shukla, K., et al. (2021). "Physics-Informed Neural Networks for Acoustic Wave Propagation." In AIAA Scitech 2021 Forum. (A direct application of PINNs for solving acoustic wave propagation.)

Thomas, D. B., & Christensen, M. G. (2014). Using Python to teach mathematics, physics, and acoustics. The Journal of the Acoustical Society of America.

Virtanen, T., et al. (2018). Computational analysis of sound scenes and events. Springer. (A foundational book on the computational analysis of sound scenes and events.)

Wei, J., Wang, X., Schuurmans, D., et al. (2022). Chain-of-Thought Prompting Elicits Reasoning in Large Language Models. arXiv.

Yang, Y. S., et al. (2021). "TorchAudio: A library for audio and speech processing." In IEEE International Conference on Acoustics, Speech and Signal Processing (ICASSP). (The official PyTorch-based library for audio and speech processing.)

Yoshida, T.: "An Attempt at Acoustics Education in the Faculty of Information and Culture", Journal of the Japan Society for Information and Culture, Vol. 12, No. 1, pp. 69-74 (2005) 6.

CLASSROOM REGISTRATION VIA THE INTERNET OF THINGS

Zhelyazko Terziyski[1], Daniela Orozova[1], Nadezhda Angelova[1] and Margarita Terziyska[2]
[1]*Department of Informatics and Mathematics, Faculty of Economics, Trakia University Stara Zagora 6000, Bulgaria*
[2]*Department of Mathematics, Physics and Information Technologies, Faculty of Economics, University of Food Technologies, 4002 Plovdiv, Bulgaria*

ABSTRACT

The use of the Internet of Things (IoT) in e-learning creates new opportunities for automating administrative tasks and enhancing interaction between teachers and students. This paper introduces an IoT-based system for automatic attendance tracking that fits into an intelligent learning environment. The system utilizes a local web server that generates a web page for registration via any Wi-Fi network, eliminating the need for an additional application. Access is provided through an address assigned by the teacher, ensuring platform independence and ease of use. Only one participant can register from each device, thereby minimizing abuse and errors. This system is convenient for both students and teachers, simplifying attendance management and easily integrating with e-learning platforms, assessment systems, and administrative portals. In addition to the educational context, it can also be used for organizing events, seminars, and remote learning sessions.

KEYWORDS

Education, Internet of Things, Classroom, Registration System

1. INTRODUCTION

As digital technologies become increasingly widespread in education, e-learning is becoming a vital part of modern learning methods. E-learning offers flexibility by removing time and space limitations, promotes self-directed learning, and provides easy access to resources across various platforms and devices (Moore et al., 2011). In this context, Internet of Things (IoT) technologies are being increasingly utilized to automate tasks and create adaptive, intelligent learning environments.

The integration of IoT in education is part of the broader concept of smart classrooms, which use sensors, mobile devices, local area networks, and data management software to enhance teaching and learning (Mohanty et al., 2016). These environments enable the collection and analysis of real-time data, supporting informed decision-making by educators and educational institutions. IoT devices can monitor parameters such as attendance, participation, noise levels, temperature, lighting, and even biometric indicators that influence learning performance (Mehta et al., 2016).

Student attendance is a key indicator of engagement and success. Although it can be tracked manually through the classic attendance form, this process is often inefficient. IoT-based solutions enable automation of this process without the need for specialized mobile apps or physical interaction with hardware, while ensuring accuracy, traceability, and protection against abuse (Xu et al., 2020).

Research shows that using IoT in education improves efficiency in managing the learning process and increases student satisfaction (Ojo et al., 2019). For example, “smart” attendance registration systems that use local Wi-Fi networks and web interfaces enable students to easily identify themselves at the start of classes, whether they are on campus or participating remotely. This is especially useful for large courses and programs with many participants, where manual verification is impractical.

Furthermore, IoT contributes to the environmental sustainability of the educational setting by promoting more efficient use of resources and reducing physical materials like paper and attendance cards (Zeeshan et al., 2013). Access and attendance management systems can be integrated with Learning Management Systems (LMS) such as Moodle, Blackboard, and Canvas, enabling centralized data management and archiving.

As a result of these trends, the need for intuitive, cost-effective, and adaptable IoT solutions for e-learning is growing more important. This research introduces a system that automates attendance tracking through a local IoT web server, without requiring special software from students. This solution not only aims to enhance efficiency but also to broaden the application of such technologies across a wide range of educational and professional settings—from university classes to conferences and online training.

This research aims to develop and empirically validate an IoT-based system for automatic student attendance registration in a classroom. The main requirements for the system include:

- Intuitiveness and accessibility without requiring additional applications to be installed.
- Minimal physical contact with the system's hardware infrastructure.
- Potential for reuse in other educational and professional settings - seminars, conferences, webinars;
- Higher accuracy and reliability compared to traditional methods of marking attendance.

2. MATERIALS AND METHODS

An IoT-based system, including a local web server, was developed to meet the requirements. The microcontroller performs the function of an IoT web server, builds its own Wi-Fi network, and allows students to register by entering the server's IP address in a web browser. The data from each registration session is stored on an SD card and can be easily transferred to other devices for subsequent processing and archiving.

Registration is carried out via any mobile or desktop device with a Wi-Fi connection – smartphone, tablet, or laptop. This allows the hardware module to be positioned flexibly in the learning environment, without requiring physical contact between students and the system. The developed system is based on a four-layer IoT architecture, presented in Figure 1a.

The Perception layer includes all the sensors and actuators of the system that communicate with the surrounding environment. In this case, these are the devices with which students log in for registration.

The network layer distributes and stores data received or sent by devices in the IoT ecosystem. It is responsible for the physical transfer of data between different devices. Various communication protocols can be used in this layer – TCP/IP, 6LoWPAN, Zigbee, LoRaWAN, Bluetooth Low Energy, etc. In this case, the TCP/IP protocol, which is the main protocol for the Internet, including IoT, was used.

The Processing layer in the IoT architecture is responsible for collecting, analyzing, and interpreting data. It includes both software and hardware components. This layer receives raw data from devices, processes it, and performs further analysis or action. In this study, an SD card was used as the hardware component, which stores the list of registered students in the course, as well as a log file with the actions of each participant and their IP address.

The Application Layer is the layer for communication with the user. It is responsible for providing the client with software resources to monitor or influence the IoT. For example, when selecting a name from the list, the application layer is responsible for providing the information to the IoT server and subsequently distributing this information to all clients connected to the local network, particularly to the specific server. For this purpose, the WebSocket protocol is used to update users' information automatically. WebSocket establishes a permanent connection between the client and the server through a WebSocket handshake process. This process allows two-way communication between the two parties using a TCP connection. This means that data can be sent from the client to the server and from the server to the client asynchronously.

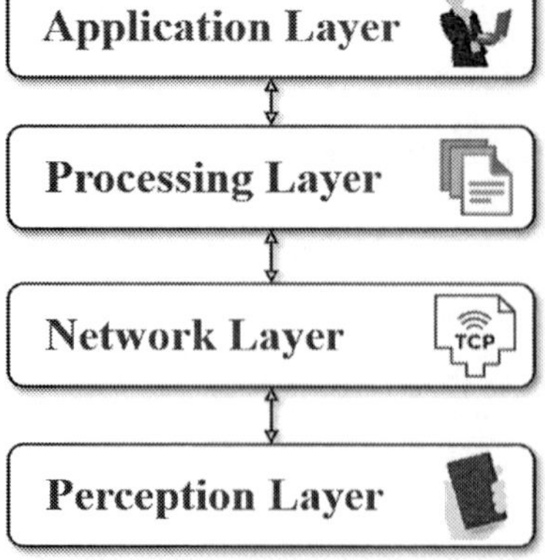

(a)

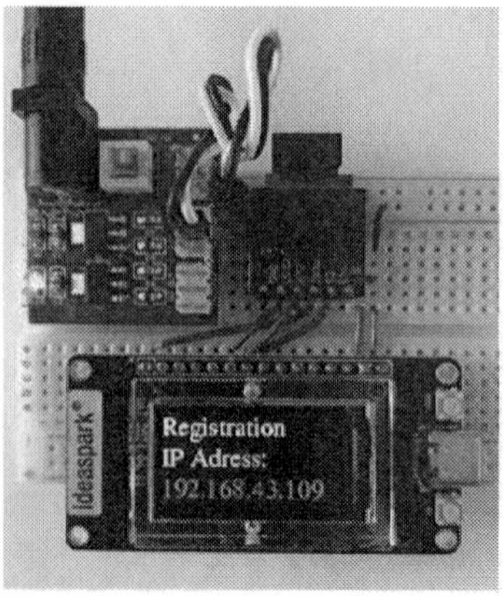

(b)

Figure 1. Architecture and hardware part of the system: (a) Proposed 4-layer IoT architecture; (b) Photo of a prototype

A prototype of the module is shown in Figure 1b. It was tested in the classes of students majoring in Software Engineering at Trakia University in Stara Zagora. The prototype has been tested for work with up to 30 participants. In theory, the maximum number of clients is determined by the possible IP addresses in the network, and their number can cover the number of seats in each hall.

The hardware used is only an ESP32 microcontroller, a display, an SD card, and a power supply. The entire hardware costs 20-25 euros, which makes the system extremely affordable and easy to configure.

The software uses several programming languages - HTML5, CSS, JavaScript, and C for the Arduino IDE development environment.

3. FLOWCHART OF THE IOT ECOSYSTEM

The system operation algorithm follows a logical sequence that includes: initialization of the local IoT server, teacher login to the system, starting an event (class), accepting and processing registration requests from participants, as well as recording and updating information on an SD card.

The entire process is visualized in Figure 2, divided into two logical flows:

(a) Lecturer Process: When the system is started, the local server is initialized and started. The system enters a mode waiting for the lecturer to log in. After a successful login, an interface with the available classes for the specific day is displayed. The lecturer selects the relevant class and starts the class session, which puts the system into an active mode for accepting registration from client devices.

(b) Participant registration process: When sending a registration request from a client device, the system checks whether:

- The device is being used for the first registration – in this case, a new entry is created in the SD card;
- A registration has already been made from the same device – then the existing entry is updated, replacing the old registration with a new one.

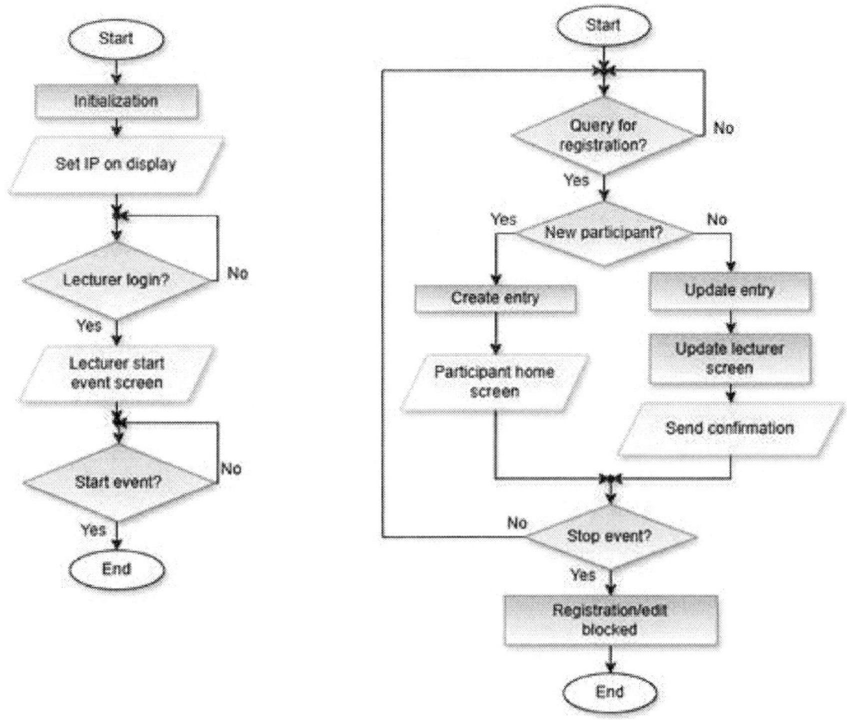

(a) (b)

Figure 2. Flowchart of the registration process via the Internet of Things: (a) Login to the system by the lecturer and start of the event; (b) Registration process

4. REGISTRATION PROCESS

When the system is turned on, it displays the server's IP address, which is used for user access. There are two types of users – lecturer and event participant. The lecturer gains access via the address <IP address>/lecturer, after which he must enter a password and username. The login data for the system is saved in the controller program and cannot be changed at this stage.

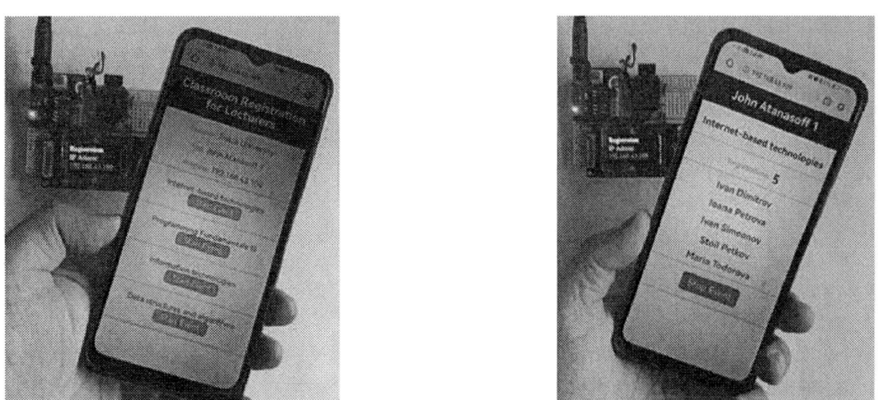

(a) (b)

Figure 3. Lecturer screen: (a) Initialization and start event screen; (b) Registration process

The lecturer starts the registration process by clicking on the button for a given event (Figure 3a). Any change or registration of a participant during the event is automatically reflected on the lecturer's page. Registration ends by selecting the "Event end" button (Figure 3b). This terminates participants' ability to perform actions on a new registration or a class participant change.

Participants can register by first connecting to the server's WiFi network. A WebSocket handshake procedure establishes a connection between the server and the participant. The participant enters an IP address into their browser; a page is displayed that includes a list of participants for registration (Figure 4a) - there is no need to enter a username and password, because the system authenticates the device by IP address. After selecting a name, the client sends a registration request to the server. The server processes the request and performs registration if this device does not already have one. It sends information about the registration to the participant and saves the new registration or change to an SD card. The participant sees the reflected change with his name, which is now associated with a specific IP address (Figure 4b).

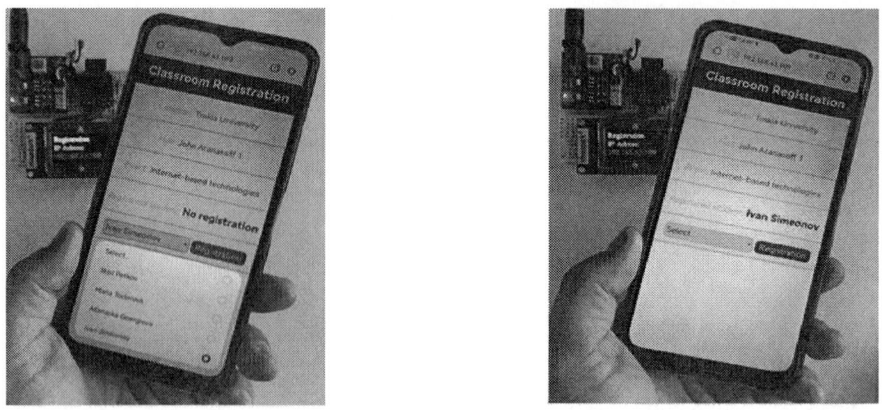

(a) (b)

Figure 4. Participant screen: (a) After connecting to the IoT server, (b) After registration

The server has information about all connected clients to the system and their corresponding IP addresses. A given device (client) always receives the same address, regardless of how often it is connected and disconnected from the local network. In this way, it is ensured that one device can only register one participant. This measure was introduced because the system is intended for use primarily in the educational process and thus prevents false registrations.

5. RESULTS

5.1 Registration Time and Errors

For the purpose of empirical evaluation, a comparison was made between the proposed IoT system and the traditional manual registration method using a paper list. The experiments were conducted in a real learning environment with different numbers of participants – 5, 10, 20, and 30 people. Ten test sessions were performed for each group, and Table 1 presents the average registration times (in seconds).

Manual registration showed increasing time with increasing number of participants and the occurrence of human errors – one error with 20 participants and three with 30. In contrast, the IoT-based system reported 100% correctness in all test sessions and showed higher time stability, regardless of the number of participants.

Table 1. Average time for registration via IoT and manual registration

Number of participants	Registration via IoT (s) /when connected to WiFi/	Manual registration
5	54	63
10	52	107
20	61	223
30	51	342

5.2 Security and Protection Against Abuse

The proposed system uses an IP-based authentication mechanism and a check for an already registered device via WebSocket communication. This eliminates the possibility of duplicate registration from the same device. A hardware-set password protects administrator access (of the teacher).

Table 2. Security analysis

Vulnerability	Potential risk	Solution
Duplicate registration	False attendances	IP-based control and WebSocket validation
Data security	Information manipulation	No close contact with the hardware module. No data is transmitted to other devices.

5.3 Durability and Reliability

To verify the reliability and resilience of the system, tests were conducted for client reconnections, server restarts, and simulated connection loss. These tests yielded the following results:

- the unique IP address of the client is preserved;
- re-registration with the same device is blocked;
- participant registration and the WebSocket connection are automatically restored.

This confirms the system's resilience to typical disruptions in a learning environment.

Similar solutions in the literature use facial recognition systems (Darshan et al, 2024), RFID systems (Nguyen et al, 2017), or mobile application-based (Anwar and Gangodkar, 2015). Compared to them, the present solution has several advantages:

- does not require application installation;
- low cost and hardware complexity;
- high flexibility and easy maintenance.

The proposed architecture uses lighter communication (WebSocket) and a simple and intuitive user interface.

In addition to the advantages, some disadvantages have also been noted, which will be addressed in the future work of the team:

- Need for an additional hardware module;
- Participants must be recorded on an SD card in advance, and the results must be downloaded manually.
- The lecturer's password cannot be changed.

6. CONCLUSIONS

In this study, an automated attendance registration system based on an Internet of Things architecture was developed, implemented, and experimentally validated in a learning environment. The system uses an ESP32 microcontroller as a web server, an SD card, and WebSocket communication, providing a low-cost, reliable, easy-to-use solution applicable to academic and organizational settings.

The results show a significantly reduced registration time compared to the traditional manual procedure and the elimination of the possibility of duplicate registration and human errors. The tests confirmed the system's resilience to interruptions and restoration of the connection, and its effectiveness with different numbers of simultaneous users. In addition, the comparative analysis against existing technologies (facial recognition, RFID, mobile applications) highlights the advantages of the proposed solution in terms of price, flexibility, simplicity, and independence from external software.

The limitations of the current prototype – the need for manual pre-loading of user data and the lack of dynamic management of administrative settings – will be overcome through future functionality expansion, including the development of a centralized management platform and cloud-based data storage.

In conclusion, the presented solution demonstrates the practical potential of IoT technologies for digitalization and optimization of processes in the educational sphere, while combining high efficiency, low complexity, and a high degree of adaptability to different environments and usage scenarios.

7. FUTURE WORK

Future development directions for the system include building a centralized cloud IoT platform to provide aggregated storage, access, and analysis of attendance data from multiple smart classrooms. The platform will automatically transfer records from local IoT devices to a remote server, eliminating the need to retrieve information from SD cards manually.

The main functionalities envisaged for integration include:

- Event archiving;
- A teacher dashboard to monitor current registrations, historical data, and anomalies;
- An analytical module based on artificial intelligence methods to analyze attendance data to detect patterns of behavior and participation habits, assess the correlation between attendance and academic success, and predict dropout or at-risk groups of students.

In the long term, it is planned to expand the hardware functionality with additional sensors for monitoring the learning environment, allowing for an even more complete assessment of the factors influencing the learning process.

Future development aims to create an innovative ecosystem for attendance management, which would not only automate administrative activities but also serve as a tool for pedagogical and strategic analysis in the context of the digital transformation of education.

ACKNOWLEDGEMENT

This work is supported by the frames of Bulgarian National Recovery and Resilience Plan, Component "Innovative Bulgaria", the Project № BG-RRP-2.004-0006-C02 "Development of research and innovation at Trakia University in service of health and sustainable well-being".

REFERENCES

Anwar, M.A. and Gangodkar, D. (2015). Design and implementation of mobile phones based attendance marking system. 2015 Communication, Control and Intelligent Systems (CCIS), pp.120–123.

Darshan, V., Kenny, D.S., Shreyas, H.R., Vinay, N. and Revathi, S. (2024). IoT Based Attendance Monitoring System Using Facial Recognition. 2024 Second International Conference on Advances in Information Technology (ICAIT), 1, pp.1–6.

Delinov, E., Orozova, D., Angelova, N. and Terziyski, Z. (2024). An approach for establishment of a Smart Classroom. International Conference on Virtual Learning, 19, pp.15–22. DOI: 10.58503/icvl-v19y202401.

Mohanty, S. P., Choppali, U., & Kougianos, E. (2016). Everything you wanted to know about smart cities: The Internet of things is the backbone. IEEE consumer electronics magazine, 5(3), 60-70.

Mehta, R., Sahni, J., & Khanna, K. (2018). Internet of things: Vision, applications and challenges. Procedia computer science, 132, 1263-1269.

Moore, J. L., Dickson-Deane, C., & Galyen, K. (2011). e-Learning, online learning, and distance learning environments: Are they the same?. The Internet and higher education, 14(2), 129-135.

Nguyen, H.K. and Chew, M.T. (2017). RFID-based attendance management system. 2017 2nd Workshop on Recent Trends in Telecommunications Research (RTTR), pp.1–6.

Ojo, O., Kareem, M. K., Odunuyi, S., & UGWUNNA, C. (2022). An internet-of-things based real-time monitoring system for smart classroom. Journal of the Nigerian Society of Physical Sciences, 297-309.

Xu, B., Da Xu, L., Cai, H., Xie, C., Hu, J., & Bu, F. (2014). Ubiquitous data accessing method in IoT-based information system for emergency medical services. IEEE Transactions on Industrial informatics, 10(2), 1578-1586.

Zeeshan, K., Hamalainen, T., & Neittaanmäki, P. (2022). Internet of Things for sustainable smart education: An overview. Sustainability, 14(7), 4293.

EXAMINING THE ROLE OF METACOGNITIVE PROMPTS ON LEARNING BEHAVIOR DURING CIRCUIT ANALYSIS PROBLEM-SOLVING IN CBLE: AN EPISTEMIC NETWORK ANALYSIS APPROACH

Jyoti Shaha, Amit Paikrao and Ramkumar Rajendran
Centre for Educational technology
Indian Institute of Technology Bombay, India

ABSTRACT

This study examines the impact of metacognitive prompts on electrical engineering students' learning behavior during problem-solving in a computer-based learning environment. This research study uses Epistemic Network Analysis (ENA) to investigate behavioral differences between students who received metacognitive prompts and those who solved problems without prompts. Thirty-two undergraduate electrical engineering students were randomly assigned to an experimental group ($n = 16$) receiving metacognitive prompts and a control group ($n = 16$) without prompts. Data collection involved interaction log data during problem-solving. We used ENA to identify differences in prominent and co-occurring actions between experimental and control groups. ENA analysis along the X-axis revealed statistically significant differences between groups. using a Mann-Whitney U test: control group (median = 0.09, $N = 16$) versus experimental group (median = -0.13, $N = 16$), $U = 247.00$, $p < .001$. The findings indicate that the control group's behaviors were oriented toward information-seeking activities, while the experimental group demonstrated greater integration of problem-solving actions with resource utilization. The results highlight the impact of metacognitive prompts on students' learning behavior during problem-solving in CBLE.

KEYWORDS

Epistemic Network Analysis, Learning Behavior, CBLE, Problem-Solving, Metacognitive Prompts, Circuit Analysis

1. INTRODUCTION

Metacognition refers to an individual's awareness of their own thinking processes and the ability to monitor and regulate these processes while engaged in a task (Ochilova, V. R., 2021). The concept of metacognition has been defined by numerous researchers. The foundational concept of metacognition was first introduced by Flavell in the 1970s, who proposed a comprehensive metacognitive model comprising four interrelated components: metacognitive goals, metacognitive experiences, metacognitive knowledge, and metacognitive strategies (Flavell, 1979). This conceptualization of metacognition was subsequently refined by Schraw and Moshman (1995), who distinguished between two core components: knowledge of cognition and regulation of cognition. Knowledge of cognition encompasses an individual's awareness and understanding of their cognitive processes across three dimensions: declarative knowledge (awareness of existing strategies), procedural knowledge (understanding of strategy application), and conditional knowledge (understanding of when and why particular strategies should be employed). Regulation of cognition, in contrast, encompasses the active processes that guide and control learning, including planning, monitoring, and evaluation.

Metacognition is essential in problem-solving because it involves awareness and regulation of one's own cognitive processes, which significantly enhances problem-solving effectiveness (Sijmkens, E. et al., 2023). It includes both knowledge about cognition (understanding one's own thinking) and regulation of cognition (planning, monitoring, and evaluating one's problem-solving strategies) (Sijmkens, E. et al., 2024). Metacognition plays a critical role in problem-solving as it helps students to understand when, why, where, and how to use their own knowledge to solve problems successfully (Güner, P. & Erbay, H.N., 2021). Metacognition enables students not only to carry out the steps of problem-solving but also to regulate and manage the entire process (Güner, P. & Erbay, H.N., 2021). Often, learners already possess metacognitive skills, but do not perform them spontaneously (Lim L. et al.,2023). Metacognitive knowledge and skills are essential for problem-solving, and active engagement in metacognitive skills during the process is equally critical (Sijmkens, E. et al., 2024).

Metacognitive prompts were established as instructional support to help students regulate their learning and problem-solving processes (Bulu, S. T., & Pedersen, S., 2012). Metacognitive prompts can be hints, clues, or questions, tools that target the learners' metacognition. There have been several studies so far that developed and analysed the impact of metacognitive prompts in problem-solving. In Kimberly's study, the prompts were provided to students through a combination of lectures and workshops. The Goldilocks Help: problem-solving workflow integrates metacognitive prompts into lectures and workshops for chemistry students. This study looks at how teaching assistants use these prompts to improve problem-solving in chemistry (Kimberly V., 2023). Similarly, BioWorld, an intelligent tutoring system, supports medical students' diagnostic clinical reasoning through metacognitive scaffolding embedded in an integrative evidence tool/panel. Metacognitive scaffolding tools support reflective activities like categorizing and prioritizing evidence. This study used descriptive statistics to overview data to examine how the frequency of different scaffolding usages predicted students' metacognitive monitoring accuracy and problem-solving efficiency (Wang, T., et. al, 2023). Sijmkens E. analyzed how discipline- and topic-specific reflective prompts, implemented as metacognitive scaffolding in an online tool Disciplinary Learning Companion (DLC), supported first-year physics students in regulating their problem-solving processes. The study investigates the relationships between interaction with the DLC (module completion) and academic achievement (Sijmkens, E., et al., 2024). Shin (2023) designed metacognitive scaffolding prompts for planning, monitoring, and reflection, which were incorporated into problem-analysis phases to guide students during programming problem-solving. Responses to these prompts were collected on paper. This study looks into how metacognitive prompting affects beginner programmers' ability to solve problems, manage cognitive load, and self-regulate their learning. The study used both quantitative data (test scores, cognitive load ratings, self-regulation scores) and qualitative process data (planning and reflection notes) to provide a comprehensive understanding of the effects of cognitive and metacognitive scaffolding in programming learning (Shin, Y., et al, 2023).

Despite the existing research on metacognitive prompts in problem-solving, there is less focus on engineering problem-solving in CBLE and unfold how learning is happening using interaction log data. In order to address this gap, the present study examines how metacognitive prompts influence students' interaction behaviors during circuit analysis problem-solving in CBLE. We chose a circuit analysis problem-solving task. Research suggests that students struggle not necessarily because they lack basic knowledge, but due to a deficiency in metacognitive skills. Metacognition is crucial for effective problem-solving in circuit analysis. Therefore, developing these metacognitive skills could lead to better student performance (Moses, K.R., 2019)

We conducted the study with 32 undergraduate engineering students. We randomly divide them into an experimental group receiving metacognitive prompts and a control group without any prompts. We analyzed the students' interaction with the CBLE to identify differences in prominent and co-occurring actions between experimental and control groups using Epistemic Network Analysis (ENA).

2. METHODOLOGY

2.1 Participants

The study was conducted with 32 second-year undergraduate Electrical Engineering students who participated voluntarily. Participants ranged from 19 to 20 years of age, with the sample comprising 7 females and 25 males. The Institutional Research Board (IRB) approved the study prior to implementation, and researchers secured informed consent from all participants. No monetary incentives were provided for participation.

To maintain consistency and minimize external distractions, the study was conducted in a controlled laboratory setting. Participants were randomly assigned to one of two groups: an experimental group ($n = 16$; 4 females, 12 males) that interacted with MetaGuru, containing embedded metacognitive prompts, and a control group ($n = 16$; 3 females, 13 males) that used the same environment without prompts.

2.2 Learning Environment

MetaGuru is a computer-based learning environment (CBLE) designed to foster metacognitive strategies through metacognitive prompts in circuit analysis problem-solving (Shaha, J., Badhe, V., & Rajendran, R. 2024). The platform was developed following instructional design frameworks proposed by Zhang (2022) and Jonassen (D.H.). The platform integrates text, video, images, and worked examples covering the topics needed for circuit analysis problem-solving, like fundamental concepts, DC circuits, and circuit theorems. Each sub-topic concludes with assessment items that provide immediate feedback. Figure 1 illustrates the screenshot of the solution page of MetaGuru. The interface includes several key features. On the left side panel, learners can navigate between different components of the environment, including access to tasks, learning materials, the highlight and annotation pages, a circuit simulator, and a calculator. This panel provides seamless navigation to support task switching and learning material. A countdown timer helps in monitoring the remaining time of the session. The central workplace displays the task, evaluation prompt and space to submit final solution.

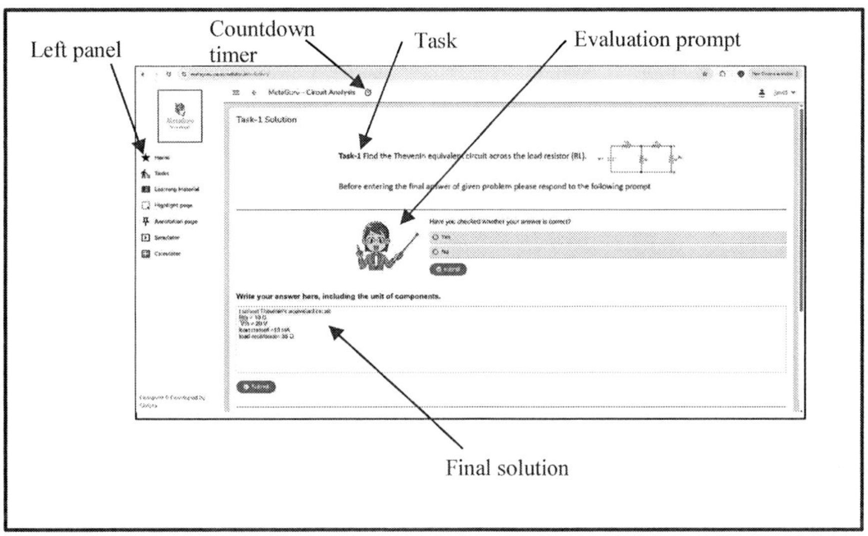

Figure 1. Screenshot of the solution page of MetaGuru

These five prompts were strategically designed to guide individuals through the orientation, planning, monitoring, evaluation, and reflection phases of problem-solving. Each prompt corresponds to a specific phase and aims to stimulate metacognitive skills throughout the problem-solving process (Shaha, J., Badhe, V., & Rajendran, R. 2024). The orientation and planning prompts are displayed on the task page, while the evaluation and reflection prompts appear on the solution page. The monitoring prompt, which helps learners assess the relevance of learning materials to the problem, is displayed as a pop-up window upon the first access of each learning resource. These prompts collectively support learners in following a systematic approach while solving three progressively challenging circuit analysis task. The tasks involve to determine the equivalent circuit and load current using methods such as Thevenin's or Norton's theorem. During problem-solving, learners use paper for calculations and circuit simplifications while simultaneously engaging with system features such as the simulator, highlighting, and annotation tools. Final answers are submitted within the platform, enabling the systematic collection of problem-solving artifacts and interaction data for analysis.

2.3 Study Design

The research study was conducted in a controlled laboratory environment over two distinct sessions, with a total experimental duration of approximately 2 hours and 30 minutes. Figure 2 illustrates the detailed block diagram of the research study design. The study employed a between-subjects experimental design comparing two groups: an experimental group that interacted with the MetaGuru featuring embedded metacognitive prompts, and a control group that used the same environment without prompts. Both groups completed study activities individually in the controlled setting.

All Participants first completed a 30-minute pre-test designed to assess their prior knowledge of circuit analysis concepts. The test included both multiple-choice and problem-solving items, establishing a baseline knowledge measure before CBLE exposure. Participants were randomly assigned to the experimental and control groups according to a predetermined randomized allocation list, ensuring unbiased distribution between the two groups. After this partition, participants received a 15-minute introduction to their respective MetaGuru CBLEs. During the subsequent 15-minute exploration phase, both groups explored their respective MetaGuru environment.

In the final 90-minute problem-solving phase, learners from both groups engaged with an identical set of three circuit analysis problems presented on the task page. Each problem required learners to determine two key aspects: the equivalent circuit of a given complex electrical network and the load current flowing through a specified load resistor. Learners could apply any appropriate circuit analysis technique, such as Thevenin's theorem, Norton's theorem, or other relevant methods, to solve these problems.

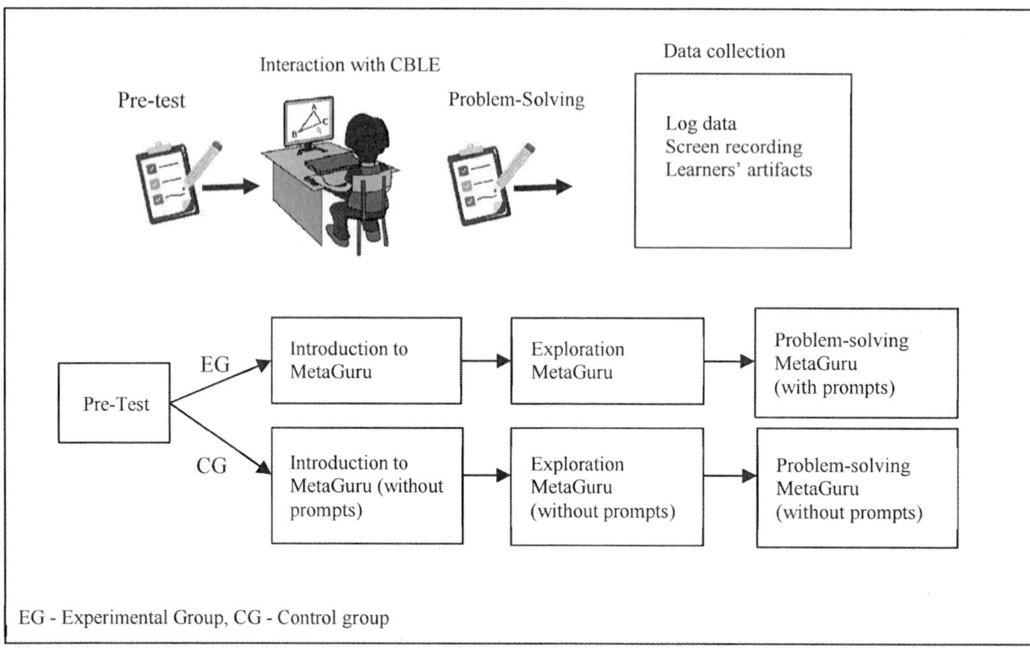

Figure 2. Block diagram of research study design

While interacting with MetaGuru, learners received paper to perform calculations and circuit simplifications. Upon completing their solutions, they submitted their final answers through the designated solution submission page in MetaGuru.

2.4 Data Collection

The MetaGuru environment automatically recorded detailed log data of learner interactions. It includes various activities such as videos watched, table of contents viewed, reading page visits, monitoring countdown timer, visits to video pages, attempted self-assessment questions, solution submissions of three tasks, visits to simulation pages, and usage of features like highlights and annotations, system login, and visits to the introduction page. Log data included the time spent on each action. Table 1 illustrates the actions captured and the description of the actions. We collected learners' generated artifacts from three problem-solving tasks. Since participants completed problem-solving activities on paper rather than within the digital environment, the MetaGuru system could not automatically capture these actions in the log data. To address this limitation, we employed screen recording technology to document problem-solving behaviors and subsequently integrated these observations into our comprehensive log dataset.

Table 1. Description of Actions captured in MetaGuru

Actions captured	Description of actions
Highlights_Annotation	The highlighting/annotating feature is used
Introduction	Visiting the Introduction of MetaGuru page
Monitoring_Time	Monitoring countdown timer
Note_taking	Note-taking from a reading page or while watching the video
Problem_Solving	Solving the problem, calculations
Reading	Reading learning material
Self_assessment	Responding to the self-assessment questions
Simulation	Interacting with the Simulation page
TOC_consulting	Visiting the Table of Contents
Video_Watching	The video is played, paused, and seek
solution-submitted	Solution of the task submitted

3. RESULTS AND DISCUSSION

To establish the homogeneity of participants' prior knowledge before the intervention, a pre-test was administered to both the experimental and control groups. The experimental group obtained a mean score of 7.63 (SD = 2.15), while the control group achieved a mean score of 6.25 (SD = 2.90). A Mann-Whitney U test was conducted to examine whether there was a significant difference in pre-test scores between the experimental and control groups. The results indicated no statistically significant difference between the two groups, $U=161.0$, $p=0.209$. This suggests that the experimental (Median=8.0) and control (Median=6.0) groups had comparable levels of prior knowledge of circuit analysis concepts.

To investigate the learners' behavior in MetaGuru during problem-solving, we used Epistemic Network Analysis (ENA). The action captured and description of actions are described in Table 1. Figure 3 illustrates the centroids of action networks for both the experimental and control groups.

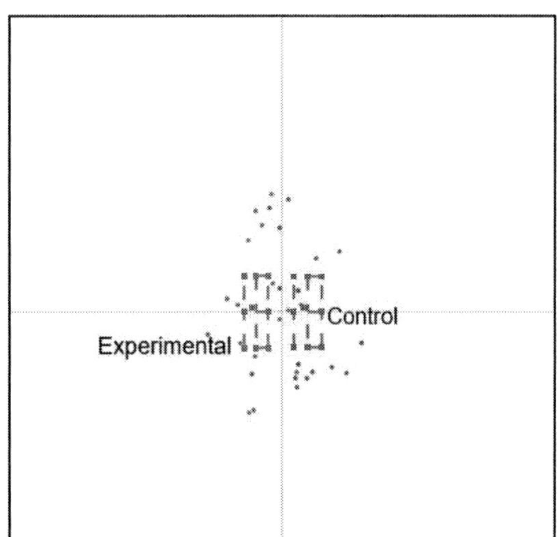

Figure 3. The ENA model of Centroids of actions of experimental and control groups

The experimental group is represented in blue, and the control group in red. Each dot represents an individual participant, while the surrounding boxes denote the confidence intervals of the group distributions. The spatial positioning of the centroids highlights the differences in action patterns between the two groups. The centroids, representing the average network for each group, are distinctly separated along the horizontal axis. This separation indicates that the metacognitive prompts led the experimental group to adopt a learning process that is statistically significantly different from the control group. Along the X axis, a Mann-Whitney test showed that the control group (Median=0.09, N=16) is statistically significantly different at the alpha=0.05 level from the experimental group (Median=-0.13, N=16, U=247.00, $p < .001$).

Figure 4 illustrates the ENA model of the comparison plot between the control and experimental groups.

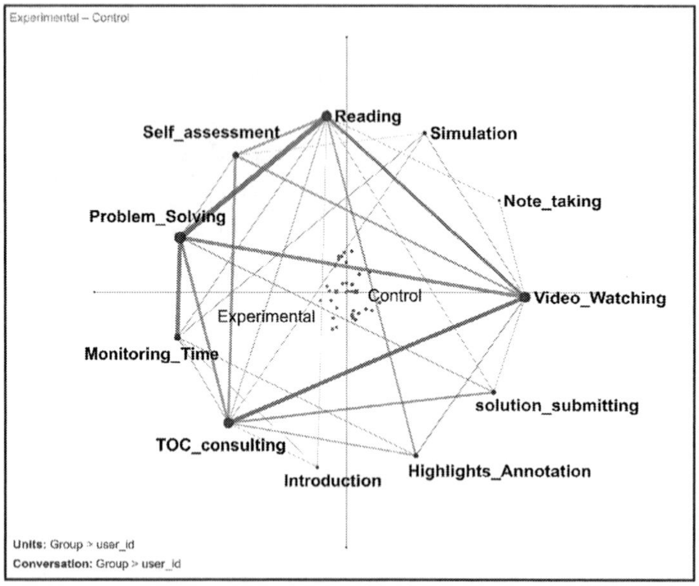

Figure 4. The ENA model of the Comparison plot between the experimental and control groups

The ENA model for the control group (in red colour) is characterized by a dominant triangular pattern between Reading, Video_Watching, and TOC_consulting nodes. The thick edges forming this triangular configuration suggest that participants without metacognitive prompts engaged primarily in repetitive cycles of information seeking. Their learning strategy involved continuous navigation between reading materials, watching videos, and consulting the table of contents, presumably to locate relevant information. While other behaviors, such as Self-assessment and Problem-solving, are present in the network, their connections to this central information-seeking loop are weaker. This pattern indicates that problem-solving and self-assessment activities remained largely disconnected from the learners' primary information-seeking processes. The observed behavioral pattern reflects a reactive approach centered on content consumption rather than problem-solving.

In contrast, the experimental group's network demonstrates a more complex and integrated behavioral pattern. While the connection between Reading and Video_Watching persists, it has been integrated into a broader network of goal-oriented actions, i.e., problem-solving actions. The model reveals several notable strengthened connections: Problem-Solving and Reading nodes exhibit stronger connectivity, suggesting that learners receiving metacognitive prompts were more likely to establish direct connections between material comprehension and problem-solving activities. The robust connection between Problem-Solving and Self-assessment indicates that the experimental group engaged in continuous evaluation of their understanding during active problem-solving phases. Additionally, the connection between Problem_Solving and Monitoring_Time highlights the integration of time management strategies directly into the metacognitive strategies. It shows that metacognitive prompts helped learners to understand the task, activate their metacognitive knowledge, plan strategies, and identify relevant information, while reducing less productive actions such as simulation use, note-taking, highlighting, and visiting the introduction page.

The ENA comparison plot further reveals differences in how each group allocated its attention to specific activities within MetaGuru. The control group displayed higher engagement in activities such as simulation use, note-taking, solution submission, highlight/annotation, and visiting the introduction page. These behaviors, while indicative of effort, are largely peripheral to solving the circuit problems. In contrast, the experimental group exhibited relatively lower engagement with these peripheral activities, but demonstrated stronger and more meaningful coordination among central cognitive and metacognitive actions—particularly problem-solving, reading, self-assessment, and monitoring time.

4. CONCLUSION

This study examined the role of metacognitive prompts in learners' interaction behaviors during circuit analysis problem-solving in a computer-based learning environment. Epistemic Network Analysis (ENA) revealed that the experimental group, supported by prompts, adopted learning processes that were statistically distinct from the control group. Using Epistemic Network Analysis (ENA), we found that learners in the experimental group demonstrated stronger connections between problem-solving actions, self-monitoring, and the use of relevant resources, whereas learners in the control group exhibited more repetitive patterns of information seeking without effective integration into circuit analysis problem-solving.

In addition, analysis of the solution-submitted action further highlighted that control group participants submitted solutions more frequently; however, many submissions were incorrect or included statements indicating an inability to solve the problem. This suggests that, without prompts, learners may attempt solutions without sufficient planning, monitoring, or reflection, resulting in less effective problem-solving outcomes. Overall, the findings suggest that embedding metacognitive prompts appeared to facilitate a shift from information seeking toward more integrated, reflective problem-solving behaviors. It is possible that the prompts encouraged learners to focus on task-oriented actions. This pattern is consistent with prior research. Wang et al. (2021) demonstrated that integrating metacognitive prompts in simulation-based inquiry environments enhances students' engagement in task-relevant activities and improves the efficiency of their problem-solving processes.

While this study provides valuable insights into learner behavior in CBLE during circuit analysis problem-solving, some limitations should be noted. The study involved a relatively small sample size (n=32), which may constrain the generalizability of the findings. Moreover, only behavioral data from log files were analyzed. Future research could strengthen these findings by triangulating ENA results with qualitative methods, such as interviews, think-aloud protocols, to capture learners' reflective processes more directly and clarify the mechanisms through which prompts influence problem-solving behavior.

The findings have implications for designing computer-based learning environments for circuit analysis problem-solving tasks. For educators and researchers, this study offers evidence to guide the integration of metacognitive prompting into CBLE to enhance student engagement in problem-solving, along with seeking relevant information.

ACKNOWLEDGEMENT

The research reported in this paper was supported in part by a TIH-IITB Travel Grant, IIT Bombay. Any opinions, findings, or conclusions expressed in this paper are those of the authors and do not necessarily reflect the views of funders

REFERENCES

Azevedo, R., Bouchet, F., Duffy, M., Harley, J., Taub, M., Trevors, G., ... & Cerezo, R. (2022). Lessons learned and future directions of metatutor: Leveraging multichannel data to scaffold self-regulated learning with an intelligent tutoring system. *Frontiers in Psychology*, 13, 813632.

Bannert, M., Sonnenberg, C., Mengelkamp, C. & Pieger, E. (2015). Short- and long-term effects of students' self-directed metacognitive prompts on navigation behavior and learning performance. *Computers in Human Behavior*, 52, pp.293-306.

Bulu, S.T. & Pedersen, S. (2012). Supporting problem-solving performance in a hypermedia learning environment: The role of students' prior knowledge and metacognitive skills. *Computers in Human Behavior*, 28(4), pp.1162-1169.

Efklides, A. (2008). Metacognition: Defining its facets and levels of functioning in relation to self-regulation and coregulation. *European Psychologist*, 13(4), pp.277-287.

Engelmann, K., Bannert, M. & Melzner, N. (2021). Do self-created metacognitive prompts promote short- and long-term effects in computer-based learning environments? *Research and Practice in Technology Enhanced Learning*, 16(1), p.3.

Flavell, J.H. (1979). Metacognition and cognitive monitoring: A new area of cognitive–developmental inquiry. *American Psychologist*, 34(10), p.906.

Greene, J.A., Moos, D.C. & Azevedo, R. (2011). Self-regulation of learning with computer-based learning environments. *New Directions for Teaching & Learning*, 2011(126).

Guo, L. (2022). Using metacognitive prompts to enhance self-regulated learning and learning outcomes: A meta-analysis of experimental studies in computer-based learning environments. *Journal of Computer Assisted Learning*, 38(3), pp.811-832.

Güner, P. & Erbay, H.N. (2021). Metacognitive skills and problem-solving. *International Journal of Research in Education and Science*, 7(3), pp.715-734.

Kumar, S.N., Lenin Fred, A., Padmanabhan, P., Gulyas, B., Dyson, C., Melba Kani, R. & Ajay Kumar, H. (2021). Multimedia-based learning tools and its scope, applications for the virtual learning environment. *Computational Intelligence in Digital Pedagogy*, pp.47-63.

Marra, R.M., Hacker, D.J. & Plumb, C. (2022). Metacognition and the development of self-directed learning in a problem-based engineering curriculum. *Journal of Engineering Education*, 111(1), pp.137-161.

Moses, K.R. (2019). June. Board 24: The effects of Mobile Circuits Tutor on students' problem-solving self-efficacy and anxiety. In *2019 ASEE Annual Conference & Exposition*.

Ochilova, V.R. (2021). Metacognition and its history. *Frontline Social Sciences and History Journal*, 1(03), pp.18-44.

Pieger, E. & Bannert, M. (2018). Differential effects of students' self-directed metacognitive prompts. *Computers in Human Behavior*, 86, pp.165-173.

Prakash, A. & Rajendran, R. (2025). Decoding learner behavior in virtual reality education: Insights from epistemic network analysis and differential sequence mining. *IEEE Transactions on Visualization and Computer Graphics*.

Schraw, G. & Dennison, R.S. (1994). Assessing metacognitive awareness. *Contemporary Educational Psychology*, 19(4), pp.460-475.

Shaha, J., Badhe, V., & Rajendran, R. (2024). Investigating the Functionality of Metacognitive Prompt during the Circuit Analysis Problem-Solving. International Association for Development of the Information Society.

Shaffer, D.W., Hatfield, D.L., Svarovsky, G.N., Nash, P., Nulty, A., Bagley, E.A. & Frank, K. (2009). Epistemic network analysis: A prototype for 21st century assessment of learning. *International Journal of Learning and Media*, 1(1), pp.1-21.

Shin, Y., Jung, J., Zumbach, J. & Yi, E. (2023). The effects of worked-out example and metacognitive scaffolding on problem-solving programming. *Journal of Educational Computing Research*, 61(6), pp.1312-1331.

Sijmkens, E., De Cock, M. & De Laet, T. (2024). September. The impact of topic-specific vs. generic self-reflection on students' metacognitive abilities, conceptual understanding, and problem-solving strategies. In *European Conference on Technology Enhanced Learning* (pp.406-420). Cham: Springer Nature Switzerland.

Utami, D.D., Setyosari, P., Fajarianto, O., Kamdi, W. & Ulfa, S. (2023). The correlation between metacognitive and problem-solving skills among science students. *EduLine: Journal of Education and Learning Innovation*, 3(1), pp.138-143.

Wang, T., Zheng, J., Tan, C. & Lajoie, S.P. (2023). Computer-based scaffoldings influence students' metacognitive monitoring and problem-solving efficiency in an intelligent tutoring system. *Journal of Computer Assisted Learning*, 39(5), pp.1652-1665.

Wang, H.-S., Chen, S., & Yen, M.-H. (2021). Effects of metacognitive scaffolding on students' performance and confidence judgments in simulation-based inquiry. *Physical Review Physics Education Research*, 17(2), 020108. https://doi.org/10.1103/PhysRevPhysEducRes.17.020108

Zhang, Q. & Lockee, B.B. (2022). Designing a framework to facilitate metacognitive strategy development in computer-mediated problem-solving instruction. *Journal of Formative Design in Learning*, 6(2), pp.127-143.

Zheng, J., Lajoie, S.P., Wang, T. & Li, S. (2023). Supporting self-regulated learning in clinical problem-solving with a computer-based learning environment: The effectiveness of scaffolds. *Metacognition and Learning*, 18(3), pp.693-709.

THE EMOTIONAL DIMENSION OF FLOW

Ehm Kannegieser[1*] and Robert Külpmann[2]
[1]*Fraunhofer Institute of Optronics, System Technologies and Image Exploitation*
Fraunhoferstraße.1, 76131 Karlsruhe, Germany
[2]*Karlsruhe Institute of Technology*
Kaiserstraße 12, 76131 Karlsruhe, Germany

ABSTRACT

Learning activities are often perceived as a tedious work tasks. To address this perception, concepts such as Gamification and Game-Based Learning have been introduced to make learning more enjoyable. Deep focus states, such as Immersion and Flow, describe situations where learners are highly focused and disregard the work aspect of the activity. To verify a hypothesis postulated in previous publications, linking an emotional aspect to the Flow Model, this paper presents a study concept, its execution and discusses the findings about the correlations between achieving a deep focus state and the learner's current emotional state.

KEYWORDS

Learning Motivation, Emotional State, Flow, Immersion

1. INTRODUCTION

The objective of this work is to explore the hypothesis that states of deep focus – i.e. Flow – inherently carry an emotional dimension. By investigating correlations between arousal, valence, and states of deep focus, adding to its quantifiability, the ultimate goal is to improve the understanding of how to elicit Flow in serious games, thereby helping to facilitate faster and more intuitive learning.

Flow, a concept defined by Csikszentmihalyi (Csikszentmihalyi, 1975), is characterized by complete involvement and enjoyment in an activity. He identified key conditions for achieving Flow: clear goals, a balance between perceived skills and challenges, and immediate feedback. Flow is characterized by intense task focus, loss of temporal and spatial awareness, and a sense of reward from the activity. Csikszentmihalyi introduced the concept of Emergent Motivation, where even mundane tasks can become rewarding when experienced in a Flow state.

Immersion which is typically discussed within gaming contexts, refers to the experience of being deeply engaged or interacting with a virtual world as if it were real (Coomans & Timmermann, 1997). Brown and Cairns (Brown & Cairns, 2004) categorized immersion into three stages: Engagement, Engrossment, and Total Immersion. Cheng later expanded this model, incorporating factors like emotional attachment and presence (see Figure 1).

To assess emotional states, various measurement methods exist, such as the Arousal/Valence model (Mandryk & Atkins, 2007), distinguishing between valence (emotional state) and arousal (physiological activity level). The Self-Assessment Manikins (SAM) developed by Lang (Lang, 1980), serves as tools for measuring these dimensions, showing correlations with other models of affect. Russell's Circumplex Model of Affect (CMA), (Russell, 1980) categorizes emotions within a circular framework (see Figure 2), aiding in the understanding of the interplay between arousal and valence.

* 0000-0001-8869-7946

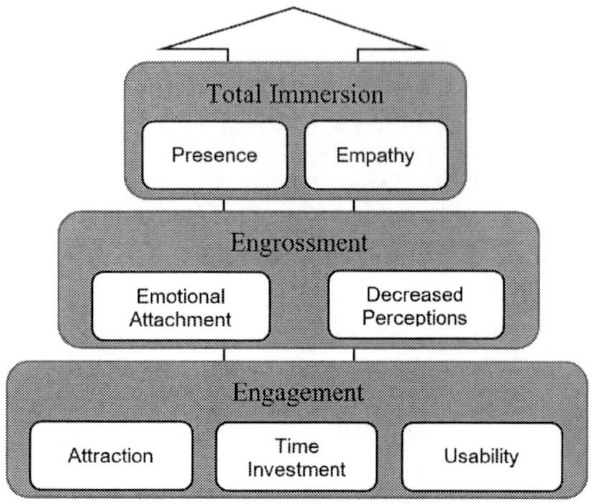

Figure 1. Hierarchical Immersion model presented by Cairns et al. and improved upon by Cheng

Figure 2. Circumplex Model of Affect by Russell

2. PREVIOUS WORK

As both Flow – characterized by optimal performance and intrinsic motivation – as well as Immersion – referring to the psychological experience of being present in a virtual environment – are traditionally assessed using subjective questionnaires, which may disrupt the experience and reduce accuracy, emphasizing the need to establish a more objective measurement framework for Flow and Immersion, potentially relying on physiological metrics alone to avoid disruptions caused by questionnaires.

To enhance measurement reliability and drawing on existing literature to identify overlapping definitions and components (Cairns et al., 2006; Csikszentmihalyi, 1991), the authors proposed a combined model of Flow and Immersion (Kannegieser et al., 2018), overlaying the Flow definition with the more fine grained levels of Immersion and its well defined criteria of sub state traversal (see Figure 3).

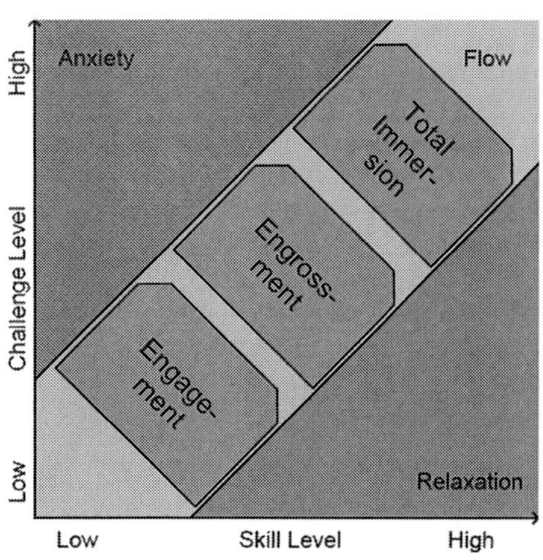

Figure 3. Combined Model of Flow and Immersion

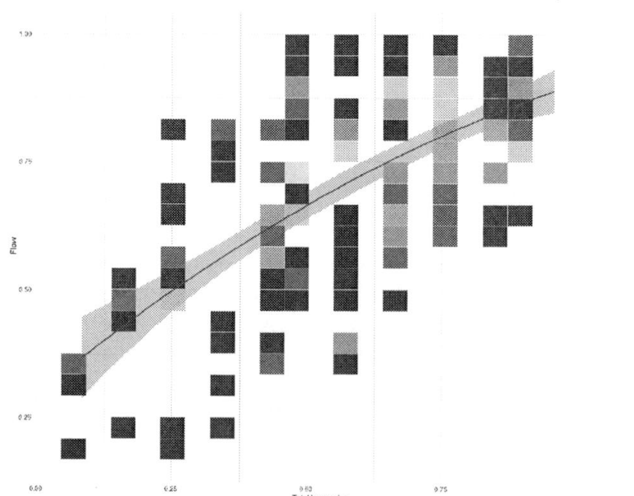

Figure 4. Scatter plot for correlation between Flow and Total Immersion, r=0.65; p<.001; conf=0.95

The hypothesis of a combined model was followed up by a study correlating questionnaire responses with physiological sensor data, such as galvanic skin response (GSR), electrocardiography (ECG), and eye tracking. The findings of this study indicated a strong correlation between Flow and Immersion (see Figure 4), suggesting that Flow may indeed be viewed as an extreme state of Immersion, supporting the hypothesis that Flow and Immersion are interrelated, although correlations between physiological data and questionnaire responses were not as significant (Kannegieser et al., 2019).

3. COMBINED FLOW/IMMERSION WITH EMOTIONAL DIMENSION

When conduction Flow surveys, the emotional state of participants had been neglected, as it wasn't part of the original Flow model, until Massimini and Carli revised Csikszentmihalyi's Flow definition into the 8-Channel model (Massimini & Carli, 1988) bearing an inherent emotional dimension.

When considering the combined model of Flow and Immersion (Kannegieser et al., 2018), incorporating emotional theory allowed for an additional dimension of features beside skill and challenge, thus making it more fine-grained and eventually more quantitative.

Emotional theory includes modeling emotions in various ways: for example, emotions are modeled as single discrete states (Tomkins & Karon, 1962) which then can be measured using facial expressions (Ekman et al., 2012). As emotions may not necessarily be discrete but overlapping, models were introduced that can be used to define emotions in a multidimensional kind of way. Looking at the The first dimension defines the subjective feeling of how attractive the current situation is perceived as. In this context, the term valence is also important, as it also refers to the attractiveness of a situation. The second dimension refers to the strength of the emotion experienced. The final dimension refers attentiveness to the emotion experienced.

Based on Wundt's classification of three emotional dimensions and their antagonists (pleasurable /unpleasurable, arousing/subduing, attain/relaxation)(Wundt, 1897) a multitude of interpretations exist:

Mäntylä (Mäntylä et al., 2016) map emotional states to a two-dimensional space where Valence describes how attractive an experienced situation appears to the subject while Arousal refers to the intensity of the experience.

Bakker (Bakker et al., 2014) defines Arousal as the emotional activation level, described as a combination of mental alertness and physical activity by using the adjectives sleep, inactivity, boredom and relaxation at the lower end and wakefulness, bodily tension, strenuous exercise and concentration at the higher end.

Lane states "Valence refers to the direction of behavioral activation associated with emotion, either toward (appetitive motivation, pleasant emotion) or away from (aversive motivation, unpleasant emotion) a stimulus" and divides it into three levels: pleasant, unpleasant and neutral (Lane et al., 1999).

A fitting foundation for the model extension is Russell's CMA (Russell, 1980) (see Figure 2): a two-dimensional model with Arousal and Valence as the dimensions, representing emotional states at any level of the two dimensions. Through the central and orthogonal positioning of the axes, four quadrants are the result portraying:

- low Arousal, low Valence with emotions like sadness, depression, and boredom,
- low Arousal, high Valence with emotions like relaxation, satisfaction, and serenity,
- high Arousal, low Valence with emotions like frustration, distress, and anxiety, and
- high Arousal, high Valence with emotions like arousal, excitement, and happiness.

When comparing Massami's eight channels Flow model to Russell's CMA, the channels' definitions can be associated to at least one of the emotions depicted in any of the CMA's quadrants. Accordingly, the Flow model may be associated with the two dimensions Arousal (which is renamed into Intensity to avoid confusion with the Flow model's channel name) (see Figure 5) and Valence (see Figure 6), resulting in an overlay of both Arousal and Valence onto the Flow dimension (see Figure 7).

As such the channels are each categorized as Valence positive / negative (see Table 2) and Intensity (Arousal) low/high (see Table 1).

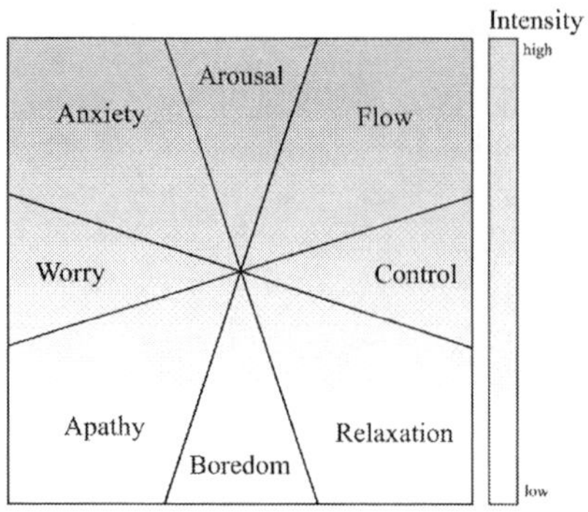

Figure 5. 8 Channel Flow overlaid with Intensity Dimension

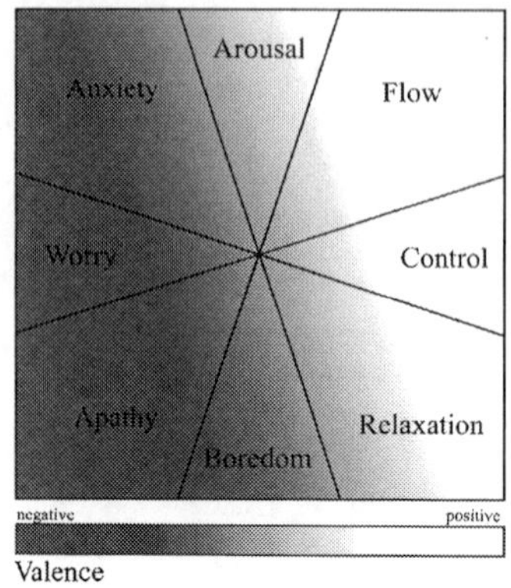

Figure 6. 8 Channel Flow overlaid with Valence Dimension

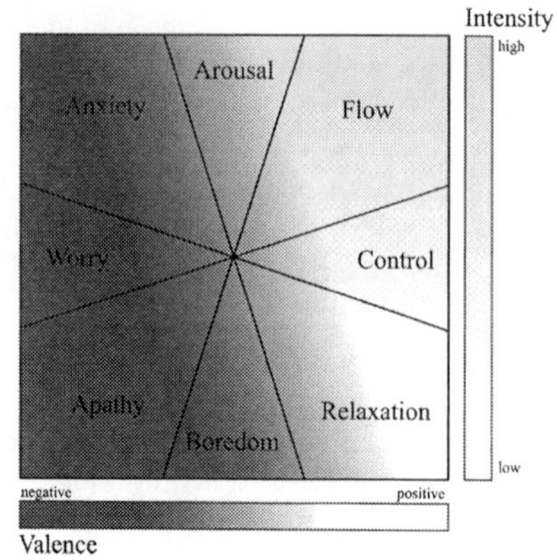

Figure 7. Combined 8 Channel Flow with Intensity/Valence Dimensions

Table 1. Flow channels, Intensity connotation

Intensity	High	Low
	Arousal	Control
	Flow	Relaxation
	Anxiety	Boredom
	Worry	Apathy

Table 2. Flow channels, Valence connotation

Valence	Positive	Negative
	Arousal	Anxiety
	Flow	Worry
	Control	Boredom
	Relaxation	Apathy

This leads to the authors' hypothesis:

— H1: There are relations between deep focus states and the additional two emotional dimensions Arousal/Intensity and Valence,

which – if found true – would greatly help quantifying deep focus states like Flow and Immersion by eliciting and examining the participants' emotional states, in regard of their Arousal/Intensity and Valence characteristics.

4. CONCEPT & STUDY

For setup and game selection the participant should be presented with a choice of pre-selected pool of games, narrowing down variability in favor of re-usability. The list of games should include titles from different genres, that might yield different depths of Immersion and Arousal/Valence. Other criteria for the game selection should be the length of the game session, control mechanisms and availability. In order to guarantee re-usability, popular but freely accessible games should be used.

After game selection, a questionnaire should be completed, eliciting gaming experience and familiarity with the selected game or genre to take into account the influence the level of familiarity might have on Arousal or Valence. Therefor a modified version of the Video Game Questionnaire was used, extending the choice of genres from eight to a total of eleven. Questions about the gaming habits in measure of hours per week in the last twelve months and before, were simplified into a self-assessment of three categories (beginner, intermediate, expert) to improve convenience.

After filling in the questionnaire, participants should play their game for about 36 minutes – because it might take some time, navigating game menus or watching intros, a period of three minutes should be added in the beginning and three in the end – which should guarantee true game play for at least 30 Minutes without any sudden interruption, improving chances for the participant to reach a state of Deep Focus.

During game play, participants would record themselves with a camera, using OBS or a similar software, to elicit additional clues off of their facial or verbal reactions during the assessment phase.

During Assessment, participants would watch their game play combined with their facial video footage as picture-in-picture. Early trials made it obvious to let the game play footage play back at twice the original speed of the original recording, to prevent participant frustration. Every three minutes real-time, or six minutes game-time, the Immersion Questionnaire (Chen et al., 2015), Flow Short Scale (Rheinberg et al., 2023), SAM (Bradley & Lang, 1994) and Affective Slider (AS), (Betella & Verschure, 2016) were answered, followed by the Game Experience Questionnaire (GEQ) at the end of assessment, giving additional information about the game experience in whole (Ijsselsteijn et al., 2013).

As general modification, all questionnaires were put into past tense to clarify that an excerpt from the past was commented on. Additionally all questionnaires were translated to German, because a German audience was expected to participate in the experiment.

To speed up the experiment process, the second half of the Video Game Questionnaire (Green et al, 2017) was replaced with a simpler self assessed experience measure (beginner, intermediate, expert).

Regarding the AS, a grayscale background instead of black and white one was used.

The original Model of the SAM was stripped of the Dominance part, under the assumption that every participant would be able to fulfill the task at hand without any problems. Additionally German translations for *calm*, *active*, *pleasant* and *unpleasant* were added to the Manikins, to reduce confusion which manifested in test runs.

The used Game Immersion Questionnaire was based on the modified version by Chen and the version by Jennett (Chen et al., 2015; Jennet et al., 2008). 4 of it's 16 questions were moved to GEQ at the end of the assessment, since they seemed to be of more general nature and therefore not suitable to be asked multiple times in rapid succession.

Regarding the AS, Betella & Verschure provided some HTML code implementations of the AS on GitHub as well as implementation instructions, but since the questionnaires were implemented in Python only the instructions and guidelines were followed, referring mostly to the visual representation of the AS and the position of certain elements.

5. STUDY RESULT

It was anticipated to gain a non-homogeneous group of 20 to 40 participants consisting of Non-Gamers, Casual Gamers and Hardcore-Gamers alike. In the end a total of 21 persons participated in the study, including 11 females, 10 males, with an age ranged from 28 to 80 with most of the participants being in their 30s. To determine and cluster the participants experience level a modified version of Green's Video Game Questionnaire as described in the previous chapter was used to place seven participants in the Beginner group, eight in the Intermediate group and six in the Expert Gamer group.

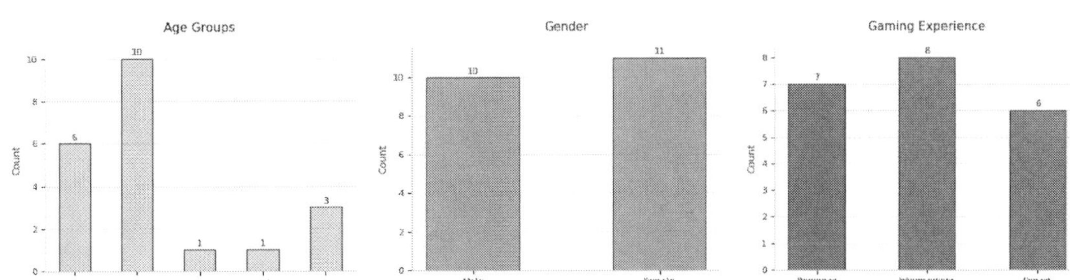

Figure 8. Participants statistics

To answer hypothesis H1 (see Chapter 3), Flow values would have to be correlated with each valence parts of AS and SAM using Spearman correlation.

Flow values were compiled over the average of all answers to the seven point likert scale of Rheinberg's Flow Short Scale, normalized to an interval between [0..1], where missing answers were replace by the low end interval value 0. Valence values for SAM, each manikin representing one point on a likert scale, were normalized to an interval between [0..1], missing answers were also replaced by the low end interval value 0.

Valence values for AS were used as provided, because they were already normalized, missing answers were replaced by the low end interval value 0.

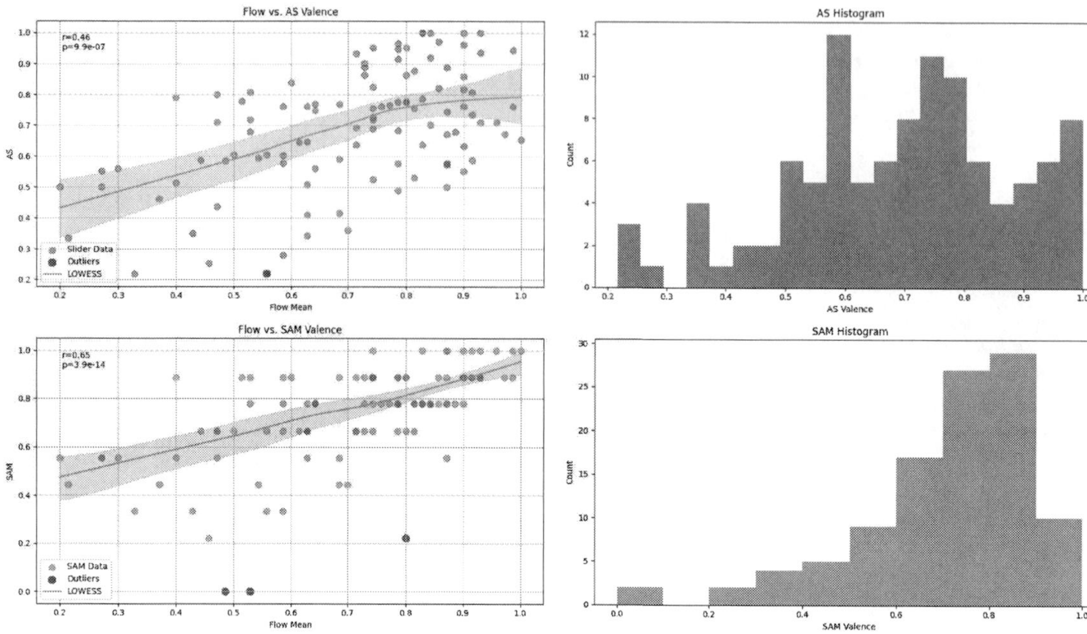

Figure 9. Spearman r correlation of Flow values and AS/SAM Valence values

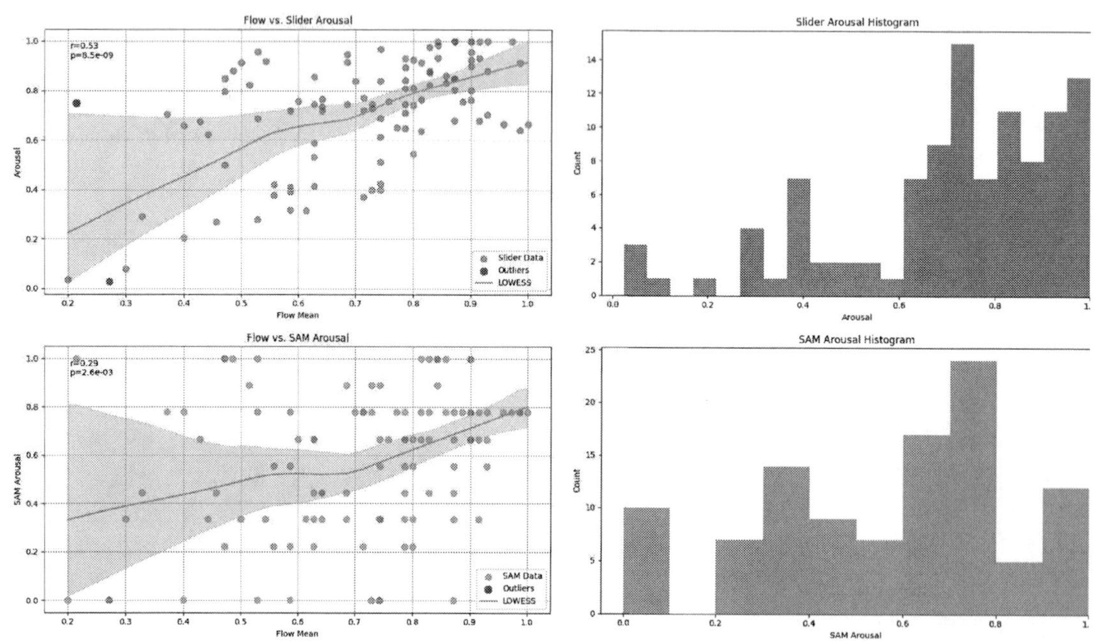

Figure 10. Spearman r correlation of Flow values and AS/SAM Arousal values

The Spearman correlation coefficient calculated as ($r = 0.46$; $p < .001$; conf = 0.95) for Flow and AS Valence, showing a medium correlation, while the Spearman correlation coefficient for Flow and SAM calculated as ($r = 0.65$; $p < .001$; conf = 0.95), showing a strong correlation (see Figure 9).

Correlations between Flow and AS / SAM Arousal turned out a bit more inconclusive: while the Spearman correlation coefficient for Flow and AS Arousal calculated as ($r = 0.53$; $p < .001$; conf = 0.95), again showing a strong correlation, the Pearson correlation coefficient for Flow and SAM Arousal calculated as ($r = 0.29$; $p < .001$; conf = 0.95), showing barely a weak correlation (see Figure 10).

Despite the fact, that there exists quit some variation in the given answers of perceived Flow and Immersion (see Figure 11), the data still shows a medium correlation with a Spearman correlation coefficient calculated with ($r = 0.52$; $p < .001$; conf=0.95), further supporting the hypothesis of the combined model of Flow and Immersion postulated in previous publications (Kannegieser et al., 2018).

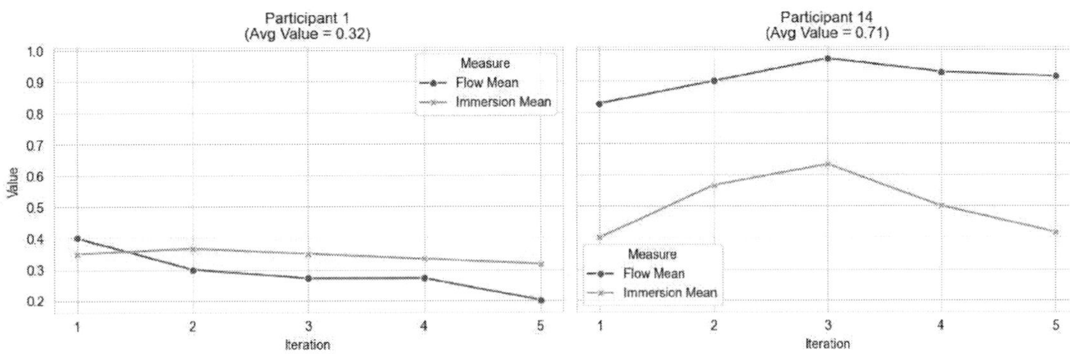

Figure 11. High/Low elicitation of Flow and Immersion

6. CONCLUSION & FUTURE WORK

The results of the performed experiment confirmed that positive emotional valence is intrinsically linked to deep focus states such as Flow in game-based tasks. By correlating Flow Short Scale scores with two independent valence measures (SAM and AS), medium to strong correlations were demonstrated, adding yet another dimension of quantifiability to Flow.

However the results of the performed experiment remained inconclusive on the nature whether or not high intensity of an emotional state (Arousal) is linked to deep focus states too, which might be due to the small amount of participants, bad usability of the study or the lack of suitability of the SAM to elicit Arousal.

In addition, the observed correlation between Flow and Immersion ($r = 0.52$, $p < 10^{-8}$) further supports the combined model, indicating that Flow can be understood as an extreme form of immersion that carries a distinct emotional signature.

Combining these results with real-time physiological sensing methods such as EEG, electrochemical skin conductance and heart-rate variability could allow for the detection of Flow onset without interruptive questionnaires.

As mentioned above, future research should touch on the topic of *Physiology of Flow*, while simultaneously expanding the participant pool and further improving the already diverse demographics to enhance the generalizability of these findings and progress towards the goal of an objective method to elicit deep focus states.

REFERENCES

Bakker, I., van der Voordt, T., Vink, P., de Boon, J. (2014) Pleasure, arousal, dominance: Mehrabian and Russell revisited. *Current Psychology, 33*, 405–421. dx.doi.org/10.1007/s12144-014-9219-4

Betella, A., Verschure, P. (2016). The Affective Slider: A Digital Self-Assessment Scale for the Measurement of Human Emotions. *PLoS ONE. 11. e0148037*. doi.org/10.1371/journal.pone.0148037

Bradley, M., Lang, P. (1994). Measuring emotion: The self-assessment manikin and the semantic differential. *Journal of Behavior Therapy and Experimental Psychiatry, 25-1*, pp. 49-59, doi.org/10.1016/0005-7916(94)90063-9

Brown, E., & Cairns, P. (2004). A grounded investigation of game immersion. *In Proceedings of the CHI'04 on Human Factors in Computing Systems* (Vienna: ACM), 1297–1300. dx.doi.org/10.1145/985921.986048

Cairns, P., Cox, A., Berthouze, N., Jennett, C., Dhoparee, S. (2006). Quantifying the experience of immersion in games. *Cognitive Science of Games and Gameplay. Cognitive Science 2006, 7*. discovery.ucl.ac.uk/149051/

Cheng, M.-T., She, H.-C., Annetta, L.A. (2015) Game Immersion Experience: Its Hierarchical Structure and Impact on Game-based Science Learning. *In: J. Comp. Assist. Learn. 31.3*, pp. 232–253., dx.doi.org/10.1111/jcal.12066

Csikszentmihalyi, M.: Flow: The Psychology of Optimal Experience. New York, NY: Harper Perennial. (1991)

Coomans, M.K.D., & Timmermanns, H.J.P. (1997). Towards a Taxonomy of Virtual reality user interfaces. *International conference on information visualisation*. doi.org/10.1109/IV.1997.626531

Ekman, I., Chanel, G., Järvelä, S., Kivikangas, J.M., Salminen, M., Ravaja, N. (2012) Social Interaction in Games: Measuring Physiological Linkage and Social Presence. *Simulation Gaming 43*, pp. 321–338. dx.doi.org/10.1177/1046878111422121

Green, C. S., Kattner, F., Eichenbaum, A., Bediou, B., Adams, D. M., Mayer, R. E., & Bavelier, D. (2017). Playing Some Video Games but Not Others Is Related to Cognitives Abilities. *Psychological Science, 28(5)*, pp. 679-682. doi.org/10.1177/0956797616644837

Ijsselsteijn, W., De Kort, Y., Poels, K. (2013). The Game Experience Questionnaire. Technische Universiteit Eindhoven

Jennett, C.I., Cox, A.L., Cairns, P.A., Dhoparee, S., Epps, A., Tijs, T.J., & Walton, A. (2008). Measuring and defining the experience of immersion in games. *International Journal of Human-Computer Studies., 66*, pp. 641-661, doi.org/10.1016/J.IJHCS.2008.04.004

Kannegieser, E., Atorf, D., Meier, J. (2018). Surveying games with a combined model of immersion and flow. *Proceedings of the International Conferences on Interfaces and Human Computer Interaction, Game and Entertainment Technologies*, pp. 353–356. doi.org/10.1007/978-3-030-77873-6_5

Kannegieser, E., Atorf, D. and Meier, J. (2019). Conducting an Experiment for Validating the Combined Model of Immersion and Flow. *Proceedings of the 11th International Conference on Computer Supported Education - Volume 2: CSEDU*, pp. 252-259. doi.org/10.5220/0007688902520259

Kannegieser, E., Atorf, D., Herold, J. (2021). Measuring Flow, Immersion and Arousal/Valence for Application in Adaptive Learning Systems. *Lecture Notes in Computer Science, 12793 LNCS*, pp. 62–78. doi.org/10.1007/978-3-030-77873-6_5

Lane, R., Chua, P., Dolan, R. (1999). Common effects of emotional valence, arousal and attention on neural activation during visual processing of pictures. *Neuropsychologia-37*, 989–997. doi.org/10.1016/s0028-3932(99)00017-2

Lang, P. J. (1980), Behavioral treatment and bio-behavioral assessment: Computer applications, in *Technology in mental health care delivery systems*, Norwood, NJ: Ablex,, pp. 119 – 137.

Massimini, F. and Carli, M. (1988) The systematic assessment of flow in daily experience, in *Optimal Experience: Psychological Studies of Flow in Consciousness*. Cambridge: Cambridge University Press, pp. 266–287. doi.org/10.1017/CBO9780511621956.016

Mandryk, R.L. and M.S. Atkins (2007). A Fuzzy Physiological Approach for Continuously Modeling Emotion During Interaction with Play Technologies. *International Journal of Human-Computer Studies 65.4*, pp. 329–347. dx.doi.org/10.1016/j.ijhcs.2006.11.011

Mäntylä, M., Adams, B., Destefanis, G., Graziotin, D., Ortu, M. (2016) Mining Valence, Arousal, and Dominance: Possibilities for Detecting Burnout and Productivity? *Proceedings of the 13th International Conference on Mining Software Repositories*. Austin, Texas: ACM, pp. 247–258. dx.doi.org/10.48550/arXiv.1603.04287

Rheinberg, F., Vollmeyer, R., Engster, S., Sreeramoju, R. (2023). FSS - Flow Short Scale

Russell, J.A. (1980). A circumplex model of affect. *Journal of personality and social psychology, 39*, 1161

Tomkins, S.S., Karon, B.P. (1962) Affect, imagery, consciousness. Vol. Volume I. New York: Springer

Wundt, W.: (1897) Outlines of Psychology. doi.org/10.1037/12908-000

QUANTITATIVE EVALUATION OF THE EFFECTS OF READING ALOUD AND SUBVOCALIZATION ON PROGRAM CODE DEBUGGING TASKS

Tetsuo Tanaka and Mari Ueda
Faculty of Information Technology, Kanagawa Institute of Technology
1030 Shimo-ogino, Atsugi, Kanagawa, 243-0292, Japan

ABSTRACT

This paper reports on an exploratory study designed to quantitatively investigate the effects of three code reading methods. We conducted an experiment with 22 university students with programming experience, who were tasked with finding and fixing bugs in C language source code using three different reading methods: "reading aloud," "subvocalization," and "silent reading." The experiment was designed as a within-subjects study, where each participant experienced all three conditions. An analysis of the experimental data using paired t-tests and other methods yielded the following findings. Overall, subvocalization showed statistically significant higher debugging performance compared to reading aloud ($p < 0.05$). However, this effect was not uniform, varying with participants' programming proficiency and their conscious ability to distinguish between the reading methods. Notably, among the group of participants who could clearly differentiate between silent reading and subvocalization, subvocalization demonstrated a statistically significant higher performance than silent reading as well ($p < 0.05$). These preliminary findings suggest that consciously controlled subvocalization may be an effective strategy for managing cognitive load and directing attention to the details of the code during debugging tasks. This paper reports these findings in detail and discusses their potential applications in programming education and practice.

KEYWORDS

Program Comprehension, Debugging, Metacognition, Subvocalization, Cognitive Load, Programming Education

1. INTRODUCTION

The role of software in modern society continues to expand, making quality assurance an issue of paramount importance. A primary factor that degrades software quality is the presence of defects, or "bugs," within the program. The process of efficiently finding and correcting these bugs during development, known as debugging, is a critical process that can determine the success or failure of a project.

At the core of debugging lies the cognitive activity of "program comprehension," where a programmer reads and understands the logical structure and behavior of the source code. Most programmers routinely perform this activity through "silent reading," reading the code without vocalization. However, when bugs are not easily found, programmers consciously or unconsciously employ various strategies. One such strategy is the externalization of thought, exemplified by "reading aloud" the code or "rubber duck debugging," where one explains the problem to an inanimate object. These methods are empirically known to help concretize thoughts and provide opportunities to notice one's own misunderstandings. On the other hand, the externalization of thought presents challenges such as the cognitive load associated with vocalization and constraints of the work environment.

We have previously researched the effects of reading aloud on programming learning. In (Ueda 2023), we reported that reading program code aloud is effective. Furthermore, in (Tanaka 2024), we reported that reading program code aloud increases cerebral blood flow (activates brain activity). As noted in that report, looking at individual data, some participants showed a significant change in brain activity indicators in the opposite direction of the overall trend. We hypothesized that this might be caused by "subvocalization," the act of articulating words internally without making a sound.

Therefore, this study focuses on "subvocalization," a cognitive activity with properties intermediate between silent reading and reading aloud. It lacks the physical constraints of reading aloud and may encourage more careful and conscious information processing than silent reading.

However, a quantitative evaluation of how these reading methods (silent reading, reading aloud, and subvocalization) specifically affect debugging performance has not been sufficiently conducted. The purpose of this study is to experimentally investigate the effects of these three reading methods on the comprehension and debugging ability of source code containing bugs and to quantitatively evaluate their effectiveness.

Given the novelty of investigating subvocalization in this context, the present work should be considered an exploratory study. Its primary aim is to gather initial evidence and generate hypotheses for future, larger-scale research, rather than to provide definitive conclusions.

To guide our investigation, we formulate the following research questions:

- **RQ1:** How do different code reading methods (silent reading, reading aloud, subvocalization) affect the debugging performance of university students?
- **RQ2:** Does the effect of these reading methods vary based on the students' programming proficiency or their self-reported ability to distinguish between the methods?

2. RELATED WORK

2.1 Cognitive Models of Program Comprehension

The process of program comprehension has been the subject of much research for many years (Brooks 1983, Schulte 2010, Hermans 2021). Early research proposed the "bottom-up theory," where programmers gradually construct the overall meaning from code fragments, and the "top-down theory," where they understand details based on hypotheses about the program's overall function. Von Mayrhauser and Vans proposed an integrated model where programmers combine top-down (from expected behavior to code) and bottom-up (from code to behavior) understanding (von Mayrhauser 1997). Debugging is an activity of searching for discrepancies between expected behavior (top-down) and the actual code (bottom-up), a situation where this integrated model is actively functioning. The reading strategies dealt with in this study are expected to directly influence the bottom-up process of extracting information from the code.

2.2 Cognitive Load in Debugging

Cognitive Load Theory posits that the amount of information human working memory can process at one time is limited. Debugging is a highly cognitively demanding task as it requires holding and manipulating numerous pieces of information—such as variable states, loop counters, and function call relationships—in working memory simultaneously. An effective debugging strategy can be described as one that appropriately manages this cognitive load, allowing working memory resources to be focused on problem-solving. In this study, "reading aloud" may increase cognitive load due to the additional task of vocalization, whereas "subvocalization" might, by structuring thought, have the effect of reducing cognitive load.

2.3 Externalization of Thought and the Self-Explanation Effect

"Reading aloud" (Ueda 2022) and "rubber duck debugging" (Thomas 2019, Lloyd 2015), which involves explaining the code to a rubber duck, are forms of thought externalization in debugging. In the field of educational psychology, it is well-known that "self-explanation," where learners explain the learning material in their own words, significantly promotes understanding (Chi 1989). Through this process, learners can discover gaps and misconceptions in their own knowledge. Debugging is also a learning process of correcting errors in one's own mental model of the program's behavior, and the self-explanation effect is thought to be effective.

2.4 The Role of Subvocalization

Subvocalization is considered to be involved in various higher-order cognitive activities such as reading comprehension, problem-solving, and planning. Particularly when processing new or complex information, subvocalization functions as an important mechanism for temporarily holding and rehearsing information (Baddeley 1992, Daneman 1980). Program code, especially in a procedural language like C, consists of sequential processes. Therefore, the act of internally vocalizing the code line by line is thought to be an extremely effective means of accurately simulating this sequential process in working memory.

Building on this background, this study holds novelty and significance in its use of a rigorous within-subjects experimental design to quantitatively clarify the effects of reading strategies, which have often been discussed qualitatively, in the specific task of debugging.

3. EXPERIMENTAL OVERVIEW

3.1 Purpose of the Experiment

To experimentally investigate the effects of reading aloud, subvocalization, and silent reading of program source code on the comprehension and debugging ability of code containing bugs.

3.2 Participants

A total of 22 third- and fourth-year undergraduate and graduate students from the Faculty of Information Technology at Kanagawa Institute of Technology participated in the experiment. All participants had prior programming experience.

3.3 Experimental Task

Language: C.

Content: Short programs composed of fundamental elements such as variables, conditional branching, loops, arrays, strings, and pointers. Each program contained multiple logical errors (bugs) that caused its behavior to differ from the expected execution result. The types of bugs included 10 typical errors that beginners are prone to, such as array index mistakes, incorrect operators, misunderstanding of integer division, and incorrect arguments for scanf.

Problem Sets: Three problem sets (a, b, and c) were used in the experiment. Each set contained four debugging problems.

3.4 Experimental Design

This experiment employed a **within-subjects design**. That is, a single participant experienced all three conditions: "reading aloud," "subvocalization," and "silent reading." This aimed to minimize the influence of individual differences in ability and to more accurately detect the differences in effects caused by the reading methods.

The order in which each participant experienced the reading methods was randomized to counterbalance order effects (such as learning effects or fatigue).

3.5 Experimental Procedure

The experiment was conducted according to the "Instructions" document distributed to the participants.

1. Explanation (10 minutes): The experimenter explained the purpose, procedure, and ethical considerations (anonymity, voluntary participation) of the experiment to the participants. Specific instructions were then given for the three reading methods.
   - Reading Aloud: Instructed to read each line of the source code out loud.
   - Subvocalization: Instructed to read each line of the source code in their head as if reading it aloud (without making a sound).
   - Silent Reading: Instructed to read the code silently, as they normally would when programming.
2. To minimize auditory distractions from participants reading aloud, all participants wore earmuffs.
3. Debugging Task (Total 55 minutes): Participants worked on the debugging tasks using the three reading methods in the randomly assigned order. Each session lasted for 15 minutes, with a 5-minute break between sessions. Participants referred to the source code and the expected execution results to find bugs, and wrote down the bugs they found and their proposed corrections on a form.
4. Post-Questionnaire (5 minutes): After all sessions were completed, participants answered a questionnaire about their confidence in programming and debugging, the ease of concentration with each reading method, and a self-assessment regarding subvocalization.

3.6 Measurement Items and Analysis Method

Objective Evaluation Metric: The total number of bugs correctly found and fixed in each session (total score).
Subjective Evaluation Metric: Self-assessment from the post-questionnaire regarding concentration, debugging achievement, and each reading method.
Analysis Method: The mean score and standard deviation for each reading method were calculated. A **paired t-test** was used to verify the significance of the difference in mean scores between the reading methods. The statistical significance level was set at 5% ($p < 0.05$).

4. EXPERIMENTAL RESULTS

This chapter objectively describes the results of the analysis of the data obtained from the experiment.

4.1 Overall Trends by Reading Method

First, the mean values and variances of the debugging performance (total score) for each reading method for all participants (N=22) were calculated (Table 1).

Table 1. Mean Scores and Variances by Reading Method

Reading Method	Mean Score	Variance
Reading Aloud	2.68	3.85
Subvocalization	3.50	4.73
Silent Reading	3.00	4.19

The mean score was highest for subvocalization, followed by silent reading, and then reading aloud.
To verify whether these differences in mean scores were statistically significant, a paired t-test was conducted (Table 2).

Table 2. t-test Results Between Reading Methods (N=22)

Comparison Pair	t-value	p-value	Significance
Subvocalization vs. Reading Aloud	2.24	0.035	**Significant**
Subvocalization vs. Silent Reading	1.28	0.217	Not Significant
Silent Reading vs. Reading Aloud	0.75	0.460	Not Significant

The result showed that the difference in mean scores between subvocalization and reading aloud was statistically significant ($p < 0.05$). On the other hand, no significant differences were found between subvocalization and silent reading, or between silent reading and reading aloud.

4.2 Analysis by Programming Proficiency

Next, participants were divided into "High," "Medium," and "Low" proficiency groups based on their total debugging scores, and we analyzed whether the effect of the reading method differed by proficiency (Table 3, Table 4). The grouping was done by dividing the total scores of all participants by tertiles.

Table 3. Mean Scores and Variances by Programming Proficiency (N=22)

Proficiency Group	Reading Aloud	Subvocalization	Silent Reading
High (N=7)	4.43 (4.95)	6.00 (0.67)	4.86 (3.14)
Medium (N=7)	2.57 (0.95)	3.43 (0.62)	3.43 (0.29)
Low (N=8)	1.25 (1.07)	1.38 (1.70)	1.00 (1.43)

Table 4. t-test Results Between Reading Methods by Proficiency Group

Comparison Pair	p-value	Significance
High: Subvocalization vs. Reading Aloud	0.111	Not Significant
High: Subvocalization vs. Silent Reading	0.268	Not Significant
High: Silent Reading vs. Reading Aloud	0.722	Not Significant
Medium: Subvocalization vs. Reading Aloud	0.045	**Significant**
Medium: Subvocalization vs. Silent Reading	1.000	Not Significant
Medium: Silent Reading vs. Reading Aloud	0.078	Marginally Significant
Low: Subvocalization vs. Reading Aloud	0.836	Not Significant
Low: Subvocalization vs. Silent Reading	0.584	Not Significant
Low: Silent Reading vs. Reading Aloud	0.649	Not Significant

In the High group, there was a trend for subvocalization to have the highest score, but the t-test results showed no significant differences between any pairs (e.g., Subvocalization vs. Silent Reading, $p = 0.268$).

In the Medium group, subvocalization and silent reading had the highest equal scores, while reading aloud had the lowest. The t-test showed a difference between subvocalization and reading aloud ($p = 0.045$) and a marginally significant trend between silent reading and reading aloud ($p = 0.078$, significant at the 10% level).

In the Low group, scores were low overall, and the differences between reading methods were small. Notably, the score for silent reading, their usual method, was the lowest, but there were no significant differences between any pairs.

4.3 Analysis Based on Post-Questionnaire Responses

Based on the post-questionnaire responses, we conducted further analysis from two perspectives.

4.3.1 Habitual Subvocalization

We divided participants into a "Habitual" group (n=12), who answered that they "do" or "think they do" subvocalize when reading text normally, and a "Non-habitual" group (n=10), who answered that they "do not" or "think they do not" (Table 5).

Table 5. Mean Scores and Variances by Subvocalization Habit (N=22)

Group	Reading Aloud	Subvocalization	Silent Reading
Habitual (N=12)	2.58 (3.90)	4.00 (3.27)	3.08 (6.27)
Non-habitual (N=10)	2.80 (4.18)	2.90 (6.32)	2.90 (2.10)

In the Habitual group, subvocalization showed a statistically significant higher score than reading aloud ($p = 0.0095$). In contrast, no significant differences were found among the three reading methods in the Non-habitual group.

4.3.2 Ability to Distinguish Reading Methods

Participants were divided into a "Distinguishable" group (n=16), who answered that they "were able" or "think they were able" to consciously distinguish between silent reading and subvocalization during the experiment, and a "Difficult to Distinguish" group (n=6), who answered that they "were not" or "think they were not" able to (Table 6).

Table 6. Mean Scores and Variances by Ability to Distinguish Reading Methods (N=22)

Group	Reading Aloud	Subvocalization	Silent Reading
Distinguishable (N=16)	3.00 (4.40)	4.13 (3.98)	3.13 (3.45)
Difficult (N=6)	1.83 (1.77)	1.83 (3.37)	2.67 (7.07)

In the Distinguishable group, subvocalization showed statistically significant higher scores compared to both reading aloud ($p = 0.0165$) and silent reading ($p = 0.0271$). This is one of the most important findings of this study.

On the other hand, in the Difficult to Distinguish group, there was a trend for silent reading to have the highest score, but no significant differences were found between any pairs.

5. DISCUSSION

In this chapter, we discuss from multiple perspectives the impact of reading methods on debugging tasks, based on the results obtained in the previous chapter.

5.1 The Effectiveness of Subvocalization

The central finding of this study is that consciously controlled subvocalization is a demonstrably effective strategy for debugging. In the overall results, subvocalization recorded the highest mean score among the three reading methods and showed a statistically significant difference compared to reading aloud.

Several cognitive factors may underlie this effectiveness.

First is the balance of load on working memory. Silent reading is fast but may lead to superficial processing of information, which may not be sufficiently retained in working memory. On the other hand, reading aloud externalizes thought but the act of vocalization itself can become an additional cognitive load, pressuring working memory. Subvocalization allows for slower and more conscious information processing than silent reading, without the load of vocalization. This is presumed to have made it easier to efficiently track short-term information such as variable values and loop states in working memory.

Second is attention control. Subvocalization has the effect of forcibly directing the programmer's attention to each line of the source code. This may have made it easier to notice logical errors hidden in the details of the code that might otherwise be skimmed over.

5.2 Individual Differences in the Effects of Reading Methods

However, the effectiveness of subvocalization was not common to all participants. The analysis revealed that its effect is strongly influenced by two factors: programming proficiency and the participant's awareness of the reading methods.

5.2.1 Influence of Programming Proficiency

The analysis by proficiency suggests that the optimal cognitive strategy differs depending on the skill level.

In the High group, subvocalization showed the highest score. This indicates that participants with high skills were able to maximize the benefits of the subvocalization technique to further enhance their abilities. Although they could already perform well with silent reading, using the more structured approach of subvocalization may have improved their ability to deal with complex bugs.

In the Medium group, the effects of subvocalization and silent reading were equivalent, and both surpassed reading aloud. This suggests that for participants in this tier, avoiding the additional cognitive load from reading aloud is important.

The results of the Low group are particularly insightful. Their performance was the lowest among the three reading methods for silent reading. This suggests that for participants who struggle with programming, their usual silent reading might be superficial and fail to sufficiently track the logic of the code. Therefore, methods like subvocalization or reading aloud, which force line-by-line processing, may have helped, albeit slightly, to prevent a decline in performance.

5.2.2 Influence of Subvocalization Habits and Awareness

The factor that most strongly influenced the effect of subvocalization was the participants' own habits and awareness regarding it.

Participants who habitually subvocalize in their daily reading showed a clear performance improvement when instructed to use the method in the experiment. This means they were able to effectively apply a cognitive skill they were already proficient into the task of debugging.

The most crucial findings of this study is that in the group of participants who could consciously distinguish between silent reading and subvocalization, subvocalization showed a statistically significant difference even against silent reading. This suggests that the effectiveness of subvocalization is not merely about careful silent reading but may be a specific, consciously controlled cognitive mode. Participants who could intentionally use this mode were able to gain a clear benefit in debugging.

Conversely, for participants who could not distinguish between the two, the instruction "to subvocalize" itself may have caused confusion and become a factor that hindered performance. For them, silent reading, performed as usual without extra instructions, yielded the best result.

5.3 Implications of This Study

From these considerations, this study offers important implications for both the practice and education of programming.

For practice, The results of this study suggest that conscious subvocalization could be a potentially effective option when stuck in debugging. This technique could be particularly helpful for programmers when they need to follow complex logic or search for simple, easily overlooked mistakes.

For education, it suggests the importance of teaching beginners effective ways to read code. Many beginners may lack a strategic approach to reading code. As seen in the low-proficiency group, their silent reading may be superficial. Training them to use "subvocalization" to track what each line of code means and how they connect to form the overall behavior, by vocalizing it in their heads, might be a promising avenue for improving program comprehension skills. However, further research is needed to validate this educational implication.

5.4 Limitations and Future Work

While this study provides initial insights, its limitations must be clearly acknowledged.

Sample Size and Statistical Power: The most significant limitation is the small sample size (N=22), which is further reduced in subgroup analyses (n=6 to 16). This small sample size limits the statistical power of our tests and prohibits the generalization of our findings. The results should therefore be interpreted with caution.

Statistical Treatment: We employed paired t-tests for our primary analysis. However, as noted by reviewers, conducting multiple t-tests can inflate the risk of Type I errors (false positives). Future research with larger samples should employ more robust statistical methods, such as mixed-effects models, which can better handle the repeated-measures nature of the data and account for individual differences. We also refrained from correcting for multiple comparisons due to the exploratory nature of this study, but this is a point to be addressed in future confirmatory studies.

Ecological Validity: The debugging tasks involved short, "toy" C programs. These tasks may not fully represent the cognitive demands of debugging large-scale, complex software systems in professional settings. Future work should aim to use more ecologically valid tasks.

Reliance on Self-Report: Our classification of participants' ability to distinguish reading methods was based on self-reporting. This introduces subjectivity and is a clear limitation. Future studies could incorporate objective measures, such as think-aloud protocols or eye-tracking, to provide a more robust validation of the cognitive processes involved.

6. CONCLUSION

This study investigated "reading aloud," "subvocalization," and "silent reading" as methods for reading source code and quantitatively evaluated their impact on debugging performance through an experiment with 22 participants experienced in programming.

The analysis revealed that consciously controlled subvocalization is an effective cognitive strategy for debugging tasks. This method resulted in statistically significant higher performance compared to other reading methods, particularly among participants who could clearly and consciously differentiate it from silent reading.

Furthermore, it became clear that the effectiveness of a reading method varies depending on the participant's proficiency and regular habits, indicating that there is no one-size-fits-all approach. While participants with high programming skills could maximize the benefits of subvocalization, it was suggested that for less proficient participants, their usual silent reading might be inefficient.

The findings of this research offer practical hints for programmers stuck on a debugging problem and also point to the potential of a new educational approach: instructing programming beginners in effective code reading strategies.

ACKNOWLEDGEMENT

We sincerely thank all the students of the Faculty of Information Technology at Kanagawa Institute of Technology who cooperated in this experiment. This work was supported by JSPS KAKENHI Grant Number JP23K02747.

REFERENCES

Baddeley, A. D. (1992). *Working memory.* Science, 255(5044), 556-559.

Brooks, R. E. (1983). Towards a theory of the comprehension of computer programs. *International Journal of Man-Machine Studies*, 18(6), 543-554.

Chi, M. T. H., Bassok, M., Lewis, M. W., Reimann, P., & Glaser, R. (1989). Self-explanations: How students study and use examples in learning to solve problems. *Cognitive Science*, 13(2), 145-182.

Daneman, M., Carpenter, P. A. (1980). Individual differences in working memory and reading. *Journal of Verbal Learning and Verbal Behavior*, 19(4), 450-466.

Hermans, F. (2021). *The Programmer's Brain.* Manning Publications.

Lloyd, J. (2015). Rubber Duck Debugging. *Journal of the Queensland Society for Information Technology in Education.* 131, 9-11.

Schulte, C., Clear, T., Taherkhani, A., Busjahn, T. and Paterson, J. (2010). An introduction to program comprehension for computer science educators. *In Proceedings of the 2010 ITiCSE working group reports (ITiCSE-WGR '10).* 65–86.

Tanaka, T., Horiuchi, R., & Ueda, M. (2024). Evaluation of the Effectiveness of Reading Aloud a Program Code in Learning Programming Based on Brain-Activity Measurements. *Proceedings of the 21st International Conference on Cognition and Exploratory Learning in the Digital Age (CELDA 2024)*, 83-89.

Thomas, D., Hunt, A. (2019). *The Pragmatic Programmer, 20th Anniversary Edition.* Addison-Wesley Professional.

Ueda, M., Ishida, N., Odagiri, K., Kasuga, H. and Tanaka T. (2022). A Proposal of Programming Learning System with Reading Aloud "ONDOKU". *Proceedings of the 12th International Congress on Advanced Applied Informatics (IIAI AAI 2022),* 260-263.

Ueda, M., Kasugay, H., & Tanaka, T. (2023). Basic study on the effectiveness of reading aloud in learning programming languages. *Acoustical Science and Technology*, 44(1), 33-35.

von Mayrhauser, A., & Vans, A. M. (1997). Program understanding behavior during debugging of large scale software. *In Papers presented at the seventh workshop on Empirical studies of programmers (ESP '97).* 157–179.

IDENTIFYING PROBLEM-SOLVING PROFILES TO INFORM SCAFFOLDING IN DIGITAL PROBLEM-SOLVING ENVIRONMENTS

Jörgen Ivar Sikk and Kairit Tammets
Tallinn University
Narva mnt 25, 10120, Tallinn, Estonia

ABSTRACT

This study investigates the development of students' problem-solving skills in technology-enhanced learning (TEL) environments, focusing on the interplay between domain knowledge, metacognitive strategies, and fading scaffolding. Through a design-based research approach, we engaged three eighth-grade classes (N=75) in a physics-based troubleshooting scenario delivered via an H5P-integrated digital platform, collecting performance data, metacognitive ratings, and process analytics. Cluster analysis of MAPS rubric scores revealed three distinct learner profiles—Expert, Novice, and Struggling—which differed significantly across all problem-solving dimensions ($p < .001$). Experts demonstrated integrated knowledge and adaptive strategies, excelling in both domain-specific application and logical progression, while Novices showed scaffold dependency and Struggling students exhibited fragmented knowledge structures. Domain knowledge emerged as the strongest predictor of problem-solving success, especially for complex tasks, with knowledge gain playing a secondary role. Metacognitive planning and monitoring were most influential among Experts, explaining 43% of variance in their problem-solving skills, but were less predictive for Novices and Struggling students. Our findings demonstrate that combining process-oriented analytics with cognitive and metacognitive measures enables early identification of learner needs and supports the design of adaptive, technology-enhanced instructional systems that foster meaningful learning across diverse student profiles.

KEYWORDS

Problem-Solving Skills, Technology-Enhanced Learning, Student Profiles, Digital Learning Resources

1. INTRODUCTION

Problem-solving skills are essential not only for academic success but also for addressing real-life challenges across all ages (Silber-Varod et al., 2019). These skills enable individuals to analyze situations, test solutions, and adapt strategies to achieve desired outcomes. In educational contexts, problem-solving skills are recognized as a cornerstone for fostering deeper learning and critical thinking. Beyond traditional learning environments, the integration of digital tools and learning analytics (LA) offers new opportunities to support the development of these skills (Wang and Chang, 2024). Virtual environments allow students to practice problem-solving by experimenting with different solutions in a low stakes setting (Chernikova et al., 2020).

Despite these affordances, several limitations remain (Bayne, 2015). The development of technology-enhanced learning (TEL) tools does not always align with sound pedagogical models or adequately consider critical factors (Wang and Chang, 2024) such as learners' prior knowledge (Simonsmeier et al., 2021). Disparities in students' prior knowledge can lead to performance gaps in problem-solving abilities (Shapiro, 2004), making the effective teaching of these skills especially challenging. Prior knowledge (Chi et al., 1981) and learners' cognitive architectures (Sweller et al., 2011) are key factors influencing problem-solving outcomes. This complexity poses difficulties for educators attempting to design instructional strategies that accommodate varying skill levels, particularly when integrating digital learning resources (Pettersson, 2018). Moreover, the dynamic nature of problem-solving skills---shifting across learners and contexts---demands refined instructional methods to foster these competencies in authentic and evolving domains (Dreyfus & Dreyfus, 1980, Geisinger, 2016).

Although adaptive methods and constructivist approaches (Kirschner et al., 2006) offer promising avenues for developing problem-solving and critical thinking skills, novices might require more explicit scaffolding before they can meaningfully engage with problem-based, project-based, or inquiry-based learning. Various digital tools have been shown to boost students' engagement and collaboration in problem-solving (Phungsuk et al., 2017, Gould et al., 2013). However, technology alone does not guarantee improved outcomes; effective implementation depends on integrating teacher expertise and scaffolding strategies (Phungsuk et al., 2017, Karumbaiah et al., 2023). Thus challenges persist in creating technology that leverages teachers' intelligence (Baker, 2016) and enables them to adapt instruction to learners' diverse profiles.

Our study explores how these challenges play out in TEL environments aimed at developing students' problem-solving skills. We conceptualize problem-solving not as a fixed trait, but as a dynamic, context-sensitive competence that evolves through interaction with tasks, tools, and supports. We theorize that problem-solving skills (PSS) emerge from an interplay of several individual characteristics, including domain knowledge, metacognitive strategies and patterns of task engagement. To design sophisticated, pedagogy-grounded learning technologies, we need more nuanced knowledge of students' problem-solving processes and the indicators that signal different levels of skill and support needs. This requires integrating process-oriented measures with cognitive and metacognitive assessments. Such insights can in turn inform more effective scaffolding strategies during classroom activities. Our guiding research questions in this intervention were:

1. Which distinct learner profiles can be identified based on students' problem-solving strategies?
2. How do these distinct learner profiles relate to students' domain knowledge, metacognitive strategies and knowledge gain?

2. RELATED WORK

2.1 Understanding Problem-Solving Skills

Problem-solving skills are abilities that enable individuals to identify, analyze, and resolve challenges effectively (Carlson et al., 2005). These skills involve a combination of domain knowledge, metacognitive strategies, and cognitive processes, forming a dynamic play of individual characteristics and task demands (Jonassen, 2011, Sweller et al., 2011). Problem-solving competence is often referred to as the ability to apply domain-specific knowledge alongside general cognitive skills such as metacognition. Metacognition, defined by Flavell (Flavell, 1979), encompasses planning, monitoring, and evaluating one's cognitive processes during problem-solving. In educational contexts, written answers often serve as indicators of metacognitive behavior (Docktor et al., 2016).

2.1.1 Effect of Domain Knowledge on Problem-Solving Skills

Domain knowledge---the specialized understanding of concepts and principles within a discipline---is foundational for effective problem-solving (Sweller et al., 2011). For instance, in physics, understanding principles like mechanics or electromagnetism enables students to recognize patterns and apply concepts effectively (Jonassen, 2011). Research highlights domain knowledge' predictive role in problem-solving success (Docktor et al., 2016, Schäfer et al., 2024). Thus, we argue, that in educational settings problem-solving is inherently domain-specific, requiring the integration of disciplinary knowledge with general cognitive abilities such as reasoning (Schäfer et al., 2024). While general cognitive skills support adaptability across tasks, domain-specific expertise reduces cognitive load by enabling efficient information processing (Sweller et al., 2011, Schäfer et al., 2024).

Thus, domain knowledge provides the specialized expertise needed to recognize and apply key principles efficiently, while metacognition - through planning, monitoring, and evaluating one's thinking - ensures that this knowledge is used effectively. Together, they help individuals manage cognitive load (Zheng et al., 2019) and adapt their problem-solving strategies (Carlson, 2005), resulting in more successful and flexible problem solvers (Schäfer et al., 2024).

2.1.2 Scaffolding Problem-Solving Skills in Technology Enhanced Learning

In TEL environments, issues such as bridging the gap between prior knowledge and its application are well observed. To tackle these issues, for example, scripted scaffolding of digital learning resources is well-established (Kollar et al., 2018) in supporting student learning and metacognition in problem-based learning scenarios (Kim et al., 2018). In general, scaffolding is a critical instructional strategy that supports learners in achieving complex tasks by providing temporary guidance tailored to their needs. Constructivist approaches such as problem-based learning emphasize authentic problem-solving scenarios where learners actively construct knowledge through exploration and collaboration (Savery, 2015). However, novice learners often require explicit scaffolding to engage meaningfully with problem-based learning tasks due to limited prior experience or domain knowledge (Jonassen, 2011). The complexity of tasks in problem scenarios and TEL environments requires scaffolding.

If effective, this scaffolding enhances learners' ability to tackle complex problems by reducing cognitive load and guiding them through structured learning processes (Van Merrienboer and Kirschner, 2017). In TEL contexts, scripted scaffolds---pre-designed prompts or feedback - help students navigate tasks systematically while fading scaffolds gradually reduce support as learners gain competence (Kim et al., 2018), allowing students to develop independence while maintaining task complexity appropriate to their skill level (Van Merrienboer and Kirschner, 2017). Technology can provide adaptive scaffolds based on learner data, but also research emphasizes the synergy between teacher expertise and technological tools (Pettersson, 2018, Karumbaiah et al., 2023). In our intervention, faded scaffolding is implemented as a component of the TEL environment to bridge the gap between students' prior domain knowledge and the complex demands of problem-solving tasks. The gradual fading of these supports is added to understand the diverse learner profiles and improve the visibility of them.

2.2 Monitoring and Differentiating Support Using Process-Oriented Learning Analytics

Monitoring learners' progress during problem-solving is essential for providing differentiated support. TEL environments enable dynamic tracking through process data such as log files and task completion metrics, capturing how students interact with tasks and make decisions (Chen et al., 2019; Greiff et al., 2016). These process data - including time on task, error rates, and task frequencies - can be transformed into pedagogically meaningful variables that guide adaptive scaffolding strategies (He et al., 2015; Ley et al., 2023).

To maintain task complexity and student engagement, it is important to assess both prior knowledge and cognitive skills, enabling the extraction of learner profiles. Modern adaptive systems build comprehensive learner models that track domain knowledge, problem-solving competencies, and metacognitive traits such as planning and self-regulation (Wang and Chang, 2024). In our physics scenario, the system tracks not only content mastery but also how students approach problems (e.g., systematic planning, revision attempts, hint usage), allowing for nuanced inferences about their strategies and needs.

Our research integrates domain-specific problem-solving principles (Jonassen, 2011) and metacognitive frameworks (Flavell, 1979; Schraw et al., 1994) to address the challenges of TEL environments. By identifying distinct learner profiles, we aim to enable more effective, individualized scaffolding for diverse learners (Wang and Chang, 2024).

3. METHODOLOGY

3.1 Study Participants and Pedagogical Design

We developed a task model to capture key influences on problem-solving development—focusing on domain knowledge and metacognitive strategies—and used these data to identify distinct learner profiles as a foundation for future adaptive interventions (Chi et al., 2014; Kim et al., 2018). Three Grade 8 classes (N = 75; ages 14–15; balanced gender mix) in a secondary school participated in an authentic classroom intervention.

Instructional Design

- **Scenario:** A troubleshooting challenge in an underground biolab during a blackout, requiring students to design a lighting system with spotlights and mirrors to maintain plant growth—aligning with Jonassen's troubleshooting framework (Jonassen, 2011).
- **Platform:** Activities delivered via a Drupal-integrated H5P "Interactive Book," structured into four cyclical phases: formulate, explore, solve, revisit (Carlson et al., 2005).
- **Task Progression:** Five tasks of increasing complexity, beginning with a multiple-choice question and culminating in an open-ended, ill-structured problem, with scaffolds that gradually faded (e.g., hint reduction) as students advanced (Kim et al., 2018).

Learning Process

1. **Individual Exploration:** Students first engaged solo to analyze the problem scenario.
2. **Artifact Creation:** Each student produced a paper-based sketch to represent their solution concept.
3. **Collaborative Refinement:** Small-group discussions enabled peer feedback and solution refinement.
4. **Revision Phase:** Students independently revised their sketches incorporating group insights.
5. **Reflection:** Each phase ended with self-reflection prompts to assess strategy use and learning .

3.2 Overview of Constructs, Variables and Data Collection

3.2.1 Constructs and Variables

To understand why some students excel at complex problem-solving tasks while others struggle, we focused on three core constructs: domain knowledge, problem-solving skill, and metacognition. Our scaffolded problem-based learning tasks were designed to trace the individual and combined effects of these constructs on student performance. Problem-solving skills were assessed using the four-item MAPS rubric, which evaluates *Useful Description, Physics Approach, Specific Application of Physics*, and *Logical Progression*, each scored on a 0–5 scale (Docktor et al., 2016). Metacognition was measured across four dimensions—*Planning, Monitoring, Self-Regulation*, and *Reflection*—using adapted rubrics from established physics education research (Flavell, 1979; Schraw et al., 1994). All scoring was completed by a single teacher to ensure consistency. For data collection, we extracted xAPI statements from students' interactions with H5P-based tasks, using custom scripts to retrieve detailed records from the Learning Locker platform. This approach provided insights into students' actions and decision-making processes, allowing us to analyze both digital log data and paper-based solution artifacts. To identify distinct learner profiles, we applied K-means clustering and ANOVA to the MAPS rubric scores, first determining the optimal number of clusters with Ward's hierarchical clustering and then refining the solution with K-means using predetermined centroids. To further understand the factors shaping these profiles, we conducted a multinomial logistic regression analysis using domain knowledge, task performance, and metacognitive skills as predictors.

4. RESULTS

In this section, we present two components of our research: (1) the role of domain knowledge in problem-solving skills across varying levels of complexity, and (2) the results of cluster analysis providing the foundation for designing adaptive scaffolding strategies.

4.1 The Role of Domain Knowledge in Problem-Solving Skills

The results from regression analyses examined the impact of domain knowledge and knowledge gain on various dimensions of problem-solving skills. Domain knowledge emerged as a significant positive predictor across all problem-solving dimensions, with the strongest effects observed for Logical Progression ($B = 4.39$) and Physics Approach ($B = 3.35$). Knowledge gain was positively associated with Useful Description ($B = 1.83$) and Logical Progression ($B = 1.29$), but showed a negative or negligible relationship with Physics Approach ($B = -0.56$) and Specific Physics Application ($B = -0.12$). The proportion of explained variance (R^2)

ranged from .10 to .26, with the highest value for Logical Progression, indicating that domain knowledge and knowledge gain together accounted for 26% of the variance in students' ability to logically organize their solutions.

4.2 Student Profiles of Problem-Solving Skills

Ward's hierarchical clustering identified three distinct learner profiles based on MAPS rubric scores (Docktor et al., 2016), with K-means refinement confirming cluster stability (average silhouette = 0.46). These empirically derived profiles—Expert (n=19), Novice (n=31), and Struggling (n=25)—differed significantly across all problem-solving dimensions (all $p < .001$). Experts demonstrated consistently high performance across all dimensions, particularly excelling in *Specific Physics Application* (M=3.47) and *Logical Progression* (M=3.37). This pattern reflects integrated conceptual understanding and strategic execution—they articulated underlying principles early, maintained coherent solution pathways, and efficiently transferred knowledge to novel contexts. Novices showed moderate competence in *Useful Description* (M=2.71) and *Physics Approach* (M=2.48), but struggled significantly with *Specific Physics Application* (M=1.90). This indicates fragmented conceptual transfer: they could outline general approaches but failed to apply domain-specific principles precisely without scaffolding. Struggling learners exhibited critical gaps, especially in *Specific Physics Application* (M=0.88) and *Logical Progression* (M=1.12). Their solutions often omitted core physics concepts, displayed disjointed reasoning, and relied on superficial feature matching rather than systematic analysis.

4.3 Student Profiles and Metacognitive Skills

We analyzed the relationship between metacognitive dimensions (Planning, Monitoring, Self-Regulation, and Reflection) and student performance metrics across the three identified clusters. One-way ANOVA revealed significant differences between clusters only for Planning, $F(2,72) = 4.45$, $p = .015$, $\eta^2 = .11$, with Expert students demonstrating the highest planning scores (M = 3.20) compared to Novice (M = 2.80) and Struggling students (M = 2.50). Monitoring showed a similar but less pronounced pattern, $F(2,72) = 3.56$, $p = .034$, $\eta^2 = .09$, with Experts (M = 3.00) outperforming Novices (M = 2.50) and Struggling learners (M = 2.40). Self-Regulation and Reflection did not show statistically significant differences between profiles. When examining clusters separately, metacognitive dimensions significantly predicted Problem-Solving Skills only for Expert students, $R^2 = .43$, $p = .048$, with Planning and Monitoring as the primary contributors. The regression models were not significant for Novice and Struggling clusters.

4.4 Profiling Learner Characteristics: Knowledge, Performance and Metacognition

To situate the clusters within the broader data landscape we computed additional indicators: (1)domain knowledge tests, (2) performance on the most ill-structured complex task (Task 4) and two metacognitive ratings (Planning, Monitoring) (Flavell 1979, Shraw et al., 1994). Expert students outperformed both Novice and Struggling groups on all measures. Knowledge gain was positive for both Experts and Novices (+.08), but slightly negative for Struggling students (–.03). Domain knowledge also showed a strong profile effect ($\eta^2 = .19$), with Experts (M = .58) surpassing Novices (.49) and Struggling students (.37). Metacognitive ratings for Planning and Monitoring followed a similar trend. Effect sizes (η^2) ranged from .07 (knowledge gain) to .31 (Task 4), underscoring that learner profile accounted for meaningful proportions of variance in both cognitive and metacognitive outcomes.

5. DISCUSSION

The identification of three distinct learner profiles - Expert, Novice, and Struggling - aligns closely with the Dreyfus model of skill acquisition (Dreyfus & Dreyfus, 1980), wherein Struggling learners operate at a rule-dependent stage, relying on explicit procedural guidance; Novices function at a context-bound stage, applying strategies situationally but lacking fluidity; and Experts demonstrate intuitive proficiency by holistically adapting their strategies to complex problems. The results underscore domain knowledge as a foundational element of students' complex problem-solving capabilities. Consistent with existing literature (Sweller et al., 2011, Jonassen, 2011), students with higher initial domain knowledge demonstrated more effective logical progression and physics-based problem-solving approaches. Interestingly, while knowledge gain positively influenced students' abilities in providing useful descriptions and logical structuring of solutions, it had a negligible or negative impact on physics-specific applications, suggesting that domain-specific competencies rely more on previously established understanding than on short-term interventions (Docktor et al., 2016).

Additionally, our investigation into metacognitive strategies revealed planning as the most influential dimension in successful problem-solving, with significant correlations between planning and problem-solving skills ($r = .29$, $p < .05$) and between monitoring and problem-solving skills ($r = .31$, $p < .01$), supporting the integration of explicit metacognitive training within learning activities (Schraw et al., 1994; Flavell, 1979). Notably, the predictive power of metacognitive skills was especially pronounced among Experts, for whom planning and monitoring accounted for 43% of the variance in problem-solving skills ($R^2 = .43$, $p = .048$), while these dimensions were less predictive for Novices and Struggling students, suggesting that lower-performing students may require more explicit instruction and scaffolding to develop these strategies effectively.

Our findings have important implications for technology-enhanced learning environments, as early identification of learner profiles using minimally invasive metrics—such as initial task performance and domain knowledge assessments—can inform targeted scaffolding strategies and support the development of adaptive digital learning resources (Wang and Chang, 2024; Ley et al., 2023). Our research demonstrates that to support meaningful learning in TEL environments, it is essential to activate students' prior knowledge, embed metacognitive prompts directly into the learning process, and use learner profiling to inform differentiated scaffolding. This can be achieved by designing tasks that provide adaptive prompts based on learners' current performance, gradually fading support as students gain competence, and using simple behavioral indicators, such as success rates on complex tasks or patterns of strategy use, to dynamically adjust scaffolding levels. This approach not only aligns with theoretical models of skill acquisition but also provides practical guidance for the design of adaptive, technology-enhanced instructional systems (Van Merrienboer and Kirschner, 2017; Kim et al., 2018), and supports recent research understanding (Brod, 2021).

6. CONCLUSION

The three-cluster solution effectively differentiated students' problem-solving approaches, highlighting Expert students as those with integrated knowledge and adaptive strategies, Novices as scaffold-dependent and contextually bound, and Struggling students as exhibiting fragmented knowledge structures (Docktor et al., 2016; Dreyfus & Dreyfus, 1980). Importantly, we view problem-solving not as a fixed state that can be easily measured, but as a context- and domain-specific cognitive construct that is observable and develops over time as learners engage with tasks and receive support tailored to their individual characteristics. Domain knowledge emerged as the strongest predictor of problem-solving success across all phases, with knowledge gain serving as a secondary factor—particularly in tasks requiring logical structuring and description, but less so in those demanding specific physics application. This research demonstrates the value of combining process-oriented data with cognitive and metacognitive measures to better understand learners' behaviors in technology-enhanced environments. By integrating performance rubrics, domain knowledge tests, and interaction traces from H5P-based activities, we constructed learner profiles that reflect not only static achievement but also how students interact with tasks, use scaffolds, and apply strategies over time (Wang and Chang, 2024; Ley et al., 2023).

This study contributes to the field by (1) confirming the critical role of domain knowledge in complex problem-solving and (2) identifying distinct learner profiles through passive task and test results that signal the need for differentiated support. Importantly, the research shows how simple authoring tools, combined with embedded process measures, can inform adaptive learning design, enabling personalized scaffolding tailored to students' evolving needs throughout different phases of learning. Future work should focus on implementing and evaluating such tailored interventions in technology enhanced environments, building on these insights to further enhance the adaptability and effectiveness of digital learning resources.

REFERENCES

Baker, R. S. (2016). Stupid Tutoring Systems, Intelligent Humans. *International Journal of Artificial Intelligence in Education*, *26*(2), 600–614. https://doi.org/10.1007/s40593-016-0105-0

Bayne, S.: What's the matter with 'technology-enhanced learning'? Learning, Media and Technology, 40, 20–35 (2015).

Brod, G. (2021). Toward an understanding of when prior knowledge helps or hinders learning. *npj Science of Learning*, *6*(1), 24.

Chernikova, O., Heitzmann, N., Stadler, M., Holzberger, D., Seidel, T., & Fischer, F.: Simulation-Based Learning in Higher Education: A Meta-Analysis. Review of Educational Research, 90, 499–541 (2020).

Carlson, M. P., & Bloom, I. (2005). The Cyclic Nature of Problem Solving: An Emergent Multidimensional Problem-Solving Framework. *Educational Studies in Mathematics*, *58*(1), 45–75. https://doi.org/10.1007/s10649-005-0808-x

Chen, Y., Li, X., Liu, J., & Ying, Z. (2019). Statistical Analysis of Complex Problem-Solving Process Data: An Event History Analysis Approach. *Frontiers in Psychology*, *10*. https://doi.org/10.3389/fpsyg.2019.00486

Chi, M. T. H., & Others, A. (1981). *Expertise in Problem Solving*. https://eric.ed.gov/?id=ED215899

Chi, M. T. H., & Wylie, R. (2014). The ICAP Framework: Linking Cognitive Engagement to Active Learning Outcomes. *Educational Psychologist*, *49*(4), 219–243. https://doi.org/10.1080/00461520.2014.965823

Docktor, J. L., Dornfeld, J., Frodermann, E., Heller, K., Hsu, L., Jackson, K. A., Mason, A., Ryan, Q. X., & Yang, J. (2016). Assessing student written problem solutions: A problem-solving rubric with application to introductory physics. *Physical Review Physics Education Research*, *12*(1), 010130. https://doi.org/10.1103/PhysRevPhysEducRes.12.010130

Dreyfus, S.E. & Dreyfus, Hubert. (1980). A Five-Stage Model of the Mental Activities Involved in Directed Skill Acquisition. Distribution. 22.

Flavell, J. H. (1979). Metacognition and cognitive monitoring: A new area of cognitive–developmental inquiry. *American Psychologist*, *34*(10), 906–911. https://doi.org/10.1037/0003-066X.34.10.906

Geisinger, K. F. (2016). 21st Century Skills: What Are They and How Do We Assess Them? *Applied Measurement in Education*, *29*(4), 245–249. https://doi.org/10.1080/08957347.2016.1209207

Gould, K. A. (2013). *Comparing changes in content knowledge between online Problem Based Learning and traditional instruction in undergraduate health professional students*. http://hdl.handle.net/11603/2064

Greiff, S., Niepel, C., Scherer, R., & Martin, R. (2016). Understanding students' performance in a computer-based assessment of complex problem solving: An analysis of behavioral data from computer-generated log files. *Comput. Hum. Behav.*, *61*, 36–46. https://doi.org/10.1016/j.chb.2016.02.095

He, Q., & Davier, M. (2015). *Identifying Feature Sequences from Process Data in Problem-Solving Items with N -Grams*. 173–190. https://doi.org/10.1007/978-3-319-19977-1_13

Jonassen, D. (2011). Supporting Problem Solving in PBL. *Interdisciplinary Journal of Problem-Based Learning*, *5*(2), Article 2. https://doi.org/10.7771/1541-5015.1256

Karumbaiah, S., Borchers, C., Falhs, A. C., Holstein, K., Rummel, N., & Aleven, V. (2023). Teacher noticing and student learning in human-AI partnered classrooms: A multimodal analysis. In *Proceedings of the 17th International Conference of the Learning Sciences* (pp. 1042–1045). International Society of the Learning Sciences.

Kim, N. J., Belland, B. R., & Walker, A. E. (2018). Effectiveness of Computer-Based Scaffolding in the Context of Problem-Based Learning for Stem Education: Bayesian Meta-analysis. *Educational Psychology Review*, *30*(2), 397–429. https://doi.org/10.1007/s10648-017-9419-1

Kirschner, P. A., Sweller, J., & Clark, R. E. (2006). Why Minimal Guidance During Instruction Does Not Work: An Analysis of the Failure of Constructivist, Discovery, Problem-Based, Experiential, and Inquiry-Based Teaching. *Educational Psychologist*, *41*(2), 75–86. https://doi.org/10.1207/s15326985ep4102_1

Kollar, I., Wecker, C., & Fischer, F. (2018). Scaffolding and Scripting (Computer-Supported) Collaborative Learning. In *International Handbook of the Learning Sciences*. Routledge.

Ley, T., Tammets, K., Pishtari, G., Chejara, P., Kasepalu, R., Khalil, M., Saar, M., Tuvi, I., Väljataga, T., & Wasson, B. (2023). Towards a partnership of teachers and intelligent learning technology: A systematic literature review of model-based learning analytics. *Journal of Computer Assisted Learning, 39*(5), 1397–1417. https://doi.org/10.1111/jcal.12844

Pettersson, F. (2018). On the issues of digital competence in educational contexts – a review of literature. *Education and Information Technologies, 23*(3), 1005–1021. https://doi.org/10.1007/s10639-017-9649-3

Phungsuk, R., Viriyavejakul, C., & Ratanaolarn, T. (2017). Development of a problem-based learning model via a virtual learning environment. *Kasetsart Journal of Social Sciences, 38*(3), 297–306. https://doi.org/10.1016/j.kjss.2017.01.001

Savery, J. R. (2015). Overview of problem-based learning: Definitions and distinctions. *Essential readings in problem-based learning: Exploring and extending the legacy of Howard S. Barrows, 9*(2), 5-15.

Schäfer, J., Reuter, T., Karbach, J., & Leuchter, M. (2024). Domain-specific knowledge and domain-general abilities in children's science problem-solving. *British Journal of Educational Psychology, 94*(2), 346–366. https://doi.org/10.1111/bjep.12649

Schraw, G., & Dennison, R. S. (1994). Assessing Metacognitive Awareness. *Contemporary Educational Psychology, 19*(4), 460–475. https://doi.org/10.1006/ceps.1994.1033

Shapiro, A. M. (2004). How Including Prior Knowledge As a Subject Variable May Change Outcomes of Learning Research. *American Educational Research Journal, 41*(1), 159–189. https://doi.org/10.3102/00028312041001159

Simonsmeier, B., Flaig, M., Deiglmayr, A., Schalk, L., & Schneider, M.: Domain- specific prior knowledge and learning: A meta-analysis. Educational Psychologist, 57, 31–54 (2021).

Silber-Varod, V., Eshet, Y., & Geri, N. (2019). Tracing research trends of 21st-century learning skills. *Br. J. Educ. Technol., 50*, 3099–3118. https://doi.org/10.1111/BJET.12753

Sweller, J., Clark, R. E., & Kirschner, P. A. (2011.). *Teaching general problem solving does not lead to mathematical skills or knowledge.*

Van Merriënboer, J. J. G. van, & Kirschner, P. A. (2017). *Ten Steps to Complex Learning: A Systematic Approach to Four-Component Instructional Design* (3rd ed.). Routledge. https://doi.org/10.4324/9781315113210

Wang, X., Maeda, Y., & Chang, H. (2024). Development and techniques in learner model in adaptive e-learning system: A systematic review. *Comput. Educ.* https://www.semanticscholar.org/paper/Development-and-techniques-in-learner-model-in-A-Wang-Maeda/868698d46df9846b00b5469de63fd5c57c4e0f09

Zheng, L., Li, X., Zhang, X., & Sun, W. (2019). The effects of group metacognitive scaffolding on group metacognitive behaviors, group performance, and cognitive load in computer-supported collaborative learning. *The Internet and Higher Education, 42*, 13–24. https://doi.org/10.1016/j.iheduc.2019.03.002

FROM CURRICULUM FOR ALL TO INCLUSIVE PRACTICE: INSIGHTS FROM A PILOT STUDY ON UDL-BASED PEDAGOGICAL TRANSFORMATION

Sara Cruz[1] and Marisa Maia[2]

[1]*Applied Artificial Intelligence Laboratory (2Ai), Polytechnic Univeristy of Cávado and Ave, Barcelos, Portugal*
Research Centre on Education (CIEd), University of Minho, Braga, Portugal
Center for Research & Innovation in Education (inED), Polytechnic University of Porto Porto, Portugal
[2]*Research Centre on Didactics and Technology in the Education of Trainers, Department of Education and Psychology of the University of Aveiro, Aveiro, Portugal*

ABSTRACT

In the context of growing demands for inclusive and flexible pedagogical practices in higher education, this study explores how university lecturers can transform their teaching through the lens of Universal Design for Learning (UDL). Grounded in a pedagogical innovation initiative, this pilot study followed four higher education lecturers over the course of one semester as they engaged in a professional development process aimed at redesigning their teaching practices based on the principles of UDL. The objective was to understand the extent to which these lecturers appropriated and applied UDL principles in their pedagogical approaches. Employing a qualitative case study methodology, the research draws on document analysis of final reflective posters produced by each participant, which synthesise the evolution of their teaching practices. The findings reveal that all lecturers successfully integrated UDL principles into different aspects of their instruction, demonstrating increased awareness and practical application of strategies to enhance accessibility, flexibility, and learner engagement. Notably, there was a clear emerging trend towards the adoption of Artificial Intelligence tools as a means to support differentiated instruction and promote inclusive learning environments. This integration of AI technologies appears to complement UDL's emphasis on multiple means of representation, engagement, and expression. The study underscores the potential of structured, reflective, and context-sensitive professional development to foster meaningful pedagogical change in higher education, while also highlighting the evolving role of AI in supporting inclusive and adaptive teaching practices. These findings offer valuable insights for institutional strategies aiming to scale inclusive education through UDL and digital innovation.

KEYWORDS

Teaching Practices, Inclusive Education, UDL, Artificial Intelligence Tools, Pedagogical Innovation, Higher Education

1. INTRODUCTION

Pedagogical innovation in higher education is a complex and ongoing process that seeks not only rhetorical change, but also a deep and sustained transformation of teaching and learning practices (Nabwire, 2016; Rege Colet, 2017). As universities face increased student diversity and rapid technological advancement, there is growing pressure to adopt flexible, inclusive, and learning-centred approaches. Despite widespread advocacy for methods such as project-based and collaborative learning, many lecturers still demonstrate limited appropriation of these strategies (Marisol, 2019), hindered by structural and cultural barriers that restrict meaningful inclusion (Fiorucci et al., 2025). Within this landscape, the Universal Design for Learning (UDL) framework has emerged as a promising approach for creating accessible and equitable learning environments (Hills et al., 2022; Schreiner et al., 2024). This article presents findings from a pilot study conducted within the scope of the Pedagogical Excellence and Innovation in Co-creation (EPIC) project, an inter-institutional initiative supporting pedagogical excellence and innovation in Portuguese higher education. Specifically, the study focuses on the "+Plural" training pathway, which supports lecturers in integrating UDL principles through a co-creation-based model. The research followed four lecturers from different universities over a semester-long training process aimed at fostering inclusive teaching practices. At the end of the intervention, each participant created a reflective poster synthesizing their pedagogical transformation. Drawing on a qualitative (Bryman, 2012), exploratory case study methodology (Yin, 2011) and document analysis of the posters, the study found that all participants appropriated UDL principles in various aspects of their teaching. Notably, a trend emerged towards the use of Artificial Intelligence tools to enhance differentiation and accessibility.

2. PEDAGOGICAL INNOVATION AND UNIVERSAL DESIGN FOR LEARNING IN HIGHER EDUCATION

Pedagogical innovation in higher education is a complex process that involves both the rhetoric of change and the sustained transformation of teaching and learning practices. According to the literature reviewed (Nabwire, 2016; Rege Colet, 2017), the technological revolution and the increase in higher education attendance have triggered transformations in teaching practices and academic identity, leading to a pedagogical revolution that reframes teaching practices to better serve student learning. Innovative pedagogical approaches, such as project-based learning, research-based learning, and collaborative learning, are increasingly adopted in higher education, yet teachers often demonstrate a limited appropriation of knowledge about these strategies, underlining the need for targeted training and sustained institutional support (Marisol, 2019). This challenge is compounded by the persistence of cultural and structural barriers that continue to limit meaningful inclusion, despite regulatory advances and policy frameworks aimed at widening access (Fiorucci et al., 2025). As noted by Gough (2005), pedagogical innovation must be understood as part of a broader transformation toward sustainable and equitable educational models. Sustainable innovations, such as the application of transformational frameworks like Theory U, offer promising directions by shifting the emphasis from content-centred to learning-centred approaches and fostering student agency (Nabwire, 2016; Rege Colet, 2017). However, disseminating ICT-based methods that require deep shifts in teaching mindsets remains challenging without well-structured professional development and institutional leadership (Agélii Genlott et al., 2019). In this regard, faculty development programmes play a pivotal role in supporting lecturers to rethink traditional teaching practices through inclusive and evidence-informed frameworks such as UDL (Fiorucci et al., 2025).

To address this point, we emphasise that UDL was selected as the guiding framework because it provides a systematic, evidence-informed approach to designing learning environments that proactively remove barriers and foster participation for diverse learners. UDL is a promising instructional approach that has the potential to support inclusion and enhance access to academic content for all students in higher education (Hills et al., 2022; Schreiner et al., 2024). The general understanding of UDL aligns with the conceptualisation and framework developed by CAST (2024), which presents UDL as a means of enhancing the teaching and learning process; mitigating barriers to learning and reducing the need for individual accommodations; and supporting curriculum design and planning aimed at developing accessible, inclusive, and flexible learning environments for all students. The UDL framework is structured around three core principles, each associated with specific neural networks involved in learning (Meyer et al., 2014): (i) Engagement - the "why" of learning – linked to the affective networks; (ii) Representation - the "what" of learning, to the recognition networks; (iii) Action and Expression - the "how" of learning, to the strategic networks.

In the context of UDL, the notion of "networks" refers metaphorically to interconnected cognitive processes that work in concert during learning. These networks operate in an integrated way during the learning process, contributing to: (i) providing means of engagement and motivation that are accessible to all students; (ii) offering information and support materials in accessible formats and (iii) ensuring varied ways for students to act upon and demonstrate their learning, suited to different needs and preferences (Meyer et al., 2014). UDL offers a comprehensive framework for creating flexible learning environments by providing multiple means of representation, engagement, and expression, thereby accommodating a wide range of learning needs (Ryder, 2019; Schreiner et al., 2024). Its implementation in higher education has been shown to improve both access and equity in learning outcomes, benefiting not only students with disabilities but also international students and other diverse learner groups (Beck Wells, 2022; Schreiner et al., 2024). However, research has pointed to considerable variability in how UDL is understood and implemented across contexts, as well as to persistent systemic challenges, including time and resource constraints, limited institutional support, and insufficient faculty understanding, which continue to hinder its widespread adoption in higher education (Hills et al., 2022;

Hollingshead et al., 2022). To overcome these barriers, scholars argue for a combination of bottom-up and top-down strategies, such as embedding UDL practices across university curricula and investing in ongoing faculty training and support, in order to foster broader and more consistent implementation of UDL principles (Hills et al., 2022).

Moriña et al. (2025) argue that the training in the UDL approach is essential to promoting a richer and more equitable educational experience for all students. Professional development that builds capacity in inclusive practice can empower lecturers to move beyond standardisation, embracing flexibility and responsiveness in course design and delivery.

3. EPIC METHOD FOR TEACHER TRAINING

The "+Plural" training pathway is one of the thematic programmes designed by the EPIC (Pedagogical Excellence and Innovation in Co-creation) consortium, a collaborative initiative involving six higher education institutions in Portugal. Embedded in a broader strategy of pedagogical transformation, it focuses on promoting accessibility and inclusion through the UDL framework. Grounded in a co-creation model, it positions teachers as reflective practitioners and students as partners. The "+Plural" course supports faculty in designing inclusive environments by fostering understanding and application of UDL principles (CAST, 2024), integrating theoretical grounding with hands-on implementation and peer collaboration.

This article reports findings from a pilot within EPIC at the introductory level of the +Plural pathway, involving short-term hybrid training sessions (e.g., inter-institutional seminars) to raise awareness of inclusive pedagogy and UDL. Digital tools played a critical role as enablers of accessibility and flexible learning. The programme aligns with international standards and emphasises transferability across disciplines.

Building on this, the present research adopted a qualitative exploratory-descriptive approach (Bryman, 2012) to examine how higher education teachers participating in a semester-long innovation programme appropriated UDL (CAST, 2024) in their practice. Data triangulation combined participants' artefacts, observation of progression, and written reflections. Content analysis followed Bardin's (1977) framework, with categories aligned to UDL principles. In line with Flick's (2004) considerations on trustworthiness, we ensured transparency and systematic documentation of corpus constitution and coding. This analytical process allowed for the triangulation of different data sources (participant artefacts, observation notes, written reflections), thereby enhancing the credibility and rigour of the findings. It also facilitated a deeper understanding of how UDL principles were interpreted, adapted, and implemented by the participants within their institutional teaching contexts.

The research unfolded in structured phases:

- Initial engagement took place asynchronously via a virtual platform, where participants shared self-presentations and explored the programme structure, schedule, and resources. This stage included the launch of Activity 1, focused on introductory reflections.
- A synchronous session offering a live walkthrough of the course, clarification of doubts, and collective discussion. This session also introduced Activity, which prompted participants to reflect on inclusion.
- Two further synchronous sessions expanded on key theoretical dimensions: (I) Session 2 explored the concept of the "myth of average" and (II) Session 3 addressed learner diversity through the lens of "a plural classroom with real characters".
- A residential retreat provided space for participants to plan a transformative teaching project, grounded in UDL. Each participant produced a pre-project proposal aligned with their teaching context.
- During the planning, participants refined their project plans asynchronously on the virtual platform, engaging in peer feedback and critical reflection.
- The implementation stage involved carrying out the projects and sharing experiences with peers via the digital platform.
- In the final, participants evaluated the process, completed a reflective questionnaire, and prepared a digital poster synthesising their learning.
- The programme concluded with a poster presentation session, in which participants collectively shared and discussed the outcomes of their transformation projects.

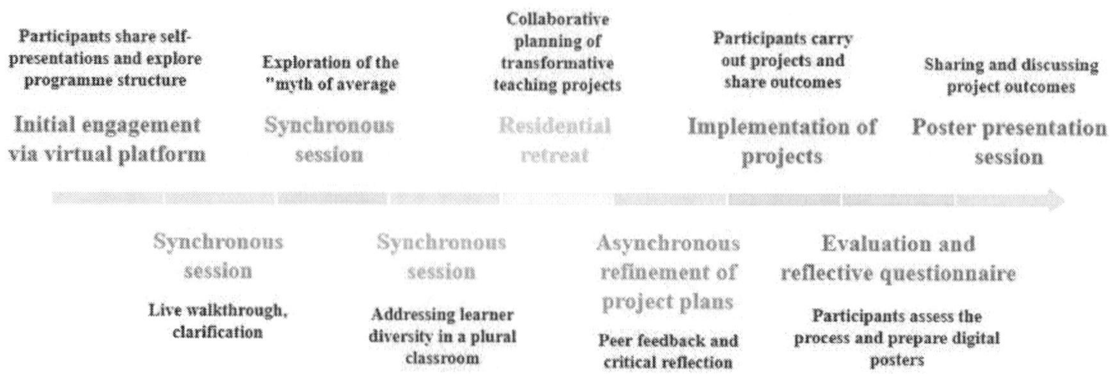

Figure 1. EPIC Transformative Teaching Programme

Throughout the training pathway, evidence was systematically collected, allowing the research team to trace the appropriation and operationalisation of UDL in real teaching contexts. The analysis focused on identifying patterns, challenges, and indicators of pedagogical transformation anchored in the UDL framework (CAST, 2024).

In this sense we bring to the discussion the practical dimension of the teacher's role, highlighting teachers' knowledge as inherently practical, a form of "knowing how" shaped by theoretical foundations and professional experience, and constructed within a specific teaching context. As Elbaz (1983) argued, such knowledge emerges from practice itself and is central to the development of new learning. The importance of reflection-in-action and reflection-on-action (Schön, 1997), combined with a diverse set of professional competencies, is seen as fundamental to advancing more reflexive and collaborative pedagogical practices that respond more effectively to the realities of the school context. Callaghan (2015) advocates for an interactive-reflective approach as a structured and productive way of engaging with the teaching–learning process. He describes teaching as a reflective activity, a form of doing in which each step is weighed, and every decision is made through deliberation. In a similar vein, the teacher can be understood as a classroom researcher, turning everyday practice into a learning laboratory where experimentation and reflection inform pedagogical choices. From this perspective, curricula are not static prescriptions but dynamic constructs, shaped in response to students' specific needs and the contextual realities of their learning environments.

This study supports a model of teacher education grounded in continuous reflection and practice-based inquiry, with action research gaining relevance. Such an approach is understood as internally co-constructed, embedded in the evolving use of new methodologies and technologies, and capable of fostering the development of interdisciplinary and transversal pedagogical projects. It promotes the image of the teacher as a reflective practitioner-researcher, who assumes authorship of their own professional knowledge (Day, 2012).

4. PILOT RESULTS AND DISCUSSION

UDL is structured around three fundamental principles: multiple forms of representation, action and expression, and engagement (CAST, 2024). Based on these principles, three pedagogical projects presented in poster format were analysed to identify how they reflect practices aligned with the UDL in higher education.

Project 1: This inter- and transdisciplinary project (developed by two teachers) promoted the co-creation of digital artistic outputs (videos, podcasts, musical compositions, graphic materials) with undergraduate and master's students. Through the integration of active learning methodologies (PBL, ABL, CBL) and accessible digital tools (Padlet, Miro, Canva, CapCut, AI), students developed a wide range of skills within a highly collaborative and inclusive learning environment.

- **Representation**: Content was explored in diverse formats (audio, image, video), enabling access to information through multiple pathways.
- **Action and Expression**: Students expressed their learning through creative and varied means, aligned with their preferences and strengths.

- **Engagement**: Motivation was fostered through connection to meaningful themes and by valuing student authorship, enhancing their sense of belonging and participation.

Project 2: This project focused on transforming an optional module to better address the diversity of the student cohort. The strategy involved active learning approaches such as the Jigsaw method, a diversification of resources, and greater flexibility in assessment (e.g., recorded lectures, subtitles, materials in English, self-assessment, digital learning diaries).

- **Representation**: Resources were made available through multiple channels, accommodating various learning styles and individual needs.
- **Action and Expression**: Students were offered diverse opportunities to demonstrate their learning, with a focus on self-regulation and formative feedback.
- **Engagement**: By incorporating collaborative and flexible approaches, the project promoted participation and reduced resistance to involvement, aligning with the principle of sustained motivation.

Project 3: This project applied UDL principles in a laboratory activity based on a guided discovery model. It was observed that many students experienced anxiety due to uncertainty around procedures and oral assessments. To address these barriers, strategies such as preparatory sessions, formative training, and dialogue opportunities were introduced.

- **Representation**: A pre-laboratory session with a quiz and clear learning objectives helped clarify expectations and enhance understanding of the procedures.
- **Action and Expression**: Group oral assessments were preceded by practice opportunities, allowing students to try out different forms of expression and build confidence.
- **Engagement**: The creation of a safe, trust-based environment contributed to reduced anxiety and an increased sense of belonging.

Each of the three posters analysed in this study reflects principles of UDL in their design, with an emphasis on creating accessible, inclusive, and equitable learning environments that accommodate student diversity.

Considering the strategies outlined in the UDL framework (CAST, 2024) and how they are being applied in higher education contexts, the analysis of the three pilot projects provides relevant insights into the pedagogical transformation currently underway in the EPIC initiative. The first project reflects the foundational principles of UDL by fostering recognition of students' expectations, emotions, and motivations; the development of self-awareness and empathy; collective reflection; and restoration of practices. These elements align with the UDL principle of engagement, which addresses the "why" of learning and is associated with the affective network (Meyer et al., 2014). The project also highlights inclusive strategies that promote active participation and collaboration, thus providing students with multiple ways of engaging meaningfully with learning tasks. Such an approach resonates with the shift described by Nabwire (2016) and Rege Colet (2017), where sustainable pedagogical innovation moves from content-centred to learning-centred models that empower student agency.

The second project demonstrates a clear alignment with the UDL framework developed by CAST (2024), recognising UDL to enhance teaching and learning while mitigating learning barriers and reducing the need for individual accommodations. Through the intentional diversification of teaching resources and assessment methods, this project supports curriculum design that fosters accessibility, flexibility, and inclusiveness for a heterogeneous student population. This aligns with findings by Schreiner et al. (2024), who emphasise the benefits of UDL in improving access and equity in higher education, particularly for international students and those with diverse needs. The project also addresses some of the structural challenges highlighted in the literature, such as the need for systematic faculty development and the embedding of UDL principles into broader curricular planning (Fiorucci et al., 2025; Hills et al., 2022).

The third project focuses on specific strategies aimed at enhancing student engagement and participation in higher education settings. These include defining clear objectives, anticipating challenges, organising content and resources, and creating iterative feedback loops. These practices align strongly with the UDL principles of action and expression, the "how" of learning, and representation, the "what", by offering students different ways of demonstrating their learning and by making content more accessible through intentional design. The project also addresses the emotional dimension of learning by acknowledging and mitigating student apprehension, particularly around assessment formats, thus supporting more equitable learning experiences.

These findings must be understood within the broader context of ongoing pedagogical transformation in higher education. The technological revolution and increased access to higher education have prompted significant shifts in academic identity and teaching practices, giving rise to what some authors describe as a "pedagogical revolution" (Gough, 2005; Marisol, 2019). Although innovative strategies, such as project-based, research-based and collaborative learning, are increasingly adopted, their implementation is often limited by faculty's basic understanding of these approaches and the lack of institutional support (Agélii Genlott et al., 2019; Fiorucci et al., 2025). This underlines the importance of targeted training programmes that build capacity in inclusive teaching and empower educators to design responsive learning environments.

UDL helps dismantle structural and pedagogical barriers, shifting the focus from standardised delivery to inclusive and learner-centred design (Schreiner et al., 2024). As Moriña et al. (2025) argue, meaningful implementation of UDL in higher education requires not only awareness of the framework but also sustained professional development that supports academic staff in rethinking teaching roles and practices.

The variability in the application of UDL across contexts, as noted by Hollingshead et al. (2022), and Hills et al. (2022), points to the need for both top-down and bottom-up strategies to ensure broader and more consistent implementation. Embedding UDL principles across institutional structures and investing in ongoing faculty development are critical steps in achieving the kind of pedagogical transformation that the EPIC project aims to promote. In addition to exploring the pedagogical integration of UDL, this study also aimed to examine how participating lecturers adopted digital technologies, particularly AI to support differentiation and inclusive teaching. The analysis of the final reflective posters revealed notable variation in the extent and pedagogical intentionality with which these technologies were applied.

The Arts4Community project stands out for its comprehensive and pedagogically integrated use of digital tools and generative AI. A variety of technologies were employed to support collaborative, artistic, and community-driven learning, such as Canva, CapCut, Audacity, Padlet, Miro, and institutional platforms (Moodle, Zoom, Microsoft 365). Of particular note is the integration of generative AI tools for music creation, positioning AI not merely as a technical novelty, but as a core resource for creative and inclusive engagement. This echoes Oyelere et al. (2020), who argue that smart learning ecosystems combining emergent technologies and inclusive pedagogies can expand access and student agency. In such ecosystems, AI and digital storytelling act as enablers of learner-centred, multimodal, and accessible educational experiences, aligning closely with the UDL principles of multiple means of representation, action/expression, and engagement.

Although the F.I.T Learning project implemented valuable inclusive practices, such as flexible assessment, diversified resources, and active learning methods, it did not reference the use of specific digital tools or AI. The transformation was focused on curriculum redesign and inclusive methodology, without a clear technological component. As Martins et al. (2019) point out, systemic barriers such as limited institutional support and digital literacy among faculty often hinder the effective implementation of technological innovations, even in contexts open to pedagogical change.

The Laboratory of Bacteriology project included a peripheral reference to AI using ChatGPT for visual content generation. While this represents an explicit use of generative AI, its application was largely illustrative, lacking deeper integration into the teaching-learning process. This reflects what Oyelere et al. (2020) describes as the "instrumental adoption" of technology, where tools are used sporadically or superficially, without being embedded in a broader pedagogical strategy aimed at inclusion or differentiation.

Table 1. Summary of Digital and AI Tool Integration in Pilot Posters

Poster	**Use of Digital Tools**	**Reference to AI**	**Type of AI Use**
Arts4Community	Yes	Yes	Generative AI used for collaborative artistic creation
Aprendizagem F.I.T.	No	No	
Laboratory of Bacteriology	Yes	Yes	AI-generated images using ChatGPT (illustrative, not pedagogical)

The comparative analysis shows that while all projects demonstrated meaningful uptake of UDL principles, the Arts4Community initiative was unique in its systematic and intentional integration of digital tools and AI, clearly aligned with the UDL emphasis on offering multiple means of engagement, representation, and expression (CAST, 2024). In line with Oyelere et al. (2020), this approach represents a move towards inclusive smart learning ecosystems, where emerging technologies enhance learner autonomy, diversity, and creativity. Conversely, the other two projects, though innovative in pedagogical terms, highlight the persistent variability and unevenness of technological adoption in higher education, as also reported by Martins et al. (2019). This underscores the need for structured, sustained professional development, such as the EPIC initiative, to build faculty capacity in both inclusive pedagogy and digital innovation. The growing presence of AI, even in exploratory or marginal uses, suggests awareness among educators of its potential to personalize learning and reduce access barriers. As digital ecosystems continue to evolve, combining pedagogical frameworks like UDL with emerging technologies such as AI, blockchain, and learning analytics (Martins et al., 2019; Oyelere et al., 2020) will be crucial to shaping inclusive, equitable, and future-ready higher education environments.

5. CONCLUSION

This study contributes to the growing body of research at the intersection of inclusive pedagogy and digital innovation by offering empirically grounded insights into how university lecturers in higher education can meaningfully appropriate the UDL framework in tandem with emerging technologies such as Artificial Intelligence (AI). Through the qualitative analysis of three pedagogical projects developed in the context of a semester-long professional development programme, the research demonstrates that UDL principles, particularly those of multiple means of engagement, representation, and expression, can be effectively embedded in diverse instructional contexts when supported by reflective, sustained, and context-sensitive faculty training (Fiorucci et al., 2025; Moriña et al., 2025).

A key finding of this study lies in the observed differentiation in the use of digital tools and AI among the participating lecturers. While all projects evidenced alignment with UDL principles, only one, the Arts4Community initiative, exemplified the systematic and pedagogically meaningful integration of generative AI technologies. This project illustrates the transformative potential of combining UDL with AI to promote learner agency, creative expression, and collaborative knowledge production, echoing the concept of "smart learning ecosystems" as articulated by Oyelere et al. (2020), where digital storytelling and emergent technologies are leveraged to foster inclusion, accessibility, and learner-centred engagement.

In contrast, the other cases revealed either limited or peripheral use of digital technologies, underscoring persistent structural and cultural barriers in higher education, such as lack of institutional support and gaps in digital literacy among faculty (Hills et al., 2022; Martins et al., 2019). These findings are consistent with broader literature on pedagogical transformation, which stresses that the mere presence of technological tools is insufficient without sustained professional development and a shift towards inclusive, learner-centred design (Nabwire, 2016; Rege Colet, 2017). The innovative character of this research rests not only in its focus on UDL appropriation but also in its attention to how digital ecosystems, particularly those incorporating AI, are beginning to reshape pedagogical practice in higher education. As noted by Oyelere et al. (2020), when properly embedded in inclusive frameworks, technologies like AI and blockchain can empower both students and educators, enhancing collaboration, multimodality, and equitable access to learning.

This study therefore advances the field by illustrating how AI can be integrated in ways that enhance, not substitute, human-centred, inclusive teaching. As higher education institutions increasingly grapple with diversity, technological complexity, and the demand for personalisation, this work offers a timely and actionable model for aligning pedagogical innovation with inclusive design. Future research should continue to explore how AI, when used critically and ethically, can serve as a catalyst for inclusive education within robust frameworks like UDL (Schreiner et al., 2024), while institutional strategies must prioritise sustained faculty development and cross-disciplinary collaboration to ensure pedagogical transformation is both equitable and scalable (Beck Wells, 2022; Hollingshead et al., 2022).

Future research should further investigate how different disciplinary contexts influence the appropriation of UDL principles in conjunction with AI and explore the long-term impact of faculty training programmes on sustaining inclusive, technology-enhanced teaching practices in higher education.

ACKNOWLEDGEMENT

We acknowledge the EPIC consortium. EPIC is part of the Impulso Mais Digital investment programme and is financially supported by the Portuguese Recovery and Resilience Plan, under the coordination of the Estrutura de Missão Recuperar Portugal and the Directorate-General for Higher Education.

REFERENCES

Agélii Genlott, A., Grönlund, Å., & Viberg, O. (2019). Disseminating digital innovation in school–leading second-order educational change. *Education and Information Technologies*, *24*, 3021-3039.

Bardin, L. (1977). *Análise de conteúdo*. Lisboa: Edições 70.

Beck Wells, M. (2022). Student perspectives on the use of universal design for learning in virtual formats in higher education. *Smart Learning Environments*, *9*(1), 37. https://doi.org/10.1186/s40561-022-00218-6.

Bryman, A. (2012). *Social Research Methods*. Oxford University Press.

CAST. (2024). *UDL Guidelines. Version 3.0*. https://udlguidelines.cast.org/more/downloads/.

Callaghan, R. (2015). Transforming teaching challenges into learning opportunities: Interdisciplinary reflective collaboration. *Africa Education Review*, *12*(4), 599-617. https://doi.org/10.1080/18146627.2015.1112145.

Day, C. (Ed.). (2012). *The Routledge international handbook of teacher and school development*. Routledge.

Elbaz, F. (1983). *Teacher thinking: A Study of Practical Knowledge*. Croom Helm.

Flick, U. (2004). *Uma introdução à pesquisa qualitativa*. São Paulo: BOOKMAN.

Fiorucci, A., Pinnelli, S., Bevilacqua, A., & Baccassino, F. (2025). Innovating University Teaching through UDL: challenges and opportunities from the DANTE-U. Project. perceptions. *Italian Journal of Health Education, Sports and Inclusive Didactics*, *9*(1). https://doi.org/10.32043/gsd.v9i1.1409.

Hills, M., Overend, A., & Hildebrandt, S. (2022). Faculty perspectives on UDL: Exploring bridges and barriers for broader adoption in higher education. The *Canadian Journal for the Scholarship of Teaching and Learning, 13*(1). https://doi.org/10.5206/cjsotlrcacea.2022.1.13588.

Gough, A. (2005). Sustainable schools: Renovating educational processes. *Applied Environmental Education and Communication*, *4*(4), 339-351. https://doi.org/10.1080/15330150500302205.

Hollingshead, A., Lowrey, K. A., & Howery, K. (2022). Universal design for learning: When policy changes before evidence. *Educational Policy*, *36*(5), 1135-1161. https://doi.org/10.1177/0895904820951120.

Marisol, E. C. (2019). Didactic trends and perceived teachers' training needs in higher education: A case study. International Journal of Cognitive Research in Science, Engineering and Education, 7(3), 71-85. https://doi.org/10.5937/IJCRSEE1903071B.

Martins, V., Oyelere, S. S., Tomczyk, L., Barros, G., Akyar, O., Eliseo, M. A., Albuquerque, C., Amato, L. H. & Silveira, I. F. (2019, November). A blockchain microsites-based ecosystem for learning and inclusion. In Brazilian Symposium on Computers in Education (Simpósio Brasileiro de Informática na Educação-SBIE) (Vol. 30, No. 1, p. 229). http://dx.doi.org/10.5753/cbie.sbie.2019.229.Meyer, A., Rose, D., & Gordon, D. (2014). *Universal Design for Learning: Theory and practice.* CAST Professional Publishing.

Moriña, A., Carballo, R., & Doménech, A. (2025). Transforming higher education: a systematic review of faculty training in UDL and its benefits. *Teaching in Higher Education*, 1-18. https://doi.org/10.1080/13562517.2025.2465994.

Nabwire, V. K. (2016). Innovative pedagogies in institutions of higher learning: Building a better future?. *European Journal of Education Studies*.

Oyelere, S. S., Silveira, I. F., Martins, V. F., Eliseo, M. A., Akyar, Ö. Y., Costas Jauregui, V., Caussin, B., Motz, R. & Tomczyk, Ł. (2020, April). Digital storytelling and blockchain as pedagogy and technology to support the development of an inclusive smart learning ecosystem. In *World Conference on Information Systems and Technologies* (pp. 397-408). Cham: Springer International Publishing. https://doi.org/10.1007/978-3-030-45697-9_39.

Rege Colet, N. M. (2017). From content-centred to learning-centred approaches: shifting educational paradigm in higher education. *Journal of Educational Administration and History*, *49*(1), 72-86.

Ryder, D. (2019). How UDL can make learning work for all your students.

Schreiner, N., Rebagay, N., & Cavendish, W. (2024). Universal Design for Learning in Higher Education to Improve Instruction in Inclusive Settings. In *The Palgrave Encyclopedia of Disability* (pp. 1-8). Cham: Springer Nature Switzerland.

Schön, D. A. (1997). Formar professores como profissionais reflexivos. In A. Nóvoa (Org.) *Os professores e sua formação*. Dom Quixote.

MEASURING SEMANTIC SIMILARITY OF LEARNING OUTCOMES: COMPUTATIONAL APPROACHES AND EDUCATIONAL IMPLICATIONS

Sorana Cimpan[1], Francesco Floris[2], Marina Marchisio Conte[2] and Sergio Rabellino[2]
[1]*University of Savoie Mont-Blanc, France*
[2]*University of Turin, Italy*

ABSTRACT

Learning outcomes (LOs) represent a pivotal component of contemporary instructional design, particularly within the context of modular and student-centred educational frameworks. However, the increasing adoption of flexible learning pathways, micro-credentials, and cross-institutional programmes has created a critical need for systematic methods to evaluate the semantic similarity between learning outcomes. This paper explores computational approaches to measuring such similarity, integrating symbolic, statistical, and hybrid methods. The SPIRAL model formalises LOs as structured, reusable entities aligned with Bloom's taxonomy. This study builds on the SPIRAL model by developing and testing a similarity metric that combines Sentence-BERT embeddings with an asymmetric adjustment based on cognitive level. A human evaluation study conducted in the domains of mathematics and physics provides a reference baseline for interpreting the results. The findings indicate that human raters consistently perceive higher similarity than the algorithm, especially in cases involving implicit conceptual or pedagogical relationships. This study makes three key contributions to the field: firstly, it advances the concept of semantic similarity as a pedagogical enabler of personalised learning pathways; secondly, it distinguishes between symmetric (equivalence) and asymmetric (implication) relations; thirdly, it promotes the use of similarity as a design driver in modular, interoperable course architectures. These contributions are instrumental in the development of intelligent educational systems that align with European frameworks, such as EQF and ESCO, while enabling scalable and meaningful personalisation of learning paths.

KEYWORDS

Learning Outcomes, Online Course Design, Personalized Learning, Semantic Similarity, SPIRAL Model, Student-Centered Learning

1. INTRODUCTION

Within the European Higher Education Area (EHEA), learning outcomes (LOs) play a pivotal role in promoting transparency, mobility, and mutual recognition of qualifications. Frameworks such as the European Qualifications Framework (EQF), the ECTS credit system, and emerging standards for micro-credentials rely on the precise articulation of LOs to support modular, flexible, and interoperable learning pathways. European policy initiatives, including the Digital Education Action Plan (2021–2027) and the Council Recommendation on micro-credentials, emphasise the importance of well-structured outcomes as the foundation for cross-institutional comparability and learner agency. This institutional vision aligns with a broader pedagogical shift toward student-centred and personalised learning. In these approaches, learners actively engage in selecting and sequencing content based on their prior experiences, goals, and preferences. This is especially true in online and hybrid environments, where students' autonomy is accentuated and instructor presence reduced. In such cases, the formulation and clarity of learning outcomes become central to effective navigation and engagement. The SPIRAL (Student centered Personalisation of Individual education through Reusable and Autonomous Learning units) model (Cimpan et al., 2024) has been developed to address this need by establishing a connection between each modular learning unit and a single, clearly defined learning outcome.

This enables the design of learning paths that are both flexible and pedagogically coherent. The model differentiates between macro and micro learning outcomes, supports reusable and autonomous units enriched with metadata (e.g. Bloom level, topic tags, and prerequisites), and allows for multiple personalised trajectories leading to equivalent competencies. This configuration enables the effective integration of instructional design and learner autonomy, thereby facilitating the dynamic generation of alternative pathways that are aligned with individual needs and prior knowledge.

Despite the centrality of LOs in both policy and pedagogy, the question of how to compare them systematically remains unresolved. It is a frequent occurrence that learners encounter overlapping competencies across different courses and platforms. However, the absence of computational methods for evaluating semantic similarity between outcomes limits the recognition of prior learning and the reusability of educational content. As digital learning ecosystems expand, the ability to detect, quantify, and interpret such similarities is crucial for supporting personalised pathways, enhancing instructional design, and fostering interoperability. Looking ahead, the SPIRAL model aims to incorporate artificial intelligence components, moving beyond static instructional design to enable the dynamic generation of adaptive, personalised learning pathways. This evolution aims to achieve the level of flexibility and scalability necessary to support the future of digital education in Europe, as outlined in the Council Recommendation on Micro-credentials for Lifelong Learning and Employability (16 June 2022). In this framework, micro-credentials are explicitly positioned as tools for empowering individuals to forge personalized and modular learning trajectories. By aligning with these policy directions and embedding inclusive design strategies, the SPIRAL model contributes to both the computational advancement of learning systems and the development of a transparent, interoperable, and learner-centred education ecosystem.

The main goal of this study is to investigate computational approaches for measuring the semantic similarity between learning outcomes, with the aim of evaluating their reliability, pedagogical plausibility, and potential integration into adaptive course design frameworks. By combining algorithmic analysis with human and AI-based validation, the study seeks to assess whether similarity metrics can support scalable, interpretable, and educationally meaningful alignment of learning outcomes. This paper is structured as follows: section 2 reviews the relevant literature and theoretical background on learning outcome similarity; section 3 outlines the methodological framework adopted for the study, including model, data and analysis procedures; section 4 presents the empirical results and section 5 offers a critical discussion of the findings, highlights their educational implications, and proposes directions for future research.

2. STATE OF THE ART

2.1 Semantic Similarity in Educational Contexts

Semantic similarity has traditionally been applied in the context of automated assessment, particularly for evaluating short constructed responses in quizzes, cloze tests, and open-ended questions (Lubis & al, 2021; de Gois, 2024). In such scenarios, similarity measures are used to compare a learner's response to an expected answer, allowing for flexible grading based on paraphrase detection and conceptual equivalence rather than exact lexical matches.

In the context of outcome-based and modular education, evaluating the semantic similarity between learning outcomes (LOs) is becoming increasingly important. This is particularly evident in scenarios about credit recognition, curriculum mapping, and the alignment of courses across institutions. Learning outcomes are not isolated statements; they encode layered pedagogical intents, typically involving a cognitive process and a disciplinary concept. Recent research has identified that human-driven comparison of LOs, as typically performed by curriculum coordinators and program managers, is both time-consuming and cognitively demanding, often requiring deep domain knowledge and pedagogical insight (Pawar & Mago, 2018). In response to this challenge, computational approaches are being explored to automate the semantic alignment of learning outcomes using tools from Natural Language Processing (NLP), Bloom's taxonomy, and domain-specific corpora. The semantic similarity between LOs can be understood along multiple dimensions: Lexical similarity, capturing overlap or resemblance in wording; Conceptual similarity, involving domain-related meaning; Cognitive-level similarity, referring to the Bloom level of the action verbs; Hierarchical or asymmetric similarity, where one LO logically presupposes another.

Pawar and Mago (2018) propose a multi-layered approach to computing semantic similarity between learning objectives. Their methodology integrates a multilayered approach that combines WordNet-based semantic similarity, used for lexical and conceptual comparison, with a Bloom Index, which quantifies the distance between the cognitive levels of action verbs through a numerical hierarchy, and domain corpus statistics, employed to disambiguate word senses and enhance context-specific accuracy.The model demonstrates the efficacy of combining symbolic and statistical methods, particularly in the context of domain-specific and syntactically concise learning outcomes. For instance, the sentence pair "Write electronic configurations of atoms" and "Describe the subatomic composition of atoms" yielded a high similarity score (≈approximately 0.85), suggesting near equivalence in disciplinary content and cognitive process despite lexical variation. It is important to note that measuring semantic similarity is not solely an exercise in classification. It is also a pedagogical enabler of personalised learning pathways. When intelligent systems can detect that two LOs are semantically close – or that one is a conceptual prerequisite of another – they can guide learners through adaptive learning trajectories. This enables students to bypass unnecessary content, earn credit for prior learning, or receive personalised recommendations tailored to their progress. Consequently, semantic similarity works not only as a technical solution for course comparison but also as a foundation for personalisation at scale, ensuring that learners engage with content that is meaningful, appropriately challenging, and pedagogically coherent.

2.2 Computational Approaches and Educational Implications of Learning Outcome Similarity

The growing modularisation of education, through micro-credentials, MOOCs, and cross-institutional programs, has increased the demand for scalable and interpretable methods to assess semantic similarity between learning outcomes. Learning Outcomes (LOs) are of pivotal importance in competency-based educational models, representing the foundation for the design, delivery and evaluation of learning experiences. According to "European Quality Framework (EQF) 2017" (European Commission, 2008), learning outcomes are defined as "*[. . .] statements of what an individual should know, understand and/or be able to do at the end of a learning process, defined in terms of knowledge, skills and responsibility and autonomy*". Existing approaches can be grouped into three main categories. *Symbolic methods* rely on structured resources such as WordNet, Bloom's Taxonomy, or OpenMath. They are interpretable and pedagogically aligned, capturing hierarchical and conceptual relationships. For example, Bloom-based comparisons assess cognitive depth, while ontologies facilitate the disambiguation of domain-specific content. *Statistical and embedding-based approaches*, such as TF-IDF, BERT, or SBERT, compute semantic similarity in vector space. These have been used to cluster micro-credentials, identify redundant content, and support recommendation systems. *Hybrid models*, like the one by Pawar & Mago (2018), combine symbolic and statistical layers to assess both surface-level and cognitive similarity. Their "Bloom Index" exemplifies how hybridisation can enhance curriculum mapping and prior learning recognition.

Building on these foundations, our study integrates symmetric and asymmetric similarity measures. While symmetric models detect redundancy, asymmetric ones highlight hierarchical or prerequisite relations -essential for adaptive learning paths. In this context, similarity is not just a technical signal but a design tool: it supports LO clustering, redundancy detection, and personalised learning path generation. Moreover, when combined with frameworks like ESCO, similarity metrics enable alignment with labour market needs, enhancing the relevance and portability of qualifications. Furthermore, semantic similarity provides a structural backbone for learning analytics systems, enabling fine-grained monitoring of learner progress, coherence analysis of course design, and the detection of misalignments between intended outcomes and actual performance patterns. In short, semantic similarity acts as an enabling infrastructure for scalable, personalised, and interoperable learning design (Floris, 2022).

3. METHODOLOGY

The definition of learning outcome (LO) presented in the preceding section serves as a foundational element within the SPIRAL model. In this framework, each LO is further enriched with a topic label that locates it within a broader thematic hierarchy, thereby supporting classification, retrieval, and reuse. Each LO is explicitly associated with a level of Bloom's revised taxonomy, which denotes the depth of cognitive engagement required. Furthermore, LOs are categorised as either macro (parent) or micro (child), depending on their function within the course structure. Macro-LOs articulate overarching educational objectives at the course level and express the competencies expected upon completion of the course. In contrast, micro-LOs are more granular and are linked to specific learning units, reflecting the competencies to be acquired upon completion of each unit. Since macro-LOs are often too broad to be assessed directly, they are operationalised through a structured set of related micro-LOs. This hierarchical relationship is formalised in the SPIRAL model through contextual parent–child mappings, enabling macro-outcomes to be decomposed into sequences of micro learning outcomes. This structured representation facilitates interoperability with international qualification frameworks, such as the European Qualifications Framework (EQF) and ESCO (European Commission, 2023), as well as micro-credentialing ecosystems. It enables the recognition of prior learning, facilitates the comparison of learning paths, and promotes cross-institutional curricular alignment. Each micro-LO is associated with a single autonomous Learning Unit (LU), enabling modular course design. This approach draws on Wiley's (2002) conceptualisation of Learning Objects while addressing known limitations regarding composability and autonomy, as outlined by Bruschi and Perissinotto (2003). The modular structure of SPIRAL supports the dynamic generation of personalised learning paths, allowing learners to select among equivalent learning units based on their existing competencies and preferences. In this context, LOs are both design elements and analytical markers. They guide the formulation of learning activities and assessments and inform learning analytics systems, which can monitor learner progress, identify design inconsistencies (e.g., mismatches in Bloom levels), and provide adaptive feedback mechanisms.

This study builds upon the SPIRAL model by investigating the semantic similarity between learning outcomes. To this end, we developed a dedicated computational pipeline designed to calculate pairwise similarity scores between LO statements. The algorithm is based on a transformer-based language model (Sentence-BERT, model "all-MiniLM-L6-v2"), which generates semantic embeddings of each LO. In order to integrate pedagogical considerations, the algorithm computes the similarity from LO_a towards LO_b by combining a semantic similarity score with a directional taxonomic factor. First, the Bloom levels of both learning outcomes are extracted; if they cannot be determined, the function defaults to a pure semantic similarity. Otherwise, the semantic similarity is computed without Bloom verbs to avoid trivial lexical overlap. The taxonomic factor T is set to 1 when LO_a is at the same or a higher Bloom level than LO_b; otherwise, it is modelled as an exponentially decreasing function of the difference between their Bloom levels, scaled by a parameter k (fixed here at 0.5). This formulation penalizes upward transitions in cognitive complexity. The final asymmetric similarity is obtained by multiplying the semantic component by T, producing a score that reflects both conceptual closeness and the directional feasibility of progressing from one outcome to another. As a result, the similarity matrix produced by the algorithm is intentionally asymmetric. For example:

- LO1: "Evaluate the validity of a mathematical proof" (Evaluate)
- LO2: "Identify the structure of a mathematical proof" (Understand)

Although these two outcomes are semantically close, they differ significantly in their cognitive demands. The direction LO1 → LO2 yields a higher similarity than LO2 → LO1, thereby reflecting the hierarchical nature of learning progression.

We conducted our analysis on mathematics and physics learning outcomes for two main reasons. First, the composition of our research group, primarily mathematicians, provided direct access to comprehensive datasets in both domains. Second, both disciplines are supported by established ontologies that can be exploited to enrich the study, allowing us to incorporate ontological distance as an additional asymmetry parameter alongside the semantic and taxonomic dimensions of similarity (Barana, 2018).

We conducted a validation protocol involving both human raters and generative artificial intelligence. A Google Forms-based questionnaire was disseminated to disciplinary experts - university instructors and researchers in mathematics and physics - who were asked to assess the degree to which one learning outcome implied another. Each participant rated a randomised, ordered pair of LOs on a five-point Likert scale (1 = "Not at all", 5 = "Fully"), based on the directional implication from LO1 to LO2. To account for subjective certainty, a confidence score was also collected for each judgment. This allowed us to compare human judgments with those generated by the algorithm. Particular attention was given to patterns of disagreement, confidence-weighted variance, and anomalies related to Bloom level transitions.

As a further investigation, we employed ChatGPT (GPT-4.5 model) to perform the same task previously assigned to human raters. After a few prompt-level adjustments, the model was asked to evaluate all 900 mathematics and physics LO pairs. The resulting scores were then systematically compared with the algorithmic output, enabling us to examine consistencies and divergences across the two approaches.

4. RESULTS

The present study aimed to evaluate the alignment between human perception and algorithmic estimation of learning outcome (LO) similarity in the domains of mathematics and physics. To this end, a dataset of pairwise similarity values was analysed. Each value represents the discrepancy between the score assigned by a panel of human raters and the score calculated by the semantic similarity algorithm. The study's results reveal several significant trends.

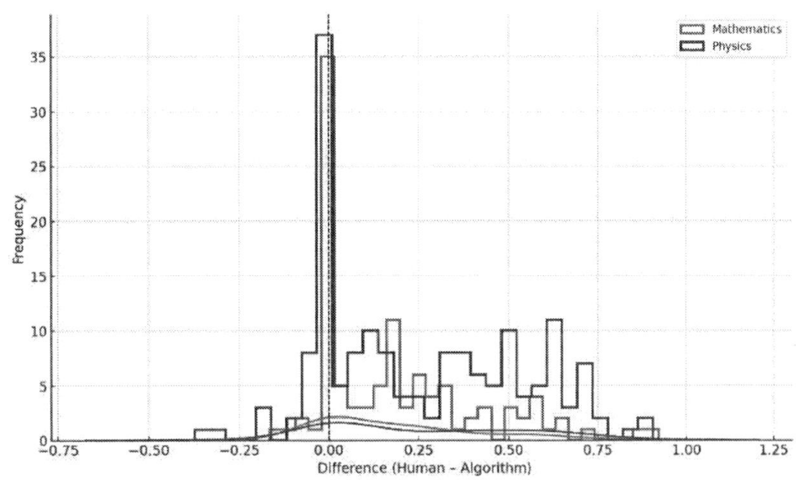

Figure 1. The histogram displays the frequency distribution of the differences between human and algorithmic similarity ratings across two disciplinary domains: mathematics (red outline) and physics (blue outline)

A comparative analysis was conducted between algorithmically computed similarity scores and human judgment on a total of 271 distinct learning outcome pairs, comprising 106 pairs from mathematics and 165 pairs from physics. The difference values were calculated as the human rating minus the algorithmic score, thereby capturing the extent and direction of divergence between the two approaches. Across both domains, a consistent trend was observed: human evaluators systematically assigned higher similarity scores than those computed by the algorithm and statistical tests (paired t-test) confirms this significant divergence. The mean difference was 0.186 in mathematics ($\sigma = 0.226$) and 0.256 in physics ($\sigma = 0.278$). This general tendency is further illustrated by the distributional patterns of the difference values, which are right-skewed in both disciplines, with dense concentrations around zero and extended positive tails (Figure 1). These patterns suggest that, although the algorithm aligns moderately with human assessments in many cases, it frequently underestimates semantic similarity, particularly in contexts that require higher-order reasoning, pedagogical interpretation, or hierarchical abstraction. Notably, while underestimation is the dominant pattern, a subset of cases revealed the opposite trend: the algorithm overestimated similarity where human evaluators perceived the two outcomes as distinct. These situations often involved lexical or structural overlap (e.g., similar verbs or repeated terminology), which the algorithm interprets as indicative of semantic proximity, even when conceptual or instructional coherence is lacking.

To explore these discrepancies further, the ten LO pairs with the largest positive and negative differences were extracted. In high-positive cases, human evaluators detected meaningful semantic alignment that the algorithm failed to capture - often due to its reliance on surface-level features. In high-negative cases, the algorithm identified similarity based on textual resemblance, whereas human experts discounted such alignment due to differences in cognitive complexity, disciplinary context, or pedagogical function. Notably, in the physics domain, human validators expressed a lower average confidence in the quality of the similarity assessments they provided. This reduced confidence may partially account for the greater divergence observed between human and algorithmic scores in that domain. These outlier cases highlight the need for hybrid systems that can integrate both semantic embedding and domain-specific reasoning to reflect expert judgment more accurately.

A complementary analysis examined the influence of differences in Bloom's taxonomy levels on the magnitude of disagreement. The results were aggregated by inter-level distance and visualised in heatmaps (Figure 2). In both cases, a clear pattern emerges: similarity judgments between learning outcomes that belong to the same Bloom level (i.e., diagonal cells) tend to exhibit more minor differences between human and algorithmic evaluations. This indicates a higher alignment when cognitive operations are comparable. By contrast, inter-level comparisons - particularly those involving greater cognitive distance, such as Remember vs. Analyse or Apply vs. Evaluate - often display more pronounced positive differences, suggesting that human raters perceive a semantic connection that the algorithm fails to detect. This may reflect the human ability to infer prerequisite or hierarchical relations that are not evident through surface-level textual analysis. Overall, the heatmaps confirm that while the algorithm performs reasonably well for LOs within the same cognitive level, it struggles to capture cross-level semantic structures that are pedagogically meaningful, particularly in more complex or less lexically aligned domains such as physics.

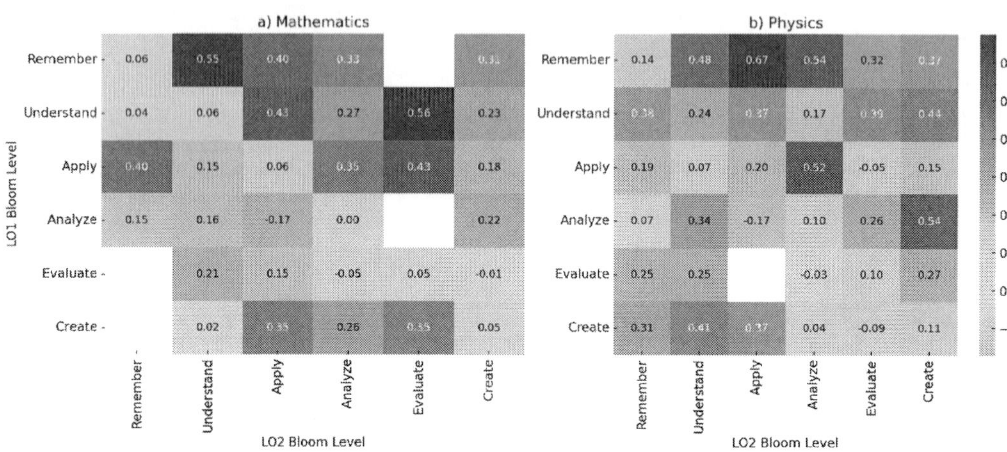

Figure 2. Mean difference between human and algorithmic similarity scores across Bloom's taxonomy levels in the *mathematics* (left) and *physics* (right) domains

To further investigate the applicability of large language models in semantic similarity tasks, we prompted Chat-GPT to evaluate the same set of learning outcomes (LO) pairs assessed by human raters. The resulting similarity scores were compared to those produced by the semantic similarity algorithm. In mathematics, the average difference between Chat-GPT and algorithmic scores was 0.051, while in physics it was 0.050, based on 900 LO pairs per domain. These small values, combined with the near-identical distributions across both domains, indicate that GPT performs in close alignment with the algorithm. This is further confirmed by an inspection of the Python code used to generate GPT's judgments, which reveals a high degree of structural and computational similarity to the algorithm's implementation. Unlike human raters, who tend to apply domain-specific interpretative strategies, GPT appears to exhibit algorithm-like behaviour.

5. DISCUSSIONS AND CONCLUSIONS

The cross-domain analysis conducted in this study, spanning both mathematics and physics, revealed consistent and meaningful patterns in the divergence between human and algorithmic estimations of learning outcome similarity. In both disciplines, human raters systematically assigned higher similarity scores than the algorithm, with mean differences of 0.186 in mathematics and 0.256 in physics. These results indicate a recurring tendency of the algorithm to underestimate semantic proximity, particularly in contexts involving conceptual or hierarchical dependencies that are not explicitly lexicalised. The right-skewed distributions of the difference values across both domains reinforce the conclusion that current semantic models adopt a conservative stance when recognising learning outcome overlap. We are also replicating the study with different models (e.g., *all-mpnet-base-v2*) to evaluate whether alternative approaches yield higher performance.

Among the most significant sources of divergence were prerequisite - objective relationships, in which one learning outcome logically or pedagogically implied the other, despite limited textual similarity. Human raters were more adept at identifying such asymmetric and hierarchical connections, whereas both the algorithm and GPT-based evaluations exhibited difficulty in doing so. Notably, GPT's judgments closely mirrored those of the algorithm - both in terms of magnitude and structure - suggesting that current LLMs, while powerful, tend to replicate rather than expand upon the logic embedded in conventional transformer-based similarity models. This observation highlights the limitations of LLMs in offering deeper, independent semantic interpretation in educational domains that require curricular reasoning and domain-specific hierarchies.

The results of this study are broadly consistent with our initial expectations. In the absence of an explicit ontological or conceptual structure, it is inherently difficult for similarity models to capture certain types of relationships - such as prerequisite chains, hierarchical dependencies, or cross-level educational implications - using only surface-level textual similarity and Bloom's taxonomy as input features. These findings highlight the limitations of purely linguistic models in addressing pedagogically meaningful but semantically implicit learning outcome relations.

The findings of this study align with and extend prior contributions in the field, most notably the work by Pawar and Mago (2018), which combined semantic similarity, Bloom's taxonomy, and corpus-based statistics for evaluating learning outcome equivalence. However, the present research moves beyond post hoc recognition and instead positions semantic similarity as a proactive design principle for the development of modular, adaptive, and personalised learning environments. In particular, this study advances the state of the art in two critical directions. First, it reconceptualises textual similarity not merely as a technical criterion for course matching or credit recognition, but as a pedagogical enabler that underpins the dynamic construction of personalised learning trajectories - especially within frameworks such as the SPIRAL model. Second, it highlights the role of semantic similarity in forward-aligned educational design, where learning outcomes are systematically linked to competence descriptors (e.g., EQF, ESCO) to foster the creation of interoperable and micro-credentialed educational offerings. Within this paradigm, semantic similarity is no longer a passive tool for alignment verification, but rather an active element in building data-informed, learner-centred educational ecosystems.

As a direction for future work, we intend to investigate whether the divergence patterns observed in STEM disciplines are also present in other domains, such as languages, history, or the humanities, which often involve different instructional logics, epistemological structures, and narrative styles. This expansion will allow us to assess the generalisability of the current findings across a broader curricular spectrum.

Furthermore, the algorithm's consistent underestimation of similarity suggests that human validation remains a crucial component in any learning outcome alignment process. While transformer-based models offer scalability and efficiency, they currently fall short in approximating expert reasoning in complex educational contexts. To address this limitation, a key objective of our future research is to integrate human evaluative judgments into the algorithmic learning loop, enabling the system to evolve through iterative validation. This approach would allow the model to converge toward increasingly accurate and pedagogically aligned similarity estimations, ultimately supporting more reliable and interpretable applications in course design and learning analytics.

This preliminary study also opened a new line of inquiry: approaching the similarity between two learning outcomes not as a single score, but as a pair of values - the difference in Bloom levels and the semantic similarity between the outcomes. Such a representation would provide richer insights into the connections between LOs (and, by extension, Learning Units) within an oriented graph, where the strength of the links could be modulated by semantic similarity and, where applicable, ontological distance, both derived from the intrinsic component of the LO (i.e., the outcome stripped of its verb).

ACKNOWLEDGEMENT

The research was conducted within Indam – Istituto Nazionale di Alta Matematica "Francesco Severi", as part of the EDVANCE Project – Digital Education Hub for Advanced Digital Culture, funded by the European Union – NextGenerationEU, Component 1, Investment 3.4 "Advanced university teaching and skills". It also falls within OPERAPlus – Mission Project 2.2 (2022–2024 Agreement), financed by the Compagnia di San Paolo Bank Foundation, and is supported by the European Alliance UNITA – Universitas Montium.

REFERENCES

Anderson, L. W., & Krathwohl, D. R. (2001). A taxonomy for learning, teaching, and assessing: A revision of Bloom's taxonomy of educational objectives: complete edition. Addison Wesley Longman, Inc.

Barana, A., Di Caro, L., Fioravera, M., Marchisio, M., & Rabellino, S. (2018). Ontology development for competence assessment in virtual communities of practice. In International Conference on Artificial Intelligence in Education (pp. 94-98). Cham: Springer International Publishing.

Bruschi, B., and Perissinotto, A. (2003). Come creare corsi online. Carocci, 2003.

Cimpan, S. et al. (2024). Student-centered personalization of individual education through Reusable and Autonomous Learning units-the SPIRAL model. In Proceedings of International Conferences e-Learning and Digital Learning 2024 and Sustainability, Technology and Education 2024 (pp. 75–82). IADIS Press.

Council of the European Union. (2022). Council Recommendation of 16 June 2022 on a European approach to micro-credentials for lifelong learning and employability (2022/C 243/02). Official Journal of the European Union, C 243, 1–7. https://eur-lex.europa.eu/legal-content/EN/TXT/?uri=oj:JOC_2022_243_R_0002

de Gois, T. S., Freitas, F. O., Tejada, J., & Freitag, R. M. K. (2024). NLP and education: Using semantic similarity to evaluate filled gaps in a large-scale Cloze test in the classroom. The Mental Lexicon, 19(1), (pp. 90-99).

Digital Education Action Plan (2021-2027), https://education.ec.europa.eu/focus-topics/digital-education/action-plan, last access 25/07/2025.

European Commission. (2017). Council recommendation on the European qualifications framework for lifelong learning and repealing the recommendation of the European Parliament and of the Council of 23 April 2008 on the establishment of the European qualifications framework for lifelong learning. Official Journal of the European Union, 60, 2017/ C 189/02:1–15.

European Commission. (2023). ESCO - European Skills, Competences, Qualifications and Occupations. Version 1.1.3. Brussels: Directorate-General for Employment, Social Affairs and Inclusion. Retrieved from https://esco.ec.europa.eu

Floris, F., Marchisio, M., Rabellino, S., Roman, F., & Sacchet, M. (2022). Clustering techniques to investigate engagement and performance in online Mathematics courses. In Proceedings of the 19th international conference on Cognition and Exploratory Learning in the Digital Age (CELDA 2022) (pp. 27-34). IADIS press.

Lubis, F. F., Putri, A., Waskita, D., Sulistyaningtyas, T., Arman, A. A., & Rosmansyah, Y. (2021). Automated short-answer grading using semantic similarity based on word embedding. *International Journal of Technology*, *12*(3), 571-581.

Miller, G. A., & Charles, W. G. (1991). Contextual correlates of semantic similarity. Language and cognitive processes, 6(1), 1–28.

Pawar, A., & Mago, V. (2018). Similarity between learning outcomes from course objectives using semantic analysis, blooms taxonomy and corpus statistics. *arXiv preprint arXiv:1804.06333*.

Wiley, D. A et al. (2002). The instructional use of learning objects. Agency for instructional technology, Bloomington, IN.

INCREMENTAL EXPERTISE: THE CONTINUUM OF EXPERTISE IN ELECTRICAL ENGINEERING GRID DESIGN THROUGH THE LENS OF EPISTEMIC FRAMES

Amit Paikrao, Jyoti Shaha, Ramkumar Rajendran and Ritayan Mitra
Centre for Educational Technology
Indian Institute of Technology Bombay, India

ABSTRACT

Modern electrical grids are becoming increasingly complex, requiring engineers who can adapt, justify their actions, and exercise sound professional judgment. Yet, many graduates struggle to demonstrate these expert traits despite strong academic performance. A key challenge in engineering education is locating where learners fall along the continuum of expertise and identifying benchmarks that mark their progression. Drawing on Epistemic Frame Theory (EFT), this exploratory study examines the epistemic frames (skills, knowledge, values, identity, and epistemology) of second-year and third-year electrical engineering students engaged in grid operation tasks. Based on a small sample, our preliminary findings suggest that second-year students' frames are dominated by skill-knowledge connections, resembling novice performance. By the third year, students maintain these links while also forming stronger connections to epistemology and identity, signaling a shift toward more integrated professional reasoning and a developing professional identity. We interpret this stage as *incremental expertise*, situated within the zone of proximal development. While limited, these findings point to the second and third year as potential milestones for guiding targeted interventions in engineering education.

KEYWORDS

Expert-Novice, Epistemic Frame Theory, Epistemic Frames, Continuum of Expertise, Electrical Engineering, Grid Design

1. INTRODUCTION AND LITERATURE REVIEW

Modern electrical grids are becoming increasingly complex with the integration of renewable energy sources and the adoption of smart grid technologies. This complexity requires engineers who can make sound decisions, adapt to rapidly changing conditions, and exercise professional judgment in real-world contexts. However, many graduates struggle to demonstrate these essential traits of expert engineers despite strong academic performance. Understanding when these challenges become visible during students' academic journey and how their thinking develops across different stages is critical. By examining the progression of students from second, third, and final years, we can better understand how expertise emerges.

A crucial step in understanding how expertise develops is to examine how experts differ from novices. Previous research shows that well-organized knowledge is the most important factor differentiating experts from novices (Paikrao, A., et al., 2025; Paikrao & Mitra, 2023; Pal S. et al., 2023). It is not only the organization of the declarative and procedural knowledge in the memory, but the connectedness of this *knowledge with* interest, identity, and associated practices (Orrill & Shaffer, 2012; Bedard and Chi 2006). Epistemic frame theory (EFT) provides a comprehensive framework for understanding these interconnections (Shaffer et al. 2006a; Shaffer, 2009; Rupp, et al., 2010). Rather than viewing knowledge as isolated facts or procedures, EFT examines how professionals think, act, and make decisions within their field. Epistemic frames represent "patterns of associations among knowledge, skills, habits of mind, and other cognitive elements that characterize communities of practice" (Shaffer, 2006b). A comprehensive epistemic frame encompasses five key components: knowledge, skills, identity, values, and epistemology. Epistemic frames guide an individual's interpretation of a situation, activating specific ways of thinking and conceptual resources (Campbell et al., 2022). They provide the essential context within which a particular situation is perceived, interpreted, and judged (Patterson & Ding, 2025).

Expertise development represents a gradual transformation of epistemic frames. The inclusion of "identity" and "values" alongside knowledge and skills offers a vibrant and holistic understanding of expertise. This development moves from more fragmented or context-dependent activations like novices to more integrated, robust, and transferable patterns of an expert (An et al., 2021; Paikrao & Mitra, 2023). This progression occurs along the continuum rather than through discrete stages focused by earlier research (Benner, P., 2022). The existing research lacks well-defined characteristics of the intermediate reference points needed to position learners along the continuum of expertise. Without such benchmarks, assessing progress and designing targeted interventions becomes challenging. Our study highlights the second-year and third-year as key milestones in the academic journey for how expertise begins to take shape. This period is particularly marked by a shift from learning foundational principles to engaging in more specialized, application-oriented work (Lantz & Dempsey, 2019).

To address this challenge of characterizing expertise development, our investigation extends beyond performance assessment. We are focusing specifically on underlying cognitive structures that guide students' actions and decisions of electrical engineering students in grid operation tasks. By exploring how elements of epistemic frames, i.e., knowledge, skills, professional identity, beliefs, and reasoning strategies interconnect, we aim to map the early stages of professional formation. This research addresses two key questions: RQ1: How do epistemic frames evolve as progress from the second year to the third year of an electrical engineering undergraduate program? RQ2: What specific epistemic frames connections most influence the transition from the second to the third year of an electrical engineering undergraduate program?

2. METHODOLOGY

To empirically investigate this continuum of expertise, ENA provides a concrete pathway to operationalize epistemic frames by mapping the connections between knowledge, skills, identity, values, and epistemology. This study enables the quantitative examination of structural changes in students' epistemic frames, offering preliminary evidence for the incremental progression of expertise.

2.1 Study Design

This study is based on a role-playing game called "The Power to the People" (https://www.rhombicogames.com/game/power-to-the-people/), replicating real-world scenarios in power system grids. Participants are tasked with designing and maintaining their power grids with a continuous power supply as cities expand and grow in number. The study involves four electrical engineering participants; two are from the second year and two are from the third year at the same university in India. All of these participants have provided consent for the use of their data for research and educational purposes. The study comprised three phases: 1. Orientation Phase: Participants were given a 15-minute demo in which they were familiarized with the game interface in detail. 2. Familiarization Phase: Participants are introduced to various checkpoints of gameplay. We have shared the checklist for the gameplay and controllers. They practice tasks such as installing generators, substations, and connecting lines. They are encouraged to play the game freely until they become accustomed to all the controls and functionalities. This phase typically lasts 15-20 minutes. Once participants feel comfortable with the gameplay, the third phase begins. 3. Data collection phase: This phase was divided into two steps. The first step was the Gamplay, in which participants were presented with the problem statement and the game's objectives before commencing gameplay. Participants engaged in gameplay, which typically lasted an average of 30-40 minutes. Tobii Pro Nano (60 Hz) eye tracker is used during this phase to track the eye gazes of the participants. The second step is interviews with eye gaze enhanced retrospective think-aloud protocol (ET-RTA) (Paikrao, A. et al., 2025). In this step, participants were shown the recorded video of their gameplay along with the eye gaze data and prompted to reflect on their gameplay experience. The purpose of this step is to get insights into their decision-making processes, strategies, and perceptions. Participants explained what they were doing, why they were doing it, and what they were thinking at those points. They were encouraged to pause the video to provide more detailed explanations. These interviews were recorded with an OBS screen recorder. These interviews lasted, on average, approximately 70-80 minutes. To maintain the novelty of the stimulus during gameplay, orientation and familiarization were conducted in regular game mode on the "Siem Reap" city in Cambodia. In the gameplay phase, "AGRA, India" city was used. Figure 1 represents the screenshot of the interview phase.

Figure 1. Screenshot of Video stimulus of designed grid in "The power to the People" during ET-RTA with fixations (red circles) and saccades (line connecting fixations)

2.2 Data Analysis

The interviews were conducted in a mixed language format, aligning with the proficiency of each participant. Later, these interviews were transcribed using Cockatoo software (https://www.cockatoo.com/login). Verbal analysis was performed on this transcription by operationalizing and contextualizing the codes by Rupp et al, (2010) for this study. Rupp's (2010) definition was developed for collaborative tasks to analyze discourse, whereas in our study, it was from the interview of a single person who performed the task on grid operations.

Table 1. Definitions of Epistemic frames codes

	Definitions by (Rupp et al., 2010; Svarovsky, 2010)	Operationalised Definitions for the study
Skill	The abilities and competencies that community members are able to perform and demonstrate.	Refers to the abilities and competencies (like ways of thinking, strategies, tactics, decision, and actions) that enable individuals to effectively engage with the system.
Knowledge	The facts and information shared by community members.	Refers to the information, facts, concepts, and principles that individuals possess and utilize within the context.
Identity	The social and cultural roles that community members view themselves as having.	Refers to how individuals understand and perceive themselves within the context, including their roles and responsibilities
Values	The opinions and beliefs held by community members that define what is important (and conversely, not important).	Refers to the ethical beliefs, principles, and priorities that guide an individual's actions and decisions within the context.
Epistemology	The justifications and methods of proof that legitimize actions and claims within the community.	Refers to justification of the actions and decisions, providing the evidence of the actions taken in the context.

Table 1 shows the original definitions and operationalised definitions of epistemic frames. The authors have validated these operational definitions with two experts from a learning sciences and learning analytics background. Further, the coded data was analyzed through the epistemic network analysis.

3. RESULTS

To answer our proposed RQ1: "How do epistemic frames evolve as progress from the second year to the third year of an electrical engineering undergraduate program?", individual ENAs for the second-year (red) and the third-year (blue) are shown in Figure 2.

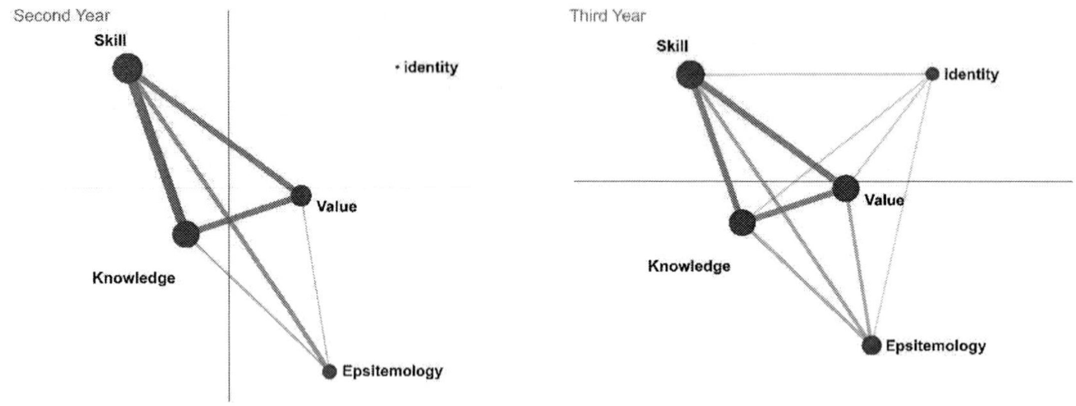

Figure 2. ENA of Second-year students (red) and Third-Year students (blue)

For second-year students (red), connections between the Skill-Value (S-V), Skill-Knowledge (S-K), Knowledge-Value (K-V), and Epistemology-Skill (E-S) have the stronger connections shown by the thick lines. The connections between epistemology-value (E-V) and epistemology-knowledge (E-K) are indicated with thin lines. However, the connections to the Identity node are entirely missing, i.e., Identity-Value (I-V), Identity-Knowledge (I-K), Identity-Skill (I-S), and Identity-Epistemology (I-E) are absent.

In the case of third-year students, network in blue color, the connections between the Skill-Value (S-V), Skill-Knowledge (S-K), Knowledge-Value (K-V), Epistemology-Skill (E-S), Epistemology-Knowledge (E-K), and Epistemology-Value (E-V) have stronger connections shown by the thick lines. The significant change here is the addition of the Identity node. This node makes clear connections with the rest of the nodes. The connection between Identity-Value (I-V), Identity-Knowledge (I-K), Identity-Skill (I-S), and Identity-Epistemology (I-E) are established in this network with thin lines. This network of third years' shows well-developed connections among all elements, suggesting that they have started developing all the essential components of the epistemic frames.

To answer our proposed RQ2: "What specific epistemic frames connections are most influential in the transition from the second-year to the third-year of an electrical engineering undergraduate program?", a comparison plot of ENA for the second-year (red) and the third-year (blue) is shown in Figure 3. This comparison plot is a subtraction network of the mean networks of the second year (red) and third year (blue). The majority of connections, i.e., Skill-Value (S-V), Epistemology-Knowledge (E-K), Epistemology-Value (E-V), Identity-Value (I-V), Identity-Knowledge (I-K), Identity-Skill (I-S), Identity-Epistemology (I-E), have a thick blue color of the third year. These connections show that they have co-occurred more frequently in third-year students than second-year students.

The only connection in red color is Skill-Knowledge (S-K), meaning the second-year students' frequency of the co-occurrences between these two nodes is more than that of the third-year students. Noticeably, Knowledge-Value (K-V) and Epistemology-Skill (E-S), these two nodes are entirely missing from the comparison plot. This missing link suggests that the second-year and third-year students have equal co-occurrences for these connections.

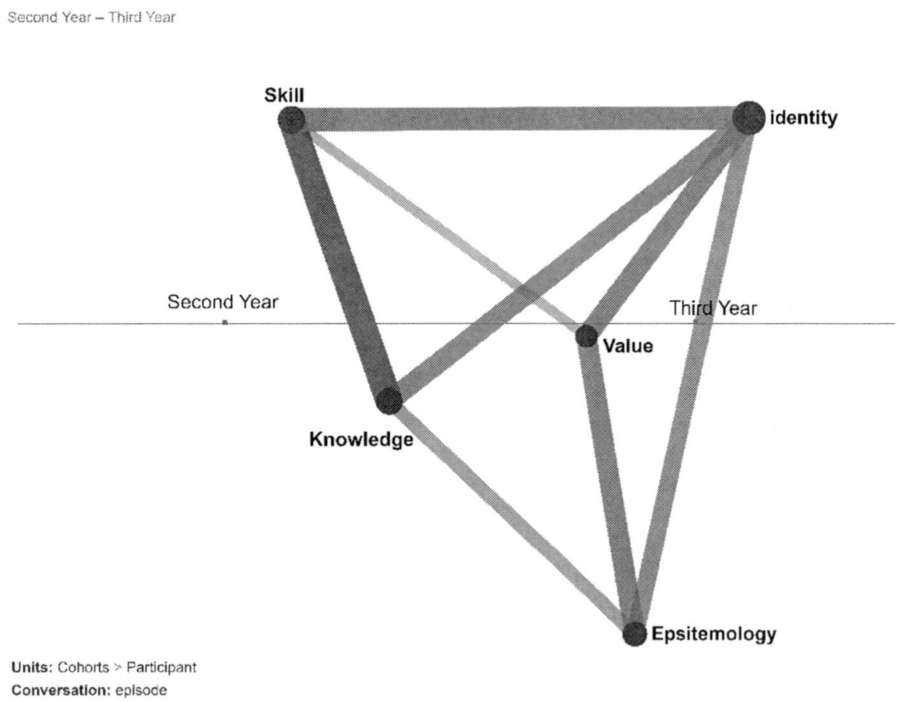

Figure 3. Subtracted network for second-year (red) and third-year (blue).

4. DISCUSSION

This study used Epistemic Network Analysis (ENA) to explore how second-year and third-year students connect the elements of an epistemic frames i.e. skills, knowledge, values, identity, and epistemology. The aim was to investigate which elements are most influential at each stage, and how the two groups differ in how they bring these elements together when solving problems.

4.1 Second-Year Students: Knowledge-Driven Performance

Second-year students demonstrate a novice-like epistemic frame characterized by fragmented knowledge application rather than integrated professional reasoning. Their networks center on Skills-Knowledge, Skills-Values, and Knowledge-Values connections, indicating that competencies arise primarily from direct application of factual information learned and beliefs they have developed during initial engineering exposure (Chi et al., 1981; Nahar., et al., 2009). This pattern reflects classic novice behavior that actions guided by declarative knowledge and explicit problem information rather than deeper conceptual principles (Paikrao & Mitra, 2023; Chase & Simon, 1973).

While these students show some capacity for justification through Epistemology-Skills connections, this integration remains incomplete. The limited links between epistemology and knowledge and values elements reveal superficial reasoning approaches typical of trial-and-error problem solving (Harsh et al., 2019). This configuration aligns with Polya's initial problem-solving phases i.e. understanding problems and devising plans, but lacks the deeper integration necessary for expert-level performance (Paikrao, A., et al., 2023). The comparison network reinforces this interpretation, as the strongest remaining connection (Skills-Knowledge) demonstrates performance-oriented thinking centered on direct knowledge application rather than conceptual understanding. This pattern underscores typical novice behavior where domain knowledge remains sketchy and superficially absorbed, preventing students from effectively reproducing key concepts when needed for complex problem-solving situations (Persky & Robinson, 2017).

4.2 Third-Year Students: Emerging Professional Integration

Third-year students exhibit emerging professional integration that represents a transitional stage between novice performance and expert competency. Building on their foundational Skills-Knowledge connections, these students develop stronger epistemic integration through enhanced Epistemology-Knowledge-Values linkages and the crucial emergence of professional identity. The appearance of an identity hub, even with thinner connections, is consistent with evidence that professional identity develops progressively through coursework and authentic experiences, and begins to organize how students justify and evaluate their actions (Vega et al., 2021; Seterra et al., 2021). This identity integration marks a fundamental shift from viewing themselves as knowledge consumers to emerging professionals whose actions, beliefs, and decisions interconnect systematically.

The strengthened epistemological connections indicate movement beyond direct knowledge application toward justification through deeper professional beliefs and identity-grounded reasoning. This transformation exemplifies Shaffer's "island of expertise" concept, where increased participation in professional community practices strengthens epistemic frame interconnections and develops organized domain-specific knowledge with multiple solution strategies, which is the key characteristics distinguishing experts from novices (Alí Fojaco, 2023; Shaffer, 2009; An et al., 2021). However, the persistence of weaker connections in the network reveals these students remain in active development rather than having achieved stable expertise.

We conceptualize this developmental stage as incremental expertise: the gradual consolidation of skills, knowledge, values, identity, and epistemology as learners progress toward expert-level thinking. From Vygotsky's perspective, third-year students operate within their zone of proximal development, having formed initial professional connections while requiring continued community support to strengthen integration (Irshad et al., 2021). This progression mirrors broader expert-novice research findings across domains, confirming that expertise development involves progressive integration of multiple knowledge types rather than simple accumulation (Balta & Asikainen, 2019). In electrical engineering contexts, where problems remain ill-structured and key concepts invisible, this epistemic integration becomes essential for advancing beyond rote learning toward authentic conceptual understanding (Chaabi & Chougui, 2021). By mapping this developmental trajectory through ENA, our study provides preliminary evidence for a measurable intermediate stage in the expert-novice continuum, offering educators concrete benchmarks for assessing and supporting professional formation in engineering contexts.

5. CONCLUSION AND LIMITATION

Our study provides a preliminary indication of incremental expertise in students' thinking. Specifically, it highlights early differences between second-year and third-year students. Second-year students display traits more consistent with novices, as their focus remains on applying knowledge and skills. In contrast, third-year students begin to demonstrate broader connections that incorporate values, epistemology, and identity within their epistemic frames. This more integrated network suggests a developmental shift, though further work is needed to confirm these patterns. For educators, these findings underscore the importance of emphasizing skills and knowledge in early years while creating opportunities for students to reflect on why those skills matter and how they shape emerging professional identity. Developing epistemic frames requires exposure to electrical engineering community practices through direct collaboration with community members. Structured reflection, peer discussion, and authentic professional tasks within these community interactions offer valuable pathways for students to strengthen broader epistemic connections earlier in their academic journey. Strengthening epistemology and identity connections is most crucial for accelerating this developmental trajectory.

5.1 Limitation

The study is based on only four participants (two per group). The small sample limits generalizability and statistical power. Findings should be seen as preliminary trends rather than conclusive patterns. The study was conducted at a single university in India. Institutional context, curriculum design, and cultural factors may influence students' epistemic frame development, limiting transferability. The role-playing game "Power to the People" offers an authentic simulation but cannot fully replicate real-world grid design tasks. Student behaviors in the game may differ from how they would act in actual professional settings.

ACKNOWLEDGEMENT

The research reported in this paper was supported in part by a TIH-IITB Travel Grant, IIT Bombay. Any opinions, findings, or conclusions expressed in this paper are those of the authors and do not necessarily reflect the views of funders.

We would like to thank Federico Casares, Founder of Rhombico Games, for permission to use "The Power to The People" game for our study.

REFERENCES

Alí Fojaco, C. (2023). Curiously: Supporting Young Children and their Caregivers Create Meaningful Learning Adventures in Nature. In: Zaphiris, P., et al. HCI International 2023 – Late Breaking Papers. HCII 2023. Lecture Notes in Computer Science, vol 14060. Springer, Cham. https://doi.org/10.1007/978-3-031-48060-7_1

An, S., Broniec, W., Rugaber, S., Weigel, E., Hammock, J., & Goel, A. (2021, June). Recognizing novice learner's modeling behaviors. In International Conference on Intelligent Tutoring Systems (pp. 189-200). Cham: Springer International Publishing.

Balta, N., & Asikainen, M. (2019). Introductory students' attitudes and approaches to Physics problem solving: Major, achievement level and gender differences. Journal of Technology and Science Education, 9(3), 378. https://doi.org/10.3926/jotse.666

Badmus, O. T., & Jita, L. C. (2024). Physics difficulty and problem-solving: Exploring the role of mathematics and mathematical symbols. Interdisciplinary Journal of Education Research, 6, 1-14.

Bédard, J., & Chi, M. T. (1992). Expertise. Current directions in psychological science, 1(4), 135-139.

Benner, P. (2022). From novice to mastery-II, The Dreyfus and Dreyfus model of skill acquisition in nursing practice. Educating Nurses.

Campbell, T., Wenner, J. A., Brandon, L., & Waszkelewicz, M. (2022). A community of practice model as a theoretical perspective for teacher leadership. International Journal of Leadership in Education, 25(2), 173-196.

Chaabi, M., & Chougui, A. (2021). Visual Analogy as a Cognitive Strategy in the Architectural Design Process: Expert versus Novice Performance. International Online Journal of Education and Teaching, 8(3), 1348-1368.

Chase, W. G., & Simon, H. A. (1973). Perception in chess. Cognitive Psychology, 4(1), 55–81. https://doi.org/10.1016/0010-0285(73)90004-2

Chi, M. T. H., Feltovich, P. J., & Glaser, R. (1981). Categorization and Representation of Physics Problems by Experts and Novices*. Cognitive Science, 5(2), 121–152.

Edwards, A. L., O'Sullivan, P. S., Rapp, J. H., Alseidi, A., Chern, H., Sewell, J. L., & Syed, S. M. (2023). Development of the Cognitive Load Inventory for Surgical Skills: preliminary validity evidence. Global Surgical Education-Journal of the Association for Surgical Education, 2(1), 102.

Harsh, J. A., Campillo, M., Murray, C., Myers, C., Nguyen, J., & Maltese, A. V. (2019). "Seeing" Data Like an Expert: An Eye-Tracking Study Using Graphical Data Representations. CBE—Life Sciences Education, 18(3), ar32. https://doi.org/10.1187/cbe.18-06-0102

Irshad, S., Maan, M. F., Batool, H., & Hanif, A. (2021). Vygotsky's Zone of Proximal Development (ZPD): An evaluative tool for language learning and social development in early childhood education. Multicultural Education, 7(6), 234-242.

Lantz, C., & Dempsey, P. R. (2019). Information literacy strategies used by second-and third-year biology students. Issues in Science and Technology Librarianship, (92).

Nahar, Y., Baillie, C., Catalano, G., & Feinblatt, E. (2009). Engineering values: An approach to explore values in education and practice. In Research in Engineering Education Symposium: Queensland, Australia.

Orrill, C. H., & Shaffer, D. W. (2012). Exploring Connectedness: Applying ENA to Teacher Knowledge.

Paikrao, A., Nath, D., Rajendran, R., & Mitra, R., (2025). Enhancing Retrospective Think-Aloud Protocols with Eye-Gaze data. In B. Jiang et al. (Eds.), Proceedings of the 33rd International Conference on Computers in Education. Asia-Pacific Society for Computers in Education.

Paikrao, A. M., & Mitra, R. (2023). Expert-Novice Differences In Electrical Circuit Analysis Based On The Order Of Attention. European Society for Engineering Education (SEFI). DOI: 10.21427/G9YB-5J15

Pal, S., Paikrao, A., & Mitra, R. (2023, October). Expert-novice differences through epistemic network analysis of eye-tracking and think-aloud data. In Fifth International Conference on Quantitative Ethnography: Conference Proceedings Supplement. International Society for Quantitative Ethnography (pp. 137-141).

Patterson, Z., & Ding, L. (2025). Epistemic framing analysis of secondary students during instruction on quantum physics. Physical Review Physics Education Research, 21(1), 010116.

Persky, A. M., & Robinson, J. D. (2017). Moving from Novice to Expertise and Its Implications for Instruction. American Journal of Pharmaceutical Education, 81(9), 6065. https://doi.org/10.5688/ajpe6065

Rupp, A. A., Gushta, M., Mislevy, R. J., & Shaffer, D. W. (2010). Evidence-centered Design of Epistemic Games: Measurement Principles for Complex Learning Environments.

Seterra D. Burleson, Debra A. Major, Xiaoxiao Hu, Kristi J. Shryock, (2021), Linking undergraduate professional identity development in engineering to major embeddedness and persistence, Journal of Vocational Behavior, Volume 128, 2021,103590, ISSN 0001-8791, https://doi.org/10.1016/j.jvb.2021.103590.

Shaffer, D. W. (2006a). Epistemic frames for epistemic games. Computers & Education, 46(3), Article 3. https://doi.org/10.1016/j.compedu.2005.11.003

Shaffer, D. W. (2006b). How Computer Games Help Children Learn. Palgrave Macmillan US. https://doi.org/10.1057/9780230601994

Shaffer, D. W. (2009). Epistemic Frames and Islands of Expertise: Learning from Infusion Experiences.

Shaffer, D. W. (2012). Models of situated action: Computer games and the problem of transfer. In Games, Learning, and Society: Learning and Meaning in the Digital Age (pp. 403–432). Cambridge University Press. https://doi.org/10.1017/CBO9781139031127.028

Shaffer, D. W. (2017). Quantitative ethnography. Lulu. com.

Shaffer, D. W., & Ruis, A. R. (2017). Epistemic Network Analysis: A Worked Example of Theory-Based Learning Analytics. In Handbook of Learning Analytics (pp. 175–187). Society for Learning Analytics Research (SoLAR). https://doi.org/10.18608/hla17.015

Siebert-Evenstone, A., Michaelis, J. E., Shaffer, D. W., & Mutlu, B. (2021). Safety First: Developing a Model of Expertise in Collaborative Robotics. In A. R. Ruis & S. B. Lee (Eds.), Advances in Quantitative Ethnography (Vol. 1312, pp. 304–318). Springer International Publishing. https://doi.org/10.1007/978-3-030-67788-6_21

Svarovsky, G. N. (2010). Exploring Complex Engineering Learning Over Time with Epistemic Network Analysis. 1(2). https://doi.org/10.5703/1288284314638

Vega, H., Irgens, G. A., & Bailey, C. (2021, January). Negotiating tensions: A study of pre-service English as foreign language teachers' sense of identity within their community of practice. In International Conference on Quantitative Ethnography (pp. 277-291). Cham: Springer International Publishing.

THE ROLE OF TECHNOLOGY-ENHANCED SIMULATIONS IN REFINING LEARNERS' MENTAL MODELS FOR COMPLEX DECISION MAKING

Jessica M. Johnson
PhD, Old Dominion University's Office of Enterprise Research and Innovation
1030 University Blvd., Suffolk VA 23435, USA

ABSTRACT

This paper explores how technology-enhanced simulations can refine K-12 students' mental models and decision-making skills within the context of maritime careers. As part of a regional initiative, over 1,300 students from multiple school divisions engaged with a suite of digital simulations interactive 360-degree environments, 3D models, and embedded game simulations. These simulations were designed to expose learners to real-world maritime concepts while addressing common misconceptions about the shipbuilding and ship repair industries. The study assessed how students' mental models shifted after interacting with the simulations and examined emerging decision-making behaviors through embedded tasks and feedback loops. Findings indicate that students not only developed more accurate understandings of maritime technologies and career pathways but also demonstrated growth in reflective and adaptive decision-making skills. The paper discusses implications for designing future adaptive simulation environments that support conceptual change and cognitive development. By aligning immersive technologies with authentic, decision-rich contexts, this work offers a promising framework for using simulation-based learning to prepare students for complex, technology-driven career domains.

KEYWORDS

Mental Model, Simulation-Based Training, Dynamic Decision-Making

1. INTRODUCTION

The maritime industry stands as a foundational pillar of national security, global trade, and regional economic development, encompassing complex systems of shipbuilding, ship repair, logistics, and advanced marine technologies. Despite this, K–12 students frequently possess outdated or limited conceptions of the field, often viewing it through the narrow lens of manual labor and failing to recognize the integral role of modern technologies such as robotics, digital twins, and automation systems. These limited mental models are reinforced by a lack of authentic engagement with the industry within formal education settings. Few students encounter curricular experiences that present the maritime sector as a dynamic, technologically rich environment, thereby diminishing both awareness and potential interest in related careers.

This study was situated within a large-scale regional initiative along the east of the US., that sought to directly address these conceptual gaps through immersive educational interventions. Developed in partnership with school districts, maritime industry stakeholders, and simulation developers, the initiative reached over 1,300 students in grades 5 through 12 across diverse urban, suburban, and rural school contexts. The program was designed to increase awareness of high-skill, high-tech maritime career pathways and to counter persistent misconceptions about the shipbuilding and repair industries.

At the heart of the intervention was a multi-modal simulation suite comprising three integrated components. First, students explored interactive 360-degree maritime environments, such as dry docks and shipyards, featuring embedded career hotspots that introduced authentic roles, tools, and tasks. Second, students engaged with 3D models of ship components and toolkits, completing blueprint-based challenges and assembly sequences. Third, game-based simulations presented design and repair scenarios constrained by time, material limits, and real-world decision-making conditions. These experiences were crafted to achieve three key learning objectives: (1) introduce modern maritime technologies and a broad spectrum of industry roles;

(2) disrupt outdated or inaccurate perceptions of maritime work; and (3) scaffold complex decision-making skills grounded in real-world industrial logic.

By immersing students in these richly contextualized environments, the study aimed to explore how technology-enhanced simulations could influence conceptual development and cognitive processes related to the maritime industry. Anchored in conceptual change theory (Vosniadou, 2002) and supported by research on simulation-based learning and systems thinking (Jacobson et al., 2016), the study investigated three guiding research questions: (1) How can technology-enhanced simulations shift student mental models about the maritime industry? (2) In what ways do simulations support adaptive, reflective decision-making skills? and (3) How can simulation design improve conceptual change in complex domains?

Ultimately, this research contributes to growing efforts to bridge the disconnect between academic learning and future workforce demands. It highlights how simulations, when intentionally designed and grounded in industry practices, can create cognitively rich learning experiences that help students navigate complexity, reason through uncertainty, and reimagine their own pathways in fields shaped by technological innovation and systemic interdependence.

2. RELATED WORK

2.1 Mental Models and Conceptual Change

Mental models are internal representations individuals use to understand and reason through complex systems and experiences (Johnson-Laird, 1983). These models shape how learners interpret information and make decisions (Norman, 1983; Seel, 2003) but often contain persistent misconceptions unless directly addressed (Gentner & Stevens, 1983; Vosniadou, 2002). Johnson-Laird (1983) described mental models as structural analogues of reality, while Gentner and Stevens (1983) emphasized analogical reasoning in revising or reinforcing them. Vosniadou (2002) argued that misconceptions are deeply embedded cognitive frameworks, not just factual errors, requiring targeted conceptual conflict for change.

Conceptual change theory suggests that learners reconstruct their models when exposed to conflicting information and given adequate support (Strike & Posner, 1992). This is particularly relevant in maritime education, where students often view shipbuilding as outdated and disconnected from digital technologies (National Research Council, 2011). In contrast, modern maritime industries use CAD, digital twins, automation, and simulations (Deloitte & The Manufacturing Institute, 2018). Immersive technologies such as VR and AR offer interactive, feedback-rich environments that promote conceptual change (Lindgren & Johnson-Glenberg, 2013; Dede, 2009). Jacobson, Kapur, and Reimann (2016) emphasize the value of simulations for sensemaking in STEM. Already used in professional maritime training (Chen et al., 2020), these tools show strong potential for K–12 applications to foster accurate mental models aligned with future careers.

2.2 Simulation-Based and Immersive Learning

Simulation-based learning environments, particularly those enhanced by immersive technologies, have demonstrated significant benefits in promoting engagement, conceptual understanding, and knowledge transfer. VR and AR create embodied experiences that reflect authentic tasks and spatial relationships, making them ideal for supporting situated cognition (Brown, Collins, & Duguid, 1989). These tools allow learners to explore systems in a way that fosters deeper conceptual integration than text or lecture-based instruction alone (Makransky & Mayer, 2022).

Theoretical models such as constructivism emphasize the role of active engagement and contextual relevance in learning. Simulations grounded in constructivist principles provide learners with the opportunity to explore problems, receive feedback, and construct understanding through action and reflection (Jonassen, 1999). The 360-degree environments and interactive decision-based tasks embedded in the simulations used in this study align with these frameworks by offering personalized, exploratory learning aligned with real-world complexity.

2.3 Decision Making in K-12 Learning Simulations

Effective decision-making is a multifaceted cognitive process involving sensemaking, reflection, and strategic thinking. In the context of K–12 education, students often have limited opportunities to practice these skills in authentic, consequence-based scenarios. Simulations offer structured environments where learners can engage in decision-making without real-world risks, allowing them to experience the outcomes of their choices and reflect on alternative strategies (Schwartz, Bransford, & Sears, 2005).

Feedback mechanisms in simulations support metacognitive growth by prompting learners to consider the implications of their decisions, revise their approaches, and generalize lessons learned to new contexts (Azevedo & Cromley, 2004). Such environments are particularly beneficial in technical domains where systems thinking, and trade-off analysis are crucial. Through simulation-based decision-making tasks, students begin to adopt frameworks used in professional settings, developing adaptive reasoning skills that are difficult to teach through traditional instruction.

3. METHODS

The study involved a total of 1,325 students across a diverse range of educational settings. Participants were drawn from urban, rural, and suburban public schools within a regional coastal district that includes both economically disadvantaged and affluent communities. The sample was intentionally stratified to reflect a cross-section of learners with varying levels of prior exposure to maritime concepts and technologies. Within this sample, 42% were female and 58% were male. Students ranged from upper elementary (grade 5) to high school (grade 12), with the majority clustered between grades 6 and 9. This broad age range enabled the research team to examine how technology-enhanced simulations influence mental model formation and decision-making across developmental stages. Recruitment was coordinated through school division liaisons and approved by participating districts under existing STEM outreach agreements. Passive parental consent protocols were used in accordance with approved guidelines, and students were informed of the voluntary nature of their participation. All learners completed the simulation experience during regular instructional hours in either classroom labs or dedicated simulation settings facilitated by trained instructors.

To comprehensively capture changes in student understanding, perceptions, and behavior, the research team implemented a multi-instrument data collection strategy. Central to this approach were pre- and post-intervention mental model surveys, which included both multiple-choice and open-ended items. These surveys also incorporated visual analogy tasks, such as prompts asking students to complete statements like "Shipbuilding is like…," as well as concept mapping activities. In these maps, students were asked to diagram the components, processes, and roles they associated with the shipbuilding and ship repair industries. This combination of items allowed researchers to assess not only factual knowledge gains but also shifts in the structural coherence and depth of students' underlying mental models. Simultaneously, the simulations themselves were equipped with built-in analytics features that tracked a wide range of learner actions. These included individual choice selections, error patterns, completion times, and the specific decision paths taken within branching scenarios. Time-on-task data was also analyzed to infer learner engagement and decision-making confidence, while variations in navigated decision points across students and grade levels provided insight into emerging strategies and learning progression. To complement the quantitative and behavioral data, students were asked to complete structured reflection prompts immediately following their simulation experience. Prompts included questions such as "What decision was hardest to make, and why?" and "What surprised you about the maritime industry?" In addition to these written reflections, a stratified subsample of 72 students participated in semi-structured interviews. These interviews probed deeper into students' cognitive and emotional reactions to the simulation and captured how their understanding of maritime roles and responsibilities had evolved.

Facilitators also contributed valuable data through structured observation logs maintained throughout each simulation session. These logs recorded behavioral cues such as frustration, collaboration, inquiry, and confidence, as well as the frequency of help-seeking behaviors and moments of spontaneous discussion around task relevance. Observers also captured contextual information, including classroom dynamics, student engagement trends, and variations in technology access that could influence the experience.

4. RESULTS

The study employed a mixed-methods analysis framework to interpret the broad array of data. For the quantitative portion, paired-sample t-tests were conducted to evaluate significant changes in survey responses, particularly in the accuracy and richness of students' mental models. Performance data from the in-game analytics, such as task completion rates and error reductions over time, were aggregated and analyzed using both descriptive statistics and inferential techniques, including analysis of variance (ANOVA) where relevant. These analyses helped identify statistically significant learning outcomes across student subgroups, grade levels, and school contexts.

Qualitative data from the open-ended responses, reflection prompts, interview transcripts, and facilitator logs were analyzed using thematic coding. An inductive coding approach was applied to generate a set of categories including "career perception," "decision awareness," "technology understanding," and "misconception correction." NVivo software supported the coding process, and inter-rater reliability was calculated to ensure consistency across coders, with Cohen's kappa exceeding 0.85 for all primary codes. To ensure analytic rigor and capture multidimensional learning outcomes, the team triangulated findings across all instruments. For example, a student's concept map development was cross-referenced with their written reflection and in-game performance to assess alignment and consistency in conceptual growth. This triangulated analysis made it possible to detect nuanced patterns in how learners internalized maritime knowledge, navigated trade-offs, and shifted their understanding of the field through simulation. By integrating multiple forms of evidence, the methodology provided both quantitative validation of conceptual change and rich qualitative insights into the learner experience, offering a robust framework for evaluating cognitive development in underrepresented educational domains such as maritime training.

4.1 Mental Model Refinement

The simulation-based learning intervention produced robust improvements in students' conceptual understanding of the maritime industry. Prior to the intervention, most students demonstrated shallow or inaccurate mental models, frequently associating maritime work solely with ship welding, manual labor, or general seafaring. Paired-sample t-tests were conducted on survey data collected before and after the simulation, revealing a statistically significant increase in the number of maritime careers students could identify ($t\,(119) = 9.83$, $p < .001$), as well as in the quality of their descriptions. **Before** the intervention, 65% of students could not name any maritime careers, and those who did often listed generic or outdated roles. **After** the simulation, over 70% of students named two or more roles, with 47% citing at least one technology-enhanced position. Students mentioned roles such as "quality assurance inspector," "automation technician," "modeling and simulation engineer," and "digital twin analyst", indicating exposure to and internalization of new industry-relevant concepts.

Concept map analysis showed not only an increase in the number of nodes but also higher connectivity between maritime systems, roles, and tools. Pre-simulation concept maps averaged 5.1 nodes with linear connections. Post-simulation maps averaged 11.7 nodes and included multi-directional links representing relationships among design, inspection, safety, and flow systems. Terms like "sensor systems," "remote inspection," "AR visualization," and "predictive maintenance" were more frequent, suggesting stronger integration of systems thinking and digital maritime workflows. Students also began situating their understanding within the ship's lifecycle, from design to build, maintain, and inspect, demonstrating refined mental models that incorporated both temporal and functional dimensions.

4.2 Misconception Disruption

Prior to the intervention, thematic coding of open-ended responses revealed a set of common misconceptions: 1) maritime careers are dirty and dangerous, 2) work consists mostly of welding or mechanical labor, and 3) the field has minimal relevance to technology or innovation. These misconceptions were prevalent across all demographics and grade levels.

Post-simulation responses indicated a dramatic shift in students' mental representations. Thematic coding using NVivo identified increased references to planning, digital inspection, system design, and quality control. For example, in post-reflection narratives, 83% of students acknowledged technology's role in modern shipbuilding and repair. One student wrote: *"I didn't know there were people who just focus on testing systems or fixing them with digital tools, I thought everything was just built by hand."*

Additionally, misconceptions were replaced with more differentiated roles such as design engineer, quality control inspector, and simulation operator, reflecting a deeper understanding of the collaborative and interdisciplinary nature of maritime careers. This conceptual shift was particularly noticeable among students who performed well on the in-game flow and pressure simulation modules.

4.3 Career Awareness Growth

The simulation modules also played a key role in shifting students' career aspirations (see Figure 1, below). A pre-survey of 122 students showed that only 32% expressed any interest in maritime careers. Post-simulation survey results showed a statistically significant increase to 72% interest ($p < .001$), with a large effect size (Cohen's $d = 1.01$). Post-simulation responses revealed that students began to see clear connections between their existing interests in science, technology, design, and engineering with roles in the maritime field. One middle school student commented: *"I like puzzles and fixing things. Now I know there are jobs that do that on ships using computer programs."* A high school student added: *"This makes me want to learn more about mechanical engineering or robotics for ships."*

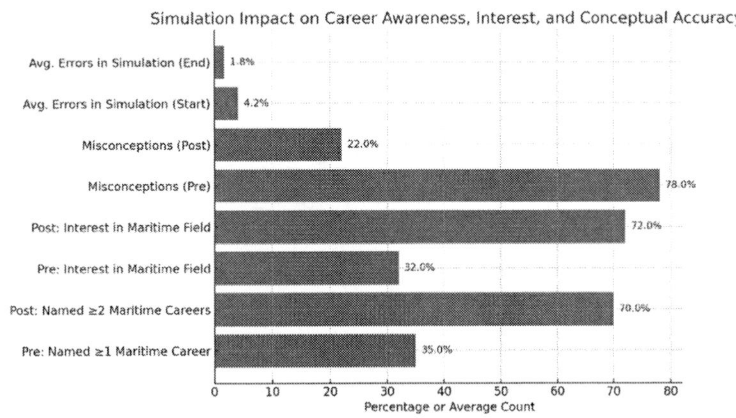

Figure 1. Simulation impact on career awareness, interest, and conceptual accuracy pre- and post- simulation exposure.

4.4 Emergent Decision Skills

Gameplay data provided insight into students' evolving decision-making strategies. Early simulation logs showed that 68% of students defaulted to trial-and-error actions without referencing blueprints, flow direction, or pressure tests. This phase was marked by rapid clicking, frequent task resets, and repeated tool cycling, behaviors indicative of exploratory but non-strategic engagement.

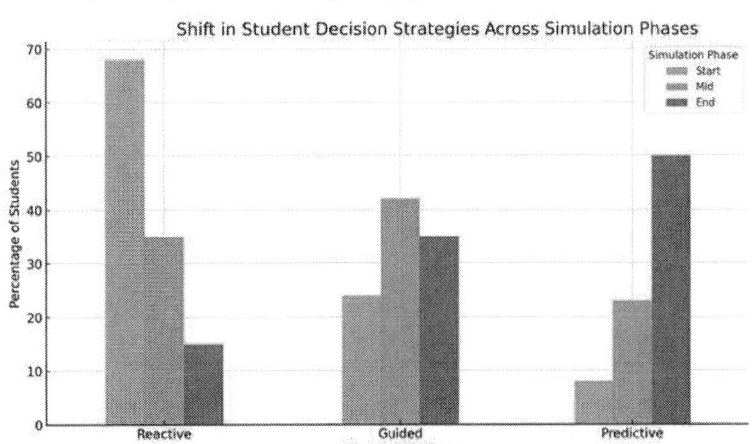

Figure 2. Emergent decision skill shifts per module phase

However, by the end of Module 3, 52% of students were consistently using forward-looking decision strategies grounded in blueprint alignment, system flow logic, and inspection outcomes. This shift was validated through log data, showing longer pause times before actions (suggesting deliberation), and a reduction in repeated errors by 41% from Module 1 to Module 3 (see Figure 2).

These findings suggest the simulations promoted **metacognitive development**, with learners adopting more reflective, structured approaches. Observational notes also recorded student "think-alouds" that demonstrated emerging understanding of interdependencies (e.g., *"If I flip this valve now, it'll stop the airflow on the other end, so I need to check the line."*).

4.5 Embedded Feedback and Learning Loops

The simulations were designed with **real-time embedded feedback** loops, including failed pressure tests, system alerts, and alignment flags. These interactive features served as in-simulation scaffolds, prompting iterative reasoning and revision. In Module 1, only 42% of students responded to feedback by revising their actions; by Module 3, 71% of students revised components based on system indicators.

The impact of these feedback loops was not only behavioral but cognitive. Reflection journals showed increased self-awareness of decision-making processes. Comments such as *"I didn't rotate the valve, so I failed the test and had to restart the whole line"* or *"The support piece didn't match the blueprint, and that's why the system didn't pass"* demonstrate growing capacity for self-monitoring and causal reasoning. Facilitator logs reinforced these trends, noting fewer help requests, more peer consultations, and more frequent use of blueprint overlays by students during the final stages of gameplay.

4.6 Cognitive Skill Gains

Cognitive growth was observed across three main domains: spatial reasoning, problem structuring, and technical vocabulary. Students who initially struggled to interpret 3D layouts or align components began referring more frequently to flow direction indicators and blueprint overlays. Spatial accuracy in mockup assembly increased by 35% by the final simulation.

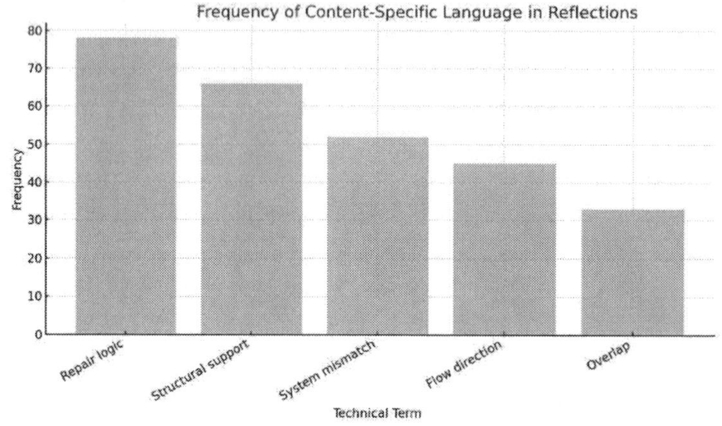

Figure 3. Content-specific frequency shifts

Technical vocabulary usage, measured through reflections, journaling, and facilitator observation, increased both in volume and accuracy. Figure 3 (see below) visualizes term frequency in student reflections, showing a marked rise in phrases like "repair logic," "system mismatch," "structural support," and "flow direction." This linguistic shift suggests not only task mastery but also development of a cognitive language toolkit needed for effective collaboration in technical environments. In addition, students began framing problems with increasing sophistication. Rather than viewing challenges as isolated tasks, they described systemic errors, inter-component relationships, and time-based dependencies. This is a strong indicator of systems thinking and problem framing, key components of macrocognitive skill development.

4.7 Triangulated Analysis and Validation

To ensure methodological rigor, data were triangulated across multiple sources: pre/post surveys, simulation logs, reflection journals, facilitator observation protocols, and concept maps. This mixed-methods integration enabled a comprehensive analysis of both the breadth and depth of cognitive and conceptual change. All qualitative data were coded in NVivo, with an inductive approach used to identify emerging categories. Coding reliability was established with Cohen's $\kappa = 0.86$ across all primary categories ("career perception," "technical understanding," "decision strategy," "technology awareness"). Patterns were validated through cross-source comparisons, for example, students who used terms like "flow mismatch" in concept maps often also revised flow configurations during gameplay and explained failures in reflections using correct terminology.

Quantitative subgroup analysis (via ANOVA) confirmed statistically significant improvements across grade levels ($p < .01$) and between schools in urban, suburban, and rural contexts, suggesting that the intervention was both **scalable** and equitable in its impacts. Together, these findings demonstrate not only the effectiveness of the simulation-based intervention in refining mental models, but also its potential to support cognitive skill development, adaptive decision-making, and career exploration in underrepresented and technologically complex fields.

5. DESIGN IMPLICATIONS

The findings from this study highlight key design principles for educational technologies aimed at reshaping mental models and fostering decision-making in complex fields like maritime trades. Immersive simulation environments proved essential in converting abstract concepts, such as flow logic, systems integration, and digital inspection, into hands-on, manipulable experiences. High visual fidelity and authentic role-based scenarios elevated learner engagement by aligning tasks with real-world maritime functions. Rather than relying on gamification alone, the simulations incorporated embedded scaffolds (blueprint overlays, diagnostics, and contextual tutorials) that reinforced domain knowledge without disrupting the learner's flow. This emphasis on cognitive fidelity ensured that scaffolding aligned with the underlying logic of maritime systems.

The study also underscores the importance of intentional challenge points and feedback loops that require strategic adaptation. Students developed metacognitive skills not because they were instructed to, but because simulation mechanics, failure prompts, branching consequences, and checkpoint logs, demanded thoughtful revision and forward planning. These patterns encouraged learners to reflect, reassess, and internalize habits essential for complex systems thinking.

Looking forward, adaptive simulations that respond to learner decision histories, misconceptions, and growth signals could personalize instruction in real time. AI-driven feedback and cognitive scaffolds tailored to individual performance could guide learners through increasingly complex problem-solving while deepening career exploration. Additionally, educator-facing dashboards that visualize indicators such as vocabulary use, reasoning patterns, and decision accuracy would offer actionable insights into conceptual development, linking simulation-based learning with broader instructional goals. Together, these implications demonstrate that immersive simulations, when designed with realism, embedded scaffolds, and adaptive feedback, can serve as powerful tools for both cognitive development and workforce readiness in underrepresented technical fields.

6. DISCUSSION AND CONCLUSIONS

This study contributes to a growing body of research demonstrating the power of immersive simulations to support conceptual change and cognitive development in K–12 learners. The use of a 360-degree, 3D, and game-based simulation suite was shown to be effective in refining students' mental models of the maritime industry, expanding their awareness of technology-integrated career roles, and supporting the development of foundational decision-making skills. By linking shifts in conceptual understanding to observable changes in cognitive strategies, such as predictive reasoning and reflective revision, the research validates immersive technology as a transformative educational tool in underrepresented domains like maritime trades. However, the study is not without its limitations. The simulation exposure occurred within a relatively short time frame, and deeper longitudinal engagement would be needed to assess the durability of conceptual shifts and the transferability of skills. In addition, disparities in technology access across participating schools may have introduced variability in the quality of student interaction, potentially influencing outcomes. While the current simulations provided strong content alignment and scaffolding, future iterations would benefit from enhanced realism, more granular performance analytics, and adaptive pathways that can respond to learner variability in real time.

Looking ahead, several future research directions emerge. One important area is the examination of long-term impacts: for instance, how early refinement of mental models through immersive simulation may shape students' academic choices, career aspirations, or persistence in STEM fields. There is also strong potential to adapt and apply this simulation-based methodology to other complex domains, such as aviation maintenance, infrastructure inspection, and renewable energy systems, fields that similarly rely on system-level reasoning and technology-integrated workflows. The integration of AI-driven personalization, including mechanisms for adjusting cognitive load and providing tailored feedback based on learner decisions and misconceptions, represents another frontier for development. Ultimately, as the education system continues to evolve to meet the needs of a rapidly changing, technologically complex world, immersive simulations represent a scalable and cognitively rich approach to engage learners, foster adaptive expertise, and support the future workforce. By grounding simulations in authentic roles, systems logic, and challenge-based learning, we can better equip students with the tools needed to navigate interdisciplinary problems and imagine new futures in high-skill, high-tech domains.

REFERENCES

Azevedo, R., & Cromley, J. G. (2004). Does training on self-regulated learning facilitate students' learning with hypermedia? *Journal of Educational Psychology, 96*(3), 523–535. https://doi.org/10.1037/0022-0663.96.3.523.

Brown, J. S., Collins, A., & Duguid, P. (1989). Situated cognition and the culture of learning. *Educational Researcher, 18*(1), 32–42. https://doi.org/10.3102/0013189X018001032.

Chen, J. C., DiBella, F. A., Moncayo, M. E., Zhang, C., & Pan, C. (2020). *Simulation-based training for shipboard damage control using mixed reality technologies.* Computers & Education, 156, 103944. https://doi.org/10.1016/j.compedu.2020.103944.

Dede, C. (2009). Immersive interfaces for engagement and learning. *Science, 323*(5910), 66–69. https://doi.org/10.1126/science.1167311.

Deloitte & The Manufacturing Institute. (2018). *The skills gap and future of work study.* https://www2.deloitte.com/insights/us/en/focus/industry-4-0/manufacturing-skills-gap-future-of-work.html.

Gentner, D., & Stevens, A. L. (Eds.). (1983). *Mental models.* Hillsdale, NJ: Lawrence Erlbaum Associates.

Jacobson, M. J., Kapur, M., & Reimann, P. (2016). Conceptual change and the design of learning environments. In R. K. Sawyer (Ed.), *The Cambridge handbook of the learning sciences* (2nd ed., pp. 95–112). Cambridge University Press.

Johnson-Laird, P. N. (1983). *Mental models: Towards a cognitive science of language, inference, and consciousness.* Harvard University Press.

Lindgren, R., & Johnson-Glenberg, M. (2013). Emboldened by embodiment: Six precepts for research on embodied learning and mixed reality. *Educational Researcher, 42*(8), 445–452. https://doi.org/10.3102/0013189X1351166.

Makransky, G., & Mayer, R. E. (2022). Benefits of immersive virtual reality in learning: A meta-analysis. *Educational Psychology Review, 34*(1), 133–164. https://doi.org/10.1007/s10648-021-09614-2.

National Research Council. (2011). *Learning science through computer games and simulations.* The National Academies Press. https://doi.org/10.17226/13078.

Norman, D. A. (1983). Some observations on mental models. In D. Gentner & A. L. Stevens (Eds.), *Mental models* (pp. 7–14). Hillsdale, NJ: Lawrence Erlbaum Associates.

Schwartz, D. L., Bransford, J. D., & Sears, D. (2005). Efficiency and innovation in transfer. In J. Mestre (Ed.), *Transfer of learning from a modern multidisciplinary perspective* (pp. 1–51). Information Age Publishing.

Seel, N. M. (2003). *Psychology of learning and instruction.* Springer.

Strike, K. A., & Posner, G. J. (1992). A revisionist theory of conceptual change. In R. A. Duschl & R. J. Hamilton (Eds.),
Philosophy of science, cognitive psychology, and educational theory and practice (pp. 147–176). State University of New York Press.

Vosniadou, S. (2002). Mental models in conceptual development. In L. Magnani & N. J. Nersessian (Eds.), *Model-based reasoning: Science, technology, values* (pp. 353–368). Kluwer Academic/Plenum.

ARE STUDENT ENGAGEMENT HIERARCHIES CONSISTENT? A RANK-BASED ANALYSIS OF ONLINE VERSUS OFFLINE ATTENDANCE RATES

Victor K. Y. Chan
Macao Polytechnic University, Rua de Luís Gonzaga Gomes, Macao, China

ABSTRACT

This paper extends the work of Chan (2023) by investigating the consistency of student attendance engagement patterns between online and offline lectures, not through direct attendance rate comparison, but through the analysis of student attendance rankings. While the previous study found no significant correlation between direct attendance rates, this research explores whether a student's relative position, or rank, within their cohort remains stable across different learning modalities. Using attendance rate data for four undergraduate courses ($n = 78$) from Macao Polytechnic University during the 2022/2023 academic year, a suite of non-parametric statistical methods were employ. The analysis reveals no statistically significant rank correlation between online and offline attendance (Spearman's $\rho = 0.192$, $p > 0.05$; Kendall's $\tau\text{-}b = 0.161$, $p > 0.05$). This indicates that the hierarchy of student engagement is not stable; a student's relative attendance rank in one modality does not predict their rank in the other. However, a Wilcoxon Signed-Rank Test shows a highly significant difference between the paired rates ($Z = -4.631$, $p < 0.001$), confirming that students systematically achieve higher attendance rates online. These combined findings suggest that while online learning provides a significant attendance boost, it also fundamentally reshuffles the student engagement hierarchy, with profound implications for identifying and supporting students in different learning environments. A word of caution is that this study targets attendance per se as opposed to attentiveness, which is a far broader concept yielding, for instance, deep learning and academic advancement.

KEYWORDS

Rank Consistency, Online Attendance, Offline Attendance, Spearman's Rank Correlation Coefficient, Kendall's Tau, Wilcoxon Signed-Rank Test

1. INTRODUCTION

The landscape of higher education has been irrevocably altered by the proliferation of digital technologies, a trend massively accelerated by the global COVID-19 pandemic. This period forced a rapid, worldwide pivot from traditional face-to-face instruction to what was often termed "emergency remote teaching" (Hodges et al, 2020). While distinct from thoughtfully designed online courses, this widespread experience has cemented online and hybrid models as enduring features of the educational ecosystem. Consequently, the academic community has intensified its investigation into the comparative efficacy and student experience of online versus offline learning. The body of literature is vast, covering pedagogical effectiveness (Edwards and Clinton, 2019), student satisfaction, and the complex relationship between attendance and academic performance (Kuzminykh et al, 2021; Pilotti and El Alaoui, 2023).

A noteworthy contribution to this field came from Chan (2023), who capitalized on a unique "natural experiment" where courses were delivered in a mixed modality due to fluctuating public health mandates. This allowed for a direct comparison of student attendance rates within the same courses and cohorts. The study's conclusions were twofold and intriguing: First, the mean online attendance rate was significantly higher than the offline rate, a finding often attributed to the greater convenience of online access (Almahasees et al, 2021). Second, and more surprisingly, there was no statistically significant Pearson correlation between an individual student's online and offline attendance rates. This suggests that a student's absolute level of attendance in one mode does not predict their attendance in the other. It is noteworthy that the study and its conclusions purposefully aimed at attendance rate online versus offline instead of attentiveness (i.e., paying attention intensively and deep learning) online versus offline, which was not the theme of the study in the first place and was left to other researches.

This paper builds directly upon the foundation laid by Chan (2023) but pivots the analytical lens from absolute values to relative positions. The former poses a different, yet complementary, question as the latter's: are student *attendance rankings* consistent across learning modalities? In other words, do the most diligent attendees in a physical classroom retain their high-ranking status when the lecture moves online or vice versa? Does the cohort of least-engaged students remain at the bottom of the attendance hierarchy, irrespective of the delivery format?

This focus on rank consistency, as opposed to direct rate consistency, is motivated by several factors. Firstly, the lack of correlation in absolute rates, as found by Chan (2023), could be a statistical artifact of a distributional shift. If the convenience of online learning provides a general uplift in attendance for most students, it could shift the entire distribution of attendance rates upwards, thereby weakening the linear relationship required for a high Pearson correlation, even if the internal ordering of students remains largely the same. Secondly, the concept of "rank effects" is a powerful one in educational and social psychology. Research suggests that a student's relative rank within their peer group can have profound impacts on their self-concept, motivation, and future academic choices, often independent of their absolute performance level (Delaney and Devereux, 2022; Devereux and Delaney, 2022). Therefore, understanding whether a student's relative standing in terms of engagement is stable is arguably as important as knowing their absolute attendance. It speaks to the persistence of individual study habits and motivational traits in the face of changing environmental conditions.

In fact, there are other literature on the relevance of ordinal rankings and the contrast between the analysis of direct quantities and that of their ordinal rankings. In recent years, scholarly work has highlighted quite some educational researches, where ranking systems often simplify complex multidimensional data into ordinal lists. For example, Li et al (2021) examined the interplay between face-to-face class attendance, virtual learning engagement, and academic performance in a blended learning environment based on both these three direct quantities and their ranks, which turned out to indicate consistent conclusions. Murphy and Weinhardt (2020) demonstrated that ordinal academic rank during primary school had lasting impacts on secondary school achievement that were independent of underlying ability. Similarly, in cross-national assessments, analyses of rankings from the Program for International Student Assessment (PISA) often lead to justification of national educational policies. Li et al (2025) noted that countries like Finland, the United Kingdom, France, Japan, and South Korea were among those countries actively responding to PISA rankings in formulating their policies despite their diverse paradigms in the responses. Breakspear (2012) even revealed that countries in making their policies tended to be more concerned or partially concerned about their PISA rankings than their individual PISA performance scores. Martens and Niemann (2013) illustrated how countries' policies responded to their disappointing PISA rankings. From another perspective, instead of ranking students or countries, Hattie's (2017) meta-analyses arrived at the rankings of the influences on student achievement and estimated the influences' effect sizes. Such findings underscore the need for researchers to critically evaluate whether rank-based analyses complement or contradict conclusions drawn from direct quantities. Please note that the PISA examples above are cited here only to make the point that rank-based analyses often, if not necessarily, matter as much as the their direct quantity counterparts in the context of education in general but not to imply in the slightest PISA being targeted in this current study.

To rigorously investigate this question of rank concordance, this study employs a suite of non-parametric statistical methods, each chosen for its specific strengths in analyzing ordinal data:

- **Spearman's Rank Correlation Coefficient (ρ or r_s):** This rank correlation statistic is the non-parametric equivalent of the Pearson correlation. It measures the strength and direction of the monotonic relationship between two ranked variables (Laerd Statistics, n.d.). Unlike Pearson's Correlation Coefficient (r), it does not assume a linear relationship, making it ideal for assessing if the ranks of one variable tend to increase or decrease as the other does, without assuming that they do so at a constant rate. Its primary purpose here is to provide a direct, well-understood measure of the overall association between the two complete attendance rankings, one online and the other offline.
- **Kendall's Tau-b (τ-b):** This rank correlation statistic also measures ordinal association but operates on a different principle. It counts the number of "concordant" and "discordant" pairs of observations (Kendall, 1938). It is often considered more robust than Spearman's ρ, particularly for smaller sample sizes and in the presence of numerous tied ranks (Number Analytics, 2025). Given that attendance

data can often have many students with perfect or identical attendance scores, Kendall's *τ-b* provides a crucial, complementary perspective on the strength of the association.

- **Rank-Biased Overlap (RBO):** Developed by Webber et al (2010), RBO is a more specialized similarity measure designed for comparing ranked lists, especially when they may be of indefinite length. Its defining characteristic is that it is "top-weighted." This means it assigns greater importance to agreement at the top of the rankings than at the bottom. This feature is exceptionally relevant to the current research question, as educators and administrators are often most concerned with identifying and understanding the behavior of the most engaged (top-ranked) and least engaged (bottom-ranked) students. By adjusting a persistence parameter p, one can explore the degree of similarity with varying emphasis on the top ranks. The larger the p, the least emphasis is placed on the top-ranks.
- **Wilcoxon Signed-Rank Test:** While the preceding methods measure association, this test is used to determine if there is a systematic difference between two related sets of observations (Nahm, 2016) by rank. It is the non-parametric alternative to the paired samples t-test. In the current context, it will test whether students, as a group, tend to systematically rank higher or lower in one modality compared to the other. A significant result would suggest that one modality inherently favors higher attendance rankings across the cohort.

By applying this comprehensive toolkit, this study seeks to move beyond the analysis of absolute attendance to uncover the deeper, underlying patterns of student engagement. The objective is to determine whether the hierarchy of student attendance is a stable, trait-like characteristic or if it is fluid and context-dependent, thereby offering a more nuanced understanding to guide pedagogical strategies in our increasingly hybrid educational future. The study's contribution is to discern students' differential attendance behaviors online and offline, which may be leveraged by subsequent studies to optimize pedagogical strategies accordingly.

2. METHODOLOGY

2.1 Materials and Data Source

The empirical foundation of this study is the dataset collected and made available through the work of Chan (2023). This dataset captures the online and offline lecture attendance records for a total of 78 senior undergraduate students. These students were enrolled across four distinct courses within the Faculty of Business at Macao Polytechnic University during the first semester of the 2022/2023 academic year, which spanned from late August to late November 2022.

The four courses included in the sample were:

- "System Analysis and Design" (E-commerce Program, Year 3, $n = 20$, English medium)
- "E-commerce Project Management" (E-commerce Program, Year 3, $n = 20$, English medium)
- "Operations Management" (Management Program, Year 3, $n = 19$, English medium)
- "Operations Management" (Management Program, Year 3, $n = 19$, Chinese-English bilingual medium)

A crucial feature of this dataset, as highlighted by Chan (2023), is that all four courses were delivered using an online-plus-offline mixed modality due to pandemic-related public health measures. Approximately one-quarter of the lectures were conducted online via the Zoom platform, with the remainder delivered in traditional, physical classroom settings. This unique "within-subject" design, where the same students in the same courses experienced both modalities, is a significant strength, as it minimizes the confounding effects of course content, instructor style, and cohort composition that often plague cross-course comparisons of online and offline learning.

The raw data consists of attendance records meticulously taken for each lecture using the university's official attendance system. Chan (2023) processed these records to calculate two key metrics for each of the 78 students:

- **Online Attendance Rate (r_n):** The proportion of online lectures the student attended for his/her course, i.e.,

$$r_n = \frac{\text{Total number of online lectures attended by the student for the course}}{\text{Total number of online lectures for the course}}.$$

- **Offline Attendance Rate (r_f):** The proportion of offline lectures the student attended for his/her course, i.e.,

$$r_f = \frac{\text{Total number of offline lectures attended by the student for the course}}{\text{Total number of offline lectures for the course}}.$$

This research utilizes these two final calculated rates (r_n and r_f) for each of the 78 students. The analysis begins by converting these two sets of continuous rate data into two corresponding sets of ordinal rank data.

2.2 Data Analysis Plan

The analytical procedure was designed to systematically address the research question of rank consistency. The primary data transformation involved ranking the 78 students based on their online attendance rate (r_n) and, separately, their offline attendance rate (r_f). In both cases, ranks were assigned from 1 (the highest attendance rate) to 78 (the lowest attendance rate). A standard approach for handling tied rates was used, where all individuals with the same rate receive the average of the ranks they would have occupied. For example, if three students are tied for the 5th highest rate, they would occupy ranks 5, 6, and 7, and each would be assigned the average rank of 6. These two resulting ranked lists—Online Attendance Rank and Offline Attendance Rank—form the input for subsequent statistical tests.

The following statistical methods were applied using the SciPy and RBO libraries in Python:

Spearman's Rank Correlation Correlation (ρ): The consistency between the two ranked lists was first measured using Spearman's ρ. The formula is equivalent to the Pearson correlation coefficient applied to the rank variables. The null hypothesis (H_0) is that there is no monotonic association between the online and offline attendance ranks ($\rho = 0$), tested against the alternative hypothesis (H_a) that an association exists ($\rho \neq 0$).

Kendall's Tau-b (τ-b): To provide a complementary and more robust measure of rank correlation, Kendall's τ-b was calculated. This method evaluates the difference between the number of concordant pairs (pairs of students who are ranked in the same order on both ranking lists) and discordant pairs (pairs ranked in opposite orders), with an adjustment for ties (the 'b' variant). The null hypothesis (H_0) is that the two rankings are independent, i.e., not rank-correlated or in different orders.

Rank-Biased Overlap (RBO): To assess top-weighted similarity, RBO was computed. RBO is calculated based on the expected overlap at increasing depths of the ranked lists, governed by a persistence parameter p (Webber et al, 2010). A higher p value (closer to 1) indicates a weaker focus on the top of the lists. RBO was calculated for three levels of p:

- $p = 0.80$: Moderately strong top-weightedness.
- $p = 0.90$: Weak top-weightedness.
- $p = 0.95$: Very weak top-weightedness.

This allows for an analysis of whether rank consistency is uniform or concentrated among the most diligent students. RBO produces a similarity score between 0 (disjoint) and 1 (identical).

Wilcoxon Signed-Rank Test: To test for a systematic difference in the central tendency of the two sets of ranks, the Wilcoxon signed-rank test was performed. This test evaluates whether the median of the differences between the paired ranks (Online Rank - Offline Rank) for each student is significantly different from zero (Statistics by Jim, n.d.). The null hypothesis (H_0) is that the median of these differences is zero. A significant result would imply that students as a group systematically rank higher in one modality than the other.

For all inferential statistical tests (Spearman, Kendall, and Wilcoxon), a significance level (alpha) of $\alpha = 0.05$ was used to determine statistical significance. P-values, 95% confidence intervals, and relevant effect sizes were calculated and reported to provide a comprehensive picture of the findings.

3. RESULTS

The key findings are summarized in Table 1.

Table 1. Summary of statistical test results ($n = 78$)

Statistical test	Coefficient / statistic	95% Confidence interval	p-value (2-tailed)
Spearman's Rank Correlation Coefficient (ρ)	0.192	[-0.038, 0.404]	0.091
Kendall's Tau-b (τ-b)	0.161	[-0.012, 0.304]	0.092
Wilcoxon Signed-Rank Test (Z)	-4.631	N/A	< 0.001**
Rank-Biased Overlap (RBO)			
• with persistence parameter $p = 0.80$	0.231	N/A	N/A
• with $p = 0.90$	0.229	N/A	N/A
• with $p = 0.95$	0.222	N/A	N/A

* $p < .05$, ** $p < .01$.
The 95% confidence intervals of both Spearman's ρ and Kendall's τ-b were estimated by Fisher's r-to-z transformation, while the standard error, if needed, was estimated by the formula proposed by Fieller, Hartley, and Pearson.
"N/A" indicates that the confidence interval or p-value was not applicable.
Among the numerous RBO implementations probably yielding varied RBO results due to different tie-breaking approaches, etc., this Table 1 adopts the Google implementation. Readers are better off viewing the RBOs here as approximations.

3.1 Rank Correlation Analysis

The Spearman's rank correlation coefficient was found to be **ρ = 0.192**. With a p-value of **0.091**, this result is **not statistically significant** at the conventional $\alpha = 0.05$ level. Therefore, the result fails to reject the null hypothesis of no monotonic association between the online and offline attendance ranks. The 95% confidence interval for the coefficient is [-0.038, 0.404], which contains zero, further supporting the lack of a statistically significant rank correlation.

Similarly, the Kendall's Tau-b analysis yielded a coefficient of **τ-b = 0.161** with a p-value of **0.092**. This, too, is **not statistically significant**. Both rank correlation measures consistently indicate that there is no discernible monotonic relationship between a student's attendance rank in an online environment and his/her rank in an offline one.

3.2 Analysis of Paired Differences

In stark contrast to the rank correlation results, the Wilcoxon Signed-Rank Test yielded a Z-score of **-4.631**, with a p-value **< 0.001**. This result is highly statistically significant. It indicates a systematic rank difference between the paired online and offline attendance rates. An examination of the ranks reveals that in 49 pairs the offline attendance rate was lower than the online rate, while in only 10 pairs was it higher (with 19 ties). This confirms that students' online attendance rates are systematically and significantly higher than their offline attendance rates.

3.3 Top-Weighted Similarity Analysis

The Rank-Biased Overlap (RBO) scores were low across all levels of top-weightedness: RBO(persistence parameter $p = 0.80$) = 0.231, RBO($p = 0.90$) = 0.229, and RBO($p = 0.95$) = 0.222. These low values corroborate the lack of rank correlation, indicating very little similarity in the rankings, even among the most diligent students.

4. DISCUSSION

4.1 Summary of Findings

The study produced two clear, yet seemingly contradictory, results. First, there is **no statistically significant rank correlation** between students' online and offline attendance ranks ($p > 0.05$ for both Spearman's and Kendall's tests). This indicates that the student engagement hierarchy is fluid and unstable across modalities.

Second, there is a **highly significant systematic difference** between the paired attendance rates by rank, with online attendance being predominantly higher than offline attendance ($p < 0.001$).

4.2 Interpretation and Comparison with Prior Work

These findings provide a powerful and nuanced extension to the work of Chan (2023). The results confirm Chan's original finding regarding the difference in mean attendance, but do so using the more appropriate non-parametric Wilcoxon test, showing that the effect is robust and systematic. More importantly, by demonstrating the lack of rank correlation, this study provides a compelling explanation for *why* Chan (2023) found no Pearson correlation between the absolute attendance rates: the students' relative positions are being fundamentally reshuffled between the two environments.

The story that emerges is one of a dual effect. The transition to online learning (1) provides a significant, systematic boost to attendance rates for the vast majority of students, and (2) simultaneously dissolves the existing engagement hierarchy. The factors that make a student a diligent attendee in a physical classroom appear to be largely different from the factors that drive attendance online. The lack of rank correlation, supported by both Spearman's and Kendall's tests and the low RBO scores, suggests that student engagement, as measured by attendance, is not a stable, monolithic trait. Rather, it is a dynamic behavior, highly sensitive to the context of the learning environment.

4.3 Implications for Educational Practice and Policy

The practical implications of these findings are substantial for educators, administrators, and instructional designers.

1. **Modality-Specific Student Monitoring:** The instability of the engagement hierarchy is a critical finding. It means that educators and support staff cannot rely on a student's attendance record in one modality to predict their behavior in another. A student who appears highly engaged in-person may be at risk of disengaging online, and vice versa, at least in terms of attendance, if not, also intensive attention and deep learning. Monitoring and intervention strategies must be tailored to, and conducted independently within, each learning environment even for the purpose of students' attention rates alone.
2. **Leveraging the "Online Boost":** The powerful and systematic increase in online versus offline attendance rates, confirmed by the Wilcoxon test, is a phenomenon to be leveraged. While it does not imply deeper learning, it does suggest that the convenience of online access (Almahasees et al, 2021) successfully removes barriers to initial participation. The challenge for educators is to convert this "presenteeism" into genuine academic and learning engagement in view of high attendance rate not being necessarily equivalent to intensive attention and deep learning.
3. **Rethinking "At-Risk" Profiles:** The concept of a single "at-risk student" profile of absenteeism may be outdated in a hybrid world. Instead, institutions may need to consider "at-risk situations," recognizing that a student's risk level changes with the educational context. Of course, such absenteeism risk is meant to be confined to that of low attendance rates as opposed to the substantially broader notion of students' inattentiveness risk, which is way more intricate and beyond this current study.
4. **Pedagogical Strategy:** For instructors, the knowledge that the engagement hierarchy is unstable across lecturing modalities can inform teaching strategies. It underscores the ongoing need for differentiated instruction and varied engagement techniques to motivate students across the spectrum, as the online environment, though being an attendance "booster," is not a "magic bullet" that equalizes student attentiveness (i.e., paying attention intensively and deep learning).

4.4 Limitations and Future Research Directions

This study, while providing valuable insights, has several limitations that open avenues for future research.

- **Generalizability:** The data is from a single institution in Macao, focusing on business undergraduates. The findings may not be generalizable to other disciplines, student demographics (e.g., first-year students versus senior students), or cultural contexts. Replicating this rank-based analysis with datasets from different universities and fields may be a critical next step.

- **Definition of Engagement:** Attendance is used as a proxy for engagement. While it is a tangible and important measure, it is an incomplete one. Future research could incorporate other behavioral data from Learning Management Systems (e.g., forum participation, resource access, time spent on tasks, etc.) to create a more holistic, multi-dimensional ranking of student engagement (Kuzminykh et al, 2021).
- **Possible Unscrupulousness in Attendance-Taking:** The student attendance, as recorded in this study's dataset, might be prone to errors due to impersonation or other dishonesty, especially in the case of online lectures despite the official and formal nature of the underlying recording process. Future research involving attendance-taking may consider even more reliable procedures.
- **Qualitative Exploration:** The quantitative analysis shows *that* ranks are unstable but not *why*. Qualitative research, such as conducting interviews with the minority of students who maintained their ranks versus the majority who significantly changed them, could provide rich insights into the personal, social, and environmental factors that drive engagement consistency or inconsistency.
- **Identifying "Shufflers":** What are the characteristics of students whose attendance ranks change most dramatically between teaching modalities? Are there patterns related to personality, home environment, or technological fluency that explain this shift? Such shuffling patterns may be worth further studies.
- **Attendance versus attentiveness:** This paper only intends to analyze attendance rates instead of the broader idea of attentiveness, which may be the true driver behind the most desirable deep learning and academic advancement. Readers are reminded that any findings and conclusions here should not be extrapolated to attentiveness.

Investigation into such areas may deserve future research albeit the non-contrived, "natural" settings for online-plus-offline blended lectures may by now be a rarity in this post-pandemic era.

5. CONCLUSION

In conclusion, this paper finds that the hierarchy of student attendance is not stable across online and offline modalities. There is no significant correlation between a student's attendance rank in the two settings, indicating that engagement behavior is highly context-dependent. Simultaneously, online learning provides a powerful and systematic boost to attendance rates across the cohort. Together, these findings depict a complex reality for hybrid education: a particular learning environment is able to not only lift overall attendance but also fundamentally reshuffle the order of who is most and least engaged. This underscores the need for educators to develop flexible, modality-aware strategies to support and engage all students effectively in the varied learning contexts of the 21st century.

ACKNOWLEDGEMENT

The original paper of Chan (2023) and the underlying data provided the foundation for this extended analysis. The author acknowledges the students and the university having participated in the original study.

REFERENCES

Almahasees, Z. et al. (2021). Faculty's and Students' Perceptions of Online Learning during COVID-19. In *Frontiers in Education, Vol. 6*, 638470. https://doi.org/10.3389/feduc.2021.638470

Breakspear, S. (2012). The Policy Impact of PISA: An Exploration of the Normative Effects of International Benchmarking in School System Performance. *OECD Education Working Papers, No. 71*. OECD Publishing. https://www.oecd.org/content/dam/oecd/en/publications/reports/2012/02/the-policy-impact-of-pisa_g17a20ec/5k9fdfqffr28-en.pdf

Chan, V. K. Y. (2023). Online vs Offline Attendance Rates: Are they Correlated and How Do they Compare? *Proceedings of the International Conferences: e-Learning and Digital Learning 2023*, Proto, Portugal, pp. 125-130. ISBN: 978-989-8704-51-1.

Delaney, J. M. and Devereux, P. J. (2022). Rank Effects in Education: What Do We Know So Far? In *Handbook of Labor, Human Resources and Population Economics*, pp. 1-38. https://papers.ssrn.com/sol3/Delivery.cfm?abstractid=4069898

Devereux, P. J., and Delaney, J. (2022). *Rank Effects in Education*. Centre for Economic Policy Research (CEPR), London, UK. https://cepr.org/voxeu/columns/rank-effects-education

Edwards, M. R. and Clinton, M. E. (2019). A Study Exploring the Impact of Lecture Capture Availability and Lecture Capture Usage on Student Attendance and Attainment. In *High Education*, Vol. 77, pp. 403–421. https://doi.org/10.1007/s10734-018-0275-9

Hattie, J. (2017). *Visible Learning: Hattie Ranking: 252 Influences And Effect Sizes Related To Student Achievement*. Retrieved September 3, 2025, from https://visible-learning.org/hattie-ranking-influences-effect-sizes-learning -achievement/

Hodges, C. et al. (2020). The Difference between Emergency Remote Teaching and Online Learning. In *Educause Review*. https://er.educause.edu/articles/2020/3/the-difference-between-emergency-remote-teaching-and-online-learning

Kendall, M. G. (1938). A New Measure of Rank Correlation. In *Biometrika, Vol. 30, No. 1/2*, pp. 81-93. https://doi.org/10.2307/2332226

Kuzminykh, I. et al. (2021). The Relationship between Student Engagement and Academic Performance in Online Education. *Proceedings of 2021 5th International Conference on E-Society, E-Education and E-Technology (ICSET 2021)*, Taipei, Taiwan, pp. 97-101. https://doi.org/10.1145/3485768.3485796

Laerd Statistics., n.d. *Spearman's Rank-Order Correlation*. Retrieved August 22, 2025, from https://statistics.laerd.com/statistical-guides/spearmans-rank-order-correlation-statistical-guide-2.php

Li, J. et al. (2025). The Effects of PISA on Global Basic Education Reform: A Systematic Literature Review. In *Humanities and Social Sciences Communications*, Vol. 12, No. 1, pp. 1-15. https://www.nature.com/articles/s41599-025-04403 -z.pdf

Li, N. et al. (2021). Investigation of Face-to-Face Class Attendance, Virtual Learning Engagement and Academic Performance in a Blended Learning Environment. In *International Journal of Information and Education Technology*, Vol. 11, No. 3, pp. 112-118.

Martens, K. and Niemann, D. (2013) 'When Do Numbers Count? The Differential Impact of the PISA Rating and Ranking on Education Policy in Germany and the US. In *German Politics*, Vol. 22, No. 3, pp. 314-332. https://doi.org/10.1080/09644008.2013.794455.

Murphy, R. and Weinhardt, F. (2020). Top of the Class: The Importance of Ordinal Rank. In *The Review of Economic Studies*, Vol. 87, No. 6, pp. 2777-2826. https://doi.org/10.1093/restud/rdaa020

Nahm, F. S. (2016). Nonparametric Statistical Tests for the Continuous Data: the Basic Concept and the Practical Use. In *Korean Journal of Anesthesiology*, Vol. 69, No. 1, pp. 8-14. https://synapse.koreamed.org/articles/1156310

Number Analytics. (2025). *Mastering Kendall's Tau: Demystifying Rank Correlation in Statistics*. https://www.numberanalytics.com/blog/mastering-kendalls-tau-statistics

Pilotti, M. and El Alaoui, K. (2023). Lessons Learned from Online and Face-to-Face Courses: To What Extent Is Students' Academic Success Just a Matter of Showing Up? In *The International Journal of Assessment and Evaluation*, Vol. 30, No. 1, pp. 15-32. https://doi.org/10.18848/2327-7920/CGP/v30i01/15-32

Statistics by Jim., n.d. *Wilcoxon Signed Rank Test Explained*. Retrieved August 22, 2025, from https://statisticsbyjim.com/hypothesis-testing/wilcoxon-signed-rank-test/

Webber, W. et al. (2010). A Similarity Measure for Indefinite Rankings. In *ACM Transactions on Information Systems, Vol. 28, No. 4*, pp. 1–38. https://doi.org/10.1145/1852102.1852106

ADAPTIVE LEARNING WITH COGNITIVE AWARENESS: AN AI MODEL FROM THE ELSEI MASTER'S PROGRAM

Zakaria Tagdimi[1], Souhaib Aammou[1] and Marina Sounoglou[2]
[1]*Abdelmalek Essaadi University, Morocco*
[2]*Aristotle University of Thessaloniki, Greece*

ABSTRACT

Personalization is often perceived as a technical problem in the context of digital education. However, it is also a cognitive challenge, requiring an understanding of how learners process information. This study presents a cognitive-based recommendation model designed and tested within the Master's program in E-learning and Intelligent Educational Systems (ELSEI) at the École Normale Supérieure (ENS) of Abdelmalek Essaadi University in Morocco. This model is based on the principles of cognitive load theory and uses artificial intelligence to adapt learning experiences in real time. The model aims to align content presentation with each learner's cognitive profile. This alignment is achieved through clustering, load classification, and hybrid recommendation techniques. This model is tested for six weeks involving 47 graduate students and has shown encouraging results: an improvement in engagement and academic performance, as well as a reduction in learning disruptions related to overload. These results suggest a broader evolution of educational AI, towards systems that are not only adaptive, but also attentive to the cognitive demands of learning.

KEYWORDS

Adaptive Learning, Cognitive Load Theory, Educational Recommender Systems, Artificial Intelligence in Education

1. INTRODUCTION

Artificial Intelligence (AI) is quickly reshaping how higher education operates—from content delivery to assessment strategies and learner support. While much of the conversation around AI in education focuses on automation or predictive analytics, its true transformative potential may lie in personalization. More specifically, AI offers a way to tailor learning experiences to the diverse cognitive profiles, motivations, and prior knowledge levels of students. Yet in many academic programs, this potential remains more theoretical than real. Effective personalization still faces challenges related to cognitive overload, learning pace, and pedagogical coherence (Long & Siemens, 2011; Pane et al., 2015).

At the Ecole Normale Superieure (ENS) of Abdelmalek Essaadi University in Morocco, the Master's in E-learning and Intelligent Educational Systems (ELSEI) provides a fertile ground for testing these ideas in practice. The program prepares future professionals in educational technology by engaging them not only with theoretical frameworks but also with hands-on AI tools. Instructors and students alike use systems for adaptive content delivery, real-time learner analytics, and intelligent feedback loops. As a result, ELSEI is both a space for professional training and a living lab for innovation in AI-enhanced pedagogy.

One of the key challenges we encountered in this context was finding the right balance between personalization and cognitive alignment. Learners don't all benefit equally from the same instructional strategies (Sounoglou, 2022). While some thrive on challenge, others risk disengagement if the material becomes too complex too quickly. Cognitive Load Theory (CLT), introduced by Sweller (1988), helps make sense of this variability by emphasizing the limits of working memory and the importance of designing learning experiences that respect those limits. When combined with real-time learner modeling, CLT can guide AI systems to recommend content that matches—not exceeds—each learner's current cognitive state.

In this paper, we introduce and evaluate a hybrid recommendation model that brings together CLT and AI to support personalized learning in graduate education. Developed and tested within the ELSEI program, the model is designed to (1) enhance student engagement, (2) increase the responsiveness of instructional sequences, and (3) improve the quality of personalization through cognitive load–sensitive analytics. Ultimately, our aim is to contribute to the development of adaptive systems that are not only intelligent in a technical sense but also attuned to the mental rhythms and needs of real learners.

2. THEORETICAL FRAMEWORK

To design adaptive educational environments grounded in learner cognition, it is essential to articulate the theoretical principles guiding personalization and AI-based decision-making. This work draws on three complementary frameworks: Cognitive Load Theory (CLT), Information Processing Theory (IPT), and recent developments in AI-driven personalization in education.

2.1 Cognitive Load Theory (CLT)

Cognitive Load Theory (Sweller, 1988; Sweller, Ayres, & Kalyuga, 2011, Sweller, 2020) posits that human working memory has limited capacity, and learning is optimized when instructional materials manage this load appropriately, is well-suited to provide guidance suggesting which educational technologies are likely to be effective and how they should be used. All of the many cognitive load effects occur because of variations in element interactivity with the vast majority being due to extraneous cognitive load (Sweller, 2023).
CLT distinguishes between:

- Intrinsic Load, inherent to the complexity of the content and the learner's prior knowledge.
- Extraneous Load, generated by the instructional design and presentation of materials, which should be minimized.
- Germane Load, the mental effort dedicated to schema construction and automation, which should be fostered.

In the ELSEI context, where students engage with advanced educational technologies, managing cognitive load becomes critical. By aligning learning content and pace to each student's working memory capacity, educators can prevent overload and promote deeper understanding.

2.2 Information Processing Theory (IPT)

Information Processing Theory conceptualizes learning as a sequence of stages: input, processing, storage, and retrieval (Atkinson & Shiffrin, 1968). Working memory serves as the cognitive bottleneck, where overload can hinder encoding into long-term memory.

AI-powered educational systems can mitigate this issue by offering real-time adjustments. For instance, a spike in incorrect responses or prolonged task durations may indicate cognitive strain. These signals can be used to simplify content or introduce supportive scaffolds aligning instructional pacing with learners' current mental bandwidth (Miller, 1956; Baddeley, 2000).

2.3 Personalization through AI

AI introduces the ability to model learners dynamically tracking patterns in performance, behavior, and preferences. Adaptive learning systems can then deliver resources that match the learner's evolving profile (Kabudi, Pappas & Olsen, 2022; Ling & Chiang, 2022; Pane et al., 2015; Romero & Ventura, 2013).

In the ELSEI program, this is implemented through:

- Learner clustering (e.g., K-means) based on interaction traces and engagement metrics.
- Cognitive load classifiers (e.g., Support Vector Machines) trained on real or simulated behavioral and physiological data.
- Hybrid recommendation engines combining collaborative filtering and semantic similarity.

This triad allows the learning system to act responsively modulating content difficulty, format, or sequencing to maximize cognitive alignment. Crucially, this form of personalization goes beyond surface-level preferences (e.g., visual vs. verbal) to engage with the learner's moment-to-moment mental workload.

By integrating CLT, IPT, and AI-driven personalization, the proposed framework aligns technological adaptivity with cognitive realism. It enables systems not just to react to learners, but to anticipate and support their cognitive state thus optimizing both learning efficiency and experience.

3. METHODOLOGY

To operationalize the integration of cognitive load theory and AI-driven personalization, a multi-layered recommendation architecture has been deployed within the ELSEI Master's program. This methodology describes the technical and pedagogical implementation of the model, its components, and its deployment context.

3.1 Context of Implementation: The ELSEI Ecosystem

The ELSEI Master's Program (E-learning and Intelligent Educational Systems) at Abdelmalek Essaâdi University serves as a living lab for testing intelligent educational interventions. The program includes courses in AI, knowledge reasoning, learning analytics, and pedagogical engineering. Students interact with a custom LMS equipped with AI-enhanced modules that log interaction traces, performance metrics, and self-reported workload measures.

This context provides an ideal environment to test adaptive systems in a real-world graduate learning setting, where learners are diverse in background, digital skills, and cognitive strategies.

3.2 The Hybrid Recommendation Architecture

The proposed model is composed of four key layers:

1. Learner Profiling via Clustering

Using K-means clustering, learners are segmented into groups based on prior knowledge (e.g., pre-test scores), learning behavior (e.g., time-on-task, task completion), and engagement metrics. This segmentation allows the system to recognize patterns and personalize content delivery accordingly.

Example: A cluster of learners who spend long durations on tasks with low completion rates may receive simplified or scaffolded resources.

2. Real-Time Cognitive Load Estimation

Cognitive load is inferred using a Support Vector Machine (SVM) classifier trained on features such as:

- Task response time
- Number of retries
- Self-reported mental effort (Likert scale)
- Navigation behavior (e.g., backtracking)

The classifier predicts whether the learner is experiencing low, optimal, or high cognitive load.

3. Content Indexing and Load Calibration

All learning objects in the platform are indexed by their intrinsic load, estimated via expert rating and historical learner data. The metadata includes content length, conceptual complexity, media format, and prerequisite dependencies.

4. Adaptive Recommendation Engine

The core module combines:

- Collaborative filtering, to suggest resources that benefited similar learners.
- Content-based filtering, to match current learner states to resource complexity.
- Cognitive alignment constraints, to ensure the content's load matches the learner's cognitive zone of proximal development.

Recommendations are re-evaluated every 15 minutes of learning activity or upon task failure.

3.3 System Workflow

The model operates as follows (figure 1):

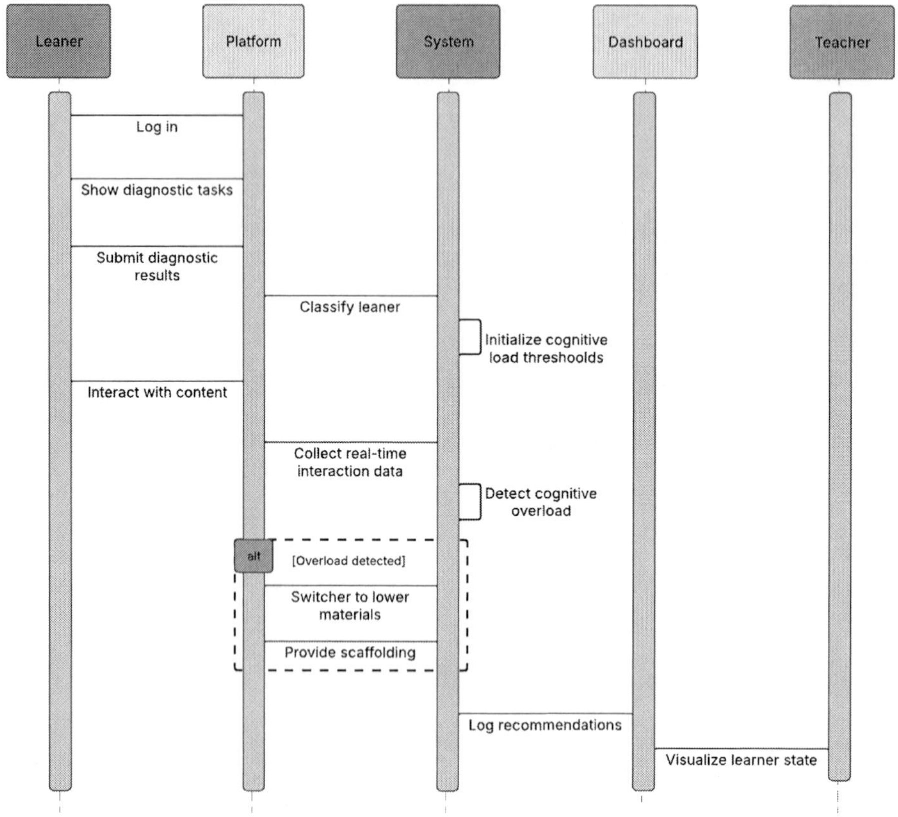

Figure 1. Adaptive learning sequence diagram illustrating system interaction and overload management

The learner begins by logging into the platform and completing a brief diagnostic task designed to assess initial knowledge and engagement characteristics. Based on this input, the system classifies the learner into a predefined cluster and initializes cognitive load thresholds that will guide subsequent adaptivity. As the learner engages with content, the system continuously collects real-time interaction data such as navigation patterns, time-on-task, and task success rates. If signs of cognitive overload are detected—based on deviation from expected thresholds—the system dynamically responds by either switching to lower-load materials or providing pedagogical scaffolding (Vygotsky, 1978), such as hints or simplified visual explanations. All recommendations and system decisions are logged and made accessible to instructors through a dedicated dashboard, enabling them to visualize learner states and intervene if needed.

3.4 Evaluation Method

To assess the system, the model was piloted in two ELSEI modules with a cohort of 47 master's students over a six-week period. The evaluation focused on several key indicators, including learner engagement, measured through session duration and page views; academic performance, assessed via quiz and project scores; and perceived usefulness, gathered through a post-module survey. Initial results—further detailed in the Results section—revealed significant improvements in both engagement and learners' perception of personalization. Additionally, the system contributed to a noticeable reduction in cognitive overload events, particularly during the more challenging phases of the modules.

4. RESULTS

The implementation of the adaptive cognitive load–aware recommendation system within the ELSEI program yielded promising results. Data were collected over six weeks across two graduate-level modules, involving 47 enrolled students. The analysis focused on three dimensions: engagement metrics, academic performance, and perceived system effectiveness.

From a behavioral perspective, students exhibited an average increase of 21% in session duration and a 19% rise in page views compared to baseline modules without adaptivity. This suggests that learners were more actively involved with the learning platform when content was aligned with their cognitive profiles.

In terms of performance, participants demonstrated an average improvement of 13% in quiz scores and a noticeable enhancement in project outcomes, as assessed by rubric-based instructor evaluations. Importantly, this improvement was more pronounced among learners initially identified in higher cognitive load clusters, indicating the model's compensatory effect.

Survey feedback collected at the end of each module highlighted the positive reception of adaptive mechanisms. Approximately 87% of students reported that recommended resources better matched their learning needs, and 76% indicated they felt less overwhelmed during complex tasks. Furthermore, overload detection events dropped by 42% after system intervention, affirming the responsiveness and efficacy of the cognitive load classification engine.

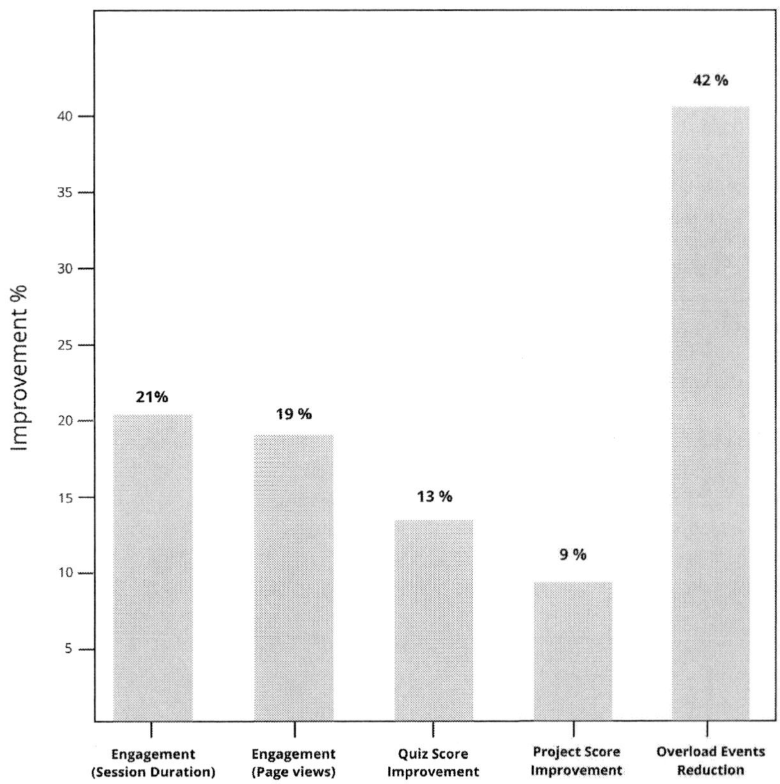

Figure 2. Impact of Adaptive System on Learner Outcomes in ELSEI Pilot

These preliminary findings support the viability of integrating cognitive load–sensitive AI systems in higher education contexts. The combination of clustering, real-time monitoring, and adaptive resource delivery appears to significantly enhance both learner experience and educational outcomes. Figure 2 illustrates the improvements observed across engagement, performance, and cognitive load indicators following system deployment.

5. DISCUSSION

The findings from this pilot suggest that bringing together cognitive load theory and artificial intelligence can make personalized learning more effective and genuinely learner-centered in higher education. Within the ELSEI Master's Program, this integration allowed us to move beyond a traditional, one-size-fits-all instructional design toward something more adaptive and attuned to how learners actually think and work.

One of the clearest signals came from the noticeable rise in learner engagement. When content was adjusted to match cognitive states more closely, students seemed not only to stay longer on the platform but also to interact more meaningfully with it. This reinforces what other researchers have pointed out: when learners feel mentally supported—neither overwhelmed or under challenged—they tend to remain more motivated and focused (D'Mello & Graesser, 2012).

Perhaps more importantly, the system appeared to help reduce moments of cognitive overload, which can be particularly discouraging in graduate-level contexts. ELSEI students often juggle complex theoretical material, hands-on projects, and professional responsibilities. In such a setting, an adaptive system that can "sense" when things are becoming too difficult and respond accordingly is more than just helpful—it's essential. This aligns with emerging perspectives on the ethical use of AI in education: intelligent systems should not merely deliver content efficiently but also support learners' cognitive and emotional well-being (Holmes et al., 2021).

Performance gains among students with higher initial cognitive load were another noteworthy outcome. The model seemed to act as a buffer, offering timely scaffolds and simplifying tasks when needed. Rather than deepening the gap between more and less advanced learners, it provided a kind of just-in-time support that leveled the playing field. In that sense, the system didn't just personalize—it helped make learning more equitable (Vygotsky, 1978).

From the results, the theoretical background and the previous research, it is clear that systems can react, predict and support the cognitive state of students optimizes the effectiveness of their learning pace, as well as their experience. The personalization of AI facilitates meaningful interactions, improve students' engagement and learning outcomes (Kabudi, Pappas & Olsen, 2022).

That said, we remain cautious about overgeneralizing these results. The study involved a relatively small group of 47 students, and the modules were limited to the ELSEI program. There's still a lot to learn about how this model might perform across different fields or in larger, more varied cohorts. Also, while our cognitive load detection relied on learner interactions and self-reported effort, it could be strengthened with more diverse data sources—such as eye-tracking, heart rate variability, or other physiological signals. Finally, one area we'd like to improve is the role of instructors. Right now, the dashboard offers helpful visualizations, but the teacher's role remains reactive. Future iterations could experiment with teacher-AI collaboration, where instructors are prompted to intervene proactively, not just observe.

In sum, these findings reinforce a key idea: if we want educational technologies to be truly adaptive, they must be cognitively informed. Designing for the mind—rather than around it—should be a priority. AI systems that understand how people think, and adjust accordingly, can turn personalization from a technical novelty into a meaningful pedagogical strategy.

6. CONCLUSION

In reflecting on this pilot experience, we found that integrating AI-driven personalization with cognitive load principles can make a real difference in how students engage with complex material. The ELSEI Master's Program offered us a unique opportunity to test this approach in an authentic academic setting, where learners come with diverse profiles and expectations.

By monitoring learners' cognitive states and adjusting content delivery accordingly, the system didn't just optimize performance metrics—it helped create a more humane learning environment. Many students reported feeling more supported, especially during high-demand moments in the course. This feedback, coupled with the performance data, suggests that adaptivity grounded in cognitive awareness is not just a technical add-on but a pedagogical shift.

One insight that emerged strongly from our observations is that personalization is most effective when it respects the learner's pace and mental bandwidth. In this sense, we believe artificial intelligence should be designed with a kind of cognitive empathy recognizing that learning is as much about timing and trust as it is about content delivery.

Looking ahead, we intend to expand the model to other modules and explore new data sources, such as physiological sensing or affective feedback, to enrich our understanding of cognitive states. We also see value in strengthening the role of teachers within the loop, enabling them to collaborate more actively with AI systems rather than observing passively from a dashboard.

Our goal is to help shape a new generation of educational technologies that understand learners not only as data points, but as whole individuals with unique rhythms, needs, and potential.

REFERENCES

Aammou, S., Tagdimi, Z., & Jdidou, Y. (2024). Leveraging Artificial Intelligence in the ELSEI Master's Program: Enhancing Educational Outcomes and Student Experience. In *Proceedings of EDULEARN24 16th International Conference on Education and New Learning Technologies* (pp. 2907-2912), Palma, Spain.

Atkinson, R. C., & Shiffrin, R. M. (1968). Human memory: A proposed system and its control processes. In K. Spence & J. Spence (Eds.), *The psychology of learning and motivation* (Vol. 2, pp. 89–195). Academic Press.

Baddeley, A. (2000). The episodic buffer: A new component of working memory? *Trends in Cognitive Sciences*, 4(11), 417–423. https://doi.org/10.1016/S1364-6613(00)01538-2

D'Mello, S., & Graesser, A. (2012). Dynamics of affective states during complex learning. *Learning and Instruction, 22*(2), 145–157. https://doi.org/10.1016/j.learninstruc.2011.10.001

Holmes, W., Bialik, M., & Fadel, C. (2021). *Artificial Intelligence in Education: Promises and Implications for Teaching and Learning* (2nd ed.). Center for Curriculum Redesign.

Kabudi, T., Pappas, I. O., & Olsen, D. H. (2022). Deriving design principles for AI-adaptive learning systems: Findings from interviews with experts. In S. Papagiannidis, E. Alamanos, S. Gupta, Y. K. Dwivedi, M. Mäntymäki & I. O. Pappas (Eds.), *The role of digital technologies in shaping the post-pandemic world* (pp. 82-94). Springer International Publishing. https://doi.org/10.1007/978-3-031-15342-6_7

Long, P., & Siemens, G. (2011). Penetrating the fog: Analytics in learning and education. *EDUCAUSE Review* (Online).

Ling, H., & Chiang, H. (2022). Learning performance in adaptive learning systems: A case study of web programming learning recommendations. *Frontiers in Psychology, 13*, 770637. https://doi.org/10.3389/fpsyg.2022.770637

Miller, G. A. (1956). The magical number seven, plus or minus two: Some limits on our capacity for processing information. *Psychological Review*, *63*(2), 81–97. https://doi.org/10.1037/h0043158

Paas, F., & Sweller, J. (2012). An evolutionary upgrade of cognitive load theory: Using the human motor system and collaboration to support the learning of complex cognitive tasks. *Educational Psychology Review*, 24(1), 27–45. https://doi.org/10.1007/s10648-011-9179-2

Pane, J. F., Steiner, E. D., Baird, M. D., & Hamilton, L. S. (2015). *Continued progress: Promising evidence on personalized learning: Executive summary*. RAND Corporation. https://doi.org/10.7249/j.ctt19w724m

Romero, C., & Ventura, S. (2013). Data mining in education. *Wiley Interdisciplinary Reviews: Data Mining and Knowledge Discovery*, 3(1), 12–27.

Siemens, G., & Long, P. (2011). Penetrating the fog: Analytics in learning and education, *EDUCAUSE Review*, 46(5), 30–40.

Sounoglou, M. (2022) Distance learning and Short Learning Program for continuous professional development: a case study of Hellenic Open University. In Ubachs, G., Meuleman, S., & Antonaci, A. (Eds), *Digital Reset: European Universities Transforming for a Changing World* (pp. 399-407). Proceedings of the Innovating Higher Education Conference 2022, EADTU, I-HE2022. Athens War Museum, Athens-Greece, October 19-21, 2022. Genève: Zenodo.

Sweller, J. (1988). Cognitive load during problem solving: Effects on learning. *Cognitive Science*, 12(2), 257–285. https://doi.org/10.1207/s15516709cog1202_4

Sweller, J., Ayres, P., & Kalyuga, S. (2011). *Cognitive load theory* (Vol. 1). Springer.

Sweller, J. (2020). Cognitive load theory and educational technology. *Educational technology research and development, 68*(1), 1-16.

Sweller, J. (2023). Discussion of the special issue on cognitive load theory. *British Journal of Educational Psychology, 93*(S2), 402-410. https://doi.org/10.1111/bjep.12606

Vygotsky, L. S. (1978). *Mind in Society: the Development of Higher Psychological Processes*. Harvard University Press.

USE OF CHUNKING STRATEGY DURING COLLABORATIVE DEBUGGING

Afaf A. Baabdullah[1] and ChanMin Kim[2]
[1]*King Saud University, Saudi Arabia*
[2]*The Pennsylvania State University, USA*

ABSTRACT

Understanding of code is critical for debugging computer programs. Chunking, breaking code into smaller parts, has been proven to be an effective strategy for analyzing code at various levels of abstraction. Novice debuggers struggle to comprehend code and recognize its underlying structure and components. They often debug code in an arbitrary and unfocused manner, potentially resulting in frustration. To facilitate the process of learning to debug, we developed a supportive tool called *Debug Space* designed to enhance the collaborative debugging process of novices. Informed by computing literature and theoretical frameworks, this tool incorporates visual cognitive resources, aiding novices in visualizing the structure and parts of code. We analyzed the conversations and actions of a pair of novices during their interactions with the tool to explore how they identified and corrected errors using visual cognitive resources and debugging strategies. The qualitative case analysis revealed that the pair underwent the subprocesses of examining debugging situations, describing discrepancies between the actual and desired code states, locating bugs, and proposing informed solutions to address the identified bugs. The results also suggest that the use of visual cognitive resources helped novices understand the configuration of the code, particularly in terms of *what* the code does and *how* it operates. This understanding enabled the pair to consider bugs and assess whether the proposed solutions can be effective. Educational implications are discussed, and future research directions are outlined in the paper.

KEYWORDS

Pair Debugging, Novice Programming Learners, Chunking Strategy, Computer-Supported Collaborative Learning (CSCL)

1. INTRODUCTION

Novice debuggers often have difficulty with a systematic review of code and understanding the structure of the code and its related parts. Struggles to construct mental representations of code make debugging difficult and frustrating (Michaeli & Romeike, 2019b) and impede the process of locating and fixing bugs (Kim et al., 2018). Many researchers have employed pair programming and debugging as potential solutions to address these challenges (Chintakovid et al., 2006; Kim et al., 2024). Despite the critical role of pair debugging in the learning process, the existing literature lacks specific guidelines on planning and structuring collaborative efforts for pairs, particularly for novice learners who lack sufficient experience (Xu & Correia, 2024). The current study engaged novice programming learners in collaborative debugging using our computer-supported collaborative learning (CSCL) tool called *Debug Space*. The tool offers guidance on debugging task structure to help novice learners transition between individual and collaborative areas, enhancing the effectiveness of both collaboration and learning. Furthermore, debugging strategies integrated in the tool, including chunking strategy, were to scaffold novice learners to study the buggy code structure, analyze its subparts in relation to each other, and make sense of the code defects. The following research questions were addressed:

1. How do pairs construct their understanding of the overall structure of block-based code?
2. How do pairs reason about bugs in code?

2. LITERATURE REVIEW

2.1 Code Understanding and Chunking Strategy

Programming and debugging present significant challenges for novices (Whalley et al., 2023). Research has explored various debugging subprocesses and their effects on debugging quality (Chintakovid et al., 2006; Park & Cheon, 2025; Prather et al., 2018). Effective debugging enhances both productivity and programming quality (Li et al., 2019). Distinctions in debugging subprocesses can differentiate more effective debugging behaviors, which lead to greater productivity, from less effective ones that hinder progress. Reviewing code in chunks is a helpful process that aids programmers in understanding the debugging situation better.

Reviewing programmed code involves examining the code to determine *what* the code does and *how* it works. This process involves understanding both the overall organization and the individual code chunks (Fitzgerald et al., 2008). By investing time in grasping the code's structure before making changes, programmers can construct an accurate conceptual model (Robillard et al., 2004). Experts understand programmed code as a system, leading to various levels of conceptual knowledge, which includes: (a) the system's main structure, (b) the components and their functions, and (c) how these components interact to produce observed results (Jonassen & Hung, 2006). In essence, expert programmers view code as a cohesive entity.

In contrast, novices typically possess surface-level knowledge of coding (Gao & Hew, 2023), often leading to misconceptions and a fragmented understanding (Bonar & Soloway, 1985). They tend to see code as isolated blocks rather than part of a cohesive structure (Corritore & Wiedenbeck, 1991). For instance, they may understand the operation of a single block, like "counter = counter + 2," but struggle to grasp how multiple blocks work together in a program. This lack of comprehension can cause confusion (Vessey, 1985), making it difficult for them to identify and fix bugs (Kim et al., 2018) and impairing their ability to form effective mental models of the program (Yoon & Garcia, 1998). As a result, novices may make random changes in hopes of fixing errors (Gao & Hew, 2023; Vessey, 1985). While trial-and-error might occasionally work, it generally does not lead to skill development and can be inefficient (Chintakovid et al., 2006). Debugging can also be a source of frustration (Michaeli & Romeike, 2019b). To improve their debugging skills, novice programmers need support in developing conceptual models of code, including both levels of abstraction, chunk and structural, but often require explicit instruction in effective strategies such as chunking (Gao & Hew, 2023). Due to time constraints, instructors often provide direct solutions or let students work on error processing independently instead of teaching debugging techniques (Michaeli & Romeike, 2019b). Research on effective debugging teaching methods is limited (Michaeli & Romeike, 2019a). While pair programming and debugging have been investigated to alleviate complexities, findings show mixed results in students' behaviors and perceptions (Sun et al., 2021), often due to a lack of guidance in collaborative task management (Xu & Correia, 2024).

2.2 Structuring Collaborative Debugging

Collaboration in small groups goes beyond individual contributions; it creates a collective understanding of the task (Barron, 2003). This process is interdependent and influenced by all group members (King, 1999). When individuals express their ideas, the cognitive process shifts from individual to group cognition (Borge et al., 2018). The group then combines the shared information into mutual knowledge, discussing to clarify collective understanding. This leads to their shared meaning development (Borge et al., 2018).

The success of collaborative learning depends on how well individuals coordinate the group learning process flow to create new meaning. Group members can influence the cognitive flow of the group process and strategically adjust their collaborative learning as needed to reach shared goals (Järvelä et al., 2019). This interaction with the surrounding social context—comprising other learners and available materials—is at the heart of effective collaboration. It necessitates reciprocal interactions and shared responsibilities among group members, both of which significantly shape the learning process (Iiskala et al., 2011). Therefore, equal and mutual participation is required (Borge et al., 2018), where all members engage in reciprocal interactions to explore each other's ideas (Goos et al., 2002). Task requirements, cognitive challenges, and desired outcomes provide vital information that guides individuals as the collaborative learning process unfolds (Järvelä et al., 2016).

Nonetheless, collaborative processes often encounter challenges that can hinder group learning and performance (Barron, 2003). Common issues include difficulty integrating ideas, failing to achieve a shared understanding, hastily accepting the first solution instead of exploring alternatives, and lacking critical analysis with supporting evidence (Borge et al., 2018). In response, Borge et al. (2018) developed a six-phase framework to enhance the quality of collaboration. The first two phases focus on individual study and reflection to clarify personal understanding. Phase three involves group discussions to foster shared understanding of complex concepts and negotiation for new insights. Phase four emphasizes individual reflection on group dynamics to identify problems, while phase five compares group strengths and weaknesses. Finally, phase six focuses on planning strategies to address issues in future discussions.

Supporting effective collaborative debugging is crucial for beginners, yet there is a lack of empirical studies in the literature. Xu and Correia's (2024) systematic literature review of pair debugging identified key factors affecting team effectiveness. The review found that individual characteristics, such as prior programming experience, skill level, gender, perceived ability, time management skills, personality traits, confidence, self-esteem, and pair compatibility, significantly influenced the success of pair programming. However, none of the studies explored the collaboration processes and their effects on debugging and learning. There is a need for more guidance on effective collaboration in pair debugging, highlighting the importance of the present study.

3. THEORETICAL FRAMEWORK

Gilmore's (1991) debugging theory posits that debuggers need to construct and reconstruct conceptual models of a debugging situation, including both the actual and desired states of code. Debuggers can construct these models in terms of *what* code does and *how* it works. According to Gilmore's theory, code comprehension can be achieved by focusing on smaller parts of the whole: forming mental representations of some parts of the code as *what* knowledge, and other parts as *how* knowledge. Debuggers need to compare their conceptual models of *what* or *how* the actual code works with their models of *what* or *how* the desired code should work. *What* knowledge can be extracted by observing the code behavior of individual programming blocks, whereas *how* knowledge requires understanding sets of blocks in the code, and *how* they interact.

4. METHODS

4.1 Participants and Context

Thirty-two undergraduate students enrolled in a general education course offered at a large public university in the northeastern United States participated in the study. The participants were paired and assigned the task of debugging Scratch code while interacting with *Debug Space* (Session 1; 12 pairs). Some of these pairs also participated in another debugging session (Session 2; 6 pairs). Debugging sessions were conducted via Zoom.

4.2 Computer-Supported Collaborative Learning (CSCL) Tool

Our computer-supported collaborative learning (CSCL) tool, *Debug Space,* contains three main phases: "Let's Debug," "Let's See How We Did," and "Let's Plan." Debugging theories (Gilmore, 1991; Gould, 1975) and a group regulation framework (Borge et al., 2018) were applied in the design of the three phases to support pairs as they collaboratively debugged code, used effective debugging strategies, reflected on their applied strategies, and planned for improvement. The "Let's Debug" phase, for example, includes cognitive resources (e.g., graphical representations of buggy code and a desired output video) to support pairs in constructing an understanding of the actual and desired states of the code at different levels of abstraction (i.e., code structure level and chunk level). These resources are likewise intended to support pairs in identifying *what* and/or *how* knowledge and applying effective strategies, such as chunking (see Figure 1), to debug the code. *Debug Space* is also designed to provide students with opportunities to individually study the code, develop related knowledge, and engage with a sense-making activity through reflection prompts. Then, *Debug Space* prompts pairs to exchange their reactions to reflection questions with each other and to develop a shared meaning of the code structure and its chunks as well as new knowledge about these abstraction levels. The scope of the present study is limited to analyzing data only from the "Let's Debug" phase to address the research questions.

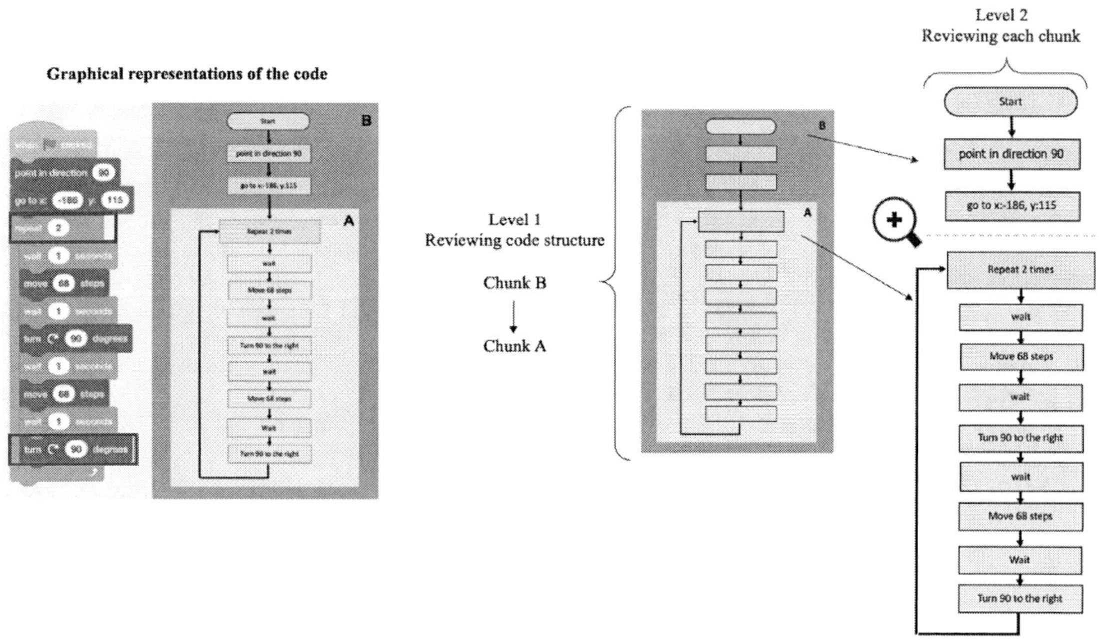

Figure 1. Graphical representations of the code in debugging session 1, illustrating two different levels: code structure level and chunk level

4.3 Debugging Task

The debugging task in Session 1 was designed to allow a sprite in Scratch to descend four steps, tracing a stair-like path. However, due to two bugs within Chunk A (see Figure 1), the sprite moved in a circular motion around the first step and then stopped. One bug in the rotation block could be fixed by replacing the second "turn to the right" block with "turn 90 degrees to the left," allowing the sprite to trace the first two steps correctly. To fix the second bug, it was necessary to change the number of repetitions from 2 to 4 to make the sprite repeat the code for the remaining steps.

4.4 Data Analysis

To thoroughly investigate how pairs tackled debugging tasks in *Debug Space*, we developed an analytical system with micro and macro methods. We transcribed Zoom recordings of debugging sessions and interviews, then identified collaborative debugging episodes (i.e., pairs' transitions through the different debugging sub-processes). We coded new ideas that emerged during conversations and actions of pairs and identified overarching ideas across their conversational turns (Namey et al., 2008). We also utilized Gilmore's (1991) debugging theory as an overriding lens to analyze how pairs reviewed the code and what types of knowledge they developed (i.e., *what* or *how* knowledge). After defining the debugging episodes, we applied a modified version of the coding scheme in Kim et al (2018) to analyze the debugging process and interview responses.

We held a series of collaborative coding sessions to review and modify coding constructs, discussed coding decisions, and resolved any disagreements. One of the authors coded debugging episodes, and then collaborative coding was done to review the coded data from 32% of the conversational turns. The disagreements were resolved during the collaborative coding sessions. The current study presents our analysis of one pair's data. We chose this pair because they were similar to other pairs in terms of their different states of code understanding, and they clearly articulated their complete understanding of the code at the different levels.

5. FINDINGS AND DISCUSSION

The pair, Savannah and Iris (pseudonyms), developed a complete understanding of the code at two different levels of abstraction (Figure 1; Gilmore, 1991). They identified the main code chunks (A and B), understood their functions and mechanisms, and analyzed *how* the chunks interacted. Initially, they reviewed the code and the cognitive resources individually. Then they spent approximately 11 minutes collaborating to discuss and clarify their understanding before making any changes. At the start of their collaborative work, they used the graphical representations on Debug Space (Figure 1) along with their knowledge of the task requirements—specifically, the desired output of the code—to actively examine the code. This active review helped them grasp the structure of the code, including the purposes of the main chunks and their interactions (as shown in Table 1, Turn 2). Savannah explained that the code was designed to position the sprite at the beginning of a stair-like path and then move it down four steps (in their dialog, they referred to Chunk A as the yellow area and Chunk B as the gray area).

After Savannah articulated her understanding, the pair used debugging strategies that involved resources such as graphical representations and the desired output video. They aimed to understand the chunk configuration of the code by mapping requirements against the code and employing forward reasoning (i.e., reviewing the code in order) and tracing (i.e., mentally simulating code execution) at the chunk level. They examined Chunk B to see how individual blocks worked together, which helped them develop a shared understanding of *what* and *how* the chunk worked (see Turns 3 and 4). As they turned their attention to Chunk A to further explore *how* the individual blocks interacted and caused the sprite's unexpected circular movement, disagreements arose (see Turns 38 and 45). Savannah described the sprite's repeated movement within Chunk A as taking different parts of a step, while Iris saw it as a whole step. These conflicting ideas led the pair to engage in collective actions. They actively examined the chunks, constructed a deeper understanding of the code, and employed effective debugging strategies to validate their ideas, resolve disagreements, and comprehend *how* the code functioned. An example of their collective actions is when Iris mapped the graphical representations of the buggy code against the desired movement in the video and traced the stair-like path. Savannah then traced the code, leading the pair to locate both bugs and accurately explain *how* Chunk A worked (see Turns 50 through 54). Such approaches to resolving cognitive conflict are critical for collaborators to create a shared conceptual understanding (Vauras et al., 2021).

Productive collaboration is a social process focused on constructing shared meaning through collaborative sense-making: teammates share their understanding of new information or artifacts, synthesize their shared understanding, and develop the new shared meaning (Borge et al., 2018; Stahl, 2006). In this study, individuals who reviewed code beforehand contributed to effective communication during collaborative sense-making, compared to pairs who did not review individually. The pre-review process helped externalize individual thinking, facilitating a transition from individual to group cognition. The transactive opportunities between individual and collaborative learning are particularly valuable when team members are unable to independently retrieve related knowledge, enabling them to seek assistance from one another to achieve their collaborative objectives (Jurkowski et al., 2024; Noroozi et al., 2013). In programming, it is crucial to switch seamlessly between individual and team tasks while managing time effectively (Cheng et al., 2003). The interaction strategies employed by the pair, such as requesting ideas (e.g., Turn 1), seeking clarification (e.g., Turn 3), and providing or asking for feedback (e.g., Turn 45), were mediated through visual representations to understand the code's functionality and underlying mechanism at the different levels of abstraction. The shared visual representations, along with negotiation processes, contributed to the development of their collective new meaning-making. The pair actively built upon each other's ideas, leading them to fully comprehend the code. They uncovered *what* the different parts of the code were and *how* they interacted to cause the sprite's unexpected circular movement. Moreover, the pair explained why the bugs occurred and how to modify the code to produce the intended movement along the stair-like path (e.g., Turns 38 and 50 through 54). Understanding the underlying mechanism of the code and its components supported their reasoning and facilitated successful problem-solving (Hindriks, 2012) as the pair fixed both bugs and achieved their programming goals on their first attempt at editing the code.

Table 1. Example data demonstrating developed knowledge at different levels of abstraction

Turns	Comprehension level	Debugging process and the type of developed knowledge
1 Iris: So, when you are looking at this [the code visual representations], what do you think is in the yellow area? **2 Savannah:** There's the initial start of the gray and then there's the yellow part which is like the actual movement from like point A to point B with like the 90 degree turns at every corner but like you gotta start it off initially and you know what I mean or else you're not gonna be able to end it. **3 Iris:** Perfect. So, you also said that then the gray area is umm, I like said it was like the main idea. But what were the words that you used?	Code structure level: Identified main structure and *how* Chunks A and B interacted	Examination the code first Active examination of the code *How* knowledge
4 Savannah: I said, start like it points in one direction first and then goes to that point.	Chunk level: Chunk B	Active examination of the code *What* and *how* knowledge
38 Savannah: So, like in the code itself. It has it turn to the right, but it can't turn to the right, it has to be able to turn left at some point to, like, I'm trying to think. So, you can wait, move, wait, turn, wait, move, wait, turn. It needs to say turn 90 to the left at the very bottom of the code like this would result in the air balloon loon being upside down.	Chunk level: Chunk A	Tracing strategy Forward reasoning Deducing a causal model *What* and *how* knowledge How to fix bugs
45 Iris: No, I see that. But remember how repeats twice? So, it means it's already doing two steps. Like, one, two, and then stops and then one two, but we needed to turn left up here, do you see what I'm saying?	Chunk level: Chunk A	Active examination of the code Mapping between the code and the desired state *What* knowledge
50 Savannah: Because that's only repeat. Because you wait at the beginning and then you're going to move 68 so you're just taking care of that first like little piece and then you're going to wait again before you turn and then you're at the very corner on the outer corner and then you're waiting and then you move again to the bottom where then you turn again. So, you only take care of one like one step. **51 Iris:** Aha.	Chunk level: Chunk A	Tracing strategy Deducing a causal model *What* and *how* knowledge *Why* knowledge
52 Savannah: So, if it's only repeating twice. It's only taking care of two them. **53 Iris:** Right. **54 Savannah:** Set of repeat four times and the bottom piece has to be turned 90 it to the left.	Chunk level: Chunk A	Active examination of the code How to fix bugs

The findings indicate that cognitive resources, such as chunking strategies, were essential for the pair's conceptual understanding of the code at various levels as well as for the development of both types of knowledge: *what* and *how*. These resources enabled them to examine and comprehend the code prior to making changes in the code. In her interview, Iris described the role of cognitive resources in her team's debugging process: "Having three different aspects [the desired output video, graphical representations, and buggy code] to look at was very helpful because it opens the opportunity for you to see the problem more clearly." Novice debuggers often require such support, as they tend to struggle with debugging (Kim et al., 2018; Şener & Umutlu, 2024) and may jump to editing code without a full understanding of the code (Prather et al., 2018). Even when they read the code first, they often perceive the code as disconnected fragments (Dong, 2022) with limited understanding of its overall structure and functionality (Sillito et al., 2008). Contextual features can help novices focus on relevant processes and engage in collaboration (Bedwell et al., 2012). For instance, cognitive resources can help programmers navigate and manage code complexity (Cabo, 2018) while effective teamwork can extend these capabilities, enabling more profound exploration of the code.

6. CONTRIBUTION AND IMPLICATIONS

The present study highlights key implementation considerations for integrating collaboration into debugging, thereby contributing to the literature by bridging a gap in understanding pair debugging and offering guidance on managing its inherent complexity. The cognitive process involved in understanding code chunks, along with the transition between individual and collaborative approaches, is essential for effective pair debugging. Instructors can support novices by engaging them in explanations of their code. These tasks guide students in expressing different types of knowledge and developing meaningful interpretations of individual commands and how they relate within a chunk. This foundational knowledge at the chunk level is vital, as it sets the stage for a more advanced level of comprehension (i.e., code structure level). Instructors can then proceed to collaborative exercises that explore relationships among different chunks, analyzing how the entire code operates as a cohesive system that influences the program's outputs. This is because collaboration in small groups thrives when individuals actively co-construct their learning processes through positive interdependence, individual and group accountability, and group processing, among other factors (Winne et al., 2010). Gilmore's theory categorizes constructed knowledge into only two types: *what* and *how*. The findings of the present study suggest the emergence of a third type: *why* knowledge. Further research is needed to further investigate this type of knowledge and the context in which participants are able to construct it. Further research is also needed on the role of emotions in pair debugging. Literature shows that the emotional component is intertwined with learning (Tan et al., 2021). Emotions can act as an initial gateway, affecting attention, stimulating thinking and complex processes, shaping interpretation, and influencing what is remembered and learned (Borge et al., 2018).

REFERENCES

Barron, B. (2003). When smart groups fail. *The Journal of the Learning Sciences*, *12*(3), 307–359.

Bedwell, W. L., Wildman, J. L., DiazGranados, D., Salazar, M., Kramer, W. S., & Salas, E. (2012). Collaboration at work: An integrative multilevel conceptualization. *Human Resource Management Review, 22*(2), 128–145.

Bonar, J., & Soloway, E. (1985). Preprogramming knowledge : A major source of misconceptions in novice programmers. *Human – Computer Interaction*, *1*, 133–161. https://doi.org/10.1207/s15327051hci0102

Borge, M., Ong, Y. S., & Rosé, C. P. (2018). Learning to monitor and regulate collective thinking processes. *International Journal of Computer-Supported Collaborative Learning*, (13), 61–92. https://doi.org/10.1007/s11412-018-9270-5

Cabo, C. (2018). Effectiveness of flowcharting as a scaffolding tool to learn python. *In 2018 IEEE Frontiers in Education Conference (FIE)*, 1–7. https://doi.org/10.1109/FIE.2018.8658891

Cheng, L. T., de Souza, C. R., Hupfer, S., Patterson, J., & Ross, S. (2003). Building Collaboration into IDEs: Edit> Compile> Run> Debug> Collaborate. *Queue*, *1*(9), 40–50.

Chintakovid, T., Wiedenbeck, S., Burnett, M., & Grigoreanu, V. (2006). Pair collaboration in end-user debugging. In *Proceedings - IEEE Symposium on Visual Languages and Human-Centric Computing, VL/HCC 2006* (pp. 3–10). IEEE. https://doi.org/10.1109/VLHCC.2006.36

Corritore, C. L., & Wiedenbeck, S. (1991). What do novices learn during Program comprehension? *International Journal of Human-Computer Interaction*, *3*(2), 199–222. https://doi.org/10.1080/10447319109526004

Dong, F. (2022). Debug education: Students debug ability assessment. *International Journal of New Developments in Education*, *4*(17), 5–12. https://doi.org/10.25236/ijnde.2022.041702

Fitzgerald, S., Lewandowski, G., McCauley, R., Murphy, L., Simon, B., Thomas, L., & Zander, C. (2008). Debugging: Finding, fixing and flailing, a multi-institutional study of novice debuggers. *Computer Science Education*, *18*(2), 93–116. https://doi.org/10.1080/08993400802114508

Gao, X., & Hew, K. F. (2023). A flipped systematic debugging approach to enhance elementary students' program debugging performance and optimize cognitive load. *Journal of Educational Computing Research*, *61*(5), 1064–1095.

Gilmore, D. J. (1991). Models of debugging. *Acta Psychologica*, *78*(1–3), 151–172. https://doi.org/10.1016/0001-6918(91)90009-O

Goos, M., Galbraith, P., & Renshaw, P. (2002). Socially mediated metacognition: Creating collaborative zones of proximal development in small group problem solving. *Educational Studies in Mathematics*, *49*(2), 193–223. https://doi.org/10.1023/A:1016209010120

Gould, J. D. (1975). Some psychological evidence on how people debug computer programs. *International Journal of Man-Machine Studies*, *7*(2), 151–182. https://doi.org/10.1016/S0020-7373(75)80005-8

Iiskala, T., Vauras, M., Lehtinen, E., & Salonen, P. (2011). Socially shared metacognition of dyads of pupils in collaborative mathematical problem-solving processes. *Learning and Instruction*, *21*(3), 379–393. https://doi.org/10.1016/j.learninstruc.2010.05.002

Järvelä, S., Järvenoja, H., & Malmberg, J. (2019). Capturing the dynamic and cyclical nature of regulation: Methodological Progress in understanding socially shared regulation in learning. *International Journal of Computer-Supported Collaborative Learning*, *14*(4), 425–441. https://doi.org/10.1007/s11412-019-09313-2

Järvelä, S., Malmberg, J., & Koivuniemi, M. (2016). Recognizing socially shared regulation by using the temporal sequences of online chat and logs in CSCL. *Learning and Instruction*, *42*, 1–11. https://doi.org/10.1016/j.learninstruc.2015.10.006

Jeffries, R. (1982). A comparison of the debugging behavior of expert and novice programmers. In *AERA Annual Meeting*. New York.

Jonassen, D. H., & Hung, W. (2006). Learning to troubleshoot: A new theory-based design architecture. *Educational Psychology Review*, *18*(1), 77–114. https://doi.org/10.1007/s10648-006-9001-8

Jurkowski, S., Mundelsee, L., & Hänze, M. (2024). Strengthening collaborative learning in secondary school: Development and evaluation of a lesson-integrated training approach for transactive communication. *Learning and Instruction*, *92*(101934), 1–9. https://doi.org/10.1016/j.learninstruc.2024.101934

Kim, C., Belland, B. R., Vasconcelos, L., & Hill, R. B. (2024). Playful programming, social resilience, and persistent actions as drivers of preservice early childhood teachers' engagement in computer science. *SAGE Open*, *14*(4). https://doi.org/10.1177/21582440241284488

Kim, ChanMin, Yuan, J., Vasconcelos, L., Shin, M., & Hill, R. B. (2018). Debugging during block-based programming. *Instructional Science*, *46*(5), 767–787. https://doi.org/10.1007/s11251-018-9453-5

King, A. (1999). Discourse patterns for mediating peer learning. In A. M. O'Donnell & A. King (Eds.), *Cognitive perspectives on peer learning* (pp. 87–115). Mahwah, NJ: Lawrence Erlbaum.

Li, C., Chan, E., Denny, P., Luxton-Reilly, A., & Tempero, E. (2019). Towards a framework for teaching debugging. In *Proceedings of the Twenty-First Australasian Computing Education Conference on - ACE'19* (pp. 79–86). Sydney, Australia: ACM. https://doi.org/10.1145/3286960.3286970

Michaeli, T., & Romeike, R. (2019a). Current status and perspectives of debugging in the k12 classroom: A qualitative study. In *IEEE Global Engineering Education Conference (EDUCON)* (pp. 1030–1038). Dubai, United Arab Emirates: IEEE. https://doi.org/10.1109/EDUCON.2019.8725282

Michaeli, T., & Romeike, R. (2019b). Improving debugging skills in the classroom - The effects of teaching a systematic debugging process. In *The 14th Workshop in Primary and Secondary Computing Education WiPSCE'19* (pp. 1–7). Glasgow, Scotland Uk: ACM. https://doi.org/10.1145/3361721.3361724

Namey, E., Guest, G., Thairu, L., & Johnson, L. (2008). Data reduction techniques for large qualitative data sets. In G. Guest & K. Macqueen (Eds.), *Handbook for team-based qualitative research* (pp. 137–161). Lanham, MD: AltaMira Press.

Noroozi, O., Teasley, S. D., Biemans, H. J., Weinberger, A., & Mulder, M. (2013). Facilitating learning in multidisciplinary groups with transactive CSCL scripts. *International Journal of Computer Supported Collaborative Learning*, *8*(2), 189–223.

Park, E., & Cheon, J. (2025). Exploring debugging challenges and strategies using structural topic model: A comparative analysis of high and low-performing students. *Journal of Educational Computing Research*, *62*(8), 2104–2126.

Prather, J., Pettit, R., McMurry, K., Peters, A., Homer, J., & Cohen, M. (2018). Metacognitive difficulties faced by novice programmers in automated assessment tools. In *ICER 2018 - Proceedings of the 2018 ACM Conference on International Computing Education Research* (pp. 41–50). Espoo, Finland.

Şener, B., & Umutlu, D. (2024). A qualitative case study:Pre-service teachers as novice programmer. *Journal of Computer and Education Research, 12*(23), 292–318.

Sillito, J., Murphy, G. C., & Volder, K. De. (2008). Asking and answering questions during a programming change task. *IEEE Transactions on Software Engineering, 34*(4), 434–451. https://doi.org/10.1109/TSE.2008.26.

Stahl, G. (2006). *Group cognition: Computer support for building collaborative knowledge*. Cambridge: MIT Press.

Sun, D., Ouyang, F., Li, Y., & Chen, H. (2021). Three contrasting pairs' collaborative programming processes in China's secondary education. *Journal of Educational Computing Research, 59*(4), 740–762.

Tan, J., Mao, J., Jiang, Y., & Gao, M. (2021). The influence of academic emotions on learning effects: A systematic review. *International Journal of Environmental Research and Public Health, 18*(18), 96–78. https://doi.org/10.3390/ijerph18189678

Vauras, M., Volet, S., & Iiskala, T. (2021). Socially-shared metacognitive regulation in collaborative science learning. In D. Moraitou & P. Metallidou (Eds.), *Trends and Prospects in Metacognition Research across the Life Span* (pp. 83–102). Cham, Switzerland: Springer. https://doi.org/10.1007/978-3-030-51673-4_5

Vessey, I. (1985). Expertise in debugging computer programs: A process analysis. *International Journal of Man-Machine Studies, 23*(5), 459–494. https://doi.org/10.1016/S0020-7373(85)80054-7

Whalley, J., Settle, A., & Luxton-Reilly, A. (2023). A think-aloud study of novice debugging. *ACM Transactions on Computing Education, 23*(2), 1–38.

Winne, P. H., Hadwin, A. F., & Gress, C. (2010). The learning kit project: Software tools for supporting and researching regulation of collaborative learning. *Computers in Human Behavior, 26*(5), 787–793. https://doi.org/10.1016/j.chb.2007.09.009

Xu, F., & Correia, A. P. (2024). Adopting distributed pair programming as an effective team learning activity: a systematic review. *Journal of Computing in Higher Education, 36*(2), 320–349.

Yoon, B. Do, & Garcia, O. N. (1998). Cognitive activities and support in debugging. In *Proceedings - 4th Annual Symposium on Human Interaction with Complex Systems, HICS 1998* (pp. 160–169). https://doi.org/10.1109/HUICS.1998.659974

CONVERSATIONS FOR LEARNING: DESIGNING PERSONIFIED HISTORICAL CHATBOTS TO ENHANCE CRITICAL THINKING IN K-12 STUDENTS

Karishma Shanghvi[1], Gurudeo Thakare[2], Alekh Velayudhan[1], Ramkumar Rajendran[3] and Lakshmi T. Ganesh[1]
[1]*Shikha Institute of Education, Mumbai, India*
[2]*Shikha Institute of Education, India*
[3]*Indian Institute of Technology, Bombay, India*

ABSTRACT

This study explores the design and implementation of personified historical chatbots for K–12 history education. Traditional history classrooms often emphasize rote memorization and factual recall, limiting opportunities for inquiry, reflection, and student engagement. To address these challenges, we developed persona-based chatbots modeled after historical figures such as Mahatma Gandhi, Albert Einstein, Benjamin Franklin, Leonardo da Vinci, and Chanakya. The system integrates large language models (LLMs) with retrieval-augmented generation (RAG) to provide contextually accurate and persona-aligned responses. Guided by dialogic pedagogy, the chatbots encourage students to ask questions, reflect critically, and engage in meaningful dialogue with historical personas. The findings from the case study of a student interaction with a personified chatbot revealed that the dialogic interactions progressed from factual inquiries to reflective, ethical, and hypothetical questions, highlighting the potential of persona-based chatbots to support curiosity, perspective-taking, and the development of critical thinking skills in history learning.

KEYWORDS

Personified Chatbots, History Education, K–12 Learning, AI in Education, GenAI

1. INTRODUCTION

History is a core subject in schools, enabling students to understand the individuals, communities, and societies that shaped the past. Learning history goes beyond memorizing facts and milestones; it involves analyzing events through a critical, historical lens while fostering future-oriented thinking. Research highlights that history education develops historical consciousness, civic responsibility, and transferable skills such as sourcing, contextualization, and corroboration (Wineburg, 2018; Nuttall, 2021; Cowgill & Waring, 2017).

Despite its significance, history teaching faces persistent challenges. Traditional approaches, including textbook-driven instruction, lecture-based delivery, and assessments focused on factual recall, often limit inquiry and reflection (Purmintasari et al., 2024; Callaway, 2020). These practices reduce opportunities for students to critically engage with historical perspectives, as history is frequently presented as fixed knowledge (Rivero et al., 2022). Teachers also encounter constraints such as large class sizes, standardized curricula, and assessment pressures, which restrict interactive and personalized learning (Rashadi & Ahmad, 2019). Consequently, history learning often becomes confined to memorization and pre-packaged narratives rather than inquiry and critical engagement.

To address these challenges, active learning strategies have been promoted to engage students in inquiry, collaboration, and problem-solving. Approaches such as game-based learning, role-play, and dialogic pedagogy have demonstrated improvements in participation, critical thinking, perspective-taking, and deeper historical understanding (Moseikina, 2022; Stack, 2023; Shargel & Katz, 2025; Prendergast, 2024). Among these, dialogic pedagogy emphasizes classroom dialogue to promote reasoning, reflection, and historical inquiry. In Taiwanese history classrooms, teachers combine monologue and dialogue through short- and long-term discussions to foster critical engagement and historical reasoning. Such approaches enhance student participation, support democratic values, and develop skills in argumentation and evaluation of truth (Alexander, 2018). However, active learning strategies, including dialogic pedagogy, face limitations.

Challenges include scaling, variability in teacher practices, classroom management, technological integration, and rigid curricula (Akçayır & Akçayır, 2018; Shulman, 2018). These limitations highlight the need for careful design, ongoing support, and balanced integration to ensure the effectiveness of active learning in history classrooms.

Recent research highlights that chatbots built on archival records can enable meaningful conversational interactions with historical figures. By drawing directly from primary and secondary sources, these systems allow learners to explore historical perspectives by asking questions in museum and educational contexts (Qian et al., 2022). The "Social bots of conviction" have been shown to promote historical empathy and perspective-taking by facilitating reflective group discussions about past events and their connections to contemporary contexts (Petousi et al., 2021). Similarly, ChatGPT simulations of historical figures, such as Simón Bolívar, have demonstrated improvements in students' critical thinking, historical understanding, and analytical abilities through dialogic interaction (Santamaria-Velasco et al., 2025). Although effective, some of these systems are limited by providing only archival text responses rather than generative dialogue, facing challenges related to information bias (Santamaria-Velasco et al., 2025). By enabling learners to interact with historical narratives in a dialogic and participatory way, personified chatbots can transform history learning from a passive exercise in memorization into an active process of critical reflection and perspective-taking.

Building on this potential, the present study explores the design of persona-based historical chatbots using Retrieval-Augmented Generation (RAG) and large language models to provide personalized, dialogic interactions while presenting information from well-integrated resources. The study also investigates how students engage with these systems and aims to contribute to the broader goal of creating effective, interactive history learning experiences that foster critical thinking

2. LITERATURE REVIEW

2.1 Teaching Learning Methodology in History

History classrooms have traditionally relied on lecture-based, textbook-centered instruction, where teachers transmit content and students are expected to recall factual knowledge. Relying on third-person narration, history is often presented as fixed and complete, limiting opportunities for students to question sources, perspectives, or interpretations (López-Fernández et al., 2023). Consequently, learners often engage passively, focusing on memorization rather than developing historical thinking skills such as contextualization, sourcing, corroboration, and perspective-taking (Rivero et al., 2022; Perrotta & Bohan, 2013). Assessment practices emphasizing factual recall further reinforce this passivity, discouraging critical analysis and independent interpretation (Purmintasari et al., 2024; Norakma Mohd Daud et al., 2015; Rashadi & Ahmad, 2019). Traditional teaching methods, constrained by standardized curricula, time limitations, and exam pressures, often fail to cultivate higher-order thinking, creativity, or meaningful engagement with historical content.

To address persistent challenges of passivity and rote learning in history classrooms, active learning strategies have been increasingly promoted as alternatives that foreground inquiry, collaboration, and reflective reasoning. Dialogic pedagogy, for instance, shifts classroom talk from recitation to purposeful questioning, argumentation, and collective meaning-making. By creating structured opportunities for students to justify claims, challenge peers, and build on ideas, dialogic teaching has been shown to improve both engagement and achievement (Alexander, 2018; Howe et al., 2019; Prendergast, 2024). In East Asian contexts, dialogic approaches further support historical thinking by encouraging students to interrogate sources and explore multiple perspectives while respecting cultural communication norms (Chang, Wegerif, & Hennessy, 2023; Geographical Association, 2025). Alongside classroom dialogue, game-based learning (GBL) has emerged as a powerful tool for making historical processes more tangible. Strategy games such as Napoleon: Total War allow learners to grapple with causation, contingency, and scale by placing them in the position of historical decision-makers (Stack, M., & Bunt, B., 2023). Students report high enjoyment and a sense of agency in such environments, though effective learning requires structured pre-briefs and reflective debriefs to connect gameplay with disciplinary reasoning (Hellerstedt A. 2025).

Research shows that role-play strategies complement digital games and can enhance empathy, perspective-taking, and moral reasoning when supported by evidence-based preparation and post-activity reflection (Khan. (2022).). Also, both in-person and virtual, have been shown to improve critical thinking, perspective-taking, and higher-level understanding of complex events (Shargel & Katz, 2025).

Collectively, the above-mentioned strategies shift history teaching from teacher-centered transmission toward student-centered inquiry. They enable learners to move beyond surface-level recall and instead engage in sourcing, corroboration, and contextualization while fostering critical thinking and analytical reasoning. Despite their benefits, active learning strategies face limitations, including high preparation demands, classroom management challenges, and technological requirements, large class sizes, rigid curricula, assessment pressures. Similarly, sustaining dialogic interaction demands skilled facilitation and cultural sensitivity.

Technology-enhanced solutions like chatbots can help address these challenges by providing personalized feedback, adaptive scaffolding, and support for self-regulated learning, thereby increasing engagement and motivation (Chang et al., 2023; Baskara, 2023). Additionally, LLM-based chatbots using Socratic questioning can foster critical thinking, reflection, and intellectual autonomy, while support introverted students and maintain privacy and accessibility (Hobert & Meyer von Wolff, 2019; Lucile, 2025).

2.2 Chatbots in Education

A chatbot is a computer program or system that engages users in human-like conversation through text or voice interfaces, often powered by artificial intelligence and natural language processing (Shawar & Atwell, 2007; Mauldin, 1994). Their primary value lies in providing real-time support, enhancing engagement, and offering personalized learning experiences (Clarizia et al., 2018). Kuhail et al. (2023) classify educational chatbots into four roles: teaching agents, peer agents, teachable agents, and motivational agents, each supporting learning in different ways.

Kuhail et al. (2022) emphasized that chatbots can act as intelligent assistants, offering real-time responses to students' queries and encouraging active engagement with the content. Similarly, Labadze, L. et. al. (2023), noted that chatbots are capable of adapting their interactions to align with individual learning preferences, thereby catering to diverse student needs. These features not only enhance access to information but also support the development of critical thinking and inquiry-driven learning.

In history education, some research studies have shown how chatbots can serve as powerful tools to enhance learning. Lee Bih Ni (2024) highlights that chatbots provide real-time, personalized responses and create immersive experiences that help students deepen their historical understanding and improve retention, particularly in K–12 contexts. Dimitra Petousi (2021) designed a "social" Bot of Conviction (BoC) for high school history education, aimed at sparking group reflection rather than just delivering information. The findings showed that the BoC effectively promoted historical empathy by encouraging perspective-taking, constructive dialogue, and linking past events to present issues.

However, many chatbots rely on scripted responses, leading to shallow dialogue and limited adaptability (Galitsky et al., 2019), while their lack of emotional intelligence reduces meaningful interaction (Wang et al., 2023). Recent developments in generative AI have begun to address these issues where language models can conduct more fluid, context-aware conversations, increasing personalization, engagement, and learner autonomy. Nevertheless, these systems introduce new challenges, including potential misinformation, ethical transparency, and student over-reliance. Hybrid models, which leverage Retrieval-Augmented Generation (RAG) to incorporate information from provided documents alongside LLM capabilities, are being explored to mitigate these risks.

3. SOLUTION APPROACH

3.1 Personified Chatbot

The proposed solution for the particular research problem is a personified educational chatbot developed by an Educational Research Lab in India, designed to embody prominent historical and polyglot personalities such as Mahatma Gandhi, Albert Einstein, Benjamin Franklin, Leonardo da Vinci, and Chanakya. The system is a web-based application that goes beyond conventional chatbots by offering an immersive dialogic experience rather than only factual responses. The chatbots are modeled as polyglot personas to represent their multifaceted knowledge and diverse expertise, allowing students to engage with each historical figure in a manner that reflects their unique worldview and interdisciplinary thinking.

3.2 Personification of Chatbot

A central feature of the design is the persona-based interaction model. In this system, a "persona" refers to a digital entity endowed with a recognizable identity, modeled after historical, fictional figures. For this prototype, the focus is on polyglot personas that symbolize linguistic diversity and intercultural competence. The persona layer defines the chatbot's tone of communication, response style, and cultural framing, ensuring that interactions feel authentic and engaging. This is implemented through prompting to the LLM, allowing the system to generate responses aligned with each persona's characteristics. By embedding personas into the chatbot, the design leverages the human tendency to anthropomorphize technology. From a human-computer interaction perspective, prior research demonstrates that systems exhibiting social presence and relatable characteristics foster stronger learner engagement, motivation, and trust (Smestad, 2019). A snapshot of the persona-based chatbot interface is presented in Figure 1 to illustrate the persona-based interaction model.

3.3 Design of the Personified Chatbot

The design architecture of the chatbot integrates Large Language Models (LLMs) with Retrieval-Augmented Generation (RAG) to balance conversational flexibility with factual accuracy (Fan, W. 2024; Yang, D., 2023). While the LLM ensures natural, context-sensitive dialogue, RAG grounds responses in curated, authoritative sources. This dual-layered design addresses the challenge of hallucinations in generative models, thereby enhancing trustworthiness and positioning the system as a reliable educational companion.

The architecture illustrated in figure 2 represents a Chatbot system design built using the large language model (LLM) and Retrieval-Augmented Generation (RAG). This particular chatbot system has two main parts: (1) retriever and (2) generator. The retriever looks for content that matches the user's query from the existing provided material, whereas the generator uses a pre-trained model (in our case, ChatGPT 3.0), and produces natural and meaningful responses. Translating to this study context, as a student interacts with the chatbot, the process starts with typing a question. For example, a student asked Gandhiji bot, "*why did you choose to fight for freedom*". This input is first handled by the retriever, which searches through a provided collection of documents. These documents are divided into smaller parts, called chunks, and each chunk is converted into a numerical representation called an embedding. Embeddings capture the meaning of the text in a form the system can compare and store in a vector database. The student's question is also converted into an embedding, and the system compares it with all stored embeddings to find the most relevant information (Church, K 2024) For this question, the retriever might select chunks related to Gandhi's experiences in South Africa, his belief in justice, and his commitment to nonviolence.

Figure 1. Interface of Persona-based Chatbot representing Gandhiji

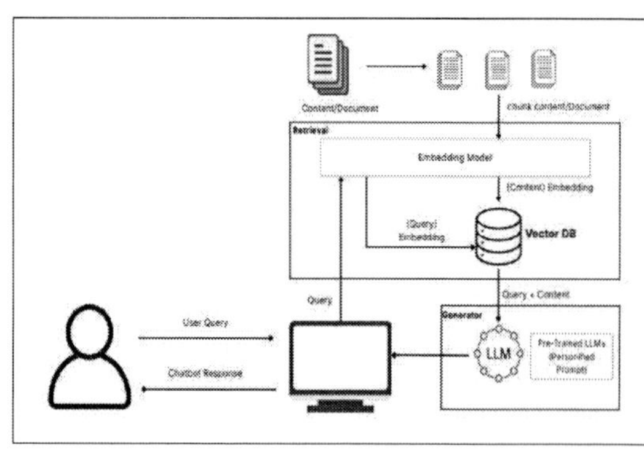

Figure 2. System Architecture of Persona-based Chatbot

Next, the generator, powered by a pre-trained large language model (LLM) such as ChatGPT, combines the retrieved information with the student's question to produce a coherent and meaningful response. In this case, the chatbot replied: "*Ah, my young friend! The fight for freedom is a journey that lies in the heart and spirit of every human being. I chose to fight for India's freedom because I....*".

This sample response demonstrates that the chatbot not only understands the question but also provides a detailed, historically accurate, and contextually rich answer. A key feature of this design is personification, allowing the chatbot to respond as a historical figure, making interactions more relatable and immersive. By merging retrieval-based accuracy with LLM-based fluency, the system supports dialogue-based exploration of historical content while maintaining reliability.

The design of the chatbot is informed by dialogic pedagogy (Alexander, 2018), which frames learning as a process achieved through meaningful conversation. Students' questions and ideas are explored interactively, allowing them to critically engage, ask follow-up "why" or "how" questions, and receive evidence-based responses. For example, when a student asks the Gandhiji chatbot, "Why did you choose to fight for freedom?" The system replies with a historically grounded, contextually rich answer, fostering joint interpretation of historical events. The designed chatbot supports six dialogic principles: collective, reciprocal, supportive, deliberative, cumulative, and purposeful talk (Alexander, 2018; Howe et al., 2019). Collective and reciprocal learning occur as knowledge is co-constructed through question-and-answer exchanges. Supportive and deliberative elements from the chatbot, emerge through empathetic language and explanations connecting principles to real-life examples, while cumulative and purposeful talk links new knowledge to prior learning and keeps discussions focused on historical understanding and ethical reasoning.

4. PLAY TESTING

Prior to the playtest, students were provided with reading materials a week in advance to build background knowledge of the historical figures, helping them pose more meaningful questions. At the start of each session, they had five minutes to review the day's material. A total of 52 middle-school students (21 from Grade 6, 18 from Grade 7, and 13 from Grade 8) from an urban English-medium school participated voluntarily with parental consent.

The playtesting aimed to explore how students engage with personified chatbot prototypes representing historical figures, including Mahatma Gandhi, Benjamin Franklin, Leonardo da Vinci, Chanakya, and Albert Einstein. Over five classroom sessions conducted during regular school hours, each day focused on a different persona, supervised by both the researcher and the classroom teacher. Students used individual devices to ensure authentic one-to-one interactions with the chatbots, which were exploratory in nature, allowing them to freely ask questions, probe ideas, and take notes on insights of interest. Each student interacted with all five chatbots across non-consecutive days to avoid cognitive overload while maintaining balanced exposure. All conversations were automatically logged by the system, capturing both student questions and chatbot responses. These logs served as the primary dataset for analysis, offering insights into the types of questions posed, the quality of chatbot responses, and the potential of the system as an engaging educational tool for learning history.

5. FINDING AND DISCUSSION

This study followed a case study approach (Tisdell E. et. al. 2025) and focused on a single student who participated over five days and interacted with each of the persona-based historical chatbots. Following the content analysis (Bengtsson, Mariette., 2016) of the student-chatbot interactions, this case demonstrates both the nature of the student's questions and how the chatbots replied, illustrating their conversational strategies and guidance.

On the first day, the student started the conversation with the Gandhi chatbot by asking about historical events and personal motivations, such as *"Why did you choose to fight for freedom?"* and *"What roles did your parents play in shaping your values?"*. The bot responded with a mix of historical context, moral reasoning, and prompts that encouraged the student to reflect personally, such as *"What do you think about that?"* or *"What values do you cherish from your own family?"*. Students asked hypothetical questions, such as *"What if you didn't face challenges in Africa?"* This invited counterfactual reasoning, enabling the student to connect historical events with choices and character, demonstrating both cognitive and emotional engagement.

On the second day, the student engaged with the Einstein chatbot. The student asked about the inspiration behind the theory of relativity, other scientific contributions, collaborative influences, and personal challenges like speech difficulties, for example, *"What inspired you to invent the theory of relativity?", "Did someone help you for this?", "You had speech problems, did you face any challenges?" ,"What are your other inventions?"* was complemented by reflective and hypothetical inquiries like *"Could this theory of relativity be used for negative purposes?"* and *"Could you say any words for the younger generation?"* The bot provided historically and scientifically grounded responses while prompting the student to consider broader social, ethical, and personal implications of scientific work, for instance, *"How do you think you would respond if faced with challenges or opportunities?", "..Keep exploring, and who knows what ideas you might come up with next!".* Likewise, after every question from the student, the bot gives the motivations, value to the student so that the student keeps asking questions.

The third-day conversation with the Benjamin Franklin chatbot also showed a mix of question types. The student began with factual queries about Franklin's role in the Revolutionary War, inventions, and writings ("Which books did you write?", "What inventions did you create?") before shifting to ethical and reflective ones ("What were your views on slavery?", "What advice would you give to the younger generation?"). The chatbot combined historical accuracy, anecdotes, and humor, recounting how he left school at ten to work in his family's candle-making business while stressing perseverance. It emphasized civic responsibility and collaboration through quotes like "An ounce of prevention is worth a pound of cure... When we share knowledge, we uplift each other." Through such storytelling and practical examples, the bot made abstract concepts like responsibility, collaboration, and self-education accessible, encouraging both intellectual and moral reasoning.

On the fourth day, the interaction with the Leonardo da Vinci chatbot included both factual and reflective exchanges. The student asked questions such as *"How did you become an artist?", "What inspired you to draw Mona Lisa?",* and *"Who supported you with all your artworks?",* to which the chatbot responded with historical details about his apprenticeship, patrons, and inspirations. As the conversation progressed, the student posed deeper inquiries like *"Why didn't you create working models of your inventions?", "Does art require mathematics?",* and *"How do you investigate a subject?",* and the chatbot replied with explanations that combined historical context, artistic philosophy, and scientific reasoning, such as *"I observed, sketched, experimented, and reflected to investigate each subject thoroughly."* When asked *"Can you give unique mediums to use for art?".* The chatbot offered motivational guidance and practical suggestions, closing with encouragement like "*Remember, experimenting with different mediums is part of the fun! Don't be afraid to try new things!"* Throughout the conversation, the bot consistently tried to encourage the student to think further by closing its replies with advice, reflection, or a moral takeaway. The responses such as, "*I painted "The Last Supper" between 1495 and 1498. It depicts the moment Jesus announces that one of his disciples will betray him*", "*When investigating a subject, I like to immerse myself in the details! ... Observation, Research, Sketching, Experimentation, Reflection.*" and "*Remember, every artist's path is unique, and curiosity is your greatest tool!*", illustrate the blend of historical fact-sharing, methodological explanation, and motivational prompting, showing an intentional design to both inform and inspire.

Finally, on the fifth day, the Chanakya chatbot encouraged historical, strategic, ethical, and practical inquiry. The student asked foundational questions ("Why are you famous?", "How can a ruler ensure equality and inclusivity?", "What are possible consequences when an economy falls?") and higher-order ones ("How to score in every subject?"). The chatbot gave structured, actionable responses combining historical examples and practical guidance, prompting strategic thinking, ethical evaluation, and reflection. Leadership weaknesses were listed as "inconsistency, lack of confidence, poor communication... and favoritism", with advice like "By organizing study, actively learning, and adapting, you can improve your results...". Historical examples illustrated governance ("I helped Chandragupta Maurya establish the Maurya Empire... teaching him about ruling wisely..."), ethical reasoning ("A ruler can maintain ethics by... promoting openness to reduce corruption..."), and strategic thinking ("Being strategic in leadership is very important... success hinges on thinking ahead..."). These responses not only informed the student about ancient statecraft but also encouraged reflection on fairness, foresight, and personal growth in modern contexts.

Overall, the interactions showed that students engaged most when the chatbots provided contextually rich, persona-driven responses paired with reflective prompts. Across all five days, the chatbots consistently combined historical, factual, and contextual information with guidance, motivational cues, storytelling, and practical suggestions drawn from the personas' own life experiences. Each bot adapted its responses to its persona and topic, blending information with prompts that encouraged reflection, exploration, and continued questioning.

By emulating historical figures, such chatbots provide students with a unique opportunity to interact with the past in a dynamic and personalized manner. For example, educators have employed AI chatbots modeled on figures like Abraham Lincoln to facilitate discussions on complex historical events, enabling students to pose questions such as, "*Why did you hesitate before issuing the Emancipation Proclamation?*" (SchoolAI, 2025). Similarly, Park et al. (2025) highlight that integrating character-specific responses and personalization features into chatbots can significantly enhance engagement and curiosity.

With this preliminary study, we focused was on documenting designing of the persona based chatbot, and how students interacted with the chatbots; however, future research will examine in greater depth the cognitive levels of student questions, the engagement trajectory over time, and the role of learner mindset in shaping the depth of inquiry.

6. CONCLUSION

The study documents the design and implementation of persona-based historical chatbots and the ways in which students interacted with them over five classroom sessions. Students engaged with chatbots representing Mahatma Gandhi, Albert Einstein, Benjamin Franklin, Leonardo da Vinci, and Chanakya. Interaction logs showed that students began with factual questions and gradually moved toward reflective, ethical, and hypothetical inquiries. The persona-based chatbots provided contextually rich responses aligned with each historical figure's communication style. Students asked mixed-level questions spanning factual understanding, ethical reasoning, interdisciplinary connections, and personal reflection. The chatbot responded with contextually rich narratives, ethical reasoning, and prompts that encouraged personal reflection, supporting iterative dialogue throughout the interaction. Such interactions can support the student to progress from basic knowledge acquisition to analytical thinking and moral evaluation, integrating factual understanding with ethical and personal application. It should be noted that the insights from the student- chatbot interactions are based on a single case study, which calls for further investigations by extending the analyses to the rest of student cases.

REFERENCES

Akcayir, G. & Akçayır, M. (2018). The flipped classroom: A review of its advantages and challenges. *Computers & Education*. 126. 10.1016/j.compedu.2018.07.021.

Ali Amer Jid Almahri, F., Bell, D., & Arzoky, M. (2019). Personas Design for Conversational Systems in Education. *Informatics*, 6(4), 46. https://doi.org/10.3390/informatics6040046

Callaway, A. "Analyzing Students' Historical Thinking Skills at Different Grade Levels" (2020). *Masters Theses. 4840.* https://thekeep.eiu.edu/theses/4840

Clarizia, F. & Colace, F. & Lombardi, Marco & Pascale, Francesco & Santaniello, Domenico. (2018). Chatbot: An Education Support System for Students: 10th *International Symposium, CSS 2018*, Amalfi, Italy, Proceedings. 10.1007/978-3-030-01689-0_23.

Hobert, S., & Meyer von Wolff, R. (2019). Say hello to your new automated tutor–a structured literature review on pedagogical conversational agents.

Kuhail, M. A., Alturki, N., Alramlawi, S., & Alhejori, K. (2023). Interacting with educational chatbots: A systematic review. *Education and Information Technologies*, 28(1), 973-1018.

Labadze, L., Grigolia, M. & Machaidze, L. Role of AI chatbots in education: systematic literature review. *Int J Educ Technol High Educ* 20, 56 (2023). https://doi.org/10.1186/s41239-023-00426-1

Lin, M. P. C., & Chang, D. (2023). CHAT-ACTS: A pedagogical framework for personalized chatbot to enhance active learning and self-regulated learning. *Computers and Education: Artificial Intelligence*, 5, 100167.

López-Fernández, C., Tirado-Olivares, S., Mínguez-Pardo, R., & Cozar-Gutierrez, R. (2023). Putting critical thinking at the center of history lessons in primary education through error-and historical thinking-based instruction. *Thinking Skills and Creativity*, 49, 101316.

Ni, L. B. (2024). The Impact of Chatbot Technology on Enhancing Historical Learning in K-12 Education. Malaysian *Journal of Social Sciences and Humanities* (MJSSH), 9(1), e002656-e002656.

Nuttall, D. (2021). What is the purpose of studying history? Developing students' perspectives on the purposes and value of history education. *History Education Research Journal*, 18(1).

Park, K., Song, H., Seo, S., Kim, J., & Suh, B. (2025, April). "Ask Sir Oliver Ingham": LLM-based Social Simulations for History Education. In Proceedings of the Extended Abstracts of the *CHI Conference on Human Factors in Computing Systems* (pp. 1-13).

Perrotta, K. A., & Bohan, C. H. (2013). " I Hate History": A Study of Student Engagement in Community College Undergraduate History Courses. *Journal on Excellence in College Teaching*, 24(4).

Petousi, D., Katifori, A., McKinney, S., Perry, S., Roussou, M., & Ioannidis, Y. (2021, June). Social bots of conviction as dialogue facilitators for history education: Promoting historical empathy in teens through dialogue. In Proceedings of the *20th Annual ACM Interaction Design and Children Conference* (pp. 326-337).

Purmintasari, Y. D., Suwarni, S., Eviliyanto, E., & Billy, J. (2024). Development of Critical Thinking Model in History Learning. HISTORIA: *Jurnal Program Studi Pendidikan Sejarah*, 12(2), 651-660.

Qian, X., Oard, D. W., & Chan, J. (2022, February). Conversational Interaction with Historical Figures: What's it good for?. In the *International Conference on Information* (pp. 32-49).

Rashadi, N. I. H. M., & Ahmad, A. R. (2019). Lesson Study: Enhancing the Teaching and Learning of History Subject. In The 2nd *International Conference on Sustainable Development and Multi-Ethnic Society* (pp. 275-279).

Rivero, P., Navarro-Neri, I., & Aso, B. (2022). Who are the protagonists of History? Exploratory study on historical relevance after completing compulsory secondary education in Spain. *Social Sciences*, 11(4), 175.

Santamaria-Velasco, J., Núñez-Naranjo, A., & Morales-Urrutia, X. (2025). Critical thinking and AI: Enhancing history teaching through ChatGPT simulations. *International Journal of Innovative Research and Scientific Studies*, 8(1), 564–575.

Shargel, R., & Katz, M. (2025). "The monument is a lie": facing difficult history through role-play in simulation. *Social Studies, Research and Practice.*

Smestad, T. L., & Volden, F. (2018, October). Chatbot personalities matters: improving the user experience of chatbot interfaces. In *International conference on internet science* (pp. 170-181).

Short Papers

INTEGRATING PODCASTING IN TEACHER PREPARATION PROGRAMS TO INCREASE TEACHER SELF-EFFICACY

Elizabeth Lapon
Franklin Pierce University, USA

ABSTRACT

A reflective practice is an essential skill for teachers to be more self-efficacious. While various approaches and strategies can be implemented to develop reflective practices, podcasting has the potential to be a beneficial form of professional development that helps teachers to learn through practical experience and inquiry. The purpose of this research is to explore if participating in a podcast about teaching practices impact teacher self-efficacy for classroom discipline and management. Findings suggest that podcasting is potentially beneficial to increase teacher candidates' confidence for classroom discipline and management and may be a useful tool to encourage meaningful reflection. Additionally, teacher candidates see the benefits in using podcasts with their future students. While further research is necessary, podcasting may be a useful instrument to encourage teacher self-development and create a valuable learning resource for all teachers.

KEYWORDS

Podcast, Teacher Preparation, Self-Efficacy, Reflective Practice, Classroom Management

1. INTRODUCTION

Reflective practice is a critical component of the teacher's experience. According to John Dewey, the purpose of a reflective practice is to change teachers' classroom practices and actions (1983). Teachers learn to become better teachers in a self-corrective process that involves experience, inquiry and reflection (Dewey, 1983). Reflective teachers are better problem solvers with a deeper understanding of themselves as they can connect discovered solutions to other ideas and experiences (Suphasri & Chinokul, 2021). Significant research demonstrates the longstanding benefits of a reflective teaching practice (Karnieli-Miller, 2020; Maksimovic & Osmanovic, 2018; Slade et al., 2019; Suphasri & Chinokul, 2021; Tiainen et al., 2018).

Bandura's theory of self-efficacy (1977) refers to a person's belief in their ability to succeed in a particular area. This theory has been widely researched in a variety of disciplines. Specifically, research in education has noted a connection between reflective practices and teacher self-efficacy. Reflective teachers view themselves as more self-efficacious (Dexter & Wall, 2021). Reflective practices promote teacher competence through planning, improving teacher performance by reconsidering strengths and weaknesses, and revisiting specific student learning needs (Huda & Teh, 2018; Cirocki & Widodo, 2019; Zahid & Khanam, 2019; Huynh, 2022). Reflective practice plays a prominent role in teacher preparation because it helps teachers review their practices, develop relevant skills, and think consciously about what is happening in the classroom, thus resulting in a higher level of reflective competence (Mohamed et al., 2022).

While various approaches and strategies can be implemented to develop reflective practices, research suggests it is preferable to reflect with others (Boud et al., 2013). Involvement of others in the reflective process is beneficial because the other person can ask reflective questions, point out underlying values and attitudes, challenge and evaluate assumptions, and provide different perspectives through one-on-one feedback (Karnieli-Miller, 2020). Learning is supported through co-constructed experiences that allow for teachers to disclose problems, receive peer feedback, make suggestions for deeper thinking, engage in pedagogically rich conversations, and promote deep examination of pedagogical practices (Blake & Gibson, 2020).

Podcasting has the potential to be a beneficial form of professional development that helps to "develop practitioners' sense of efficacy, connection, and commitment with the profession" (Turner, 2020). For example, the Güler & Özkan (2018) study observed how the implementation of podcasts to preservice teachers increased content comprehension, raised their consciousness, led to critical thinking, and enhanced collaborative learning. Additionally, podcasting has the potential to serve as a highly accessible tool for purposeful and meaningful exchanges among those in teaching (Turner, 2020). The specific value added by the podcast format compared to similar, unrecorded discussions is the potential for global reach, community building, creating a sense of belonging, highlighting shared experiences, and making learning more accessible (Scriven, 2022).

Classroom discipline and management is considered one of the most challenging components of teaching and can be especially trying for new teachers. The purpose of this research is to explore whether participating in a podcast about teaching practices impacts teacher self-efficacy, particularly in the arena of classroom discipline and management.

2. METHODOLOGY

This research study utilized the thematic analysis research method to identify and interpret patterns or themes in a data set to lead to new insights and understanding (Naeem et al., 2023). By utilizing teacher candidate responses to open-ended questions, a more in-depth, realistic understanding of the impact of podcasting to increase teacher self–efficacy could be unearthed. However, because the research study had a small number of participants from the same institution, the findings in this study serve as a starting point for further investigation. By introducing triangulation with multiple sources of data, additional research methods, or different researchers to analyze the data, it may increase the credibility, validity, comprehensive understanding, and generalizability of the initial findings of this study.

2.1 Participants

The subjects invited to participate in this study are second-year education teacher candidates from a small, private university in the northeastern region of the USA. All ten participants were taking the course: Design and Management of the Classroom Environment. Participation in the study was voluntary. All participants could withdraw or leave the study at any point without any obligation to continue or negative consequences for their refusal to participate. No personally identifiable data was collected, and participants knew the purpose behind the study before they agreed or declined to join. The study went through Institutional Review Board (IRB) review and approval.

2.2 Data Collection and Analysis

Participants in the study were required to spend 15 hours observing in a local elementary or high school classroom as part of the course. Based on these observations, participants were asked to write a one paragraph description on a challenging or innovative discipline or management situation that they observed in their host classroom. Participants were then asked to participate in a 10-minute podcast with their professor where they would read the prepared classroom discipline or management situation that they saw in the field. Professor and participant then discussed different ways to handle the situation and ideas for strategies to try to manage the situation described. By using an interpretivist paradigm, professor and participant were able to describe, understand, and interpret the participant's experience together(Merriam & Tisdale, 2015, p. 12). After the podcast, participants were then asked to respond to four open-ended questions. The podcasts created could potentially be used as a learning tool for education courses both domestically and internationally, and for all teachers confronting these issues.

Initially, the researcher reviewed each teacher candidate's open–ended response to get an overall sense of the participants' experiences and perspective. Next, with the research questions in mind, codes were formulated to reveal patterns and themes. When coding, the participants' words, perceptions, and opinions were paramount in the analysis. Miles et al. (2014) advised two cycles of coding to derive patterns and explain the meaning of the data collected by assembling it into analyzable units. A second code is useful to add detail, enrich the meaning of the first code, and identify particular qualities that may emerge (Miles et al., 2014). The researcher was mindful not to insert their opinions and to make sure that the voices of the participants were upheld throughout the process. The researcher wrote analytic memos to reflect on the responses and the themes that emerged as they coded. Engaging in reflexivity about perspectives by writing analytic memos throughout the analysis process was an important validation strategy (Creswell & Poth, 2016). As suggested by Miles et al. (2014), the researcher utilized a mix-and-match method that used descriptive, in vivo, and process coding to help organize, classify, and categorize the information. Specifically, the researcher looked for repetitions in phrasing or content, categories explicitly offered by the participants, analogies or metaphors used, similarities and differences in their responses to the questions posed.

2.3 Findings

After appearing on the podcast, participants were asked to respond to the following four questions:

a. Describe your confidence in addressing the classroom discipline or management situation that you saw in the field before appearing on the podcast.

b. Explain how appearing on the podcast impacted your confidence to address the classroom discipline or management situation that you saw in the field. Be specific. Was it helpful/not helpful? Explain, why or why not?

c. Do you think being on a podcast is a useful strategy for encouraging reflection about classroom discipline or management? Explain, why or why not?

d. From having participated in this experience, do you think you will use podcasts as a teaching strategy with your future students? Explain, why or why not? If yes, how do you see yourself using podcasts with your future students?

In response to question A, participants expressed they lacked confidence in their ability to manage the situation they observed in the classroom. For example, one participant stated, "I felt I would have handled the situation differently, but I didn't know the correct steps to take to correct the behavior." Another participant expressed, "Before appearing on the podcast, I struggled with addressing classroom discipline, especially when students displayed disrespect." With one exception, students articulated an overall lack of confidence around classroom discipline, with some expressing anxiety concerning this aspect of teaching.

In response to question B, participants reported a significant boost in their confidence to handle classroom discipline and management situations. For example, one participant explained, "Discussing my approach openly and receiving positive feedback confirmed that my strategies had merit and were feasible for real situations. Hearing additional ideas from others also broadened my perspective on possible solutions." Teacher candidates also reported the value in working through these situations with someone who has significant teaching experience.

In response to question C, participants believed podcasting was a very useful tool for reflection. Although some participants did express their nervousness and initial discomfort about being on a podcast. Overall, participants found discussion to be an effective tool for reflection, meaning making, and "deeper thinking." For example, one participant communicated, "Discussing with other people makes it encouraging to see what you can figure out together." Another participant explained, "Observing how the teacher reacts to different situations allows me to get a better idea of how I want to react as a teacher." Several participants also expressed that they preferred being on the podcast to writing as a means of reflection.

In response to question D, overall participants believed podcasts were a highly effective teaching strategy that they would want to use with their future students. Ways participants suggested to implement podcasting included: "to engage students in meaningful analysis and reflection," as "presentation for research projects," so "students think about their learning and share ideas," to "assess student understanding," and for students to "express their creativity."

3. CONCLUSION

While this study provides insight into the potential benefits of integrating podcasts in teacher preparation programs to increase teacher self-efficacy for classroom discipline and management, a larger confirmatory study is needed for greater validity and generalizability of this study's findings. Future research could investigate when is the most meaningful time in a teacher preparation program to introduce teacher candidates to podcasting, if integrating podcasting would be a meaningful tool for reflection in other methods courses, and what if any are the potential harms to podcasting. Additionally, researchers could explore the usefulness of teacher candidates in teacher preparation programs listening to podcast recordings made by other teacher candidates.

Findings suggest that podcasting is potentially beneficial for increasing teacher candidates' confidence for classroom discipline and management and may be a useful tool for encouraging meaningful reflection. Additionally, teacher candidates see the benefits in using podcasts with their future students. Because podcasting encourages active participation and critical thinking, it could constitute part of a reflective practice, which research has shown benefits teacher candidates by encouraging them to adapt and adjust both their thinking and actions (Dewey, 1983). While further research is necessary, podcasting may be a useful instrument for encouraging teacher self-development and may serve as a valuable learning resource for all teachers.

REFERENCES

A. Dexter, C., & Wall, M. (2021). Reflective functioning and teacher burnout: the mediating role of self-efficacy. *Reflective Practice,* 22(6), 753–765. https://doi.org/10.1080/14623943.2021.1968817

Bandura, A (1977). Self-efficacy: Toward a unifying theory of behavioral change. *Psychological Review. 84* (2): 191–215. https://educational-innovation.sydney.edu.au/news/pdfs/Bandura%201977.pdf

Blake, J., & Gibson, A. (2021). Critical friends group protocols deepen conversations in collaborative action research projects. *Educational Action Research, 29*(1), 133-148.

Boud, D., Keogh, R., & Walker, D. (2013). *Reflection: Turning experience into learning.* Routledge.

Cirocki, A., and Widodo, H. P. (2019). Reflective practice in English language teaching in Indonesia: shared practices from two teacher educators. Iran. J. Lang. Teach. Res. 7, 15–35. doi: 10.30466/ijltr.2019.120734

Creswell, J. W., & Poth, C. N. (2016). *Qualitative inquiry and research design: Choosing among five approaches.* Sage publications.

Dewey, J. (1983). *How we think: A restatement of the relation of reflective thing in the educative process.* New York, NY: D.C. Heath.

Güler, S., & Özkan, Y. (2018). Podcast Applications in Pre-service Language Teacher Education from a Constructivist Perspective. *World Journal on Educational Technology: Current Issues, 10*(3), 131-141.

Huda, M., and Teh, K. S. M. (2018). "Empowering professional and ethical competence on reflective teaching practice in digital era," in Mentorship strategies in teacher education. eds. K. Dikilitas, E. Mede and D. Atay (IGI Global), 136–152.

Huynh, H. T. (2022). Promoting professional development in language teaching through reflective practice. Vietnam J. Educ. 6, 62–68. doi: 10.52296/vje.2022.126

Karnieli-Miller, O. (2020). Reflective practice in the teaching of communication skills. *Patient Education and Counseling, 103*(10), 2166-2172

Maksimovic, J., & Osmanovic, J. (2018). Reflective practice as a changing factor of teaching quality. *Research in Pedagogy, 8*(2), 172-189.

Merriam, S. B., & Tisdale, E. J. (2015). *Qualitative research: A guide to design and Implementation* (4th ed.). Wiley.

Miles, M. B., Huberman, A. M., & Saldaña, J. (2014). *Qualitative data analysis: A methods sourcebook* (4th ed.). SAGE Publications.

Mohamed, M., Rashid, R. A., & Alqaryouti, M. H. (2022). Conceptualizing the complexity of reflective practice in education. *Frontiers in psychology, 13,* 1008234.

Naeem, M., Ozuem, W., Howell, K., & Ranfagni, S. (2023). A step-by-step process of thematic analysis to develop a conceptual model in qualitative research. *International journal of qualitative methods, 22,* 16094069231205789.

Scriven, R. (2022). Making a podcast: Reflecting on creating a place-based podcast. *Area, 54*(2), 260-267.

Slade, M. L., Burnham, T. J., Catalana, S. M., & Waters, T. (2019). The Impact of Reflective Practice on Teacher Candidates' Learning. *International Journal for the Scholarship of Teaching and Learning, 13*(2), 15.

Suphasri, P., & Chinokul, S. (2021). Reflective practice in teacher education: Issues, challenges, and considerations. *Pasaa, 62*(1), 236-264.

Tiainen, O., Korkeamäki, R. L., & Dreher, M. J. (2018). Becoming reflective practitioners: A case study of three beginning pre-service teachers. *Scandinavian Journal of Educational Research, 62*(4), 586-600.

Turner, M. W. (2020). Podcasting: Spaces for connection and development. In P. Clements, A. Krause, & R. Gentry (Eds.), Teacher efficacy, learner agency. Tokyo: JALT. https://doi.org/10.37546/JALTPCP2019-05

Zahid, M., and Khanam, A. (2019). Effect of reflective teaching practices on the performance of prospective teachers. Turk. Online J. Educ. Technol. 18, 32–43.

STUDY ON AUTOMATIC GENERATION OF LECTURE VIDEOS BASED ON CONTENT ANALYSIS OF LECTURE SLIDES

Kota Mizukami[1], Daisuke Deguchi[1], Tomoki Toda[1], Hiroshi Murase[1],
Haruya Kyutoku[2] and Tsubasa Minematsu[3]
[1]*Nagoya University, Japan*
[2]*Aichi University of Technology, Japan*
[3]*Kyushu Institute of Technology, Japan*

ABSTRACT

With the spread of online education, the demand for lecture videos in which instructors read aloud from slide decks has been increasing. However, creating such videos entails significant labor and cost. This study proposes a method that automatically generates lecture videos—including narration audio and highlighted text—using the slides themselves as input. First, the slide content is analyzed with large language models and optical character-recognition. Based on the extracted information, narration speech is synthesized and key text within the slides is highlighted to enhance learners' understanding. Experiments using real presentation slides confirmed that the proposed method can automatically generate lecture videos.

KEYWORDS

Automatic Lecture Video Generation, Text Highlighting, Large Language Model

1. INTRODUCTION

Online and hybrid learning have greatly increased the need for video-based teaching materials.

Lecture videos—where instructors read aloud from slides—can enhance learning by combining verbal and visual information (Mayer and Anderson, 1991). However, producing such content requires significant time for recording and editing. To reduce this burden, we propose a method that automatically generates lecture videos from slide decks. The system analyzes slide content using language and image processing, then outputs a narrated slide show with synchronized highlights. This automation benefits both academic and corporate education. Our method consists of: (i) generating narration text, (ii) synthesizing narration audio, and (iii) highlighting the narrated slide content. Section 2 reviews related work; Section 3 explains our method; Section 4 presents experiments; Section 5 concludes.

2. RELATED WORK

Ando and Ueno (2011) showed that synchronizing pointers with narration and visual elements enhances learner comprehension by directing attention to relevant screen areas. This supports the use of pointer-based emphasis in AI-generated lecture materials.

Xu et al. (2024) combined OCR, LLMs, and TTS to construct a pipeline that produces lecture videos in which an avatar delivers synthetic speech based on slide content. A user study comparing these AI-generated lectures to conventional recordings suggested improved memory retention in English language learning. However, their system lacks the mechanisms for highlighting slide elements.

Optical character recognition (OCR) extracts textual content from images. Modern approaches like CRAFT (Baek et al., 2019) apply deep learning to enhance detection accuracy.

Text embedding represents text as numerical vectors in a semantic space, allowing similarity comparisons. Sentence-BERT (Reimers & Gurevych, 2019) is widely used for this purpose.

Large language models (LLMs) are pretrained neural networks capable of handling diverse natural-language tasks. Models like ChatGPT also support multimodal inputs (OpenAI, 2022).

Text-to-speech (TTS) systems synthesize speech from text. Modern TTS services such as Google Text-to-Speech (gTTS) use deep learning for natural-sounding output (Google, 2025).

3. PROPOSED METHOD

We propose a pipeline that takes a slide deck as input and automatically (i) generates narration text and speech, (ii) highlights relevant text on each slide, and (iii) produces a lecture video combining these elements. As shown in Figure 1, each slide is rasterized into an image, denoted I_i, and processed using OCR. Narration is generated via ChatGPT, speech via TTS, and highlights are selected by comparing OCR text with the narration using Sentence-BERT embeddings. Details of each stage are described in Sections 3.1–3.3.

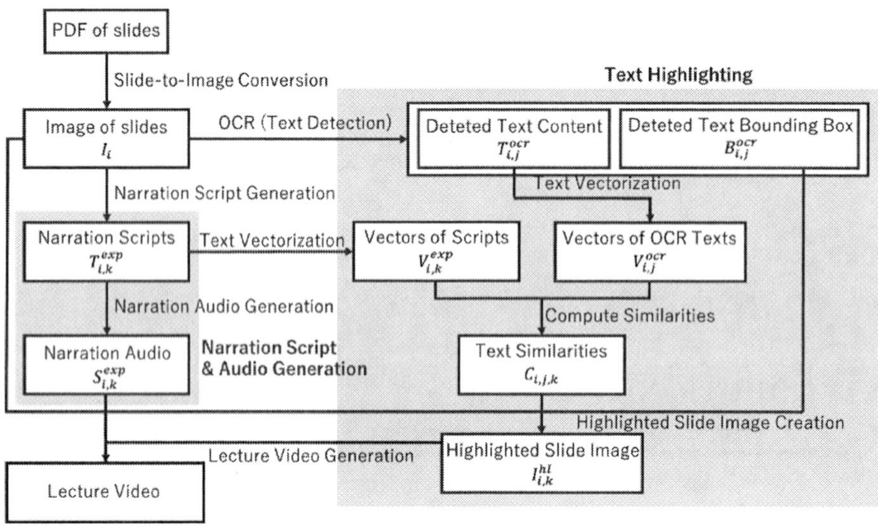

Figure 1. The workflow of proposed method

3.1 Generation of Narration Script and Audio

To obtain the script spoken in the lecture video, each image of slides is supplied to ChatGPT. ChatGPT is prompted with the following three-stage sequence:

Precondition confirmation and overall task instructions – a prompt provides ChatGPT with information essential for narration generation and an overview of the entire task.

Grasping the entire slide deck – all slide images are then presented so that ChatGPT can understand the structure and progression of the presentation and devise a strategy that avoids biased or redundant narration.

Generating narration for each page – finally, the slide images are fed one by one, and ChatGPT outputs the narration text for each page.

Table 1 lists the full prompt sequence used to instruct ChatGPT in the narration-generation process.

Table 1. The full prompt sequence

Stage	Prompt Text	Associated Input
Precondition confirmation and overall task instructions	You are a university professor. Please think about what to say in the class using the slides I will give you. Please meet the following conditions. 1. Return only the content to be spoken 2. Do not include control characters such as titles and line breaks 3. Combine the amount of information in the slides with the amount of information in the text. For example, do not speak for a long time on title slides or scene transition slides. 4. In the closing slide, summarize what has been said so far. 5. Be aware that research and other materials in the document may not be the presenter's achievements. 6. Pay special attention to numbers and letters in formulas and tables. 7. Do not speak about things that are not written on the slide. 8. Do not read the page number of the slide.	No input
Grasping the entire slide deck	First, I will give you all the pages of the slides. Please make a plan for what to say while minimizing what you say.	Entire slide PDF
Generating narration for each page	This is page {page_num}. Please give a presentation while looking at this page.	Image of each page

As a result, executing these steps for the i-th slide image I_i yields the page-level narration text T_i^{exp}. And then, T_i^{exp} is split at punctuation; each fragment $T_{i,k}^{exp}$ is converted to speech via TTS, yielding $S_{i,k}^{exp}$.

3.2 Text Highlighting

First, OCR detects all text regions on I_i, obtaining both the bounding boxes $B_{i,j}^{ocr}$ and their corresponding strings $T_{i,j}^{ocr}$. Next, Sentence-BERT embeds $T_{i,k}^{exp}$ and $T_{i,j}^{ocr}$ to produce vectors $V_{i,k}^{exp}$ and $V_{i,j}^{ocr}$. Then, for each narration fragment $T_{i,k}^{exp}$ on i-th slide, we compute cosine similarities $C_{i,j,k} = \cos(V_{i,k}^{exp}, V_{i,j}^{ocr})$ between its embedding $V_{i,k}^{exp}$ and the embeddings $V_{i,j}^{ocr}$ of all OCR-detected strings on the same slide. Among all candidate strings, only the one with the highest cosine similarity is selected as the highlighted text. Formally, we define $j_{i,k}^* = \arg\max_j C_{i,j,k}$: the index of the single text region with the highest similarity. Finally, the bounding box B_{i,j^*}^{ocr} chosen in the previous step is drawn onto the original slide image I_i to produce the highlighted frame $I_{i,k}^{hl}$.

3.3 Video Generation

All speech segments $\mathrm{S}_{\mathrm{i,k}}^{\mathrm{exp}}$ and highlighted images $\mathrm{I}_{\mathrm{i,k}}^{\mathrm{hl}}$ are concatenated to produce the final lecture video that synchronizes narration with visual emphasis.

4. EXPERIMENTS

To evaluate the practical effectiveness of our method, we conducted a focused case study using a representative English-language slide. We extracted text regions from the slide using optical character recognition (OCR) and assigned each region to a unique bounding box (BBox) number. For each narration fragment generated by ChatGPT, our method selected the most semantically similar OCR region based on Sentence-BERT cosine similarity. Figure 2 shows the slide image with numbered bounding boxes, along with a table listing each narration fragment and its corresponding BBox number. We subjectively evaluated whether highlighted regions matched the narration. In general, they were judged contextually appropriate. However, in cases where no appropriate pointing target exists on the slide for a given narration fragment, the system still selects a text region to highlight. For example, as shown in Figure 2 short narration text "First," was incorrectly assigned to Slide component (5). This behavior may distract learners by drawing attention to irrelevant content, revealing a limitation of the proposed method. Therefore, future improvements should consider allowing the system to refrain from highlighting when no semantically appropriate region is found.

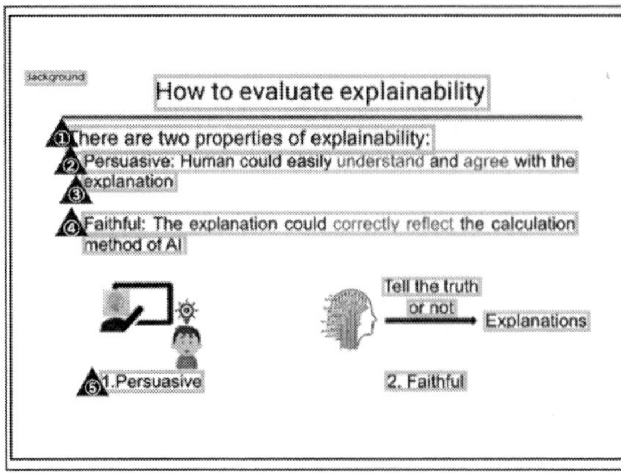

Narration Fragment	Highlighted OCR Text
Evaluating explainability involves two key properties.	①
First,	⑤
persuadability ensures that humans can easily understand and agree with AI explanations.	②
Second,	③
Faithfulness checks if the explanations accurately reflect the AI's actual computational methods.	④
Both aspects are essential for building trust in AI systems.	④

Figure 2. Slide image annotated with OCR-detected text regions (BBox numbers) and their corresponding narration fragments generated by ChatGPT. The table on the right shows each narration fragment and the matched bounding box ID selected by the proposed method

5. CONCLUSION

We proposed a method that takes lecture slides as input, analyzes their content with an LLM and OCR, generates narrated speech and text highlights, and automatically outputs a lecture video. Experiments confirmed that the proposed method can generate lecture videos automatically. Future work includes extending the highlight-generation process to support not only text but also figures and tables. Additionally, we aim to develop a method that incorporates temporal constraints—such as avoiding repeated pointing to content that has already been explained—to improve the coherence and instructional quality of the generated video. Furthermore, we plan to conduct user studies to evaluate the perceived clarity, usefulness, and educational effectiveness of the generated videos.

ACKNOWLEDGEMENT

This research was partially supported by CREST, JPMJCR22D1.

REFERENCES

Ando M. and Ueno M. (2011). Effect analysis of pointer presentations on multimedia e-learning materials based on dual channel model. *Educational Technology Research*, 34(1-2), pp.59-73.

Baek Y. et al. (2019). Character Region Awareness for Text Detection. *Proceedings of the IEEE/CVF Conference on Computer Vision and Pattern Recognition (CVPR)*. Long Beach, USA, pp. 9365–9374.

Google. (2025). Google Cloud Text-to-Speech. Available at: https://cloud.google.com/text-to-speech (Accessed 16 February 2025).

Mayer R.E. and Anderson R.B. (1991). Animations need narrations: An experimental test of a dual-coding hypothesis. *Journal of Educational Psychology*, 83 (4), pp. 484–490.

OpenAI. (2022). ChatGPT: Optimizing Language Models for Dialogue. Available at: https://openai.com/blog/chatgpt (Accessed 16 February 2025).

Reimers N. and Gurevych I. (2019). Sentence-BERT: Sentence Embeddings using Siamese BERT-Networks. *Proceedings of the 2019 Conference on Empirical Methods in Natural Language Processing and the 9th International Joint Conference on Natural Language Processing (EMNLP-IJCNLP)*. Hong Kong, China, pp. 3982–3992.

Xu T. et al. (2024). From recorded to AI-generated instructional videos: A comparison of learning performance and experience. *British Journal of Educational Technology (Early View, published 28 October 2024)*. DOI: 10.1111/bjet.13530.

USER EXPERIENCE TESTING OF AN IMMERSIVE AR APPLICATION WITH AI COMPANION: EXPLORATIVE USER STUDY IN AN EDUCATIONAL CONTEXT

Thomas Keller and Felix Bauer
ZHAW – Institute of Business Information Technology
Winterthur, Switzerland

ABSTRACT

This paper explores the development and evaluation of an immersive Augmented Reality (AR) application featuring an AI-based companion designed to enhance independent learning within educational contexts. The research aimed to assess user experience (UX) across dimensions of attractiveness, usability, controllability, and motivation, along with evaluating the perceived clarity and effectiveness of the companion's guidance. Utilizing a mixed-methods approach, the application underwent iterative user-centered design processes followed by rigorous testing involving 18 secondary school students. The results indicate that the AR application significantly improved learner engagement and motivation, achieving high scores in attractiveness and stimulation. However, companion interactions revealed variability, particularly in transparency and originality, highlighting specific areas for improvement. Overall, the immersive AR application, combined with the AI-driven companion, demonstrates considerable potential for enhancing autonomous learning, provided targeted refinements in interaction transparency, flexibility, and thematic precision are implemented.

KEYWORDS

Augmented Reality, Education, Virtual Tutor, User Experience Testing

1. INTRODUCTION

Emerging technologies increasingly transform learning processes in educational contexts. Digital content, particularly interactive learning resources, is gaining significance (Ahn et al. 2018; Dreesbach et al. 2023). Augmented Reality (AR), by integrating digital content with the physical world, opens new avenues for educational methods. A crucial success factor for these applications is the User Experience (UX), influencing motivation, understanding, and effectiveness of digital educational tools significantly (Graser, Kirschenlohr, and Böhm 2024; Hammer, Egger-Lampl, and Möller 2018; Minge and Thüring 2018). This study addresses the development and evaluation of an immersive AR application supplemented by an AI-based companion. The objective is to evaluate user experience, specifically focusing on understandability, usability, controllability, motivation, and overall impression. Empirical data were collected through a laboratory experiment involving 18 students, providing insights into the UX and suitability for independent learning within the third cycle of Curriculum 21 (D-EDK 2016).

2. OBJECTIVES AND METHODOLOGY

The primary objective was to develop an immersive AR application incorporating an AI-based virtual companion and evaluate the user experience (UX). The research questions aimed at assessing the UX of the AR application regarding comprehensibility, usability, controllability, motivation, and overall impression. Additionally, the study examined the perceived usefulness and clarity of the Companion's assistance and the impact of its fixed spatial location.

Prototyping of the AR application was iterative, employing user-centered design principles and continual user testing. The evaluation was executed through structured laboratory experiments using standardized User Experience Questionnaires (UEQ). Two separate UEQs were used to for evaluation. One for the immersive AR application without companion and the other to specifically evaluate the companion. The UEQ enables the differentiated recording of six dimensions of the user experience: attractiveness, efficiency, perspicuity, dependability, stimulation and novelty. These scales cover both pragmatic and hedonic aspects of use and thus allow a comprehensive assessment of the application and the Companion from the user's perspective (Schrepp et al., 2014, p. 385). Additionally, following questions were asked with a 7-point Likert scale:

- I found the fixed location of the Companion helpful during use (Location is helpful).
- The fixed location of the Companion had a positive influence on my user expe-rience (Location has a positive influence).
- I would like to be able to choose the location of the Companion flexibly (Desire for more flexible location).
- I can imagine using this immersive AR application for independent learning (Can imagine using AR for learning).
- I would like to use this immersive AR application for independent learning (Would like to use AR for learning).

3. RELATED WORK

Research on AR in educational contexts reveals significant advantages in learning performance and engagement through interactive visual elements. Criollo-C et al. (2021) demonstrated AR's efficacy in improving learning outcomes and reducing cognitive load. In their study, learners using a mobile AR application significantly outperformed peers using traditional methods in both learning outcomes and task completion speed, attributing these advantages to high-quality visualizations and intuitive interactions.

Similarly, Parras-Burgos et al. (2020) explored AR applications in technical drawing, demonstrating that visual AR elements significantly enhance spatial comprehension and learner motivation. In their evaluation, 99.47% of participants reported improved spatial reasoning capabilities, highlighting the cognitive support provided by graphical interactions with 3D models.

Evaluation of UX in AR applications predominantly utilizes quantitative methods like UEQ. Graser et al. (2024) emphasized through their systematic literature review that positive UX significantly impacts both pragmatic and hedonic qualities of AR educational tools. Notably, UX evaluations frequently highlight usability and motivational strengths but also identify technological limitations such as visual constraints or limited interactivity as recurring issues affecting overall UX negatively.

In related UX evaluations, Maulana et al. (2022) conducted a systematic UX assessment of an AR application designed for educational purposes, employing the ADDIE model and the UEQ. Their results showed positive ratings across all UX dimensions, particularly in attractiveness and pragmatic quality. They emphasized that while functional aspects like efficiency and ease of use are crucial, emotional and stimulating qualities of AR significantly enhance sustained learner engagement and motivation.

Pedagogical agents in AR, e.g., AI Companions, conceptualized through theories like Social Agency Theory, demonstrate mixed but generally positive influences on learner motivation. Atkinson et al. (2005) suggest that social cues provided by agents activate social interaction patterns, potentially increasing cognitive processing and learning depth. However, Domagk (2010) highlighted through experimental evidence that neither agent presence nor attractiveness consistently improved learning outcomes, indicating the complexity and contextual dependency of effective agent design.

Empirical findings regarding chatbot-based agents in education by Huang et al. (2025) and Hobert et al. (2023) suggest generally positive impacts on motivation and learning engagement. Huang et al. (2025), through their extensive scoping review, found that chatbot use frequently enhanced learner motivation by providing interactive and adaptive learning support. Additionally, Hobert et al. (2023) emphasized the motivational advantages of interactive and dialogue-based chatbot interactions over passive formats, underscoring the relevance of conversational interactions in educational AR applications.

Further supporting this, Chiu et al. (2023) indicated that additional human support combined with chatbot interactions significantly benefits learners with low digital proficiency, highlighting the importance of tailored support mechanisms based on learners' digital literacy.

Overall, the reviewed literature underscores the significant potential of AR and AI Companions to enhance motivation, cognitive engagement, and learning outcomes in educational settings. However, the effectiveness of these technologies depends heavily on thoughtful UX design, comprehensive user evaluation, and context-sensitive adaptation of learning support mechanisms.

4. CONCEPTUALIZATION OF THE LEARNING APP

The immersive AR application developed using Unity included functionalities such as interactive 3D visualization of chemical compounds and structures (e.g., water, carbon dioxide, lactose) (Kurzweil 2023). It leveraged the Meta XR All-in-One SDK for AR integration and Convai (Convai 2024) for AI-driven interactions. The UI design included intuitive touch interactions and visualizations (Figure 1) such as the ball-and-stick model (Nkosi and Mnguni 2020), significantly aiding cognitive understanding. The Companion, powered by the Gemini Flash language model[1], provided verbal interaction capabilities, assisting learners in formulating precise queries. Users could interact verbally with the Companion, adding chemical structures via a touch interface, manipulating these structures within the virtual environment, and disposing of unnecessary components using an integrated virtual bin.

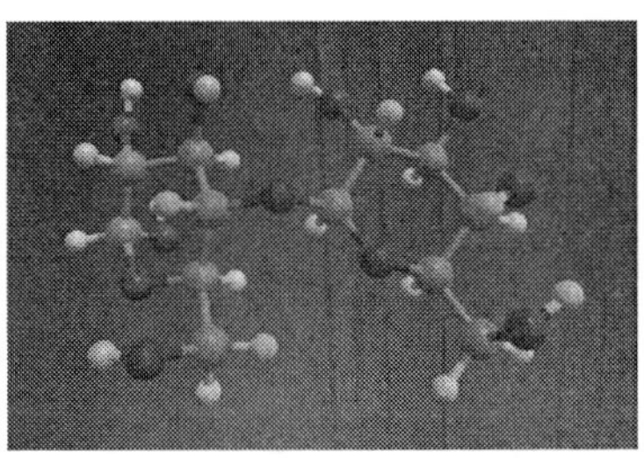

Figure 1. Ball and stick model

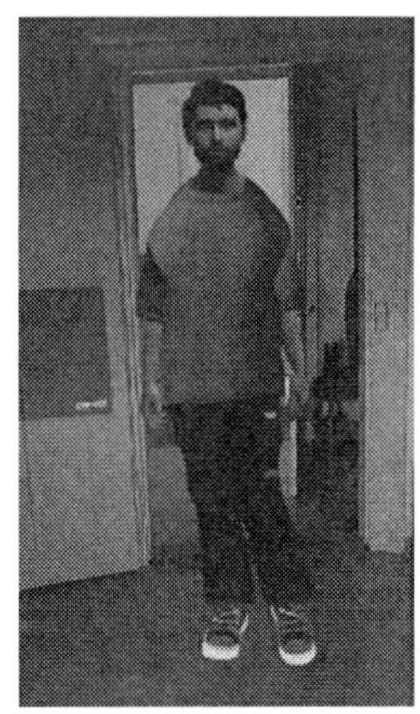

Figure 2. AI Companion

To ensure a design that is conducive to learning, this application deliberately uses a realistic, yet stylistically reduced avatar. Comic-like avatars are often associated with leisure or entertainment in a school context, which can potentially have a negative impact on the learning focus (Zhang, 2023, p. 247). The chosen companion avatar in Figure 2 conveys a certain degree of credibility and social presence without being irritating due to excessive realism. The aim is to draw attention to the learning content.

The technological infrastructure, primarily based on Unity and Convai's integration of Gemini Flash, facilitated the intuitive operation and meaningful educational interactions within the AR environment.

The design decisions also addressed the target group's developmental considerations, such as adjustable interfaces to accommodate varying physical heights among adolescents. Moreover, the Companion featured a clearly defined and visually distinct avatar to foster a sense of social presence and credibility, thus enhancing learner engagement and interaction effectiveness (Chandra et al. 2024; Fidan and Gencel 2022; Tinwell and Sloan 2014).

[1] https://deepmind.google/models/gemini/flash/

5. USER EXPERIENCE STUDY

The laboratory experiment involved 18 students from a rural secondary school in Switzerland. Participants interacted with the AR application in a controlled setting, evaluating both general UX and specific Companion interactions. Results (Bauer and Keller 2025) indicated a positive UX regarding attractiveness and stimulation (Figure *3*). However, Companion interactions showed mixed results, particularly lower scores in transparency and originality (Figure *4*).

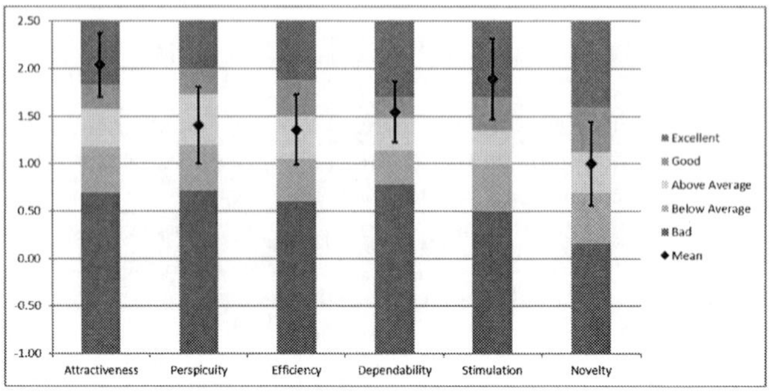

Figure 3. Benchmark without AI companion

Additional data showed the fixed spatial location of the Companion significantly helped inexperienced AR users by providing structure and orientation, although some experienced users preferred more flexibility. Correlation analysis reinforced that perceived helpfulness of the fixed location correlated strongly with willingness to use the application, especially among AR novices.

The detailed evaluation results (Bauer and Keller 2025) from the UEQ indicated that the general UX of the AR application without the Companion received high scores in attractiveness ("excellent") and stimulation ("excellent"), suggesting a strong motivational impact. However, originality scored slightly lower, reflecting the conventional aspects of the design. The pragmatic qualities of efficiency, transparency, and controllability were consistently rated positively, indicating high usability.

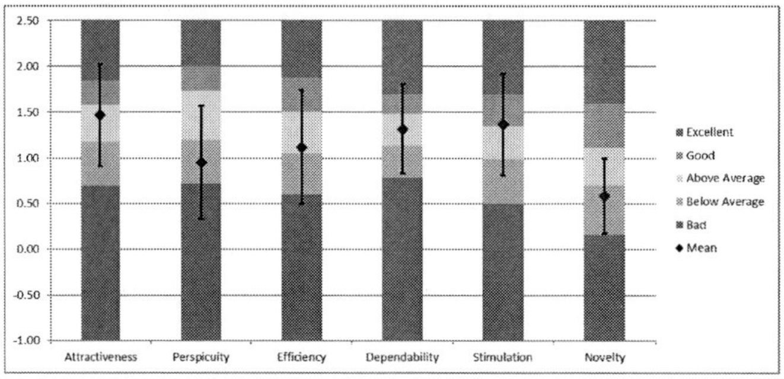

Figure 4. Benchmark for the AI companion

The Companion-specific UEQ results were more nuanced (Figure *4*). The Companion scored highly in attractiveness, showing general approval, but lower in transparency, which indicated potential comprehension or interaction difficulties. Efficiency and controllability had moderate positive ratings, suggesting overall usefulness but with room for improvement. The hedonistic aspects showed a clear divide, with good stimulation scores but relatively low originality scores.

Additional Likert-scale questions (Figure *5*) reinforced these findings, particularly highlighting the beneficial aspect of the Companion's fixed spatial location for inexperienced AR users, facilitating better orientation and structure within the immersive environment. Conversely, experienced AR users expressed a desire for more flexible positioning options, reflecting varying preferences based on user familiarity with AR technology.

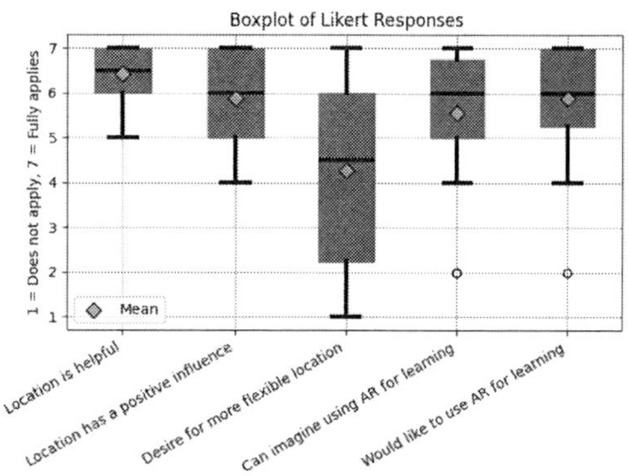

Figure 5. Boxplot of Likert Responses

These detailed results suggest a generally positive perception of the AR application's UX, with specific areas for enhancement, particularly in improving the Companion's transparency and interaction flexibility.

6. CONCLUSION

The immersive AR application was well-received, highlighting its significant potential in educational contexts, particularly concerning motivation, cognitive activation, and active engagement with learning materials. Users reported a highly positive overall user experience, emphasizing the application's attractiveness, usability, and stimulating visual interaction. The application's capability to facilitate independent exploration and modeling chemical structures aligns closely with the competence goals set by Curriculum 21, demonstrating its practical relevance and effectiveness in supporting self-directed learning.

However, while the general UX received high ratings, several critical areas were identified that require targeted improvements. Firstly, transparency and comprehensibility of the AI-driven Companion need enhancement, as users occasionally experienced difficulties in interpreting its functionalities and communications. Secondly, greater flexibility in interactions would significantly improve the Companion's effectiveness, particularly regarding its responsiveness to non-verbal cues and more intuitive dialogue capabilities. Thirdly, more precise thematic limitations for the Companion's responses are necessary to prevent misinterpretations and ensure consistent educational focus.

A crucial recommendation from this study is the incorporation of automatic evaluation mechanisms for chemical models constructed by learners. Implementing such a feature would greatly enhance the educational accuracy of the AR application by promptly identifying and correcting learner-generated errors, thus preventing misconceptions from being reinforced. This automated assessment capability is essential to leverage the application's full potential as an accurate and reliable educational tool.

Future research could explore several promising directions to further advance the development and integration of immersive AR applications within educational settings. Investigating adaptive learning pathways tailored by the AI Companion based on real-time learner interactions could offer insights into personalized learning enhancement. Additionally, examining longitudinal effects of immersive AR use on learner engagement, retention, and academic performance would provide robust evidence of long-term educational benefits. Comparative studies assessing immersive AR against traditional and other digital teaching methods could further validate its efficacy and refine its implementation strategies.

In conclusion, this study affirms immersive AR combined with an AI-driven Companion as a promising educational tool. With targeted improvements and expanded research, this innovative approach holds substantial potential to significantly enhance autonomous learning experiences, promoting deeper understanding and sustained motivation within the structured curriculum framework of Curriculum 21.

REFERENCES

Ahn, J.-W., Chang, M., Watson, P., Tejwani, R., Sundararajan, S., Abuelsaad, T., and Prabhu, S. (2018). "Adaptive Visual Dialog for Intelligent Tutoring Systems." Pp. 413–18 in *Artificial Intelligence in Education*. Vol. 10948, *Lecture Notes in Computer Science*, edited by C. Penstein Rosé, R. Martínez-Maldonado, H. U. Hoppe, R. Luckin, M. Mavrikis, K. Porayska-Pomsta, B. McLaren, and B. Du Boulay. Cham: Springer International Publishing.

Atkinson, R. K., Mayer, R. E., and Merrill, M. M. (2005). "Fostering Social Agency in Multimedia Learning: Examining the Impact of an Animated Agent's Voice." *Contemporary Educational Psychology* 30(1):117–39. doi:10.1016/j.cedpsych.2004.07.001.

Bauer, F., and Keller, T. (2025). "Virtual Tutor UX."

Chandra, R. L., Castermans, K., Berkaoui, D., Querl, P., and Heribert, N. (2024). "Creating Realistic Human Avatars for Social Virtual Environments Using Photographic Inputs." *Journal of Information Systems and Informatics* 6(3):2110–29. doi:10.51519/journalisi.v6i3.842.

Chiu, T. K. F., Moorhouse, B. L., Chai, C. S., and Ismailov, M. (2023). "Teacher Support and Student Motivation to Learn with Artificial Intelligence (AI) Based Chatbot." *Interactive Learning Environments* 1–17. doi:10.1080/10494820.2023.2172044.

Convai. (2024). "Welcome | Documentation." https://docs.convai.com/api-docs.

Criollo-C, S., Abad-Vásquez, D., Martic-Nieto, M., Velásquez-G, F. A., Pérez-Medina, J.-L., and Luján-Mora, S. (2021). "Towards a New Learning Experience through a Mobile Application with Augmented Reality in Engineering Education." *Applied Sciences* 11(11):4921. doi:10.3390/app11114921.

D-EDK. (2016). "Gesamtausgabe Des Lehrplan 21."

Domagk, S. (2010). "Do Pedagogical Agents Facilitate Learner Motivation and Learning Outcomes?: The Role of the Appeal of Agent's Appearance and Voice." *Journal of Media Psychology* 22(2):84–97. doi:10.1027/1864-1105/a000011.

Dreesbach, T., Krutikov, S., Vogel, J., and Thomas, O. (2023). "Metaverse als Business-Chance – Perspektiven aus der Wirtschaftsinformatik." *Wirtschaftsinformatik & Management* 15(3):224–32. doi:10.1365/s35764-023-00469-z.

Fidan, M., and Gencel, N. (2022). "Supporting the Instructional Videos With Chatbot and Peer Feedback Mechanisms in Online Learning: The Effects on Learning Performance and Intrinsic Motivation." *Journal of Educational Computing Research* 60(7):1716–41. doi:10.1177/07356331221077901.

Graser, S., Kirschenlohr, F., and Böhm, S. (2024). "User Experience Evaluation of Augmented Reality: A Systematic Literature Review."

Hammer, F., Egger-Lampl, S., and Möller, S. (2018). "Quality-of-User-Experience: A Position Paper." *Quality and User Experience* 3(1):9. doi:10.1007/s41233-018-0022-0.

Hobert, S., Følstad, A., and Law, E. L.-C. (2023). "Chatbots for Active Learning: A Case of Phishing Email Identification." *International Journal of Human-Computer Studies* 179:103108. doi:10.1016/j.ijhcs.2023.103108.

Huang, W., Jiang, J., King, R. B., and Fryer, L. K. (2025). "Chatbots and Student Motivation: A Scoping Review." *International Journal of Educational Technology in Higher Education* 22(1):26. doi:10.1186/s41239-025-00524-2.

Kurzweil, P. (2023). "Periodensystem der Elemente (PSE)." Pp. 31–43 in *Chemie*. Wiesbaden: Springer Fachmedien Wiesbaden.

Maulana, F. I., Wijaya, I. B. A., Azis, B., Harjo, A. A., Suwondo, L., and Livianty, V. (2022). "Evaluation of User Experience on the Augmented Reality Glovic Cafe and Bakery Jember Application to Maximize User Experience." Pp. 270–74 in *2022 8th International Conference on Education and Technology (ICET)*. Malang, Indonesia: IEEE.

Minge, M., and Thüring, M. (2018). "Hedonic and Pragmatic Halo Effects at Early Stages of User Experience." *International Journal of Human-Computer Studies* 109:13–25. doi:10.1016/j.ijhcs.2017.07.007.

Nkosi, T., and Mnguni, L. (2020). "The Impact of Physical Molecular Models on Students' Visuo-Semiotic Reasoning Skills Related to the Lewis Structure and Ball & Stick Model of Ammonia." *Journal of Baltic Science Education* 19(4):594–604. doi:10.33225/jbse/20.19.594.

Parras-Burgos, D., Fernández-Pacheco, D. G., Polhmann Barbosa, T., Soler-Méndez, M., and Molina-Martínez, J. M. (2020). "An Augmented Reality Tool for Teaching Application in the Agronomy Domain." *Applied Sciences* 10(10):3632. doi:10.3390/app10103632.

Tinwell, A., and Sloan, R. J. S. (2014). "Children's Perception of Uncanny Human-like Virtual Characters." *Computers in Human Behavior* 36:286–96. doi:10.1016/j.chb.2014.03.073.

DIGITAL INNOVATIONS IN EDUCATIONAL TEXTBOOKS

Joan Ann Swanson
Franklin Pierce University, Rindge, New Hampshire, USA

ABSTRACT

This study utilizes a systematic literature review to explore empirical studies focused on innovations embedded in digital textbooks. These revolutionary innovations take many forms and have the potential to enhance student engagement and learning. Accessibility and affordability of digital texts serve to meet many student needs, however, the empirical study of such digital text use with innovations, lags compared to the construction of digital text advancements. Faculty hesitation for digital text use may be due to inexperience and lack of professional development.

KEYWORDS

Digital Textbooks, Innovation, Place-Based Education, Pedagogy

1. INTRODUCTION

While textbooks have been the anchor of both secondary and post-secondary level education (Murray & Pérez, 2011), the age of assigning a print textbook in an educational context may be waning. Digitization of textbooks is increasingly fueled by pedagogical goals. Yet, instructors report students are not reading texts and thus seek more ways to engage students in their course materials (Grönlund et al., 2018). The delivery method of textbooks is being revolutionized with the onset of digital and mobile technologies. Research shows "E-textbooks are advancing from mere portable document format (PDF) versions of hard-copy books to interactive multimedia tools" (Roberts, Benson, & Mills, 2021, p.329). The revolution and adoption of new ideas, such as a digital textbook is often challenging and is considered an innovative practice. Innovation, as defined by Agélii Genlott et al. (2023, p. 4171) "is an idea, or a practice, perceived as new among the adopters", often met with implementation challenges, but has potential to provide transformational impact. This supports Rogers' (2003) theory of innovation which purports that innovation involves relative advantage, compatibility, complexity, trialability and observability within a social system.

While the trend to use digital text is on the rise, there little empirical study on the best pedagogical practices related to digital texts or innovative technologies increasingly incorporated into these texts. This study seeks to survey the empirical study of innovations incorporated in digital texts and address the related pedagogical implications. The research questions that guide this study are: 1) What is the scope of empirical study on digital textbook innovations since 2020, and 2) What are the current digital textbooks trends in educational settings?

2. DIGITAL TEXTBOOK REVOLUTION

The innovations surrounding textbook advancements mirror the drive to have more technology enhanced classrooms which enable increased active, learner-focused, collaborative learning and are dubbed future learning spaces (FLS) (Eyal & Gil, 2020; Hod, 2017). Virtual spaces are now learning environments which can foster a sense of place and community (Aragaki, 2025). The digital textbook enhanced with current innovations is a gateway into virtual space- and place-based learning.

The surge of digital texts is apparent and reflected in less paper in library holdings (Thornton et al., 2024). Projections for digital market publishing indicate an expansion "from \$186.77 billion in 2023 to \$367.19 billion by 2031", and "video to be the fastest growing content type, followed by text and audio" (Fan, 2024 p. 28). Educational textbook companies are quickly responding to the shift in textbook publications. AI has catapulted the speed of the production process in the publication business because of copyediting, glossary-making, proofreading, and indexing have become faster and more efficient with the help of AI-driven automation tools (Fan, 2024). However, along with the tremendous AI advancements also has come some problematic situations such as AI-based plagiarism. "Alarm bells are going off about the use of AI in the publishing community" (Fan, 2024, p.28). Publication of textbooks using AI is newly charted territory, so while educators and publishers are embracing this move forward, they are also desperately trying to grasp AI capabilities, benefits, and dangers.

The move to digital text for an educational institution is reflective of overall system changes. "Scaling up digital innovation requires changes in work processes, investment in technical systems to share across schools, education of teachers, leadership to make sure changes are implemented, monitoring of effects of changes, and corrective action when necessary" (Agélii Genlott et al., 2023, p.4171). While studies show flipped classrooms, integrating multimodal digital resources and multimedia, tend to improve students' experience, engagement and learning performance (Xiao & Adnan, 2022), the systematic change is quite daunting.

2.1 Variability in Digital Textbook Content and Use

There are multiple perspectives as to what defines a digital or e-textbook. Emerging is a generation of collaborative digital textbooks, far different than the digital replicas of existing textbooks (Grönlund et al., 2018). For this study, we utilize Cavanaugh's (2005) definition of e-textbooks as computer technology enabling books to be displayed via text, image, or sound. Recent renditions of digital textbooks have embedded technological innovations to demonstrate or enhance the ability to understand the concepts through animations, simulations, VR, or gamification. Many digital texts are also designed for collaboration and digitally enable involvement between the learners, teachers, and the content (Grönlund et al., 2018).

Digital textbook acceptance and preferences vary. Many college students prefer printed textbooks over electronic (Baron, 2015), however, those preferences can be swayed by discipline and purpose (Swanson et al., 2017). For example, students in health science are increasingly utilizing electronic devices with embedded animations (Gillum et al., 2014). Walston (2007) found students favored print text over e-books but postulates e-book preference for research due to searchability features. Other digital text elements which found favor among student users included personal support functions such as quizzes (Grönlund et al., 2018).

Since students' lives today are immersed in a digital world, there is an assumption that they automatically are adept with the use of anything digital. "Digital natives", those who have grown up in a digital era (Prensky, 2012) are not always knowledgeable about the tools embedded in digital texts (Grönlund et al., 2018) or able to transfer or adapt their technological skills to an educational realm (Swanson et al., 2017).

2.2 Benefits and Drawback of Digitization of Textbooks

Numerous benefits exist with the use of digital textbooks including cost savings, convenience, accessibility, increased motivation, engagement, as well as visual appeal. Some researchers note today's student has an increased expectation for digital content to be available on hand-held devices (Murray & Pérez, 2011, Roberts, Benson, & Mills, 2021). Students note the convenience of using digital texts enables all their books and assignments on one device, thus alleviating losing papers and carrying heavy loads of books and materials (Grönlund et al., 2018).

A systematic literature review to determine elements of usability for digital textbooks (Wan & Mustafa, 2020) revealed usability factors including ease of use, efficiency, accessibility, and engagement, all of which typically increase learning. These usability factors additionally align with Universal Design for Learning principles, known to be effective for inclusive education (Shlasko & Pacheco, 2024). The innovations and technological developments related to digital content have remarkably enhanced access solutions for those with disabilities (e.g., text to speech, eye-tracking navigation, Hover text, and customization of sounds for hearing impaired) (Fan, 2024). Additionally, digital textbooks are often personalized to accommodate students' learning style preferences or instructional needs (Wang & Hartsell, 2017).

Wide variability in text capabilities offered in digital textbooks constitutes a problem when measuring their effectiveness and usability. Textbook digitization covers a continuum of digital content ranging from scanning an article to having all instructional materials digital (Grönlund et al., 2018; Wang & Hartsell, 2017). More recent innovations involve highlighting ability, interactivity, animations, simulations, media and web links. While positive assessments of digital textbook use have occurred, Dobler (2015) also reported some users claim they were distracted while on their device, struggled with eye strain and felt overwhelmed.

Some instructors hesitate to commit to using digital textbooks because they feel inadequately prepared, lack resources, or technical support. Additionally, some teachers use digital text in the same didactic manner as traditional print texts. To further understand the hesitancy pattern to adopt digital technology, Zheng and colleagues (2019), investigated teachers' adoption of digital technology through a longitudinal study involving a digital textbook platform. They found lower levels of use and adoption when there was a lack of experience sharing and peer demonstrations. Modeling and professional development in this realm is essential. Additionally, digital texts aren't always available for specific content (Wang & Hartsell, 2017).

3. METHODS AND RESULTS

This study utilized a systematic literature review to investigate the use of innovative technology in digital textbook publication. This review followed guidelines outlined by the Preferred Reporting Items for Systematic reviews and meta-Analyses (PRISMA), (Page, 2021). The goal of the review was to assess the scope of empirical work related to the latest trends in digital textbook publication.

3.1 Research Question 1: What is the Scope of Empirical Study on Digital Textbook Innovations Since 2020?

Multiple search terminology combinations were utilized which led to the determination that very little empirical research exists on the innovations included in current digital textbook publishing. The most useful approach to finding literature on this topic was to conduct a multi-faceted terminology approach: one search stream leading to another, building a larger pool of information. Artificial intelligence, augmented reality (AR) and virtual reality (VR), were highlighted in the search as well. Multiple database searches were conducted with little yield: search terms included variations and combinations of "textbook publishing" and "augmented reality/AR" and "virtual reality/VR", "mixed reality", and "innovations in digital textbooks", and "digital publishing trends". The final searches utilized the following terminology combination: "interactive digital textbook publishing and innovations", "publishing and augmented reality or AR and virtual reality or VR textbook publishing" and "textbook innovation". In all these search combinations, only one review of innovations in digital textbooks was found and it was an editorial publication, thus not counted in the empirical data (Tan 2024).

The combined yield from the searches provided a scope of articles to review (n=509). Once duplicates were removed the number became (n=438) and the final number after delineation was (n=50). The articles chosen for this study covered a methodological spread consisting of qualitative (n=33), mixed methods (n=4) and quantitative (n=13). One third of the qualitative studies reported on case studies (n=12). To be considered for this study, the articles had to be in the past twenty years (2005-2025) because digital text innovations are a recent development. Inclusion criteria requirements included empirical research reported in English, between 2020 and 2025, and included innovations within the texts. Editorials, book and conference proceedings were excluded.

As studies were determined eligible for the review, they were entered into a database. The following categories were established for each article: author, article title, publication source, date, research type, methodology utilized, and then the main and secondary concepts of the study. Lastly, a list of innovations related to digital textbooks was created which included the following: multimedia content, interactive materials such as quizzes and simulations, annotative/mark-up tools, AI summarizing tools, iBooks replacing lectures, multimedia-enhanced lectures, hyper-textuality, scaffolding and adaptability of materials, linked podcasts, student engagement tracking, linked materials such as illustrations, pronunciations and definitions, and means for collaborative communication. Only eight studies focused on AR or RV, which revealed a significant need for more study.

3.2 Research Question 2: What are the Current Digital Textbooks Trends in Educational Settings?

An analysis of the authors reporting on these empirical studies reveals a vast spread. Only one author was recorded more than once. Additionally, research represented digital textbook use at the higher education level, primary schools and alternative education situations. Countries noted in studies were Canada, China, Ireland, Lithuania, Palestine, United States, South Africa, Sweden, and the United Kingdom. There were 50 publishing outlets represented. Topics spread among disciplinary content (health sciences, history, music, journalism, and literacy). Some recorded innovations were data visualizations, animations, AR, immersive journalism, storytelling, Geographic Information Systems and Technology (GIS&T), interactive multi-media, online quizzes, and embedded gamification. The topic of open textbooks and open educational resources were foci for many articles. Some of these texts highlight concepts related to social justice, affordability, and usability of digital educational materials. Additionally, several articles encourage the use of theoretical perspectives. Diffusion of Innovation Theory was highlighted, as was the Levels of Use (LoU) theory.

4. DISCUSSION AND CONCLUSION

While benefits of digital or e-textbooks are numerous and include features to advance student learning at a reduced economic cost, a wide gap still exists in standardization of format and offerings within e-textbooks. No specific author, research team or research institution is leading the charge in the study of innovations in digital textbooks. The lack of empirical study connected to digital texts innovations is concerning and was a clear limitation in this study. We are living in an age where our daily lives are intricately connected to technological innovations and that should be more significantly reflected in our instructional tools.

One of the greatest impediments to digital textbook adoption is faculty hesitation. More professional development is needed. While it is critical for students to acclimate to the use of new digital tools, it is even more so for faculty (Van Horne et al., 2016).

A new design pattern is needed for the development of technologically innovative educational texts in multiple content areas to enable a learning shift from a static page to multi-modal, technologically based text. More research is also needed to understand the full impact of digital design patterns in the FLS environment. Leveraging new creativity by unleashing technological innovations in the textbook body opens the door to a new brand of place-based education. Within this new pedagogical context, dynamic opportunities avail for instant access to a variety of information sources, increased visualization, animated interactions, and experiential digital practice. VR, AR, and AI-designed simulations meld into new models for student engagement in specially designed content. AR and VR technologies in higher education have limited implementation at this time and are scarce when considered as in conjunction with e-textbooks.

Finally, the challenge for stakeholders, including educational institutions, is to seriously consider the use of digital textbooks and the potential for future learners to take advantage of the advancements. As noted by Wang and Hartsell, (2017). The more publishers understand instructional needs and the factors influencing decision-making for text adoption, students will be better served. Digital tools cannot replace the teacher (Grönlund et al., 2018) but can enhance student engagement and the instructional environment. Student success in a digital world is tied to encouraging faculty to explore these digital tools and publishing companies expanding their development of innovative texts. This study challenges educational researchers to take action. The digital realm is a space in which a new era of place-based education should be considered and studied in more depth.

REFERENCES

Agélii Genlott, A., Grönlund, Å., Viberg, O., & Andersson, A. (2021). Leading dissemination of digital, science-based innovation in school – a case study. Interactive Learning Environments, 31(7), 4171–4181. https://doi.org/10.1080/10494820.2021.1955272

Aragaki, W. (2025). The importance of place-based learning in digital spaces. Digital Promise, https://digitalpromise.org/2025/03/27/the-importance-of-place-based-learning-in-digital-spaces/#:~:text=Places%20are%20sites%20of%20knowledge,How%20does%20this%20translate%20virtually?

Cavanaugh, T. (2005). The digital reader: Using ebooks in k-12 education. Eugene, OR: International Society for Technology in Education (ITSE).

Eyal, L., & Gil, E. (2020). Design patterns for teaching in academic settings in future learning spaces. British Journal of Educational Technology, 51(4), 1061–1077. https://doi-org.ezproxy.franklinpierce.edu/10.1111/bjet.12923

Gillum, S., Garner, M., Walson, D. and Dexter, N. (2014), Interactive E-Textbooks: Millennial Medical Students' Learning Preferences, available at: http://dcdm.doody.com/2014/01/interactive-e-textbooks-millennial-medical-students-learning-preferences/

Grönlund, Å., Wiklund, M. & Böö, R. (2018). No name, no game: Challenges to use of collaborative digital textbooks. Education and Information Technologies, 23, 1359–1375. https://doi.org/10.1007/s10639-017-9669-z

Murray, M., & Pérez, J. (2011). "E-Textbooks Are Coming: Are We Ready?" The Journal of Issues in Informing Science and Information Technology, 8: 49-60. Retrieved from https://www.researchgate.net/publication/292408156_E-Textbooks_Are_Coming_Are_We_Ready

Page, M. J., McKenzie, J. E., Bossuyt, P. M., Boutron, I., Hoffmann, T. C., Mulrow, C. D. et al. (2021). The PRISMA 2020 statement: an updated guideline for reporting systematic reviews. BMJ (372) 71. https://doi:10.1136/bmj.n71

Prensky, M. (2012). The emerging online life of the digital native. In The emerging online life of the digital native (pp. 86-100). Corwin Press, https://doi.org/10.4135/9781483387765.n7

Rogers, E. (2003). Diffusion of innovations. Free Press.

Roberts, K., Benson, A., & Mills, J. (2021). E-Textbook technology: Are instructors using it and what is the impact on student learning? Journal of Research in Innovative Teaching & Learning, 14(3) 329-344. https://doi.org/10.1108/JRIT-04-2021-0028

Shlasko, D. & Pacheco, R. (2024). Applying universal design for learning (UDL) supports inclusive education. Retrieved from https://www.learningforjustice.org/magazine/applying-universal-design-for-learning-udl-supports-inclusive-education.

Swanson, J. A., Renes, S. L., & Strange, A.T. (2017). I might not be as tech as you think: Digital versus print preferences. The14th International Conference on Cognition and Exploratory Learning in the Digital Age (CELDA), Vilamoura, Algarve, Portugal.

Tan, F. (2024). Pathways for innovation development of digital textbooks in higher education in China. Frontiers in Digital Education, 1(3), 267-270.

Thornton, L., Rose-Wiles, L. M., ^ Shea, G. (2024). Will print books survive? Print book circulation and in-house use at a mid-sized academic library. The Journal of Academic Librarianship, 50(6) Article 102979. https://doi.org/10.1016/j.acalib.2024.102979

Van Horne, S., Russell, J.-E. & Schuh, K. L. (2016). The adoption of mark-up tools in an interactive e-textbook reader. Educational Technology Research & Development, 64, 407–433. http://doi.org/10.1007/s11423-016-9425-x

Xiao, J; & Adnan, S. (2022). Flipped anatomy classroom integrating multimodal digital resources shows positive influence upon students' experience and learning performance. Anatomical Sciences Education, 15(6), 1086-1102.

Zheng, L., Gu, X., & Gibson, D. (2019). Understanding the process of teachers' technology adoption with a dynamic analytical model. Interactive Learning Environments, 27(5/6), 726–739. https://doi-org.ezproxy.franklinpierce.edu/10.1080/10494820.2019.1610457

TREASURE: A CUSTOMISABLE SERIOUS GAME FRAMEWORK FOR SCHOOL CULTURE LEARNING

Ziliang Wang and Jingyun Wang
Durham University
Stockton Road, Durham DH1 3LE, United Kingdom

ABSTRACT

This study addresses the challenges faced by foreign guardians in navigating unfamiliar educational practices by proposing a serious game framework called TREASURE (a cusTomisable seRious gamE frAmework for School cUltuRe lEarning). This framework outlines key design principles for serious games aimed at multicultural education, including multilingual support, a customizable user dashboard, gender-specific pronunciations, at least one multimedia-based exploration mode for accessing structured school event information, and a quiz mode with immediate feedback to enhance learning through interaction and visual reinforcement. Moreover, to illustrate the key components and design structure of TREASURE, a prototype game was elaborately implemented.

KEYWORDS

Serious Games, Customizable Game Design, Game-Based Learning, Cross-Cultural Education, School Culture

1. INTRODUCTION

As global mobility increases, more and more families are raising children in countries different from their own. Guardians living abroad often face unfamiliar school cultures that require active parental involvement, such as understanding the significance of school events, appropriate behaviour, or what materials to bring. Even when language is not a barrier, implicit cultural expectations can create confusion and stress for foreign guardians. However, there is a lack of tailored educational support which can greatly enhance foreign guardians' ability to navigate school culture more effectively. Therefore, cross-cultural educational support is urgently needed to bridge these gaps and facilitate smoother cultural integration (Banks and Banks, 2010; Berry, 2005). Studies have shown that when newcomers receive culturally responsive guidance and resources, it significantly enhances both their sense of belonging and their children's academic success (UNESCO, 2016a). However, there remains a lack of readily accessible, tailored materials that can effectively support guardians in understanding the "why" and "how" behind school activities.

To address this, this research proposes to leverage game-based learning which fosters user engagement and facilitates deeper understanding through interactive and adaptive experiences (Plass, Homer, and Kinzer, 2015). Additionally, by integrating real-life scenarios and cultural nuances into the gameplay, serious games can effectively bridge cultural gaps and enhance learners' comprehension of context-specific norms (Tazouti, Boulaknadel, and Fakhri, 2019). This approach is expected to support guardians to better understand the significance of various school events, the required preparations, and their roles in these activities.

Therefore, a cusTomisable seRious gamE frAmework for School cUltuRe lEarning (named TREASURE) is designed to support navigating school-related cultural norms in diverse educational settings. To evaluate the effectiveness of TREASURE, we also implemented a well-designed serious game which consolidates essential information about school culture and events, and will conduct some experiments with foreign guardians to investigate two research questions: (1) How effective is the educational game designed based on TREASURE in enhancing foreign guardians' understanding of cultural practices and school-related knowledge? (2) What specific design improvements can optimise the balance between educational content and engaging gameplay?

This work contributes to the design of the first serious game framework addressing school culture – TREASURE. By leveraging customizable elements, TREASURE accommodates a diverse range of users, including guardians from various cultural and linguistic backgrounds, through interactive learning environment and ensures adaptability by delivering educational content tailored to different learning needs, in contrast to traditional educational games that typically target a single, fixed demographic. Furthermore, the integration of real-life scenarios and cultural nuances enhances its effectiveness in bridging knowledge gaps, fostering deeper engagement, and promoting a better under-standing of cross-cultural educational practices.

2. EDUCATIONAL GAME THEORY AND CUSTOMIZABLE GAME DESIGN PRINCIPLES

The creation of educational games (often referred to as "serious games") is grounded in theories suggesting that digital game-based instruction can outperform traditional teacher-led models in engagement, motivation, and adaptability (Aldrich, 2005; Kapp, 2021). Foundational work highlight that elements such as challenge, curiosity, and control foster intrinsic motivation and active exploration (Malone, 1981; Malone and Lepper, 1987). Game-oriented approaches also embed rapid feedback, clear goals, and interactivity, which encourage deeper cognitive processing (Kapp, 2021). Specifically, educational games allow flexible, modular learning that fits into short time slots, such as commutes or breaks, making them suitable for busy guardians (Prensky, 2003; Hug, 2005). Such micro-learning supported by game mechanics lowers barriers and strengthens retention. In addition, many game-based solutions feature adaptive difficulty, avatar customization, and real-time analytics to sustain motivation for diverse adult learners (Kapp, 2021; Moreno and Mayer, 2007). Such features align with research on autonomy, relevance, and feedback as key to adult learning (Moore and Kearsley, 2011). Overall, educational games offer an effective alternative to traditional teaching by combining rigour with flexible, engaging experiences.

Customisation enhances users' sense of control and identity, boosting immersion, engagement, and motivation (Cuthbert et al., 2019). For learners, two common types of customisation in game are aesthetic customisation (e.g., avatar creation) and functional customisation (e.g., adjusting difficulty or abilities), which enhance control, identity, and motivation (Cuthbert et al., 2019). For instructors, some game frameworks allow fine-grained customisation of learning content and game element placement, helping keep the experience relevant and up to date (Wang et al.,2022). Building on this, our TREASURE framework emphasises customisation and personalisation, enabling users to adapt the game to their own preferences and interests.

3. A CUSTOMIZABLE FRAMEWORK FOR LEARNING SCHOOL CULTURE THROUGH GAME-BASED METHODS

A customizable serious game framework TREASURE is proposed to facilitate cultural understanding of school systems for guardians in cross-cultural contexts. To showcase its practical application, we developed a game prototype that transforms school-related cultural knowledge into an engaging, interactive format.

3.1 The Customizable Game Function Settings

Firstly, to accommodate the diverse linguistic backgrounds of foreign guardians, TREASURE framework suggests serious games should include multiple language options. This multilingual approach seeks to enhance accessibility and inclusivity, ensuring that participants can engage with learning content in a language they are most comfortable with. Research has indicated that offering instruction in one's preferred or native language can significantly boost motivation, comprehension, and overall learning efficacy (UNESCO, 2016b). Upon logging in, users may select their desired language from the main menu as shown in Figure 1(a), granting them immediate access to all core functionalities. By integrating multiple language options, the prototype game appeals to a broader range of cultural and linguistic backgrounds, reducing potential language barriers and enabling users to optimise their learning process.

Secondly, TREASURE framework proposes serious games incorporates a personalised dashboard as shown in Figure 1(b) to demonstrate users' progress and accomplishments. Gamified achievement systems have been proven to effectively boost motivation and long-term user engagement (Hamari and J. Koivisto, 2015). Each user has a dedicated profile where they can track achievements, view in-game statistics, and monitor performance, fostering a sense of achievement and self-efficacy. Additionally, users can personalise their gaming experience further by uploading and updating the profile photo of their avatars. This feature allows users to express their identity and style, which is consistent with the findings that self-expression enhances user satisfaction (Hassenzahl, 2008).

Thirdly, TREASURE framework proposes serious games provide gender specific pronunciation for supporting inclusion learning. Studies indicate that providing users with voice options tailored to their preferences can enhance learning engagement and comfort in interactive settings (Nass and Brave, 2005). In both the learning modes described in section 3.2, users can select their preferred gender-specific pronunciation for vocabulary, audio prompts and instructions, as shown in Figure 1(c). This feature ensures an engaging and personalised learning experience, enhancing overall effectiveness.

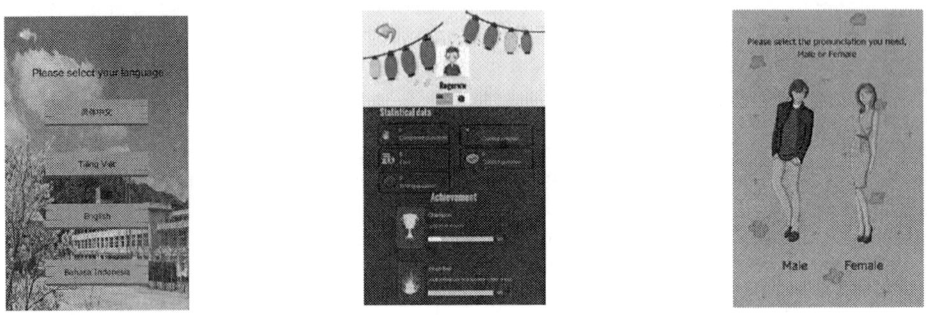

(a) Multiple language support   b)User Dashboard   (c) Gender-specific pronunciation

Figure 1. The customizable game settings

3.2 Multimedia Learning Modes

TREASURE framework proposes serious games should at least provide one multimedia exploring mode for access to well-organized school events, and one quiz mode with immediate feedback tailored to enhance learning through direct interaction and visual aids.

3.2.1 School Culture Exploring mode

This research implemented a prototype system with an exploring mode which allow the users to access to all the events of school organized by term periods. For examples, in Japanese school culture, there are 3 terms: spring/autumn/winter, in total 26 events. Figure 2(a) shows the 12 sprint events, with navigation arrows below to jump to winter or autumn categories. Once a user views an event, its corresponding button turns green to track progress. To ensure the relevance and authenticity of the content, the details regarding school culture was supported by insights and cultural guidance from a local expert.

(a) Main interfaces   (b) School activity   (c) Items to Bring Notes

Figure 2. An example of the culture exploring mode

The following three features are designed to offer practical guidance and cultural insights, enhancing the user's engagement and confidence in navigating school activities effectively. (1) **Activity Pronunciation and Background Explanation**: When users click on a specific school event in one term, they are presented with comprehensive information with a visual list of corresponding items to ensure their understanding and preparedness for the event as demonstrated in Figure 2(b). The detailed background explanation of the activity offers contextual information about its significance within the educational system. Meanwhile, users are greeted with an audio pronunciation of the event's name in Japanese (as shown in the top of Figure 2(b)), allowing them to familiarize themselves with its correct pronunciation. This dual approach to auditory and textual learning aids in language acquisition and cultural understanding. (2) **Special Instructions**: Beneath the activity description, any special instructions or noteworthy points related to the event are highlighted in red. These instructions may include cultural customs, expected behaviours, or specific protocols to be followed during the activity. By providing this information upfront, users can better prepare for the event and avoid potential misunderstandings or faux pas. (3) **Items to Bring and Attention Notes**: In the bottom of Figure 2(b) displays the items that participants need to bring to a specific event. Clicking on any listed visual item expands the display to reveal a larger image of the item as shown in Figure 2(c), accompanied by its name in Japanese and Romanized characters. In additional, its translation in the user's preferred language and a brief explanation is provided, detailing the item's purpose or significance in the activity's context. This feature enables users to understand what to bring and why each item is necessary or advisable.

3.2.2 Quiz Mode

Early feedback from two foreign guardians indicated that the initial exploration-only mode was monotonous, as working through 26 events in one sitting maybe dull and hard to sustain. In response, a quiz-based mode was introduced, providing just-in-time links to relevant content upon incorrect answers, supporting a "learning by doing" approach (Kolb, 1984) to help foreign guardians navigate all the events more effectively. The quiz mode features two primary types of questions aimed at preparing guardians for their active participation in school events. The first type focuses on identifying the items necessary for various school activities as shown in Figure 3(a). The second type in Figure 3(b) concentrates on the expected actions and behaviours during these events. Each question is presented with a set of four picture options, among which only one is correct. Beneath each question, an image of the activity is displayed, accompanied by the activity's name in Japanese (together with the pronunciation in Japanese) and translations (depending on the mother language of the user). This feature is designed to familiarise users with the visual and linguistic aspects of the events, aiding in both language acquisition and cultural comprehension. All these features not only make the game accessible but also engaging, helping them visually connect with the material. Moreover, feedback is delivered immediately after an answer submission. A correct answer triggers a confirmation message (Figure 3(b)). For an incorrect answer, the correct solution is presented alongside a button (Figure 3(a), bottom right) that links to a comprehensive explanation within the exploring mode, illustrated in Figure 2(b).

(a) Things need to bring: feedback to incorrect answer

(b) Things need to do: feedback to correct answer

Figure 3. The examples of questions and two types of feedback in quiz mode

4. CONCLUSION

In this paper, we presented a customizable framework TREASURE aimed at supporting foreign guardians in understanding school-related cultural norms through interactive serious game design. Through the development of a functional game prototype, we demonstrated how educational content can be transformed into an interactive and engaging format to address cross-cultural challenges. The accompanying description in section 3 illustrated the core components and structure of the framework, highlighting its flexibility and potential for adaptation to various cultural contexts.

To answer the two research questions in this research, future work will investigate whether our prototype is a valuable tool in supporting cross-cultural understanding and parental engagement in diverse educational contexts. Firstly, we aim to incorporate representative samples to capture the diversity of foreign guardians' experiences. Secondly, we will include school culture of more countries to widen the diversity of the culture content. Finally, we may refine the game mechanics in TREASURE to make it more engaging, which may involve introducing additional learning modes to increase the game's appeal and minimize the monotony of the learning process.

ACKNOWLEDGEMENT

We acknowledge Dr. Li Xiaoyan (Kyushu University) for her insights into Japanese culture.

REFERENCES

Aldrich, C. (2005). *Learning by Doing: A Comprehensive Guide to Simulations, Computer Games, and Pedagogy in e-Learning and Other Educational Experiences*. Pfeiffer.

Banks, J.A. and Banks C.A.M. (2010). *Multicultural Education: Issues and Perspectives*. 7th ed. Wiley.

Berry, J.W., (2005). Acculturation: Living successfully in two cultures. *International Journal of Intercultural Relations*, 29(6), pp.697–712.

Cuthbert, J. *et al.* (2019). The effects of customisation on player experiences and motivation in a virtual reality game. *Proceedings of the 31st Australian Conference on Human-Computer Interaction (OzCHI 19)*. Australia, pp.221–232.

Hamari, J. and Koivisto, J. (2015). Working out for likes: An empirical study on social influence in exercise gamification. *Computers in Human Behaviour*, 50, pp.333–347. https://doi.org/10.1016/j.chb.2015.04.018

Hassenzahl, M. (2008). User experience (UX): Towards an experiential perspective on product quality. *Proceedings of the 20th Conference of the Computer-Human Interaction Special Interest Group (CHISIG) of Australia on Computer-Human Interaction: Designing for habitus and habitat (OZCHI '08)*. Australia, pp.11–15.

Hug, T. (2005). Micro learning and narration. *Media in Transition (Workshop)*. Innsbruck University Press.

Kapp, K.M. (2012). *The Gamification of Learning and Instruction: Game-Based Methods and Strategies for Training and Education*. Pfeiffer.

Kolb, D.A. (1984). *Experiential Learning: Experience as the Source of Learning and Development*. Prentice Hall.

Malone, T.W. (1981). Toward a theory of intrinsically motivating instruction. *Cognitive Science*, 5(4), pp.333–369.

Malone, T.W. and Lepper, M.R. (1987). Making learning fun: A taxonomy of intrinsic motivations for learning. *Aptitude, Learning and Instruction*, 3, pp.223–253.

Moreno, R. and Mayer, R.E. (2007). Interactive multimodal learning environments. *Educational Psychology Review*, 19(3), pp.309–326.

Moore M.G. and Kearsley G., *Distance Education: A Systems View of Online Learning*, 3rd ed., Cengage Learning, 2011.

Nass, C. and Brave, S. (2005). *Wired for Speech: How Voice Activates and Advances the Human-Computer Relationship*. MIT Press.

Plass, J.L. et al. (2015). Foundations of game-based learning. *Educational Psychologist*, 50(4), pp.258–283. https://doi.org/10.1080/00461520.2015.1122533

Prensky, M., (2003). Digital game-based learning. *Computers in Entertainment (CIE)*, 1(1), pp.21.

Tazouti, Y., Boulaknadel S., and Fakhri Y. (2019). ImALeG: A serious game for Amazigh language learning. *International Journal of Emerging Technologies in Learning (iJET)*, 14(12), pp.121–133. https://doi.org/10.3991/ijet.v14i12.10991

UNESCO, (2016a). *Global education monitoring report 2016: Education for people and planet*. https://en.unesco.org/gem-report/report/2016/education-people-and-planet (accessed Apr. 12, 2025).

UNESCO, (2016b*). If you don't understand, how can you learn?* Global Education Monitoring Report Policy Paper, No. 24.

Wang, J., Hodgson, R. and Cristea, A.I. (2022). *MEMORABLE:* A multi-player customisable serious game framework for cyber-security learning. *In: S. Crossley and E. Popescu, eds. Intelligent Tutoring Systems. Cham: Springer*, pp.313–322. https://doi.org/10.1007/978-3-031-09680-8_29

A CASE REPORT ON THE IMPLEMENTATION OF A WEBXR PLATFORM FOR TEACHING AND LEARNING IN THE CHINESE LANGUAGE ENHANCEMENT PROGRAMME (HKU)

Ming Wai Chung* and Chi Ming Chan*
CLEP, School of Chinese, The University of Hong Kong, Hong Kong
**Dr.*

ABSTRACT

The WebXR technology creates a dynamic, accessible, and engaging learning environment that enhances students' educational experiences. It is adopted by educational institutes worldwide. This paper is a case report on the establishment and deployment of a WebXR platform by the Chinese Language Enhancement Programme (CLEP) at the University of Hong Kong, aims at improving students' proficiency in Chinese language communication through immersive virtual reality (VR) experiences. We explore the integration of generative AI-powered avatars that promote interactive learning and deliver real-time feedback on language usage and presentation skills, as well as the pedagogical impacts of this technology and discuss challenges encountered during implementation.

KEYWORDS

Virtual Realty(VR), WebXR, Immersive Learning, AI-powered Avatar, Pedagogy Shift

1. INTRODUCTION

In the past decades, VR technology has been integrated into various aspects of life. (Onyesolu, M. O., & Eze, F. U., 2011) From the simple augmented reality (AR) which used QR codes to trigger videos or 3D animations (Kan, T. W., Teng, C. H., & Chen, M. Y., 2011), to the use of optical devices to offer immersive environments for users to engage in exciting novel scenarios and activities. (Rubio-Tamayo, J. L., Gertrudix Barrio, M., & García, F., 2017) VR technology has been widely adopted in game industry, products sale, and in the educational sector. Multiple research studies have shown the use of VR in classroom and in self-learning. (Young, G. W., Stehle, S., Walsh, B. Y., & Tiri, E., 2020; Geng, J., & Wu, X., 2021) This technology promotes engaging, multi-channel learning experiences, and gives teachers and students opportunities to interact with the world in a different way. (Xin, Y., 2022)

VR technology also changes our perception of teaching and learning by re-shaping the role of teachers and learners. (KAHE, C., 2025, p.42; Oliveira, A., Feyzi Behnagh, R., Ni, L., Mohsinah, A. A., Burgess, K. J., & Guo, L., 2019; Mystakidis, S., Berki, E., & Valtanen, J. P., 2021) This innovative experience transformed the traditional pathways of knowledge dissemination and the methods of understanding and constructing knowledge. (Strielkowski, W., Grebennikova, V., Lisovskiy, A., Rakhimova, G., & Vasileva, T., 2025). This transformation brings new challenges to teachers, urging them to adapt new methods in teaching and preparation of teaching materials and activities. (Harron, J. R., & Mason, L. I. N. D. S. E. Y., 2020; Graeske, C., & Sjöberg, S. A., 2021) To obtain effective teaching and learning results, tools like the Meta Quest or Apple Vision that provides rich immersive experiences are good choice. However, these devices are costly, making it a barrier for many schools. In contrast, WebXR is a technology that allows users to create and access virtual reality (VR) and mixed reality (MR) experiences directly in web browsers via smartphones, tablets, and computers, without the need for app downloads, thus makes it a more cost-effective way to set up a VR environment.

The Chinese Language Enhancement Programme (CLEP) of the University of Hong Kong aims at enhancing students' Chinese language communication proficiency through latest technology. Starting from 2022, CLEP has used WebXR technology to develop a virtual learning platform for its courses. In this paper, we will share our experiences on the building and deployment of WebXR technology for teaching and learning.

2. OBJECTIVES AND FEATURES OF CLEP'S WEBXR PLATFORM

Our WebXR platform aims at enhancing students' language skills through immersive virtual reality experiences. We have designed and created several virtual classrooms for students to have their language classes in VR environments.

Figure 1. VR classrooms

The WebXR platform also provides an interactive learning environment with the support of generative AI. We have introduced generative AI-powered avatars on the platform to help students engage more deeply. These avatars served as supportive companions for students to learn Chinese language knowledge and practice various communication skills. For example, we have created a virtual dentist clinic with a virtual dentist for dental students to practice verbal communication skills with patients.

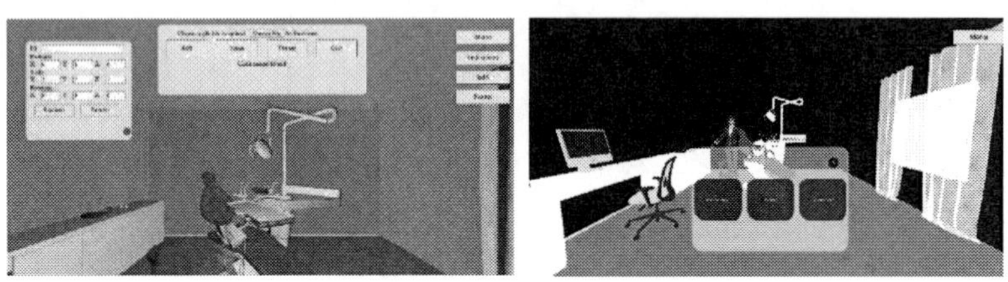

Figure 2. VR dental clinic with AI-powered avatar

The WebXR platform can immediately assess students' performance in dialogues, interviews, and speeches, and give useful feedback. The AI-powered avatars can deliver instant evaluations and feedback on students' language usage and presentation skills. This instant feedback helps students understand their performances in an effective way and in time so they can quickly refine their verbal communication skills. This feature ensures that every student receives timely support.

Figure 3. Example of real time feedback

3. PEDAGOGICAL IMPACTS

CLEP's implementation of the AI-powered WebXR platform sets a new standard for collaboration across disciplines. Students can strengthen their subject-related Chinese language skills through hands-on practice which is not available in the past. The platform's features of student-designed virtual learning spaces, real-time feedback, and self-training rooms, not only improve the learning experience but also extend its relevance to various academic and professional areas. The immersive VR simulations can enhance discipline-specific learning outcomes by allowing the integration into fields like healthcare, business, and cultural studies.

Over the past three years, course materials have had 49,550 views from 1,255 students across 12 fully operational virtual rooms. In a user survey conducted in 2025 regarding the benefits of the VCLLC (Virtual Chinese Language Learning Centre) WebXR virtual learning environment, 89% of students cited quick access to information and resources as a major advantage. Furthermore, 72% acknowledged the platform's ability to enhance learning and comprehension of complex topics through its immersive and interactive features.

For students, the WebXR classroom also provides exciting new experiences. In our school focus interview, one student said, " He found that WebXR to be very interesting because it offers an immersive experience that makes them feel as if they are in a classroom, watching Dr. Chan or other professors teaching. This is like the concept of online courses but much more engaging and interesting than simply watching a video."

4. CHALLENGES

Several challenges related to adoption, integration, scalability, data security, access to VR technology, and server capacity during the deployment of the VR platform are needed to solve. The first challenge is the server's performance issues caused by increased number of users. Starting from merely 100 students at the pilot stage to the full-scale support of over 3000 students per year, we have to upgrade the server infrastructure to maximize the capacity of usage and conduct regular monitoring to minimize the operational errors of the platform. A dedicated IT officer is also crucial for managing server operations, troubleshooting technical problems, and ensuring system reliability.

We also need to address teachers' hesitation and unfamiliarity with AI tools. To help them gain confidence and encourage their engagement, we need to offer comprehensive workshops, hands-on training, user-friendly guides, and ongoing feedback mechanisms.

The protection of student data and prevention of unauthorized access to students' work are top priorities in our IT policy. However, the frequent changes in security access or update of existing systems may cause integration challenges, such as login or document embedding issues. Therefore, it is important to collaborate with IT Service department to work out an effective solution to enact the easy access of the platform while implementing strict security protocols to safeguard user information.

5. CONCLUSION

CLEP's WebXR platform attempts to build a dynamic VR environment that enhanced students learning experiences across diverse disciplines. The development of the WebXR-based teaching and learning environment with AI-powered avatars is a significant advancement in integrating technology into our courses. It shows our efforts in adopting immersive virtual reality and generative AI to enhance language proficiency, giving students a self-directed learning environment that transcends traditional boundaries.

As shown in the user survey, 90% of students expressed support for integrating AI language models into the VCLLC WebXR virtual learning environment. This strong endorsement highlights the increasing demand for AI-driven tools to enhance the learning experience. We are soon set to develop the next generation of a virtual AI environment, where students can directly interact with AI agents through both text and voice. This feature is designed to provide personalized assistance, answer questions in real-time, and offer tailored learning support. By incorporating advanced AI capabilities, the platform will foster a more dynamic and interactive educational experience, helping students engage more effectively with their studies. This innovation will enrich students' learning journeys across various disciplines.

REFERENCES

Bodorik P. et al. (1991). Deciding to Correct Distributed Query Processing. *In IEEE Transactions on Data and Knowledge Engineering*, Vol. 4, No. 3, pp 253-265.

Graeske, C., & Sjöberg, S. A. (2021). VR-Technology in Teaching: Opportunities and Challenges. *International Education Studies*, *14*(8), 76-83. Source: https://eric.ed.gov/?id=EJ1309404

Geng, J., & Wu, X. (2021). Application of virtual reality technology in university education. In *2021 2nd International Conference on Artificial Intelligence and Education (ICAIE)*, IEEE, pp. 472-475.

Harron, J. R.,et al. (2020). Creating virtual spaces: Using eXtended reality and transformative technologies to prepare teachers to thrive in an ever-changing world. *What teacher educators should have learned from*, 213-228. Source: https://www.learntechlib.org/primary/p/219088/ebook_219088.pdf#page=214

KAHE, C. (2025). Education at Crossroads: A Paradigm Shift and Emerging Methodologies in Teaching-Learning. *Emerging Methodologies In Teaching And Learning: A Contemporary Overview*. P.37-45.

Kan, T. W. et al. (2011). QR code based augmented reality applications. In *Handbook of augmented reality* (pp. 339-354). New York, NY: Springer New York.

Mystakidis, S. et al. (2021). Deep and meaningful e-learning with social virtual reality environments in higher education: A systematic literature review. *Applied Sciences*, *11*(5), 2412. Source: https://www.mdpi.com/2076-3417/11/5/2412/pdf?version=1615280078

Oliveira, A. et al. (2019). Emerging technologies as pedagogical tools for teaching and learning science: A literature review. *Human Behavior and Emerging Technologies*, *1*(2), 149-160.

Onyesolu, M. O. et al. (2011). Understanding virtual reality technology: advances and applications. *Adv. Comput. Sci. Eng*, *1*, 53-70.

Rubio-Tamayo, J. L.,.et al. (2017). Immersive environments and virtual reality: Systematic review and advances in communication, interaction and simulation. *Multimodal technologies and interaction*, *1*(4), 21.

Strielkowski, W., Grebennikova, V., Lisovskiy, A., Rakhimova, G., & Vasileva, T. (2025). AI-driven adaptive learning for sustainable educational transformation. *Sustainable Development*, *33*(2), 1921-1947. Source: https://onlinelibrary.wiley.com/doi/full/10.1002/sd.3221

Xin, Y. (2022). Influence of learning engagement on learning effect under a virtual reality (VR) environment. *International Journal of Emerging Technologies in Learning (iJET)*, *17*(5), 226-237.

Young, G. W. et al. (2020). Exploring virtual reality in the higher education classroom: Using VR to build knowledge and understanding. *Journal of Universal Computer Science*, (8), 904-928.

EASING TECHNOSTRESS AMONG TEACHERS: WHAT FACTORS MAKE A DIFFERENCE?

Maria Grazia Diana[1], Pierpaolo Zivi[2], Gianluca Malatesta[3],
Maria Lidia Mascia[4], Cristina Cabras[1], Alberto Di Domenico[3], Massimiliano Palmiero[2]
and Maria Pietronilla Penna[1]
[1]*Department of Pedagogy, Psychology, Philosophy, University of Cagliari, Cagliari, Italy*
[2]*Department of Communication Sciences, University of Teramo, Teramo, Italy*
[3]*Department of Psychology, University "G. D'Annuzio" of Chieti-Pescara, Chieti, Italy*
[4]*Department of History, Human Sciences and Education, University of Sassari, Sassari, Italy*

ABSTRACT

The increasing use of ICT in education has heightened technostress among teachers, affecting their well-being and performance. This study examined whether cognitive emotion regulation and divergent thinking predict technostress in 322 Italian secondary school teachers. Using the Technostress Creator Scale, Cognitive Emotion Regulation Questionnaire, and Alternative Uses Task, hierarchical regression analyses showed that maladaptive strategies were linked to higher technostress (overload, invasion, complexity), while adaptive strategies reduced techno-complexity. Unexpectedly, higher divergent thinking was associated with greater techno-invasion, possibly due to overconfidence and increased tech use. These results highlight the need for interventions that reduce maladaptive coping and guide creative potential. To mitigate technostress, schools should implement training programs aimed at fostering adaptive emotional regulation and encouraging mindful technology use, especially among teachers characterized by high divergent thinking. Furthermore, establishing support networks may promote the exchange of effective strategies and contribute to improved well-being.

KEYWORDS

Technostress, Cognitive Emotion Regulation, Divergent Thinking

1. INTRODUCTION

Recent technological advancements, accelerated by the COVID-19 pandemic, have profoundly transformed the educational sector, leading to increased workload and a blurring of personal and professional boundaries for teachers (Korzynski et al., 2021; Wang et al., 2024; Bruggeman et al., 2022). Above all the Italian educational system, especially in more recent years, has undergone a gradual but significant digital transformation. Ministerial initiatives and collaborative school networks have actively promoted technology-enhanced teaching practices and specific training, marking a clear step forward in educational innovation. Despite these systematic efforts, research consistently reports a gap between teachers' recognition of the pedagogical value of digital technologies and their self-assessed ability to use them effectively (Toto & Limone, 2021; Xu, 2022; Cataudella et al., 2024).

This pervasive integration of digital technologies has contributed to the rise of technostress, defined as psychological stress resulting from prolonged or problematic use of ICT, manifesting in anxiety, frustration, and difficulty adapting to technological changes—ultimately impairing teachers' well-being and job performance (Tacy, 2016; Cuadrado et al., 2024; Cataudella et al., 2024; Tarafdar et al., 2019; Dragano & Lunau, 2020). Tarafdar and colleagues (2007) identified five core technostress creators: techno-overload (pressure to work faster/longer), techno-invasion (blurring of work-life boundaries), techno-complexity (difficulty learning new technologies), techno-insecurity (fear of being replaced), and techno-uncertainty (constant changes). Given the already high-stress nature of teaching, educators are particularly susceptible to these pressures, which have been linked to reduced job satisfaction (Ogakwu et al., 2024; Chou & Chou, 2021).

While research has increasingly explored both environmental and individual determinants of technostress, factors like age, gender, and education show inconsistent associations (Bruggeman et al., 2022; Soares & Nursalam, 2023; Facchini & Sala, 2019; Rašticová et al., 2025; Marchiori et al., 2019; La Torre et al., 2020). According to the transactional theory of stress, stress emerges from a perceived imbalance between environmental demands and an individual's coping capacity, with cognitive appraisal and coping mechanisms serving as key mediators of this process (Lazarus & Folkman, 1987). Scholars have further distinguished between cognitive and behavioral dimensions of emotion regulation, which encompass conscious and unconscious processes that modulate emotional responses to specific events (Garnefski, Kraaij, & Spinhoven, 2001; Campbell-Sills & Barlow, 2007). The cognitive dimension—especially relevant when behavioral responses are constrained, as with ICT-related stressors—facilitates awareness and reappraisal of emotional reactions before acting (Garnefski, Kraaij, & Spinhoven, 2001).

In line with Lazarus' transactional theory, cognitive appraisal significantly influences whether stressors are perceived as challenges or threats, which in turn affects adaptive responses and the stimulation of creative thinking. Creativity, often operationalized as divergent thinking—i.e., the capacity to generate multiple, novel solutions to open-ended problems—is linked to positive psychological outcomes such as well-being, resilience, and enhanced cognitive functioning (Runco & Acar, 2012; Palmiero et al., 2019; Palmiero et al., 2020; Mendes et al., 2020). Thus, creativity may function both as an outcome of effective coping and as a resource that enables individuals to reframe stressors and maintain psychological flexibility.

This study examines cognitive factors underlying technostress in secondary school teachers, aiming to identify vulnerability and resilience profiles to inform targeted support strategies.

H1: Divergent thinking and cognitive emotion regulation will significantly predict levels of technostress among secondary school teachers.

2. Methods

2.1 Procedure

A cross-sectional online survey on technostress was conducted among secondary school teachers using non-probabilistic snowball sampling. Informed consent was obtained from all participants prior to their participation in the study. The questionnaire, distributed via various digital and institutional channels, was part of a broader research project. The study was carried out in accordance with the ethical principles of the Declaration of Helsinki and adhered to the Ethical Code of the Italian Association of Psychology (AIP). Ethical approval was obtained from the Institutional Review Board of Psychology (IRBP) at the Department of Psychology, University 'G. D'Annunzio' of Chieti-Pescara (Protocol No. 24026, approved on November 22, 2024). This study is part of a broader research project (Zivi et al. 2025).

2.2 Participants

The sample is composed by 325 participants, 322 teachers (mean age 44.3 years, SD = 9.8, range 24–66) identifying as male or female were included in the analysis.

2.3 Measures

(1) Participants completed a socio-demographic questionnaire collecting personal and professional data.

(2) The Technostress Creators Scale (TCS; Tarafdar et al., 2007) measured five technostress dimensions on a 5-point Likert scale. In this study we focused on three specific dimensions: techno-overload; techno-invasion and techno-complexity. The average score for each of these technostress creators was computed. Cronbach's Alpha for the three subscales ranged from .801 to .875, which are commonly considered as indicating high good to high internal consistency in this sample.

(3) The Italian version of the CERQ-Short (Mannila et al., 2018) assessed adaptive and maladaptive emotion regulation strategies. Strategies were grouped into adaptive (e.g., positive reappraisal, planning) and maladaptive (e.g., rumination, catastrophizing) categories. The average score for each of these two strategies was computed. Cronbach's Alpha for CERQ-A was 0.769 and for CERQ-M was 0.758, indicating also in this case a high internal consistency in this sample.

(4) The Italian version of the Alternative Uses Task (Sprini & Tomasello, 1989) evaluated verbal and visual divergent thinking. It allows collecting fluency (the number of relevant ideas), flexibility (the number of categories encompassing the relevant ideas) and originality (the quality of ideas). The inter-rater correlations (intra-class coefficient, absolute agreement) were computed for each parameter. Then, the scores for fluency, flexibility and originality are defined by the average of the ratings of the three evaluators. This evaluation method has shown satisfactory reliability, with Cronbach's alpha between .82 and .99 and ICC between .77 and .99.

3. RESULTS

A hierarchical linear regression analysis was performed to examine whether cognitive emotion regulation and divergent thinking predict perceived technostress among secondary school teachers. In Model 1, socio-demographic variables were entered, including age, gender, and educational level. Model 2 introduced cognitive emotion regulation, differentiating between its adaptive (CERQa) and maladaptive (CERQm) components. Finally, Model 3 incorporated divergent thinking.

Techno-overload

Model 1 was not statistically significant, $F(3, 318) = 0.14$, $p = .934$, $R^2 = .001$; Adjusted $R^2 = -.008$. With the inclusion of Model 2, the overall model became significant, $F(5, 316) = 3.38$, $p = .005$, $R^2 = .051$; Adjusted $R^2 = .036$; $\Delta R^2 = .049$, $F(2, 316) = 8.23$, $p < .001$. Only CERQm was a significant predictor ($\beta = .203$, $p < .001$). After adding Model 3, the overall model remained significant, $F(6, 315) = 3.48$, $p = .002$, $R^2 = .062$; Adjusted $R^2 = .044$; $\Delta R^2 = .011$, $F(1, 315) = 3.84$, $p = .051$. CERQm remained a significant predictor ($\beta = .199$, $p < .001$).

Techno-invasion

Model 1 was not statistically significant, $F(3, 318) = 1.37$, $p = .252$, $R^2 = .013$; Adjusted $R^2 = .003$.

With the addition of Model 2, the overall model became significant, $F(5, 316) = 5.51$, $p < .001$, $R^2 = .080$; Adjusted $R^2 = .066$; $\Delta R^2 = .067$, $F(2, 316) = 11.58$, $p < .001$. Only CERQm was a significant predictor ($\beta = .261$, $p < .001$). Model 3 remained significant, $F(6, 315) = 5.62$, $p < .001$, $R^2 = .096$; Adjusted $R^2 = .079$; $\Delta R^2 = .016$, $F(1, 315) = 5.74$, $p = .017$. However, both CERQm ($\beta = .256$, $p < .001$) and divergent thinking ($\beta = .052$, $p = .017$) were significant predictors.

Techno-complexity

Model 1 was statistically significant, $F(3, 318) = 8.04$, $p < .001$, $R^2 = .070$; Adjusted $R^2 = .062$. Age ($\beta = .017$, $p = .003$) educational attainment ($\beta = -.164$, $p = .009$), and gender ($\beta = -.395$, p = .008) were significant predictors. Model 2 remained significant, $F(5, 316) = 12.67$, $p < .001$, $R^2 = .167$; Adjusted $R^2 = .154$; $\Delta R^2 = .096$, $F(2, 316) = 18.31$, $p < .001$. Significant predictors included: age ($\beta = .023$, $p < .001$), educational attainment ($\beta = -.149$, $p = .013$), gender ($\beta = -.332$, $p = .018$), CERQa ($\beta = -.158$, $p = .002$), and CERQm ($\beta = .273$, $p < .001$). Model 3 remained significant, $F(6, 315) = 10.68$, $p < .001$, $R^2 = .169$; Adjusted $R^2 = .153$; $\Delta R^2 = .002$, $F(1, 315) = 0.78$, $p = .376$. The same predictors remained significant: age ($\beta = .023$, $p < .001$), educational attainment ($\beta = -.139$, $p = .023$), gender ($\beta = -.338$, $p = .017$), CERQa ($\beta = -.158$, $p = .002$), and CERQm ($\beta = .2754$, $p < .001$).

No statistically significant models were found for techno-uncertainty and techno-insecurity. A forest plot summarizing the significant predictors of Model 3 for each technostress creator is reported in Figure 1.

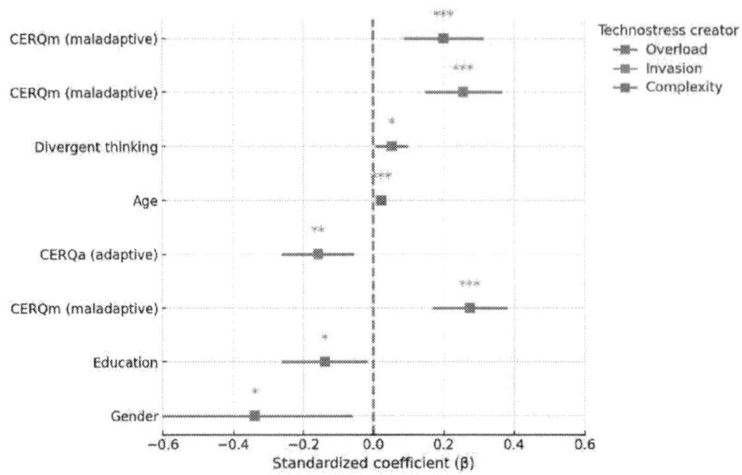

Figure 1. Model 3: significant predictors of technostress. Forest plot of standardized coefficients (β) with 95% CIs. Squares are point estimates; the vertical line marks β=0. Colors denote Overload, Invasion, and Complexity. Only predictors with $p<.05$ are shown. Asterisks: * $p<.05$; ** $p<.01$; *** $p<.001$

4. DISCUSSION

The findings offer important insights into the psychological mechanisms underlying technostress among secondary school teachers, underscoring the roles of cognitive emotion regulation and divergent thinking. Maladaptive strategies (e.g., rumination, catastrophizing) were positively associated with all dimensions of technostress, suggesting that ineffective emotional coping increases vulnerability to digital demands. Conversely, adaptive strategies (e.g., reappraisal, planning) negatively predicted techno-complexity, indicating a protective effect through enhanced coping and self-efficacy. These results are consistent with previous research (Gaudioso et al., 2024; Levante et al., 2025). A novel and unexpected result emerged in the positive association between divergent thinking and techno-invasion. While creativity is often regarded as a resource for psychological well-being (Palmiero et al., 2020; Mendes et al., 2020), in this context it may foster greater technological engagement and blurred boundaries, thereby amplifying stress. This finding suggests that creativity, when insufficiently regulated, may exert unintended adverse effects.

These results call for a more nuanced understanding of creativity's role in digital contexts and highlight the importance of promoting adaptive coping strategies. Schools and school leaders should implement targeted training programs aimed at enhancing teachers' emotional regulation strategies, fostering the adoption of adaptive approaches to reduce technostress. Specifically, psychological support interventions and dedicated workshops on managing technology-related stress can assist teachers in recognizing and adjusting maladaptive strategies, thereby alleviating feelings of overload, invasion, and perceived complexity associated with technology use. Moreover, given the unexpected link between divergent thinking and the phenomenon of techno-invasion, it is essential to provide clear guidelines and training aimed at promoting a mindful and balanced use of digital tools. This would help prevent overconfidence that could lead to compulsive or inappropriate use of technology. The guidance of experienced coaches or mentors could further support a sustainable creative orientation, turning innovative potential into a positive resource without increasing the technological burden. Finally, schools should consider creating spaces for peer exchange and collaboration among teachers, to encourage mutual support and the sharing of best practices in managing technostress. Such initiatives would contribute to fostering a more positive and sustainable working environment.

5. CONCLUSION

In conclusion, this study underscores the critical role of individual psychological resources in shaping secondary school teachers' experiences of technostress. Maladaptive forms of emotion regulation were found to heighten vulnerability across all dimensions of technostress, highlighting the detrimental impact of ineffective coping on teachers' capacity to manage digital demands. Conversely, adaptive strategies, particularly reappraisal and planning, emerged as protective factors that mitigate perceptions of techno-complexity, pointing to the value of fostering emotional resilience and self-efficacy in digital contexts. Notably, the finding that divergent thinking was positively associated with techno-invasion adds a novel dimension to the literature, suggesting that creativity, while generally regarded as a psychological asset, can under certain circumstances contribute to excessive technology engagement and blurred work–life boundaries. Taken together, these findings emphasize the need for a more nuanced understanding of creativity's dual role in digitalized educational environments, functioning both as a potential resource and as a possible risk factor. From an applied perspective, teacher training and professional development programs should prioritize the cultivation of adaptive coping strategies and emotional regulation skills, while also supporting creativity in ways that acknowledge and safeguard against its possible unintended consequences.

Several limitations warrant consideration. The sample lacked demographic balance, and the cross-sectional design precludes conclusions regarding changes over time or causal relationships.

Future research should build upon these results by examining the mechanisms through which creativity exerts its protective or detrimental effects, with particular attention to mediators such as overconfidence, boundary management, and digital self-regulation. Longitudinal and experimental designs will be especially valuable for disentangling causal pathways and for assessing changes in technostress responses over time. Expanding demographic diversity in future samples will further enhance the generalizability of findings and provide a more comprehensive picture of how psychological resources interact with the challenges of digitalization in education. Research of this kind aims not only to deepen our understanding of the factors that can make the relationship between teachers and technology problematic, but also to inform the design of technological solutions developed through multidisciplinary collaboration. By integrating principles of usability and user-centered design, such efforts can help normalize the everyday use of digital tools in educational settings while minimizing the stress associated with their adoption.

ACKNOWLEDGEMENTS

This study was funded by the Ministry of University and Research (MUR) of Italy – Prin 2022 PNRR (p202259mea_01).

REFERENCES

Bruggeman, B., Garone, A., Struyven, K., Pynoo, B., & Tondeur, J. (2022). Exploring university teachers' online education during COVID-19: Tensions between enthusiasm and stress. Computers and Education Open, 3, 100095. https://doi.org/10.1016/j.caeo.2022.100095

Campbell-Sills, L. & Barlow, D. H. (2007). Incorporating Emotion Regulation into Conceptualizations and Treatments of Anxiety and Mood Disorders. in Handbook of emotion regulation 542–559 (The Guilford Press, New York, NY, US, 2007)

Cataudella, S., Mascia, M. L., Agus, M., Ifenthaler, D., Tomczyk, Ł., &Penna, M. P. (2024). A pilot study on individual and contextual factors influencing teachers' digitalisation process. Contemporary Educational Technology, 16. https://doi.org/10.30935/cedtech/15189

Chou, H. L., & Chou, C. (2021). A multigroup analysis of factors underlying teachers' technostress and their continuance intention toward online teaching. Computers and Education, 175. https://doi.org/10.1016/j.compedu.2021.104335

Cuadrado, D., Otero, I., Martínez, A., París, T., & Moscoso, S. (2024). Predicting technostress: The Big Five model of personality and subjective well-being. PloS ONE, 19. https://doi.org/10.1371/journal.pone.0313247

Dragano, N., & Lunau, T. (2020). Technostress at work and mental health: and research results. In Current Opinion in Psychiatry (Vol. 33, pp. 407–413). Lippincott Williams and Wilkins.https://doi.org/10.1097/YCO.0000000000000613

Facchini, C., & Sala, E. (2019). Anziani e nuove tecnologie. Rischi e opportunità. https://doi.org/10.1447/95862

Garnefski, N., Kraaij, V. & Spinhoven, P. (2001). Negative life events, cognitive emotion regulation and emotional problems. Personal. Individ. Differ. 30, 1311–1327 (2001)

Gaudioso, F., Turel, O. & Galimberti, C. (2017). The mediating roles of strain facets and coping strategies in translating techno-stressors into adverse job outcomes. Comput. Hum. Behav. 69, 189–196. https://doi.org/10.1016/j.chb.2016.12.041

Korzynski, P., Rook, C., Florent Treacy, E., & Kets de Vries, M. (2021). The impact of self-esteem, conscientiousness and pseudo-personality on technostress. Internet Research, 31, 59–79. https://doi.org/10.1108/INTR-03-2020-0141

La Torre, G., De Leonardis, V., & Chiappetta, M. (2020). Technostress: how does it affect the productivity and life of an individual? Results of an observational study.Public Health, 189, 60–65. https://doi.org/10.1016/j.puhe.2020.09.013

Lazarus, R. S. & Folkman, S. (1987). Transactional theory and research on emotions and coping. Eur. J. Personal. 1, 141–169 (1987)

Levante, A., Petrocchi, S., Bianco, F., Castelli, I. & Lecciso, F. (2025). Emotional exhaustion faced by Italian female teaching staff during COVID-19 pandemic: A sequential mediation model applying coping strategies, self-efficacy for online teaching, and technostress. Int. J. Educ. Res. Open 8, 100403. https://doi.org/10.1016/j.ijedro.2024.100403

Mannila, L., Nordén, L.-Å. & Pears, A. (2018). Digital Competence, Teacher Self-Efficacy and Training Needs. in Proceedings of the 2018 ACM Conference on International Computing Education Research 78–85 (Association for Computing Machinery, New York, NY, USA, 2018). doi:10.1145/3230977.3230993.

Marchiori, D. M., Mainardes, E. W., & Rodrigues, R. G. (2019). Do Individual Characteristics Influence the Types of Technostress Reported by Workers? International Journal of Human-Computer Interaction, 35, 218–230. https://doi.org/10.1080/10447318.2018.1449713

Mendes, A., Câmara, J., Caires, A. L., Garcês, S., & Pocinho, M. (2020). Creativity and cognitive reserve in old age: An exploratory study in the Portuguese population. PSICOLOGIA, 34, 229–235. https://doi.org/10.17575/psicologia.v34i1.1518

Ogakwu, N. V., Ede, M. O., Manafa, I. F., Okeke, C. I., & Onah, S. O. (2024). Quality of Work-Life and Stress Management in a Rural Sample of Primary School Teachers: An Intervention Study. Journal of Rational - Emotive and Cognitive -Behavior Therapy, 42, 135–161. https://doi.org/10.1007/s10942-022-00494-8

Palmiero, M., Nori, R., Piccardi, L., & D'Amico, S. (2020). Divergent Thinking: The Role of Decision-Making Styles. Creativity Research Journal, 32, 323–332. https://doi.org/10.1080/10400419.2020.1817700

Palmiero, M., Piccardi, L., Nori, R., Palermo, L., Salvi, C., & Guariglia, C. (2019). Editorial: Creativity: Education and rehabilitation. In Frontiers in Psychology (Vol. 10). Frontiers Media S.A. https://doi.org/10.3389/fpsyg.2019.01500

Rašticová, M., Šácha, J., Lakomý, M., & Mishra, P. K. (2025). Technostress Among Older Workers: A Central European Perspective. Psychology Research and Behavior Management, 18, 1211–1225. https://doi.org/10.2147/PRBM.S508500

Runco, M. A., & Acar, S. (2012). Divergent thinking as an indicator of creative potential. Creativity Research Journal, 24(1), 66–75. https://doi.org/10.1080/10400419.2012.652929

Soares, D., & Nursalam. (2023). The use of digital technology in health learning during the COVID-19 pandemic: A systematic review. Journal of the Pakistan Medical Association, 73, S135–S139. https://doi.org/10.47391/JPMA.Ind-S2-32

Sprini, G., & Tomasello, S. (1989). Torrance tests of creative thinking (Test di pensiero Creativo). (Firenze: Giunti O.S. Organizzazioni Speciali).

Tacy, J. W. (2016). Technostress: A Concept Analysis: OJNI. https://doi.org/https://www.proquest.com/scholarly-journals/technostress-concept-analysis/docview/1984361812/se-2

Tarafdar, M., Cooper, C. L., & Stich, J. F. (2019). The technostress trifecta - technoeustress, techno distress and design: Theoretical directions and an agenda for research. In Information Systems Journal (Vol. 29, Issue 1, pp. 6–42). Blackwell Publishing Ltd. https://doi.org/10.1111/isj.12169

Tarafdar, M., Tu, Q., Ragu-Nathan, B. S., & Ragu-Nathan, T. S. (2007). The impact of technostress on role stress and productivity. Journal of Management Information Systems, 24, 301–328. https://doi.org/10.2753/MIS0742-1222240109

Toto, G. A., & Limone, P. (2021). Motivation, Stress and Impact of Online Teaching on Italian Teachers during COVID-19. *Computers*, *10*(6), 75. https://doi.org/10.3390/computers10060075

Wang, Q., Zhao, G., & Yao, N. (2024). Understanding the Impact of Technostress on University Teachers' Online Teaching During the COVID-19 Pandemic with the Transactional Theory of Stress (TTS). Asia-Pacific Education Researcher, 33, 187–198. https://doi.org/10.1007/s40299-023-00718-0

Xu, J. (2022). A person-centered approach to teacher motivation towards information technology: Integrating achievement goals and expectancy-value perspectives. Educational Technology Research and Development, 70, 397–417. https://doi.org/10.1007/s11423-022-10085-0

Zivi, P, Malatesta, G, Mascia, M. L., Diana, M. G., Di Domenico, A., Penna, M. P., Palmiero, M. (2025). Protective factors against technostress in secondary school teachers. Sci Rep 15, 35554 (2025). https://doi.org/10.1038/s41598-025-19604-4

UNLOCKING METACOGNITION THROUGH COMPUTATIONAL THINKING

Giulia Paludo
University of Trento, Department of Information Engineering and Computer Science
Via Sommarive 9, 38123 Povo (TN), Italy

ABSTRACT

Computational Thinking (CT) is the mental process of formulating problems and their solutions in such a way that allows a third actor, whether human or machine, to effectively implement them. It includes a set of underlying processes such as decomposition, abstraction, algorithmic thinking, and solution evaluation. The cognitive underpinnings of CT involve advanced cognitive abilities, Higher Order Thinking Skills (HOTS) such as analysis, planning, evaluation and creativity which are highly supported by metacognition which plays a pivotal role in enhancing learning and problem solving processes. With this purpose, a scoping review was performed and from the literature retrieved, CT and metacognition appear to have a strong connection, however this relationship is still little explored. This contribution investigates, through a scoping review, the bidirectional relationship between CT and Metacognition, also in regard to educational practices.

KEYWORDS

Computational Thinking, Metacognition, Educational Design, Problem Solving, Self-Regulated Learning

1. INTRODUCTION

The growing necessity for Computer Science (CS) Education as well as new technologies has called for a more structured reflection on the foundations, implementation and implications of bringing CS even in pre-school settings. In the Information Era, merely using computers and software instrumentally has become obsolete, implying a paradigm shift in how the educational system has to address the development of such skills. Among the essential transversal skills for the 21st century, Computational Thinking (CT) as well as problem solving (PS) and many others, have been acknowledged to play a crucial role especially in regard of technologies even if transferable also to other "unplugged" settings (Tabesh, 2017). The relationship between CT and metacognition, defined as the awareness and regulation of one's thinking processes (Cornoldi, 1990) is particularly relevant (Da Silva, 2024). In the realm of learning, metacognition is widely acknowledged to be a powerful resource to enhance the learning process quality (Üzümcü, 2023) with high transferability across domains. It enables individuals to better plan, monitor and assess their processes. These skills, especially in relation to PS, are highly valuable for the different CT components requiring flexibility, error detection, and iterative refinement. On the same line, CT tasks offer stimulating settings for practicing and both becoming aware and developing metacognitive strategies. In light of this theoretical alignment questions about the bidirectional relationship between CT and metacognition arise: *does engaging in CT activities enhance metacognitive skills by prompting reflection and strategy use? Or do pre-existing metacognitive abilities better equip learners to tackle CT tasks effectively?* To address these questions a scoping review with the PRISMA flow process was performed on peer-reviewed reports published between 2015 and 2025 available in Scopus and Web of Science according to the keywords *computational thinking, metacognition* and *algorithmic thinking*.

2. COMPUTATIONAL THINKING IS NOT ONLY PROGRAMMING

When talking about CS, the focus goes to the instrumental aspect of programming which is about creating instructions for the computer to follow for accomplishing an envisioned goal. This task is based on CT, the mental process engaged by the programmer "(…) *formulating problems and expressing solutions in a way that they can be effectively executed by an external agent*" (Wing, 2011). This definition elevates PS by involving a third agent for the solution execution. Programming becomes a PS challenge since the key objective becomes also expressing correctly the solution in a given language which employs a specific syntax (Igelnik, 2011). The final outcome is a structured articulation of both the problem and the solution: the initial task is broken down into smaller components which, once abstracted and reconducted to known patterns, allow to design the algorithm iteratively adjusted through debugging.

2.1 Expressing Solutions and Debugging

As mentioned in the previous section, CT brings conventional problem solving to an upper level by requiring solutions to be explicitly formulated in a clear, executable sequence. The *expression* component implies making the reasoning processes explicit, and, more importantly, articulating them in order to achieve coherence and clarity so another agent can correctly reach the same results. Indeed, translating a solution into an algorithm requires careful examination and reflection on the PS process, which may not occur in other contexts. Articulating each step taken clearly and reviewing the entire sequence, including the implicit one, prompts awareness of one's own cognitive and PS processes (Swanson et al., 2024). Providing a concrete and visible translation of the solution (Igelnik, 2011), supports this process through a form of embodied metacognition, where the visual and interactive representation of thought processes aids reflection and understanding. Repeated exposure to such practices gradually fosters the generalization of metacognitive strategies, such as self-monitoring and revision, across different tasks and learning settings. Similarly, debugging draws explicit attention to evaluation and monitoring, often overlooked tasks in educational contexts that focus solely on production without encouraging revision. Debugging supports the acquisition of transferable monitoring strategies by requiring learners to locate the specific step that prevents the solution from working (Cervera et al 2020). This form of targeted revision creates a context in which the translation of thought into action is questioned and refined through alternative strategies that call for adjustment and adaptation, two central components of metacognitive regulation (Veenman et al, 2006).

2.2 CT Training: Tools, Platforms and Approaches

CT training in K-12 is increasingly recognized as an essential part of transversal skills training. Consequently, numerous tools both plugged and unplugged have been developed to support a smoother integration in exisiting curricula. *Block based programming* with tools like Scratch (https://scratch.mit.edu/) and Code.org (https://code.org/) is a key component of CT activities providing programming languages and development environments in which students experience (Tonbuloğlu, 2024). While these platforms require autonomy and independence, they have the potential in providing a setting able to stimulate sequential reasoning and the employment of metacognitive strategies is notable (Yadav, 2022). Another pillar is constituted by *physical computing tools*, such as educational robotics kits able to provide a hands-on experience enhancing the engagement and understanding of CT principles especially with preschoolers and early primary school (Tonbuloğlu, 2024). Different types of robots can be introduced in classrooms' practices and literature has demonstrated their effectiveness in accomplishing the CT learning goals set (Cervera et al, 2020). In this scenario, CT activities can provide a powerful setting for exploring and understanding how to take advantage of metacognitive strategies since most of the aforementioned activities require expression and debugging components. Plugged and digital tools are more effective in engaging metacognitive processes related to CT, as they support greater learner autonomy, partly thanks to real-time feedback and a reduced focus on producing a "correct answer," as would typically be expected in a paper-and-pencil task. This allows students to engage more freely, encouraging individual revision and fostering the gradual internalization of these strategies, which might not happen if constantly mediated by a teacher. Peer collaboration can still serve as a valuable middle ground: the presence of a third agent, not sharing prior knowledge or implicit understanding with the learner, makes the translation process more necessary and meaningful, while also increasing motivation to revise and debug one's reasoning.

3. CT AND METACOGNITION: A BIDIRECTIONAL RELATIONSHIP

The relationship between CT and metacognition is significant and powerful. Metacognitive skills such as planning, monitoring and evaluation can support CT's components while CT on its side can be enhanced by stronger metacognitive abilities (Veenman et al., 2006). Practicing CT can foster the development of metacognitive awareness by training in the explicit formulation of PS strategies. More in detail, scientific literature provides evidence of a positive correlation between CT skills and both metacognitive knowledge and regulation (Cervera et al., 2020). In fact, higher metacognitive awareness appears to be facilitating CT tasks by providing strategies to better managing both ambiguity and complexity (Zhang et al., 2024). In this connection, metacognitive performance was reported as predictive for CT: metacognitive components, such as planning and evaluation, account for a significant portion of the variance in CT abilities (Üzümcü, 2023). These findings highlight the foundational role that metacognitive skills play in learning CT and arise the discussion on how designing holistic training able to engage both constructs. This synergy is further supported by contextualization within socio-constructivist educational frameworks: as discussed by Silva et al (2024), drawing from Vygotskian principles, integrating metacognitive strategies into classroom activities boosts CT development by encouraging reflective thinking and collaborative PS. Similarly, Zhang et al. (2024) propose that CT mediates the relationship between metacognitive skills and other higher-order abilities, implying that CT could have downstream benefits on other learning domains. This hypothesis brings CT's role from an underlying part of programming to that of a more transversal cognitive tool. In this regard, Cox et al. (2022) introduced the concept of computational metacognition, proposing that the combination of metacognitive awareness and structured CT processes can enhance PS, learning, and adaptation to best manage complexity and ambiguity and it can be observable through indicators such as strategy monitoring during algorithm design, reflective abstraction when debugging, and iterative self-assessment in problem decomposition. This construct can be also be envisaged as a forma mentis, a way of thinking which, by providing a computational structure to PS, leaves more space and resources for other processes such as creativity. However, this relationship has counter hypotheses telling that this connection may be influenced by factors such as age, with younger students benefiting differently than adolescents or adults as effective metacognitive processes requires more developed HOTS (Tsarava et al., 2019). Moreover, the subject domain plays a role, as CT integrated in mathematics may activate distinct metacognitive processes (Montuori et al., 2024). Pragmatically speaking, as illustrated in Figure 1, the relationship between CT and metacognition can be outlined as a continuous interplay between two closely related domains. Metacognition encompasses knowledge (regarding the task and strategies) and regulatory processes (planning, monitoring, and reflection). Conversely, CT involves core components such as decomposition, pattern recognition, abstraction, and algorithmic thinking, as well as iterative and modular practices such as testing, remixing, and optimization. At the top centre of the diagram, these areas are linked by what we may refer to as *computational metacognition* (Cox et al. 2022), where reasoning about one's own PS process becomes explicit and structured through computational strategies. This integration supports not only PS but also fosters self-regulated learning and strategies application in different contexts. The potential educational implications of this interplay span from CT activities and the inclusion of CT components in other activities across disciplines. In this context, decomposition and algorithm design can effectively mirror metacognitive processes like planning and sequencing. Incorporating these elements can elicit computational metacognition and reflection on one's own solution processes (Yadav et al., 2022).

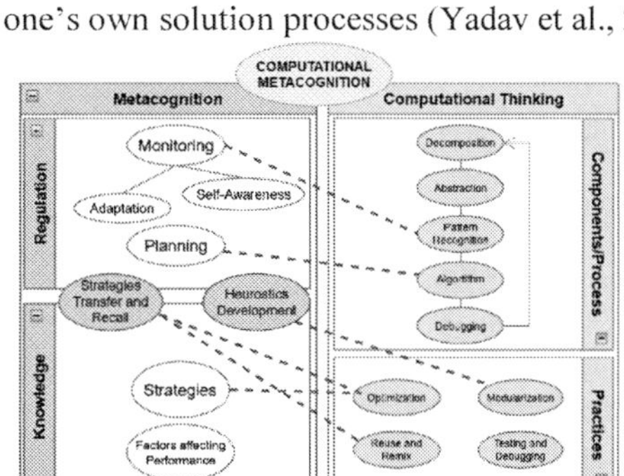

Figure 1. Interactions between metacognition and CT. Engaging in CT tasks engages metacognitive awareness, while CT provides a structured environment where metacognitive strategies can be practiced, made visible, and transferred

4. DISCUSSION AND CONCLUSIONS

Leveraging the connection between CT and metacognition enables to design activities providing a structured lens through which learners can develop and apply metacognitive skills, leading to deeper, more flexible problem solving capacities. Recalling the initial questions, both directions, CT enhancing metacognition and vice versa, remain plausible. It is evident is that CT tasks, especially those requiring the translation of an intuitive solution into a sequence of explicit, reproducible steps, create a context that encourages metacognitive reflection. This translation process requires learners to make their reasoning visible and aware of steps that would otherwise remain implicit. Moreover, the debugging phase shifts the focus from performance to revision, centering attention on monitoring, evaluation, and adaptation often overlooked. CT offers a tangible and embodied approach to metacognition development with practices such as block-based environments, providing concrete supports to externalize thinking. These applications are successful in first scaffolding learning and secondly fostering the gradual integration of metacognitive strategies in different tasks and contexts. Repeated exposure to this kind of activities can support the cultivation of computational metacognition which prompts self-regulation, evaluation, and iterative improvement. In this light, CT is not just the mental process behind programming; it becomes a tool for metacognitive development while benefitting from metacognition itself. Future research should build on this synergy to guide educational design with CT's potential as a domain-specific competence and as a driver of metacognitive growth. Beyond this theoretical perspective, a pilot study is envisioned for exploring CT interventions and metacognitive regulation in learning. On a final note, this bidirectionality can lead to new approaches not only to CS education but also in transversal skills training for digital and non-digital settings.

REFERENCES

Cervera, N., Diago, P. D., Orcos, L., & Yáñez, D. F. (2020). The Acquisition of Computational Thinking through Mentoring: An Exploratory Study. *Education Sciences*, *10*(8), Articolo 8. https://doi.org/10.3390/educsci10080202

Igelnik, B. (A c. Di). (2011). *Computational Modeling and Simulation of Intellect: Current State and Future Perspectives*. IGI Global. https://doi.org/10.4018/978-1-60960-551-3

Rodrigues Da Silva, D., Kurtz, F. D., & Araújo, M. C. P. D. (2024). Metacognition and Computational Thinking in Vygotsky's Historical-Cultural Perspective. *Revista Espaço Pedagógico*, *30*, e15264. https://doi.org/10.5335/rep.v30.15264

Sharif University of Technology, & Tabesh, Y. (2017a). Computational Thinking: A 21st Century Skill. *OLYMPIADS IN INFORMATICS*, *11*(2), 65–70. https://doi.org/10.15388/ioi.2017.special.10

Swanson, H. J., Ojutiku, A., & Dewsbury, B. (2024). The Impacts of an Academic Intervention Based in Metacognition on Academic Performance. *Teaching and Learning Inquiry*, *12*. https://doi.org/10.20343/teachlearninqu.12.12

Tonbuloğlu, İ. (2025). Tools and Resources for K-12 Computer Science Education: In S. B. Kert (A c. Di), *Advances in Educational Technologies and Instructional Design* (pp. 349–372). IGI Global. https://doi.org/10.4018/979-8-3693-4542-9.ch013

Üzümcü, Ö. (2023). Computational thinking scale: The predictive role of metacognition in the context of higher order thinking skills. *Journal for the Education of Gifted Young Scientists*, *11*(3), 423–437. https://doi.org/10.17478/jegys.1355722

Veenman, M. V. J., Van Hout-Wolters, B. H. A. M., & Afflerbach, P. (2006). Metacognition and learning: Conceptual and methodological considerations. *Metacognition and Learning*, *1*(1), Articolo 1. https://doi.org/10.1007/s11409-006-6893-0

Yadav, A., Ocak, C., & Oliver, A. (2022). Computational Thinking and Metacognition. *TechTrends*, *66*(3), Articolo 3. https://doi.org/10.1007/s11528-022-00695-z

Yeni, S., Grgurina, N., Saeli, M., Hermans, F., Tolboom, J., & Barendsen, E. (2023). Interdisciplinary Integration of Computational Thinking in K-12 Education: A Systematic Review. *Informatics in Education*. https://doi.org/10.15388/infedu.2024.08

Zhang, D., Bin Ahmadon, M. A., & Yamaguchi, S. (2022). Human-AI Pair Programming by Data Stream and Its Application Example. *2022 IEEE International Conference on Consumer Electronics-Asia (ICCE-Asia)*, 1–4. https://doi.org/10.1109/ICCE-Asia57006.2022.9954649

INTELLIGENT TUTORING SYSTEMS MEET GENERATIVE-AI CHATBOTS TO CRAFT PERSONALIZED LEARNING PATHS: A PHENOMENOLOGICAL STUDY REVEALS 7 KEY DESIGN ISSUES

Michele Norscini, Lucio Monterubbiano and Chiara Moroni
Skilla.com
Via Alessandro Volta, 5/9,
62012 Civitanova Marche (MC), Italy

ABSTRACT

In asynchronous online learning, integrating Large Language Models (LLMs) into Intelligent Tutoring Systems (ITSs) opens up new possibilities for delivering conversational support to guide learners through content-rich course libraries.
In this study, we present a phenomenological investigation of user experiences with a generative-AI-powered chatbot capable of recommending a personalized learning path at the end of an exploratory conversation. Using the think-aloud protocol, we collected data on users' interactional experiences, and through phenomenological analysis, we explored their perceptions and expectations.
Findings indicate overall user satisfaction with the chatbot's ability to provide tailored orientation within an extensive training library, particularly in terms of interactional fluency and personalization. Nonetheless, each participant highlighted at least one critical issue—ranging from unclear recommendation logic and occasional mismatches to limitations in planning support and concerns about tone or metaphor use.
Building on these insights, we identified seven key design issues that should inform the development of educational conversational agents.

KEYWORDS

Intelligent Tutoring System, Large Language Model, Chatbot, Learning, Think-aloud, Phenomenology

1. INTRODUCTION

Over the past fifteen years, Intelligent Tutoring Systems (ITSs) have emerged as a compelling solution to personalize asynchronous online learning, thanks to their student modeling capabilities, real-time diagnosis of learner difficulties, and adaptive feedback (VanLehn, 2011; Azevedo et al., 2016; Mousavinasab et al., 2018; Behera et al., 2020). However, despite their potential, ITSs have consistently faced the limitation of scripted and rigid conversations, preventing the learner from engaging in an authentic dialogue with a knowledgeable and supportive figure (Laurillard, 2012; Ji & Yuan, 2022; Yildirim-Erbasli & Bulut, 2023). This limitation intersects with another typical challenge in online learning: the overwhelming volume of content available in digital libraries, which often hinders learners from quickly and independently identifying the most relevant resources, resulting in cognitive and educational overload (Nabizadeh, 2020; Amicucci, 2021; Gupta et al., 2025).

The integration of Large Language Models (LLMs) into ITSs could radically change this scenario. LLMs' ability to understand context and simulate human-like language allows them to transform ITSs into systems capable of conducting authentic conversations (Ji & Yan, 2022; Wang et al., 2025; Zhu et al., 2025). Within a chatbot interface, AI-powered agents can serve as dialogue partners, enabling learners to interact as if a real teacher were present. In this dialogic mode, generative-AI tutors can perform many of the teacher's functions: monitoring learner progress, explaining concepts, reformulating examples, or proposing tailored exercises (Mousavinasab et al., 2018; Lui et al., 2024; Wang et al., 2025). Among these functions, one stands out as critical: providing orientation within increasingly vast digital learning libraries (Ng & Fung, 2024; Abu-Rasheed, 2025; Wang et al., 2025). By engaging in dialogue and interpreting users' challenges, goals, and preferences, the conversational agent can sift through the vast content and recommend personalized learning paths, explaining its choices in real time (Abu-Rasheed, 2025; Wang et al., 2025).

In other words, technological innovation today can offer a solution to two of the main challenges of asynchronous online learning: the absence of authentic tutoring dialogue and the difficulty of navigating increasingly vast content libraries. This study explores how users experience these new possibilities, focusing on a conversational chatbot named Ariadne, which combines dialogic tutoring (Ji & Yuan, 2022) with personalized course recommendation (Wang et al., 2025), in order to highlight its strengths and, above all, its main critical issues.

2. CONTEXT & METHOD

The study was conducted in the context of asynchronous online corporate learning. Specifically, it investigated a digital library comprising over 300 courses on the most in-demand soft and digital skills in the workplace. The library is accessible via a Learning Management System (LMS), where a GPT-4o-powered chatbot named Ariadne was integrated. The name, inspired by the mythological Ariadne, metaphorically represents a guiding thread that prevents learners from getting lost in the maze of available courses.

The chatbot itself references this myth and its symbolic elements—thread and labyrinth—throughout the dialogue. It was designed with an open-ended conversational structure: responses and recommendations are generated dynamically via GPT-4o. Its behavior is guided by a system prompt written by us, the authors, which defined tone, metaphor, and interaction rules. Some constraints are intentional—for example, the mandatory steps of the conversation or the limit of ten recommended courses.

We decided to structure the conversation with Ariadne in multiple steps. It begins with a profiling phase, in which the chatbot asks the user about their job, daily challenges, perceived causes of their difficulties, and professional goals. After collecting this information, Ariadne summarizes it and requests confirmation, ensuring an accurate understanding of the learner's needs. Upon confirmation, the chatbot proposes a curated course playlist, providing justifications for each recommendation (e.g., "I suggest this course because..."). Users can continue the dialogue, requesting replacements, elaborations, or additional resources until the playlist fully reflects their preferences. Only then is the playlist "locked" and made accessible for consumption within the LMS.

Our research, implemented in this context, sought to answer a deliberately broad question: How do users perceive their interaction with the Ariadne chatbot? To address this, we adopted a phenomenological approach (Husserl, 1936; Giorgi, 1992; Smith, 2004, 2011; Sità, 2012), which allowed us to suspend prior assumptions (*epochè*) and prioritize the lived experiences of users.

Seven corporate employees—first-time users of Ariadne—were remotely observed and video-recorded during their interaction with the chatbot. We employed the concurrent think-aloud protocol (level 2) (Ericsson & Simon, 1980, 1998; Chang & Johnson, 2021), which involved users verbalizing their thoughts in real time, without guided questions or interruptions. Sessions were conducted via Microsoft Teams, recording screen, audio, and chat logs synchronously to ensure alignment between commentary and actions.

Transcripts of the recordings were segmented into self-contained meaning units (Giorgi, 1992). As an example, consider the following excerpt during the profiling phase: "I'm not sure what to answer here... These questions are too abstract. I wish they were rooted in my professional context". This was treated as a self-contained meaning unit, as it expresses a coherent reflection on the perceived lack of contextual relevance in the chatbot's questions. A total of 236 meaning units were identified across the seven sessions.

The analysis of the meaning units followed an integrated approach combining eidetic reduction (Husserl, 1936; Giorgi, 1992; Smith, 2011) and thematic analysis (Braun & Clarke, 2006), applied in an iterative and coordinated manner. Through eidetic reduction, we identified the meaning units that expressed elements of experience essential to the emergence of a negative or positive user perception. If those elements had not been present, the negative or positive experience would not have taken place. In the example above, the participant's frustration stemmed directly from the abstract nature of the chatbot's questions; without this mismatch in contextual relevance, the negative experience would likely not have occurred.

Thematic analysis then provided an operational method to group the selected meaning units into inductive categories. The categories were compared and refined through collaborative discussion among us, the authors. In the case of the excerpt above, the analysis contributed to defining the category "Contextualized Questions", later identified as one of the seven key design elements.

Eidetic reduction and thematic analysis allowed us to isolate the structural elements that characterized the quality of the interaction and to link these elements to actionable design issues.

3. FINDINGS

Overall, the seven participants evaluated the chatbot experience positively: all reported feeling "guided," "listened to," and that the time needed to find relevant courses in a "very large" library had been reduced. The primary value attributed to the tutor was its ability to provide rapid, personalized guidance, crafting tailored learning paths based on expressed needs.

However, each participant highlighted at least one critical element. Through eidetic reduction and thematic analysis, we distilled seven critical design issues, each exemplified by a user comment:

1. Clarity of Recommendations – User 1 requested that the system "explain more clearly why a course is being recommended"; a lack of transparent rationale undermines trust.
2. Scope of the Library – User 2 emphasized the need for "guardrails and clarity on what is not available"; the chatbot should clearly indicate when a requested topic is outside the library, avoiding false expectations.
3. Contextualized Questions – User 3 found the chatbot's questions "too abstract" and asked for prompts "rooted in my professional context," signaling a gap in the profiling depth.
4. Scheduling Support – User 4 appreciated the suggestions but wished the tutor could "help schedule the learning path," integrating it into a concrete timeline.
5. Tone Personalization – User 5 felt the chatbot's tone was overly compliant: "that way of talking to me gets on my nerves," revealing a mismatch between tone and user preference.
6. Metaphor/Character Choice – User 6 did not resonate with the Ariadne metaphor: "this metaphor doesn't convince me," showing that culturally specific references may alienate some users.
7. Recommendation Accuracy – User 7 received a course suggestion "based solely on word similarity," such as a course for managers rather than one on becoming a manager, exposing semantic ambiguity issues.

These seven issues highlight areas requiring improvement: clarity and accuracy of recommendations, library boundaries, scheduling features, and personalization of tone, questions, and narrative framing. While arising from individual experiences, eidetic reduction revealed that these were perceived as systemic—not incidental—issues, and thus represent essential leverage points for improving chatbot design and interaction quality (see Table 1).

Table 1. Key Design Issues Identified Through User Feedback

User	Transcript Excerpt	Design Issue	Design Implications
User 1	"Explain more clearly why a course is being recommended."	Clarity of Recommendations	Improve recommendation clarity
User 2	"There should be guardrails and clarity on what is not available."	Scope of the Library	Explain library boundaries
User 3	"These questions are too abstract... I wish they were rooted in my professional context."	Contextualized Questions	Ask more contextual questions
User 4	"It would be helpful if the tutor could help schedule the learning path."	Scheduling Support	Add scheduling functionality
User 5	"That way of talking to me gets on my nerves."	Tone Personalization	Adapt tone to user
User 6	"This metaphor doesn't convince me."	Metaphor/Character Choice	Use accessible metaphors
User 7	"I got a course recommendation just based solely on word similarity…"	Recommendation Accuracy	Improve the accuracy of the recommendation

4. CONCLUSION

The generative-AI-powered conversational chatbot already offers two concrete benefits: it bridges the gap of dialogic tutoring in asynchronous learning and assists learners in navigating extensive course libraries, significantly reducing search time. However, user feedback reveals seven critical issues that must be carefully addressed in the design process, as they can significantly impact the user experience.

Among these, minimizing recommendation errors and clarifying the reasoning behind suggestions are especially crucial. This importance is confirmed by similar findings in related studies (Ji & Yan, 2022; Wang et al., 2025). When these two issues are not adequately addressed, the chatbot no longer functions as an effective learning aid.

The study also highlights the importance of adapting tone, metaphors, and questions to the learner's expectations and context. It further points to the need for functional improvements, such as clarifying the scope of the library and supporting learners in scheduling the recommended training activities.

However, the study is limited by a small, homogeneous sample and the absence of quantitative data. These constraints call for a cautious interpretation of the findings and underscore the need for broader validation.

Future work will refine the prototype and test it with more diverse users, combining qualitative insight with behavioral metrics such as search time, course adoption, and completion.

In summary, generative-AI-powered tutors show great promise, but their effectiveness hinges on their ability to combine pedagogical mediation, deep personalization, and robust follow-up tools that support learners throughout their educational journey.

REFERENCES

Abu-Rasheed, H., Abdulsalam, M.H., Weber, C., Fathi, M. (2024). Supporting Student Decisions on Learning Recommendations: An LLM-Based Chatbot with Knowledge Graph Contextualization for Conversational Explainability and Mentoring. https://doi.org/10.35542/osf.io/ervym

Amicucci, F. (2021). *Apprendere nell'infosfera*. FrancoAngeli, Milan.

Azevedo, R., Martin, S.A., Taub, M., Mudrick, N.V., Millar, G.C., Grafsgaard, J.F. (2016). Are Pedagogical Agents' External Regulation Effective in Fostering Learning with Intelligent Tutoring Systems?, in: Micarelli, A., Stamper, J., Panourgia, K. (Eds.), *Intelligent Tutoring Systems, Lecture Notes in Computer Science*. Springer International Publishing, Cham, pp. 197–207. https://doi.org/10.1007/978-3-319-39583-8_19

Behera, A., Matthew, P., Keidel, A., Vangorp, P., Fang, H., Canning, S. (2020). Associating Facial Expressions and Upper-Body Gestures with Learning Tasks for Enhancing Intelligent Tutoring Systems. International Journal of Artificial Intelligence in Education. *International Journal of Artificial Intelligence in Education* 30, 236–270. https://doi.org/10.1007/s40593-020-00195-2

Braun, V., Clarke, V. (2006). Using thematic analysis in psychology. *Qualitative Research in Psychology* 3, 77–101. https://doi.org/10.1191/1478088706qp063oa

Chang, C.-C., Johnson, T. (2021). Integrating heuristics and think-aloud approach to evaluate the usability of game-based learning material. *J. Comput. Educ.* 8, 137–157. https://doi.org/10.1007/s40692-020-00174-5

Ericsson, K.A., Simon, H.A. (1980). Verbal reports as data. *Psychological Review* 87, 215–251. https://doi.org/10.1037/0033-295X.87.3.215

Ericsson, K.A., Simon, H.A., (1998). How to Study Thinking in Everyday Life: Contrasting Think-Aloud Protocols With Descriptions and Explanations of Thinking. *Mind, Culture, and Activity* 5, 178–186. https://doi.org/10.1207/s15327884mca0503_3

Giorgi, A. (1992). Description versus interpretation: Competing alternative strategies for qualitative research. *Journal of Phenomenological Psychology* 23, 119–135. https://doi.org/10.1163/156916292X00090

Gupta, A., Siddiqui, M., Smith, G., Reddig, J., MacLellan, C. (2025). Intelligent Tutors for Adult Learners: An Analysis of Needs and Challenges. https://doi.org/10.48550/arXiv.2412.04477

Husserl, E. (1936). Die Krisis der europäischen Wissenschaften und die transzendentale Phänomenologie. Meiner, Hamburg.

Ji, S., Yuan, T. (2022). Conversational Intelligent Tutoring Systems for Online Learning: What do Students and Tutors Say?, in: *2022 IEEE Global Engineering Education Conference (EDUCON)*, pp. 292–298. https://doi.org/10.1109/EDUCON52537.2022.9766567

Laurillard, D. (2012). *Teaching as a Design Science: Building Pedagogical Patterns for Learning and Technology*. Routledge, Abingdon, UK.

Lui, R.W.C., Bai, H., Zhang, A.W.Y., Chu, E.T.H. (2024). GPTutor: A Generative AI-powered Intelligent Tutoring System to Support Interactive Learning with Knowledge-Grounded Question Answering, in: *2024 International Conference on Advances in Electrical Engineering and Computer Applications (AEECA)*. IEEE, Dalian, China, pp. 702–707. https://doi.org/10.1109/AEECA62331.2024.00124

Mousavinasab, E., Zarifsanaiey, N., R. Niakan Kalhori, S., Rakhshan, M., Keikha, L., Ghazi Saeedi, M. (2021). Intelligent tutoring systems: a systematic review of characteristics, applications, and evaluation methods. *Interactive Learning Environments* 29, 142–163. https://doi.org/10.1080/10494820.2018.1558257

Nabizadeh, A.H., Leal, J.P., Rafsanjani, H.N., Shah, R.R. (2020). Learning path personalization and recommendation methods: A survey of the state-of-the-art. *Expert Systems with Applications* 159, 113596. https://doi.org/10.1016/j.eswa.2020.113596

Ng, C., Fung, Y. (2024). Educational Personalized Learning Path Planning with Large Language Models. https://doi.org/10.48550/arXiv.2407.11773

Sità, C. (2012). *Indagare l'esperienza. L'intervista fenomenologica nella ricerca educativa*. Carocci editore, Rome.

Smith, J.A. (2004). Reflecting on the development of interpretative phenomenological analysis and its contribution to qualitative research in psychology. *Qualitative Research in Psychology* 1, 39–54. https://doi.org/10.1191/1478088704qp004oa

Smith, J.A. (2011). Evaluating the contribution of interpretative phenomenological analysis. *Health Psychology Review* 5, 9–27. https://doi.org/10.1080/17437199.2010.510659

VanLehn, K. (2011). The Relative Effectiveness of Human Tutoring, Intelligent Tutoring Systems, and Other Tutoring Systems. *Educational Psychologist* 46, 197–221. https://doi.org/10.1080/00461520.2011.611369

Wang, T., Zhan, Y., Lian, J., Hu, Z., Yuan, N., Zhang, Q., Xie, X., Xiong, H. (2025). LLM-powered Multi-agent Framework for Goal-oriented Learning in Intelligent Tutoring System. https://doi.org/10.48550/arXiv.2501.15749

Yildirim-Erbasli, S.N., Bulut, O. (2023). Conversation-based assessment: A novel approach to boosting test-taking effort in digital formative assessment. *Computers and Education: Artificial Intelligence* 4, 100135. https://doi.org/10.1016/j.caeai.2023.100135

Zhu, Y., Ye, Z., Yuan, Y., Tang, W., Yu, C., Shi, Y. (2025). AutoPBL: An LLM-powered Platform to Guide and Support Individual Learners Through Self Project-based Learning, in: *Proceedings of the 2025 CHI Conference on Human Factors in Computing Systems*. ACM, Yokohama Japan, pp. 1–26. https://doi.org/10.1145/3706598.3714261

FOSTERING CONCEPTUAL UNDERSTANDING OF PARALLEL CIRCUITS BEHAVIOUR BY CONSTRUCTING QUALITATIVE REPRESENTATIONS

Tessa Hoogma[1], Marco Kragten[1] and Bert Bredeweg[1, 2]
[1]*Faculty of Education, Amsterdam University of Applied Sciences, Amsterdam, The Netherlands*
[2]*Informatics Institute, Faculty of Science, University of Amsterdam, Amsterdam, The Netherlands*

ABSTRACT

Understanding the behaviour of parallel circuits is challenging for many students. In this paper, we present a lesson designed to support students in learning about parallel circuits by constructing a qualitative representation. Qualitative representations are non-numerical models that focus on causal relationships and system states, aligning closely with human reasoning. The lesson consists of three units that help students understand both the specific system behaviour of parallel circuits and develop general qualitative reasoning skills. Students are guided through the modeling process using a structured workbook containing explanations and reflection prompts, and by built-in support functions within the modelling software. Results show that students make frequent use of these support functions and that most students are able to successfully construct a correct qualitative representation by the end of the lesson. This approach illustrates how learning through model construction can deepen conceptual understanding of system behaviour.

KEYWORDS

Qualitative Representations, Parallel Circuits, Support Functions

1. INTRODUCTION

Understanding electrical circuits is essential in secondary school physics. However, students often struggle with the causal relationships between the quantities involved such as current, resistance and voltage (Adeduyigbe et al., 2024; Shipstone et al., 1988; Viard & Khantine-Langlois, 2001). As a result, they tend to plug numbers into formulas (e.g., Ohm's Law) without developing a deeper conceptual understanding of electrical system behaviour (Cohen et al., 1983; Quezada-Espinoza, 2023). This emphasizes the need for an instructional approach that fosters causal reasoning.

Constructing qualitative representations is an effective way to develop a conceptual understanding of system behaviour. Qualitative representations are non-numerical descriptions of systems that focus on causal relationships and system states (Forbus, 2019). Simulations can be run to investigate system behaviour. In this paper, we present a lesson in which students learn about the behaviour of parallel circuits by constructing a qualitative representation. At the same time, they gain general skills in qualitative reasoning about system behaviour – skills that can be applied to understand systems beyond the domain of circuits (Bredeweg et al., 2023b, Kragten et al., 2022). In this paper, our focus is on the instructional scaffolds provided to support students' learning.

2. REPRESENTATING THE PARALLEL CIRCUIT – THE LESSON

DynaLearn (2025) software enables users to construct and simulate qualitative representations of dynamic systems (Bredeweg et al., 2013a). It offers five levels, with higher levels enabling the description of more complex system behaviour. For the lesson discussed in this paper, level 3 was used. There are four built-in support functions available in DynaLearn (discussed below).

Constructing a qualitative representation is guided by a workbook that provides information about parallel circuits and the qualitative vocabulary used in DynaLearn. Students construct their qualitative representation step by step. They gradually add new domain concepts while simultaneously learning the qualitative vocabulary. Each step is followed by a simulation and reflection guided by targeted questions.

The lesson presented in this paper is divided into three units, each addressing a specific aspect of the domain knowledge and the qualitative reasoning learning goals (Table 1).

Table 1. Learning goals

Unit	Domain knowledge	Qualitative reasoning
1	Relationship between resistance, voltage and current in an electrical circuit	System behaviour in linear causal chains
2	Adding devices in a parallel circuit decreases resistance	Causes of ambiguity
3	Inverse relationship between values of resistance and current in a parallel circuit	Co-occurrence of values, system states and boundaries

Unit 1. This part of the lesson focuses on the concepts of voltage, resistance, and their effects on current in a closed circuit. Figure 1 shows the qualitative representation students construct step by step. They begin by adding the entity *Circuit*, followed by the quantities *Current* and *Resistance*. Entities represent physical objects or abstract concepts. Quantities are measurable properties of entities and include a derivative (δ) that represents their direction of change. **Video support** (icon left in canvas) provides guidance on how to create ingredients.

Based on information in the workbook, students must add the appropriate causal relationships between the quantities: a positive causal relationship (+) indicates that a change in the causing quantity results in a change in the affected quantity in the same direction; a negative causal relationship (−) indicates that the affected quantity changes in the opposite direction.

To run a simulation, students set the initial direction of change for the starting quantities of the causal chain. The **scenario advice** alerts students to missing or redundant settings via a blue exclamation mark on the right side of the canvas; clicking it provides a hint. Figure 1 shows a simulation result (with one state, as displayed in the state graph on the right side) where *Resistance* is set to increase but *Voltage* has no initial change. Consequently, it cannot be determined how *Current* will behave. The scenario advice suggests setting an initial change for *Voltage*. Students are then prompted to reflect with questions such as "If the resistance increases and voltage stays constant, then current *decreases/stays the same/increases*.".

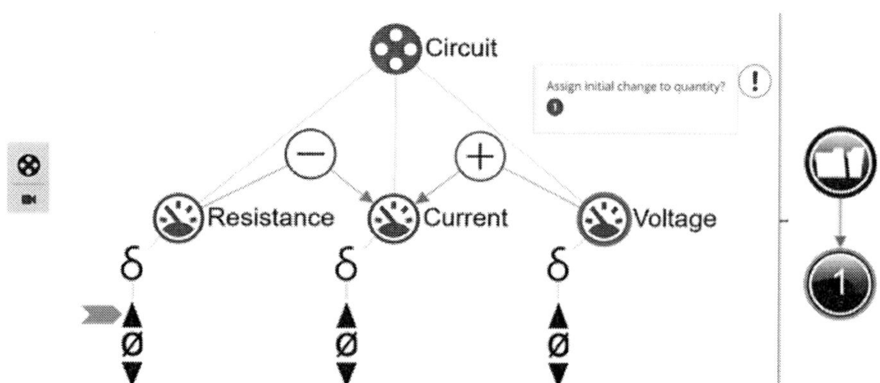

Figure 1. Simulation result with a missing initial setting for Voltage. Hence, the behaviour of Current cannot be determined, and the scenario advice gives an alert (see exclamation mark, which says: "Assign initial value to quantity?")

Unit 2. In parallel circuits, adding more devices decreases the total resistance. If voltage remains constant, the total current increases. Students add the entity *Device* and relate it to *Circuit* through a configuration (i.e., *connected to*), which describes their structural relationship. They also add the quantity *Number of* to the entity *Device*. The **norm-based support** assist students throughout the lesson by comparing their representation to a predefined norm. Deviations are flagged with a red question mark, which offers hints when clicked.

Next, students are asked to add the correct causal relationship between *Number of* and another quantity. Drawing on their knowledge from the workbook, students should recognize that a negative causal relationship between *Number of* and *Resistance* is required. Figure 2 shows a representation with an incorrect causal relationship, flagged by the norm-based support. Students can still run a simulation, where *Number of* is set to increase and *Voltage* to decrease. This results in an ambiguous outcome for *Current* (decrease, remain steady or increase). Students may also encounter ambiguous system behaviour with correct representations, as the workbook prompts them to run simulations with different initial settings and reflect on the outcomes.

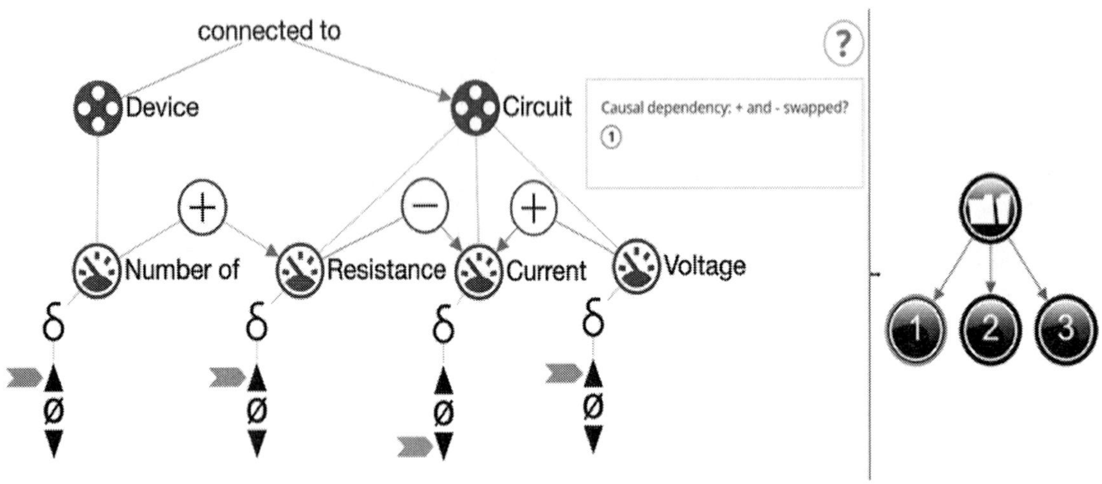

Figure 2. Ambiguous simulation results, and thus three states (right-hand side). State #1 selected. An incorrect causal relationship is flagged by the norm-based support, which says: "Causal dependency: + and – swapped?")

Unit 3. In a parallel circuit, adding devices lowers resistance and raises current – up to a maximum determined by fuses or the internal resistance of the battery. An open circuit makes resistance insurmountably, preventing any current from flowing.

Students first add quantity spaces to the quantities *Current* and *Resistance*. *Quantity spaces* define the possible values of a quantity by point values and intervals. *Current* receives a quantity space with a zero point (*0*), an interval (+) and a maximum (*Max*), while *Resistance* receives a quantity space with a minimum point (*Min*), an interval (+), and a maximum point (*Insurmountably*). To complete the representation, a direct reverse correspondence between these quantity spaces must be added because the quantity spaces of *Resistance* and *Current* are inversely related. *Correspondences* specify co-occurring values between quantity spaces, and therefore between quantities.

Once possible states are defined, a continuous change is required to show the full system behaviour. Exogenous influences can exert such a continuous effect (i.e., decreasing, steady, or increasing) from outside the system. Students run a simulation with two exogenous influences: *Number of* devices is set to increase and *Voltage* is constant. The initial value of *Resistance* is *Insurmountably*. Figure 3 shows the simulation results with three successive states: in state 1, *Resistance* is *Insurmountably* and decreasing while *Current* is *0* and increasing; in state 2 (not shown), *Resistance* and *Current* are both + and continue to decrease and increase, respectively; in state 3 (not shown) *Resistance* is *Min* and *Current* is *Max*. The **progress bar** (canvas bottom) shows per ingredient type how many have been added, how many are required, and how many are incorrect. When all required ingredients of a type are correctly added, the numbers in the progress bar turn green.

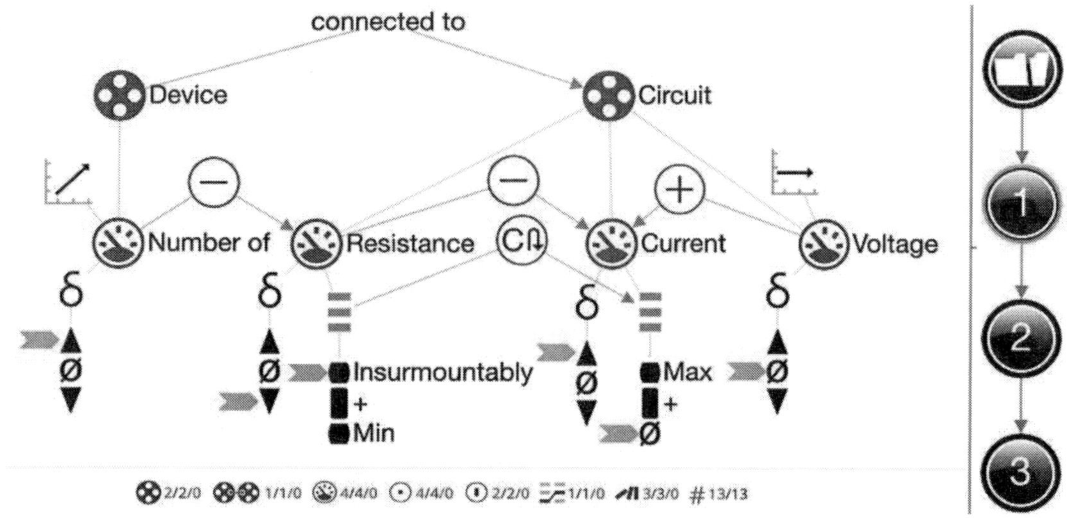

Figure 3. Simulation results of the full qualitative representation of a parallel circuit with state #1 selected. The progress bar at the bottom of the canvas shows that the representation is complete

3. RESULTS

The lesson was evaluated in two upper secondary education classes, with a total of 32 students participating. Students had no experience with constructing qualitative representations. They had 100 minutes to complete the lesson, during which 27 students fully completed the representation. Two students were missing the correspondence between the quantity spaces for *Resistance* and *Current*. One student was missing seven ingredients and had one incorrect ingredient. Two students were each missing 11 ingredients, with one of them also having one incorrect ingredient.

To gain insight into students' working time, their use of the built-in support and the number and types of errors they made during the construction process, we analysed the action log generated by the software (Table 2 and 3). Table 2 presents the time students spent in the software constructing their representation and their use of built-in support. Note that the use of the progress bar is not included, as it requires no interaction and thus leaves no trace in the log. These results show that the allotted time was sufficient for most students to complete the lesson and that they frequently used the built-in support. Table 3 presents the type of errors made during the construction process. It reveals that most mistakes occurred when establishing causal relationships between quantities.

Table 2. Summary of student activities and support use

Measure	M	SD
Construction time	57 minutes	19
Norm-based support	4.6	4.9
Videos support	5.8	4.8
Scenario advice	0.9	1.6

Table 3. Summary of errors during construction process

Errors	M	SD
Total	17	12
Entity	1.6	2.2
Configuration	1.5	2.0
Quantity	1.4	2.6
Causal relationships	10.2	6.4
Quantity space	3.4	4.9
Correspondence	0.1	0.3

4. CONCLUSION AND DISCUSSION

In this paper, we present a lesson in which students learn about parallel circuit behaviour by constructing a qualitative representation. The lesson is divided into three units, each with learning goals focused on domain knowledge and qualitative reasoning. Students are guided by a workbook and built-in support that scaffold the modeling process. These support mechanisms promote active learning by guiding accurate understanding and preventing misconceptions.

Results show that most students are able to construct the correct representation. During the construction process, they make a range of errors. Constructing correct causal relationships providing to be the most challenging. To address these difficulties, student frequently use the built-in support to correct their representation. These findings suggest that the lesson effectively supports students in constructing qualitative representations of parallel circuits.

A follow-up study could investigate the effect of the lesson on understanding domain knowledge of parallel circuits. Previous studies have shown that constructing qualitative representations has a positive effect on learning domain knowledge and qualitative reasoning skills (Kragten & Bredeweg, 2024).

Overall, the lesson presented in this paper demonstrates an approach to support conceptual understanding of dynamic systems by constructing qualitative representations in physics. The approach is also suitable for exploring other topics that involve dynamic systems, such as in biology, economics, and geography. Many more examples of such lessons can be found in our online repository, which currently includes over 40 lessons.

REFERENCES

Adeduyigbe, A., Ukoh, E.E., & Okeke, U.K. (2024). Influence of school type on senior secondary school physics students' learning difficulties and misconceptions about electricity in Ondo West Local Government, Ondo State, Nigeria. *African Journal of Teacher Education* 13(3), 192–207.

Bredeweg, B., Kragten, M., Holt, J., Kruit, P., van Eijck, T., Pijls, M., Bouwer, A., Sprinkhuizen, M., Jaspar, E., & de Boer, M. (2023a). Learning with Interactive Knowledge Representations. *Applied Sciences*, *13*(9), 5256.

Bredeweg, B., Kragten, M., Holt, J., Vaendel, D., Hanse, J., & Bloemen, S. (2023b). Stargazing live! inspiring with real data in a mobile planetarium and learning through conceptual modelling. In C. Frasson, P. Mylonas, & C. Troussas (Eds.), *International Conference on Intelligent Tutoring Systems*. LNCS 13891, 257-269.

Bredeweg, B., Liem, J., Beek, W., Linnebank, F., Gracia, J., Lozano, E., ... & Mioduser, D. (2013). DynaLearn – An intelligent learning environment for learning conceptual knowledge. *Ai Magazine*, *34*(4), 46–65

Cohen, R., Eylon, B., & Ganiel, U. (1983). Potential difference and current in simple electric circuits: A study of students' concepts. *American Journal of Physics* 51(5), 407–412.

DynaLearn (2025) *DynaLearn*. Available at: https://dynalearn.nl/ (Accessed 19 June 2025). The presented lesson is available via https://create.dynalearn.nl. Select 'Login with code' using TCX64D (English) or XL4S4V (Dutch).

Forbus, K.D. (2019). *Qualitative representations: How people reason and learn about the continuous world*. MIT Press.

Kragten, M., & Bredeweg, B. (2024). Calcium Regulation Assignment: Alternative Styles in Successfully Learning About Biological Mechanisms. In A. M. Olney, I.-A. Chounta, Z. Liu, O. C. Santos, & I. I. Bittencourt (Eds.), *International Conference on Artificial Intelligence in Education*. LNAI 14829, 220–234.

Kragten, M., Jaspar, E., & Bredeweg, B. (2022). Learning Domain Knowledge and Systems Thinking using Qualitative Representations in Secondary Education (grade 10-12). In *35th International Workshop on Qualitative Reasoning* – Co-located at International Conference on Artificial Intelligence, 13–22.

Quezada-Espinoza, M., Dominguez, A., & Zavala, G. (2023). How Difficult are Simple Electrical Circuit Conceptions? New Findings. *European Journal of Educational Research*, 12(3), 1269–1284.

Shipstone, D.M., Rhöneck, C.V., Jung, W., Kärrqvist, C., Dupin, J.J., Johsua, S., & Licht, P. (1988). A study of students' understanding of electricity in five European countries. *International Journal of Science Education*. 10(3), 303–316.

Viard, J., & Khantine-Langlois, F. (2001). The concept of electrical resistance: How Cassirer's philosophy, and the early developments of electric circuit theory, allow a better understanding of students' learning difficulties. *Science & Education* 10(3), 267–286.

UNDERSTANDING WHAT STUDENTS LEARN FROM AUTHENTIC SCIENCE AND ENGINEERING PRACTICES

Nancy Butler Songer, Julia Calabrese, Holly Cordner and Daniel Aina
The University of Utah, USA

ABSTRACT

Even as professional scientists and engineers have identified a set of steps for problem-solving in authentic settings, pre- university curricular programs that combine science and engineering towards solutions are not common. We present research studies that implemented and evaluated the assessment of student learning (ages 10-14) associated with curricular programs that followed a new instructional approach integrating science and engineering to design solutions to authentic problems. We evaluated student learning outcomes using assessment instruments that presented strong validity arguments. Utilizing Design-Based Research (DBR), we studied student learning with 554 adolescents over three cycles. Outcomes include validated assessment instruments that provide evidence of science and engineering learning, as well as statistically significant, yet varied, outcomes in each cycle. Conclusions reflect on what was learned from the design of curricular programs and assessment tasks that integrate science and engineering.

KEYWORDS

Science, Engineering, Problem-Solving, Secondary Students, Assessment

1. INTRODUCTION

Recent research has shown that professional scientists and engineers follow a common set of interrelated decisions when solving problems authentic problems in the sciences and engineering. A study by Price et al. (2021), based on interviews with professionals across a wide range of scientific and engineering disciplines, identified a consistent decision-making process used in authentic contexts. This process consists of interconnected and iterative decisions that draw on background knowledge and practices from both the sciences and engineering resulting in a series of steps to provide tested solutions for real-world challenges.

However, even as we understand how problem solving occurs by professionals, many pre-university instructional programs do not provide opportunities for our youth to deepen their learning through iterative decisions in science and engineering toward the creation of solutions. This is true even though national standards, such as those in the United States (NGSS Lead States, 2013), explicitly discuss how problem solving naturally involves iterative and interconnected thinking from the sciences, mathematics and engineering. This kind of knowledge that is fostered through the practices of both science and engineering can be described as three-dimensional science (3D, NRC, 2014). In programs that foster 3D science, the dimensions are fostered simultaneously and consist of: disciplinary core ideas, crosscutting concepts, and science and engineering practices. One of the challenges is assessment of learning (Gotwals & Songer, 2013). In other words, even if programs foster 3D science, the design and evaluation of assessment instruments that provide evidence of this learning is difficult. This paper addresses these challenges through research studies that describe a learning model that fosters 3D science for youth 10-14 and provides evidence of student outcomes.

2. INSTRUCTIONAL MODEL, RESEARCH STUDIES AND OUTCOMES

2.1 A New Instructional Model

Our research goal was to design and evaluate an instructional model that provides youth ages 10-14 with multiple opportunities to conduct problem solving that mirrors the work of professionals in the design of solutions to local environmental problems. Our instructional model, Iterative Science and Engineering (ISE), draws from existing instructional models in the sciences and engineering (e.g., Bybee et al, 2006) and fosters problem solving in science and engineering in an iterative, creative, and mutually beneficial process. In our instructional approach, instructional activities systematically provide science investigation and engineering design iterations over multiple weeks, with each iteration informing the next step. This design was created to mirror how professionals apply scientific and engineering knowledge in a beneficial and iterative process.

As outlined in Table 1 and illustrated in Figure 1, activities in ISE are grounded in an interdisciplinary phenomenon introduced in the first Engage phase, such as an invitation from the Department of Agriculture to study local invasive insects. This phase is followed by Explore that include multiple rounds of data collection including, for example, data collected on the number and kinds of invasive insects in their region. Explore is followed by Explain, which focuses on the analysis of student-generated data and the construction of arguments that utilize student data as evidence. In Engineer, students draw from their analysis in a multi-step engineering design process leading to multiple designs, and, in some cases, physical building of insect traps to mitigate local invasive insect populations. In any enactment of the full ISE model, students cycle between phases emphasizing science (e.g., Explore and Explain) and engineering design (Engineer) up to three times.

Table 1. Phases of the Iterative Science & Engineering Instructional Model. Bold text indicates steps that are iterations

Engage: Students ask questions and obtain a purpose for their study.
Explore: Students collect data to use as evidence to understand their problem.
Explain: Students analyze their data, construct arguments & consider a solution.
Engineer: Students design and build a solution that meets specific design criteria.
Explore: Students collect data to evaluate their first build (solution).
Explain: Students analyze data and revise their solutions.
***Engineer:* Students revisit their design and build a second design.**
***Explore:* Students collect data on the effectiveness of their solutions.**
***Explain:* Students analyze data and determine solution effectiveness.**
Educate: Students synthesize data and educate others.

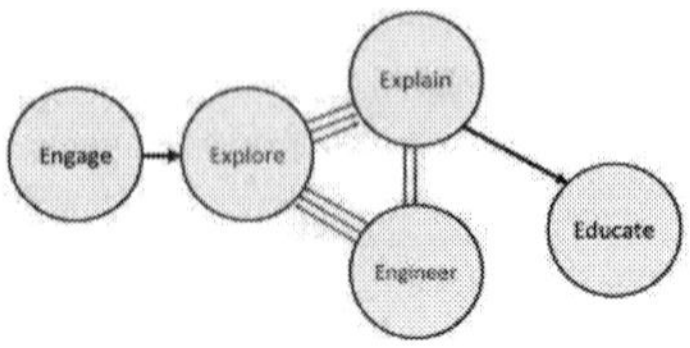

Figure 1. The Iterative Science and Engineering Instructional Model

We designed a six week, field-based curricular unit that manifested the ISE learning model called Invasive Insects. In this curricular unit, students conducted a series of activities to study and design traps to mitigate the populations of one local invasive insect that was harmful to ecosystem stability and/or local agriculture. In the final phase of the unit, students summarized what they had learned and created infographics to share designs.

2.2 Research Materials and Methods

Our question is: What evidence of 3D science and engineering do adolescents demonstrate in association with the Invasive Insect science and engineering curricular unit as measured by pre-post assessment?

To ensure we had an assessment instrument that provided valid and reliable information of student outcomes, we designed an identical pre and posttest instrument following recommendations on developing assessments that provide evidence of three-dimensional (3D) problem solving knowledge and student proficiency in science. We also built on our previous work in the design and validity evaluation of science assessments to create tasks that mirrored many of the activities conducted during the six weeks of classroom instruction but with scaffolds or hints diminished or removed. These assessment tasks with limited scaffolds or hints were designed to provide evidence of students' 3D science and engineering knowledge with limited assistance. After task design, we conducted cognitive interviews with ten students to provide validity information that provided evidence that the items elicited information about the intended construct.

We implemented our curricular program over three design-based research (DBR) cycles (Design-Based Research Collective, 2003) with a total of 554 adolescents in five classroom settings in the mountain states of the United States (for more details on the research program associated with these studies, see Songer et al., 2024). We selected DBR as a research approach as it was an excellent fit to our studies focused on the design, enactment, and revision of an innovation in an early phase of research and design.

In all DBR cycles, the pre/post-test was worth 21 points. Constructing 3D scientific arguments was nine points, and the remaining short answer items accounted for 12 points. In the three multi-part constructing scientific argument questions, students were required to complete scientific arguments with limited scaffolds. The remaining questions included a variety of constructed response items that mirrored 3D learning in the unit, including construction of food webs and improvements to a trap designed to mitigate invasive insects. Figures 2 and 3 provides samples of assessment tasks on the identical pre and posttests.

Two researchers scored each of test. Codes were compared to compute interrater reliability ($k = 96.2\%$). To examine accuracy, we conducted 80 spot checks (100% accuracy). We conducted a Kolmogorov-Smirnov test for normality before evaluating any pretest/posttest or between-group differences. In all cases, results indicated that the data were not normally distributed ($p < 0.05$). Therefore, to calculate changes between the pretest and posttest, we used a Wilcoxon Sign Rank test. Finally, to examine the magnitude of the effects of changes between groups, we calculated r^2 by dividing the square of the Z statistic by the sample size.

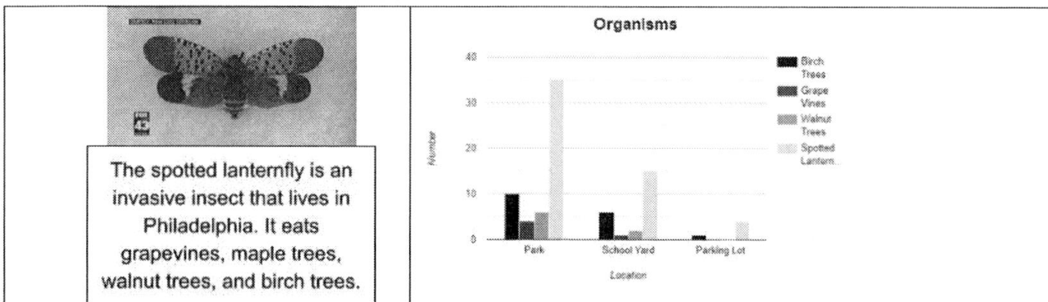

Write a Claim-Evidence-Reasoning (CER) argument to answer the scientific question, "Would placing traps in the park reduce the number of spotted lanternflies?"

Figure 2. Example scientific argument constructed response item (with no scaffolds) from the pre and posttest

Rowan and Lily built the trap below to catch an invasive insect in our schoolyard. They are going to place the trap on a mountain trail to catch insect eggs in February.

What are three suggestions you have to improve Rowan and Lily's trap?

Figure 3. Example engineering design constructed response item from the pre and posttest

2.3 Results

Student learning outcomes demonstrated significant pre-post improvements in each of the three DBR cycles, even as the results varied by cycle and population. For example, Cycle 1 students demonstrated significant improvement on 3D scientific argument questions ($p < .001$, $r^2 = 0.57$). This was true for both of the subparts as well, i.e., scientific argument ($p < 0.001$, $r^2 = 0.44$) and other constructed response items ($p < 0.001$, $r^2 = 0.48$). even as Cycle 1 students did not demonstrate significant improvement on engineering design tasks. In reflection, we realized that the version of the Invasive Insects unit used by Cycle 1 students including only one time for each of the Explore-Explain-Engineering phases and students did not physically construct any insect traps. As a result, even as we kept the unit length to six weeks, we implemented a few changes to our curricular program in advance of Cycle 2 including expanding pieces of the Engineer phase so that some student teams had time to build insect traps. Nevertheless, our student outcomes in Cycle 2 were similar to those in Cycle 1 where students demonstrated statistically significant differences ($p < .001$) from the pretest to the posttest in 3D scientific argument questions and other constructed response items but did not demonstrate significant improvement on the assessment tasks associated with engineering design ($p = .100$).

Upon reflection of these outcomes, we realized that that to understand the engineering design cycle completely, students needed to not only physically build one trap but they also needed to provide peer critique of each other's trap designs and subsequently build a second trap that incorporated the improvements. This emphasis on introducing more iterative cycles through the phases of the ISE learning model (Figure 1 and Table 1) facilitated more time for students to reflect on the pros and cons of their first trap build prior to physically building a second version of their trap. In addition, the changes to the Cycle 3 unit facilitated student learning associated with a new and important 3D Science Standard, "MS-LS2-5 Evaluate competing design solutions for maintaining biodiversity and ecosystem services" (NGSS Lead States, 2013).

Cycle 3 student outcomes reflected the importance of these changes, as Cycle 3 students were the only group that demonstrated statistically significant improvements on the engineering design tasks. In other words, student outcome results demonstrated statistically significant improvements ($p < .01$) by students from pretest to posttest in all categories. Student outcomes in engineering design were not only statistically significant, but they represented the largest change (0.56 points out of 3; 90.3% improvement.)

3. CONCLUSION

We presented research studies associated with the implementation and study of student learning with curricular programs following the ISE instructional approach in three research cycles. We evaluated student learning outcomes using assessment instruments that presented strong validity arguments. While student outcomes demonstrated significant improvement from pre to posttest in some areas in all three cycles, we saw the strongest improvements in Cycle 3 after reflecting on outcomes from two prior cycles and adjusting the ISE unit to emphasize more iteration of science and engineering. While our design-based research data do not allow any causal connections between curricular changes and student outcomes, we believe that the curricular changes that fostered more time for 3D engineering design, reflection, and re-building allowed students opportunities to conduct integrated scientific problem-solving and engineering design more similar to that commonly practiced by professional scientists and engineers.

We developed these research studies recognizing that problem-solving and designing solutions for authentic, real-world problems are not simple, and curricular programs that iterate between science and engineering are not standard in pre-university settings. If we expect citizens of the future to be comfortable with science-influenced engineering design and the critique and improvement of solutions, these kinds of programs must become a central component of pre-university instruction.

REFERENCES

Bybee, R., Taylor, J. A., Gardner, A., Van Scotter, P., Powell, J., Westbrook, A., and Landes, N. (2006). The BSCS 5E Instructional Model: Origins and Effectiveness. A report prepared for the Office of Science Education NIH. https://www.researchgate.net/publication/281412517_The_BSCS_5E_instructional_model_Origins_and_effectiveness

Design-Based Research Collective. (2003). Design-Based Research: An Emerging Paradigm for Educational Inquiry. *Educ. Res.*, 32, 5–8.

National Research Council [NRC] (2014). *Developing Assessments for the Next Generation Science Standards*. Pellegrino, J.W., Wilson, M.R., Koenig, J.A., Beatty, S.A., Eds.; The National Academies Press: Washington, DC, USA.

NGSS Lead States. (2013). *Next Generation Science Standards: For States, by States.* The National Academies Press: Washington, DC, USA.

Price, AM, Kim, CJ, Burkholder, EW, Fritz, AV, Wieman, CE. (2021). A Detailed Characterization of the Expert Problem- Solving Process in Science and Engineering: Guidance for Teaching and Assessment. *CBE Life Sci Educ. 2021 Sep;20(3)*:ar43. doi: 10.1187/cbe.20-12-0276. PMID: 34388005; PMCID: PMC8715817.

Songer, N.B.; Calabrese, J.E.; Cordner, H.; Aina, D. (2024). Usable STEM: Student Outcomes in Science and Engineering Associated with the Iterative Science and Engineering Instructional Model. Educ. Sci. 2024, 14, 1255. https://doi.org/10.3390/educsci14111255

DETECTING AI-ASSISTED CHEATING IN ONLINE EXAMS THROUGH BEHAVIOR ANALYTICS

Gökhan Akçapınar
Department of Computer Education and Instructional Technology
Hacettepe University Beytepe, 06800, Ankara, Turkey

ABSTRACT

AI-assisted cheating has emerged as a significant threat in the context of online exams. Advanced browser extensions now enable large language models (LLMs) to answer questions presented in online exams within seconds, thereby compromising the security of these assessments. In this study, the behaviors of students (N = 52) on an online exam platform during a proctored, face-to-face exam were analyzed using clustering methods, with the aim of identifying groups of students exhibiting suspicious behavior potentially associated with cheating. Additionally, students in different clusters were compared in terms of their exam scores. Suspicious exam behaviors in this study were defined as selecting text within the question area, right-clicking, and losing focus on the exam page. The total frequency of these behaviors performed by each student during the exam was extracted, and k-Means clustering was employed for the analysis. The findings revealed that students were classified into six clusters based on their suspicious behaviors. It was found that students in four of the six clusters, representing approximately 33% of the total sample, exhibited suspicious behaviors at varying levels. When the exam scores of these students were compared, it was observed that those who engaged in suspicious behaviors scored, on average, 30–40 points higher than those who did not. Although further research is necessary to validate these findings, this preliminary study provides significant insights into the detection of AI-assisted cheating in online exams using behavior analytics.

KEYWORDS

Online Exams, AI-Assisted Cheating, Cheating Detection, Behavior Analytics, Academic Integrity

1. INTRODUCTION

Large language models (LLMs) based on generative artificial intelligence have demonstrated high performance across various domains in benchmark studies (Ali and Xie, 2025). While these capabilities may present significant potential for educational purposes, they also pose substantial risks to assessment, which is a critical component of the educational process. Recent studies have highlighted that students frequently use AI tools such as ChatGPT for cheating purposes (Kazley et al., 2025). Furthermore, specialized AI tools have been developed specifically to facilitate cheating in online exams. These tools operate as browser extensions and are capable of rapidly detecting questions either from text or screenshots, generating answers within seconds. This represents a significant threat to the security of online assessments. However, the extent to which these tools are used by students remains unknown.

It is observed that most studies on the detection of cheating in online exams primarily focus on proctoring and identifying cheating based on students' physical behaviors (Wang et al., 2025, Leong, 2025). On the other hand, research addressing AI-assisted cheating has largely concentrated either on detecting AI-assisted plagiarism (Steponenaite and Barakat, 2023) or on pedagogical strategies aimed at preventing AI-assisted cheating (Leaton Gray et al., 2025). The commonality among these studies is the recognition that generative AI technologies, such as large language models, constitute a significant threat to academic integrity.

It is noteworthy that there are very few studies aiming to detect AI-assisted cheating in online exams based on students' exam-taking behaviors. On the other hand, previous studies have shown that students' exam logs provide valuable insights into their exam-taking behaviors (Yıldırım et al., 2023). Therefore, this study investigates whether it is possible to identify behaviors related to AI-assisted cheating by analyzing students' online exam-taking behaviors.

2. METHOD

In this study, exam data from 52 students were analyzed. The data were collected from first-year undergraduate students enrolled in the Department of Computer Education and Instructional Technology during the final exam of the Introductory Programming course. The students took the exam using a web-based exam tool developed by the author. The exam consisted of 25 multiple-choice questions. To enhance exam security, both the order of the questions and the order of the options were randomized for each student. Questions were presented one at a time on the students' screens, and navigation between questions was not permitted. Additionally, the time allowed for each question was limited to 90 seconds. When the allotted time expired, the system was configured to automatically proceed to the next question. The exam was administered in a computer laboratory under the supervision of the course instructor. Students participated in the exam either using computers available in the laboratory or their personal computers. Prior to the exam, students were informed about the academic integrity policy regarding cheating. Students were instructed not to navigate to any page or application other than the exam page during the exam.

In addition to student responses, the developed exam system also recorded students' interactions while answering questions. These interactions included mouse clicks, text selection, loss of page focus, copying, pasting, and so on. Within the scope of this study, three metrics that could serve as indicators of AI-assisted cheating were utilized: the number of text selections (TSC), the number of right-click actions (RCC), and the number of times the page focus was lost (FLC). These metrics were determined by examining popular browser extensions commonly used for cheating, such as AnswerAI.

During the data preprocessing stage, these metrics were calculated for each question individually, and then aggregated totals were obtained for the entire exam. Subsequently, the data were analyzed using clustering method. Clustering analysis is an unsupervised machine learning approach employed to group similar patterns within the data (Demšar and Zupan, 2024). The k-Means clustering algorithm was used for this purpose. All analyses were conducted using the Orange Data Mining software (Demšar et al., 2013). The optimal number of clusters was then determined by evaluating silhouette scores (Rousseeuw, 1987) across a range of 2 to 8 clusters. In other words, the data mining tool tested different cluster solutions on the normalized data and selected the number of clusters that yielded the highest silhouette score as the optimal solution.

3. RESULTS

As a result of the clustering analysis, the optimal number of clusters was determined to be six, and students were subsequently grouped into six distinct clusters based on their suspicious behaviors during the exam. Figure 1 presents a graph displaying the cluster means for the variables used in the clustering process. The distribution of students across the clusters is as follows: Cluster 1 (C1) included 3 students, Cluster 2 (C2) included 34 students, Cluster 3 (C3) included 6 students, Cluster 4 (C4) included 4 students, Cluster 5 (C5) included 1 student, and Cluster 6 (C6) included 4 students.

An examination of the cluster means presented in Figure 1 indicates that students were divided into distinct groups based on the type and frequency of suspicious behaviors exhibited during the exam. Students in Clusters 1 (C1), 4 (C4), and 6 (C6) demonstrated similar behavioral patterns, characterized by frequent occurrences of text selection, focus loss, and right-click actions—all considered suspicious behaviors. In contrast, students in Cluster 2 (C2) did not exhibit any suspicious behaviors. Students in Cluster 3 (C3) displayed a low frequency of text selection, did not use right-click actions, but frequently lost focus on the exam page. The single student in Cluster 5 (C5) exclusively engaged in a high number of text selections, without exhibiting right-click or focus loss behaviors.

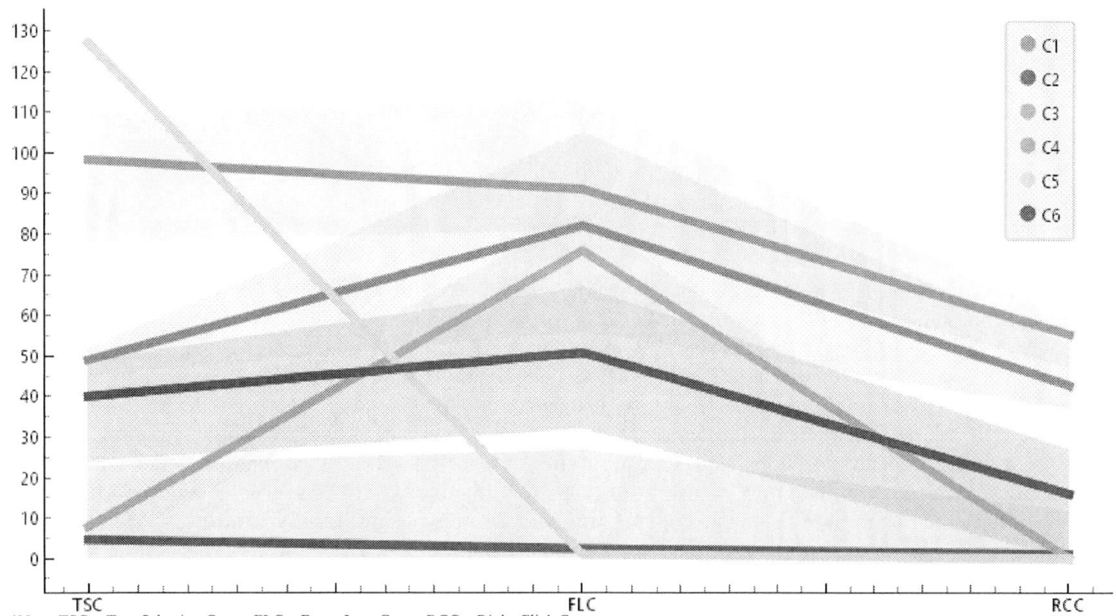

*Note: TSC = Text Selection Count; FLC = Focus Loss Count; RCC = Right-Click Count.

Figure 1. Cluster means*

Descriptive statistics regarding the exam scores of students in each cluster were presented in Table 1. According to these results, students in Cluster 2 (C2), who did not exhibit any suspicious behaviors, achieved an average score of 40.94. In contrast, students in Clusters 1 (C1), 4 (C4), and 6 (C6), who demonstrated high frequencies of suspicious behaviors, obtained average scores of 82.67, 77.27, and 57.00, respectively. Students in Cluster 3 (C3), who only showed a high frequency of focus loss, had an average score of 72.00, while the single student in Cluster 5 (C5), who exhibited only a high number of text selection actions, scored 32.00.

Table 1. Descriptive statistics for exam scores

Cluster	*N*	*Mean*	*Std.*	*Median*
C1	3	82.67	7.54	88.00
C2	34	40.94	18.36	42.00
C3	6	72.00	10.83	70.00
C4	4	77.27	4.95	76.54
C5	1	32.00	0.00	32.00
C6	4	57.00	9.11	54.00

4. DISCUSSION AND CONCLUSION

AI cheating extensions that can be installed on web browsers typically operate as follows: first, the user selects the question text; next, they right-click to open the context menu and choose the extension from the menu. The extension then pops up a window on the right side of the page, providing an answer along with some explanations. Another method of cheating, without using a browser extension, involves copying or taking a screenshot of the question and submitting it to AI tools such as ChatGPT or Gemini. In order to use such cheating methods, students must engage in behaviors such as text selection, right-clicking, and loss of page focus when using browser extensions, or copying and taking screenshots when submitting questions to AI tools. In standard exam-taking behavior, there is no situation that would require the constant, simultaneous use of all three behaviors. However, students in Clusters 1 (C1), 4 (C4), and 6 (C6) (N = 11) demonstrated all three of these suspicious behaviors, though at varying levels. The exam scores of students in these clusters were also substantially higher than those of students in Cluster 2 (C2), who did not exhibit any suspicious behaviors. Therefore, there is a strong likelihood that students in C1, C4, and C6 made use of such AI extensions.

For Cluster 3 (C3), the six students exhibited high rates of focus loss, but did not demonstrate text selection or right-click behaviors. Frequent focus loss indicates that these students were often switching between the exam screen and other tabs or applications during the exam. Such behavior is also inconsistent with standard exam-taking practices, particularly as students were explicitly instructed prior to the exam not to navigate away from the exam page. Notably, the average exam scores of students in this cluster were approximately 35 points higher than those in the non-suspicious group (C2). This raises suspicions that these students may have used AI tools such as ChatGPT in another tab or window during the exam.

On the other hand, the student in Cluster 5 (C5) performed a high number of text selections, but did not engage in right-clicking or focus loss behaviors. This student's exam score was also significantly below the average. It was observed during the exam that some students tend to select text while reading the questions, employing it as a reading strategy. Therefore, text selection alone is not necessarily indicative of cheating.

The likelihood that students cheated using sources other than AI is quite low, as the structure of the exam system presented all questions and answer options to each student in a random order. Students were prevented from returning to previous questions, and the time they could spend on each question was limited. Therefore, the possibility of students copying from one another is significantly reduced. As a result, although these results alone may not be sufficient to conclusively prove cheating, the findings clearly indicate that AI-based cheating constitutes a significant threat to the integrity of online exams. Even in a proctored, face-to-face exam setting, 32.69% of students exhibited suspicious behaviors potentially related to AI-assisted cheating. This study also contributes to future research by identifying behavioral indicators that may be associated with AI-assisted cheating.

REFERENCES

Ali, M. & Xie, B. (2025). Automated Benchmarking Infrastructure: Moving Toward Robust Investigations of Gen AI in Computing Education. *ACM Inroads,* 16, 46–51.

Demšar, J., et al. (2013). Orange: data mining toolbox in Python. *the Journal of machine Learning research,* 14, 2349-2353.

Demšar, J. & Zupan, B. (2024). Hands-on training about data clustering with orange data mining toolbox. *PLOS Computational Biology,* 20, e1012574.

Kazley, A. S., et al. (2025). Is use of ChatGPT cheating? Students of health professions perceptions. *Medical Teacher,* 47, 894-898.

Leaton Gray, S., et al. (2025). AI-Based Digital Cheating At University, and the Case for New Ethical Pedagogies. *Journal of Academic Ethics.*

Leong, W. Y. (2025). Enhancing Academic Integrity in E-Exams Through AI-Driven Proctoring Technologies. 14th International Conference on Educational and Information Technology (ICEIT), 14-16 March 2025, 392-396.

Rousseeuw, P. J. (1987). Silhouettes: a graphical aid to the interpretation and validation of cluster analysis. *Journal of computational and applied mathematics,* 20, 53-65.

Steponenaite, A. & Barakat, B. (2023). Plagiarism in AI Empowered World. *In:* ANTONA, M. & STEPHANIDIS, C., eds. Universal Access in Human-Computer Interaction, 2023// 2023 Cham. Springer Nature Switzerland, 434-442.

Wang, P., et al. (2025). Smart proctoring with automated anomaly detection. *Education and Information Technologies,* 30, 9269-9288.

Yıldırım, D., et al. (2023). The Effects of Exam Setting on Students' Test-Taking Behaviors and Performances: Proctored Versus Unproctored. *International Review of Research in Open and Distributed Learning,* 24, 174-193.

ENGAGEMENT ANALYTICS: FIRST RESULTS OF A SYSTEMATIC LITERATURE REVIEW

Prosper Sanou, Eric Bittar and Bart Lamiroy
CReSTIC - Reims Champagne-Ardenne University
UFR Sciences Exactes et Naturelles - Moulin de la Housse - BP 1039 - 51687 Reims CEDEX 2 - France

ABSTRACT

This paper presents preliminary findings from a systematic literature review on learner engagement in digital learning environments, conducted in the context of developing a national public health educational platform in France. The study investigates how to support learning in open platforms, the nature of learner engagement, and methods to measure and foster it. Engagement is examined both as an indicator of learning and as a predictor of success, with various conceptualizations identified in the literature, including behavioral, cognitive, emotional, and academic dimensions. The review analyzed 608 articles across ten scientific databases, narrowing down to 79 relevant publications after filtering by discipline and publication date. The findings highlight diverse approaches to measuring engagement—through activity quantity, time investment, and quality of learner behavior—and provide a theoretical basis for defining meaningful engagement indicators. These results will inform the design of trace collection and analytics tools for the forthcoming digital learning platform.

KEYWORDS

Learning Analytics, Engagement, Systematic Literature Review

1. INTRODUCTION

The French national public health institute is preparing a nationwide campaign aimed at developing the psychosocial skills of the French population. This initiative targets two main audiences: adults in educational roles (such as parents, teachers, educators, and nurses), and young people aged 16 to 25 from diverse social backgrounds. As part of this campaign, a publicly accessible digital learning platform will be developed.

Our role is to collect, with users' consent, digital traces of activity on this platform and to construct indicators that reflect user engagement, with the dual aim of assessing the platform's relevance and providing recommendations for its improvement. The platform is still in the design and deployment phase. At this preparatory stage, we have undertaken a broad exploration of learner engagement within digital learning environments.

While numerous studies have examined engagement in higher education—where learners are typically motivated by the prospect of earning a degree—our context differs in that users may be either young people or adults, and the platform offers only a certificate of participation upon completion.

Our research questions are as follows:

1. How can learning be supported in an open digital platform?
2. What are the key characteristics of learner engagement?
3. How can engagement be measured and promoted in an open learning environment?

We address the first question in the next section, while the remaining two are explored through a systematic literature review (SLR), the methodology and initial findings of which are presented subsequently. To provide a coherent account, the literature reviewed is organized along three analytical axes: (a) how engagement is conceptualized (indicator vs predictor), (b) how it is measured (quantity, time, quality), and (c) how multidimensional models inform digital trace design.

2. LEARNER ENGAGEMENT TO SUPPORT LEARNING

Dehaene, as cited by (Treuillier and Boyer 2022), emphasizes that student engagement is essential for ensuring a high-quality learning process. Similarly, (Tang 2014), cited by (Willans et al. 2019), explains that engagement is widely regarded as a desirable attribute in learners. Engagement plays two major roles: it serves both as an indicator of learning and as a predictor of success.

Engagement as a Learning Indicator. (Iksal 2012) defines an indicator as a pedagogically meaningful observable, calculated or inferred from observed data, which reflects the quality of interaction or learning activity. Indicators can focus on pedagogical tools, learning content, or on users such as learners and teachers. As a specific learning indicator, engagement relies on various sub-indicators such as presence, participation, perseverance, and performance, that help to establish engagement profiles (Soussia 2022).

Engagement as a Predictor of Success. Learner engagement is recognized as a critical factor in educational achievement (Rozo 2019) and academic success (Tzimas and Demetriadis 2021). However, definitions of success vary across educational projects. While high levels of engagement are generally associated with better learning outcomes, the concept of engagement remains multifaceted and context-dependent.

Some of the articles cited in this section 2 come from our preliminary research, others come from the SLR which we present below. These definitions highlight the types of digital traces that may be relevant for our platform (presence, participation, perseverance) and point to the need for multi-indicator engagement profiles.

3. SYSTEMATIC LITERATURE REVIEW ON ENGAGEMENT

Our SLR focuses on learner engagement within digital learning contexts. We selected English-language peer-reviewed scientific publications within the fields of Learning Analytics (LA), Educational Data Mining (EDM), and Artificial Intelligence in Education (AIED).

The review targets research related specifically to learning contexts, including Massive Open Online Courses (MOOCs), Learning Management Systems (LMS), and Intelligent Tutoring Systems (ITS). It emphasizes key concepts such as engagement, motivation, and behavior, in relation to learners or students, and aims to identify relevant indicators and predictors of engagement. To narrow the scope, we limited our search to articles published from 2014 onward.

The query below was run across ten major academic search engines and repositories. Table 1 presents the results.

("learning" OR "MOOC" OR "LMS" OR "ITS") AND ("Learning Analytic" OR "Educational Data Mining" OR "Artificial Intelligence in Education") AND ("engagement" OR "motivation" OR "behavior" OR "behaviour") AND ("student" OR "learner") AND ("indicator" OR "predictor")

Table 1. Quantitative results of the request

Library or search engine	Results
JLA (Journal of Learning Analytics)	13
JEDM (Journal of Educational Data Mining)	4
IJAIE (International Journal of Artificial Intelligence in Education)	7
CJLT (Canadian Journal of Learning and Technology)	6
ERIC (Education Resources Information Center)	133
ACM (Association for Computing Machinery)	163
Web of Science	16
Science Direct	164
Wiley	34
Scopus	68
Total	**608**

After removing duplicate entries, the dataset included 593 unique articles. We then filtered these based on disciplinary relevance by scanning for specific keywords in the abstracts using Zotero, a bibliographic management tool:

Abstract ["Learning Analytics" OR "Educational Data Mining" OR "Artificial Intelligence in Education"]

This filtering yielded 115 articles: 63 conference papers and 52 journal articles. For this initial stage of our study, we retained all 52 journal articles and selected 27 conference papers published from 2021, resulting in a corpus of 79 articles.

Here we include articles from the SLR, and also important articles cited by articles from the SLR.

4. APPROACHES AND DIMENSIONS OF LEARNER ENGAGEMENT

The articles reviewed in our systematic literature review reveal multiple conceptualizations of learner engagement. It is often regarded both as an indicator of learning and a predictor of success, and is measured through activity levels, time investment, or qualitative attributes of the learning process. Across the different studies, three main approaches to measuring engagement emerge.

First, several authors treat it as the quantity of actions. According to (Fredricks et al. 2004), engagement involves students performing acts, participating, and being involved in learning activities. In this sense, engagement is measurable through the quantity of activities, actions, or events. Similarly, (Pirot and De Ketele 2000), mention that only actions can be considered truly engaging. Engagement is thus conceptualized as the frequency or quantity of observable behaviors.

Second, other authors focus on time investment. (Jennings and Angelo 2006) assert that student engagement typically refers to the time and effort students dedicate to their academic experiences. (Ma et al. 2015), notes that since effort is difficult to quantify, time becomes the primary metric for evaluating engagement.

Third, a growing body of work emphasizes the quality of learning behaviour. (Kuh et al. 2007) define engagement as a combination of access, compliance, and investment. (Fredricks et al. 2004) also emphasize compliance, defining behavioral engagement as "doing the work and following the rules." Other researchers highlight the qualitative aspect of learner behavior. For instance, (D'Mello et al. 2017) describe behavioral engagement as active participation in learning, encompassing effort, persistence, and focus. (Newmann 1992) define engagement as psychological investment and effort directed toward learning, understanding, mastering knowledge, and developing competencies or skills. From this perspective, engagement reflects the purposeful quality of a learner's behavior.

Finally, multidimensional models integrate these perspectives. (Fredricks et al. 2004) present a three-dimensional model: behavioral, cognitive, and emotional. Behavioral engagement relates to observable actions, while cognitive engagement refers to intellectual investment, such as concentration, attention, and learning strategies. The emotional dimension—sometimes referred to as motivational—concerns learners' affective reactions toward the institution or instructor (Gérard et al., 2020).

(Reschly and Christenson 2006) propose a four-dimensional model, adding an academic dimension, which refers to extrinsic motivation, driven by institutional requirements or constraints.

5. CONCLUSION

Taken together, the studies reviewed provide a conceptual foundation to address our research questions. First, they clarify how learning can be supported in open platforms (RQ1) by emphasizing the importance of designing environments that foster behavioral, cognitive, and emotional engagement. Second, they contribute to identifying the key characteristics of engagement (RQ2), showing that engagement is both a dynamic process and a multidimensional construct that can be described through observable actions, invested time, and qualitative learning behaviors. Third, they suggest various methods for measuring and encouraging engagement (RQ3), from tracking frequency of actions to analyzing motivation and persistence.

This analysis identified a variety of definitions and dimensions of engagement, but did not seek to empirically validate or rank these models. The findings imply that future engagement analytics must adopt adaptive, context-sensitive approaches, supported by flexible platform design and interdisciplinary collaboration. Only then can trace-based systems meaningfully capture and promote the multifaceted nature of learner engagement in open digital environments.

In conclusion, this initial exploration of engagement, based on a systematic literature review, highlights the diverse metrics used to assess engagement—ranging from activity counts to time spent and the quality of learners' involvement. It will guide the development of engagement indicators adapted to the construction of trace-based learner profiles. Forthcoming work will now focus on three core dimensions of engagement: behavioral, cognitive, and affective, in relation to the specific context of our national educational platform.

REFERENCES

D'Mello, S., Dieterle, E., and Duckworth, A. (2017). 'Advanced, Analytic, Automated (AAA) Measurement of Engagement During Learning'. *Educational Psychologist* 52 (2): 104–23. https://doi.org/10.1080/00461520.2017.1281747.

Fredricks, J. A., Blumenfeld, P. C., and Paris, A. H. (2004). 'School Engagement: Potential of the Concept, State of the Evidence'. *Review of Educational Research* 74 (1): 59–109.

Iksal, S. (2012). 'Ingénierie de l'observation basée sur la prescription en EIAH'. Thesis, Université du Maine. https://theses.hal.science/tel-00991970.

Jennings, J. M., and Angelo, T. A. (2006). 'Student Engagement : Measuring and Enhancing Engagement with Learning.' Student Engagement : Measuring and En... | Items | National Library of New Zealand | National Library of New Zealand, Wellington, N.Z. : New Zealand Universities Academic Audit Unit, 2006., January 1. https://natlib.govt.nz/records/21618700.

Kuh, G. D., Kinzie, J., Buckley, J. A., Bridges, B. K., and Hayek, J. C. (2007). 'Piecing Together the Student Success Puzzle: Research, Propositions, and Recommendations. ASHE Higher Education Report, Volume 32, Number 5'. *ASHE Higher Education Report* 32 (5): 1–182. https://doi.org/10.1002/aehe.3205.

Ma, J., Han, X.,Yang, J., and Cheng, J. (2015). 'Examining the Necessary Condition for Engagement in an Online Learning Environment Based on Learning Analytics Approach: The Role of the Instructor'. *The Internet and Higher Education* 24 (January): 26–34. https://doi.org/10.1016/j.iheduc.2014.09.005.

Newmann, F. M. (1992). *Student Engagement and Achievement in American Secondary Schools*. Teachers College Press, 1234 Amsterdam Avenue, New York, NY 10027. https://eric.ed.gov/?id=ED371047.

Pirot, L., and De Ketele, J.-M. (2000). 'L'engagement académique de l'étudiant comme facteur de réussite à l'université Étude exploratoire menée dans deux facultés contrastées'. *Revue des sciences de l'éducation* 26 (2): 367–94. https://doi.org/10.7202/000127ar.

Reschly, A. L., and Christenson, S. L. (2006). 'Prediction of Dropout Among Students With Mild Disabilities: A Case for the Inclusion of Student Engagement Variables'. *Remedial and Special Education* 27 (5): 276–92. https://doi.org/10.1177/07419325060270050301.

Rozo, R. C. (2019). 'Monitoring learners' engagement in mind mapping activities from interaction traces'. Phdthesis, Université de Lyon. https://theses.hal.science/tel-02159628.

Soussia, A. B. (2022). 'Analyse prédictive des données d'apprentissage, en situation d'enseignement à distance'. Phdthesis, Université de Lorraine. https://hal.univ-lorraine.fr/tel-04056797.

Tang, R. (2014). 'Fostering Student Engagement in an Academic Writing Class through an Electronic Academic Writing Survey'. *Asian Journal of the Scholarship of Teaching and Learning* 4 (3): 142–53.

Treuillier, C., and Boyer, A. (2022). 'A New Way to Characterize Learning Datasets'. In *International Conference on Computer Supported Education, CSEDU - Proceedings*, edited by Cukurova M., Rummel N., Gillet D., McLaren B., and Uhomoibhi J., vol. 2. Science and Technology Publications, Lda. Scopus. https://doi.org/10.5220/0010982500003182.

Tzimas, D., and Demetriadis, S. (2021). 'The Impact of Learning Analytics on Student Performance and Satisfaction in a Higher Education Course'. In *Proc. Int. Conf. Educ. Data Min., EDM*, edited by Hsiao I.-H., Sahebi S., Bouchet F., and Vie J.-J. International Educational Data Mining Society. Scopus. https://www.scopus.com/inward/record.uri?eid=2-s2.0-85174841452&partnerID=40&md5=574cf60fabfe0850682c3534830c6fbf.

Willans, F., Fonolahi, A., Buadromo, R., Bryce, T., Prasad, R., and Kumari, S. (2019). 'Fostering and Evaluating Learner Engagement with Academic Literacy Support: Making the Most of Moodle'. *Journal of University Teaching and Learning Practice* 16 (4). https://eric.ed.gov/?id=EJ1230070.

STUDENT-CENTERED LEARNING AND PEDAGOGY IN THE AGE OF AI

Alexander Williams and Ngozi Harrison
University of California, Los Angeles
405 Hilgard Avenue, Los Angeles, CA 90095, USA

ABSTRACT

This short paper aims to discuss student-centered learning in the wake of generative AI and large language models (LLMs). Students are using AI to supplant their ability to think critically and analyze. Increasingly, teachers and educators are concerned about what the future of the classroom will look like in the midst of rapid technological change. There is a need for innovative approaches that reaffirm the value of creativity, critical thinking, and student agency. In response, we offer examples from our teaching experiences informed by our own pedagogical frameworks for continuing to center student learning and experiential learning in the face of AI. Our approach reflects our respective disciplinary training in Information Studies, Literature, Hip Hop Studies, and Critical Data Studies.

KEYWORDS

Student-Centered Learning, Pedagogy, Artificial Intelligence, Hip-Hop Pedagogy, Constructivism, Writing

1. INTRODUCTION

As researchers, scholars, and instructors, it is our responsibility to examine and review our educational practices and frameworks for the betterment of our students and profession. We conduct this evaluative work using frameworks that require us not to avoid but to embrace the most vexing problems that students face in the pursuit of education. With the growing integration of education and AI, large language models (LLMs), and other advanced technologies, these problems continue to present complications within and beyond the classroom. In the humanities, AI is often framed as a threat to classroom learning or as the future of education. Some claim that AI will provide every student with a chatbot tutor, making instructors obsolete, while others warn about the danger of overreliance on LLMs. Recent work published by a research team at Microsoft has shown that generative AI does have an impact on the cognitive skills and critical thinking skills of frequent users (Lee *et al.*, 2025). Lee e*t al.* conclude, based on a survey of knowledge workers, that while generative AI may improve productivity, overreliance can lead to less critical engagement to ensure the quality of work and diminished skill for independent problem solving. As teachers constantly seeking to utilize paradigms and practices with demonstrated impact and efficacy, my co-researcher and I hope this preliminary report will reinforce the need for student-centered learning and demonstrate pedagogies in the digital age from two different disciplinary perspectives. The goal of our approach is to reaffirm experiential learning as the foundation for developing critical reading, writing, and thinking skills that empower our students to critically and confidently engage with the evolving technologies shaping their world.

2. BODY OF PAPER

Arts-based research methods center diverse modalities in inquiry processes (e.g., drawing, painting, dance, film, poetry), thereby centering "affective experiences, senses, and bodies, and imagination and emotion as well as intellect" in knowledge-making (Finley, 2008). By inviting expansive ways of knowing and being into processes of knowledge production, arts-based methods center student experience, creativity, and previous knowledge silos in their learning. Even as scholars have begun to theorize the liberatory potentials of arts-based research methods in education and in the learning sciences more broadly (Cahnmann-Taylor and Siegesmund, 2017), we argue that there is still more work to be done to implement these methods in classrooms across academic disciplines, particularly given more ubiquitous student use of AI. Many of the technologies that are referred to as AI are shrouded in hype and mythology (Kapoor and Narayanan, 2024). Tools such as ChatGPT, diffusion models, agentic AI, and predictive AI are changing the way we think about the role of automation in society. Corporations market AI tools to students, universities, and faculty members and argue that AI will make many aspects of traditional education obsolete. While AI tools can be remarkably effective, there are a number of ethical, environmental, and social concerns that must be addressed. In addition, the role that AI plays within the academy should not be defined by corporations but instead should be in service of students and the learning environment. We argue that instead of blind acceptance of AI tools within the academy, the goal of teaching students in our contemporary moment should be to instill within them frameworks to critically think about technology. The classroom can be a space to practice the skill of critically analyzing claims about artificial intelligence, learning what AI systems can and cannot do, and learning how to design and build the kind of sociotechnical futures we would like to see. Alongside this critical engagement with technology, there is a need to affirm the kinds of experiential education and artistic expression. The following example from the hip-hop studies co-author demonstrates his pedagogical experience using arts-based research methods and hip-hop pedagogy to prompt student-centered learning and critical engagement with technology.

Research on hip-hop pedagogy (Stovall 2006, Alim 2007, Petchauer 2009) has established how this framework models an intellectually rich set of practices in which to frame multi-disciplinary learning. Recent studies, such as the Lyripeutics Storytelling Project (Nzinga *et al.*, 2023) have conducted multiple interventions to collect qualitative and quantitative data on these arts-based inquiries and methodologies. To test this research in the classroom, one co-author observed how hip-hop pedagogy facilitates the acquisition of expertise, life-long learning, and student-centered learning within a literary learning environment. While teaching a creative writing course, the co-author implemented a lesson plan exposing their students to hip-hop and its use as a method of self-reflection, critical analysis, and reading comprehension. To provide their students with a theoretical foundation before participating in the lesson, they assigned three readings articulating the use of poetic devices in hip-hop, hip-hop's importance in literature, and the body's role in producing hip-hop. To accompany student engagement with the lesson's critical texts, they assigned the students several songs spanning multiple subgenres to introduce them to a variety of flows, rhyme schemes, and lyrical approaches the students themselves could incorporate into the upcoming assignment. The co-author's theoretical background in hip-hop pedagogy, comprised of Alim, Stovall, Petchauer, Emdin, and others, guided their construction of the lesson plan's learning objectives and its intersecting components centering the student within each organizational element. The assignment was simple:

> "Using the information from our class readings and the week's assigned songs, craft a verse to be rapped to the beat provided in the Week 9 module. The verse should demonstrate a keen attention to detail regarding syncopation and rhythm. Below are some elements that may prove helpful in thinking through when crafting your verses. I am not expecting these verses to be perfect, but I do want you to try your best and to have fun!"

To prepare the students in writing their lyrics, the co-author led an in-class exercise exposing their students to the production technologies and techniques used to create hip-hop instrumentals and linked this musical work to the writing exercises and tools developed throughout the quarter. As the co-author demonstrated the techniques producers employ in making drum loops, bass lines, and the like, they articulated this work as a method of brainstorming akin to how one would generate critical observations and ideas about a text or poem. By demonstrating the musical and literary elements of hip-hop with their students in real time, the co-author empowered them to pursue the themes, flow, and content that spoke to them as individuals, writers, and participants of a deep cultural artform. After spending time on their own and wrestling with their lyrics, the students returned to the classroom the following week and performed their raps to each other as a ritual of community formation, student-centered learning, and kinship. Using a "holistic approach…incorporating theory and practice" (Alim 2007), the lesson plan was designed to showcase how dynamic writing can be as a process and technology's place inside and out of the classroom. If one of these students, after completing the aforementioned lesson, were to enter the assignment prompt into ChatGPT they would have the necessary tools to critically engage with ChatGPT's output by testing the output's rhyme scheme, flow, and use of other poetic devices. As educators living in the wake of AI's integration with learning, we can teach students how to critically engage with both the output of Large Language Models and the technology itself by explaining how these models work, providing space in class to explore and demystify these technologies while also discussing their social implications. In our pedagogies, we, the authors, understand that critically engaging with technology is an extension of the reading, writing, and critical thinking skills we develop and equip them with in the classroom.

Techno-determinism is a theory that holds that technology proceeds on a linear path and technological disruption is inevitable (Dunbar, 2023). For example, the claim that AI will inevitably replace artists and writers is a techno-determinist narrative. This framework is limited because it obscures the many societal factors that inform how technologies evolve and denies human agency. Our critique of techno-determinism is informed by the disciplinary training of one of our co-authors within Critical Information Studies, Critical Data Studies, and the emerging field of Critical AI Studies (Noble 2018, Klein & Posner 2020, Raley & Rhee, 2023). Giving students the tools to critically analyze technologies helps them to identify the politics, harmful social effects, and asymmetrical power relations embedded in the tech we use every day. One example of these critical socio-technical frameworks being used in an educational context is the pedagogical approach of *critical race algorithmic literacy* (Tanksley 2024). This framework bridges critical race theory in education, critical race technology theory, and abolitionist pedagogy. Instead of a blind embrace of AI, students begin to think critically about their own position in relation to technological systems and how they might want to change those systems. Technical knowledge is a part of this process, but there is also a need for writing, reflection, and arts-based methods that span traditional disciplinary boundaries

In an *Introduction to Critical AI Studies* course, one co-author designed an assignment that incorporated both technical learning and reflective writing, titled a "Technical Autoethnography." The co-author led an in-class tutorial teaching students how to set up a local Large Language Model on their personal computers using the AI platform Ollama. After completing this tutorial, students wrote an autoethnography reflecting on their experience. Alongside this assignment, students were assigned several readings that provided a theoretical framework to critically consider how LLMs work, what data was used to train the model, and who owns and develops the model. The goal of this assignment was multifaceted. First, having students learn how to set up their own LLM demystifies AI and exposes students to using AI models outside of the traditional ecosystem of large corporations. Second, asking students to reflect on this process provides them a space to practice their writing, creative expression, and fluency in discussing technical topics. Third, this assignment also challenges students to think about who owns the technology they use and what decisions are made in its development. AI presents a new set of challenges for educators, and we believe that there is a need to develop new pedagogical tools and frameworks to continue to center student learning in the face of a changing technological environment.

3. CONCLUSION

The purpose of this short paper is to offer pedagogical insight from two distinct disciplinary classrooms where student-centered learning was the key instructional methodology, supplementing student use of technology. Using arts-based methods, both researchers sought to instill foundational silos of knowledge within their students that those students could then apply in their utilization of technology. At multiple stages of instruction, both researchers utilized writing as a process of reflection, integration of new knowledge, and conversation with texts and scholars to reinforce student agency. For the hip-hop studies author, reinforcing student agency meant foregrounding their voices and experiences within knowledge production processes as they were introduced to hip-hop technologies and applications. For the critical information studies author, centering student learning meant building the students' capacity to exercise agency over their relationship to artificial intelligence. This was done by using various critical technology frameworks to design student learning experiences that demystify AI, challenge techno-determinist narratives, and affirm writing expression as a way to imagine alternative socio-technical futures. For students, generative AI seems seductive as an educational tool because it promises to remove the labor and frustration required to write. Our classroom instruction should reinforce that the point of writing is not simply to produce a document and get a grade. As a pedagogical tool, writing helps to spark a process of reflection, integration of new knowledge, and conversation with texts, scholars, and helps students develop their own ideas. Student-centered learning means that our pedagogical approach should center writing as a process and expression. In order to help students to develop these skills, we must equip them with the kinds of knowledge that will challenge them to exercise agency over their relationship to technology and not replace the process of writing and critical thinking with seemingly efficient substitutes.

ACKNOWLEDGEMENT

The authors of this paper would like to thank their students for their hard work and dedication in the classroom and beyond.

REFERENCES

Alim, H. S. (2007). Critical hip-hop language pedagogies: Combat, consciousness, and the cultural politics of communication. Journal of Language, Identity, and Education, 6(2), 161–176.

Cahnmann-Taylor, M., & Siegesmund, R. (2017). *Arts-Based Research in Education: Foundations for Practice*. Routledge.

Dunbar, A. W. (2023). Every information context is a CRiTical Race information Theory opportunity: Informatic considerations for the information industrial complex. Digital Transformation and Society, 2(4), 356–375. https://doi.org/10.1108/DTS-02-2023-0013

Finley, S. (2008). Arts-based research. In J. G. Knowles & A. L. Cole (Eds.), *Handbook of the arts in qualitative research: Perspectives, methodologies, examples, and issues*, (pp. 71-81).

Nzinga K., Palomar M., O'Neal S., Williams A. (2023)."Publishing and production as student empowerment: Facilitating knowledge through community sites of cultural transmission"., Sensorial Attunement: Intergenerational Justice-oriented Learning Across Community-based Approaches and Methodologies. International Society of the Learning Sciences.

Kapoor, S., & Narayanan, A. (2024). AI Snake Oil: What Artificial Intelligence Can Do, What It Can't, and How to Tell the Difference. Princeton University Press. https://doi.org/10.1353/book.129007

Klein, L., & Posner, M. (2020). Data. In B. Burgett & G. Hendler (Eds.), Keywords for American Cultural Studies, Third Edition (Vol. 11, pp. 82–85). NYU Press. https://www.jstor.org/stable/j.ctv11vcb5n.24

Lee, H.-P. (Hank), Sarkar, A., Tankelevitch, L., Drosos, I., Rintel, S., Banks, R., & Wilson, N. (2025). The Impact of Generative AI on Critical Thinking: Self-Reported Reductions in Cognitive Effort and Confidence Effects From a Survey of Knowledge Workers. Proceedings of the 2025 CHI Conference on Human Factors in Computing Systems, 1–22. https://doi.org/10.1145/3706598.3713778

Noble, S. U. (2018). *Algorithms of oppression: How search engines reinforce racism*. New York University Press.

Petchauer, E. (2009). Framing and Reviewing Hip-Hop Educational Research. Review of Educational Research, 79(2), 946–978.

Raley, R., & Rhee, J. (2023). Critical AI: A Field in Formation. American Literature, 95(2), 185–204. https://doi.org/10.1215/00029831-10575021

Stovall, D. (2006). We can Relate Hip-Hop Culture, Critical Pedagogy, and the Secondary Classroom. Urban Education, 41(6), 585–602.

Tanksley, T. C. (2024). "We're changing the system with this one": Black students using critical race algorithmic literacies to subvert and survive AI-mediated racism in school. English Teaching: Practice & Critique, 23(1), 36–56. https://doi.org/10.1108/ETPC-08-2023-0102

WHAT DRIVES EMPLOYEES TO ENGAGE IN CONTINUING EDUCATION? IMPLICATIONS FOR COURSE RECOMMENDER SYSTEMS – A SYSTEMATIC LITERATURE REVIEW

Floris K. Scherb[1] and Dirk Ifenthaler[1, 2]
[1]*Learning, Design and Technology, University of Mannheim, Germany*
L 4, 1, 68161 Mannheim
[2]*UNESCO Co-Chair on Data Science in Higher Education Learning and Teaching, Curtin University, Australia*

ABSTRACT

This research presents a systematic literature review (SLR) investigating motivational factors that drive employees to engage in continuing education and derives design implications for recommender systems (RS). Following PRISMA guidelines, 11 empirical studies published between 2010 and 2025 were analyzed using qualitative content analysis grounded in Self-Determination Theory. Findings reveal that intrinsic motivations—such as personal professional development and skill acquisition—are predominant, while extrinsic motivations (e.g., employer requirements) also play a role. Based on these insights, three design implications for RS are proposed: support for self-regulated exploration, accuracy for mandatory learning contexts, and explanation features for career-oriented users. These findings contribute to the user-centered design of continuing education RS by aligning recommendations with learners' motivations, potentially increasing system usefulness, user satisfaction, and reuse intention.

KEYWORDS

Systematic Literature Review, Course Recommender System, Motivation

1. INTRODUCTION

Continuing education plays a pivotal role in the modern workforce, which is facing new skill requirements, such as AI-related competences and skills, in an ever-changing labor market (Leopold et al., 2025). However, the German continuing education market alone has more than an estimated 18,000 private and public actors (OECD, 2021a, p. 63), offering a vast number of courses. This abundance can make it difficult for employees to find the most suitable course, potentially overwhelming them during their search (Scheibehenne et al., 2010).

To support employees navigating this overwhelming and diverse course landscape, recommender systems (RS) can be deployed. These systems match individuals with personalized recommendations from a broad range of available options based on users' explicit or implicit data input (Burke, 2002; Resnick & Varian, 1997). However, this raises the question: on what data a continuing course RS should base its recommendations to ensure both accurate and actionable options?

To investigate this question, the *ResQue* framework from Pu et al. (2011) provides the dimension of perceived usefulness, which reflects how well recommendations align with users' goals, predicting user satisfaction and potential reuse of the RS. Because perceived usefulness is tied to users' goals, it is inherently linked to their motivation to use the RS (Venkatesh, 2000). Therefore, if perceived usefulness increases when recommendations match learning motivations, then identifying and classifying these motivations is a necessary first step.

2. MOTIVATION ENGAGING IN CONTINUING EDUCATION

Deci et al. (1996) describe the Self-Determination Theory (SDT) as a model of motivation along a continuum from intrinsic (driven by personal interest) to extrinsic (driven by external rewards or pressures). Intrinsic motivation supports high self-regulation and autonomy, while extrinsic motivation is linked to lower self-regulation. SDT is particularly relevant for continuing education, where motivation is both essential for participation and learning outcomes (Mavropoulos et al., 2021; Pang & Lee, 2013).

Mlambo et al. (2021) conducted a systematic literature review (SLR) on nurses' professional development, highlighting motivation as a key factor. For instance, maintaining up-to-date knowledge of nursing practices was the primary driver, followed by maintaining formal certification and engaging in social networking.

In contrast, Hemmler et al. (2023) categorized workplace learning goals and aligned them with goal-sensitive educational RS across professions, providing key inspiration for this SLR. Finally, Scherb et al. (2025) evaluated a continuing education course RS with guidance counselors and contributed practical design insights. However, this SLR focuses on two main objectives: (1) exploring motivational reasons that drive employees to engage in formal or non-formal continuing education, and (2) deriving design implications for continuing educational course RS. These objectives lead to two research questions (RQs):

1. What motivates employees to engage in continuing educational course programs?
2. Which design implications for a continuing course RS accounting for employees' motivation towards continuing education can be derived?

3. METHOD

A SLR was conducted to answer the research questions. The established PRISMA guideline for reporting systematic literature reviews were followed (Page et al., 2021). The ERIC database was selected to retrieve relevant papers. The time frame for document retrieval spanned from 2010 until March 2025. The starting point 2010 was chosen to capture the worldwide disruption of the labor market caused by the financial- and economic crises in 2008 / 2009 (Bell & Blanchflower, 2011).

The search query was adapted from Hemmler et al. (2023) and modified for this review: ("*goal*" OR "*objective*" OR "*motivation*") AND ("*professional training*" OR "*professional development*" OR "*vocational training*" OR "*workplace learning*" OR "further education" OR "*continuing education*" OR "*lifelong learning*" OR "*skills development*" OR "*adult education*").

Following inclusion and exclusion criteria were predefined and rigorously applied in the screening process: The Study (1) was written in English or German, (2) was published between 2010-2025, (3) was published in a peer-reviewed journal, (4) has an abstract available, (5) shows empirical findings, (6) was excluded, if it was a literature review, scoping review or meta-analysis, (7) is written in the context of continuing education / professional development, (8) shows findings on actively employed individuals, (9) is not focused on continuing education in the form of community of practice, (10) focused on formal, non-formal or curricular based continuing educational courses.

Nine duplicates were removed from an initial 2,554 documents retrieved from the ERIC database. After screening titles and abstracts, 116 full-text papers were assessed. Of these, 52 met the inclusion criteria, and 11 were ultimately selected for this short-paper SLR. The ultimately selected papers were chosen based on employee background, so that for instance not only employees from a teaching background are in the sample.

The extracted bibliographic metadata included authors, year of publication, and country of origin. Additionally, extracted information included study design, continuing educational program details, sample size, participants' employment background, and their motivations for engaging in continuing educational programs. Qualitative content analysis was conducted based on Mayring (2014) to code the motivations identified in the selected papers. Deductive coding categories were derived from the dimensions of workplace learning goals proposed by Hemmler et al. (2023), which are grounded in SDT (Deci et al., 1996). Additional inductive categories were added during the coding process to capture emerging themes.

4. FINDINGS AND CONCLUSION

Regarding RQ 1: Studies mention that employees had high intrinsic motivation to participate in continuing education because they were motivated by their own internal interests (Anghel et al., 2024; McMillan et al., 2016; Truong & Murray, 2019), or because they wanted to expand their current knowledge (Anghel et al., 2024; Støren, 2013). Most findings indicate that the rather intrinsic motivation for personal and professional development is the most expressed motivation for continuing education. The most expressed motivations are a general desire to develop professionally (Anghel et al., 2024; Barker et al., 2024; Botham, 2018; Egloffstein & Ifenthaler, 2017; Jacobbe et al., 2013; McMillan et al., 2016), developing new specific skills for the current job (Anghel et al., 2024; Bautista & Ho, 2021; Bouwma-Gearhart, 2012; Pong et al., 2023), develop self-esteem in ones' own professional abilities (Barker et al., 2024; Bautista & Ho, 2021; Bouwma-Gearhart, 2012; Pong et al., 2023) or social-oriented motivations e.g. meeting other professionals (Anghel et al., 2024; Bouwma-Gearhart, 2012; Jacobbe et al., 2013; Pong et al., 2023). In contrast, some employees indicated that external requirements set by the employer drove their participation and were therefore extrinsically motivated (Botham, 2018; McMillan et al., 2016; Truong & Murray, 2019). But also developing one's career opportunities (Bautista & Ho, 2021; Botham, 2018; Egloffstein & Ifenthaler, 2017; McMillan et al., 2016), obtaining a certificate (Anghel et al., 2024; Bautista & Ho, 2021) were motivational factors. Regarding RQ2: A one-size-fits-all approach to RS design is unrealistic due to the range of motivations in self-regulated learning. Therefore, this SLR focuses on three main design implications.

First, as intrinsic motivation for engaging in continuing education is prevalent, RS should support self-regulated learners by recommending not only accurate but also diverse and novel courses to enhance perceived usefulness (Pu et al., 2011). This should allow employees to not only find the right course but also the opportunity to explore courses or a series of courses in the form of skill paths.

Second, a RS that only recommends required courses should limit exploration and focus on job-specific courses tailored to the organizational job-role required needs. This, in turn, means that this kind of RS must focus on providing accurate courses to increase its perceived usefulness (Pu et al., 2011).

Third, career-oriented motivations can be addressed through RS-generated explanations, such as explained career or certification benefits, which may help employees assess recommendation relevance and quality and support informed decision-making (Tintarev & Masthoff, 2007). In conclusion, these design implications may enhance a RS's perceived usefulness, user satisfaction, and employees' reuse intention (Pu et al., 2011).

However, two key limitations must be discussed in this short SLR: ***first***, only $N = 11$ out of $N = 52$ papers were analyzed, offering only a snapshot of this SLR; ***second***, while data on employees' professional background, country, and training programs was collected, it was not further discussed in the context of this SLR.

ACKNOWLEDGMENT

This work results from the project *KISMET-AI: Continuing Education Recommendations with the KISMET-AI*. This project was partially financed by *Invest BW BW1_3064*.

REFERENCES

Anghel, E., Littenberg-Tobias, J., & Von Davier, M. (2024). Educators' motivation in mass open online courses for professional development. *Education and Information Technologies*, *29*(14), 1-25. https://doi.org/10.1007/s10639-024-12590-6

Barker, H., Lee, H., Kellogg, S., & Anderson, R. (2024). The Viability of Topic Modeling to Identify Participant Motivations for Enrolling in Online Professional Development. *Online Learning*, *28*(1). https://doi.org/10.24059/olj.v28i1.3571

Bautista, A., & Ho, Y. L. (2021). Music and Movement Teacher Professional Development: An Interview Study with Hong Kong Kindergarten Teachers. *Australasian Journal of Early Childhood*, *46*(3), 276-290. https://doi.org/10.1177/18369391211014759

Bell, D. N. F., & Blanchflower, D., G. (2011). Young people and the Great Recession. *Oxford Review of Economic Policy*, *27*(2), 241-267. https://doi.org/10.1093/oxrep/grr011

Botham, K. A. (2018). An analysis of the factors that affect engagement of Higher Education teachers witch an institutional professional development scheme. *Innovations in Education and Teaching International, 55*(2), 176-189. https://doi.org/10.1080/14703297.2017.1407664

Bouwma-Gearhart, J. (2012). Research University STEM Faculty Members' Motivation to Engage in Teaching Professional Development: Building the Choir Through an Appeal to Extrinsic Motivation and Ego. *Journal of Science Education and Technology, 21*(5), 558-570. https://doi.org/10.1007/s10956-011-9346-8

Burke, R. (2002). Hybrid Recommender Systems: Survey and Experiments. *User Modeling and User-Adapted Interaction, 12*(4), 331–370. https://doi.org/10.1023/A:1021240730564

Deci, E. L., Ryan, R. M., & Williams, G. C. (1996). Need satisfaction and the self-regulation of learning. *Learning and Individual Differences, 8*(3), 165–183. https://doi.org/10.1016/S1041-6080(96) 90013-8

Egloffstein, M., & Ifenthaler, D. (2017). Employee Perspectives on MOOCs for Workplace Learning. *TechTrends, 61*(1), 65–70. https://doi.org/10.1007/s11528-016-0127-3

Hemmler, Y. M., Rasch, J., & Ifenthaler, D. (2023). A Categorization of Workplace Learning Goals for Multi-Stakeholder Recommender Systems: A Systematic Review. *TechTrends, 67*, 98–111. https://doi.org/10.1007/s11528-022-00777-y

Jacobbe, T., Hartlaub, B. A., & Whitaker, D. (2013). Motivation for and Benefits from Attending the AP Statistics Reading. *Journal of Education and Training Studies, 1*(2), 32–37. https://doi.org/10.11114/jets.v1i2.135

Leopold, T., Di Battista, A., Játiva, X., Sharma, S., Li, R., & Grayling, S. (2025). *Future of Jobs Report 2025*. World Economic Forum (WEF). https://www.weforum.org/publications/the-future-of-jobs-report-2025/

Mavropoulos, A., Pampouri, A., & Kiriatzakou, K. (2021). Adults' motives and barriers of participation in mixed and asynchronous learning training programs. *Journal of E-Learning and Knowledge Society, 17*(1), 29-38. https://doi.org/10.20368/1971-8829/1135256

Mayring, P. (2014). *Qualitative Content Analysis: Theoretical Foundation, Basic Procedures and Software Solution*. Beltz. https://nbn-resolving.org/urn:nbn:de:0168-ssoar-395173

Mlambo, M., Silén, C., & McGrath, C. (2021). Lifelong learning and nurses' continuing professional development, a metasynthesis of the literature. *BMC Nursing, 20*(1), Article 62. https://doi.org/10.1186/s12912-021-00579-2

OECD (2021a). *Getting Skills Right: Continuing Education and Training in Germany*. OECD. https://doi.org/10.1787/1f552468-en

Page, M. J., McKenzie, J. E., Bossuyt, P. M., Boutron, I., Hoffmann, T. C., Mulrow, C. D., Shamseer, L., Tetzlaff, J. M., Akl, E. A., Brennan, S. E., Chou, R., Glanville, J., Grimshaw, J. M., Hróbjartsson, A., Lalu, M. M., Li, T., Loder, E. W., Mayo-Wilson, E., McDonald, S., … Moher, D. (2021). The PRISMA 2020 statement: An updated guideline for reporting systematic reviews. *BMJ, 372*, n71. https://doi.org/10.1136/bmj.n71

Pang, V., & Lee, P.L. (2013). Motivational Factors in Continuing Education an Academic Achievement of Adult Learners. *Malaysian Journal of Learning and Instruction, 10*. https://doi.org/10.32890/mjli.10.2013.7651

Pong, H.-K., Leung, C. H., & Cheung, H. Y. (2023). Development and validation of an instrument to measure Chinese post-secondary and part-time students' motivation to learn accounting in Hong Kong. *Journal of Adult and Continuing Education, 29*(2), 318-342. https://doi.org/10.1177/14779714231169687

Pu, P., Chen, L., & Hu, R. (2011). A User-Centric Evaluation Framework for Recommender Systems. RecSys '11: Proceedings of the fifth ACM conference on Recommender systems, USA, IL, Chicago, 157-164. https://doi.org/10.1145/2043932.2043962

Resnick, P. & Varian, H. (1997). Recommender Systems. *Communications of the ACM, 40*(3), 56-58. https://doi.org/10.1145/245108.245121

Scheibehenne, B., Greifeneder, R., & Todd, P. M. (2010). Can There Ever Be Too Many Options? A Meta-Analytics Review of Choice Overload. *Journal of Consumer Research, 37*(3), 409-425. https://doi.org/10.1086/651235

Scherb, F. K., Ifenthaler, D., Von Bachmann, P., & Diestelkämper, R. (2025). A User-Centric Evaluation of a Continuing Education Course Recommender System. *2025 IEEE Global Engineering Education Conference (EDUCON)*, London, United Kingdom. https://doi.org/10.1109/EDUCON62633.2025.11016659

Støren, L. A. (2013). Who attends work-related training five years after graduation? A comparison across European countries. *International Journal of Lifelong Education, 31*(2), 165-189. https://doi.org/10.1080/02601370.2012.733972

Tintarev, N., & Masthoff, J. (2007). A Survey of Explanations in Recommender Systems. *2007 IEEE 23rd International Conference on Data Engineering Workshop*, Istanbul, Turkey,801-810. https://doi.org/10.1109/ICDEW.2007.4401070

Truong, M. T., & Murray, J. (2019). Understanding Language Teacher Motivation in Online Professional Development: A Study of Vietnamese EFL Teachers. *The Electronic Journal for English as a Second Language, 24*(3), 1-22.

Venkatesh, V. (2000). Determinants of Perceived Ease of Use: Integrating Control, Intrinsic Motivation and Emotion into the Technology Acceptance Model. *Information Systems Research, 11*(4), 342-365. https://doi.org/10.1287/isre.11.4.342.11872

MOBILE EDUCATION SYSTEM FOR EFFICIENT LEARNING OF CIRCUIT CONSTRUCTION FOR ULTRASONIC SENSING

Atsushi Takemura
Tokyo University of Agriculture and Technology
2-24-16, Naka-cho, Koganei-shi, Tokyo 184-8588, Japan

ABSTRACT

This study proposes a novel mobile education system designed to assist students in efficiently learning how to construct electronic circuits that incorporate sensors and integrated circuits. The proposed system sequentially recognizes circuit images and identifies errors and inappropriate parts as each circuit element is connected. In addition, it provides guidance to learners on how to correct these errors and rectify any inappropriate parts in their constructed circuits. The effectiveness of the system was evaluated through experiments in which 20 undergraduate students built an ultrasonic object-detecting circuit. Comparative tests between two groups, one using the proposed system and the other not, demonstrated the system's efficacy.

KEYWORDS

Mobile Education System, Experiment, Circuit Construction, Ultrasonic Sensor

1. INTRODUCTION

Education in science and technology requires teaching students about electronic circuits and conducting experiments related to their construction. Recently, various educational systems have been developed to help students grasp the theories and analyses of electronic circuits, including a system for learning theoretical analysis (Ortega-Alvarez, 2018) and simulator-aided reflective learning (Dickerson, 2022). To facilitate remote learning of experiments involving circuit operation and laboratory equipment, several remote laboratory systems have been developed, such as the step-by-step learning of an induction motor (Hayashi, 2023) and project-based learning aimed at enhancing students' professional skills (Fukumoto, 2025). Conversely, hands-on experience with physical components in a real laboratory is crucial for increasing students' capabilities in research and development. To address this need, an educational system for experiments involving circuit construction has been developed (Takemura, 2024). This system can automatically detect incorrect and inappropriate parts (e.g., redundant and hazardous wiring) in a constructed circuit using image-recognition techniques This automated detection of erroneous and inappropriate parts reduces the workload of instructors who must verify numerous circuits with various layouts and compositions and help prevent accidents (e.g., electric shocks or fires). However, the image recognition technique applies only to images captured after the whole circuit is constructed. To enhance the efficiency of circuit construction, a new system is needed that allows learners to sequentially correct errors and rectify inappropriate parts while building a circuit. To tackle this problem, this study developed a novel technique for sequential processing and incorporated it into a new mobile education system for experiments focused on electronic circuit construction. In addition, the study demonstrated the effectiveness of the proposed system through experiments involving the construction of an ultrasonic object-detecting circuit using ultrasonic sensors and integrated circuits (ICs).

2. TECHNICAL FEATURES OF THE PROPOSED SYSTEM

Figure 1 illustrates the technical features of the proposed system for learning circuit construction. This system comprises the individual learners' tablet PCs and a remote analysis system. During the experiment, learners use their tablet PCs to transmit images of their circuits to the remote analysis system as needed, regardless of whether the entire circuit is completed. The analysis system employs image recognition techniques to automatically detect errors and inappropriate parts (e.g., redundant and hazardous wirings) in the circuit and instruct the learner to correct or improve them. This study presents a new technique for sequential instruction based on the following processes (a)–(f):

(a) The remote system utilizes image processing techniques to identify the components and wirings in the circuit. as well as to detect the connected positions of the terminals of each component. If an inappropriate part is identified using the technique developed in the previous study (Takemura, 2024), the system instructs the learner to make improvements.

(b) The analysis system compiles a list of constructed circuit information, which includes device categories and the connected positions of each device's terminals within the circuit under construction. The list is updated as the learner connects new components.

(c) The analysis system sequentially organizes the information in the list (b) to partially generate the SPICE netlist (a standard circuit simulation program) for the circuit being constructed.

(d) The analysis system sequentially compares the partially generated SPICE netlist obtained from (c) with the complete SPICE netlist stored in the system's database. Any discrepancies between the learner's circuit under construction and the complete circuits help identify erroneous parts in the learner's circuit.

(e) If an erroneous part is detected in process (d), the system instructs the learner to correct it.

(f) Once the entire circuit is completed, the analysis system provides the learner with a simulation of the functionality of his or her constructed circuit based on the automatically generated SPICE netlist.

The automated techniques for detecting errors and inappropriate parts in a constructed circuit, as well as translating the complete circuit into a SPICE netlist, were developed in the previous study (Takemura, 2024). To enhance the efficiency of circuit construction, this study introduces a new technique for sequential processing encompassing processes (a)–(e).

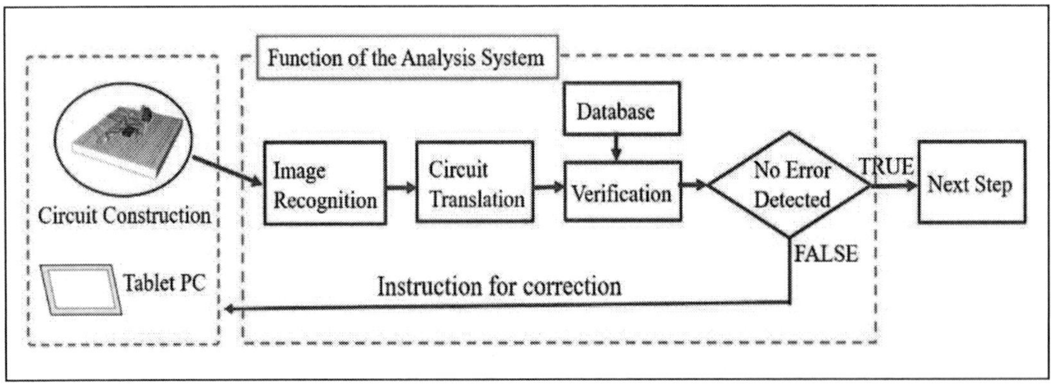

Figure 1. Schematic of the functions and workflow of the proposed system

3. METHODOLOGY FOR EVALUATING THE PROPOSED SYSTEM

The effectiveness of the proposed system was assessed through a comparative study involving two distinct groups of students (Group-1 and Group-2) aged 19–21 years at the Tokyo University of Agriculture and Technology. Each group consisted of ten students tasked with constructing an ultrasonic object-detecting circuit, which includes a pair of ultrasound transmitters and receivers. This circuit is essential for detecting the presence of an object between the two ultrasonic sensors, making it a vital component for understanding fundamental sensing techniques and their applications, such as in robotics. Figure 2(a) shows the diagram of this circuit to be constructed for this experiment. Group-1 performed circuit construction using the conventional method prevalent in 2023. Meanwhile, Group-2 performed the same task but implemented the new system in 2024. Prior to the experiments, students completed questionnaires to assess their experience with circuit construction. Based on their responses, they were categorized into three groups:

A: Experienced in circuit construction using active devices (e.g., ICs) and sensors, in addition to practice exercises at school.

B: Experienced in circuit construction and practice exercises at school, but with no experience using active devices and sensors.

C: No experience in circuit construction aside from practice exercises at school.

Figure 2(b) shows the number of students in each experience category, revealing that the majority were classified as category C.

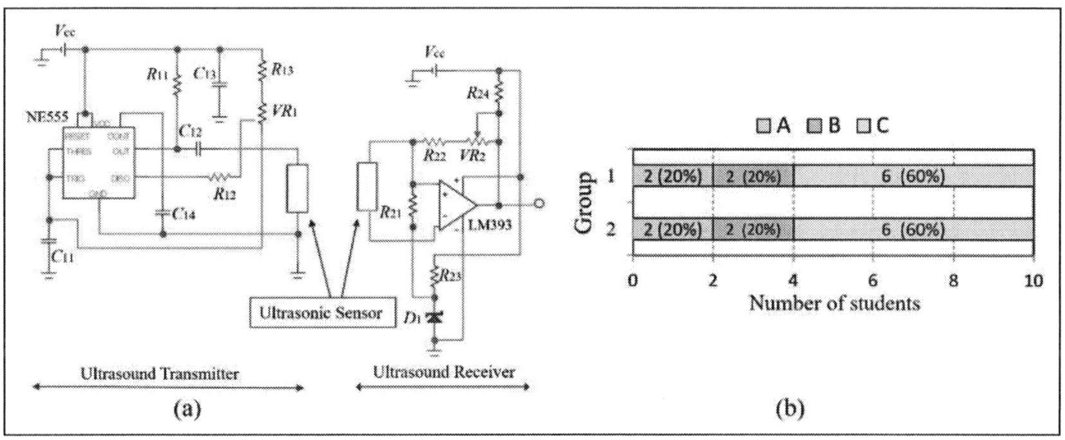

Figure 2. (a) Diagram of the ultrasonic object-detecting circuit to be constructed in the experiments, and (b) grouping of students for the evaluation of the proposed system, along with the proportion of students in each experience category

Students in Group-1 followed the traditional method for constructing circuits, which includes the following steps (T1)–(T4):

(T1) Lecture on the theory and methods for constructing the circuits from the instructor.

(T2) Circuit construction in the laboratory using the necessary components.

(T3) Submission of the constructed circuits to the instructor for inspection. If errors or issues are identified, students are guided to correct them.

(T4) After completing the circuit construction, students learn the workings of the circuit using experimental equipment.

The students in Group-2 were tasked with constructing the same circuits as those in Group-1, but they utilized the newly proposed system according to the following processes. Group-2 completed tasks (T1), (T3), and (T4) as well. However, task (T2-G2) for circuit construction by Group-2 differed from task (T2) for Group-1 as follows:

(T2-G2) In this task, students constructed the circuit using the necessary components in the laboratory. If needed, the student used his or her mobile PC to transmit an image of the circuit under construction to the system and then received feedback. If the system identified errors or inappropriate parts in the circuit, the student corrected or improved the circuit based on system instructions.

4. RESULTS AND DISCUSSION

Figure 3 presents the test results for Group-1 and Group-2, illustrating the effects of the proposed system on the experiment described in Section 3. Figures 3(a) and (b) display the correctly constructed circuits of the ultrasound transmitter and receiver by a student in Group-2.

Figure 3(c) shows that the average time required for circuit construction in Group-2 was less than that in Group-1. This result suggests that the use of the system reduces the time needed for circuit construction.

Figure 3(d) shows the number of students who received instructions to correct errors and inappropriate parts in their constructed circuits during step (T3). This result shows that only one student of Category A in Group-1 (10% of students) successfully constructed the circuit, whereas nine (90% of students) were instructed by the instructor to correct errors or replace inappropriate parts at least once. By contrast, nine students in Group-2 (90% of students) constructed correct circuits using the new system, demonstrating its effectiveness. However, one student in Category C from Group-2 (10% of students) constructed a circuit with errors despite using the system, and this student was directed to correct the mistakes by the instructor. This false negative originated from an incorrect detection of the wiring connections in the constructed circuit. Future studies must focus on improving the techniques for capturing and recognizing circuit images and evaluate them using the circuits constructed by more experimenters.

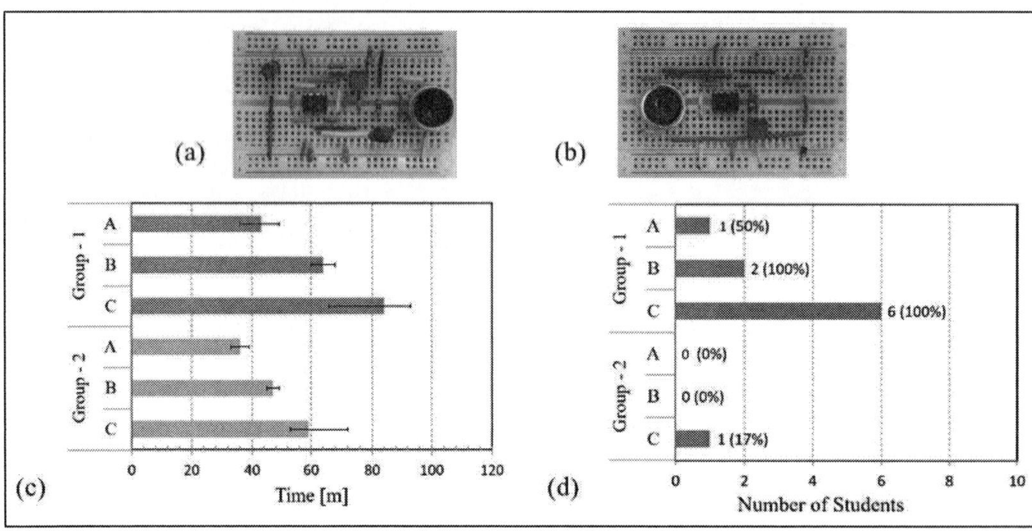

Figure 3. Results of the comparison test between Group-1 and Group-2: (a) correct circuit of an ultrasound transmitter constructed by a student in Group-2; (b) the correct circuit of an ultrasound receiver built by the same student who constructed circuit (a); (c) the average time and range required for circuit construction by group and level of experience; and (d) the number of students whose constructed circuits included errors and inappropriate parts discovered at the process (T3)

During the evaluation process, positive feedback and suggestions for improvement were received from the instructor, further validating the effectiveness of the proposed system. Their comments emphasized the following key points:

- In general, constructing circuits with ultrasonic sensors and ICs involves complicated wiring, making it challenging even for experienced students to build the circuits correctly. This new system aids students in constructing accurate circuits regardless of their level of experience.

- The system effectively reduces the instructor's workload in validating circuits with various layouts and compositions constructed by numerous students and helps prevent accidents caused by operating incorrect circuits.
- To minimize false negatives in automated circuit recognition, improvements are needed in the techniques used for capturing and recognizing circuit images.

In addition, students in Group-2 provided positive feedback regarding the proposed system's usefulness, stating that

- The new technique for sequential detection of errors and inappropriate parts in a circuit under construction is beneficial for efficiently building an accurate circuit.

However, the methods for sequentially capturing and recognizing circuit images require further enhancement. Future studies should implement the following improvements:

- Multi-directional image capture of circuits.
- Enhanced image recognition techniques (e.g., using AI).
- Evaluation using more circuits and experimenters

5. CONCLUSIONS

This study presented a novel mobile education system aimed at facilitating the efficient construction of electronic circuits. The proposed system allows students to iteratively improve circuits containing errors and inappropriate parts by following the system's instructions. The effectiveness of this system was demonstrated through experiments involving the construction of an ultrasonic object-detecting circuit, comparing two groups of university students. By improving the techniques for the capture and automated recognition of circuit images, the overall effectiveness of the educational system could be significantly enhanced.

ACKNOWLEDGMENTS

This study was partially supported by a Grant-in-Aid for Scientific Research (KAKENHI) 23K02629 from the Japan Society for the Promotion of Science.

REFERENCES

Dickerson, S. J., et al. (2022). Use of SPICE circuit simulation to guide written reflections and metacognition, *In IEEE Transactions on Education*, vol. 65, no. 3, pp. 471–480.

Fukumoto, H., et al. (2025). Development and evaluation of remote laboratory system for simulated induction motor, *In IEEE Transactions on Education*, vol. 68, no. 1, pp. 79–85.

Hayashi, V. et al. (2023). Implementation of PjBL with remote lab enhances the professional skills of engineering students, *In IEEE Transactions on Education*, vol. 66, no. 4, pp. 369–378.

Ortega-Alvarez, J. D., et al. (2018). Exploring undergraduate students – computational modeling abilities and conceptual understanding of electric circuits, *In IEEE Transactions on Education*, vol. 61, no. 3, pp. 204–213.

Takemura, A. (2024). Mobile education system for enhancing the efficiency of physical circuit construction and its application to laboratory experiments, *Proceedings of IADIS International Conference CELDA 2024*, pp. 353–358.

DESIGNING CHATBOT-RESISTANT INTERACTIVE QUESTIONS FOR COMPUTER SCIENCE ASSESSMENT

Johannes Knaut, Michael Wiehl and Mike Altieri
Ostbayerische Technische Hochschule Amberg-Weiden
Kaiser-Wilhelm-Ring 23, 92224 Amberg, Germany

ABSTRACT

The rise of generative AI tools such as ChatGPT has introduced new challenges for digital assessment in higher education, particularly in programming lectures. This paper presents a practical approach to designing automatically assessed questions to reduce susceptibility to AI-generated answers while promoting deeper student engagement. Three programming questions in a university-level online competency test were redesigned using three pedagogically grounded principles: interactive exploration, dynamic process encoding and contextual specificity. Evaluation using performance data from two student cohorts and direct testing against an AI model showed that the redesigned questions led to lower average scores but more code runs per question, indicating increased student engagement and reduced reliance on automated solutions. This work contributes actionable strategies for maintaining assessment integrity in an AI-rich learning environment.

KEYWORDS

AI-Resistant Assessment, Interactive Learning, Computational Thinking, Programming Education, Chatbot Misuse

1. INTRODUCTION

The rise of large language models (LLMs) like ChatGPT presents new challenges for digital assessment in higher education. While these tools can support learning, they also allow students to bypass critical learning processes by generating complete answers to practice tasks and formative assessments. This is especially concerning in programming education, where automated feedback systems and text-based question formats are particularly vulnerable to AI-generated responses. There is a growing need to redesign digital assessments to encourage genuine engagement and limit superficial solution strategies. This paper outlines a design-based approach to creating chatbot-resistant, automatically assessed questions in computer science. Three programming questions from a university-level online test are redesigned to discourage copy-paste solutions. Their effectiveness is evaluated using performance data and AI resistance testing. The aim is to offer practical strategies for preserving the pedagogical integrity of digital assessments in an AI-rich environment.

2. BACKGROUND

A recent systematic review by Bittle & El-Gayar (2025) examined 41 studies from 2021 to 2024, uncovering dual effects of generative AI in higher education. While these tools enhance engagement and learning efficiency, they also significantly increase risks of academic dishonesty, particularly ghostwriting and automated cheating.

The challenge of LLM-enabled academic misuse is vividly displayed in programming contexts. Savelka et al. (2023) documented that GPT-4 is now capable of completing standard code assignments with high accuracy. Denny et al. (2023) found that GitHub Copilot could solve about half of evaluated coding problems on its first attempt and handle many of the rest with just minor tweaks to the problem description.

McDanel & Novak (2025) propose specific strategies for crafting "LLM-resistant" programming tasks, such as limiting the solution space, incorporating visual components and adding details about required environment configurations.

In response to AI's increasing capabilities, Cipriano et al. (2024) introduced a diagram- and video-based notation for OOP exercises, aiming to foster deeper engagement and reduce reliance on LLM solutions. Their classroom study (n=56) showed that students engaged more with visual content and were less inclined to use GPT-4 or Bard for code generation.

Visualizations, animations, and diagrams have been shown to facilitate deeper learning by engaging multiple cognitive channels, a concept known as dual-coding theory. This approach aligns with broader principles of active learning, which have been shown to significantly improve student performance and engagement compared to traditional lecturing (Freeman et al., 2014). A study by Grissom et al. (2003) found that students who engaged interactively with algorithm visualizations, such as responding to integrated questions during their exploration, demonstrated greater learning gains than those who merely viewed the visualizations passively. Similarly, a study of Hosseini et al. (2016) suggests that animated examples are more engaging than static code examples. Open-source tools like JSXGraph (Gerhäuser et al., 2010), STACK (Sangwin, 2015), and CodeRunner (Lobb & Harlow, 2016) can be used to support active involvement via integration of interactive applets and individualized feedback (Gailer et al., 2024; Knaut et al., 2022).

3. DESIGN OF CHATBOT-RESISTANT QUESTIONS

In response to the concerns about the integrity and effectiveness of online assessments, three questions in the computer science section of a university-level online competency test—used for applicants to a master's program—were redesigned or replaced to reduce susceptibility to AI-generated answers. The redesign was guided by three core principles: interactive exploration, dynamic process encoding and contextual specificity.

3.1 Design Principles

The first principle, **interactive exploration**, aims to shift the student's role from passive responder to active investigator. Instead of providing complete textual task descriptions, redesigned questions include dynamic elements that require students to explore the task requirements in an interactive way. This approach encourages pattern recognition, conceptual understanding, and elaborative reasoning. Moreover, it is harder to outsource to AI tools as relevant information can only be revealed by interaction.

The second principle, **dynamic process encoding**, involves tasks where learners must observe a dynamic process—often presented visually or spatially—and then encode that process into a formal representation, such as a data structure, algorithm, or symbolic expression. It requires students to mentally simulate a process and express it in a structured, often textual or symbolic, format.

The third principle, **contextual specificity**, reduces the likelihood that a chatbot can generate a correct answer without access to a specific context. Optimally, the context is only retrievable within a closed environment, such that AI tools without platform access cannot provide a complete solution.

3.2 Question Design

These principles were applied to three programming questions (Q6, Q7 and Q9). The programming questions are all implemented with CodeRunner and students can press a check button to run their code as often as they want during their attempt of the competency test and see one or two, but not all test cases. When pressing "check" the students are also informed if there are hidden test cases that have failed.

Question 6 asks students to write a Python function that generates a staircase-like output based on two parameters, "a" and "b". Before the redesign, the question included an explanation and static examples of the required pattern. In the revised version (Figure 1), the pattern is not explained but must be found by active exploration of an interactive applet, implemented with JSXGraph. By using sliders, the students can explore all valid function outputs for different parameter values. This requires students to observe patterns and derive logic from multiple examples.

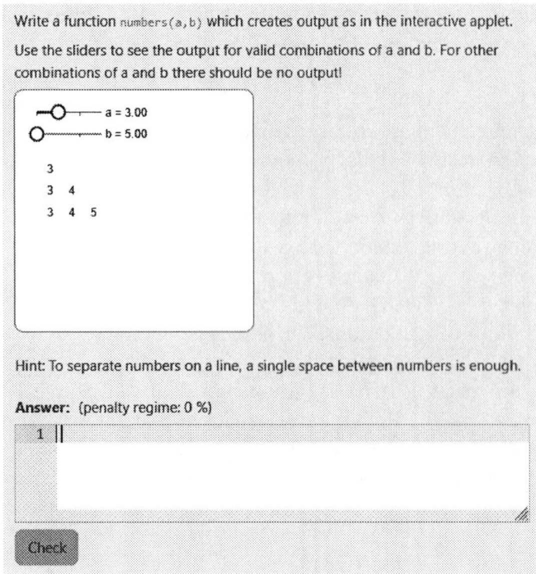

Figure 1. Question 6 (Staircase with sliders)

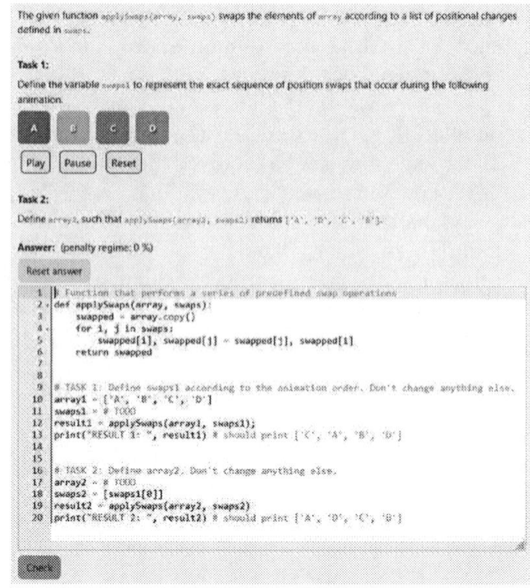

Figure 2. Question 7 (Animation-based swaps)

Question 7 was replaced entirely. The original task involved generating a specific output pattern, which could be easily solved by a chatbot. The new version (Figure 2) includes a simple animation with four boxes that are swapped in a specific sequence according to a given function. Students must start the animation and write down the exact swap order in a form that is accepted by the function. In a second subtask the student must use the first swap operation of the animation to find the initial sequence from a given output sequence.

Question 9 retained its original structure—a Python class implementation—but added a requirement for an additional method that printed a specific word found on a Moodle page. The word itself was only accessible within the closed Moodle platform. This ensured that students had to interact with the platform directly, satisfying the principle of platform-dependent access.

Anecdotal evidence suggests that the three redesigned questions were not inherently more difficult to solve than the original versions, although they posed greater challenges for AI systems.

4. RESULTS

To evaluate the effectiveness of the redesigned questions, we compared performance data from two cohorts of students who completed the time-restricted open-book online competency test as part of their application to a master's program in artificial intelligence. The baseline cohort (n = 204) completed the original version of the test using only static question texts, while the intervention cohort (n = 179) completed the version with three redesigned questions. To ensure comparability, the analysis was limited to programming tasks only.

4.1 Quantitative Results

Figure 3 shows the average scores for all programming questions before and after the redesign of the three targeted questions (Q6, Q7, Q9). Questions 6 and 7 saw a clear decrease in scores after redesign, likely due to the higher engagement required by the strengthened AI resistance, while Question 9 maintained a similar average. Participant-level analysis confirms these trends: for the redesigned questions, students' average scores decreased by 2.6 points (Cohen's $d = -1.13$, $p < .001$), whereas the unchanged questions showed a slight increase of 1.4 points (Cohen's $d = 0.73$, $p < .001$).

Figure 4 shows the average number of code runs per question. Question 6 had by far the most executions, with Questions 7 and 9 also checked more often than before, suggesting stronger engagement with all redesigned questions. On average, students executed 2.17 more runs on the changed questions (Cohen's $d = 1.27$, $p < .001$) and 0.17 more runs on the unchanged questions (Cohen's $d = 0.21$, $p = .041$).

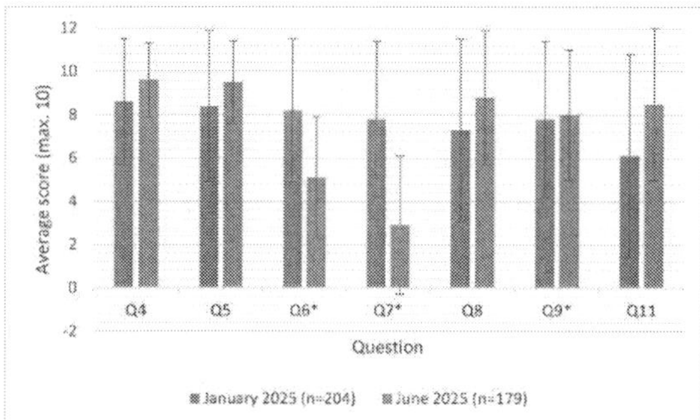

Figure 3. Average score per question (±1 SD)

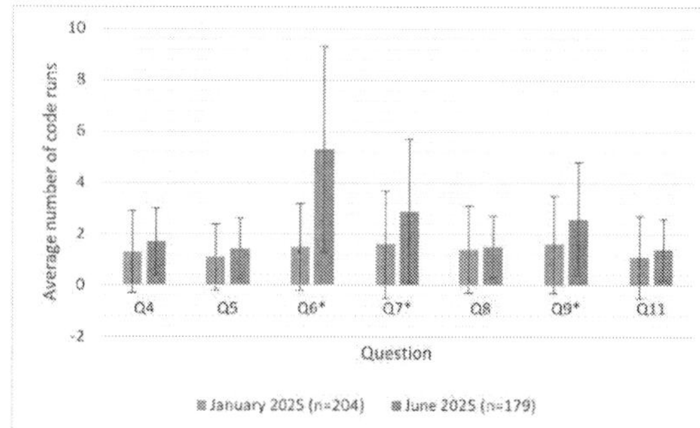

Figure 4. Average code runs per question (±1 SD)

4.2 AI Resistance

To assess the effectiveness of the redesigned questions in resisting AI-generated solutions, we conducted a controlled test using GPT-4o, a publicly available version of ChatGPT. Each question was submitted as a screenshot along with the prompt: "Solve the following question.". The responses were then manually entered into the Moodle system to determine the score achieved. For comparison, the original versions were also tested.

Table 1. Results produced by LLM-model GPT-4o

Questions	Score (max. 10)	Key observations
Q6 (original)	10	Correct answer
Q6 (redesign)	**3.33**	Alternative slider settings were ignored
Q7 (original)	10	Correct answer
Q7 (redesign)	**2.5**	Animation steps were ignored
Q9 (original)	10	Correct answer
Q9 (redesign)	**8.33**	Context-specific word was not printed

The results in Table 1 suggest that the redesigned questions successfully disrupted the typical copy-paste workflow used with AI tools. For Question 6 the model generated the correct base algorithm but completely ignored all edge cases. Question 7 demonstrated strong AI-resistance as well, as the model could not access or interpret the animation. Question 9 showed that even a simple dependency on a closed platform provides the model with incomplete information, that can only be resolved through involvement by the learner.

5. CONCLUSION

This study addressed the challenge of AI-assisted answer generation in digital assessments by redesigning three programming questions with principles of interactive exploration, process encoding, and contextual specificity. The redesigned items produced lower average scores and more code runs, and were less easily solved by ChatGPT, suggesting reduced reliance on AI and stronger student engagement. All three principles result in incomplete information for the AI and require interaction with the visual elements or with the learning environment. The work is limited by its small scope—only three strategies applied to three questions within a Moodle-based test—and by the absence of direct measures of student perceptions or cognitive load.

Future research should extend these principles to other examples and domains, explore additional design strategies, and investigate how AI resistance interacts with task difficulty.

REFERENCES

Bittle, K. and El-Gayar, O. (2025). Generative AI and Academic Integrity in Higher Education: A Systematic Review and Research Agenda. *Information*, Vol. 16, No. 4, pp. 296.

Cipriano, B. P. et al. (2024). A Picture Is Worth a Thousand Words: Exploring Diagram and Video-Based OOP Exercises to Counter LLM Over-Reliance. *European Conference on Technology Enhanced Learning*, pp. 75–89.

Denny, P. et al. (2023). Conversing with copilot: Exploring prompt engineering for solving cs1 problems using natural language. *Proceedings of the 54th ACM technical symposium on computer science education V. 1,* pp. 1136-1142.

Freeman, S. et al. (2014). Active learning increases student performance in science, engineering, and mathematics, *Proceedings of the National Academy of Sciences*. Vol. 111, No. 23, pp. 8410-8415.

Gailer, B. et al. (2024). Automatic assessment of the geometric performance of basic operations with complex numbers: An example question using STACK and JSXGraph. *Proceedings of the International Meeting of the STACK Community 2024*, pp. 1–16.

Gerhäuser, M. et al. (2010). JSXGraph-Dynamic Mathematics with JavaScript. *International Journal for Technology in Mathematics Education*, Vol. 17, No. 4.

Grissom, S. et al. (2003). Algorithm visualization in CS education: comparing levels of student engagement. *Proceedings of the 2003 ACM symposium on Software visualization*, pp. 87-94.

Hosseini, R. et al. (2016). Animated examples as practice content in a java programming course. *Proceedings of the 47th ACM technical symposium on computing science education*, pp. 540-545.

Knaut, J. et al. (2022). A Theory-Based Approach of Feedback in STACK-Based Moodle Quizzes Taking into Account Self-Regulation and Different Proficiency of Learners. *International Journal of Emerging Technologies in Learning (iJET),* Vol. 17, No. 23, pp. 38–55.

Lobb, R. and Harlow, J. (2016). Coderunner: A tool for assessing computer programming skills. *ACM Inroads*, Vol. 7, No. 1, pp. 47–51.

McDanel, B. and Novak, E. (2025). Designing LLM-Resistant Programming Assignments: Insights and Strategies for CS Educators. *Proceedings of the 56th ACM Technical Symposium on Computer Science Education V. 1*. Pittsburgh, PA, USA, pp. 756-762.

Sangwin, C. (2015). Computer aided assessment of mathematics using STACK. *Selected regular lectures from the 12th international congress on mathematical education*, pp. 695-713.

Savelka, J. et al. (2023). Thrilled by Your Progress! Large Language Models (GPT-4) No Longer Struggle to Pass Assessments in Higher Education Programming Courses. *Proceedings of the 2023 ACM Conference on International Computing Education Research,* Vol. 1, Chicago, IL, USA, pp. 78–92.

NEUROSCIENCE AND NEURO-PEDAGOGICAL INSIGHTS: ENHANCING ENGLISH LANGUAGE LEARNING THROUGH MULTIPLE INTELLIGENCES AND AI-SUPPORTED DIAGNOSTIC MODELS

Jessica Vanessa Balderas Villafranca, Olga Laura Rosas Sánchez
and Hugo Ernesto Vargas Rodríguez
Escuela Normal Lic. J. Guadalupe Mainero
Matamoros, Tamaulipas, Mexico

ABSTRACT

This short paper reports the findings of a semester-long intervention with 60 pre-service teachers of the Bachelor in Preschool Education at the Escuela Normal Lic. J. Guadalupe Mainero, Matamoros, Tamaulipas. The study explored the integration of Multiple Intelligences (MI), neurocognitive principles, and AI-driven diagnostics in English as a Second Language (ESL) learning, using the Cambridge Interchange 1 textbook (Units 1–5). Students, initially diagnosed at CEFR A2 level, engaged with AI tools designed to enhance specific neurocognitive functions (working memory, sustained attention, visual-spatial processing, auditory processing) aligned with their MI profiles. AI-driven apps such as Socratic, Reflectly, ThingLink, Elsa Speak, and LyricsTraining were used to personalize grammar, vocabulary, listening, and speaking activities. Results indicate that 65% of participants progressed to B1 level, with significant gains in listening and speaking, and increased motivation and self-regulation. This study highlights the potential of combining neuroscience, AI, and MI theory for personalized ESL instruction in teacher education.
The increasing convergence between cognitive neuroscience and artificial intelligence is reshaping the way we approach language education. This short paper builds on a previously implemented pedagogical intervention that combined Howard Gardner's Multiple Intelligences Theory and AI-driven diagnostics in English as a Second Language (ESL) classrooms in Mexico. In this extended phase, the focus shifts to how neurocognitive principles—specifically, executive functions and working memory—can further personalize learning experiences and enhance student motivation and performance.
Preliminary findings indicate significant gains in student engagement and progress, especially among those previously categorized as low-level learners. This approach promotes just-in-time learning and reinforces self-regulation—critical for language acquisition. The paper reflects on practical implications and future pathways for integrating neuroscience, AI, and differentiated pedagogies in teacher education programs.

KEYWORDS

Multiple Intelligences, Artificial Intelligence, Neuroscience, ESL, Personalized Learning, Teacher Training

1. INTRODUCTION

The convergence of neuroscience, artificial intelligence (AI), and multiple intelligences (MI) provides a powerful framework for innovating language education. Neurocognitive functions are defined as the mental skills related to information processing, including working memory, sustained attention, auditory and visual processing (Diamond, 2013). Neuroeducation design elements refer to pedagogical strategies that adapt learning tasks to these cognitive processes, enhancing engagement and retention (Tokuhama-Espinosa, 2011).

Previous research has demonstrated the promise of AI-driven adaptive learning in second language acquisition (Zawacki-Richter et al., 2019; Beatty, 2013). However, few studies combine AI with MI and neurocognitive design in the context of teacher training programs in Latin America. This paper presents an intervention with Mexican Normal School students located in the northeast on the border with the United States of America, the state of Texas specifically aiming to provide evidence on how AI-driven MI-based activities aligned with neurocognitive principles can foster ESL development.

This paper continues a line of research previously presented in EDUTEC Spain and national conferences in Mexico, with a focus on the application of MI theory and AI tools in English as a Second Language (ESL) classrooms. The current phase integrates neuroeducation design elements to enhance the personalization and cognitive alignment of the learning process

2. METHODOLOGY

This study adopted a mixed-methods exploratory design. Participants were 60 pre-service teachers (average age 20; all female) from two groups of the Bachelor in Preschool Education program at the Escuela Normal Lic. J. Guadalupe Mainero. The intervention lasted from August to December 2024, covering Units 1–5 of Cambridge Interchange 1. The course was divided into three evaluation periods, including quizzes, digital activities, and a collaborative project.

2.1 Instruments

Students completed an MI inventory. A CEFR-aligned placement test online on EF Education. AI tools were integrated according to neurocognitive functions:

Socratic (working memory + logical-mathematical).
Reflectly (sustained attention + intrapersonal).
ThingLink (visual-spatial).
Elsa Speak (pronunciation, auditory processing).
LyricsTraining/Voicemod (musical intelligence).

2.2 Procedure

Each unit integrated AI+MI tasks:

Unit 1: Where are you from? → Socratic for WH-questions and *verb to be*.
Unit 2: What do you do? → Reflectly journaling on routines and time expressions.
Unit 3: How much are these? → ThingLink for interactive vocabulary maps on shopping and clothing.
Unit 4: Do you play the guitar? → LyricsTraining and Voicemod to practice listening and speaking through songs.
Unit 5: What an interesting family! → Elsa Speak for pronunciation and present continuous in family contexts.

2.3 Data Collection

Quantitative data: Pre/post CEFR placement tests and AI log files (accuracy, time on task).
Qualitative data: Reflective journals, classroom observation, and surveys.

This project was implemented with pre-service primary school teachers in a Mexican Normal School. The methodological approach was mixed, incorporating qualitative observation and quantitative AI-generated data. Students first completed an MI inventory and a diagnostic language placement test.

3. NEURO-PEDAGOGICAL FRAMEWORK

Table 1. Relationship between neurocognitive domains, multiple intelligences, and types of AI-driven tasks used in the intervention applications

Unit	Topic	MI Type	AI App	Results/Impact
Unit 1: Where are you from?	WH-questions, verb to be, subject pronouns	Logical-Mathematical	**Socratic**	Improved grammar accuracy, stronger reasoning in sentence building
Unit 2: What do you do?	Jobs, workplaces, simple present, time expressions	Intrapersonal	**Reflectly**	Increased motivation, deeper reflection on daily routines, improved writing fluency
Unit 3: How much are these?	Shopping, prices, clothing, colors	Visual-Spatial	**ThingLink**	Enhanced vocabulary retention, creative use of visual maps, better recall of functional expressions
Unit 4: Do you play the guitar?	Music, TV, yes/no + wh-questions, comparisons	Musical	**LyricsTraining / Voicemod**	Significant gains in listening and pronunciation, higher engagement with authentic content
Unit 5: What an interesting family!	Family members, present continuous, quantifiers	Auditory/Verbal	**Elsa Speak**	Improved pronunciation, fluency in present continuous, confidence in oral interaction

4. RESULTS AND OBSERVATIONS

The intervention yielded measurable language gains: 65% of students progressed from A2 to B1, with an average CEFR gain of 0.5. Speaking fluency and listening comprehension improved significantly, especially in Units 4 and 5. Students demonstrated a 30% increase in engagement with AI-based tasks compared to traditional workbook assignments. Journals revealed heightened motivation, particularly when tasks matched MI profiles. The integration of neuro-pedagogical elements showed a measurable improvement in learner motivation and English proficiency gains. The most notable progress occurred among students initially assessed as A1–A2 (CEFR), particularly in listening and speaking skills. AI-generated reports enabled timely intervention and personalized support.

5. DISCUSSION

The integration of neuroeducational design with AI and MI theory provided a personalized learning experience. The findings align with previous research highlighting the benefits of AI in adaptive ESL instruction (D'Mello & Graesser, 2015; Beatty, 2013). The use of neurocognitive functions ensured tasks were cognitively aligned, reducing overload and promoting motivation.

Nevertheless, limitations include the absence of a control group, the relatively small sample, and reliance on self-reported data. Future research should incorporate neurofeedback tools and affective computing to refine adaptive learning pathways.

6. CONCLUSION AND FUTURE WORK

This short paper demonstrates that integrating neuroscience, AI, and MI in ESL classrooms enhances student motivation, self-regulation, and proficiency. The study contributes original insights by applying this approach in Mexican teacher education, a context underrepresented in the literature.

Future work will expand with larger samples, longitudinal designs, and neurofeedback-based tools to deepen personalization. The intervention fostered higher engagement and self-directed learning. Future work will expand the scope to include neurofeedback-based apps and real-time affective analysis to refine adaptive learning pathways in ESL contexts. The future plan contemplates the creation of AI algorithms within a custom-built digital platform that tracks learning patterns and recommends tasks suited to their dominant intelligences and neurocognitive profiles (working memory load, attention span).

REFERENCES

Beatty, K. (2013). *Teaching & researching: Computer-assisted language learning.* Routledge.

D'Mello, S., & Graesser, A. (2015). *Feeling, thinking, and computing with affect-aware learning technologies. In S. Schroeder & C. Pea (Eds.), The Cambridge Handbook of Computing Education Research* (pp. 419–451). Cambridge University Press.

Diamond, A. (2013*). Executive functions. Annual Review of Psychology*, 64, 135–168.

Tokuhama-Espinosa, T. (2011). *Mind, brain, and education science: A comprehensive guide to the new brain-based teaching.* W.W. Norton.

Zawacki-Richter, O., Marín, V. I., Bond, M., & Gouverneur, F. (2019). *Systematic review of research on artificial intelligence applications in higher education.* International Journal of Educational Technology in Higher Education, 16(39), 1–27.

Beck, K. and Ralph, J., 1994. Patterns Generates Architectures. *Proceedings of European Conference of Object-Oriented Programming.* Bologna, Italy, pp. 139-149.

STUDENT ENGAGEMENT, DEVELOPING CRITICAL THINKING SKILLS AND THE USE OF AI

John W. Hatcher III, Jamie Davis, Bevann Dubuisson and Steele Russell
Southeastern Louisiana University SLU 10549, Hammond, LA, 70402, USA

ABSTRACT

This qualitative study explores the intersection of student engagement, the development of critical thinkings, and the use of artificial intelligence (AI) in teaching and learning. Drawing on the perspectives of higher education faculty, the research examines how AI can be integrated into instruction to support the cultivation of critical thinking at both undergraduate and graduate levels. Data were collected through a survey and a focus group, during which participants shared strategies for effectively engaging students and fostering analytical and evaluative thinking through AI-assisted activities. The study identifies key approaches and considerations for leveraging AI as a tool to promote higher-order thinking and deeper cognitive engagement. Findings highlight both the opportunities and challenges of incorporating AI in instructional contexts and offer insights to inform best practices. This research contributes to the ongoing discourse on the role of emerging technologies in education by providing guidance for educators seeking to enhance student participation and critical thought through AI integration.

KEYWORDS

Student Engagement, Critical Thinking, Artificial Intelligence (AI)

1. INTRODUCTION

Student engagement has long been recognized as a critical component of the teaching and learning process, and this remains true in contemporary educational settings. Similarly, the development of critical thinking skills continues to be a central objective for educators seeking to prepare students for complex problem-solving and lifelong learning. The integration of artificial intelligence (AI) into instructional practice represents a novel and potentially transformative innovation. This development requires educators to adopt nuanced approaches to the intersection of student engagement, critical thinking skill development, and the application of AI across various academic disciplines. In higher education, fostering engagement and promoting critical thinking are essential for academic success and the cultivation of intellectual autonomy. However, traditional instructional strategies often fall short in supporting sustained engagement and deep cognitive processing among diverse student populations. The rapid advancement of educational technologies has introduced AI as a promising tool to enhance teaching and learning. AI-powered applications offer capabilities such as personalized instruction, real-time feedback, and the creation of dynamic learning environments each of which may support the dual goals of increasing student engagement and promoting critical thinking. Despite the potential of these technologies, limited empirical research exists on their effective integration into higher education contexts. This gap in the literature underscores the need to explore how AI can be intentionally embedded in pedagogical design to support student learning and cognitive development. This study carries personal, practical, and intellectual significance for both the researchers and the broader educational community. Personally, it reflects the researcher's commitment to improving teaching practices in higher education. As an educator addressing the challenges of engaging diverse learners and nurturing critical thinking, the researcher is motivated to explore innovative strategies that align with 21st-century learning demands. The integration of AI into instructional design provides an opportunity for professional growth and pedagogical advancement, with the potential to improve teaching efficacy and student learning outcomes. Practically, this study responds to an urgent need for evidence-based strategies guiding the use of AI in higher education. As institutions increasingly implement AI technologies, there is a growing demand for informed policies and instructional frameworks that ensure effective and ethical application. The findings of this research may offer valuable guidance to administrators, faculty, and instructional designers in creating practices that promote engagement and critical thinking through AI-enhanced instruction. These insights may contribute to improved student retention, academic performance, and institutional success. Intellectually, the study adds to the growing body of literature on technology-enhanced learning by examining the intersection of AI, student engagement, and critical thinking. While these topics have been explored independently, few studies have investigated their convergence within the context of higher education. This research seeks to deepen the understanding of how AI tools can be purposefully designed and implemented to foster active learning and cognitive skill development. By generating new insights into pedagogical design and learning theory, the study contributes to ongoing scholarly discourse regarding the role of emerging technologies in postsecondary education. The overarching question that is guiding this study is, what are the perceptions of higher education educators about how to engage undergraduate and graduate level students in developing critical thinking skills and the role of AI in the learning process? In order to address this essential question, the following research questions were used to guide this study:

R1. How do you define critical thinking in the context of your teaching?
R2. Why do you believe it is important for students to develop critical thinking skills?
R3. What challenges, if any, do you face when trying to promote critical thinking among students, and how do you address those challenges?
R4. What specific strategies have you found most effective in engaging students in developing critical thinking?
R5. What are your perceptions of the role of artificial intelligence (AI) in supporting or hindering students' development of critical thinking skills? Can you share any experiences where AI tools have impacted your teaching or student learning?
R6. Can you share any experiences where AI tools have impacted your teaching or student learning?

The development of critical thinking skills in students begins with the foundational step of engagement and the question "why." Before learners can analyze, synthesize, evaluate, or create, they must first be emotionally and intellectually invested in the material. Faculty play a critical role in fostering this engagement using available tools and strategies. In today's educational landscape, artificial intelligence (AI) has emerged as a transformative tool with the potential to reshape teaching and learning in significant ways. This literature review explores how AI can enhance student engagement and, in doing so, support the development of critical thinking skills. Drawing on Bloom's Taxonomy, learning is conceptualized as a progression from foundational knowledge acquisition to higher-order thinking skills such as analysis, synthesis, evaluation, and creation (Momen et al., 2023). Within Bloom's model, engagement serves as the entry point to cognitive development. Klein's (2005) theory of interdisciplinary learning further emphasizes the importance of collaboration, contextual relevance, and real-world problem solving. Together, these perspectives underscore the need for intentional, interdisciplinary, and AI-supported strategies to guide students from surface-level engagement to deep critical thinking. Such approaches foster reflective thinking and prepare students for academic success and career readiness in an increasingly complex world.

2. STUDENT ENGAGEMENT

Student engagement is a key predictor of meaningful learning and critical thinking in higher education. Fredricks et al. (2004) identify three dimensions of engagement: emotional (feeling safe, valued, and connected), cognitive (effort and persistence with challenging content), and behavioral (active participation in learning activities). Without engagement, students are less likely to develop higher-order thinking skills. Disengagement can result in missed assignments, poor comprehension, and low performance on assessments. Long-term consequences may include academic failure, probation, or dropout. According to the Gardner Institute (Koch, 2024), nearly 28% of college students drop out after their first year. Although disparities exist based on racial and socioeconomic factors, research consistently shows that students who feel seen, heard, and supported by their institutions are more likely to persist. Faculty play a vital role in cultivating engagement through effective teaching practices, meaningful relationships, and, increasingly, the use of educational technologies such as AI. Research indicates that blended learning environments promote emotional, behavioral, and cognitive engagement by balancing structured instruction with student-centered approaches (De Bruijn-Smolders & Prinsen, 2024). AI adds a powerful new dimension to these efforts. For instance, AI-generated feedback that includes motivational language that has been shown to reduce students' negative emotional responses, such as frustration or disengagement, thereby improving emotional engagement and perceptions of learning (Alsaiari et al., 2024). AI tools can also identify student emotions and enable real-time instructional adjustments, enhancing personalized learning support (Salloum et al., 2025). Conversational AI platforms, such as ChatGPT, have been found to increase student participation and attention when thoughtfully integrated into teaching (Heung & Chiu, 2025). Additionally, Godsk and Møller (2025) found that AI tools clarified assignment expectations, leading to increased student motivation and participation. Real-time feedback and personalized support further contribute to student autonomy (Nguyen et al., 2024). AI can also promote inclusivity by addressing diverse learning needs and preferences (Yaseen et al., 2025). Students familiar with AI-enhanced platforms tend to demonstrate greater persistence and engagement in their learning processes. Overall, AI-integrated strategies support more equitable, participatory, and cognitively rich educational experiences.

3. CRITICAL THINKING

Critical thinking has been defined as the ability to understand, judge, and solve problems and is widely regarded as a core objective of higher education (Stassen et al., 2011). The researchers are defining critical thinking as one's ability to engage the higher-order thinking skills (of analyzing, synthesizing, evaluating, & creating) to resolve and address real world problems, challenges, and issues. It is essential not only for academic achievement but also for informed decision making in professional settings (Kalinowski & Kitto, 2019). However, students do not develop these skills automatically. Critical thinking must be taught intentionally and scaffolded through targeted instructional strategies that depend on student engagement and sustained cognitive effort. AI tools can support the development of critical thinking by promoting deep understanding and self-regulated learning (Lan & Zhou, 2025). Self-regulation, a foundational component of critical thinking, can be enhanced when students have access to tools that help track their learning, manage tasks, and make informed decisions (Lan & Zhou, 2025). Intelligent tutoring systems, for example, scaffold complex problem-solving by guiding students through steps and offering feedback and explanations (Sajja et al., 2023). These systems are particularly effective in helping students move from surface learning to deep understanding. However, Pratama et al. (2023) caution that faculty must carefully frame the use of AI in the classroom. Without proper guidance, students may misuse AI tools as shortcuts, potentially undermining their development of critical thinking. Thoughtful integration of AI, when aligned with Bloom's taxonomy, can enhance rather than replace cognitive effort by fostering analytical, evaluative, and reflective thinking (Wang & Fan, 2025; Yaseen et al., 2025).

4. ARTIFICIAL INTELLIGENCE

Artificial intelligence has come to prominence in the public eye recently due to its impact on popular culture. What was once the purview of scientists and engineers has now become a consideration or concern for almost every discipline in higher education. Defining AI can be challenging depending on the audience. Warwick & Shah (2015) define artificial intelligence as getting machines to do things that only humans were previously capable of. The eponymous Turing test was once the standard for judging artificial intelligence (Warwick & Shah, 2015); another is the ability of a machine to defeat a chessmaster (Campbell et al., 2002). Both of these standards have been achieved. The recent advances in artificial intelligence are primarily due to three factors: 1) increased computational power via Graphics Processing Units; 2) improved algorithms, in particular the development of the Rectified Linear Unit (ReLU); and 3) availability of large data sets for training and validation (Alabi, 2025; Chopra, 2024; Krizhevsky et al., 2017; Nair, V. & Hinton, G. E. 2010). Research in artificial intelligence has been characterized by periods of intermittent feast and famine (Haenlein & Kaplan, 2019). How long this current golden age continues is uncertain but it is certain to have both positive and negative impacts on society.

5. INTERDISCIPLINARY LEARNING

Interdisciplinary learning connects ideas across subject areas, promoting relevance and purpose in education. Klein (2005) argues that interdisciplinary approaches challenge students to synthesize knowledge across domains, solve complex problems, and consider multiple perspectives. These activities deepen understanding and foster critical thinking by encouraging flexible and integrative thought. AI's potential is amplified in interdisciplinary learning environments. When embedded in design-based learning across departments, AI fosters a shared intellectual culture that reinforces critical thinking expectations in various contexts (Kalinowski & Kitto, 2019). Alignment of outcomes and the strategic use of AI across disciplines help students transfer knowledge and thinking strategies between contexts—an essential skill for navigating the complexities of the modern world. AI-enhanced platforms are particularly well suited for interdisciplinary learning, as they adapt across subject areas while supporting personalized learning (Nguyen et al., 2024). These tools allow students to explore problems from diverse perspectives, interact with tailored content, and engage in real-time collaboration that reflects disciplinary nuance. Student engagement, critical thinking, artificial intelligence (AI), and interdisciplinary learning function most effectively when integrated into a unified instructional approach. Engagement draws students into the learning process; critical thinking enables them to interpret, analyze, and apply knowledge; AI provides scaffolding and responsive feedback; and interdisciplinary learning fosters relevance, adaptability, and transfer of skills. AI-driven tools, in particular, offer emotionally responsive feedback, reduce cognitive overload, and promote student confidence (Alsaiari et al., 2024; Salloum et al., 2025). This is especially valuable in higher education, where learners are expected to develop autonomy while navigating increasingly complex content. Interdisciplinary approaches further ground learning in real-world applications and enhance critical thinking across academic domains. When combined, these elements empower students to take ownership of their education and develop the cognitive flexibility and problem-solving abilities necessary for success in a rapidly evolving world. For faculty, ongoing engagement with contemporary pedagogical practices is essential to prepare students for the demands of modern education and the global workforce.

6. METHODOLOGY

This research study employed a qualitative methodology using a descriptive and exploratory approach to gain insight into the perceptions of higher education educators regarding effective strategies for engaging undergraduate and graduate students in developing critical thinking skills, as well as the perceived role of artificial intelligence (AI) in the learning process. Data collection was completed through a semi-structured focus group and online questionnaire. The study utilized a purposive sample of 49 faculty and staff members from diverse disciplines at a state university, it includes 22 focus group participants and 27 survey respondents representing 12 different departments. Both modalities offered participants an opportunity to engage in an in-depth exploration of their experiences, instructional practices, and perspectives on student engagement, critical thinking, and AI use. The online questionnaire focused on participants providing their individualized responses through the open-ended research questions, while the focus group encouraged dialogue and the exchange of ideas among participants utilizing the same open-ended research questions. The focus group was audio-recorded and transcribed for analysis. A thematic analysis was used to identify patterns and key themes that emerged from the data, ensuring that the voices of participants are central to the interpretation of findings. AI technology did not contribute to the conceptualization or substantive writing of this article. Its use was confined to secondary support functions such as spellcheck.

7. FINDINGS

Data were collected through a semi-structured focus group, which included six guiding questions designed to explore faculty perceptions of student engagement, critical thinking, and artificial intelligence (AI). All responses were transcribed verbatim to preserve the authenticity of participants' perspectives. The analytic process followed an inductive thematic analysis approach (Braun & Clarke, 2006). The analysis began with repeated readings of the transcripts to build familiarity with the content. Initial codes were developed to capture key ideas and recurring patterns. These codes were then grouped into broader themes that reflected shared meanings in the data. Themes were examined within each question and across the dataset, with attention to the core areas of student engagement, critical thinking, and AI. To ensure transparency and rigor, the process emphasized clear connections between raw data and interpretation. Verbatim excerpts were used to illustrate themes and demonstrate how codes were grounded in participant responses. A preliminary and general overview of the results produced a brief narrative and descriptive account of how participants perceived AI as both an opportunity and a challenge in higher education. The findings highlight the potential duality of AI use as a tool of support and a crutch to potentially undermining student engagement and critical thinking. The following section presents a synthesis of participant's responses, with exemplar quotes to illustrate key themes of each research question.

R1. How do you define critical thinking in the context of your teaching?
Critical thinking was mostly defined as the application of knowledge in a real-world context, It also involves a foundational skill of evaluating information.
"I want them (students) to actually take what they've learned and apply it in a real-life scenario."

R2. Why do you believe it is important for students to develop critical thinking skills?
Critical thinking is to cultivate autonomous, resourceful, and effective problem-solvers.
"It helps them (students) to ask the right questions. Answering the how, how can I solve this problem?"

R3. What challenges, if any, do you face when trying to promote critical thinking among students, and how do you address those challenges? Student disposition and preparation.
"Students don't have very much background research, especially freshmen."

R4. What specific strategies have you found most effective in engaging students in developing critical thinking? Effective strategies center on active, collaborative, and experiential learning.
"I love to role play."

R5. What are your perceptions of the role of artificial intelligence (AI) in supporting or hindering students' development of critical thinking skills? Perceptions of AI are complex. While participants acknowledge AI's potential to support critical thinking through effective prompting, it can lead to bigger issues.

R6. Can you share any experiences where AI tools have impacted your teaching or student learning?
AI has impacted teaching by offering innovative, personalized, and practical learning tools.
"If you're using AI and you're using it well, you're having to think critically to do so because it's all about writing that prompt."
"My big issue is the copyright... the ethics of the use of the vast ones that they are using."

The analysis of faculty perspectives revealed interconnected themes regarding strategies for enhancing student engagement, development of critical thinking, and the complex role of AI in higher education. Three primary themes emerged: (a) the strategies employed to engage students effectively, (b) the importance of cultivating critical thinking skills, and (c) the perceived benefits and challenges of AI in support of or the hindrance of developing critical thinking skills.

8. CONCLUSION

Overall, the findings indicate that faculty view critical thinking as a central educational goal, closely linked to active, experiential engagement strategies. AI presents both opportunities and challenges, acting as a potential enhancer of analytical skills when used ethically and intentionally, but also posing risks if misapplied. The interplay among critical thinking, engagement, and AI highlights the importance of deliberate instructional design and faculty support in fostering higher-order cognitive skills in students. Future research should examine strategies for integrating AI in ways that strengthen, rather than diminish, critical thinking and student engagement. Studies exploring faculty development, equitable access to AI tools, and the redesign of assessments to emphasize reasoning and process would be especially valuable. Multi-institutional research could also clarify how instructional context, policy frameworks, and disciplinary differences shape the impact of AI in higher education, which would help ensure that AI integration aligns with the broader mission of cultivating independent thinkers and engaged learners.

REFERENCES

Alsaiari, O., Baghaei, N., Lahza, H., Lodge, J., Boden, M., & Khosravi, H. (2024). Emotionally enriched feedback via generative AI. *arXiv*. https://doi.org/10.48550/arXiv.2410.15077

De Bruijn-Smolders, M., & Prinsen, F. R. (2024). Effective student engagement with blended learning: A systematic review. *Heliyon, 10*, https://doi.org/10.1016/j.heliyon.2024.e39439

Fredricks, J. A., Blumenfeld, P. C., & Paris, A. H. (2004). School engagement: Potential of the concept, state of the evidence. *Review of Educational Research, 74*, 59-109. https://doi.org/10.3102/00346543074001059

Gardner Institute (Koch, J. V.). (2024). *Undergraduate retention and student success: First-year dropout trends*. Retrieved from https://www.jngi.org/

Godsk, M., & Møller, K. L. (2025). Engaging students in higher education with educational technology. *Education and Information Technologies, 30*(2), 2941–2976. https://doi.org/10.1007/s10639-024-12901-x

Heung, Y. M., & Chiu, T. K. F. (2025). How ChatGPT impacts student engagement from a systematic review and meta-analysis study. *Computers and Education: Artificial Intelligence, 8*, 100361. https://doi.org/10.1016/j.caeai.2025.100361

Kalinowski, J., & Kitto, K. (2019). Promoting critical thinking in higher education. *Studies in Higher Education, 44*(5), 799–800. https://doi.org/10.1080/03075079.2019.1586322

Klein, J. T. (2005). Integrative learning and interdisciplinary studies. *Peer Review*, 7(4), 8–10. https://www.juniata.edu/academics/departments/integrated-media-arts/media/integrative-learning-and-interdisciplinary.pdf

Koch, A. (2024, March 18). *Because that's where the highest levels of attrition and inequitable student performance gaps are*. John N. Gardner Institute for Excellence in Higher Education. https://gardnerinstitute.org/why-transform-the-first-two-years-of-college/

Kvale, S. (1996). *InterViews: An introduction to qualitative research interviewing*. Sage Publications.

Lan, M., & Zhou, X. (2025). A qualitative systematic review on AI empowered self-regulated learning in higher education. *npj Science of Learning, 10*(21). https://doi.org/10.1038/s41539-025-00319-0

Momen, A., Ebrahimi, M., & Hassan, A. M. (2023). Importance and Implications of Theory of Bloom's Taxonomy in Different Fields of Education. In M. A. Al-Sharafi, M. Al-Emran, M. N. Al-Kabi, & K. Shaalan (Eds.), *Proceedings of the 2nd International Conference on Emerging Technologies and Intelligent Systems (ICETIS 2022)* (Vol. 573, pp. 696–707). Springer, Cham. https://doi.org/10.1007/978-3-031-20429-6_47

Nguyen, A., Kremantzis, M., Essien, A., Petrounias, I., & Hosseini, S. (2024). Enhancing student engagement through artificial intelligence (AI): Understanding the basics, opportunities, and challenges. *Journal of University Teaching and Learning Practice, 21*(6). https://doi.org/10.53761/caraaq92

OpenAI. (2025). ChatGPT (Sept 15 version) [Large language model]. https://chat.openai.com

Pratama, Y. E., Huang, W., & Bustinza, O. F. (2023). Facilitator or hindrance? The impact of AI on university students' learning engagement. *International Journal of Educational Technology in Higher Education, 20*(1), 34. https://doi.org/10.1186/s41239-025-00534-0

Punch, K. F. (1994). *Politics and ethics in qualitative research*. In N. K. Denzin & Y. S. Lincoln (Eds.), *Handbook of qualitative research* (pp. 83–97). Sage Publications.

Ramos, F. (1989). *Some ethical implications of qualitative research*. In International Conference on Qualitative Research in Education. University of Georgia.

Sajja, R. S., Sermet, Y., Cikmaz, M., Cwiertny, D. M., & Demir, I. (2023). Artificial intelligence–enabled intelligent assistant for personalized and adaptive learning in higher education. *Information, 15*(10), 596. https://doi.org/10.3390/info15100596

Salloum, S. A., Alomari, K. M., Alfaisal, A. M., Aljanada, R. A., & Basiouni, A. (2025). Emotion recognition for enhanced learning: Using AI to detect students' emotions and adjust teaching methods. *Smart Learning Environments, 12*(1), 21. https://doi.org/10.1186/s40561-025-00374-5

Stassen, M. L. A., Herrington, A., & Henderson, L. (2011). 10: DEFINING CRITICAL THINKING IN HIGHER EDUCATION. *To Improve the Academy, 30*(1), 126–141. https://doi.org/10.1002/j.2334-4822.2011.tb00653.x

Wang, J., & Fan, W. (2025). The effect of ChatGPT on students' learning performance, learning perception, and higher-order thinking: Insights from a meta-analysis. *Humanities and Social Sciences Communications 12*, 621. https://doi.org/10.1057/s41599-025-04787-y

Yaseen, H., Mohammad, A. S., Ashal, N., Abusaimeh, H., Ali, A., & Sharabati, A.-A. A. (2025). The impact of adaptive learning technologies, personalized feedback, and interactive AI tools on student engagement: The moderating role of digital literacy. *Sustainability, 17*(3), 1133. https://doi.org/10.3390/su17031133

LEVERAGING SOCIAL MEDIA TO REALISE THE MODE 3 UNIVERSITY

Amy Zidulka
Royal Roads University
2005 Sooke Road
Victoria, British Columbia, Canada

ABSTRACT

This paper explores the potential to leverage social media's affordances to operationalize the mode 3 university vision of greater entanglement between higher education institutions and the wider world. While the mode 3 concept reimagines universities as more porous and engaged with society, there is currently an execution gap in translating this vision into transformative institutional change. The paper argues that social media, despite its well-known issues, offers affordances for learning and connection that universities are not fully leveraging. It proposes that rather than rejecting social media, universities should innovate its governance to harness its capabilities for fostering education and societal good, in the spirit of a mode 3 vision. This paper's concepts provide the foundation for an empirical action research project that ultimately aims to bring into being a university-owned social media platform. This research seeks to bridge conceptual work on the mode 3 university with social media's practical affordances to explore pathways for transformative institutional change in higher education.

KEYWORDS

Informal Learning, Social Media, Mode 3 University, Ecological University, Educational Technology

1. INTRODUCTION

The term "mode 3 university"— what Barnett (2017) has called "the ecological university" and Nørgård, Mor, and Bengtsen (2019) the "networking university"—has been employed to describe a reimagination of the university as an institution that, through greater entanglement with the world outside its walls, can better influence individual and societal learning and change. The mode 3 vision suggests that the university would not only further extend itself into the world but also make itself more porous to the influence of world outside its walls (Canals et al. 2018; Lee & Bligh 2023; Matthews, 2023). It is a vision in which "the institution, society, teachers, researchers, students, employees, workers, and societal citizens enter into closer dialogues and partnerships.... to co-create future knowledge and societal value" (Nørgård et al. 2019, p. 74). To take this vision seriously is to entertain radical institutional transformation, in which power to decide what is learned and how becomes shared among those inside and outside the institution. It is a hopeful vision, which would allow the university to move into a position of greater influence to impact societal good and serve as a force of reason and connection in an increasingly polarized world.

Currently, an execution gap exists in the mode 3 literature. While mode 3 champions have suggested multiple tactics for its operationalization, these tactics tend to be classroom innovations such as "education flashmobs" involving student public self-organization (Nørgård et al. 2019) that exist within the current university structures. While worthwhile innovations, these tactics hinge on pathways between the university and society being forged and reforged by select motivated individuals, without suggesting a transformation of institutional architecture so that entanglement with the world becomes the university's default state. Consequently, they do not necessarily open a path to the institutional change needed to fulfill the mode 3 promise of "radical transformation" (Barnett 2017, p. 49).

This short paper outlines a research project in process, whose goal is to explore the potential of a university-owned social media (SM) platform to operationalize a mode 3 vision. This research rests on the premise that SM have affordances for learning and connection that currently are not being deployed by universities. Moreover, it suggests that an appropriate response to SM's well known negative impacts would be not their rejection but a reimagining of their governance. Indeed, given the prominent role that SM have come to play in the public sphere, universities, those institutions best equipped to foster education in service of societal good, have a responsibility to not abdicate their control to profit-motivated corporate interests. These foundational ideas will be used to further link the mode 3 vision and the affordances of social media and launch an empirical action research project at the author's institution.

2. THE AFFORDANCES OF SOCIAL MEDIA

Educational research suggests that, if "social media platforms are, at best, 'accidental' civic spaces" (Zuckerman 2022a, p. 38), they nonetheless have proven impactful in fostering meaningful learning and change. Studies of diverse populations, including professional groups, students, and citizen scientists using a diversity of platforms, such as Facebook, Tiktok, and Reddit, have shown that SM sites are offering new ways to learn through networks of connection, co-create knowledge with others, engage in flexible self-directed learning (González-Sanmamed et al. 2020). In fact, SM can be understood as offering expanded means to learn in ways that educational scholars have long championed, for example through constructivist and community-of-practice approaches (González-Sanmamed et al. 2020). Particularly compelling is the work of social movement scholars who demonstrate that movements like Black Lives Matter, Me Too, Occupy Wall Street, and the Arab Spring nurture the acquisition of subject-matter expertise, development of process-oriented capabilities such as in organising for social change, capacity for self-reflection, personal transformation such as increased belief in their ability to shift political systems, and material change in the world (Careless, 2015; Falter & Forbes, 2020; de Veer & Valdivia-Vizarreta, 160; Lozano-Diaz & Fernandez-Prados, 2020; Mercea & Yilmaz, 2018; Schroeder et al., 2020; Simões, Amaral, & José Santos, 2021). It would appear undeniable that, in good ways and bad, people are learning through online engagement, with SM having become spaces of public pedagogy (Freishtat & Sandlin, 2010).

Universities largely have relegated SM use to the marketing departments or to adoption at the classroom level, with some individual instructors asking students, for example, to post on SM platforms. In so doing, they have not transformed to a degree commensurate to the societal transformation wrought by the advent of the social web. When universities were invented, information was scarce, accessing it meant convening in specialized spaces, and the classroom thus was "an information architecture…[that] practically made sense" (Cope and Kalantzis, 2009: n.p.). Today, however, information is abundant, accessible across space and time, its production emerges from a multiplicity of interconnected sources and, consequently, "the inflexibility of institutionally provided space is increasingly incongruous, being at odds with commonplace open and connective behaviours that exploit SM to make, share, and curate knowledge" (Middleton, 2018: 105). In our era, for the university to maintain a primary identity as a purveyor of classes is to risk decreased relevance, as all around people turn to other, fluid and ubiquitous forms of learning.

Given the many negative impacts of SM, its further adoption within the university context would come with significant risk. However, this research project aligns itself with those pursuing new governance models to leverage SM's affordances for learning and connection, for example, former director of the MIT Center for Civic Media Ethan Zuckerman, who has engaged in advancing a "Good Web" movement (Zuckerman 2020b), as well as by organizations like the Dutch PublicSpaces, committed to virtual ecosystems that "serve the common interest and do not seek profit" (PublicSpaces Foundation 2021). A university platform could learn from these projects while building on the university's distinct strengths. At a time when low trust in platforms like X is precipitating a search for alternatives (Tenbarge & Collier, 2024), universities are uniquely positioned to leverage their societal role as producers and disseminators of credible knowledge. Moreover, the ways in which students, alumni, faculty, and staff are already connected both to each other and to the university's digital ecosystem suggests a university platform could quickly benefit from the network effect, which other startup platforms struggle to seed (Srinivasan, 2023).

As articulated by González-Sanmamed et al. (2020), SM can be understood as "continuously connected, decentralised and open social structures that transcend territorial boundaries, overcome physical and temporal barriers, and dramatically expand possibilities for mobilisation, intervention and resistance" (pp. 87-88). They thus potentially could serve as foundational architecture to further connect the university with the world. The potential for SM supporting a mode 3 vision, in which the university is more entangled with the world outside its walls, seems worthy of exploration.

3. NEXT STEPS

The next phase of this research will be empirical, with the aim of contributing to knowledge on education futures while creating a working prototype of a university-owned SM platform. The action research cycle of iteratively doing, learning, and adapting, which is appropriate when one seeks both to foster practical change and to contribute to theoretical understanding (Huxham & Vangen, 2003), will be adopted. Because launching a university-managed platform would be a complex and risky proposition, the author also will be guided by the design thinking principle of iterative prototyping—launching small-scale experiments for the purpose of learning and, ultimately, to come to a scalable proof of concept (VanGronigen et al., 2023). Research will be guided by the question, "How can a university-owned social media platform be governed and designed to operationalize the mode 3 university's aims of porous, reciprocal engagement between the institution and wider society?" The prototype will build on the work of multiple scholars who have theorized their use of informal SM communities in educational settings, including Dron and Anderson (2014) who designed a university-wide virtual commons and Liberatore et al. (2018) who adapted for the virtual world Wenger et al.'s (2002) principles for cultivating communities of practice.

This research would contribute to operationalization of the mode 3 university and yield a scalable model for other institutions to adopt or adapt, paving the way for deeper societal integration of higher education. Limitations would include the fact that prototype results from a single university may not generalize, given that different universities adopt different stances to digital transformation and exist within different legal, cultural, and funding contexts.

4. CONCLUSION

This paper introduced the mode 3 university and suggested that SM's affordances could potentially support its advancement. It represents the conceptual building blocks the author will use to advance an empirical action research project, in which she will prototype its ideas, with the aim of ultimately designing a university owned and managed SM platform. The research project's goal is to bridge conceptual work on the mode 3 university with social media's practical affordances to explore pathways for transformative institutional change in higher education.

REFERENCES

Barnett, R. (2017). *The Ecological University: A Feasible Utopia.* Routledge, London.

Canals, L., et al. (2018). International journal of educational technology in higher education, 15(6).

Careless, E., (2015). Social Media for Social Justice in Adult Education: A Critical Theoretical Framework. *Journal of Teaching and Learning*, 10(1).

Cope, B. and Kalantzis, M. (2009). Ubiquitous Learning: An Agenda for Educational Transformation. *Ubiquitous Learning*, pp. 3–14.

de Veer, V. and Valdivia-Vizarreta, P. (2021). Approaching informal learning about# feminism on Twitter. *On the Horizon*, *29*(4), pp.160-173.

Dron, J. and Anderson, T. (2014). Filling the Gaps With a Virtual Learning Commons at an Online University. In: ECSM 2014 University of Brighton, Brighton, UK, 10–11 July 2014, pp. 144–151.

Falter, M.F. and Forbes, M.D. (2020). Amplifying Teacher Voices Through Instagram: Subversive Teaching Meets the 21st Century. In: Dyches, J., et al. (eds) *Acts of Resistance: Subversive Teaching in the English Language Arts Classroom*. Myers Education Press, Maine, pp. 79–94.

Freishtat, R.L. and Sandlin, J.A. (2010). Facebook as Public Pedagogy: A Critical Examination of Learning, Community, and Consumption. In: Kidd, T.T. and Keengwe, J. (eds) *Adult Learning in the Digital Age: Perspectives on Online Technologies and Outcomes*. IGI Global, pp. 148–162.

Huxham, C. and Vangen, S. (2003). Researching Organizational Practice Through Action Research: Case Studies and Design Choices. *Organizational Research Methods*, 6(3), pp. 383–403.

Lee, K. and Bligh, B. (2023). Transformative Networked Learning: An Expanded Design Framework for Individual, Group, and Social Perspective Transformations. In: Dohn, N.B., et al. (eds) *Sustainable Networked Learning*. Research in Networked Learning. Springer Nature, Switzerland, pp. 169–187. Available at: https://link.springer.com/10.1007/978-3-031-42718-3_10 (accessed 19 February 2024).

Liberatore, A., Bowkett, E., MacLeod, C.J., et al. (2018). Social Media as a Platform for a Citizen Science Community of Practice. *Citizen Science: Theory and Practice*, 3(1). Available at: https://doi.org/10.5334/cstp.108 (accessed 16 Sept 2025).

Lozano-Díaz, A. and Fernández-Prados, J.S. (2020). Educating Digital Citizens: An Opportunity from Critical and Activist Perspectives of Sustainable Development Goals. *Sustainability*, 12(18), p. 7260.

Matthews, A. (2023). The Mode 3 Network University and Design: A New Materialist Perspective. In: Dohn, N.B., Jaldemark, J., Öberg, L.-M., et al. (eds) *Sustainable Networked Learning*. Research in Networked Learning. Springer Nature, Switzerland, pp. 189–209.

Mercea, D. and Yilmaz, K.E. (2018). Movement Social Learning on Twitter: The Case of the People's Assembly. *The Sociological Review*, 66(1), pp. 20–40.

Middleton, A. (2018). *Reimagining Spaces for Learning in Higher Education*. Bloomsbury Academic Press, London.

Nørgård, R.T., Mor, Y. and Bengtsen, S.S. (2019). Networked Learning In, For, and With the World. In: Littlejohn, A., et al. (eds) *Networked Professional Learning*. Springer, Cham, Switzerland, pp. 71–88.

PublicSpaces Foundation, n.d. *PublicSpaces Manifesto*. *PublicSpaces International*. URL https://english.publicspaces.net/publicspaces-manifesto (accessed 16 Sept 2025).

Schroeder, S., et al. (2020). "Like, Share, Comment," and Learn: Transformative Learning in Online Anti-Trump Resistance Communities. *Adult Education Quarterly*, 70, pp. 119–139.

Simões, R.B., et al. (2021). The New Feminist Frontier on Community-Based Learning. Popular Feminism, Online Misogyny, and Toxic Masculinities. *European Journal for Research on the Education and Learning of Adults*, 12, pp. 165–177.

Srinivasan, R., (2023). *Platform Business Models for Executives, Management for Professionals*. Springer Nature, Singapore. https://doi.org/10.1007/978-981-99-4910-6

Tenbarge, K. and Collier, K. (2024). X Sees Largest User Exodus Since Musk Takeover. *NBC News*.

VanGronigen, B.A., Bailes, L.P. and Saylor, M.L. (2023). "Stuck in This Wheel": The Use of Design Thinking for Change in Educational Organizations. *Journal of Educational Change*, 24, pp. 699–725.

Wenger, E., McDermott, R. and Snyder, W. (2002). *Cultivating Communities of Practice*. Harvard Business Press, Cambridge, MA.

Zuckerman, E. (2022). How Social Media Could Teach Us to Be Better Citizens. *Journal of e-Learning and Knowledge Society*, *18*(3), pp.36-41. https://doi.org/10.20368/1971-8829/1135818

Zuckerman, E., (2022b). *The Good Web*. 30 Jun. *Stanford Social Innovation Review*. Available at: https://ssir.org/articles/entry/the_good_web . (accessed: 16 Sept 2025).

Reflection Papers

CAPTURING THE RESEARCH BASE: FRAMING A LITERATURE SEARCH ON DIGITAL COMPETENCES

Annika Wilmers[1], Carolin Keller[1], Pia Sander[2], Alexander Christ[1], Tanja Mayer[2] and Katja Buntins[2]
[1]*DIPF | Leibniz Institute for Research and Information in Education, Germany*
[2]*University of Duisburg-Essen, Germany*

ABSTRACT

This paper reflects how the broad concept of digital competences can be translated into a search strategy to capture relevant research literature in the field using research synthesis methodology. Two key areas of interest are the transfer of existing definitions and understandings of digital competences into search criteria and terms, and the planning process involved in conducting a literature search on broad and interdisciplinary research topics while using PRISMA-SEARCH. The chosen review type is an overview of reviews, defined as a review based on existing research syntheses, which is particularly well-suited to mapping broader areas such as digital competences.

KEYWORDS

Digital Competences, Research Synthesis, Overview of Reviews, Literature Search, PRISMA-S

1. UNDERSTANDING AND CLUSERING A FIELD WITH REVIEW METHODOLOGY

Research into digital competences, also discussed as digital skills or media literacy among other terms, has increased significantly in recent years (Kreuder et al., 2024). This growth has been driven by the necessity to define, frame, and implement competences for a digitalized world, and by rapid technical developments. Maintaining an understanding of this field of research is challenging, and an overview of reviews can be a useful method. Overviews of reviews, also referred to as reviews of reviews, meta-reviews or umbrella reviews, point to research syntheses that generate their findings based on research syntheses (Sutton et al., 2019). Overviews of reviews are close to systematic reviews procedures while dealing with multiple study levels: the level of the overview, of the included reviews and of the underlying primary studies (Polanin et al., 2017). Overviews generally cover broader questions or thematic areas, which corresponds to the aim of capturing developments in the research field by reviewing existing research syntheses (e.g. Pollock et al., 2023; Lunny et al., 2017).

This reflection paper provides insights into how a broad literature search in the field of digital competences can be designed while the exact procedure as well as results regarding the efficacy of the search are discussed elsewhere. Special attention will be drawn to the question of the transferability of the PRISMA-S guidelines, which were originally developed for the medical field (Rethlefsen et al., 2021). The documentation of the literature search can be accessed via the Research Data Center for Education at the DIPF | Leibniz Institute for Research and Information in Education.

2. THEORETICAL FRAMING: DEFINING THE TOPIC AND THE TARGET GROUP

The term 'digital competence' as a collective term for the ability to act competently in a digital world is the subject of controversial debate in research. In particular, there is criticism that it is primarily understood as a technological term, which may overlook reflective and critical skills in dealing with digitality (see Kerres,

2023). But even when understanding the term more broadly, digital' competences present definitional challenges: Firstly, they encompass many different sub-aspects (e.g. information literacy), and secondly, the distinction between digital and non-digital competences is not clear-cut, as many underlying abilities (e.g. problem-solving) are relevant in both contexts. Another difficulty arises from the diversity of terms such as digital skills, or media literacy, which are used inconsistently and sometimes interchangeably. This inconsistency further increases in multilingual contexts where translations do not always align precisely.

In this situation we initially decided to consider competences that are explicitly linked to 'digitisation' only, so that general competences such as 'critical thinking' were not taken into account. The understanding of digital competences underlying this overview is based both on relevant literature in the field (e.g. Fraillon, 2024) and on a comparison of national and international strategies and frameworks for digital education (e.g. KMK, 2021; EC, 2019; BMBF, 2019). As a basis for determining and clustering digital competences we chose UNESCOs differentiated 'Digital Literacy Global Framework' from 2018, which is an extension of the European Digital Competence Framework for Citizens (DigComp 2.0 from 2016; updated in 2022). The UNESCO Digital Literacy Global Framework defines digital literacy as "the ability to access, manage, understand, integrate, communicate, evaluate and create information safely and appropriately using digital technologies to create employment, decent jobs and entrepreneurship. It includes competences variously referred to as computer literacy, ICT literacy, information literacy and media literacy." (UNESCO, 2018, p. 6)

The target group includes all learners aged six to 27 years in formal and non-formal settings and in different stages or transitions within the education system using the definition of "young people" found in international contexts, in the sociological context and in German legislation.

3. DEFINING THE SCOPE OF THE LITERATURE SEARCH

In line with the considerations above, the literature search was not dominated by a specific research question but rather mapped the range of current research syntheses on the topic of digital competences of young learners. In this context, we chose a limited number of inclusion and exclusion criteria for the literature search. Included languages were German and English and the search covered literature from the year 2000 onwards.

Instead of using an analytical framework like the PICO model which structures the literature search according to specific criteria (e.g. population or intervention) but risks limiting searches with a broader and/or qualitative approach (Cooke et al., 2012; Methley et al., 2014), we identified core elements of the research topic and separated these into individual blocks (block search). These blocks consist of (1) types of research syntheses, (2) digital competences and (3) the target group of young learners.

4. DATABASE SEARCH AND ADDITIONAL SEARCH TACTICS

For each of these blocks search terms were collected in English and German, for example for types of research syntheses the selection of terms was based on the English-language classification of review types by Sutton et al. (2019). In addition, German terms were also used to identify research syntheses, if these are commonly used in the German literature. To determine keywords for 'young learners', we used terms that covered both the target group and the learners' educational stages. To determine digital competences, keywords were grouped in a phrase search.

Reflecting the heterogeneous and interdisciplinary nature of education research, searches were conducted in the following databases in the areas of education, psychology and social sciences: German Education Research Portal - Fachportal Pädagogik (including the German Education Index FIS-Bildung, ERIC (Education Resources Information Center), "EBSCOhost ebooks", the FID national licenses as well as education areas of the "Library of Congress" and the BASE (Bielefeld Academic Search Engine) database), ERC (Education Research Complete), APA PsychInfo, APA PsychArticles, Scopus, Web of Science (Core Collection) and PubPsych. Additionally, we manually searched the publication lists of central institutions (Campbell Collaboration, the EPPI Center and the What Works Clearinghouse) and a list of relevant journals from the fields of e-learning, knowledge management and media didactics. After removing duplicates and titles published in other languages 4,871 studies were included in the screening process.

5. ASSESSMENT OF THE APPLICABILITY OF PRISMA-SEARCH

The extension developed by PRISMA for complete documentation of literature searches, PRISMA-Search, contains 16 criteria which are divided into four subject areas: Information Sources, Search Strategies, Peer Review and Managing Records. These categories can be applied to all complex search strategies, regardless of the type of review or research discipline except for researching study registries. In educational research, studies from different disciplines may be relevant to the synthesis. Comprehensive study registries in which central topics can be researched are lacking in both education and social sciences. Similarly, research syntheses in educational research are not centrally registered, as is the case with the Cochrane Library or PROSPERO. This leads to more time-consuming searches for research syntheses in education sciences, as these are distributed across various data sources. For the same reason, nuanced search strategies that can be applied to various research contexts (e.g. different database systems or different use of vocabulary in subdisciplines) are essential for capturing all of the relevant literature. In our experience, the PRISMA-S approach can therefore be transferred to other disciplines. However, this does not change the fact that a literature search such as the one we conducted in our case on digital competences must still be very broad in scope and grounded in a theoretical context in order to cover all facets of the subject matter.

ACKNOWLEDGEMENT

This research is funded by BMBFSFJ under the funding numbers 01JD2300A and 01JD2300B.

REFERENCES

Bundesministerium für Bildung und Forschung (BMBF). (2019). *Digitale Zukunft: Lernen. Forschen. Wissen. Die Digitalstrategie des BMBF.* Berlin.

Cooke, A., Smith, D., & Booth, A. (2012). Beyond PICO: the SPIDER tool for qualitative evidence synthesis. *Qualitative health research, 22*(10), 1435–1443. https://doi.org/10.1177/1049732312452938

European Commission (2019). *Key competences for lifelong learning.* Publications Office.

Fraillon, J. (2024). *An international perspective on digital literacy. Results from ICILS 2023.* IEA.

Kerres, M. (2023). Bildung in der digitalen Welt: (Wie) Kann digitale Kompetenz vermittelt werden? In N. McElvany, R. Lorenz, M. Becker, H. Gaspard, & F. Lauermann (Eds.), *IFS-Bildungsdialoge: Vol. 6. Lernen in und für die Schule im Zeitalter der Digitalität – Chancen und Herausforderungen für Lehrkräfte, Unterricht und Lernende.* Waxmann.

Kreuder, A., Frick, U., Rakoczy, K., & Schlittmeier, S.J. (2024). *Digital competence in adolescents and young adults: a critical analysis of concomitant variables,* methodologies and intervention strategies. *Humanities and Social Sciences Communications, 11*(48). https://doi.org/10.1057/s41599-023-02501-4

Kultusministerkonferenz (KMK) (2021). *Lehren und Lernen in der digitalen Welt. Die ergänzende Empfehlung zur Strategie „Bildung in der digitalen Welt".* Berlin and Bonn.

Lunny, C., Brennan, S. E., McDonald, S., & McKenzie, J. E. (2017). Toward a comprehensive evidence map of overview of systematic review methods: Paper 1-purpose, eligibility, search and data extraction. *Systematic Reviews, 6*(1), 231.

Methley, A. M., Campbell, S., Chew-Graham, C., McNally, R., & Cheraghi-Sohi, S. (2014). PICO, PICOS and SPIDER: a comparison study of specificity and sensitivity in three search tools for qualitative systematic reviews. *BMC health services research, 14*, 579. https://doi.org/10.1186/s12913-014-0579-0

Polanin, J. R., Maynard, B. R., & Dell, N. A. (2017). Overviews in Education Research. *Review of Educational Research, 87*(1), 172–203. https://doi.org/10.3102/0034654316631117

Pollock, M., Fernandes, R. M., Becker, L. A., Pieper, D [D.], & Hartling, L. (2023). Chapter V: Overviews of Reviews. In J. P. T. Higgins, J. Thomas, J. Chandler, M. Cumpston, T. Li, M. J. Page, & V. A. Welch (Eds.), *Cochrane book series. Cochrane handbook for systematic reviews of interventions* (Version 6.4). Wiley-Blackwell.

Rethlefsen, M. L., Kirtley, S., Waffenschmidt, S., Ayala, A. P., Moher, D., Page, M. J., Koffel, J. B., & PRISMA-S Group (2021). PRISMA-S: an extension to the PRISMA Statement for Reporting Literature Searches in Systematic Reviews. *Systematic reviews, 10*(1), 39. https://doi.org/10.1186/s13643-020-01542-z

Sutton, A., Clowes, M., Preston, L., & Booth, A. (2019). Meeting the review family: exploring review types and associated information retrieval requirements. *Health Information & Libraries Journal, 36*(3), 202–222.

UNESCO (2018). *A Global Framework of Reference on Digital Literacy Skills for Indicator 4.4.2. Information Paper No. 51.* UIS/2018/ICT/IP/51. https://uis.unesco.org/sites/default/files/documents/ip51-global-framework-reference-digital-literacy-skills-2018-en.pdf

COMPUTATIONAL THINKING IN MATHEMATICS EDUCATION: BETWEEN CURRICULAR EXPECTATIONS AND TEACHING PRACTICES

Marcela de Seabra[1], António Domingos[2] and Manuel Vara Pires[1]
[1]Centro de Investigação Transdisciplinar em Educação e Desenvolvimento (CITeD), Instituto Politécnico de Bragança, Portugal
[2]FCT NOVA, EDUNOVA.ISPA, CICS.NOVA, Universidade NOVA de Lisboa, Portugal

ABSTRACT

This paper examines the gap between curricular expectations for the integration of Computational Thinking (CT) and its implementation in mathematics education. Through a reflective analysis that intersects literature with classroom experience, we argue that teachers' fragmented understanding stems not merely from training deficits but from deeper tensions between pedagogical innovation and systemic constraints. We contend that traditional mathematical competencies already implicitly incorporate core elements of CT. Instead of introducing CT as external knowledge, we propose a reconceptualization of teacher education to value existing mathematical practices as a foundation for CT development, thereby avoiding curricular overload and fostering an organic integration that empowers teachers to recognize the CT already present in their classrooms.

KEYWORDS

Computational Thinking, Mathematics Education, Teacher Training, Problem Solving, Reflective Practice

1. INTRODUCTION

Mathematics education faces a contemporary paradox. Computational Thinking (CT), defined by Wing (2006) as decomposition, pattern recognition, abstraction, and algorithm design, shares deep conceptual affinities with mathematical reasoning (Grover & Pea, 2013). Decomposing problems, identifying regularities, abstracting, and constructing algorithms are intrinsic to mathematical work. Yet, despite this proximity, many teachers feel insufficiently prepared to explicitly integrate CT into their practices (Kong & Abelson, 2019; Ye et al., 2023), revealing a tension between the potential for innovation and classroom reality. This contradiction transcends mere technical training issues. As Brennan and Resnick (2012) warned, theoretical compatibility does not guarantee effective pedagogical translation. The challenge involves school culture, curricular policies, and professional identity. Weintrop et al. (2016) identified practices at the mathematics-computing intersection that are already part of teachers' repertoires. However, these practices are seldom recognized as contributions to CT, remaining pedagogically invisible, which fosters the belief that CT is foreign knowledge demanding an additional workload.

2. MATHEMATICS TEACHING AND THE IMPLICIT PRESENCE OF CT

The supposed simplified views of CT held by teachers (Zahid, 2025) deserve an empathetic analysis. Rather than knowledge gaps, this may represent a pragmatic adaptation to educational ecosystems marked by dense curricula and assessment cultures focused on standardized outcomes. Traditional pedagogical practices already tacitly incorporate the pillars of CT. Vygotsky's (1978) seminal work on higher cognitive skills emerging through contextualized social interaction resonates with Papert's (1980) later ideas on the connections between mathematics and programming.

Explicit CT integration faces structural barriers. The pressure to cover extensive curricula and prepare students for exams that historically favor calculation over open-ended problem-solving is a documented constraint (Fullan, 2007; Darling-Hammond, 2010). This tension extends globally. While countries like Finland and Estonia have achieved remarkable cross-curricular integration, many educational systems struggle between innovative discourse and traditional assessment metrics, which rarely value algorithmic efficiency (Bocconi et al., 2016). International approaches vary, with Denmark emphasizing data and programming and Sweden focusing on instructions and commands (Elicer et al., 2023), highlighting the tension between the depth of CT and the pressures of testing.

3. FROM IMPLICIT TO INTENTIONAL PRACTICE: A CONCRETE EXPERIENCE

Effective CT integration emerges when teachers recognize existing practices. Consider a lesson on first-degree equations. When faced with a problem like $3x + 5 = 14$, a student, unknowingly, is delving into CT. First, they decompose the problem: 'I need to isolate x.' This decomposition leads to a sequence of steps. The student recognizes a pattern: in similar problems, operations are inverted to maintain equivalence. This abstraction allows them to create a mental algorithm: 1. Subtract the constant term (5) from both sides. 2. Divide by the coefficient of x (3). This procedure is not just a calculation; it is the design of a systematic and efficient solution. The pedagogical bridge occurs when the teacher intervenes, not to teach a new topic, but to name what has already been done: 'The sequence of steps you created is an algorithm. You are thinking like a computer scientist.' This linguistic bridge transforms a mathematical routine into an explicit CT competency, reinforcing both student and teacher self-efficacy without adding new content.

This approach, which values practical knowledge, is more powerful than the mere introduction of technology. Tools like GeoGebra or Scratch have potential but are often used to mechanize procedures rather than to explore modeling (Ertmer & Ottenbreit-Leftwich, 2010). CT transcends the digital. Euclid's algorithm or the Fibonacci sequence are historical examples of "unplugged" algorithmic reasoning (Bell et al., 2009).

To help teachers access this knowledge, professional development should focus on three concrete strategies: **1. Recognition Activities:** Teachers analyze their own lessons to identify where they already promote the pillars of CT; **2. Linguistic Bridges:** Developing a common vocabulary to legitimize existing skills, explicitly calling procedures "algorithms" or problem-solving divisions "decomposition."; **3. Collaborative Communities**: Creating spaces to share examples and design organic integrations, as demonstrated by Gadanidis et al. (2017).

This aligns with constructivist theories (Piaget, 1977) and the complexities of TPACK (Koehler & Mishra, 2009), suggesting that sustained change occurs through the evolution of practice, not its replacement (Guskey, 2002).

4. CONCLUSION

CT represents a unique opportunity to renew mathematics education, but its successful integration requires a paradigm shift. Instead of an external imposition on overloaded curricula, CT must be recognized as intrinsic to mathematical thinking itself. Our reflection, supported by literature and an analysis of practice, concludes that the primary challenge is to create the conditions for teachers to recognize, name, and enhance the multiple ways they already practice CT.

This evolutionary approach values teachers as experienced professionals (Hargreaves & Fullan, 2012) and builds upon the foundations of mathematics education. Bridging the gap between curricular expectations and classroom reality requires valuing knowledge derived from practice (Cochran-Smith & Lytle, 2009).

Ultimately, recognizing that mathematics teachers are already CT practitioners creates the conditions for authentic and sustained change.

ACKNOWLEDGEMENT

This work is supported by FCT – Foundation for Science and Technology through the individual research grant: 2024.01567.BD.

REFERENCES

Bell, T., Alexander, J., Freeman, I., & Grimley, M. (2009). Computer science unplugged: School students doing real computing without computers. *The New Zealand Journal of Applied Computing and Information Technology, 13*(1), 20–29.

Bocconi, S., Chioccariello, A., Dettori, G., Ferrari, A., & Engelhardt, K. (2016). *Developing computational thinking in compulsory education.* European Commission, JRC Science for Policy Report. https://data.europa.eu/doi/10.2791/792158

Brennan, K., & Resnick, M. (2012). New frameworks for studying and assessing the development of computational thinking. *Proceedings of the 2012 Annual Meeting of the American Educational Research Association*, Vancouver, Canada, 1–25.

Cochran-Smith, M., & Lytle, S. L. (2009). *Inquiry as stance: Practitioner research for the next generation.* Teachers College Press.

Darling-Hammond, L. (2010). *The flat world and education.* Teachers College Press.

Elicer, R., Tamborg, A. L., Bråting, K., & Kilhamn, C. (2023). Comparing the integration of programming and computational thinking into Danish and Swedish elementary mathematics curriculum resources. *LUMAT: International Journal on Math, Science and Technology Education, 11*(3), 77–102. https://doi.org/10.31129/LUMAT.11.3.1940

Ertmer, P. A., & Ottenbreit-Leftwich, A. T. (2010). Teacher technology change: How knowledge, confidence, beliefs, and culture intersect. *Journal of Research on Technology in Education, 42*(3), 255–284. https://doi.org/10.1080/15391523.2010.10782551

Fullan, M. (2007). *The new meaning of educational change* (4th ed.). Teachers College Press.

Gadanidis, G., Cendros, R., Floyd, L., & Namukasa, I. (2017). Computational thinking in mathematics teacher education. *Contemporary Issues in Technology and Teacher Education, 17*(4), 458–477. https://www.citejournal.org/volume-17/issue-4-17/mathematics/computational-thinking-in-mathematics-teacher-education/

Grover, S., & Pea, R. (2013). Computational thinking in K–12: A review of the state of the field. *Educational Researcher, 42*(1), 38–43. https://doi.org/10.3102/0013189X12463051

Guskey, T. R. (2002). Professional development and teacher change. *Teachers and Teaching, 8*(3), 381–391. https://doi.org/10.1080/135406002100000512

Hargreaves, A., & Fullan, M. (2012). *Professional capital: Transforming teaching in every school.* Teachers College Press.

Koehler, M. J., & Mishra, P. (2009). What is technological pedagogical content knowledge (TPACK)? *Contemporary Issues in Technology and Teacher Education, 9*(1), 60–70. https://citejournal.org/volume-9/issue-1-09/general/what-is-technological-pedagogicalcontent-knowledge

Kong, SC., Abelson, H., Lai, M. (2019). Introduction to Computational Thinking Education. In: Kong, SC., Abelson, H. (eds) *Computational Thinking Education*. Springer, Singapore https://doi.org/10.1007/978-981-13-6528-7_1

Papert, S. (1980). *Mindstorms: Children, computers, and powerful ideas*. Basic Books.

Piaget, J. (1977). *The development of thought: Equilibration of cognitive structures*. Viking Press.

Vygotsky, L. S. (1978). *Mind in society: The development of higher psychological processes*. Harvard University Press.

Weintrop, D., Beheshti, E., Horn, M., Orton, K., Jona, K., Trouille, L., & Wilensky, U. (2016). Defining computational thinking for mathematics and science classrooms. *Journal of Science Education and Technology, 25*(1), 127–147. https://doi.org/10.1007/s10956-015-9581-5

Wing, J. M. (2006). Computational thinking. *Communications of the ACM, 49*(3), 33–35. https://doi.org/10.1145/1118178.1118215

Ye, H., Liang, B., Ng, O. L., & Chai, C. S. (2023). Integration of computational thinking in K-12 mathematics education: A systematic review. *International Journal of STEM Education, 10*(1), Article 3. https://doi.org/10.1186/s40594-022-00404-3

Zahid, M. Z. (2025). Mathematics teachers' perceptions of computational thinking and its integration into mathematics education. *LUMAT: International Journal on Math, Science and Technology Education, 13*(1), 1–24. https://doi.org/10.31129/LUMAT.13.1.2696

AUTHOR INDEX